THE HUMANITIES

Louise Dudley
Austin Faricy

Revised by

James G. Rice
Department of Humanities
Stephens College

Sixth Edition

McGRAW-HILL BOOK COMPANY

New York St. Louis San Francisco Auckland Bogotá Düsseldorf
Johannesburg London Madrid Mexico Montreal New Delhi
Panama Paris São Paulo Singapore Sydney Tokyo Toronto

This book was set in Palatino by Monotype Composition Company, Inc.
The editors were Robert P. Rainier and Susan Gamer;
the designer was Joan E. O'Connor;
the production supervisor was John F. Harte.
The drawings were done by J & R Services, Inc.
The jacket serigraph print was done by Joan E. O'Connor.
Von Hoffmann Press, Inc., was printer and binder.

Note: Acknowledgments for quoted material and illustrations
appear at the appropriate places in the text. Copyrights are included
on this page by reference.

THE HUMANITIES

1 2 3 4 5 6 7 8 9 0   VHVH   7 8 3 2 1 0 9 8 7

Library of Congress Cataloging in Publication Data

Dudley, Louise, date
   The humanities.

   Bibliography: p.
   Includes index.
   1. Arts. I. Faricy, Austin, joint author.
II. Rice, James G. III. Title.
NX440.D82 1978   700'.1   77-22110
ISBN 0-07-017971-9

Printed in the Philippines
by JMC PRESS, INC.
with special agreement with
McGraw-Hill, Inc.

CONTENTS

PART FOUR   STYLE

PREFACE

*The social sciences attempt to see human beings in the
mass, as subjects for generalizations, their behavior
being a fit subject for prediction. The individual tends to be
buried in the mass, of which he forms an element. The
humanities, on the other hand, are far more concerned
with the individual, and especially with unique creations
of the individual imagination which we call works of art.*

—Frank Willett*

Today we think of the humanities as a loosely defined group of
cultural subject areas rather than as scientific, technical, or even
socially oriented subjects. Thus, by the term *humanities* we generally
mean art, literature, music, and the theater—areas in which human
values and individual expressiveness are celebrated.

The humanities engage both our intellectual and our intuitive,
emotional selves. They do so intentionally and without apology. It is
this which sets them apart from those areas which aim at being rig-
idly empirical, objective, factual. Delight and pleasure in the arts can
arise from casual sensualism in the aural, tactile, or visual experiences they evoke. But the knowledge of how the works which afford
us these pleasures come into being, the understanding of the artist's
use of a medium in making a personal statement, and the sharing of
that experience—these deepen and broaden our enjoyment at both
the level of understanding and the level of feeling.

* Frank Willett, "African Arts and the Future: Decay or Development?" in *African Themes*
(Northwestern University Studies, 1975), p. 213.

That is what this book is about. It is not a history of the arts, setting out neatly defined periods, influences of one artist on another, or even influences of one art on another. It is not simply a book of illustrations which engage our senses. It focuses, rather, on that most human act, an artist interacting with an experience or subject, translating it into a medium, using the elements of the medium and the techniques for working in it to produce the finished work. This is the critical moment in the experience of the humanities. If the artist is unequal to creating that which was felt or if we, as the artist's audience, are unequal to recreating what is presented to us, communication fails, community is diminished, our humanity is untouched.

In a sense, this book may be looked upon as a check on poorly rationalized surveys or histories of the humanities. It hopes to place the reader in a position of examining with some sophistication the primary materials from which scholars' categories and historical periods have been derived.

The approach to the study of the humanities in this edition is the one pioneered by Dr. Louise Dudley many years ago. It is perhaps even more significant for students now than it was then. Developments in the humanities since the first edition was published some thirty years ago have made it even more necessary that students acquire, keep, and use the information that allows them to examine works of art personally and at first hand, and to make their own evaluations and judgments of them.

The originality of Dr. Dudley's approach consists of (1) studying all the arts together, stressing those principles which they have in common and those aspects which separate and make them uniquely special kinds of expression; (2) centering attention on individual works of art themselves and the ways in which the experience of an artist, interacting with a medium, becomes significant for us; (3) cultivating students' confidence in their personal responses and perceptions rather than in learned canons of aesthetics, categories, period styles, and the like, from which they deduce what they are supposed to think and feel; (4) outlining a process of interacting with the arts in which students can start with their own observations and intuitive responses and enter into a dialogue with the arts, beginning with surfaces and pursuing their study as deeply and widely as they can.

Historians have always known that historical writing, whether of the arts, the sciences, or politics, is a mere matter of selection and arrangement in some elegant scheme which has coherence and is satisfying to the writer and his or her immediate public. In the past two decades, however, two dramatic instances have made this insight common knowledge: all histories have had to be rewritten, and the events upon which they were based reevaluated, to integrate the contributions of blacks to our culture; and at the moment they are being rewritten again to reflect the new assessment of women's contributions to all aspects of civilization. Now, therefore, more than ever students need to be able to examine and evaluate the facts and artifacts of the humanities on their own—for understanding, for enjoyment, and as a safeguard against accepting too readily whatever generalizations and formulations concerning human activity have been or will be made.

The approach and framework of this sixth edition of *The Humanities* are the same as in previous editions. However, many new materials have been added to bring the sixth edition abreast of the times and to increase its appeal and usefulness. Some of the changes made are as follows:

1 Greater emphasis has been placed on the combined arts of film, dance, and opera.
2 For the first time, photography is included among the visual arts.
3 Twentieth-century arts are dealt with in more detail, and more illustrations of them have been included.
4 The chapters on music have been completely revised, with sensitivity to the fact that music is always a difficult subject for students and teachers who have not studied it previously.
5 Marginal quotations from a variety of sources have been included where they provide a kind of dialogue with the text, reinforce a point made in the text, or shed light on particular illustrations.
6 A Glossary has been added for ready reference to technical terms and matters touched upon only lightly in the text proper. Since its purpose is sensory recognition as well as cognition, wherever possible it refers to specific illustrations in the text.
7 The Bibliography has been completely updated, and the section on teaching materials has been expanded and updated.
8 A students' workbook and a complete teachers' resource manual, with suggestions for tests, have been prepared to accompany this edition.

Professor James Shirky, my colleague at Stephens College, has my special thanks for revising the chapters on music. I wish also to thank the following persons, who provided me with useful comments as this revision progressed: Robert Douglas, Anchorage Community College; Homer F. Edwards, Jr., Wayne State University; Arthur R. Bassett, Brigham Young University; Faye-Ellen Silverman, Peabody Conservatory; Glenda Jones, Lake City Junior College; Peter Gano, The Ohio State University; Elmore Giles, Community College of San Francisco; Richard Byrne, University of Minnesota; and Carl Sclarenco, Indiana State University.

James G. Rice

1 INTRODUCTION

REMINDERS AND ASSUMPTIONS

Basic human needs stand at the center of the art experience. What these needs are may be debated and rationalized, but their existence cannot be questioned. The need for a sense of identity reinforced by signs and symbols, the need for confirmation of our inner perplexities, the need to be reassured that inner ambivalences, doubts, and anxieties can be given shape: these needs are so much a part of our humanity that they function at an unconscious level.

This book has to do with the understanding and enjoyment of the arts—a subject which concerns all of us, for every day we are consciously and unconsciously having our values shaped by the art around us, and every day we make decisions and judgments that are determined by our understanding of the arts and our sensitivity to them.

In diverse situations connected with our work and other activities, we encounter the arts in various forms; and to the extent that we respond to them, liking or disliking one or another art object, we are all critics of the arts. We pass judgment, express opinions about art; but because we do not know the principles with which works of art may be judged, we are likely to feel somewhat insecure in doing so, knowing our preferences are personal, but not feeling confident that they are valid in terms of art criticism.

Figure 1-1. I. M. Pei (1917–), American architect. Everson Museum of Art, Syracuse, N.Y. (1961–1968). (Bush-hammered reinforced concrete using cantilever construction principle. 60,000 square feet, 120 by 255 feet below grade, 130 by 140 feet above grade.)

The three buildings shown in Figures 1-1, 1-2, and 1-3 are well known examples of some current trends in architecture made possible by the development of new building materials, engineering principles, and prevailing aesthetic tastes in the culture. You have probably seen photographs of them, and you have certainly seen buildings with profiles similar to them in many, many places. Perhaps you simply dismissed them as "modern architecture," as "different," without reflection on what made these new shapes on the landscape

Figure 1-2. Buckminster Fuller (1895–), American architect. United States Pavilion at Expo 67, Montreal. (Geodesic dome constructed of steel tubes and covered with transparent acrylic; 250 feet in diameter. Canadian Consulate General, New York.)

Figure 1-3. Jocern Utzon (1918–   ), Danish architect. Sydney Opera House, Australia (1959–1972). (Reinforced concrete shell construction. Australian Tourist Commission.)

possible, on the many, many decisions made in adapting the materials and techniques to creating living-working spaces for particular functions, or on the aesthetic decisions involved in arriving at the proportions and relationships of the various parts. Still, such buildings are a part of our everyday environment; they are a part of the artificial environment of shapes, textures, and colors which is our daily living space on earth.

Most people know that they are not getting all the pleasure they could from art. They know others who are getting greater pleasure than they from concerts, paintings, plays, and poetry; and whether or not they realize it, they would like to share these pleasures themselves. In the realm of art, they feel like the inhabitants of the world before Prometheus brought them the divine fire:

Though they had eyes to see, they saw to no avail; they had ears, but understood not; but, like to shapes in dreams, throughout their length of days, without purpose they wrought all things in confusion.

—Aeschylus (fifth century B.C., Greek dramatist), *Prometheus Bound*, 447–451 B.C., Trans. Herbert Weir Smyth

For many of us such feelings are justified. Rudolf Arnheim, the most important perceptual psychologist of our century, has called us "a generation that has lost touch with its senses":

We have become callously and casually blind. More broadly, you might say we suffer from perceptual pellegra—a disease caused by the deficiency of our sensory experience. . . . A child who enters school today faces a 12-20-year apprenticeship in alienation. He learns to manipulate a world words and numbers, but he does not learn to experience the real world.

To become whole again, we must learn to use and enjoy o senses. An education in the arts is an education of the senses. Artis have always known this. Joseph Conrad makes his purpose as novelist quite clear:

My task which I am trying to achieve is, by power of the written word, make you hear, to make you feel—it is, before all, to make you *see*.[2]

And D. W. Griffith, the great American film director whose life w devoted to developing motion pictures into a significant art forr is reported to have summed up his life work in a simple sentenc "What I am trying to do above all is to make you see."

Indeed, our culture and society have not created an environme in which we have been encouraged to feel and experience sponta eously. This is especially true in the arts. We have been condition and educated to feel that the world of art is a kind of magic circ which only the initiated can penetrate.

We are alienated from the arts as a source of personal enjoymer They are felt to be the remote and mysterious province of an éli element in our society, of a technically trained coterie of critics wl accept without modesty, perhaps even with pride, the designatio "arbiters of public taste," with the authority to say what is art ar what is not. Further, our education system tends to deal with a which has been so designated and with official statements about Art is thereby removed from the activities and enjoyment of tl average person in the street, rather than being continuous with tl experiences and activities of all humankind. We should, therefor constantly remind ourselves that so-called "good art" and "bad ar are not really kinds of arts, but simply categories representing th judgment of some person or groups of persons.

With the development of mass communications and trave people are no longer so isolated from the arts and culture generally they used to be. In the course of reading, traveling, and conversir with friends and acquaintances, people come into contact with mar different artistic stimuli that provoke questions they are not alwa able to handle or feelings they do not necessarily understand.

Never have the opportunities for coming to know and appr ciate the arts been greater. Fine reproductions of masterpieces of a

[1] Quoted by James R. Peterson in "Eyes Have They, but They See Not: A Conversation wi Rudolf Arnheim," *Psychology Today*, June 1972, p. 65. Reprinted by permission of Psycholo, Today Magazine. Copyright © 1972 Ziff-Davis Publishing Company.
[2] Quoted in George Bluestone, *Novels into Film* (Baltimore, Md.: The Johns Hopkins Press, 195; preface.
[3] Reprinted with the permission of Farrar, Straus & Giroux, Inc. (New York), from *Against I terpretation* by Susan Sontag, copyright © 1961, 1962, 1963, 1964, 1965, 1966 by Susan Sontag.

and recordings of the world's great music have put us into a position of veritably living in a museum or a concert hall in which we have at our fingertips the great art and music of the world.

The mass media, particularly magazines and television, stress more and more the importance, even the newsworthiness, of what is going on in the arts. A significant feature of both *Time* and *Newsweek* magazines is the in-depth articles they carry about exhibits, concerts, art movements, artists, and art events, frequently accompanied by several pages of quite good color reproductions. One of the best short histories of photography as an art was a twenty-page illustrated article in *Newsweek*. The inauguration of a new museum by I. M. Pei in Syracuse, New York (Figure 1-1), becomes the occasion for an article; a new school of artists—the color-field painters—is worth a feature article; the British Broadcasting Corporation in England cooperates with American television (with help from the Xerox Corporation) to produce an outstanding cultural program, "Civilisation" (1971–1972), featuring the distinguished art critic Kenneth Clark. Undoubtedly, such events are of great cultural and artistic importance, for mass media are eager to take advantage of them. But for many people, young and old, these very occasions raise as many questions as they answer. Kenneth Clark and his views do not interest everybody, and although presented with the best will in the world, his erudition cannot reach the so-called "average person," in spite of its enormous value. Similarly, color-field painting will not mean the same thing to every person who sees the articles in *Time* and *Newsweek*, and to many readers it will mean scarcely anything at all. Pei's "brutalist" museum in Syracuse will have a different impact on different people, and on many people it will have very little impact. These various reactions suggest that there are still many people who cannot participate fully and confidently in the culture of which they are a part.

This book has to do with the appreciation of the arts as normal human activity—not as puzzles to which a few people who label themselves "critics" have the key. But before beginning our formal examination of the arts, some reflection on the role which art has played in all cultures and among all people should reassure us of our right and privilege to enjoy the arts as the very human creations of very human beings like ourselves.

The Universality and Importance of Art

The psychologist J. C. Flugel, in his book *The Psychology of Clothes*,[5] has concluded that "the three basic motives for clothing ourselves are for *protection*, for *modesty*, and for *decoration*." Amassing evidence

Technology is not going to remove our deep-seated need for order and harmony; or the feeling of sympathy for our fellow creatures, both human and animal; or the belief, for which we have no rational grounds, that some part of us is immortal.

—Kenneth Clark[4]

---

[4] Kenneth Clark, "In the Beginning: The Mystery of Ancient Egypt," *Readers Digest*, June 1975, p. 91; condensed from a television script.
[5] London: The Hogarth Press, Ltd., 1950.

from various geographical regions and primitive peoples, he finds—surprisingly—that the most important of these three motives decoration. By "important" he means pervasive. There are many e amples of clothing worn in severe climates which is not protectiv and *modesty* is an extremely relative term—dress considered mode in one culture or geographic region is frequently considered in modest or indecent in another. This line of reasoning leads Flugel the conclusion that when the wish to be attractive—that is, to ador oneself in keeping with the aesthetic ideals of one's society—come into conflict with the need for comfort and protection, it is the im pulse to decoration that wins. Similarly, Franz Boas, in his boc *Primitive Art*, points out that "there are no people known to the ar thropologist, no matter how close to the level of mere survival, th do not put into art energies that they can ill afford to subtract from their struggle against nature."[6]

The arts constitute one of the oldest and most important mear of expression developed by human beings. Even if we go back t those eras called "prehistoric" because they are older than an periods of which we have written records, we find works to whic we give an important place in the roster of the humanities. In 1879 Spaniard, accompanied by his little daughter, was exploring a cav in Altamira, in northern Spain. Suddenly she began to cry, "Bull Bulls!" He turned his lantern so that the light fell on the ceiling of th cave, and there he saw the pictures of wild boar, hind, and biso which we now know as the Altamira cave paintings (Figure 1-4

[6] Quoted from Eliseo Vivas, "The Function of Art in the Human Economy," in Julian Har (ed.), *The Humanities: An Appraisal* (Madison: The University of Wisconsin Press, 1962), p. 128

Figure 1-5. *Apollo with Kithara,* Greek lekythos from the middle of the fifth century B.C. (Red-figured lekythos. Terracotta. Height: 15 inches. New York, Metropolitan Museum of Art; gift of Mr. and Mrs. Leon Pomerance, 1953.)

Since that time, some similar paintings have been found in other caves, and the experts have given their judgment that these belong to the Upper Paleolithic Age, 10,000 to 20,000 years before Christ.

Even at this early stage, one senses the basic rooting of art in the human psyche: the seeking and making of external images for inner feelings and emotions. Sitting in a cave in flickering firelight, the early artist sees or finds—taking shape in the shadows playing along the rough, rocky walls—images from daily activities. Outlining with charcoal or other colored material helps define these forms so that they become recognizable to all. In some of the cave paintings, jutting rocks serve as hip-bones, heads, or other parts of animals; in flickering light, they give the paintings a sense of movement and three-dimensionality. Our need to give objective, physical form to what we dream, feel, or imagine is the source of creativity. The development and use of skills in doing this give us art.

Throughout history, artists of whatever degree of sophistication have frequently found that the impulse to compare visually similar things is a spur to creating satisfying objective images for their feelings.

In almost every country the earliest art goes back to prehistory. The Greek Homeric epics, the *Iliad* and the *Odyssey*, probably date back to a time before the beginning of recorded history. These poems may have been put together between the twelfth and the ninth centuries B.C., but it is generally believed that they are collections of earlier tales which were known and sung for many years before that time.

We do not have any examples of music and dancing at such early dates, because for a long time there were no adequate means of notation for these arts; but we do know that music and dance were important very early in human history. In 586 B.C., for example, the Greeks held a festival or competition at which one man played a composition for the aulos—a double-pipe reed instrument. There are pictures of instruments and dancers on early Greek vases. On a lekythos (oil container) from the middle of the fifth century B.C., there is a painting of Apollo holding a kithara (Figure 1-5)—the most important of the Greek instruments and the precursor of the modern harp.[7] And copies of two drawings of dancers from Greek vases are reproduced in this book. Figure 1-6 depicts two dancers in movements which seem similar to those seen in folk dances of our time; and Figure 16-1 shows a follower of Dionysus in a religious dance.

The Old Testament refers often to musical instruments. In II Samuel 6:5 we are told that when the ark was brought home, "David

[7] Donald J. Grout, *A History of Western Music,* (New York: W. W. Norton & Company, Inc., 1964), pp. 5–7.

and all the house of Israel were dancing lustily before the Eternal and
singing with lutes, with lyres, with drums, with rattles, and with
cymbals" (Moffatt translation). Moreover, the Hebrews had a song
book, the Psalms, which in its present form probably dates from the
second century B.C., though many of the songs are older. It is divided
into five books, each closing with a doxology. Often there are definite directions as to how the song is to be sung. Psalm 9 is to be sung
by a choir of boy sopranos. Psalm 12 is for bass voices. Psalms 54,
55, and 67 are to be accompanied by stringed instruments. Psalm 5
is to have a flute accompaniment. At times the tune is given; and a
favorite tune may be used for several poems, as at the present time.
Psalms 57, 58, 59, and 75 are to be sung to the tune "Destroy it not"
(Moffatt translation).

Not only is art found in all ages; it is found also in all the countries of the world. Stonehenge (Figure 4-2) is in England; the beautiful head of Nefertiti (Color Plate 1; Color Plates 1 through 10 follow
page 56) is from Egypt; Aesop's *Fables* are Greek, as is this little
song of Sappho, a poet of the fifth century B.C.:

Mother, I cannot mind my web today
All for a lad who has stolen my heart away.[8]

[8] Translated by Marjorie Carpenter.

The *Arabian Nights* tales, which came to us from Persia or one or the other of the Arabic-speaking countries, eventually go back to ancient India. The *Rubaiyat* of Omar Khayyam, from the eleventh century after Christ, is Persian, though it is best known to us in the quatrains of FitzGerald, of which the following is possibly the most famous:

A Book of Verses underneath the Bough,
A Jug of Wine, a loaf of Bread—and Thou
    Beside me singing in the Wilderness—
Ah, Wilderness were Paradise enow!

It seems very modern, as does this later short poem from the Chinese:

What life can compare with this? Sitting quietly by the window,
I watch the leaves fall and the flowers bloom, as the seasons
    come and go.[9]

No matter what age or country we consider, there is always art. And this art is not good because it is universal, but universal because it is good. Old songs and stories, old pictures and statues, have been preserved because they are alive, because they meet the needs of people, because they are liked. There is a timelessness about art which makes us feel it is not old; that is, it does not grow old.

When we recite the Psalms—"The Lord is my shepherd; I shall not want," or "By the rivers of Babylon, there we sat down, yea, we wept, when we remembered Zion"—we do so because we find in them something that fits our needs.

A familiar tune is the one to which we sing both "We won't go home until morning" and "For he's a jolly good fellow." Early French lyrics of the song began: "*Malbrouk s'en va-t-en guerre*" ("Marlborough is off to the wars"); these lyrics date from about 1709, when the Duke of Marlborough was fighting in Flanders. The song is said to have been a favorite of Marie Antoinette about 1780. It was introduced into Beaumarchais's comedy *Le Mariage de Figaro* in 1784. The tune itself, however, is much older. It was well known in Egypt and the East, and is said to have been sung by the Crusaders. But none of us who sing it today think of these aspects of the song. We sing it because we like the song, because it fits our mood when we want a jolly, rollicking air.

Suppose it is a more modern poem we are thinking about:

[9] Quoted from the Chinese of Seccho by Aldous Huxley, *The Perennial Philosophy* (Freeport, N.Y.: Books for Libraries Press, 1972), p. 63.

Márgarét, áre you grieving
Over Goldengrove unleaving?
Leáves, like the things of man, you
With your fresh thoughts care for, can you?
Áh! ás the heart grows older
It will come to such sights colder
By and by, nor spare a sigh
Though worlds of wanwood leafmeal lie:
And yet you *will* weep and know why.
Now no matter, child, the name:
Sórrow's springs aré the same.
Nor mouth had, no nor mind, expressed
What heart heard of, ghost guessed:
It ís the blight man was born for,
It is Margaret you mourn for.

—Gerard Manley Hopkins (1844–1889, British poet),
"Spring and Fall: To a Young Child" (between 1876 and 1889)[10]

In reading poetry of this kind, dealing as it does with universal feelings, one does not care much when it was written, or where, or by whom.

In the final evaluation of any work of art, age and nationality as such are matters of comparative indifference. Bach, Beethoven, and Brahms lived in different centuries, and all composed great music; the final evaluation depends on the music alone. The bust of a pharaoh's consort, *Queen Nefertiti* (Color Plate 1), made more than 3,000 years ago, is as contemporary in feeling as the portrait of Anna Zborowska which Amedeo Modigliani painted in 1919 (Figure 1-7). The Egyptian artist, in producing for the pharaoh's enjoyment what may be the first true portrait in the history of art, has abandoned the priestly canons of the monumental and funeral art of the time. Without the pomp and circumstance usually accorded semidivine personages, the artist has given us a mature, graceful woman in a style that is both modern and archaic, and therefore timeless.

An important point about the humanities, then, is that art has been created by all people, at all times, in all countries, and that it lives because it is liked and enjoyed. A great work of art is never out of date. This point has been stated in many different ways by different people. Some speak of the intrinsic worth of art: its value is in itself. Bernard Berenson, the art critic and historian, talks of the "life enhancing" value of art. Whatever words are used, the fact remains that we like art for itself, and the value of art, like all spiritual values, is not exhausted. Art is used, but it is not used up. It does not grow

[10] From W. H. Gardner and N. H. MacKenzie (eds.), *The Poems of Gerard Manley Hopkins*, 4th ed. (New York: Oxford University Press), 1967.

old. A good expression of this is found in a quotation from President John F. Kennedy's speech of November 1962, on behalf of the National Cultural Center in Washington, D.C.:

Aeschylus and Plato are remembered today long after the triumphs of imperial Athens are gone. Dante outlived the ambitions of thirteenth-century Florence. Goethe stands serenely above the politics of Germany; and I am certain that after the dust of centuries has passed over our cities, we, too, will be remembered not for victories or defeats in battle or in politics, but for our contribution to the human spirit.

By the same token, a painting by Rembrandt of a seventeenth-century dignitary is great even though we may know little or nothing of the person portrayed. It is not the social or political importance of the sitter that makes the portrait significant, but the artistic effort, which has outlasted the contemporary significance of its subject.

THE THREE LANGUAGES AND THE ARTS

There is nothing occult or mysterious about the arts. They use two languages. The primary language is built into us as a part of our human heritage. Jacquetta Hawkes, in her introduction to the massive *History of Mankind*, noted:

While civilizations have come and gone we are still born to the identical equipment of body and limbs already shaped a hundred thousand years or more ago—yes, down to our scratching nails and that tendency to long canine teeth. . . .

What it will prove most important to remember is that our species did not only inherit from the past its bodily equipment, dominated by its subtly elaborated brain, but also highly charged emotional centres and all the strange ancient furniture of the unconscious mind. . . . Today some of us believe (while others do not) that among the elusive and yet the most precious heirlooms of all were shadowy deep-seated memories of the experience of the evolving animal line during the vast stretches of its history; memories which enrich and unite modern men by throwing up from the unconscious the images and ideas that inspire our arts and help to make them universally evocative. Memory of this kind, if it exists, not only unites men at a very profound level of their being through their common response to its images, but also can serve to make us aware of their old kinship with all life and all being—that blessed and also truthful sense of oneness of which our intellect, if granted too much power, quickly deprives us.[11]

This is the language of the arts, to which we are all heir and can all respond, given the chance and some reassurance of its validity. It is built into the very center of our humanity, and when it lies uncultivated and becomes "foreign" to us, we become less than human:

The cultivation of the arts is an education of the sensibilities, and if we are not given an education of this kind, if our hands remain empty and our per-

[11] Jacquetta Hawkes and Leonard Wooley, *History of Mankind*, vol. I: *Prehistory and the Beginnings of Civilization* (New York. Harper & Row, Publishers, Inc., 1963, p. 4.

ception of form is unexercised, then in idleness and vacancy we revert to violence and crime. When there is no will to creation, the death instinct takes over and wills endless, gratuitous destruction. [12]

The secondary language of the arts is made up of the conventions, the traditions, the styles, which have accumulated over the ages. The greater the number of works of art we come to know intimately, the larger our vocabulary of these conventions.

There is, of course, a third language, which is *about* the arts. It is the language in which this and other books on the arts are written. It is not intended to put obstacles between the student and art, nor is it intended as a substitute for looking. One of the joys that come to us from experiencing the arts comes through our sharing the experience with other people. To do this, we need some ability to talk about the arts meaningfully, expressively, and in ways which communicate. A certain amount of terminology therefore becomes necessary, not for its own sake, but for enhancing our pleasure through sharing.

The distinction between objects as external reality and theories, constructs, and sciences dealing with them is simple enough on reflection. It is, nonetheless, an important distinction in studying the arts.

Northrop Frye puts the matter neatly:

Physics is an organized body of knowledge about nature, and a student of it says that he is learning physics, not that he is learning nature. Art, like nature, is the subject of a systematic study and has to be distinguished from the study itself, which is criticism. It is therefore impossible to "learn literature": one learns about it in a certain way, but what one learns, transitively, is the criticism of literature. Similarly, the difficulty often felt in "teaching literature" arises from the fact that it cannot be done: the criticism of literature is all that can be directly taught. [13]

We can, nonetheless, place ourselves in the presence of literature and the other arts. We can cultivate our perceptions and discernment with the guidance of teachers and books such as this. Encouraged by an awareness of our basic humanity, we can value the experience of perceiving and come to enjoy reflective dialogue and constructive speculations about our responses to the arts.

By coming first to the arts with our wholeness, we guard and nurture it, our potential humaneness; doing so is the beginning of becoming an aesthetician, a critic. If we cultivate openness, we can

[12] Herbert Read, "Art and Life," *The Saturday Evening Post*, Sept. 26, 1959. Reprinted from *The Saturday Evening Post*, © 1959 The Curtis Publishing Company. Used by permission of David Higham Associates Limited, London.
[13] "The Archetypes of Literature," *Kenyon Review*, Winter 1951; this essay was incorporated in *Anatomy of Criticism* (Princeton, N.J.: Princeton University Press, 1957).

become persons who are sensitive yet confident in our authentic responses and who therefore need not be timid, awed, or uncertain as we later meet the grand systems of aesthetics, criticism, and philosophy.

ART AND EXPERIENCE

It has been said that art is experience, because all art demands experience; but probably it is clearer to say that all art involves experience, that there can be no appreciation of art without experience.

When we say that art involves experience, we mean by *experience* just what we always mean by the word: the actual doing of something. If you have talked on television, you know that experience. If you have never ridden a horse or fallen in love, you do not know those experiences. You may have always wanted to see the home of Washington at Mount Vernon; you may have read much about it and have seen pictures of it; but you do not have the experience of the place until you see it for yourself. It is one experience to sing a song and a different experience to hear it. It is an experience to read a story or see a play, just as it is an experience to write the story or act in the play. But just to hear *about* the story, the song, or the play is not an experience of it.

Each person must know a work for himself or herself. The dramatist may write a good play, which may be presented by skillful actors, but it is lost to the critics unless they see it for themselves. The poet and the painter may write their poems and paint their pictures, but you cannot know or judge them unless you have heard and seen them for yourself, not as fact or information but as experience. On the lowest level, this means that since a work of art is always something to be seen or heard, we must see it or hear it, or see *and* hear it, if we are to know what it is. We must hear the music and see the painting if we are to know them. Years ago, Gertrude Stein was asked why she bought the pictures of the then unknown artist Picasso. "I like to look at them," said Miss Stein. After all, what can you do with a picture except look at it? A painting is something to be looked at; a poem or a piece of music is to be heard. Many of the people who say they do not like poetry have never heard it; they read a poem as they would a stock market report or a telephone directory.

It is interesting and valuable to learn about any work, to know what the critics have said or what the conditions were under which it was produced. But unless one knows the work itself, has experience of it, one knows little. The first and last demand of art is *experience*.

It is because of this physical appeal of art that we like to dwell on individual works. We look at a painting or a statue though we have seen it a thousand times. We drive a block out of the way every morning to see a building we admire. We continue to get pleasure from looking at Queen Nefertiti even though we have known this statue for years. We wear out a record playing a favorite piece of music over and over, and if we are alone or among friends, we hum bits of it. When we have heard a poignant melody, even casually, as we may hear the love theme from Franco Zeffireli's film *Romeo and Juliet* or the theme from Mozart's Twenty-first Concerto used in Bo Widerberg's film *Elvira Madigan*, we may be humming it not only all the next day but for a long time after that. Many people quote poetry to themselves and to others, although this custom of a slower and gentler time has tended to fall into disuse. And it is not at all uncommon, even today, to quote lines from, say, Shakespeare make a point:

All the world's a stage
And all the men and women merely players . . .

Some people will automatically convert a real-life situation into an occasion for quoting something "appropriate." A personal setback may evoke Shakespeare's sonnet beginning "When in disgrace with fortune and men's eyes. . . ." And of course poetry is still, as ever, a source for expressions of love. For several generations, lovers have cherished Elizabeth Barrett Browning's sonnet beginning

How do I love thee?
Let me count the ways . . .

Young people of today are more apt to use songs as quotations or as love references; everyone is familiar with the cliché "They're playing our song."

Scientists typically have no such love for the manner in which a scientific idea is expressed. They do not walk down the street repeating happily to themselves, "The square of the hypotenuse is equal to the sum of the squares of the other two sides," or "The distance of the sun from the earth is some 90 millions of miles." Such ideas may be, and are, just as exciting as those of poetry, but the idea and the words are not the same; to the scientist the physical presentation of an idea is not important. To the poet the idea and the words are the same. Change a word and you have changed the poem. It is this quality of experience that the American poet Archibald MacLeish must have had in mind when he said:

A poem should not mean
But be.[14]

All the arts *are* more truly than they *mean*.

Before leaving this discussion, we may note two characteristics of experience. First, the experience of art is personal and individual, it depends on what you are, what you have inside you. In the last analysis your experience will not be exactly the same as that of any other person. Do not expect to agree with everyone; all you can do is be honest and straightforward.

Second, every artistic experience is accompanied by some emotion, or emotional reaction. You like it or you do not like it. As you react, you think it is "wonderful," "frustrating," "fine"; or you say, "Lord, what fools these mortals be!" Your feeling may be changed markedly when you have closer acquaintance with that work or artist, but there is always some feeling that is a part of the experience.

One of the most instructive aspects of experiencing works of art has to do with new types of art, which genuinely baffle many observers, even those who really want to appreciate them. A recent, and very telling, instance was the abstract expressionist movement of the late 1940s and the 1950s (for example, see Figure 1-8 and Color Plate 10). The early exhibitions by Jackson Pollock, Willem de Kooning, Franz Kline, Robert Motherwell, and others were a disconcerting experience to many people. They simply did not understand the art and were generally told something like "You have to *feel* it"—a notion that many took to be an evasion or intellectual snobbery. The fact is, however, that repetition of exposure to such art, together with a receptive attitude, *has* resulted for many in greater understanding and enjoyment.

ART AND NATURE

Many books have been written about art, and many learned theories have attempted to explain it. Some of them are good, some are poor; sometimes they agree, often they disagree. But on one point there is universal agreement. Art is not nature. Art is made by human

[14] Concluding lines of "Ars Poetica," from *Collected Poems 1917–1952* by Archibald MacLeish. Copyright 1952 by Archibald MacLeish. Reprinted by permission of Houghton Mifflin Company (Boston).

Figure 1-8. Franz Kline (1910–), American painter. *Mahoning* (1956). Oil on canvas. Size: 80 by 100 inches. Gift of the Friends of the Whitney Museum of American Art, New York. Photograph by Geoffrey Clements.)

beings. Artists frequently find their inspiration and subject matter in nature, and artists do use nature as a medium, but art is itself not nature. Landscaping has been practiced as an art for thousands of years. The elaborately planned and executed grounds and gardens of eighteenth-century mansions reflect the same aesthetic ideals characteristic of the architecture, music, sculpture, and painting of the period. Although today we may marvel more in wonder than in aesthetic admiration at trees and shrubs grown and shaped like animals or trained into unnatural symmetrical forms, a little reflection will reveal that they share an aesthetic with the other arts of the century. Japanese gardens and bonsai trees are so closely tied to Oriental aesthetics that we recognize the cultural origins of even very bad imitations. More recently, sophisticated, heavy earth-moving machinery has been used to sculpture mountains, valleys, streams, and lakes into waste areas of garbage and sand. In all these instances, nature is the medium, not the finished art. Even so-called "found objects" of some twentieth-century artists are not nature. True, they are sometimes natural objects found *in* nature or objects made by human beings for some other purpose; but when they are placed in a frame, organized into sculpture, or otherwise isolated, they are experienced in a new way, given a new significance. What is art is not nature; what is nature is not art.

There is a story that a woman looking at a painting by Matisse said, "I never saw a woman who looked like that!" and Matisse replied, "Madam, that is not a woman; that is a painting." A woman must be looked at as a woman, and a painting as a painting. In the final scene of *Hamlet* the dying hero enjoins his friend Horatio:

If thou didst ever hold me in thy heart,
Absent thee from felicity a while
And in this harsh world draw thy breath in pain
To tell my story.

No dying man ever said such a thing.

Art is made by human beings, and no matter how close it is to nature, it always shows that it was made by human beings. Therefore we have a right to ask of any work of art: Why did the artist make it? What did the artist want to show? What experience was he or she trying to make clear? What had intrigued the artist so much that sharing it with others seemed important?

As children, probably most of us thought an artist learned how to paint very much as other people learned to sew on buttons, to drive a car, or to write on a typewriter. We supposed that when the artist found a scene to paint, he or she sat down and painted it. In this view, the artist was a kind of human camera to reproduce a scene. Poetry and music seemed as easy, if one "knew how" to write them. The artist needed only to find words to rhyme or notes to form melodies, and that was all. Such a view is, of course, nonsense.

The artist sees or learns something impressive, wants to put it into some form so that others may understand it too, and starts to make a picture, a poem, or a piece of music according to present inspiration and previous training. The artist does not worry much about beauty but wants desperately to get it "right," to have it express just the point he or she has in mind.

Suppose, for instance, that a poet is feeling the intoxication and freshness of the varied and continually changing world, especially as seen in the creatures of earth, air, and water. The words come out in a rush, bringing opposites together in a joyous jumble. And then suppose that the poet wants us to wonder at the creating of these varied forms by an unchanging creator. When Gerard Manley Hopkins has finished, we feel he has captured his experience of awe and delight:

PIED BEAUTY

Glory be to God for dappled things—
    For skies of couple-colour as a brinded cow;

For rose-moles all in stipple upon trout that swim;
Fresh-firecoal chestnut-falls; finches' wings;
   Landscape plotted and pieced—fold, fallow, and plough;
      And áll trádes, their gear and tackle and trim.

All things counter, original, spare, strange;
   Whatever is fickle, freckled (who knows how?)
      With swift, slow; sweet, sour; adazzle, dim;
He fathers-forth whose beauty is past change:
                           Praise him.[15]

   Cézanne painted a landscape which he called *Well and Grinding Wheel in the Forest of the Château Noir* (Figure 1-9, page 20). It looks very much like scenes we have observed, and we would say Cézanne had copied nature. However, we have a photograph of the exact scene (Figure 1-10), and we are able to compare the actual appearance of the landscape with Cézanne's version. First we notice the amount of detail. Cézanne gains unity by paying no attention to the textures of the trees, the grass, or the stones; he paints them all in similar fashion. Next is the arrangement. In the painting the trees on the right are smaller, and there are more of them. The well and the grinding weel in the center are made larger and more important. The path to the well is left out. And while he has kept the curling branches of the trees on the left, Cézanne has made them into a curved pattern which draws the eye to the trees on the right, and with them makes a circular movement which encloses the entire design. In the painting, also, the contrasts between light and dark are made much less pronounced than in the photograph. In the painting we see what Cézanne has done with the landscape, or we see Cézanne's reaction to the landscape. He has changed details from the way they were in nature, and by doing so he has made a design that we want to look at and study. By his deliberate changes the painter has created a new artistic reality in which the various elements are most closely related to one another both intellectually and visually, creating at the same time a new kind of tight space as the elements come forward. It is not nature, but art.

OUR PERCEPTION OF THE WORLD

When we say that art is not nature and that we should not expect to find in art exactly what we find in nature, we assume that all of us see the same things in nature and that our vision is accurate. But only a little study proves the opposite. We may look first at the statue of a bull that was found in front of an ancient Assyrian palace (shown in

[15] From W. H. Gardner and N. H. MacKenzie (eds.), *The Poems of Gerard Manley Hopkins,* 4th ed. (New York: Oxford University Press), 1967.

Figure 1-9. Paul Cézanne (1839–1906), French painter. *Well and Grinding Wheel in the Forest of the Château Noir* (1895–1900). (Oil. Size: 25½ by 31½ inches. Merion, Pa.; Barnes Foundation.)

Figure 1-10. Photograph of location of *Well and Grinding Wheel*, Figure 1-9. (Courtesy of Erie Loran, *Cézanne's Composition*, University of California Press.)

Figure 1-11. *Winged Bull with Five Legs* (ninth century B.C.) (From the Palace of Ashurnasirpal II. Limestone. Height: 11½ feet. New York, Metropolitan Museum of Art; gift of John D. Rockefeller, Jr., 1932.)

Figure 1-12. *Nekaühor and his Namesake Son*, Egyptian, Fifth Dynasty (ca. 2500 B.C.). False door (detail) from offering chamber in tomb of Nekaühor. (Limestone, painted relief. New York, Metropolitan Museum of Art; Rogers Fund, 1907.)

Figure 1-11); it is usually referred to as the "Guardian of the Palace." He is an important animal, large and stately, a very impressive bull. He should be capable of guarding anything that needs to be guarded. But if you look carefully, you can see that this bull is not like nature: he has five legs. There are four on the side, as you would see them if you were looking at him from the side. But come around in front; if you meet a quiet bull head-on, you expect to see two legs; one leg would look queer by itself, and so another leg was added.

Or turn to the Egyptians. We are all familiar with the Egyptian paintings of men and women, with their thin straight bodies, stiff but graceful (Figure 1-12). We like them, but they do not follow nature. We notice first the eyes. If you look straight at a person's face, you see the eyes roughly as oval. If you look at a face in profile, the shape is entirely different. But when drawing a face, the Egyptians made the head in profile with the eyes as of a full face. Moreover, the body was presented facing you, but the arms and legs were in profile. In those cases the artists were, of course, as were the makers of the Assyrian bull, portraying what they knew, what they thought of as the total appearance instead of the actual look of things.

We have come to accept such distortion when we are familiar with it through tradition, as with Egyptian figures. But when a new artist distorts, that is likely to arouse ridicule or anger. The early works of Beethoven were thought to be the ravings of an upstart, and the orchestras of Wagner's time protested that his scores could not be played. The twelve-tone works of the composer Alban Berg, dating from the 1920s and 1930s, were greeted with violent protests because the twelve-tone scale was such a startling departure from the traditional seven-tone scale; it produced a music that sounded "unnatural."

We are all inclined to see and hear only what we know is there, what we have been taught to see and hear. The artist opens our eyes and ears so that we can see the world more clearly. Through the artist, we open our eyes and ears to new visions of life. And it is amazing how quickly we do learn to see what the artist is trying to show us. A few years ago, students looking at Van Gogh's *Landscape with Cypresses* (Color Plate 2) protested that nature never looked like that; now they sit back with general content: "Ah, Van Gogh's *Landscape with Cypresses!*" The revolutionary experiments of Picasso and Braque, known as "cubism," in which a simultaneous presentation is made of different aspects of a form, have by now become part of the common contemporary vocabulary of art (see Figure 2-9). Cubism and its later variants have found their way into the industrial arts—advertising and packaging, for example—where we accept them without a second thought. The wide acceptance of even abstract expressionism, a still more radical movement, has already been mentioned. By the time the abstract expressionists were at work,

however, the question of how far artists should move from natur
had given way to the question of their right to express themselve
however they wished. Since World War II, the various movement
that have evolved—such as hard-edge painting, color-field painting
pop art, op art, minimal art, and impossible art—have seldom bee
practiced with great fidelity to nature.

THE THEORETICAL BASIS OF THIS BOOK

This book is written for people who wish to know more about th
arts—how they are made and how they work—and who wish to b
able to experience them more deeply with confidence that the ex
perience has integrity, that they are not simply projecting their ow
feelings into works of art or trying to feel what they are told the
should feel about art.

This book cannot teach appreciation and it does not pretend to
Appreciation cannot be taught. Appreciation comes from experience
and experience can only be lived. Consequently, our primary ma
terial for a study of the arts should always be works of art themselves
We will show you some of the bases of appreciation, some of th
qualities of art that others have enjoyed, and some of the basic prin
ciples that underlie all the arts. This book invites you to open you
eyes and ears; it is a guide to what you can see and hear in the arts
but it is not a substitute for your very personal looking, listening
and responding.

The process of coming to know a work of art in a very persona
way, of coming to understand it, of arriving at an interpretation of
can be intellectually divided into two kinds of activity: observing an
responding.

Observing may be considered as gathering data. This consists o
taking inventory, noting what is immediately presented to the sense
in the work of art, gathering facts and impressions—the "data" o
analysis—in an orderly way. Naturally, the more experienced on
becomes in doing this, the more information the work of art wi
yield. At the same time that this activity is going on, one become
aware of feelings and attitudes which the handling of the variou
elements evokes. One also begins to speculate about their relation
ships to one another, and to feel out how they may fit into som
structure, some formal organizational pattern. While the orderly
intellectual, observing activity takes place, the reacting, speculative
feeling-out process accompanies it almost unconsciously.

Responding to what is observed is a kind of synthesizing ac
tivity. The more one responds to objective analysis as it reveals mor
and more about the work to the senses, the more one is able to brin

To look at any thing,
If you would know that thing,
You must look at it long:
To look at this green and say
"I have seen spring in these
Woods," will not do — you must
Be the thing you see:
You must be the dark snakes of
Stems and ferny plumes of leaves,
You must enter in
To the small silences between
The leaves,
You must take your time
And touch the very peace
They issue from.

—John Moffitt[16]

the aspects into a converging focus. Even at the analytical stage, several possible explanations of the work may suggest themselves. One tests them in the responding phase by reviewing the sensory data and their tendency to organize themselves. What one becomes more and more aware of is a predominating principle of organization accounting for the dominant effect which the work itself presents. Thus, answers to "What does it all mean?" "What are its themes?" and "What problems—artistic as well as intellectual—has it effectively presented or resolved?" should become apparent (if it is indeed a work of art).

Interpreting a work of art as a human document involves discovering the tendency toward meaning implicit in the work and only then reflecting on its subject as significant for human interest in terms of value. It is this terminal phase of becoming aware of works of art as expressing human concern within particular contexts which makes the study of art a humanistic study. Although it may appear to be obvious or of little significance, we should note that the study of a work of art has a temporal dimension. The longer we expose ourselves openly and inquiringly to it, the stronger is the impression the sensory data make on the mind as "significance." As one becomes thoroughly skilled in this kind of detailed, objective analysis, insights into the expressed values in particular works of art will come more quickly. In the beginning, however, the more time spent in reflective, speculative analysis, the more insightful will be the interpretation.

THE PLAN OF THIS BOOK

The plan of the book is to start with the most nearly obvious principles of art and proceed to those that are less obvious. The first two questions asked of any work are usually: What is it about? and What is it for? The first question concerns the subject, the second the function, of a work of art. Accordingly, subject and function will be discussed first. Subject and function, however, are not essential to all art; there are works without subject and works without function. For this reason, subject and function are grouped together as background.

The next question asked of a work of art is: What is it made of? The answer indicates its medium. Medium, of course, is essential to all art, since any work of art must be presented in some medium.

The next question is: How is it put together? This question is important because it has to do with organization. The elements of an

[16] © 1961 by John Moffitt. Reprinted from his volume *The Living Seed* by permission of Harcourt Brace Jovanovich, Inc. (New York).

art, whether shapes, tones, colors or words, must be arranged according to some pattern to express meaning; in brief, they must b organized before they can become a work of art.

The two remaining questions are in the nature of a comment c the finished creation. One is: What is the personality, the indivic uality, of this work? This brings up the matter of style. The other i How good is it? This is judgment.

If these items are arranged in order, we have the outline of th book:

1. Background
   a. What is the work of art about? (*subject*)
   b. What is it for? (*function*)
2. What is it made of? (*medium*)
3. How is it put together? (*elements and organization*)
4. What is its mood, temper, personality? (*style*)
5. Is it good? (*judgment*)

Admittedly, analyzing a work of art in this way may seem a artificial as dissecting a cadaver in order to find the secret of life. An analysis *can* obscure the fact that the relations among the parts are i fact more important than the totality of individual parts, as is tru of any organic whole. But it is only in sensual perception that this : so. Indeed, there is nothing for the mind which is not first somethin that invites the senses vitally: feeling is the *interplay* between min and the senses which critics have aptly called the "sensuous dia logue." It follows that all the questions in this series overlap. An one of them, pursued in depth, will finally involve all of them. But we were to investigate each question independently, we would hav to reenact the whole history of the study of art.

The very essence of education is to telescope and recapitulate a quickly as possible the investigations which have gone before These, then, are the questions which students of the arts, afte years of inquiry, have arrived at as the most basic, comprehensive and fruitful ones to ask in becoming acquainted with, and unde standing, works of art.

In this plan of approaching works of art with questions and i speaking of our reactions to what is found in the works as responses we have hinted that a meaningful encounter with the arts is a kin of dialogue. Now we state this point directly. These questions ar "openers" in a dialogue in which the works of art, in response to ou questions, ask questions of us. Sometimes they may not give u direct, simple answers, but may refuse to answer, or may preser us with ambiguous answers; they may even appear to want to chang the rules of the game. Nonetheless, the responses—if we have pu

[17] "Engaging Art in Dialogue," *Saturday Review*, July 15, 1967, p. 74.

sued the questions open-mindedly enough and with enough imagination—are a part of the work of art and have meaning. As we shall see, not all art is intended to satisfy or to please or to entertain us; it may challenge us, may disturb us, may pose questions to which there are still no answers.

Subject, function, medium, organization, style, judgment: Considering these, we need to remind ourselves that they are categories—groupings for the many questions we can ask about the arts. They are mere conveniences for calling attention to ways of looking at art. They are not even so separate and distinct as they may appear to be. For the richest and most enjoyable experience with the arts, we must try to read back into these terms the variety which is generalized in them.

When we are considering "subject" and ask "What is it about?" we must remember that any answer given will not be completely satisfactory except in a mere factual sense, for it is the very nature of art not to be caught in words; it is itself. In some art we will find that the subject seems to be the medium itself, its potentialities, the feeling it generates. Other paintings have no representational subject, but record subjective experiences which the painter has had in applying paint to a canvas in a particular way. Such paintings are sometimes called "action painting": the artist records the process of creating them and permits us to share in his or her "acting" in a particular medium. Cézanne once remarked, "The subject of art is paint," and a contemporary artist, Lawrence Weiner, is quoted as saying, "I really believe the subject matter of my art is—art."[18]

When John Cage listed in a concert program a piece entitled "4'33"," and at that point in his concert entered the stage ceremoniously, seated himself attentively at the piano, and sat in absolute silence for the allotted time, he used the medium of music—sound and silences—as his subject. For our heightened attention, he "framed" *silence*, which we usually do not even notice except by its absence.

Nor should we assume that these terms imply judgments about the work of art. If there is no nameable subject in the work, we are not to think it inferior on this count, for, indeed, if it speaks to us at unnameable levels, the artist has succeeded in expanding our experience beyond words and traditional grammar.

Similarly, when we consider "organization" in the arts, we must always be aware of the range of ordering and what the term *ordering* encompasses—from the utterly chaotic at one end of a continuum to the strictly mechanical geometric at the other. Different points on the continuum evoke different feelings and emotions in us. The artist orders the work to record a particular emotion and to elicit

[18] Quoted in Lucy Lippard, *Six Years: The Dematerialization of the Art Object from 1966–1972* (New York: Praeger Publishers, Inc., 1973), p. 130.

that particular emotion in us. We must not therefore fall into th
unthinking attitude that symmetry and carefully contrived balanc
are always virtues in a work and that varying patterns of disorder ar
bad. All the possibilities of arrangements are expressive and poten
tially appropriate, depending on the artist's need for them in creat
ing a particular work.

For example, it may appear from a first glance at *Mahonin*
(Figure 1-8) that Kline has haphazardly painted black lines across th
canvas with a heavily saturated brush. However, each of the irregula
black bars crossing the surface is formed by numerous brush stroke
varied in character and density, and the off-white shapes which forn
the background are as carefully painted as the black bars. Balance i
the painting is created by the thrust and counterthrust of triangula
black and white shapes between the vertical sides of the picture
What appears at first to be completely spontaneous organization will
on examination, reveal a careful repetition of shapes and placemen
of lines to create a strong, stable composition.

Similarly in music, dissonances or so-called "discords" ma
sound unpleasant and meaningless by themselves, but may be ver
eloquent and essential in particular emotional contexts.

THE SECRETS OF ART

There is always more in a work of art than is consciously, deliber
ately, put into it by the artist.

No matter how carefully we analyze a work of art, studying it
parts and their relationships and comparing it with other works, i
we have indeed experienced the work, we will in the end feel dis
satisfied, feel that somehow its secret magic has slipped through ou
rational nets. This is one characteristic which distinguishes human
istic expression from scientific expression and mathematical expres
sion, which work within closed systems. The feeling has its tru
origins in forgotten, never completely known, parts of our being anc
seeks through mediums and techniques to establish itself objectively
No matter what our beliefs, our religion, or our philosophy, ther
always remain questions.

Whatever we experience, whatever part of our experience we ar
able to share with others, questions seem to persist as a part of ou
humanity, however many certainties we accumulate. What is reality
What is the meaning of life? What are we about?

Art is about experience. More than that, it is born in experience
it is an artifact of the artist's experience of a reality. It is more authen
tic than expository language because it does not force experience intc
words and a grammar which conceal as much as they reveal. It i
more intimate and personal than such exposition because the life o

impulse, the vibration of our senses, imprints itself on a medium. Art is as uniquely individual as a footprint in wet sand or a fingerprint in clay. It is so personal that artists are usually hesitant to talk about their art, fearing that in attempting to translate it into words, they will add or subtract from the experiences recorded.

Artists, like the rest of us, live in a culture, in a place, and at a time in history. Whether they are Egyptians making bas-reliefs in a stone cliff or our own contemporaries welding pieces of old automobiles together to create unique forms in a landscape, they are making statements which probe concepts of life and reality. Such concepts have come to them in part through the common wisdom and accepted ideas of the time, but, more importantly, through personal experiences and feelings which resonate against contemporary conditions.

It is a part of our humanity that we are forever organizing our reality, ordering the events we experience and our feelings about them, placing ourselves and our environment in some great scheme of things. Art has always been a way of making nonverbal statements about the reality we experience, about what we perceive as real, about what we hope is real, and about what we feel ought to be real. One way of approaching art, therefore—especially in our century, when we have come to distrust the very appearances of the world as reality—is to examine it as a representation of statements by artists about the reality they have known.

One of the reasons why art has been produced by all people, however primitive—and certainly a reason why we value art and seek it out—is the experience consciously and unconsciously documented in it. The arts speak to us at our most human levels of feeling and responding. Although art does not answer our questions about life, authentic art does probe questions and does give us insight into the search by other human beings for answers. Many critics have commented upon the similarity of works of art to dreams. They form themselves in the deep matrix of our unconscious selves. We cannot deny their relevance even when we do not understand them, even when we are unable to explain them in words. How many of us, when we have told someone a dream, have felt that we have communicated it as it really was? The arts have these qualities in greater or lesser degree; they satisfy our psychological needs in a confirming sort of way, though they may or may not have a practical function in a workaday world.

As we study works of art, therefore, coming to understand how they "work," how they are put together, we should not close ourselves to the secrets they reveal to us—sometimes as unconsciously as they hold them.

[19] *Film and the Critical Eye* (New York: Macmillan, 1975), p. 12. Copyright © 1975 by Macmillan Publishing Company, Inc.
[20] Quoted in Denis Thomas, *Abstract Art* (New York: E. P. Dutton and Company, 1976), p. 4.

SUMMARY

1. The human need for art and its importance to life among all peoples at all times have been attested to by historians, sociologists, and anthropologists.

2. The arts existed and were appreciated long before they became objects for study and long before there was a technical terminology for discussing them. The basic language of the arts is built into us biologically and psychologically. As human beings, we are all "critics" of the arts and potential creators of arts.

3. The best preparation for study of the arts is "openness," the willingness to place ourselves in the presence of a work of art, to experience it personally. Our tools in coming to know the arts intimately and to have informed judgments about them are our senses. Our sensitivities and observational acuity are best cultivated by giving attention to art objects themselves. Teachers as guides to our observing and textbooks which focus our attention on particular aspects of art for reflection about their significance are helpful at all stages in the study of art, but they are not indispensable.

4. It is our personal experience with the arts which is important. Anything which hinders experiencing them personally and fully is antithetical to them. Such experience frequently bypasses verbalization and intellectualization.

5. Art is not nature. Because of our familiarity with the camera and its ability to record detailed images of nature and persons when placed in a proper location, we sometimes have a tendency to judge visual art by its verisimilitude, its accuracy in realistically representing objects, persons, and environments. Sometimes this fact leads us to consider "truth to nature" as an important criterion in judging a work of art; but even representational art is not and cannot be nature. Individual artists have their own very personal ways of seeing. They work in a medium and organize elements of the art in the medium to express their personal perceptions and feelings.

6. Analysis of a work of art—however careful, detailed, and technical—often leaves us with the frustrated feeling that the essence, the thing which makes it a work of art, has somehow slipped through our net. The feelings which have been generated or heightened by analysis are, in the end, something different from it, or more than it. They are the work of art given its full freedom and power to move us, to delight us beyond the abstraction of words and our grammar of linear rationality.

ONE
BACKGROUND

The origin of art:
The discrepancy between physical fact and psychic effect

The content of art:
Visual formulation of our reaction to life

The measure of art:
The ratio of effort to effect

The aim of art:
Revelation and evocation of vision

—Josef Albers*

* From Eugene Gomringer (ed.), *Josef Albers: His Work as a Contribution to Visual Articulation in the Twentieth Century* (New York: Wittenborn Art Books, Inc., 1967). By permission of Wittenborn and Anni Albers.

2 SUBJECT

What is the subject of the following two selections? The first is from the contemporary American poet Elizabeth Bishop; the second is from one of the leading modern American novelists, Saul Bellow.

Think of the storm roaming the sky uneasily
Like a dog looking for a place to sleep in,
listen to it growling.

Think how they must look now, the mangrove keys
lying out there unresponsive to the lightning
in dark coarse-fibred families . . .

    —Elizabeth Bishop (1911–   , American poet),
    "Little Exercise"[1]

Hard work? No, it wasn't really so hard. He wasn't used to walking and stair-climbing, but the physical difficulty of his new job was not what George Grebe felt most. He was delivering relief checks in the Negro district, and although he was a native Chicagoan this was not a part of the city he knew

---

[1] Reprinted with the permission of Farrar, Straus & Giroux, Inc. (New York), from *The Complete Poems* by Elizabeth Bishop, copyright 1946 by Elizabeth Bishop, copyright renewed 1973 by Elizabeth Bishop. "Little Exercise" appeared originally in *The New Yorker*.

much about—it needed a depression to introduce him to it. . . . He coul
find the streets and numbers, but the clients were not where they wer
supposed to be. . . .

—Saul Bellow (1915– , American novelist),
"Looking for Mr. Green"[2]

WHAT IS SUBJECT?

Subject is the term used for whatever is represented in a work of art
In Cézanne's *Well and Grinding Wheel* (Figure 1-9) the subject is th
landscape. In the poem quoted above, the subject is a storm; in th
prose selection, the subject is a welfare investigator looking for hi
clients. Each of the caryatids (columns sculptured in human shape
on the famous Porch of the Maidens on the Erechtheum (Figure 2-1
represents a young woman. The short piano composition by Rave
called "The Fountain" shows the rise and fall of the water in a foun
tain. In brief, the subject of a work of art answers the question: Wha
is it about?

Not all arts have subjects. Those arts without subject are callec
"nonobjective"; they do not represent anything. They are what they
are without reference to anything in the natural world. The caryatids
of the Erechtheum represent maidens, but the other columns of the
building do not represent anything at all. Bach's cantata *Christ Lag ir
Todesbanden* has a subject, as the title indicates—"Christ Lay in the
Bonds of Death"—but his Brandenburg Concertos do not have a subject. Subject is not essential to art.

SUBJECT IN THE ARTS

Not only do some works of art have subject while others do not, but
in the matter of subject we find characteristic differences between
one art and another. Architecture, for example, is essentially an art
which is not representational. Occasionally we will see buildings
made to look like ice cream freezers or coffeepots, if they are used for
selling ice cream or coffee, but they are recognized as freakish examples, and fortunately they are rare. A building is constructed for
a certain purpose (a home, a factory, an office); and it may be in a
definite style (classical, Gothic, Romanesque); but usually it has no
subject. A building may, however, show details that are representational, as we saw in the Erechtheum, although as a whole it has no
subject.

[2] Excerpt from "Looking for Mr. Green" from *Seize the Day* by Saul Bellow. Copyright 1951 by
Saul Bellow. Reprinted by permission of The Viking Press, Inc. (New York).

Figure 2-1. Erectheum, Porch of the Maidens (420–393 B.C.). (Pentelic marble. Height of each caryatid: 7 feet, 9 inches. Athens, Acropolis. Photograph, Office of Press and Information, Embassy of Greece.)

. . . The sensitive observer of sculpture must learn to feel shape simply as shape, not as description or reminiscence. He must, for example, perceive an egg as a simple single solid shape, quite apart from its significance as food, or from the literary idea that it will become a bird. And so with solids, such as a shell, a nut, a plum, a pear, a tadpole, a mushroom, a mountain peak, a kidney, a carrot, a tree trunk, a bird, a bud, a lark, a lady-bird, a bulrush, a bone. From these he can go on to appreciate more complex forms or combinations of several forms.

—Henry Moore[3]

If architecture is the art where subject is least common, literature is the one where it is most common. When we read words we expect them to be *about* something. There are so-called poems and bits of prose which have no subject, but they are rare. So important is subject in literature that we usually name any piece of writing by its content: "a novel of adventure," "a psychological novel," "a literary essay," "a poem about nature."

Traditional sculpture and painting usually have subject. In looking at a painting or a statue, we expect to recognize the subject, to know what it is about: a man, a horse, a landscape. And as in literature, painting and sculpture are classified according to subject. Paintings are identified as, for example, landscapes, seascapes, portraits, figure paintings, paintings of animals. Statues are classified as portraits, single or group figures, animals, etc.

There is however, a great deal of sculpture and painting without subject. The sculptor or the painter, like the architect, may make a design which is interesting in itself and which expresses the artist's idea though it has no subject. Examples of this type of art are Henry Moore's *Two Forms* (Figure 2-2) and Piet Mondrian's *Composition with Blue and White* (Color Plate 3). In works such as these the artists do not expect the critic to imagine any specific subject. In Moore's sculpture, for example, we perceive shapes common in nature, a larger one hovering over a smaller one, the smaller inclining toward the larger. We sense a relationship, but is it protection, love, the act

[3] Quoted in Philip James, *Henry Moore on Sculpture* (New York: The Viking Press, Inc., 1966), p. 64.

Figure 2-2. Henry Moore (1898–   ), British sculptor. *Two Forms* (1934). (Pynkado wood. Height: 11 inches. New York, Museum of Modern Art; Sir Michael Sadler Fund. Photograph, Soichi Sunami.)

of separating? The group is unified and richly evocative, but deliberately ambiguous. Even the Mondrian can perhaps be related to some stimulus form and color which the artist reduced to the final, completely nonobjective forms we see here.

Of the combined arts, theater and opera always have subjects, dance may or may not have subject. The minor arts, such as textiles, metalwork, and pottery, sometimes have subject and sometimes do not; in these arts the subject is often a matter of indifference. One may eat with a spoon for months without ever noticing whether the design on the handle represents grapes or roses, or whether it has any subject. Even in wallpaper and dress materials, where the design is more conspicuous, subject is of little importance. Choice is often made on the basis of design and color rather than subject.

Music occupies a position about halfway between literature and architecture. A great deal of music has no subject: the sonata, the étude, the symphony, etc. On the other hand, much music has subject; we have already mentioned "The Fountain" and *Christ Lag in Todesbanden*. Music without subject is called *"absolute music"*; music with subject is called *"program music."*

Sometimes a distinction is made between program music which actually imitates the subject and that which merely sets the mood and suggests the story or picture the composer had in mind. "The Fountain" obviously belongs to the former group: it imitates the motion of the fountain, its ceaseless flow, its constant change, and its monotony. An example of the latter group is the composition called *Pictures at an Exhibition.* As the title indicates, Moussorgsky represents himself as visiting an art exhibit and looking at one picture after another. There are eleven pictures, with such different subjects as "The Old Castle," "Children in the Tuileries Gardens," and "Two Polish Jews." There is also a theme which represents the artist walking from one picture to the next. In this composition Moussorgsky tries to give the mood of each picture—romantic or gay, comic or quarrelsome—but he does not imitate the subject itself.

Music is unique among the arts in that it cannot make its subject clear. Even when the music is definitely imitative, as in Rimsky-Korsakov's "Flight of the Bumblebee," the subject is not always clear. If the music is played with no clue to the subject given, many people will not recognize what it is about. One person, hearing the piece about the bumblebee, realized that the music had subject, but decided that it represented a blizzard.

SUBJECT AND CONTENT

The first question which comes to mind when we encounter a work of art for the first time has to do with its subject: What is it about? In other words, we want to know what it represents, what its theme is. This is a question which asks about the *who, what, when,* and *where* of the work. It is the question which we have been discussing, but obviously there is more to a work of art than recognizing what is or is not represented in it. To stop at this point is like assuming that one understands a sentence when one has identified its subject or that one understands a piece of literature when one has defined all the nouns used in it. Information of this kind does not move us very far in understanding or experiencing the art. Later questions, therefore, have to do with what the effects of works of art are and how they have been achieved—the *why* and *how* of them. Finally, we come to the questions: What does it mean? How do I feel about it? How do I relate to it? How do I value it?

Subject, therefore, is sometimes used in two ways in discussing works of art. It is used to refer to the thing represented, the immediately perceived subject matter when the work is first brought into focus of attention; that is the sense in which we will be using it in this text. However, *subject* is also sometimes used to refer to the larger, total meaning of the work after one has entered into dialogue with it and has considered it in detail. We shall refer to this broader meaning of *subject* as "content."

Beyond the question of subject (What is it about?), the other questions we shall be asking will constitute one side of a dialogue. Your increasingly accurate and incisive observations and heightened awareness of your feelings as you attend to a work and what these responses tell you will constitute the other. Their integration will be the content of the work for you.

These two levels of meaning in works of art, what we shall call subject and content, can be illustrated from Arthur Miller's play *The Crucible.* The play presents an account of the witch trials in Salem, Massachusetts, in 1692. This account, presented dramatically, is the nominal, ostensible subject matter of the play. However, *The Crucible* was written during the McCarthy era in the early 1950s, a time when unrestrained, vicious, and at times irresponsible, accusations of "communism" were being made against many people. A disturbing aspect of the situation was that accused persons were frequently accepted as being guilty before the charges could be proved or disproved. With such incidents so widespread, it is doubtful that any person at a performance of the play missed the parallels in fantatical self-righteousness, false accusations, rampant suspicion, and the distrust and misery caused by them. It is a demonstration of the presence of such destructive possibilities in persons who believe themselves unconditionally right which makes up the content of the play. In 1967, long after McCarthyism had run its course, when Miller reworked the play for a special CBS television broadcast, he made this larger meaning clear in one sentence he added to the narrator's speech at the end of the play: "Wherever men have lost all faith in one another, the ancient cry of 'witch' still hovers on the wind, and it can still destroy."

Let us examine a second and more difficult example of the difference between simple identification of what is represented and the insights that emerge from analysis, using the other questions outlined in Chapter 1 (page 24). Consider *Woman I* (Color Plate 4), painting by Willem de Kooning, usually considered one of the important painters of our time. (*Woman V*, another painting in de Kooning's "Woman" series, was bought in 1974 by the Australian National Gallery for more than $750,000, the largest amount ever paid for a painting by a living artist.)

What is de Kooning's *Woman I* about? A first glance at the painting tells us that it represents a seated woman. That is a first answer: "De Kooning's painting is of a seated woman, somewhat strangely abstractly represented."

As we look more closely, we see that she is quite large, overweight, with very large, pendulous breasts; that, even so, she has trim ankles but swollen feet, and is wearing ridiculous spike-heeled shoes; that her skirt is inappropriately short for her size and age; that her knees sprawl apart; that she has shrunken cheeks; that she wears too much makeup; and that her smile is a leer. Considering these points, we conclude the treatment is consistently one of burlesque, of exposing bizarre foibles of a siren who is now old but is desperately clinging to a self-image that is no longer realistic. We arrive at an answer which accounts consistently for more of the painting: "With a mixture of violent brush strokes of pure paint and delicately mixed flesh colors, the artist has presented us with a burlesque of a once seductive woman now grown old, but displaying herself as if she still had her youth and attractiveness."

As we examine the treatment of the medium, the mixture of quickly brushed areas and the carefully modeled portions, we become aware that what seemed at first to be hasty, spontaneous, even careless painting is probably painstakingly done for purposes of communication. We study the colors, seek reasons for their placement on the canvas, play our observations against the tentative conclusions we have reached. Suddenly, to the left of the woman's face, we see an eye. Another face? It is facing the older woman. It must be a face—there is a body; the breasts double as the shoulder of the central figure; the second figure is wearing a yellow dress. Could this be the shadow image of the older woman as a younger woman? Is de Kooning showing us woman at different stages in her life? Suddenly we notice a strange area of yellow-blond to the right of the woman's right breast. Is this the back of a head of long hair? We check. There is a body—of a child. She is sitting on the knee of the older woman, looking at her, it seems. Childhood, young womanhood, old womanhood! Considering the care with which certain areas of the painting have been done, the way in which the background is broken into multicolored areas, the clearly recognizable eye, the distortions which fuse the woman's and the young girl's body, we conclude that they were either put there or left there deliberately. Thus we arrive at another level in answering the question; What is it about? At this level, the answer becomes almost unphrasable. We are back with the title: *Woman*, not "A Woman," not the name of some particular woman. (One of de Kooning's paintings is, for example, titled *Marilyn Monroe*.) Although the burlesque and satiric aspects of the painting when first seen may suggest a vicious dislike of women, or of *a* woman, a more careful study of it leads us to conclude the opposite. The artist is projecting the contradictions he saw in many women of his time—thus, the generalized title *Woman*—the image as seen by the artist and the self-image which is a synthesis of memories of childhood and youth and an internalized cultural ideal of the female. In the way he projects these contradictions, he is expressing indignation at such discrepancies.

If any reassurance is needed that we have not been irresponsible in our responding to the painting, it comes from the various accounts de Kooning has given us of his way of working, of "participating" in his paintings as they developed; of finding images, generating images, destroying images; and of how the paintings changed as he experienced them. Further, in this particular instance, we are told by Harold Rosenberg that de Kooning worked on *Woman I* for two years, during which the painting changed many times; and Thomas Hess tells us that it was painted literally hundreds of times.[4] For a while it showed a girl in a yellow dress seen on Fourteenth Street; later, it came to contain mothers de Kooning had passed on East Side park benches and other women.

Traces of these stages in the creation of the work are still to be found in it, and some of them seem to have been integrated as shadow images suggesting stages in the life cycle of the contemporary female.

[4] Thomas Hess, *De Kooning* (New York: Harry M. Abrams, Inc., Publishers, 1974), pp. 30 ff.

This kind of analysis clearly goes beyond answering the question: What is the subject? It enters into dialogue with the way the
subject has been presented, how the medium, elements, and organization have been used to give the work "content" beyond simply
representation.

WAYS OF PRESENTING THE SUBJECT

Realism, Abstraction

Realism   As we have said, no art is ever like nature. Even when
artists choose a subject from nature, they change, select, and arrange
details to express the ideas they want to make clear. Often the presentation of details and the organization of them in the work are so
nearly obvious, and seem so natural, that we do not notice that the
work is not like nature, as in Cézanne's *Well and Grinding Wheel* (Figure 1-9). When this is the case, we say the work is "realistic."
Another level of reality may be seen in the Italian Renaissance painting by Domenico Ghirlandajo, *Old Man and Boy* (Color Plate 11; Color
Plates 11 through 16 follow page 88) or in Jan van Eyck's *Annunciation* (Color Plate 28; Color Plate 28 is in the group following page 216).
Ghirlandajo and van Eyck have utilized very detailed elements from
nature, photographic touches that bring us closer to nature itself.
Such works we call "naturalistic" rather than realistic.

Figure 2-3. Constantin Brancusi
(1876–1957), Roumanian sculptor. *Bird
in Space* (1925). (Polished bronze,
marble and oak base. Height: 50¼
inches. Philadelphia Museum of Art;
The Louise and Walter Arensberg
Collection. Photograph, A. J. Wyatt,
staff photographer.)

Abstraction   Abstraction is another way of presenting a subject.
Sometimes an artist becomes so interested in one phase of a scene or
a situation that the subject is not shown at all as an objective reality,
but only as the artist's idea of it or feeling about it. For example,
Brancusi is impressed by the grace of a bird in flight, by the sweep
of its body as it flies thruogh the air, so he tries to represent those
qualities in his statute *Bird in Space* (Figure 2-3). It does not look like
a bird, and it is not supposed to look like a bird. It is supposed to
convey an impression of a bird's grace and speed.
Mondrian called one of his paintings *Broadway Boogie-Woogie*
(Color Plate 5). Again, it does not look like Broadway, or boogie-
woogie, yet it suggests characteristics of several things we associate
with dance: the perforated roll of the mechanical player piano,
monotony of beat, strong accent, improvisation, and the bright lights
of the city. Probably none of us could recognize the subject by ourselves, but once it has been suggested, we can see the connection.
This painting looks very much like the Mondrian painting we saw
earlier, *Composition with Blue and White* (Color Plate 3). But that has
no apparent subject, and this has. Both types are commonly called
abstract; for the one without subject, however, a more exact term is
nonobjective.

Josef Albers's woodcut *Aquarium* (Figure 2-4) can be enjoyed as a pure abstraction in which dark shapes and negative shapes—that is, the white spaces between the dark ones—are put together to create a sense of movement within an oval contained in a rectangular frame. We can enjoy the play between the small vertical oval at the left and the large horizontal ovals in the center and at the right, and the repetition of the small vertical triangle on the left in a vertical position at the right. We may even notice a tendency for the solid and negative spaces to change places as we study the painting. However, when we know that Albers called the woodcut *Aquarium*, we can see that the black bar across the top is the surface of water, that the rounded corners at the bottom outline an aquarium, and that the in-and-out movement of the dark and white spaces creates an impression of a fish swimming.

Since the subject often would not be known without the title, question is frequently raised about giving a name to a picture or a musical composition that in no way bears any likeness to the object named. Would it not be better to consider all such works nonobjective? Probably not. The title, as in Albers's *Aquarium* (Figure 2-4), usually helps one to understand what the artist had in mind. In some cases, as in Brancusi's sculpture *Bird in Space* (Figure 2-3), Honegger's composition "Pacific 231," or Ravel's "Fountain," the name offers a real explanation of the artist's purpose and idea. In others, as in Picasso's *Ma Jolie* (Figure 2-9) or Moussorgsky's *Pictures at an Exhibition*, the title gives the source for the original inspiration.

Between abstraction and realism there are many ways of presenting the subject. Henry Moore's *Reclining Figure* (Figure 2-5) is fairly

Figure 2-5. Henry Moore. *Reclining Figure* (ca. 1935). (Elm wood. Size: 19 inches high, 35 inches long, 17¼ inches wide. Buffalo, N.Y., Albright-Knox Art Gallery, Room of Contemporary Art Fund.)

It might seem from what I have said of shape and form that I regard them as ends in themselves. Far from it. I am very much aware that associational, psychological factors play a large part in sculpture. The meaning and significance of form itself probably depend on the countless associations of man's history. For example, rounded forms convey an idea of fruitfulness, maturity, probably because of the earth, women's breasts and most fruits are rounded, and these shapes are important because they have this background in our habits of perception. I think the humanist organic element will always be for me of fundamental importance in sculpture, giving sculpture its vitality.

—Henry Moore[5]

close to an abstraction; El Greco's *Resurrection* (Color Plate 6), on the other hand, is close to realism. As in many of El Greco's painting the bodies are unnaturally long. El Greco was illustrating that part of the Apostles' Creed which says that Christ "was crucified, died, and was buried. He descended into hell. The third day he rose again from the dead." In his picture El Greco wanted the body of Christ to rise and it does seem to rise from the mass of writhing bodies around it. A body of normal size would have seemed dumpy, stodgy, and still. For works like the El Greco (or like the Van Gogh shown in Color Plate 2) which are close to realism, the term *expressionist* has been used, and for works that approach abstraction, like Moore's *Reclining Figure* (Figure 2-5), the term *organic* is sometimes used. The use of these or other terms, however, is unimportant. It is important to realize that each artist presents a subject in accordance with his or her idea of that subject. For instance Picasso's *Old Guitarist* (Figure 2-6) seems more distorted when compared with his realistic *Blue Boy* (Figure 2-7) than when compared with his *Fernande* (Figure 2-8). And *Fernande* seems almost realistic when put by the side of *Ma Jolie* (Figure 2-9), in which the woman has disappeared into a series of straight-edged, transparent planes which overlap and penetrate one another in the typical cubist fashion.

Sign and Symbol

When we drive down a street and see a red light suspended over an intersection, we know that the light means "Stop." A musician opens a piece of music, sees a certain sign, and knows that the notes which

[5] Quoted in Philip James, *Henry Moore on Sculpture* (New York: The Viking Press, Inc., 1966), p. 6

Figure 2-6. *Far left:* Pablo Picasso (1881–1973), Spanish painter. *The Old Guitarist* (1903). (Oil on wood. Size: 47¾ by 32½ inches. Courtesy of the Art Institute of Chicago.)

Figure 2-7. *Near left:* Picasso. *Blue Boy* (1905). (Gouache. Size: 40 by 22½ inches. Private collection, U.K.)

Figure 2-8. *Below left:* Picasso. *Fernande* (1909). (Oil on canvas. Size; 24½ by 16¾ inches. *Fernande*, Pablo Picasso, © S.P.A.D.E.M., Paris, 1977.)

Figure 2-9. *Below right:* Picasso. *Ma Jolie (Woman with a Guitar)* (1911–1912). (Oil on canvas. Size: 39⅜ by 25¾ inches. New York, Museum of Modern Art; acquired through the Lillie P. Bliss Bequest.)

follow are in the treble clef. These are signs; each of them conveys very specific bit of information. However, when the poet writes "M love is like a red, red rose," although we may know what each wor signifies in isolation, together they clearly hint at something beyon the word-thing meaning. The one-to-one relationship between th separate words and the things signified in *context* are no longer *signs* but *symbols*. This distinction is important in studying the arts.

Signs have a literal quality. Symbols combine them with an ab stract or suggestive meaning. Symbols, in this sense, mean mor than they say. A "crucible" was a medieval vessel in which metal could be separated from the less valuable materials which becom liquid at a specific temperature. "Crucible" is in this sense a sign When Arthur Miller writes a play dealing with the religious an social pressures of a community struggling against delusion an hysteria and entitles the play *The Crucible*, the word becomes sym bolic. Shells have beautiful, mathematically symmetrical shapes an curves. Throughout history, they have been admired. When Jocer Utzon, the Danish architect, uses a group of shell shapes to enclos an opera house at water level on a finger of land, the result suggest sails or gulls or breaking waves and becomes symbolic in evokin feelings and suggestions beyond shell shapes. (See Figure 1-3.) Eer Saarinen uses a shape suggesting the spread wings of a bird in fligh for the TWA Terminal Building at Kennedy Airport (see Figur 14-36).

A sign has a one-to-one reference to what it signifies; it poin to something in some context other than its own. The individu shapes in a configuration of shapes; the letters in a word; the tone in a melody and the notes signifying them; the two-dimensiona planes of a three-dimensional volume in a configuration defining face, as in Picasso's semiabstraction *Fernande* (Figure 2-8)—these ar all signs carrying bits of information which enter into perception a a meaningful whole. Therefore, *one* sign to *one* information bit sig nifies, points; a configuration of signs taken together has meanin We literally read the signs of any language—a script, notation, body language cue—in a time and space context, linearly, scanning th bits (as we do letters) in groups. In this way the signs (attributes) i the de Vries statue shown in (Figure 2-10) must be taken together t identify it as a representation of the messenger of the gods, Mercur —winged cap and sandals, hand pointing to the sky (divine mes senger), staff and intertwined snakes (healer). The caduceus—th staff entwined with snakes—was thought to have magical power over sleeping, waking, and dreaming, and so became identified wit healing. It is now the symbol of the medical profession and, by adop tion, of the Army Medical Corps.

A sign or group of signs becomes symbolic when it expresse

Figure 2-10. Attributed to Adriaen de Vries. *Mercury* (ca. 1574). (Bronze. Height: 5 feet, 9 inches. Washington, D.C., National Gallery of Art; Widener Collection.)

more than it strictly signifies. It has literal meaning *and* suggestive meaning—i.e., denotation *and* connotation. It is information charged with emotion. In Picasso's *Fernande* (Figure 2-8), the planes are cues which help us read a human face to which we react with at least the emotion that accompanies recognition.

Unlike signs in a one-to-one relationship, symbols do not have definite meanings. Their meanings are as broad as the range of emotions they elicit, that is, their connotations. In the Christian tradition, S. Peter is represented with keys (a sign) whose meaning can be understood only within the biblical tradition. To the Hindu, of course, this context is not as rich or meaningful as it is for a Christian, to whom it is the representation by a highly emotional symbol of spiritual power "on earth as it is in heaven." Similarly, the head in Figure 3-24 can be identified as the Buddha by the four attributes of the usual Indian representation: the "bump of wisdom," here covered with a topknot of hair; the tuft of hair between the eyes, sometimes called "the eye of knowledge," which his followers imitate with cosmetics (the *urnao*); the eyes lowered in humility; the pendulous earlobes with long slits made by the princely jewelry he once wore but abandoned in renouncing his worldly life. But even with this identification the meaning is not as rich to a Christian as to a Hindu. Only a scholar would recognize Dionysus (Bacchus) in the vase painting by Execias (Figure 2-11), which brings together the attributes of a wine harvest god (the grape clusters of Bacchus) with the adventures of a sea god (the dolphins), thus blending two mythological sources into one narrative. The legend is that one day while in a drunken sleep, Bacchus was kidnapped by pirates to be sold into slavery. Waking from his stupor in the hold of a ship, he demanded to be taken to Naxos. When his kidnappers refused, he change< them into dolphins, while vines laden with grapes sprang from th< mast. Thus the legend and the oral tradition from diverse sources ar< visually brought together in a new configuration of emblems to ex< plain how and why a harvest god became a sea god.

There are many symbols of the Christian church: Peter is repre< sented with a key because of Christ's saying that he gave Peter th< keys of the kingdom of heaven (Matthew 16:19). Paul is often repre< sented as a bald old man carrying a sword. The symbols of the fou< Evangelists Matthew, Mark, Luke, and John were commonly used i< the Middle Ages and are frequently found today: Matthew is sym< bolized as a winged man, Mark a winged lion, Luke a winged ox< and John an eagle. We see these in a characteristic setting in th< tympanum—the curved space above the door—of the cathedral a< Chartres (Figure 14-23).

There are also private symbols in art; often only the artist know< what a private symbol represents. The parables of the New Testa< ment are such symbols; the disciples often had to ask Jesus to explai< them, as in this case:

Behold, a sower went forth to sow. And when he sowed, some seeds fell b< the wayside, and the fowls came and devoured them up: Some fell upo< stony places, where they had not much earth: and forthwith they sprun< up, because they had no deepness of earth: And when the sun was up, the< were scorched; and because they had no root, they withered away. An< some fell among thorns; and the thorns sprung up, and choked them. Bu< other fell into good ground, and brought forth fruit, some an hundredfold< some sixtyfold, some thirtyfold.

—Matthew 13:3–8

The hidden meanings here are obvious when we see that certai< parallels—between preaching and sowing, between diversity of so< and climate and acceptance of the Word, between harvest and salva< tion—are carried out consistently in the context of the metaphor.

The parable of the sower is prophetic of a revolution in culture< when the New Testament becomes the source of a new system o< social and moral values with new signs. An example is the whit< banner, signifying victory over the flesh, in El Greco's *Resurrectio<* (Color Plate 6). The Word is triumphant over earthly powers, sig< nified by military arms and the consternation of the soldiers guard< ing the empty tomb. We can read such signs because a certain part o< our cultural heritage, expressed in holy images charged with emotio< (icons), makes us literate in these graphics. But we need outsid< information to read a comparable icon from another cultural traditio< (see Figure 2-23).

Sometimes one is not certain whether a symbol is intended, a< in Robert Frost's poem "Stopping by Woods on a Snowy Evening."

Whose woods these are I think I know.
His house is in the village though;
He will not see me stopping here
To watch his woods fill up with snow.

My little horse must think it queer
To stop without a farmhouse near
Between the woods and frozen lake
The darkest evening of the year.

He gives his harness bells a shake
To ask if there is some mistake.
The only other sound's the sweep
Of easy wind and downy flake.

The woods are lovely, dark and deep,
But I have promises to keep,
And miles to go before I sleep,
And miles to go before I sleep.

—Robert Frost (1857–1963, American poet),
"Stopping by Woods on a Snowy Evening" (1923)[6]

Here no separate literary image—snow filling up the neighbor's woods, the habit-ridden horse, the contemplative drive—carries a specific meaning in the way the whole does in expressing a definite mood. Frost as a poet gives us a concrete picture to express an abstraction, a way of expressing a feeling in the aesthetic form of poetic language which a prose paraphrase of the subject would not reveal. The poem itself is therefore symbolic to whoever has had a similar experience which can be recreated from images in memory. But, again, how would one who had never seen snow understand such a poem? A prose translation would give all the information contained implicitly in Frost's poem, but it would miss the significance, even if one had an encyclopedia at hand with the same explicit information but lacked the simple experience. The meaning would be as hidden (parabolic rather than symbolic) as the metaphor of Jesus concerning the coming of the kingdom of heaven.

In Sandburg's "Grass," the grass that covers all is clearly a symbol; the poem means more than that grass grows on battlefields:

Pile the bodies high at Austerlitz and Waterloo.
Shovel them under and let me work—
I am the grass; I cover all.

And pile them high at Gettysburg
And pile them high at Ypres and Verdun.
Shovel them under and let me work.
Two years, ten years, and passengers ask the conductor:
What place is this?
Where are we now?

I am the grass,
Let me work.

    —Carl Sandburg (1878–1967, American poet),
      "Grass" (1918)[7]

The grass in this poem symbolizes time, oblivion, human forgetful
ness of the sacrifices of soldiers. A somewhat similar symbolism is
used by the contemporary American Robert Lowell, in *For the Union
Dead* (1964). The symbolism here is much more complicated, how
ever, and the theme is how values for which people die may be
ignored by others:

". . . One morning last March
I pressed against the new barbed and galvanized

fence on the Boston Common. Behind their cage,
yellow dinosaur steamshovels were grunting
as they dropped up tons of mush and grass
to gouge their underworld garage . . .
shaking over the excavations, as it faces Colonel Shaw
and his bell-cheeked Negro infantry
on St. Gaudens' shaking Civil War relief,
propped by a plank splint against the garage's earthquake . . .

Shaw's father wanted no monument
except the ditch,
where his son's body was thrown
and lost with his 'niggers.'

The Aquarium is gone. Everywhere,
giant-finned cars nose forward like fish;
a savage servility
slides by on grease."

    —Robert Lowell (1917–   ), American poet),
      from *For the Union Dead*[8]

[7] From *Cornhuskers*, by Carl Sandburg, copyright, 1918, by Holt, Rinehart and Winston, Inc.; copyright, 1946, by Carl Sandburg. Reprinted by permission of Harcourt Brace Jovanovich, Inc.
[8] Reprinted with the permission of Farrar, Straus & Giroux, Inc. (New York), from *For the Union
Dead* by Robert Lowell, copyright © 1960 by Robert Lowell.

Lowell's poem is somewhat more sharply focused than Sandburg's, which refers to the world and all time. Lowell, a Bostoner himself, is interested in the disrespect offered to the monument of an Abolitionist who led the first Negro regiment in the Civil War. Two months after it marched through Boston, this regiment had been cut in half; not only do people forget this, says Lowell, but they offer us a parking lot instead of the memory.

The great dramatists of the ancient Greeks, like Euripides, often go far beyond the tale itself to give their audience an interpretation of the human being's struggle against life, the gods, and the environment. Thus Medea, in the play of that name by Euripides, becomes a symbol of womankind outraged, of jealousy so great (it drives her to the murder of her own children) that it transcends the emotion of any one woman.

In visual art we may see relatively clear symbols, as in Munch's expressionist painting *The Shriek* (Figure 2-12)—a comment on psychological dislocation—or Kandinsky's *Improvisation #30*, which symbolizes a foreboding of World War I (Color Plate 9). We also may find more abstruse symbols in such work as Beckmann's *Departure* (Figure 2-13). Here the much more private nature of the painter's expression necessitates some sort of translation by the critic. We may guess—and it is no more than a guess—that the side panels symbolize the tyranny of Nazism and the central panel reflects the artist's liberation from it.

Figure 2-12. Edvard Munch (1863–1944), Norwegian painter and printmaker. *The Shriek* (1896). (Lithograph, 20⅝ by 16¹³⁄₁₆ inches. Collection, Museum of Modern Art, New York; Matthew T. Mellon Fund.)

Figure 2-13. Max Beckmann (1884–1950), German painter. *The Departure* (1932–1933). (Oil on canvas, triptych. Size: center panel 84¾ by 45⅜ inches; side panels each 84¾ by 39¼ inches. Collection, Museum of Modern Art, New York. Given anonymously.)

Figure 2-14. Marc Chagall (1887–), Russian painter. *I and My Village* (1911). (Oil on canvas. Size: 85⅝ by 59⅝ inches. New York, Museum of Modern Art; Mrs. Simon Guggenheim Fund.)

Dreams and the Subconscious

During the 1920s artists developed ways of presenting the subjects that have to do with dreams and the subconscious. Under the influence of Freudian psychology, the subconscious has come to be recognized as important in human conduct, and naturally it has found expression in art.

Subjects of this sort attempt to show the inside of the human mind as well as the appearance of the outside world. They try to reveal thoughts and dreams that are not controlled by reason or any conscious order. The work which results is like its subject; it may be clear and vivid, but it is not necessarily logical. Events and people are shown together in unrelated and therefore irrational combinations. The reality of such scenes can best be understood if we remember our own thoughts and dreams; we find ourselves taking part in actions under circumstances which probably have to do with our ordinary life, but which are combined in forms that are strange and irrational. Paintings of this kind belong to the type called "surrealism"—that is, "super" realism. Indeed, it seems that they have to be photographically "real" if their apparent illogicality is to be convincing.

Chagall's painting *I and My Village* (Figure 2-14) presents a rural scene. The two important characters are the man and the cow. Their faces are bound together in a circle and they look at each other with sympathy. The man holds a spray for the cow to eat. The cow is thinking of being milked, as we can tell from the small figures painted on her jaw. In the background are the other objects of the village—a workman with a scythe, a woman, and a row of the village houses—some of them right side up and some, upside down. The cross at the top of the picture and the ring on the man's hand are symbols we recognize which help us to understand the man and the entire situation. Probably the most famous surrealist picture is *The Persistence of Memory*, by Salvador Dali (Figure 2-15). The four limp watches symbolize the relativity, flexibility, and destructibility of time.

In addition to this figurative and relatively naturalistic surrealism, there is another type known as "abstract" surrealism and represented by Joan Miró, Max Ernst, and Roberto Matta (Color Plate 7). The works of these artists have a less photographic character. Their playfulness—even absurdity—and deliberate lack of logic again suggest the dream world.

In literature, the desire to locate and hold the subconscious is found in the stream-of-consciousness novel, in which the author attempts to trap every thought or feeling that passes through the mind of a character. Time, naturally, becomes confused in the process. Joyce's *Ulysses* is one of the well-known examples; Proust's

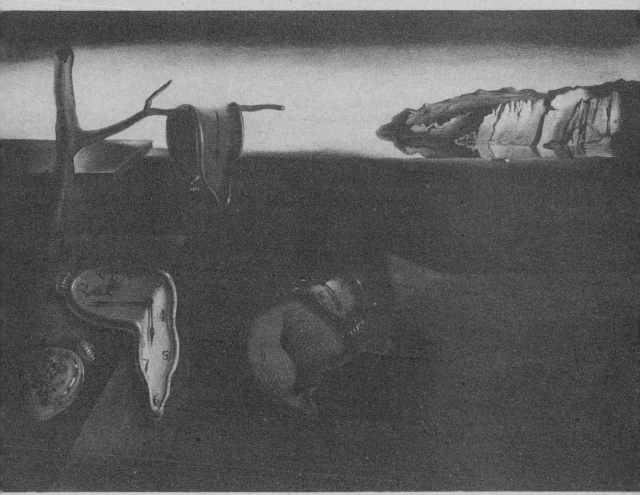

Remembrance of Things Past is perhaps even more celebrated. In poetry, surrealism can be felt in such a poem as Karl Shapiro's "Love for a Hand." Here the dream world is explicit, and every stanza contains some symbol of the relationship of the man to the woman. The figure of speech and the implications in the last words, "his hand eats hers," are a culmination of the mysterious atmosphere created by the light moving in the room, the ominous references to "little animals that prowl," and the image of drowning.

Two hands lie still, the hairy and the white,
And soon down ladders of reflected light
The sleepers climb in silence. Gradually

They separate on paths of long ago,
Each winding on his arm the unpleasant clew
That leads, live as a nerve, to memory.

But often, when too steep her dream descends;
Perhaps to the grotto where her father bends
To pick her up, the husband wakes as though
He had forgotten something in the house.
Motionless he eyes the room that glows
With the little animals of light that prowl

This way and that. Soft are the beasts of light
But softer still her hand that drifts so white
Upon the whiteness. How like a water plant
It floats upon the black canal of sleep,
Suspended upward from the distant deep
In pure achievement of its lovely want!

Quietly then he plucks it and it folds
And is again a hand, small as a child's.
He would revive it, but it barely stirs,
And so he carries it off a little way
And breaks it open gently. Now he can see
The sweetness of the fruit, his hand eats hers.

> —Karl Shapiro (1913–   , American poet)
> "Love for a Hand"[9]

In Visconti's film version (1971) of Mann's novel *Death in Venice*
the scene is sometimes the present and sometimes the past. When
the main figure, a composer, begins thinking about the past, it is
acted out before him; then, just as in actual thought, time shifts back
to the present. The composer himself is seen both as a young man
and an older one; his relationships with his wife and friends are not
shown in terms of the "now" of the story but as they developed over
the years and as part of the explanation for his illogical behavior of
the fictional present. Narratives like this and like those of Joyce and
Proust resemble surrealism because they break from the "normal" by
jumping back and forth in time, and in their preoccupation with the
workings of thought they naturally become involved with the role of
the subconscious. But they should be distinguished from "surrealism" in the sense in which the term is applied to something like
Dali's *Persistence of Memory*, which uses visual symbols, natural-
istically portrayed, to indicate the reality hidden in the subconscious.
    Analogous to the surrealist's attempt to discover "truth" in this
way is the attempt of the expressionists to change the physical appearance of external reality. To this end they made violent use of

[9] Copyright 1952 by Karl Shapiro. Reprinted from *Poems 1940–1953*, by Karl Shapiro, by permission of Random House, Inc. (New York).

color, form, and space. This is also an attempt to get at the essential truth which one sees inwardly and feels. The Norwegian Edvard Munch, who came to Germany at the end of the nineteenth century, became the spiritual and artistic inspiration of the expressionist movement. His lithograph *The Shriek* (Figure 2-12) conveys a sense of terror through its omission of naturalistic details and its distortion and twisting of what it shows. Munch and the other expressionists change form, space, and color for the sake of expressiveness and emotionality.

A contemporary type of expressionism is known as *abstract expressionism*. In paintings of this school, the colors are slapped, dribbled, or sometimes thrown onto the canvas. The effects are at times accidental, but the artist feels that the creative act itself is a work of art. Kandinsky (Color Plates 8 and 9) has many of the characteristics of this school even in his earlier works, which already have a certain explosive force. The mature paintings of Kandinsky clearly prefigure the endless motion of the abstract expressionist movement since the late 1940s, as seen in the works of Jackson Pollock (Color Plate 10) and others. Typically, expressionist artists throw themselves into the work, losing themselves in its ceaseless motion and expressiveness.

BEAUTIFUL AND UGLY SUBJECTS OF ART

The last consideration in this chapter on subject has to do with the artist's choice of subject. What are fit subjects for art? Are there certain subjects that are not allowed in art? Almost instinctively, some will answer these questions by saying that the noble, the lovely, the beautiful, the distinguished, and the unusual are the proper subjects for art. "The Fountain" and the caryatids of the Erechtheum seem to have appropriate subjects for works of art, and usually we have something of this kind in mind when we call a subject "artistic." By this same impulse, subjects that are ugly, undignified, or commonplace would not seem proper subjects for art.

But when one turns from theory to practice, this idea is not borne out. Some of us might turn away in disgust if we actually met the old man with a diseased nose painted by Ghirlandajo (*Old Man and Boy*, Color Plate 11). But the old man's concern for the boy and the boy's adoration of the man are so great that we forget the man is old and ugly. William Carlos Williams, the well-known American poet, refers to Brueghel's *Parable of the Blind* (Color Plate 42; Color Plate 42 is in the group following page 440) as "this horrible but superb painting" and in the rest of the poem explains what he means by his description. Study the painting and read his poem on the same page, then see if you agree with him.

Even far more specifically and violently "ugly" subjects—like Orozco's mural painting in the Governor's Palace at Guadalajara in Mexico (Color Plate 13), where the great liberator of Mexico, Hidalgo y Costilla, sets the nation aflame with revolt and violence—may move us to pity, enthusiasm, and admiration as well as horror. Whatever reaction—or combination of reactions—we have, the result is a great experience. We can have such an experience from any violent confrontation artistically and dramatically presented. Actually, with works like this, the question of ugliness fades into the background. Only those who are committed to the cult of beauty for its own sake will object to what Orozco has shown.

Shakespeare has painted a very clear picture of winter in a short lyric in *Love's Labour's Lost*. The muddy roads, the greasy, sweaty cook, the nose "red and raw," are not beautiful details; yet, this is one of the most charming moments in all Shakespeare's writings, and very few moments in all literature leave us with an equal sense of winter's beauty.

When icicles hang by the wall
    And Dick the shepherd blows his nail
And Tom bears logs into the hall
    And milk comes frozen home in pail,
When blood is nipp'd and ways be foul,
Then nightly sings the staring owl,
       "Tu-whit; tu-who!"
       A merry note,
While greasy Joan doth keel the pot.

When all aloud the wind doth blow
    And coughing drowns the parson's saw
And birds sit brooding in the snow
    And Marian's nose looks red and raw,
When roasted crabs hiss in the bowl,
Then nightly sings the staring owl,
       "Tu-whit; tu-who!"
       A merry note,
While greasy Joan doth keel the pot.

    —William Sakespeare (1564–1616, British poet and dramatist),
    Love's Labour's Lost, V, ii, 922–938 (ca. 1590)

Emphatically, art is not limited to subjects that in themselves are beautiful or agreeable. The beautiful and the agreeable are subjects of art, but they are not the only ones. Any subject may be a subject of art. We may like in art what we do not like in nature, because we see the subject as it has been interpreted for us by the artist.

This last sentence answers the question of the relationship of subject to *value* in a work of art. Does the choice of subject help to determine the final judgment as to whether a work may be counted good or bad, great or mediocre? Can we say that a work of art is good if it has a certain subject, and poor if it has another? A "beautiful" subject does not necessarily produce a good work of art, nor an "ugly" subject a poor one; a noble subject does not mean a noble work of art, nor an ignoble subject an ignoble work. The value of art lies not in the subject but in what the artist does with that subject. The greatness of art comes not from the subject but from the artist. Thus a beautiful woman will not necessarily give us a great portrait, nor will a portrayal of God inevitably culminate in a noble result.

Rubens's *Judgment of Paris* (Figure 2-16), painted in 1638, and Picasso's *Demoiselles d'Avignon* (Figure 2-17), painted more than 250 years later, are interesting as regards the problem of the ugly and the

Figure 2-16. Peter Paul Rubens (1577–1640). *The Judgment of Paris* (1638–1639). (Oil on canvas. Size: 57⅛ by 76⅜ inches. National Gallery, London.)

Figure 2-17. Picasso. *Les Demoiselles d'Avignon* (1906). (Oil on canvas. Size: 96 by 92 inches. Collection, Museum of Modern Art, New York; acquired through the Lillie P. Bliss Bequest.)

beautiful in art. Both are famous paintings, both are studies in representing feminine beauty, both have as their subject seduction and the judging and appreciation of feminine beauty. But there the similarities end. Rubens selected as his subject the popular myth of Paris choosing the most beautiful of the goddesses. Picasso chose the parlor of a brothel on the *carrer d'Avinyo* ("alley of Avignon") in Barcelona, where prostitutes displayed themselves to prospective customers. To present the feminine ideal from all points of view, Rubens painted one goddess from the front, one from the back, and one in profile; Picasso—more interested in the technical problems of doing this than in realism and taking his cue from African masks, in which he was interested at the time—attempted to present all sides at once: see especially the figure at the right. Rubens has given his idyllic scene aesthetic distance by placing it in a secluded meadow with trees and by having the characters interested in one another. Picasso has deliberately kept his figures near the canvas level and even seems to play with its surface in ambiguous ways; it is almost as though the canvas is being pulled apart so that the women can stare brazenly at us. Here we are presented with a contrast in ideals of physical beauty and a contrast in painting styles. Probably most of us would find the figures to the left in Picasso's painting more attractive physically than the buxom goddesses in Rubens's work; but we may find Picasso's stylistic experiments in representing the human figure unattractive or even distasteful. To dismiss either as ugly on these grounds, however, would be not only to fail in understanding the differences in what they were attempting, but to rob ourselves of the enjoyment to be found in each. For example, since Eve tempted Adam with fruit, and Paris will award a golden apple to the most beautiful seductress, there is probably a bit of witticism in Picasso's including fruit in his seduction scene. Moreover, the little still life is of a type which had become almost a cliché among his fellow painters.

The Beckmann triptych (three-part painting) mentioned earlier, *The Departure* (Figure 2-13), is in itself far from a beautiful or pleasant subject. But the result of the contrast between horror and release from horror, the serenity of the central panel as a symbol of overcoming the forces of fate, provides the spectator with a purging of the emotions. Daumier's *Rue Transnonian* (Figure 3-3) is as shocking a subject as one could wish to find, but the subject has here become a source of tragedy. The same is true of Picasso's *Guernica* (Figure 3-4).

In literature also there are moments of supreme brutality and horror which nevertheless constitute great art. Euripides's *Medea*, which we have already mentioned, is an example: a spiteful, brutal, and terrifying act is the occasion for supreme tragedy. Shakespeare's plays are filled with violence of various kinds, from the multiple deaths marking the end of *Hamlet* to the murders in *Macbeth* and the suicides in *Romeo and Juliet*. Yet each of these plays in its own way is a milestone in the history of the humanities, filled with noble sentiments and great imagery. In the works of contemporary dramatists like Beckett and Ionesco, the so-called "theater of the absurd," the interest is not in delineating noble sentiments, but rather, in demonstrating futility. What is shown may not be uplifting in the manner of older plays, but plays like *The Chairs* and *The Bald Soprano* by Ionesco or Beckett's *Waiting for Godot* have a great deal to say concerning the modern world and its problems, and they say it well.

SUMMARY

A very good book on understanding poetry[10] uses as titles of the firs
three sections of its opening chapter these unqualified assertions:

The subject of a poem may be anything whatever.
The subject of a poem is not the same thing as the theme.
The meaning of a poem is not the same thing as its subject c
its theme.

These three statements are true of all the arts. Art may be abou
anything, although some subjects seem to be more effective in on
medium than another. And the nominal representational subject c
a work of art is not the same thing as its theme. Finally, and this i
most important, the content of a work of art—its significance, value
and importance to us—is more than its subject and theme. Indeed, :
is the very nature and essence of art that it is more than all its parts
that holistically it reaches us in ways that are not merely rational, tha
bypass the intellectual and affect us in intimate, personal ways.

[10] Robert W. Boynton and Maynard Mack, *Introduction to the Poem* (New York: Hayden Book Con
pany, Inc., 1973).

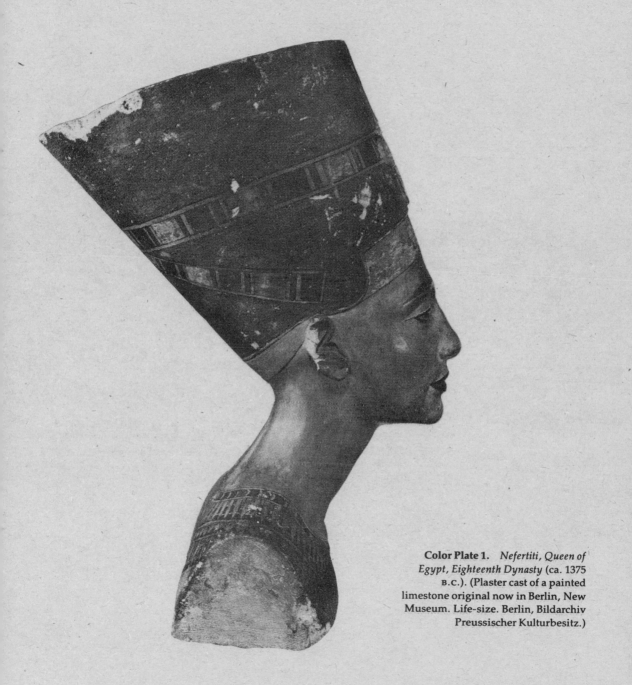

Color Plate 1. *Nefertiti, Queen of Egypt, Eighteenth Dynasty* (ca. 1375 B.C.). (Plaster cast of a painted limestone original now in Berlin, New Museum. Life-size. Berlin, Bildarchiv Preussischer Kulturbesitz.)

Color Plate 2. Vincent Van Gogh (1853–1890), Dutch painter, etcher, and lithographer. *Landscape with Cypresses* (1889). (Oil on canvas. Size: 28½ by 35¾ inches. London, National Gallery.)

Color Plate 3. Piet Mondrian (1872–1944), Dutch painter. *Composition with Blue and White* (1936). (Oil on canvas. Size: 41 by 38 inches. Hartford, Connecticut, Wadsworth Atheneum.)

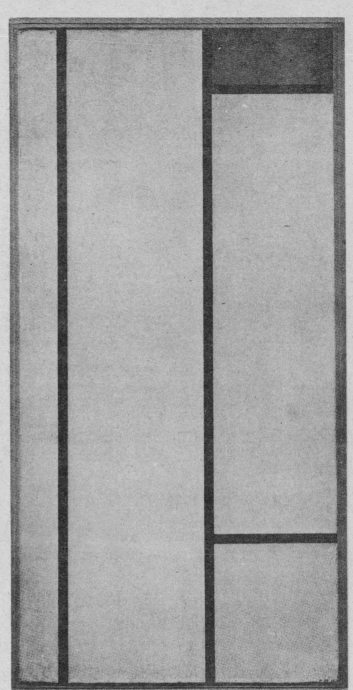

Color Plate 4. Willem de Kooning (1904–   ), American painter. *Woman* . (1950–1952). (Oil on canvas. Size: 6 feet 3⅞ inches by 4 feet 10 inches. Collection, Museum of Modern Art, New York. Purchase.)

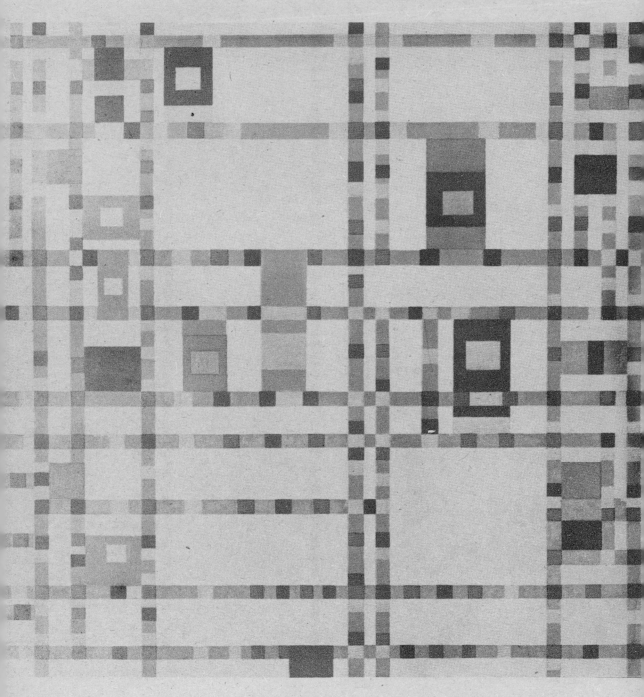

Color Plate 5. Piet Mondrian. *Broadway Boogie Woogie* (ca. 1942–1943). (Oil on canvas. Size: 50 by 50 inches. New York, Museum of Modern Art. Given anonymously.)

Color Plate 6. El Greco (1541–1614), Spanish painter. *Resurrection* (ca. 1597–1604). (Oil on canvas. Size: 108¼ by 60 inches. **Madrid**, Prado. Photograph by Alinari.)

Color Plate 7. *Above:* Roberto Matta (1912–   ), Chilean painter. (Fresco. Paris, UNESCO Building.)

Color Plate 9. *Above:* Vasily Kandinsky (1866–1944), Russian painter. *Improvisation #30 (Warlike Theme)* (1913). (Oil on canvas. Size: 43¼ by 43¾ inches. Chicago, Art Institute of Chicago; Arthur Jerome Eddy Memorial Collection.)

Color Plate 8. *Opposite page, bottom:* Vasily Kandinsky. *Light Picture, #188* (1913). (Oil on canvas. Size: 30¾ by 39½ inches. New York, Solomon R. Guggenheim Museum.)

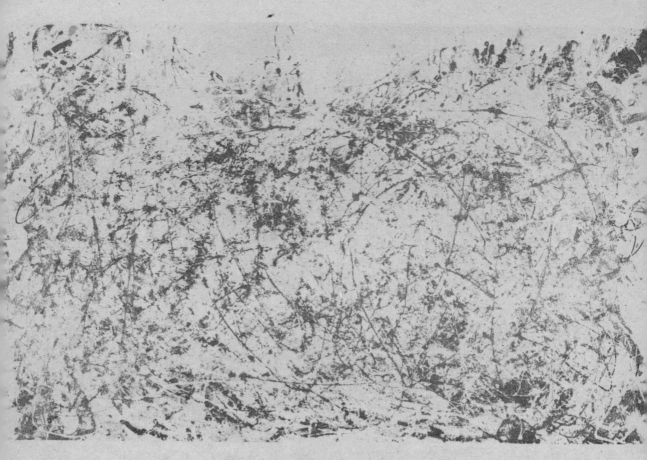

Color Plate 10.   Jackson Pollock (1912–1956), American painter. *Number 1* (1948). (Oil on canvas. Size: 68 by 104 inches. New York, Museum of Modern Art.)

3 SOURCES OF ART SUBJECTS

When I consider how my light is spent
Ere half my days in this dark world and wide,
And that one Talent which is death to hide
Lodged with me useless, though my soul more bent
To serve therewith my Maker, and present
My true account, lest He returning chide,
"Doth God exact day-labour, light denied?"
I fondly ask. But Patience, to prevent
That murmur, soon replies, "God doth not need
Either man's work or his own gifts. Who best
Bear his mild yoke, they serve him best. His state
Is kingly: thousands at his bidding speed,
And post o'er land and ocean without rest;
They also serve who only stand and wait."

   —John Milton (1608–1674, British poet and essayist),
      "On His Blindness" (ca. 1655)

The subjects used in art are usually clear and obvious. They need no explanation other than the work itself. Rimsky-Korsakov's bumble-bee and Elizabeth Bishop's storm are self-explanatory. Cézanne gives the name of the forest in which he found the well and grinding wheel that attracted his attention, but it is of no real importance in our understanding of the picture. On the other hand, there are many works of art which depend for their understanding upon some knowledge of the subject. When Tchaikovsky calls his suite *Romeo and Juliet*, he takes it for granted that we know the story of Shakespeare's young lovers.

Figure 3-1. Michelangelo (1475–1564), Italian painter, sculptor, architect, and poet. *David* (1501–1503). (Marble. Height: 18 feet. Florence, Academy. Photograph by Alinari/Scala.)

Milton's sonnet "On His Blindness" tells the facts essential f an understanding of the poem: that the poet lost his eyesight wh he felt his greatest work lay before him, and that through this expe ence he learned patience and submission to the will of God. Ho ever, one understands the poem better and enjoys it more if o knows, even vaguely, the story of the poet's life. Milton lost his sig in the service of his country before he had written the great poe which he had always wanted to write and which he knew he cou write, the poem he did write later in spite of his blindness, *Parad Lost.*

Similarly, anyone can see that Michelangelo's *David* (shown Figure 3-1) is a statue of a young man, a very beautiful young m with a serious, determined expression on his face. He is standi with his left arm raised and his right arm by his side. Anyone c identify the subject to this extent and can get a great deal of pleasu from the statue with no other information. But the sculptor h named the young man David, and we understand the statue better we know the story Michelangelo expected us to know. It tells, I Samuel 17, how David, a mere boy, killed the giant Goliath with pebble from his slingshot.

The examples given so far can all be enjoyed without any know edge of the subject. But Botticelli's *Birth of Venus* (Color Plate 12) very obscure if one accepts it at its face value. The young woman very beautiful, but why should she be standing naked on the edge a shell? Why does not the shell topple over? Who are the people each side of her? What are they doing? Botticelli assumed that tho who looked at his picture would know that Venus, the goddess love and beauty, was born from the foam of the sea, and his patro did know. In the picture, she is being blown to the shore by t winds, while one of the Horae (seasons) is waiting on the bank receive her.

When we talk about the sources of art subjects, we are thinkir primarily of subjects like those just mentioned, those which demar some knowledge on the part of the critic who wishes to get the id the artist had in mind.

The number of subjects used in this way is limitless. Any arti may use any subject from any source, and it is impossible ever know all the subjects of art. Even the scholar who has devoted a lif time to their study never expects to know all of them. There ar however, a few sources which are part of the background of eve cultivated person. For convenience they may be grouped under the six headings:

1. Nature
2. History, including legend, folklore, and current events
3. Greek and Roman mythology

4. The Judaeo-Christian tradition
5. Oriental sacred texts
6. Other works of art

NATURE

In Chapter 1, we have made the point that art is not nature and is not intended to be nature. This fact is worth noting again because aspects of nature—animals, people, landscapes—have been the most common inspiration and subject matter for art. It is obvious that nature can be the subject or content of both literary and visual art (for example, Brueghel's *Fall of Icarus*, Figure 3-27, and Auden's and Madden's poems with the same subject, page 85), and that nature is the root metaphor of much poetic diction and visual imagery (for example, Shakespeare's "When icicles hang by the wall," page 52, and Frost's "Birches," page 306). Nevertheless, we will concentrate here on nature in the visual arts.

From what we now know, it appears that animals painted on the walls of caves by prehistoric peoples were the very first subject matter (see Figure 1-4). Some human figures were included in this earliest art, but they were not so carefully presented as animals were. However, from the time when we have accurate records of art, the human male and female figures—idealized during the Greek period and individualized from the Roman period on—have been used by artists in all mediums as subject matter. It can, in fact, be stated categorically that the representation of the human figure in painting and sculpture vastly outnumbers that of any other subject in art. So vast is this treatment that some critics subdivide it into three parts: single and group figures, the portrait, and the religious image. It would be quite possible to do a complete history of Western culture by concentrating on any one of these subdivisions. Indeed, there are examples of each from every period in the somewhat limited number of illustrations in this book. Here, of course, we are considering them chiefly from the point of view of what may be called their formal aesthetic qualities: how they have come into being and how they affect us. They can, however, be studied from the point of view of how humankind saw itself, its interests, and its ideals, and how human beings relate themselves to a society and to the universe. For example, Michelangelo's *David* (1501–1503) (Figure 3-1) tells us much about Florence at that time—its ideals; its sense of youthful vigor, strength, and pride; and its defiance of the "giant" countries which surrounded it.

Next to animals and people and their activities, nature as landscape has been the most common subject of art. In landscape painting, human beings have documented their regard for nature, their

feelings toward it, and their sense of a relationship to it. Kenne[
Clark states quite succinctly a motivation which seems to be involv[
in landscape painting and its role in culture:

We are surrounded with things we have not made and which have a life a[
structure different from our own: trees, flowers, grasses, rivers, hills, clou[
For centuries they have inspired us with curiosity and awe. They have be[
objects of delight. We have re-created them in our imagination to reflect o[
moods. And we have come to think of them as contributing to the idea whi[
we call nature. Landscape painting marks the stages in our conception [
nature.[1]

When animals, men and women, and landscapes are the subje[
in art, we have no difficulty at a first level of understanding in kno[
ing what the art is about. However, a closer examination of lan[
scapes will reveal that not only are they different in technique a[
style, but they also disclose quite different attitudes toward natu[

HISTORY

In one sense, all art is conditioned by the historical period in whi[
it is created. The dress, the houses, the manner of living, t[
thoughts of a period are necessarily reflected in the work of the arti[
Such general references, however, may be taken for granted, and [
do not call a subject historical unless it refers to specific places, pe[
sons, or events.

Such subjects are numerous. One obvious reason is that rule[
like to have themselves and the great deeds of their time perpetuate[
consequently, statues and paintings of the great are found in ea[
civilization. In these, artists often have a double duty, in that they a[
supposed to give a flattering likeness of the subject and at the sam[
time display their own skill. An exception to this general rule [
found in the portraits of the Spanish court painted by Goya. A fir[
look at the portrait of Maria Luisa of Parma (Figure 3-2) shows her [
a royal person in all her royal finery; a second look, however, gives[
telling commentary on her character and disposition. Goya seems [
mock her pretentious elegance. The painting tells us that she is ug[
and vain.

Another reason for the use of historical subjects is that artists a[
sensitive to the events taking place in the world around them. In R[
Transnonian (Figure 3-3), Daumier was voicing protest against soci[
injustice. In a street skirmish a shot from one of the windows [
number 12, rue Transnonain, wounded an officer; the soldiers ther[

Figure 3-2. Francisco Goya (1746–1828), Spanish painter, etcher, and lithographer. *Maria Luisa of Parma* (ca. 1790–1792). (Oil on canvas. Size: 43⅝ by 33⅝ inches. New York, Metropolitan Museum of Art; bequest of Mrs. H. O. Havemeyer, 1929, H. O. Havemeyer Collection.)

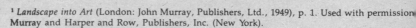

[1] *Landscape into Art* (London: John Murray, Publishers, Ltd., 1949), p. 1. Used with permission[
Murray and Harper and Row, Publishers, Inc. (New York).

Figure 3-3. Honoré Daumier (1808– 1879), French lithographer and caricaturist. *Rue Transnonain* (1834). Lithograph. Size: about 11½ by 17½ inches. New York, Metropolitan Museum of Art; Rogers Fund, 1920.)

Figure 3-4. Pablo Picasso (1881–1973), Spanish painter. *Guernica* (1937). (Oil on canvas. Mural 11 feet, 6 inches, by 25 feet, 3 inches. Collection of the artist, on extended loan to the Museum of Modern Art, New York, from the artist's estate.)

upon rushed into the building and killed all its inhabitants. Daumier's lithograph depicts the scene when they had left. A similar protest is found in Picasso's painting *Guernica* (Figure 3-4), which was inspired when an unarmed Basque city was bombed by the Fascists in the Spanish Civil War (1936–1939). Today many artists are more exclusively concerned with aesthetics, but similar examples may still be found. The pop artist Robert Rauschenberg, among

others, has produced some art of social protest directed against tl
war in Vietnam (Figure 3-5).

Historical subjects as such can be identified and recognized wi
little trouble; records are kept, histories are written, and referenc
are usually clear and easy to find. In quite a different class is legen
the progenitor of history. Legend may be defined as history that
not or cannot be authenticated: the facts are not verifiable. We can
sure of few, if any, facts about King Arthur or King Lear, and tho
facts do not correspond with the legends about them. Often a legei
gets attached to a historical person; for example, Charlemagne is

historical king of France, but the exploits of his nephew Roland are legendary. Many artists, writers, and composers have made use of legend. Till Eulenspiegel, the legendary bad boy of medieval Germany, is the hero of Richard Strauss's tone poem *Till Eulenspiegel's Merry Pranks*. Wagner used legend for the subject of his great cycle of four operas, *The Ring of the Nibelungs*. In it he tells the saga of the Nibelung gold from the time it was stolen until it was restored to the Rhine maidens. Wagner based the *Ring* cycle on Norse myths and on a twelfth-century poem, "The Song of the Nibelungs," which was a reflection of the historical struggles between Huns and Burgundians during the Dark Ages.

GREEK AND ROMAN MYTHOLOGY

Greek and Roman mythology has been a very important source for subjects in art. The stream of its influence on Western cililization may be traced primarily to two sources. First are the works of Greece and Rome during the period of Greek and Roman civilization, from the sixth century before Christ to the fifth century after Christ. Those arts are so well known that they count as a definite part of our inheritance: architecture, drama, poetry, sculpture, and painting. Second are the arts of Europe during the Renaissance, the period of revived interest in things Greek and Latin between the fourteenth and sixteenth centuries. During this period, poets, painters, and sculptors drew largely from Greek and Roman sources for subjects. Of the examples already mentioned, the poems of Homer and Sappho, the Erechtheum, and the vase painting *Dionysus Sailing the Sea* belong to the first period; Botticelli's *Birth of Venus* belongs to the second.

Stories from Greek and Roman mythology center on the deities and the heroes. Each of the deities had his or her own province and was known by some symbol. Jupiter, for example, the king of the gods, was known by his thunderbolt. Bacchus, god of wine, was shown with grapes and grape leaves.

About each of the gods and goddesses there clustered many stories. We have already noted a story about the birth of Venus. Another goddess, Proserpine, the daughter of Ceres (Demeter) was carried off by Pluto to be queen of the underworld. Ceres implored Jupiter to restore her daughter to her, and at last a compromise was made whereby Proserpine would forever spend half her time with her mother and half with her husband. It is summer when Ceres has her daughter with her.

In addition to the stories of the gods, there are many tales of the heroes, who were mortal men in close touch with the gods, and in whose exploits the gods themselves assisted. Each of these heroes became the nucleus for a series of stories to which any author might

Figure 3-6. *Laocoön* (ca. 40 B.C.). School of Rhodes. (White marble. Height to right hand of Laocoön: 8 feet. Rome, Vatican Museum. Photograph by Alinari/Scala.)

add additional tales as the fancy struck. Among the heroes a Perseus, who killed the Gorgon (monster) Medusa and saved the li of Andromeda; Oedipus, who was doomed to kill his father ar marry his mother; and Theseus, who killed the Minotaur with the a of Ariadne and then, tiring of her, deserted her on the island Naxos, where she was met and loved by Bacchus. Titian's painti *Bacchus and Adriadne* (Color Plate 14) shows Bacchus leaping from h chariot to console Ariadne, who has just been forsaken by Theseu she has gathered up her skirts, preparing to flee, when she looks ba at the god—and stays.

The greatest of all Greek stories, however, are about the Troja War, which was fought over Helen, whose face "launched a tho sand ships, and burnt the topless towers of Ilium." We find mar references in art to one or another story connected with Troy—su as the judgment of Paris, when a shepherd boy had to choose whi of three goddesses was the most beautiful, or the use of a wood horse by the Greeks to obtain entrance to Troy. The *Laocoön* (Figu 3-6) represents the punishment inflicted by the gods on the Troja priest who urged the Trojans not to take the Greeks' wooden hor into the city.

The three great classical epics are concerned with the Troja War. Homer's *Iliad* tells of the war itself, beginning with the anger Achilles and narrating the events through the death of Hecto Homer's *Odyssey* describe the wanderings of Ulysses after the wa and Vergil's *Aeneid* describes the adventures of Aeneas and t founding of Rome, also after the war.

THE JUDAEO-CHRISTIAN TRADITION

Religion and Art

Anyone who has taken a trip to Europe has probably seen innume able museums and churches. Many travelers see so many that the become discouraged. Tourists who are taken about by guides are given the same set table d'hôte cultural diet. Catholics and no Catholics, the religious and the nonbelievers, all see the same mon ments of art, and much of this art is religious art. Obviously, religic has played an enormous role in inspiring works of visual a music, architecture, and literature through the ages. In fact, it no exaggeration to say that in some periods, such as the prehi toric and the medieval, there was really no difference between r ligion and art. The painters of the caves at Altamira in northe Spain (see Figure 1-4) probably had no notion of themselves as artis in our sense; they were performing a religious rite that was suppos to help them in hunting. Similarly, the artisans of the Middle Ag (we are not using the word *artists* yet) were part of a reverenti age of faith in which religion permeated the totality of experience, as something which could not be separated from any other aspect of living. In modern culture, religion is separate to an immeasurably greater extent, so much so that it is hard for us to grasp how everything for medieval people was part of religion. It was the Church which was the source of education, entertainment, most social occasions, and, of course, faith. This faith was both expressed in and strengthened by the carvings on church portals and the colorful designs in stained-glass windows. Such carvings and designs told people the things the Church felt they should know. For the illiterate people of that age the portal carvings and window pictures were a kind of text—they have often been called "the poor man's Bible." The artisans who had produced them were unimportant, and indeed most often anonymous.

It was during the Renaissance of the fifteenth and early sixteenth centuries that the European artisans became "artists" and conscious of their role in a way that had never been true before (in the Far East, artists had arrived at this point somewhat earlier). With this change of attitude in the artist, art itself changed from the spontaneous expression of a universal feeling—whose visible symbol was the cathedral of the Middle Ages—to a more studied, artificial, and individual expression: the art of the Renaissance.

As religious art became self-conscious and individual, it also became more intellectual and philosophical; the Sistine Chapel frescoes, which are discussed below, are an excellent example, It also took on a new set of values and dimensions. In the first place, it became, far more than ever before, a kind of private status symbol. The individual sponsor, or patron, became hugely important. For example, Giotto's Arena Chapel frescoes (fourteenth century; Figure 3-21) were done for a wealthy Paduan who sponsored them in memory of his father. The church of S. Maria Novella, designed by Alberti in the fifteenth century (Figure 3-7), was sponsored by a wealthy Florentine family. More important, however, religious art during the Renaissance reflected the new intellectual currents of the time. Thus Michelaneglo's frescoes in the Sistine Chapel sum up the combination of pagan neo-Platonic philosophy with Christian belief that is typical of the sixteenth-century Renaissance. Finally, and perhaps most important, with the greater individualism and intellectuality exercised by this new breed of artists, religious art took on broader meaning. Now individual artists wandered somewhat from biblical texts to produce increasingly humanistic interpretations. The scene in the Sistine Chapel where God is shown creating Adam (Color Plate 15) is a long, but interesting, distance from the biblical text: "And the Lord God formed man of the dust of the ground, and breathed into his nostrils the breath of life; and man became a living soul" (Genesis 2:7). Both the Old Testament text and Michelangelo's

Figure 3-7. Leone Battista Alberti (1404–1472), Italian architect. Church of S. Maria Novella, Florence. (Photograph by Alinari/Scala.)

Figure 3-8. *Romanesque Madonna and Child* (twelfth century). (Oak, polychromed. Height: 31 inches. New York, Metropolitan Museum of Art; gift of J. Pierpont Morgan, 1916.)

interpretation have their own poetic quality. The simple indirectio of the former statement leaves the painter a great deal of room, whic he readily takes. Ghiberti has interpreted this moment different (Figure 4-5) in his bronze doors for the Baptistery in Florence: in very simple fashion he shows God raising Adam to his feet (this also a departure from the text). Michelangelo's depiction is muc more dramatic. The figure of God is rushing through the air as approaches the figure of Adam, who is lying on the ground with or are raised languidly and supported by the knee. God does not qui touch Adam; he merely extends his "strong hand and outstretche arm," willing the languid figure into life, as the life-giving energ seems to flow from the divine figure to the human one. Whe Ghiberti has given us a calm lyrical scene, Michelangelo gives an ir terpretation that produces a sense of mystical yearning; the man wh longs to be born, is gazing toward his Creator, the symbol of irr sistible force and creativity.

As we study the development of art in the Renaissance perioc we are able to see how each generation or century interprets biblic texts differently, and how in each case the interpretation reveals th basic attitude of the period. Let us take, for example, the way i which successive generations have treated the Virgin Mary, either a a devotional object or as a work of art—or as something in betwee

The French *Madonna and Child* of the twelfth century—th Romanesque period—at the Metropolitan Museum of Art (shown i Figure 3-8) is a highly stylized, formal, and unemotional representa

Figure 3-9. *La Vierge Dorée* (ca. 1280). Amiens Cathedral. Height: 120 inches. Caisse Nationale des Monuments Historiques et des Sites, Service Photographique, Archives Photographiques, Paris.)

tion. It seems to convey the quality of a feudal society and a religion whose dominant form was monasticism. There is nothing warm or "human" about this portrayal. Human reality has been omitted altogether, or at least completely subordinated to the concentric lines that flow over the entire surface of the sculpture. The result is a highly abstract, impersonal image or icon.

The *Vierge Dorée* ("Gilded Virgin") of the cathedral of Amiens (shown in Figure 3-9) is a product of the thirteenth century (the Gothic period) and the growth of town life during that time. This is a

Figure 3-10. *Christ and S. John* (*Johannes an der Brust Christi;* Swabia, Germany, ca. 1320). (Gilded polychrome oak carving. Size: 34½ by 17½ inches. Skulpturengalerie, Staatliche Museen Prussischer Kulturbesitz, West Berlin.)

humanized and warm representation. Here the mother looks te derly at her child, a more real infant than the rather large figure s ting on the Madonna's lap in the Romanesque example we have ju discussed. The Virgin is now all sweetness and smiles, unlike t somber, even severe, expression of the earlier figure. (For an examp of the sensitive humanizing of a different subject in the later part this period, see the sculpture *Christ and S. John*, Figure 3-10, and t discussion of it on page 78.)

Giotto's *Madonna Enthroned*, a work of the early fourteenth ce tury (Color Plate 16), is conceived monumentally and is almc classically Roman. Giotto, who is famous for his convincingly scul turesque forms, here projects a new and heroic ideal of humanit

This is an ideal that may be related in general terms to the classical
background of Italy, which was being consciously revived at this
point, particularly by the middle class: we are now in the Renaissance ("revival") period.

Botticelli's *Madonna of the Magnificat* (shown in Figure 3-11) is an
example of the more developed and intellectual classicism that was
widely practiced during the fifteenth-century Renaissance. Botticelli's *Birth of Venus* (Color Plate 12), which uses elaborate literary
allegories and references from classical literature, is one side of the
coin; the warm-blooded, sensuous portrayal of a holy figure such as
the Virgin is the other side. As has already been noted, the Renaissance tried constantly to reconcile the values of paganism with those
of Christianity.

During the last phase of the Renaissance, in the early sixteenth
century, we find the heroic conception of humanity and the idealization of all figure carried to their logical conclusions. The *Madonna of
the Book*, by Michelangelo, from the Bargello National Museum in
Florence (shown in Figure 3-12), exemplifies the heroic idealization
of the human form. This was also typical of Raphael and Leonardo da
Vinci—Michelangelo's contemporaries. All are characterized by a
sense of contained power, and by placement of the figures within a
geometrical framework.

Figure 3-12. Michelangelo. *Madonna of the Book*. (Marble. Florence, Bargello Museum. Photograph by Alinari/Scala.)

The Madonna and Child continues as a subject down to our own time. Each period which has treated this subject has given it the stamp of a particular age. With the Protestant Reformation of the sixteenth century, the number of countries in which religious art was supreme decreased. The new Protestant countries included a large part of Germany, the Netherlands, the Scandinavian countries, Britain, and Switzerland. In the United States, which has always been predominantly Protestant, there has been little religious art of importance. Indeed, as the general influence of religion has diminished in modern times, its influence on art has also diminished. One obvious exception should be noted: religious folk art, for example in France, Germany and Spain, in which untrained artists express themselves in emotionally effective terms. But although religious themes in art have diminished in importance, it is not to be supposed that they have disappeared. In the visual arts, in literature, and in music, examples are still to be found today.

T. S. Eliot, for example, in his poem "Journey of the Magi," writes a monologue in which an old man tells of his journey as a young man to find the star, the difficulties and disappointments of his long trip, and at last his finding of the child. Now as an old man he ponders on the meaning.

JOURNEY OF THE MAGI

'A cold coming we had of it,
Just the worst time of the year
For a journey, and such a long journey:
The ways deep and the weather sharp,
The very dead of winter.'
And the camels galled, sore-footed, refractory,
Lying down in the melting snow.
There were times we regretted
The summer palace on slopes, the terraces,
And the silken girls bringing sherbet.
Then the camel men cursing and grumbling
And running away, and wanting their liquor and women,
And the night-fires going out, and the lack of shelters,
And the cities hostile and the towns unfriendly
And the villages dirty and charging high prices:
A hard time we had of it.
At the end we preferred to travel all night,
Sleeping in snatches,
With the voices singing in our ears, saying
That this was all folly.

Then at dawn we came down to a temperate valley,
Wet, below the snow line, smelling of vegetation;
With a running stream and a water-mill beating the darkness,
And three trees on the low sky,
And an old white horse galloped away in the meadow.
Then we came to a tavern with vine-leaves over the lintel,
Six hands at an open door dicing for pieces of silver,
And feet kicking the empty wine-skins.
But there was no information, and so we continued
And arrived at evening, not a moment too soon
Finding the place, it was (you may say) satisfactory.

All this was a long time ago, I remember,
And I would do it again, but set down
This set down
This: were we led all that way for
Birth or Death? There was a Birth, certainly,
We had evidence and no doubt. I had seen birth and death,
But had thought they were different; this Birth was
Hard and bitter agony for us, like Death, our death.
We returned to our places, these Kingdoms,
But no longer at ease here, in the old dispensation,
With an alien people clutching their gods.
I should be glad of another death.

   —T. S. Eliot (1888–1965, American poet)[2]

[2] From *Collected Poems 1909–1962*, by T. S. Eliot, copyright 1936 by Harcourt Brace Jovanovich, Inc.; copyright 1963, 1964, by T. S. Eliot. Reprinted by permission of the publishers.

Another modern artist, the painter Georges Rouault, has painted a head of Christ in which he shows clearly the physical suffering and at the same time the calm of spirit which not only overcomes the suffering but is compassionate (Color Plate 17; Color Plates 1 through 26 follow page 152).

In these two examples, as in *Modern Migration of the Spirit*, by the Mexican painter Orozco (Figure 6-12), it is noteworthy that we are no longer dealing with the glorifications or direct religious references of earlier art. In these works, and indeed in most modern Western treatments of religious themes, the writer, artist, or composer uses the subject as an occasion for the expression of his or her own feelings and philosophy of life. Eliot's "Journey of the Magi" is a very personal treatment of the theme: the old man's ruminations are on his own experiences and reactions; the motif is "we" rather than "he." Rouault's art is definitely that of a Christian socialist at the beginning of our century; but the artist is using the sufferings of Christ to express his personal melancholy as he considers the sufferings of mankind in general. His painting *The Holy Face* (Color Plate 17) with its decorated borders suggests a scarf and recalls medieval depictions of the legend of S. Veronica. The legend is that S. Veronica wiped the face of Christ on the way to Calvary; the natural imprint of the sweat and blood was left on the cloth and thereby the image of Jesus was preserved. The legendary original cloth is preserved in Rome; but many, many copies were made and held sacred. The reference to this legend in *The Holy Face* and the heavy black outlines and brilliant hues suggesting a stained-glass cathedral window contribute to the effectiveness of Rouault's personal statement. Orozco goes even further, using the story of Christ to accuse humanity of unthinkingly destroying itself; Christ seems to act as an avenger, to wrest back his cross from those who have used it for their own ends. What strikes Orozco as a humanitarian is the fact that Christ's name has been so constantly invoked to defend and support acts of war and destruction—as the weapons in the background of the picture show.

The fact that modern pictorial art has become increasingly abstract has been another reason for the decline of traditional religious subject matter. But a few examples of very nearly traditional religious subjects can be found. Salvador Dali's *Last Supper* (1955), in the National Gallery in Washington, is one—but even this work is filled with the painter's own symbolism (Figure 3-13).

In music there has been a revival of religious subjects. Rock hymns, such as "Put your hand in the hand of the Man who calms the sea," are one example; another example is Leonard Bernstein's *Mass* (1971), a serious work attempting to present the traditional Roman Catholic Mass in modern terms. Although there are conflicting opinions about the effectiveness of *Mass*, it is nevertheless significant that an important contemporary musician has utilized this ancient material to express a new viewpoint.

ure 3-13. Salvador Dali (1904–   ),
panish painter. *The Sacrament of the
st Supper*. (Oil on canvas. Size: 65⅝
by 105⅛ inches. Washington, D.C.,
ational Gallery of Art; Chester Dale
Collection.)

Judaeo-Christian Sources of Art

The Bible   The Protestant Bible, as is commonly recognized, is not a single book but a library. The books of the Bible may be grouped as follows:

I. Old Testament (39 books)
    A. History (Genesis through Esther). The historical books give the story of the Jews from the creation to the Babylonian exile.
    B. Poetry (Job through the Song of Songs). Job is a poetic drama; Proverbs is a collection of wise sayings and epigrams. The Song of Songs and Ecclesiastes are, respectively, a group of marriage songs and a statement of gently cynical philosophy.
    C. Prophecy (Isaiah through Malachi). The prophets were not soothsayers, but practical men who judged and interpreted the affairs of their own times. They were patriots, reformers, preachers, and teachers.
II. New Testament (27 books)
    A. History. The four Gospels: Matthew, Mark, Luke, and John; the Acts of the Apostles.
    B. Letters. The epistles written by Paul and others to the Christian churches that were just starting in the various parts of the world.
    C. Apocalypse. The Revelation of S. John.

Any consideration of the Bible in relation to art must take into account the fact that the Bible itself is great art. For the English-

Figure 3-14. William Blake (1757–1827), English poet, painter, and engraver. *When the Morning Stars Sang Together* (ca. 1825). (Engraving. Size: 6 by 7½ inches. New York, Metropolitan Museum of Art. Gift of Edward Bennet, 1917.)

speaking peoples, the Bible has the additional advantage of bei available in the King James version, probably the greatest translati ever made. So the Bible not only is a source of art, but is itself ar

The most frequently used subjects from the Bible are taken fro the life of Jesus. The accounts of his birth and death are most oft used; the Madonna with the baby Jesus, the Annunciation, the vi of the Magi and the shepherds, from the stories of his birth; ar from his death, the betrayal by Judas, the scourging, the Crucifixio deposition, and entombment. In the Old Testament, the stories the Creation are probably more important than any others, thoug reference is frequent to the great figures of the Old Testament: A raham, Jacob, Moses, Samson, David, Elijah, and others.

The influence of the poetry and prophecy of the Old Testame is found chiefly in music. *The Messiah* by Handel takes its text in pa from the prophets. The opening tenor recitative uses the words Ihaiah, Chapter 40, "Comfort ye, comfort ye, my people." A oratorio on King David was written by Honegger. Blake's engravir *When the Morning Stars Sang Together* (shown in Figure 3-14) is take from the Book of Job. The Lord, answering Job out of the whirlwin asks:

Where wast thou when I laid the foundations of the earth?
Declare, if thou hast understanding.
Who hath laid the measures thereof, if thou knowest?
Or who hath stretched the line upon it?
Whereupon are the foundations thereof fastened?
Or who laid the corner stone thereof;
When the morning stars sang together,
And all the sons of God shouted for joy?

—Job 38:4–7

The Sistine Ceiling. It has been a not uncommon practice to tell stori from the Bible in a series of pictures. One of the greatest of these w made by Michelangelo to decorate the ceiling of the Sistine Chap (Figure 3-15). The chapel is a long, narrow room, about 155 by feet. In painting this space, Michelangelo chose to divide it into number of small areas.

Down the center of the ceiling is a series of nine rectangles tel ing the story of the Creation through the time of Noah (Color Plate and Figures 3-15 through 3-20):

1. Separation of Light from Darkness
2. Creation of Sun and Moon
3. Creation of Land and Water
4. Creation of Adam
5. Creation of Eve

6. Temptation and Expulsion
7. Sacrifice of Noah
8. The Deluge
9. The Drunkenness of Noah

Michelangelo began to paint this vast room with its 40-foot-high ceiling at the far end (at the left of our picture here) so as to leave the altar free as long as possible. Thus the pictures were actually done from number 9 to number 1, reversing the biblical sequence and ending with the monumental and mystical *Separation of Light from Darkness* (Figure 3-17). This is a huge and almost frightening single figure far different from the complex and detailed narratives at the left of the picture.

Each of these panels shows sculpturally decorative and classically conceived nude male figures (this is Michelangelo the sculptor expressing himself) that project in a general way the mood of the panel (Figure 3-18).

The subject of the series is the fall of man and redemption through the coming of Christ. For that reason the artist shows in the corners scenes representing God saving the chosen people; for example, *The Hanging of Haman* (not shown) is from the story of a beautiful Hebrew girl who was made queen by the Persian king Artaxerxes. When the king's evil minister, Haman, plotted against the Hebrews, Queen Esther and her uncle Mordecai managed to defeat him and save their people.

Forming a border around the entire ceiling is a row of figures representing the prophets of the Old Testament and the sibyls (prophetesses) of classical mythology (Figure 3-19 shows one), who foretold the birth of Christ. The Old Testament prophets who forecast the coming of a redeemer or savior are also included. Figure 3-20

Figure 3-15. Michelangelo. Ceiling of the Sistine Chapel (1508–1512). (Fresco. Length: 132 feet; width: 45 feet. Vatican City. Photograph by Alinari/Scala.)

Figure 3-16. Michelangelo. *Temptation and Expulsion,* detail of Sistine Chapel ceiling. (Photograph by Alinari/Scala.)

Figure 3-17. *Left:* Michelangelo. *Separation of Light from Darkness,* detail of Sistine Chapel ceiling. (Photograph by Alinari/Scala.)

Figure 3-18. *Right:* Michelangelo. *Decorative Nude,* detail of Sistine Chapel ceiling. (Photograph by Alinari/Scala.)

Figure 3-19. *Left:* Michelangelo. *Libyan Sibyl,* detail of Sistine Chapel ceiling. (Photograph by Alinari/Scala.)

Figure 3-20. *Right:* Michelangelo. *Isaiah,* detail of Sistine Chapel ceiling. (Photograph by Alinari/Scala.)

Figure 3-21. Giotto (1266–1336), Italian painter. *Joachim Returning to the Sheepfold* (ca. 1305). (Fresco, Height of figures: 3½ feet. Padua, Arena Chapel. Photograph by Alinari/Scala.)

shows the prophet Isaiah: "Behold, a virgin shall conceive, and bear a son, and shall call his name Emmanuel" (the Hebrew word *Emmanuel* means "God is with us").

The Apocrypha   The Apocrypha are those books of the Bible which were not accepted in the official Old and New Testaments: for example, the three Hebrew narratives Judith, Susanna, and Tobit. Judith is the story of a beautiful young woman who saved her nation when it was besieged by Holofernes. She followed him into his own tent and persuaded him to go to sleep. Then she cut off his head and carried it back to her home. Inspired by her feat, the Israelites fought and drove away their enemies. Botticelli painted a picture of her as she goes home, her servant carrying the head of Holofernes in a bag.

The New Testament Apocrypha comprise early stories of the lives of Jesus and Mary. Those that have had the greatest influence on art are the ones that have to do with the birth and death of the Virgin.

In the Arena Chapel at Padua, Giotto has painted a cycle of frescoes depicting the life of the Virgin. *Joachim Returning to the Sheepfold* (Figure 3-21) shows the dejection of Joachim, who was later to be the father of Mary, after his offering had been refused because he was still childless. In his sadness, he does not even realize that he has reached the sheepfold. The shepherds hold back in doubt and in fear of intruding, but the little dog recognizes his master and runs to meet him.

Legends and lives of the saints   The saints are those people formally recognized by the Christian church because of the exceptional holi-

Figure 3-22. Albrecht Dürer (1471–1528), German painter, engraver, and woodcarver. *S. Jerome in His Cell* (1514). (Engraving. Size: about 9¾ by 7½ inches. New York, Metropolitan Museum of Art; Fletcher Fund, 1919.)

ness and piety of their lives. About them many stories have bee told which have found their way into the arts. There is, for instanc the story that one day when S. Jerome was teaching, a lion walke into the room and lifted up its paw. All the students fled, but S Jerome, noticing that the lion was wounded, pulled a thorn from i paw. After that the lion was Jerome's constant companion. In Dürer engraving *S. Jerome in His Cell* (shown in Figure 3-22), the saint pictured working in his study; the scene is one of scholarly quiet an order, and in front is a large lion, sleeping peacefully.

In the polychromed oak statue *Christ and S. John* (Figure 3-10 John, the disciple "whom Christ loved," is depicted as a young ma sleeping peacefully with his head on the shoulder of Christ, an old man. Its scriptural source is a passage in the account of the Last Supper, John 13:23 (King James version):

Now there was leaning on Jesus' bosom one of his disciples, whom Jesus loved.

From this brief passage a legend grew over the centuries that the tremendous vision of things to come, described by John when, as an old man on the isle of Patmos, he wrote the Book of Revelation, had been given to him as a dream precisely at the moment at the Last Supper when he had fallen asleep leaning on Christ's shoulder. The utter peace and trust of the youthful S. John and the protective, affectionate concern of Christ in the statue depicting that moment reflect a changing religious attitude in the later part of the Middle Ages when the idea of a vengeful God to be feared was being replaced by belief in a loving God to be loved. In the words of S. Bernard of Clairvaux, the greatest spokesman of this attitude: "God has become your brother."

Ritual   The ritual of the church has been of great importance in art. The prayers and the words of the responses are beautiful. Through constant repetition they have become familiar to almost everyone, and they have had great influence on language and speech patterns. Just as important has been the influence on music; the various rituals were early set to music, and the composers of each generation wrote new music for the services. The most important of all the rituals of the church is the Mass, which is the celebration of the Holy Communion. It is regularly in five parts (only the opening words are given):

> Kyrie: "Lord, have mercy upon us."
> Gloria: "Glory be to God on high."
> Credo (Creed): "I believe in one God."
> Sanctus: "Holy, holy, holy."
> Agnus Dei: "O Lamb of God, that takest away the sins of the world."

We have already mentioned Leonard Bernstein's *Mass*, a modern version of this traditional ritual.

Oriental Sacred Texts

As we have become more and more familiar with Eastern art through travel and modern reproductions of art, the importance of Oriental sacred tests has become apparent. The countries of the Orient, especially China, Japan, and India, have all produced sacred texts of one kind or another, and these have inspired various kinds of art. Most

Figure 3-23. *Siva as Nataraja* (southern India, ca. 1800). (Copper. Boston, Museum of Fine Arts; Marianne Brimmer Fund.)

fruitful have been the texts and traditions of Hinduism an
Buddhism.

Among the principal deities of the Hindu system are Vishnu
Siva, and the goddess Devi. Vishnu is one of the oldest of Hind
gods; worship of Vishnu, which goes back into the earliest recorde
periods, is inspired by the sacred books known as the Vedas, wher
he appears as a kind of solar god. A later book, known as th
Mahābhārata, is an epic in which Vishnu is identified as the divin
hero-teacher. In the famous *Bhagavad-Gita* ("Song of the Blessed"
a section of the *Mahābhārata* and perhaps the most widely read re
ligious book of India, Vishnu is identified with Krishna, the god o
caste duty who is only one of the many incarnations of Vishnu. Du
ing the earliest Vedic times, the god Siva was worshipped as pa
of—or identical with—Rudra, the storm god. Unlike the beneficer
Vishnu, Siva is associated with the darker powers of nature. He i
the divine dancer who creates and destroys. His eternal movement i
the rhythm of the universe itself. The example from the Museum o
Fine Arts in Boston, shown in Figure 3-23, depicts him as Lord of th

Dance (Nataraja), the cosmic dancer, with his complement of four hands, each of which represents one of the aspects of his being and his importance. The universe is his theater and he himself both actor and audience. He holds in his upper hands the symbols of creation (a hand drum) and of destruction (fire), while his lower hands are posed in gestures of protection and assurance. He is enclosed in a ring of fire (the manifest world), and in his dance he crushes the evil dwarf of ignorance, Apasmara. In his headdress are a crescent moon, a human skull, cobras, and flowers. In his right ear is a man's earring; in his left, a woman's.

The Buddhist religion, which is perhaps the most widespread and influential in the Oriental world, began in India and spread from there into most of the other countries of East. Its artistic representations are almost without number, and many of them have their inspiration in the "Jataka" tales from the life of the Buddha. A fine example of an Indian head of the Buddha is shown in Figure 3-24, which displays quite clearly the attributes by which Indian representations of him can be recognized: the "bump of wisdom," tuft of hair between the eyes, lowered lids, and pendulous earlobes with long slits. (See page 43 for a fuller discussion of these symbols.) The Lohan, or disciple of Buddha, from the T'ang period of ancient China (Figure 6-6), is one of many thousands of examples of the acceptance of Buddhist ideas from India by the various other countries of the Far East.

Of all the Buddhist religious figures commonly stylized in Oriental arts, perhaps none is more intrinsically moving without knowledge of its religious source than the Kuan Yin, a seated female bodhisattva, that is, a follower of Buddha who has attained enlightenment but who postpones Nirvana in order to help others attain it. The example in Figure 3-25 is typical in stressing the qualities associated with her—repose and compassion. She sits in a relaxed position known as "royal ease," suggesting the informal affability of royalty; part of her weight rests on one arm, while the other is extended across a raised knee. The relaxation of the hand, the downcast eyes, the soft, warm coloring, the perfect distribution of weight communicate a sense of complete peacefulness and quiet.

Not only do all the great religions of the East have their particular texts to furnish narrative religious material, but there are also historical books and handbooks which tell the artist how to work. An example of narrative text is the well-known Persian *Shah-Nama* ("Book of Kings") of the fourteenth century, a narrative of the Moslem Persian monarchs frequently illustrated in Persia (Color Plate 33; Color Plate 33 is in the group following page 216). An example of the handbooks for artists is the one known as the "Six Canons" (that is, laws) of the painter and critic Hsieh-Ho, from around A.D. 500. In this book the author prescribes, as the necessary qualities of the successful painting, such things as "rhythmic vital-

Figure 3-24. *Head of Buddha* (Gandhara, India, ca. fifth century). (Stucco. Height: about 11½ inches. London, Victoria and Albert Museum.)

Figure 3-25. *Kuan Yin Bodhisattva* (Chinese, 1115–1254 to Early Yuan Dynasty). (Polychromed wood. Height: 7 feet, 11 inches. Nelson Gallery of Art, Atkins Museum, Kansas City, Missouri. Nelson Fund.)

ity," "the law of bones and brushwork" (composition and line "harmonious coloring," and "finish."

In India we find a remarkable book on the technique of t drama, called the Fifth Veda, the *Natya Sastra*, or the Theater Ved Indian acting and dance are covered by the same word, *Natya*, a the sharp distinctions we make in the West do not exist. (Compa *Nataraja*, Lord of the Dance.) This book not only lays down speci rules for the training of the actor in a seven-year apprenticeshi but has detailed instructions for constructing the stage or playir area and making costumes. The playing area, although it is hard more than a square separated from the spectators by a border, " nonetheless considered a sacred precinct, and upon entering it the performer invokes the deity."[3] From our earliest records the ideas of theater and dance have been congenial to Hindu thought and religion, in which the phenomenal world is seen "not as a battlefield of principles but as a theater for the display of natural forces created by the divinities."[4] We have already spoken of the "divine dancer," Siva Nataraja, who dances the manifest world into existence, sustains it with dance, and finally dances it to nonexistence. Some scholars now think that Indian theater was established as an art at least a thousand years before it was so recognized elsewhere. There is, for example, a Greek legend that Dionysus, whose religious rites are the beginning of Greek theater, came to Greece from the Far East. There are also Indian texts on the plastic arts, known as the *Silpa Sastras*, which prescribe rules for sculpture and architecture. These very specific injunctions about how one acts, dances, paints, and carves all date from the Gupta dynastry of A.D. 320 to A.D. 535—about the same time as the early Christian period in the West—in their written form, but scholars agree that they represent oral traditions which date back hundreds of years.

SUBJECTS DERIVED FROM OTHER WORKS OF ART

A last category of subjects may be found in those works that take their subject directly from other works of art.

It is worth observing what the poet adds over and above the description when a painting is the source of information. Anne Sexton gives us vivid images of the power in the revolving constellations in Van Gogh's *Starry Night* (Figure 3-26). The strong verbs, the powerful comparison of the cypress tree to the hair of a drowning woman, the many images of heat and movement all prepare us for the dramatic short lines conveying her personal identification with the powers of nature and her urge to lose herself in those powers and die. In a way she has gone beyond the painter.

The town does not exist
except where one black-haired tree slips
up like a drowned woman into the hot sky.
The town is silent. The night boils with eleven stars.
Oh starry night! This is how
I want to die.

It moves. They are all alive.
Even the moon bulges in its orange irons
To push children, like a god, from its eye.

[3] Jacques Burdick, *Theatre* (New York: Newsweek Books, 1974), p. 98.
[4] *Ibid.*, p. 97.

Figure 3-26. Vincent Van Gogh (1853–1890), Dutch painter, etcher, and lithographer. *The Starry Night* (1889). (Oil on canvas. Size 29 by 26¼ inches. Collection, Museum of Modern Art, New York. Acquired through the Lillie P. Bliss Bequest.)

The old unseen serpent swallows up the stars.
Oh starry, starry night! This is how
I want to die:

Into that rushing beast of the night,
sucked up by that great dragon, to split
from my life with no flag,
no belly,
no cry.
   —Anne Sexton, (1928–   American poet),
     "Starry Night"[5]

[5] From *All My Pretty Ones* (Boston: Houghton Mifflin Company, 1963). Copyright © 1961, 19
1963 by Anne Sexton. Reprinted by permission of Houghton Mifflin Company and The Sterli
Lord Agency, Inc.

Brueghel used the subject of Icarus for one painting, and Auden and Madden have been inspired by the painting to write poems. The Greek myth tells that Icarus, the son of Daedalus, the great artisan, was given wings by his father. Since the wings were fastened on by wax, Daedalus warned the boy not to fly too near the sun. But the boy, exulting in his new power, could not restrain himself; soon the wax melted, he fell into the sea, and he was drowned.

In Brueghel's painting *The Fall of Icarus* (Figure 3-27) the boy is almost submerged; only one of his legs is seen as it disappears into the water. Nearby is a luxurious ship, and on a slight rise a farmer is plowing with a horse; below is a shepherd who is looking up at the sky, his sheep all around him.

Auden gives his poem the name of the museum in which the painting is found.

Figure 3-27. Pieter Brueghel the Elder (ca. 1525–1569), Dutch painter. *The Fall of Icarus* (ca. 1554–1555). (Tempera on canvas. Height: ca. 2 feet, 4 inches. Patrimoine des Musées Royaux des Beaux-Arts, Brussels.)

MUSEE DES BEAUX ARTS

About suffering they were never wrong,
The Old Masters: how well they understood

Its human position; how it takes place
While someone else is eating or opening a window or just walking dully
                                                                        along;

How, when the aged are reverently, passionately waiting
For the miraculous birth, there always must be
Children who did not specially want it to happen, skating
On a pond at the edge of the wood:
They never forgot
That even the dreadful martyrdom must run its course
Anyhow in a corner, some untidy spot
Where the dogs go on with their doggy life and the torturer's horse
Scratches its innocent behind on a tree.

In Brueghel's *Icarus*, for instance: how everything turns away
Quite leisurely from the disaster; the ploughman may
Have heard the splash, the forsaken cry,
But for him it was not an important failure; the sun shone
As it had to on the white legs disappearing into the green
Water; and the expensive delicate ship that must have seen
Something amazing, a boy falling out of the sky,
Had somewhere to get to and sailed calmly on.

—W. H. Auden (1907–1973), British poet)[6]

Charles Madden finds a very different emphasis; he is less **philo-**
sophic about the theme, using it rather as a means of evoking **a poetic**
mood.

THE FALL OF ICARUS
(From Brueghel's painting)

The bulging sails by a riotous wind caught
pull the ships and their rigging nets toward shore
to be emptied. The sailors quickly will calm their floors
and their houses in the evening light will melt into the mountains.

And on the hill with one foot planted in the earth
his plowing almost done, his eyes cast down and fully shielded
from the sun which now is growing shadow, the farmer
turns in soil and toil the final circles of the day.

Below him a quiet pastoral: on lichen-bearing rocks
the feeding sheep, the quiet watching dog, the silent shepherd

so stalking with his eyes the homing flight of birds
that neither he nor the intent fisherman closer to the shore,

none has seen the silent fall of Icarus
through the riotous wind and the shadows of the coming evening light,
nor do they hear his sigh, both of pity and delight
of his remembered waxed and winged flight.

—Charles F. Madden (1921–   , American poet, teacher)[7]

We have mentioned Tchaikovsky's suite based on Shakespeare's play *Romeo and Juliet*. Debussy's *Afternoon of a Faun* is based on a poem by Mallarmé, and the ballet of the same name is based on both. Rimsky-Korsakov's *Scheherazade* finds its source in *The Arabian Nights*. Browning's poem "Fra Lippo Lippi" was inspired by the painting *The Coronation of the Virgin* by Fra Filippo Lippi. Strauss takes his subject *Don Quixote* from the novel by Cervantes. Maeterlinck's play *Pelléas et Mélisande* was used by Debussy for his opera of the same name.

There are many instances of paintings or graphics inspired by poetry. Generally, however, these works of graphic art are illustrative in character, although they may very well give an added dimension to the poem itself. In principle, a painter is not likely to devote a serious work of art to illustrating or embellishing a single poem, if for no other reason than that such a task is both difficult and unrewarding. On the other hand, longer works of literature have engaged a great many artists from the Renaissance forward; the plays and poetry of Dante, Milton, Shakespeare, Molière, and Byron are examples. Among the outstanding works of visual art derived from literature are the series of lithographs done by the French painter Eugène Delacroix (1798–1863) for the great verse drama *Faust* by the German poet Johann Wolfgang von Goethe, who was quite ready to admit that the artist had contributed something to the poetry. Much more recently (1931) Picasso did a series of illustrations for an edition of the *Metamorphoses* of Ovid (a collection of poems of the first century after Christ). The thirty etchings which illustrate this great collection of love poetry (Figure 3-28) are marvelously expressive of its sensuous paganism, although they are far removed in character from any plastic art produced by the ancients themselves. By attaching his own interpretation of the pagan to these poems, Picasso has given them an added dimension, as Delacroix did for Goethe's *Faust*. The painting derived from literature must not merely illustrate if it is to be successful—just as the poem derived from a painting must not

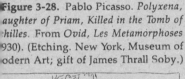
Figure 3-28. Pablo Picasso. *Polyxena, Daughter of Priam, Killed in the Tomb of Achilles.* From *Ovid, Les Metamorphoses* (1930). (Etching. New York, Museum of Modern Art; gift of James Thrall Soby.)

[7] From *Northwest Review*, University of Oregon, 1960. Used by permission of Charles F. Madden.

merely describe. The source must be a point of departure for the artist's own creativity.

Dramas are often based on novels, and operas on plays; many cinema plots are taken from dramas or novels. Works that derive from other works of art are always individual and can never be classified or grouped together. Therefore, it is sufficient for our purpose merely to note that works of art often are so derived.

Color Plate 11. Domenico Ghirlandajo (1449–1494), Italian painter. *Old Man and Boy* (ca. 1480). (Oil on wood. Height: 2 feet, ³⁄₈ inches. Paris, Louvre. Photograph by Alinari.)

Color Plate 12. Sandro Botticelli (1444–1501), Italian painter. *Birth of Venus* (ca. 1485). (Tempera on canvas Height: 5 feet, 3¼ inches. Florence Uffizi Gallery. Photograph by Scala New York.

Color Plate 13. José Clemente Orozco (1883–1949), Mexican painter. *Don Miguel Hidalgo y Costilla* (1936–1939). (Detail from frescoes in the Governor's Palace, Guadalajara, Mexico.)

Color Plate 14. Titian (1477–1576), Italian painter. *Bacchus and Ariadne* (ca. 1520). (Oil on canvas. Size: 60 by 75 inches. London, National Gallery. Reproduced by courtesy of the Trustees.)

Color Plate 15. Michelangelo (1495–1564), Italian painter, sculptor, architect, and poet. *Creation of Adam*, detail of Sistine Chapel ceiling, Vatican City. (Length of Adam 10 feet. Photograph by Scala, New York.)

Color Plate 16. Giotto (1266–1336).
Italian painter. *Madonna Enthroned*
(ca. 1310). (Tempera on wood. Height:
10 feet, 8½ inches. Florence, Uffizi
Gallery. Photograph by Scala,
New York.)

4 FUNCTION

DEFINITION

Benvenuto Cellini, the famous goldsmith, made an elaborate little bowl for Francis I, King of France (Figure 4-1). It is made of gold on a black ebony base; on it are two figures: a woman representing the land and a man representing the sea. We identify the man by his trident (a three-pronged spear), which is the symbol of Neptune, the god of the sea. As we look at the bowl and marvel at its exquisite workmanship, we ask: What is it for? The answer to this question gives the *function* of an article. Cellini made his bowl as a container for salt, and because of its function it is called a saltcellar. As used in this book, the word *function* will be reserved for those arts whose medium is itself directly practical and useful.

Many of the works cited in Chapter 3 were made primarily for their function. The lekythos on which was represented Apollo with his kithara is primarily a vessel for holding oil. It has a long neck to make it possible to pour the oil slowly. The painting by Execias called *Dionysus Sailing the Sea* is in the bottom of a cylix, a shallow drinking cup. These paintings, like the figures on the saltcellar, are decorative and without any actual function, but it should be noted that with the Greeks, as with Cellini and other later artists, the decorations are related to the function of the vessel. Bacchus, the god of wine, is clearly related to the function of the cylix; Cellini uses Neptune, the god of the sea, to symbolize salt.

These are clear examples of functional art; but sometimes we do not know, or are not sure of, the original function of an object. Since the Altamira cave paintings predate the use of writing, we have to

Figure 4-1. Benvenuto Cellini (1500–1572), Italian sculptor and goldsmith. *Saltcellar of Francis I* (ca. 1545). Gold and enamel. Height: about 8 inches. Vienna, Kunsthistorisches Museum.)

make assumptions about their function, which undoubtedly ha
something to do with hunting. By analogy with magical practic
among primitive people today, we conclude that the pictures we
designed to ensure a successful hunt—what we now call "symp
thetic magic." Apparently the caves were in more or less constant u
as sanctuaries or holy places, since successive generations of painte
have superposed their paintings on others. It is therefore fairly sa
to say that these paintings had a practical function.

Stonehenge (shown in Figure 4-2) is also prehistoric, but of it v
have more definite knowledge. Its characteristic feature is a series
circles of huge stones set upright in the ground and capped wi
lintels. Toward the center are two broken rings of stones and at tl
center a large slab which may have served as an altar. One lon
established fact has seemed most significant. Stonehenge is oriente
so that its axis passes through a 35-ton marker stone and poin
directly to the spot on the northeast horizon where the sun rises
the summer solstice, the longest day of the year. The place may hav
had some ceremonial or other religious purpose. Certainly it w
built with one eye on the calendar. Astronomical calculations prov
that Stonehenge was in use about 1500 B.C.

Many works are cherished for themselves after their functior
have ceased, and these have the right to be considered as artistic. Tl
Altamira paintings are a case in point. The war speeches of Church
are now being widely printed and read as works of literature. Tl
lithographs by Daumier which appeared for forty years in the perio
ical *Charivari* as cartoons making social comment are now collecte
and reproduced for their own sake.

Figure 4-2. Stonehenge (ca. 1800–1400 B.C.), Salisbury Plain, Wiltshire, England. (Diameter of circle: 97 feet; height of stones above ground: 13½ feet. Photograph, Central Office of Information, London.)

FUNCTIONAL AND NONFUNCTIONAL ARTS

Obviously, function plays a larger part in some arts than in others. Architecture is directly and almost entirely functional: buildings are always built for some special use. The applied arts also are almost entirely functional. In fact, they are called "applied" arts because they have function. Metalwork such as gates, lamps, grilles, Chinese ritual bronzes, Christian religious objects, armor, weapons, tools, and coins; ceramics; glassware; stained glass; mosaic and tilework; textiles; enamelwork; furniture; and books are among the many types of applied arts, or crafts. Each of these examples is made for some definite and specific use. Moreover, in the applied arts, as in architecture, function is so important that it, rather than the name of the art, is used to identify individual works. Examples of those arts are ordinarily known by their direct function; although we speak of a painting, a poem, or a statue, we do not usually speak of a building or a piece of ceramics or metalwork; we say, instead, "a school," "a church," "a plate," "a saucer," "a suit of armor" (Figure 4-3).

If architecture and the applied arts are most directly functional, literature and painting are probably least functional, though there are many examples of writing and painting with a definite purpose. Picasso's *Guernica* and Daumier's *Rue Transnonain* were protests against abuses of their time. *Uncle Tom's Cabin* was written for the definite purpose of fighting slavery, and it did much to arouse anti-slavery sentiment before the Civil War. Oliver Wendell Holmes's short poem "Old Ironsides" was written to protest a naval order that the frigate *Constitution* be destroyed. This ship, known as "Old Iron-sides," was famous for its exploits during the War of 1812. Holmes's poem—which begins with the familiar line, "Aye, tear her tattered ensign down!"—aroused so much response that the order to scrap the old ship was countermanded; her tattered flag was not torn down.

Expository and argumentative writing is indirectly functional insofar as it is designed to accomplish some definite end. Newspaper stories and pictures are also indirectly functional; they want to make clear the news. All advertisements, whether in words or in line and color, are functional in that they are designed to influence people.

FUNCTION IN MUSIC

Music in its origins was primarily functional, its two sources being dance and religion. The earliest people seem to have invoked their gods by beating the drum and singing, and from that time to the present, music has been of paramount importance in worship.

Figure 4-3. Italian suit of armor (ca. 1400). (Armor for man. New York, Metropolitan Museum of Art; The Bashford Dean Memorial Collection, gift of Helen Fahnestock Hubbard, 1929, in memory of her father, Harris C. Fahnestock.)

Dancing is also very ancient. As it has evolved, modern danc music includes the ballet and tunes for social and folk dances, such a the jig, waltz, minuet, fox trot, polonaise, mazurka, rumba, tango and cha-cha. Rock is the most recent development. In dance, music i essential to mark the rhythm and so to keep the dancers together. I also sets the mood of the dance—lively, warlike, gay, courtly graceful.

Closely akin to dance music are marches, work songs, and gam songs. A march serves the same purpose as a dance in that it mark the time for people walking in a procession, whether it be a militar occasion, a wedding, or a funeral. Work songs mark the rhythm o work. Chanteys are sung by sailors when lifting anchor or loadin cargo. The popular Russian folk song "The Volga Boatman" helpe the tow-men in their struggle against the current of the river. Gam songs are about halfway between dance and work songs. In "Th Farmer in the Dell" or "London Bridge Is Falling Down," the son is sung as the game is played, and the song is an essential part of th game.

Certain compositions become identified with certain specifi occasions. One march, "Hail to the Chief," is used as a salute to th President of the United States. Another, Handel's "Dead March' from *Saul*, is used for the funerals of the royal family in England. Th Wagner and the Mendelssohn marches are so universally used i America for weddings that the wits have wondered if weddings ar legal without them.

With the development of musical instruments, music outgrew its narrow dependence on dancing and ritual, and we now have much music that has no connection whatever with either dance o religion, such as symphonies, sonatas, and operas. On the othe hand, many musical compositions retain a connection with thei functional origin though they are no longer functional. Few of the polonaises and mazurkas of Chopin, for example, could be used a accompaniment for a dance, but they are still given the names o dances and resemble these dances in certain ways. Bach's great Mass in B minor is too long to be used for church services, but it retains the form of the Mass designed for church ritual. Lullabies and serenades may also be dissociated from their original use, yet they retain certain characteristics: the lullaby has a sweet melody and swaying rhythms; the serenade connotes night and love.

FUNCTION IN SCULPTURE

Sculpture is much more *functional* than painting or literature. Re ligion has for ages made great functional use of sculpture. The bronze doors which Ghiberti made for the Baptistery at Florence (Figures

4-4 and 4-5) are a magnificent example. They are so faultless that when Michelangelo saw them he exclaimed, "They are so beautiful that they might fittingly stand at the gates of paradise"—and they have been called the "Gates of Paradise" ever since.

In the Medieval and Renaissance church, sculpture was frequently used for instructional purposes. The panels of the "Gates of Paradise," for example, record scenes from the Old Testament. In the first panel, as has been mentioned, the subject is the Creation. Several different scenes are presented; in the lower left-hand corner God is bringing Adam to life while the angels rejoice; in the center of

Figure 4-5. *Above:* Lorenzo Ghiberti. *The Creation,* detail c "Gates of Paradise" (1425–1452). Height of detail: 3 feet, 10 inches. Photograph by Alinari/Scala.)

Figure 4-6. *Left: Signs of the Zodiac,* with corresponding occupations (first half of the thirteenth century). Details, basement of west façade. (Stone. Height of each quatrefoi 2½ feet. Amiens Cathedral. Photograph, Caisse Nationale des Monuments Historiques, Paris.)

the panel is the creation of Eve, with a circle of angels surroundin the figures. On the left, behind the creation of Adam, is the Tempta tion: Adam and Eve stand under a tree with the serpent coile around it. On the right is shown the Expulsion: Adam and Eve hav been driven from the garden by an angel, and God is seen far back i the heavens.

On one wall of the Gothic cathedral at Amiens is a calenda showing the signs of the zodiac. Each of the signs is represented b its symbol, and under it is a relief, of the same size and shape, whicl illustrates a typical occupation for that sign or month. The first of th three signs in our photograph (Figure 4-6) pictures a goat, the sign o Capricorn, which corresponds roughly to the month of December Shown under it is a man hanging meat for the winter. The middle relief shows a man pouring water—Aquarius—who stands fo January. Under him is a table at which is seated a man with two heads who, like the month of January (from Latin *Janus,* the name o this two-headed personage), looks to both the new and the old year February, the last of three signs, is represented by two fish, the sigr

being Pisces, "fish." Under them is a monk trying to keep warm. He has taken off his shoes and is warming his hands and feet before the blazing fire.

Another important function of sculpture is the commemoration of individuals or events. The Lincoln Memorial in Washington, D.C., is an example of the former; the Gateway Arch in St. Louis, of the latter (Figure 4-7). Perhaps the most impressive monument of our century, the Gateway Arch was built "to commemorate the role St. Louis played in our epic surge westward and to honor those soldiers and pioneers, from Lewis and Clark to the homesteaders, who moved the national boundaries 2,000 miles to the Pacific." Not only the graceful shape and impressive size—a 630-foot arch suggesting a gateway—but the dramatic uses of new mediums and principles of construction are symbolic of its commemorative, celebrative significance. (See page 360 for more details.) Often a statue records an event of importance: *The Charioteer* (Figure 6-3) probably commemorates a victory. Among sculptures that are not connected with architecture, fountains take an important place. The fountain is frequently used as a medium for telling a mythological or allegorical story; for example, the fountain by Carl Milles opposite the Union Station in St. Louis represents the union of the Missouri and the Mississippi Rivers. A more recent monument of this type is the

Monument for a Devastated City by Ossip Zadkine, commemoratin[g] those who died in the bombing of Rotterdam at the beginning [of] World War II (Figure 4-8).

The tombstone is one of the opportunities for sculpture that [is] too frequently disregarded. But tombstones can and should [be] beautiful. Figure 4-9 shows an American tombstone of the coloni[al] period, from New England. In Figures 4-10 and 4-11 we have tw[o] examples from different ages: one is Greek of the fifth century B.C.[,]

Figure 4-8. Ossip Zadkine (1890–1967), Dutch sculptor. *Monument for a Devastated City* (1953). (Rotterdam, Netherlands. Netherlands National Tourist Office, New York.)

Figure 4-9. Tombstone of Samuel Green (1759). (Detail. Lexington, Mass. From Graebner, Fite, and White, *A History of the American People*, 2d ed., McGraw-Hill, New York. Used with permission of McGraw-Hill Book Company.)

gure 4-10. Hegeso stele (late fifth century B.C.). (Pentelic marble. Height: 4 feet, 10½ inches. Athens, National useum. Photograph by Alinari/Scala.)

the other is nineteenth-century American, the work of Augustus Saint-Gaudens.

Another functional use of sculpture is the coin. Every coin shows a relief: the Lincoln penny, the Jefferson nickel, the Franklin Roosevelt dime, and the Washington quarter. In the United States we are now paying more attention to the designs on coins than we did fifty years ago. It is interesting to note how the spirit of a country is reflected in the designs on its coins. Ancient Greek coins are as important artistically as ancient Greek monumental sculpture and as typical of their times (Figure 4-12.)

FUNCTION IN ARCHITECTURE

Architecture is the only one of the major arts that is directly functional. It is also the art in which the proper performance of function is most important. Buildings are large and expensive, and they cannot easily be replaced. If a chair is not comfortable, we can buy

Figure 4-12. Greek coin (fifth century .c.). (Silver, New York, Metropolitan useum of Art; gift of J. Pierpont Morgan, 1905.)

another and use the uncomfortable one only when we have company
But we cannot treat architecture in any such way. If a building doe
not function, we have to put up with an inconvenient and inefficier
structure. Therefore it is in architecture that we see most clearly th
influence of functional demands. These can be traced to demand
that arise from climate and those that come from social conditions

Factors Influencing Function in Architecture

Climate With central heating, structural steel, and air conditionin
it is possible to live in any kind of house in any climate; nevertheles
climate is still a factor of which everyone is acutely conscious. Is th
climate wet or dry, hot or cold, sunny or dark, even or variable
windy or calm? In countries where there is strong wind, the house i
planned with windbreaks and the living rooms are put in protecte
areas away from the wind, whereas in warm climates with tem
perate winds, the house is planned to take advantage of the prevai
ing breeze. In a cold climate, emphasis is placed on building fo
warmth; in a warm climate, it is placed on the attempt to keep coo
When the climate is mild, the primary function of the wall is to er
sure privacy and to keep out the sun and rain; hence, it may be
very light material. In China and Japan, for instance, the walls ar
merely sliding screens.

The size and number of the doors and windows are likewis
determined largely by climate. In hot southern countries where th
sun is blinding, the object is to shut out the light; accordingly, i
Spain and in Egypt the windows are small and few. In the norther
countries, where there is much rain and the winters are long an
dark, the demand is for more light, and the windows are large an
numerous. The shape of the roof depends primarily on the amount
rain and snow. A flat roof is found in warm, dry countries, as i
Egypt and Greece, where the roof can be used as an extra sitting roor
or as a bedroom on warm nights. But a flat roof is practical only in
dry climate. Where there is rain, it is usually found best to tilt th
roof to make it easier for the water to run off. The degree of slope i
determined partly by the amount of rain. In countries where ther
is much rain, the roofs are more steeply pitched than in countries tha
have only a little rain. The amount of snow is an important facto
also. Snow is very heavy; a large quantity will break through a roo
hence, in mountainous countries where there is a great deal of snow
the roofs are very steeply pitched and are left unbroken by window
so that the snow will slide off. The steeply pitched, broken roofs tha
are found on the châteaux are useful in France, where there is muc
rain and little snow, but they would not be practical in the Alps. I
China there are very heavy rains during the monsoons. Accordingly

the roofs are steeply pitched and project over the house; at the eaves they are turned up to admit light.

Here in the United States, both the northern and the southern states have beautiful examples of the colonial type of architecture. But there are interesting differences due primarily to differences in climate. In the South there are many more verandas than in the North. And in the South the columns of the porch often extend to the roof in order to shade the windows of the second story. There is a difference, too, in the arrangement of the buildings. In New England, because of the cold and the snow, the barns and the other outbuildings were often attached to the main residence so that the men of the house could do the chores without going out in the cold. In the South, with its mild winters, the outbuildings were scattered all around the yard as separate structures. Even a rather modest house would have a smokehouse (for meat), a hen house, a carriage house, probably an ice house (for storing ice), and a cellar (for keeping food cool), as well as the barns.

Social Factors The term *social factors* is used here to mean all those elements in architecture that are determined by people in contrast with those that are governed by nature. A first consideration in any building is the use to which it is to be put, its function in the narrower sense of the term. A building is designed for a special purpose: it may be an office building, a church, a residence, a garage, and so on. These primary functions are influenced by the physical conditions—climate, as we have just seen, and terrain—but they are even more dependent on social forces. In olden times there was always need for protection. Castles and fortifications were made with very thick, strong walls, as defense against the enemy. Palaces had to be strong enough to ward off possible attack. The palace which Michelozzo built for Cosimo de' Medici served both as palace and fortress (Figure 4-13).

Another example of social influences on architecture can be found by comparing buildings designed as places of worship (Figure 4-14). To Christians a church or a cathedral is primarily a place where large numbers of people can assemble, because corporate worship is an integral part of the Christian faith. Hence the cathedral at Amiens is large, the construction is open, and it will hold many people. The Greeks, on the other hand, had no service in the same sense; their gatherings for religious purposes were infrequent and were held out-of-doors. For them the temple was basically a shrine for the statue of the god, and in consequence their temples were small, accommodating only a few people at a time. The Parthenon, though large for a temple, is only about one-fourth the size of the cathedral at Amiens. And small as the Parthenon is, it was divided into two rooms: a large room in which the statue of Athena was kept, and a smaller one for

Figure 4-13. Michelozzo (1396–1472), Italian architect. Medici-Riccardi Palace, Florence. (Stone. Length: 300 feet; height: 90 feet. Photograph by Alinari/Scala.)

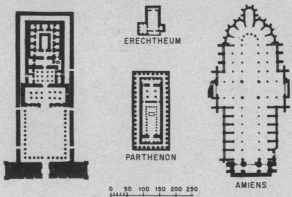

Figure 4-14. Floor plans showing relative size of the Erechtheum, the parthenon, the temple at Edfu, and Amiens Cathedral.

the treasures. The Erechtheum, another Greek temple, is even smaller. The Egyptian temple had a different arrangement because the ritual was different. In Egypt the temple was fundamentally a sanctuary which could be visited only by the Pharaoh and the priest. In front of the sanctuary was a series of rooms to which other people were admitted according to their rank. An Egyptian temple, such as that at Edfu, consisted of four parts: first, the pylon, a huge gateway covering the entire front of the building; second, a large open court accessible to everyone; third, a hall, or hypostyle, with many large, decorated columns. This hall, which was dimly lighted because the columns were very closely spaced, was reserved for dignitaries who occupied a position midway between the people and the Pharaoh. And finally, there was a small inner sanctuary for only the priest and the king.

Sometimes the government steps in with laws which affect architecture, though these may not be directly concerned with building as such. A tax on the number of windows, for instance, will result in houses with fewer windows. It is supposed that a tax on the number of stories of a house had much to do with the development of the mansard roof, which gave all the space of an extra story though technically it was only an attic. One interesting example of this type is to be found in the zoning law of New York City. This law was made necessary by the skyscrapers, for if very tall buildings are placed on each side of a street, the street between will be dark, like a very narrow canyon. The purpose of the law is to ensure that a street should always have the proper amount of air and sunshine, and it accomplishes this end by regulating the height of a building in proportion to the width of the street and the size of the lot. An imaginary triangle is drawn with the lot as its base, and the law requires that the building should not project beyond that triangle, except for a tower not to exceed one-fourth the area of the plot. In order to utilize their plots to the best advantage, some builders have designed structures in which the upper floors are set back from the lower floors, as in the building in the background in Figure 4-15; but a different solution has been used in Lever House, in the foreground. The height of the tower is not restricted by law in either case.

In the latter part of the nineteenth century and the first half of our century, function became the most important principle in guiding American architects and the prime criterion in judging architecture. As a reaction against architecture in which the relationship between the aesthetic and the functional had been all but lost, Henry Hobson Richardson, Louis Sullivan, and Frank Lloyd Wright designed buildings in which they aimed at more "honest" exteriors and more functional, flexible interiors. The functionalist style they pioneered was further refined at the famous German art school, the Bauhaus. The two directors of the school, Walter Gropius and Ludwig Mies van der Rohe, reduced the urban building to a basic

framework of steel, a skin of glass, and an open interior in which "curtain walls" could be moved around to suit the purposes of the user.

Both Gropius and Mies van der Rohe later came to the United States, where their ideas and buildings created what has come to be called the "international style." Wright, however, while he continued to champion functionalism, continued also to insist that a building should grow from the site and should provide congenial pleasant, attractive spaces for those working and living in it, a point of view which came to be called "organic" style (see page 357). Currently, the rigorous, functional international style is being modified toward something more inviting than the steel skeleton with "glass skin" of the Bauhaus. But buildings have a long life, and New York and other large cities will for many years have architectural monu ments to the vitality of this rigorous, pure, sterile functionalism of the first half of the twentieth century.

Although there are many individual styles in architecture today, all of them tend to combine concern for mere function with other qualities—variety in shape, color, carefully coordinated proportions, texture, symbolism, and many more. Important in all these is an aim to create buildings which not only "work," but are for people—to delight in as they pass them, to live in, to work in, to create in, to enjoy. There is, too, a return to the concern for the expressive qualities of buildings, as in the TWA Terminal Building (see Figure 14-36.)

In Chapter 14, Organization in Architecture, we have chosen Eero Saarinen and his way of working to exemplify the typical approach of architects in the latter half of our century. Here we quote him in paragraphs which summarize the thinking of one important architect on the importance of function, "organic" form, and "structural honesty," as well as the roles which time, place, and meaning assume in his buildings:

I am a child of my period. I am enthusiastic about the three common principles of modern architecture: function, structure, and being part of our time. The principle of respecting function is deeply imbedded in me as it is in others of this period. But, like others, I do not look to it to solve my architectural problems. Sometimes, however, the problem and the time are ripe for an entirely new functional approach to a problem (as in the new jet airport for Washington), and at such moments function may become the overwhelming principle in directing the formula of design.

The principle of structure has moved in a curious way over this century from being "structural honesty" to "expression of structure" and finally to "structural expressionism." Structural integrity is a potent and lasting principle and I would never want to get far away from it. To express structure, however, is not an end in itself. It is only when structure can contribute to the total and to the other principles that it is important.

The third common principle of modern architecture—the awareness of the thinking and technology of our time—is for me an ever-present challenge. I want always to search out the new possibilities in new materials of our time and to give them their proper place in architectural design.

Yes, I am dedicated to these three basic principles of modern architecture. But it seems to me they are not necessarily the only pillars one's work must rest on. The great architecture of the past did not rest on these alone. There are other principles equally or more important.

When I approach an architectural problem, I try to think out the real significance of the problem. What is its essence and how can the total structure capture that essence? How can the whole building convey emotionally the purpose and meaning of the building? Conveying significant meaning is part of the inspirational purpose of architecture and, therefore, for me, it is a fundamental principle of our art.

The conviction that a building cannot be placed on a site, but that a building grows from its site, is another principle in which I believe. I see

Figure 4-16. Murphy and Mackey (now Murphy, Downey, Wofford and Richman), architects. The Climatron, (1960), Missouri Botanical Garden, St. Louis, Mo. (Aluminum structural frame and suspended grid system which contains the transparent plastic "skin." Diameter: 170 feet; height: 70 feet. Photograph, Hedrich-Blessing.)

architecture not as the building alone, but the building in relation to surroundings, whether nature or man-made surroundings. I believe ve strongly that the single building must be carefully related to the whole in t outdoor space it creates. In its mass and scale and material it must become enhancing element in the total environment. Now this does not mean th the building has to succumb to the total. Any architecture must hold its he high. But a way must be found for uniting the whole, because the total e vironment is more important than the single building.

The external form of my work varies greatly. But inside the solution every problem there are underlying principles that hold it together and jo each building I have done to every other one. In fact, if it didn't sound t pompous, I would say that the common denominator of my work is the co stant philosophy—the constant respect for the principles in which I believe

Sometimes the development of a new medium or an inventic makes it possible to meet a need which could not be met before. A interesting example is the Climatron (Figure 4-16; see also Figure 1-2 in which the geodesic dome principle developed by Buckminst Fuller is used to provide a large, completely unobstructed interi and a high level of natural light for the artificial creation and contr of a wide range of climatic conditions for growing tropical plant This application of the geodesic dome principle to climate control h proven to be practical and functional, and Fuller has himself pr

[1] Aline B. Saarinen (ed.), *Eero Saarinen on His Work* (New Haven, Conn.: Yale University Pre 1962), pp. 6–8.

posed a climate-control dome for New York City large enough to cover some two miles of midtown Manhattan.

FORM FOLLOWS FUNCTION

Whenever art has function, the function influences and often determines the form. This is just another way of stating the obvious fact that if an object is made for a certain function, it should be made in such a way that it can perform that function. As the function changes, the form changes, and if there are many functions, there will be many forms. Take an object of everyday use, such as a spoon. There are spoons for babies and spoons for adults, spoons for cooking, spoons for eating, spoons for serving, deep spoons and shallow spoons, spoons with long handles, and spoons with short handles. Even a rather small household will have a variety of spoons because there are a variety of functions to be served by them. Door keys offer another interesting example. Keys are now carried by many people, and one person often has to carry more than one key; accordingly, keys are small. But when gates and doors were in the charge of special porters who were always in attendance, keys were large and massive; they were, in fact, a visible symbol of the power and importance of the place to be locked.

These examples have been taken from the industrial arts, but instances may be cited from any art that is functional. A lullaby must have a rocking rhythm to soothe the baby. A march or a jig must keep the time exactly so that one may march or dance in time to it. A coin must be small and flat, and any decoration on it must also be flat.

FUNCTION AND BEAUTY

Some arts are functional and some are not. Is there any relationship between function and value as art? Can we say that functional arts are greater or less great than arts that are not functional? The value of any work of art depends on the work itself, not on its being functional or nonfunctional. Architecture, which is always functional, is not superior or inferior to painting or poetry, which are usually nonfunctional. In the evaluation of two works of art, the presence or absence of function, just like the presence or absence of subject, is a matter of no consequence. If one were asked to name the world's greatest works of art, one could certainly include the plays of Aeschylus and Shakespeare, the cathedrals at Chartes and Amiens, and the symphonies of Brahms. The plays have subject but no function; the cathedrals have function but no subject; the symphonies have neither subject nor function.

Figure 4-17. Skidmore, Owings and Merrill, architects. John Hancock Building (1968–1969), Chicago. Height: 100 stories. Photograph © Ezra Stoller/ESTO.)

In the evaluation of functional art, however, the problem is different. Obviously the function should be known if the work is to be understood; if it is a birdbath or a saltcellar, it should be known as a bath for birds or as a container for salt when it is judged. It cannot be adequately judged just as a shape.

But when the function is understood, is there any relationship between the function of a work and its value as art? Yes; in a general way there is. There has been a great deal of discussion on this point, and any statement may be contradicted by excellent examples to the contrary, but it will usually be granted that a functional object is not beautiful unless it can perform its function adequately and acceptably. If it is desirable for people to see and hear in church, a church should be constructed so that they can see and hear in it. A chair that is uncomfortable is not so good as one that is comfortable. A residence should be so planned that the business of housekeeping may be carried on in it with the maximum of ease and efficiency. A beautiful teapot that is useless is like a beautiful bridge one cannot cross or a beautiful car that will not run.

In this respect we must admit that the saltcellar of Cellini fails if considered as a saltcellar. The figures are well conceived and executed, but the whole is too elaborate for its function. On the other hand, it was a custom at this time to have on the table a large and elaborate saltcellar known as "the salt." The salt was placed before the master of the house, between him and the guest of honor, serving to indicate rank: for this social use the Cellini saltcellar was admirably adapted. For a modern example, it is interesting to consider the John Hancock Building (Figure 4-17). Are its 100 stories functional as living and working space; that is, does its impressive height serve its function?

Adequate performance of function usually tends to produce beauty of design. Why this should be true we do not know, but it is true. The shapes in nature that are the most beautiful are also the most efficient, as the wings of a bird. Practical design offers many examples; everything is eliminated except what is essential, and the result is beautiful. Examples of such shapes are found in the canoe, the canoe paddle, the handle of an ax or a scythe, the blades of an electric fan.

Nevertheless, it is true that, although efficiency does make for beauty, efficiency and beauty are not the same. An article that adequately performs a function is not necessarily beautiful. Art demands something beyond function, something in addition to efficiency and proper performance of function. The shape of a spoon may be the best possible for its particular function, but the spoon is not for that reason a work of art. In the economy of nature, the best shape for an object's use *tends* to be the most beautiful, but it is our pleasure in the shape and not its usefulness that makes us consider it as akin to art.

TWO
MEDIUM

*Each property of Matter is a school for the understanding—
its solidity or resistance, its inertia, its extension, its figure,
its divisibility. The understanding adds, divides, combines,
measures, finds nutriment and room for activity. . . .*

—*Ralph Waldo Emerson*

5 MEDIUM— GENERAL CONSIDERATIONS

DEFINITION

Many widely diverse objects go under the name of art. A song, a sonata, a symphony, a statute, a skyscraper, a tapestry, a tragedy, a teapot, a poem, a painting, a palace, an oratorio, a cathedral, a chest, an etching, an engraving, an epic, a dance, a novel, a lyric—all these and more are classed as art. A single reading of this list, however, is sufficient for certain obvious classifications. The song, the symphony, the sonata, and the oratorio belong to the art of music; the cathedral, the palace, and the skyscraper are examples of architecture; the poem, the tragedy, the epic, the lyric, and the novel are literature. The basis for these classifications is, first of all, the way the artist has communicated an idea to us—the medium. The word *medium*, which comes from the Latin word *medium*, "means," denotes the means by which an artist communicates an idea; it is the stuff out of which a work of art is created. Architecture makes use of wood, stone, brick, concrete; sculpture makes use of steel, marble, bronze, wood; painting makes use of colored pigments on wood or canvas.

Medium is essential to art. Subject and function, as we have seen, are not essential. There is art without subject and there is art without function, but there is no art without medium. A work can exist only in some medium. And the names we use to designate both the art and the artist are derived from the medium. The poem we have examined by Elizabeth Bishop (Chapter 2) and Wagner's *Flying Dutchman* were both inspired by the idea of a storm. Bishop, who used words in poetic form to express her idea, is called a poet; Wagner, who used tones, is called a musician or composer.

On the basis of medium, the arts are primarily classified as *visual* and *auditory*. Painting, sculpture, architecture, tapestry, and glassware are examples of visual arts; they are seen. Music and literature are auditory arts; they are heard. Even when reading a musical score or a page or poetry silently, one hears the sound in one's mind. Also on the basis of medium, the arts are classified as *time arts* and *space arts*. The visual arts are space arts. The auditory arts are time arts. Theater, opera, and cinema are known as *combined arts*, being both visual and auditory, existing in both space and time. Though dance is largely visual, it is classed with the combined arts because it exists in both time and space.

By a third classification on the basis of medium, the arts are divided into *major* and *applied*, or *minor*, arts. The five major arts are music, literature, painting, sculpture, and architecture. The applied, or minor, arts are metalwork, weaving, ceramics, glass, furniture, photography, lettering, bookmaking, and the like. The terms *major* and *minor*, however, are of no importance in determining the value of any single work of art. A good piece of porcelain is better than a poor painting; a beautiful Oriental rug is better than a poor statue; a good saltcellar is better than a poor building. The five great arts deserve the name *major*, not because there is anything necessarily superior about them as such, but because more very great works have been made in those mediums than in the arts that are designated as "minor." Another distinction between the major and the minor arts is that the major arts generally express an emotion or idea—or both—whereas the applied arts generally do not. It is important to note that any work of art is great or not great in and of itself and should be judged thus, without consideration of its classification.

THE ARTIST AND THE MEDIUM

An artist chooses the medium that can best express what he or she wants to convey. Often an artist will use more than one medium. William Blake, for instance, used words in some of his works, as in "The Sick Rose."

O Rose, thou art sick!
The invisible worm
That flies in the night,
In the howling storm,

Has found out thy bed
Of crimson joy,
And his dark secret love
Does thy life destroy.

> —William Blake, British poet and artist (1757–1827),
>   from *Songs of Experience* (1794)

He also created visual art, as in his print *When the Morning Stars Sang Together* (Figure 3-14), where the medium is engraving. He also used a third medium, watercolor. In each case he chose the medium that seemed right for the idea he was expressing. Thus it is quite safe to say that the idea expressed in "The Sick Rose" is essentially verbal and poetic, that it would be rather difficult to express it visually. In the print, he has admittedly taken a difficult poetic image to illustrate, but the presence of the host of stars and the division of the different types of beings into rows or levels have made it possible for him to express the idea in pictorial terms.

However, the words *choice* and *selection* used in connection with the determination of medium give a false impression, for they imply that the artist makes a deliberate choice. This is not so. The artist does not make a conscious, reasoned choice of a medium; the selection of medium is a part of the artistic inspiration. The idea which Blake put into a poem came to him as an idea for a poem. The idea which he put into the engraving came to him as an idea for an engraving. He did not start with an idea out of which he might make a poem or an engarving. When the unknown Greek sculptor of the fifth century before Christ made the bronze statue of Zeus now at the National Museum in Athens (Figure 5-1), he chose sculpture because

Figure 5-1. *Zeus* (from Cape Artemision, ca. 470 B.C.). (Bronze Height: 82 inches. National Museum, Athens.)

what he wanted to convey demanded volume and strength. And h
chose bronze because the posed, commanding figure with arms ou
stretched to throw a thunderbolt would have been quite impractic
and vulnerable had it been attempted in marble. A poet is a po
rather than a painter because he or she thinks in terms of words. *
one poet said, "When I enjoy a scene, I find myself hunting for word
that will exactly express the impression it has made on me."

The artist thinks in terms of a specific medium. Two of Dürer
great prints are of horsemen: for one, the artist has used engravin;
for the other, woodcut. He chose each medium to express the exa
idea he wanted to make clear in that print. The engraving (shown
Figure 5-2) is called *The Knight, Death, and the Devil*. The knig
probably represents the Christian who is not led astray by tempt
tions. A very serious and praiseworthy person, he rides across th
picture apparently bound for the ideal city shown against the sky. H
pays no attention to his companions: Death, who holds an hourglas

Figure 5-2. Albrecht Dürer (1471–1528), German painter and engraver. *The Knight, Death, and the Devil* (ca. 1513). (Engraving. Size: 9¾ by 7¼ inches. New York, Metropolitan Museum of Art, Harris Brisbane Dick Fund, 1943.)

Figure 5-3. Dürer. *The Four Horsemen of t Apocalypse* (ca. 1498). (Woodcut. Size: 15¹³⁄₁₆ by 11 inches. Boston, Museum of Fine Art

before him, and the Devil, half pig and half wolf. The woodcut is called *The Four Horsemen of the Apocalypse* (Figure 5-3). According to a passage in the New Testament (Revelation 6), the first horse is white, and its rider, who carries a bow, "went forth conquering, and to conquer." Some think Christ is this conquering rider. The second horse is red and symbolizes war; its rider, who carries a sword, drives peace from the earth. The third horse, which is black, represents famine; the scales in the hands of its rider show that food is scarce and must be weighed. Last is a pale horse, "and his name that sat on him was Death."

A sculptor plans a statue not for wood in general but for oak or mahogany. The architect does not plan a house and then decide whether it shall be of brick, wood, or stone; the demands of brick, wood, and stone are different, and the house must be designed according to the material. The jeweler does not imagine a design and then say, "Shall I make it in copper or gold?" It is a design for gold or a design for copper. The artist thinks and feels in terms of the medium.

Moreover, artists love and respect a medium for itself; they use it because it has certain qualities, and they try to bring out and emphasize those qualities. The sculptor gives life to a statue not by denying that it is wood or stone, but by incorporating the qualities of wood or stone into the meaning of the sculptured piece. In the statues of Henry Moore, we are always conscious of the texture of wood as wood, or bronze as bronze. To the poet the words are the poem. They are not one of many ways the poet has found to express an idea; they *are* the idea. The poem cannot be separated from the words it is made up of.

In studying any work of art, therefore, it is always worthwhile to ask why the artist "chose" (in our qualified sense) the medium in question. Why did Wagner give the sword theme to the trumpet? Why did the sculptor of the statue of Zeus want it in bronze? Why did Dürer use engraving for *The Knight, Death, and the Devil* and woodcut for *The Four Horsemen of the Apocalypse?* How do these works suit the inherent qualities of the medium chosen? We can surmise that Dürer used engraving for *The Knight, Death, and The Devil* to show the variety of nature and man; he also wanted to achieve a high degree of light and shadow to give the man and the horse a sculptural effect. Both these aims are easier to achieve with engraving than with woodcut. *The Four Horsemen of the Apocalypse* produces an emotional and dynamic effect for which the generalized technique of the woodcut is far more suitable. Wagner's sword theme was probably given to the trumpet because the trumpet symbolizes war. The Greek sculptor may have used bronze because a free-standing marble figure would have been impossible: the weight of the body would have broken the legs.

Figure 5-4. Pablo Picasso (1881–1973), Spanish painter. *Outdoor Sculpture* (1967). (Steel and concrete. Height: 50 feet. Chicago Civic Center. Photograph © Pub. Bldg. Comm., Chicago.)

We must remember, of course, that traditional sculpture was f more influenced by medium than contemporary scultpure is. We c say that sculptors like Michelangelo and the Greeks were influenc by the availability of marble (although they occasionally cho bronze, as in the case of the Greek Zeus). Traditional sculpture w far more closely tied to the availability of Carrara or Pentelic marb and to the needs of architectural decoration than is the case toda When Picasso does one of his "public sculptures" (Figure 5-4), he responding more to his own staylistic evolution than to the availabi ity or desirability of sheet metal.

It is interesting, and important, to note that today the hard-an fast distinctions between certain mediums are breaking down. F example, the distinction between free-standing sculpture, such Michelangelo's *David*, and relief sculpture, such as the *Ludov Throne* shown in Figure 5-5 and discussed below, is no longer alwa valid. How is a mobile by Calder (his *Lobster Trap and Fish Tail*, di cussed below, is shown in Figure 5-6) to be classified, for exampl Moore's *Two Forms* (Figure 2-2), tends to demolish the idea of sol masses as a necessary characteristic of sculpture.

THE DISTINCTIVE CHARACTER OF MEDIUM

If what is said in one medium cannot be said in another, it follov that no work can ever be translated from one medium to anothe There is no argument about this point if it is a question of two di ferent arts. A description of a scene and a painting of the same scer do not tell the same story; inevitably, what they say is different. Ar

Figure 5-5. *Ludovisi Throne* (ca. 460 B.C.). (Marble. Height at center: 3 feet, 4½ inches. Rome, Terme Museum. Photograph by Alinari/Scala.)

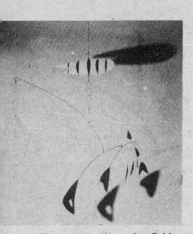

Figure 5-6. Alexander Calder (1898–1976), American sculptor. *Lobster Trap and Fish Tail* (1939). (Mobile. Steel wire and sheet aluminum. Size: 8½ feet high, 9½ feet in diameter. New York, Museum of Modern Art; commissioned by the Advisory Committee for the stairwell of the Museum.)

the same is true, though to a lesser degree, when it is a question of two mediums within a single art. If the artist's intuition demands a statue of marble, it follows that a copy of the statue in bronze will miss something which the artist considered essential to the original.

It is in music and literature that the problem of translation arises most often. Music that was written for the orchestra is arranged for piano, and music written for piano is arranged for orchestra. Works in foreign languages are translated into English, and English works are translated into foreign languages. In this kind of translation, something of the original is always lost or changed. Every time Stokowski transcribes the music of Bach, the result is Stokowski as well as Bach. Gilbert Murray's translations of Euripides show us Euripides plus Gilbert Murray. The orchestral score of *The Afternoon of a Faun* transcribed for piano has lost something that was essential to the music. Even when a great artist like Casals plays a Bach prelude on the cello, we have lost something of the original conception.

On this point, however, a caution is necessary. It is better to know a Greek play in translation than not to know the play. It is better to hear Bach arranged by Stokowski than not to hear Bach. It is better to know the famous masterpieces of painting and sculpture in reproductions than not to know them at all. One should strive not to be too much of a purist, on the one hand, or too easily pleased, on the other; one should not refuse to know Bach's music as played by the orchestra, but one should hear it on the harpsichord if given the opportunity. It is well to study the works of Botticelli in reproductions until one has a chance to see the originals. One should read translations from the Greek but remember that Sophocles and Euripides are best understood when their plays are read in the original Greek.

The problem of adapting a work of art from one medium to another is perhaps most familiar to us in the form of literature made into film drama. Examination of a film adaptation of a literary work will also show some of the differences between the art of writing and the art of film. This will serve as an example of what distinguishes one medium form another, and of what sort of artistic and social value an adaptation may have. To a certain extent, the film version of a literary work spoon-feeds the viewer. More demands are made on someone reading a literary work than on someone watching a film, in general; for example, the reader may have to use imagination to fill in details. Yet a panoramic novel like Tolstoy's *War and Peace* may be brought to new life by means of film, which can use costume, landscape, architecture, and interior design to recreate the portrait of early nineteenth-century Russia. A psychological novel, though, may suffer very much in "translation" to film, as is shown by Luchino Visconti's film treatment of Thomas Mann's *Death in Venice*, which has been mentioned already. (The film was a prize winner at the

Cannes film festival.) Those who are familiar with Mann's short evocative novella of the twentieth century, with its subtle atmosphere of a doomed city, may well find unbearable the panoplies costume movie set in a fashionable watering place and the endless self-recriminations of its hero. The whole idea and purpose of Mann's *Death in Venice* have been changed. Where the original leaves us with a feeling of irremediable regret and nostalgia, the end of the film leaves us with a feeling of pity for the guilt-ridden but still innocent hero who has gotten nowhere near the object of his forbidden love, a beautiful Polish boy. Mann's hero (a writer, not a composer as in the film) is committed to an unending search for ideal beauty rather than beautiful boys. His discussions of this problem with a colleague, typically abstract in the fasion of that time and that intellectual level, make good sense in the novella. In the more factual medium of the film, however, it becomes difficult to take these two quite seriously. In the book, they did not have to be as "forceful" or even as "interesting" as it seems film characters must be. Another point is that Mann's novella is not as long or elaborate as a feature film. A poetic vignette like *Death in Venice*, perhaps, ought to stay in the form in which it was created. This is not meant to imply that literature should not be translated into film. The comments on the film version of *War and Peace* have suggested that film can add to the reader's enjoyment. Novels of this kind, which evoke a whole period of history, tend to make good films. Such novels include Hemingway's *For Whom the Bell Tolls*, a story of the Spanish Civil War of the 1930s, and the more recent treatment (1971) by Paolo Pasolini of Boccaccio's *Decameron*, a lusty reconstruction of fourteenth-century Florence during an outbreak of the Black Death. Where the original literary work is a play, the film version may offer to the average viewer the advantage of widening the confines of the play. In the film versions of *Romeo and Juliet*, we lose the most subtle moments of the play, but the films seem to bring the period and its people to life in a way that must prove very valuable to the modern viewer. Lawrence Olivier's film version of Shakespeare's *Henry V* (Olivier also performs the title role) is an excellent evocation of the importance of Agincourt in the conflict between the English and French. Many people who have never shown any interest in Shakespeare come away from the film version of *Henry V* with their first real idea of what he is all about.

One must, moreover, be cautious in judging a work of art which has the same story as another work of art as an attempt to "translate" the work. In the first place, individual artists may understand the story differently—that is, as having different themes—or they may want to emphasize different aspects of the story to make a different point. The story of Romeo and Juliet, best known to us in Shakespeare's play, has been used by many artists, usually with some adherence to Shakespeare's version, or at least a dependence on our knowing that version, but with no attempt to "translate" the play in any literal sense. Leonard Bernstein's *West Side Story* has its inspiration in Shakespeare's play, but, beyond the central situation of two people from enemy groups being deeply in love and the tragic outcome of that love, *West Side Story* cannot be judged as an attempt to "translate" Shakespeare's play into a musical. Prokofiev made the Romeo and Juliet story into a ballet, Tchaikowsky used it in his popular *Romeo and Juliet Fantasie Overture* (to an opera he never finished), and the nucleus of the story has been used by many other artists. Similarly the story of Faust, a scholar-student of the occult who in old age bargains with the devil for youth and riches in exchange for his soul, has been used by many artists in different mediums. Goethe used it for his play, Gounod for an opera, Liszt for a symphony. A similar situation exists in relation to Voltaire's satire *Candide*. The story is that of a naive youth who is taught that "this is the best of all possible worlds"—a seriously held philosophical position in Voltaire's time—and through a series of adventures which should have convinced him of its absurdity, continues to believe what he was taught. The story was used by Terry Sutherland in a satiric, pornographic novel, *Candy*. The central character, now female, named for Candide, has been taught perversely a different truth—the greatest virtue is to "comfort those whose needs are greatest"—which she maintains throughout the novel. Leonard Bernstein's successful Broadway musical *Candide* has the hero accept Voltaire's "truth," which becomes one of the important songs, "The Best of All Possible Worlds"; but here Bernstein selects and adjusts to contemporary conditions the instructive adventures which should convince Candide of its falseness.

An especially instructive example of the difference between *interpreting* a story and *translating* a story from one medium to another is to be found in a book by the critic and scholar of dance Selma Jeanne Cohen, *The Modern Dance: Seven Statements of Belief.*[1] In preparing the book, she asked seven outstanding modern choreographers to describe what they would do if commissioned to develop a dance from the biblical story of the Prodigal Son. The seven essays, relating their proposals, give us not only seven different interpretations of the story, but seven individual approaches to dance as a medium.

To summarize, in these instances in which artists have taken subject matter from other works but developed it to suit their individual purposes and in the many, many other instances which could be cited, we must judge each new work on its own merits, not on its faithfulness to the originals. As in the use of Greek myths by artists, the originals serve merely as inspiration or a starting point or an analogy; the artist's purpose is not to "translate" them, but to use them.

[1] Middletown, Conn.: Wesleyan University Press, 1965.

Sculpture

The nature of the medium inevitably influences the type of subject
can portray. Traditionally, sculpture in the round has tended t
emphasize mass and weight, and its subjects are objects of defni
form and solidity. The qualities we associate with metal—strength
weight, durability—can heighten the effect the sculptor desires
their physical attributes are incorporated into the subject, as in th
Artemision bronze god (Figure 5-1) poised on one foot; or these ver
qualities, such as the weight of bronze, may be finely balanced at th
center of gravity to heighten the effect of a subject caught in motior
as in the *Flying Horse of Kansu* (Figure 6-4). Trees and clouds are nc
common in sculpture. Moreover, the sculpture of the past has bee
limited almost entirely to the bodies of animals and especially to th
bodies of human beings. It has emphasized not only the human bod
but, in large measure, the nude human body. We do not suppos
that David really was naked when he fought Goliath; but the body c
David is more nearly ideal when it is naked, and therefore bette
suited to the meaning and purpose of the statue. When clothes ar
used, we want them to be simple and straightforward, as in th
figures of the caryatids of the Erechtheum.

Sculpture in relief, unlike sculpture in the round, has a backgroun
to which figures are attached, and therefore it can show more kind
of subjects with more varied backgrounds. On the background ma
be carved many subjects not so appropriate to sculpture in the rounc
trees, clouds, birds, fish. In the famous "Gates of Paradise," Ghi
berti seems almost as free as a painter in his choice of subject. In th
so-called *Ludovisi Throne* (shown in Figure 5-5), which is supposed t
portray the birth of Venus, the goddess is being lifted from the wate
by two attendants. The representation of cloth, especially the way :
delineates the form seen through the cloth, is exceptionally fine.

With the interest in abstract art there have developed new styles
as we have seen in Moore's *Two Forms* (Figure 2-2). This sculptur
differs from older forms in treatment of medium as well as in subjec
Whereas older sculpture is solid, today's sculpture is often hollow
playing up concave as well as convex surfaces. Thin strips of meta
are combined with plastic or glass, even with wood and wires, t
make interesting arrangements. Often they are suspended wher
they can move, and one gets various lights and shadows from them
Such sculptures, called "mobiles," are associated primarily with th
name of Alexander Calder. An example is *Lobster Trap and Fish Ta*
(shown in Figure 5-6), which hangs in the stairwell of the Museur
of Modern Art in New York City. Of his mobiles Calder said in 1951
"The idea of detached bodies floating in space, of different sizes an

densities, perhaps of different colors and temperatures, . . . some at rest, while others move in peculiar manners, seems to me the ideal source of form."[2]

Although abstract, *Two Forms* and *Lobster Trap and Fish Tail* are still tied to concrete subject matter, as their titles show. In some works more recent than these, sculptors have produced entirely subjectless art—pure exercises in form and space.

Painting

Traditional painting has a much wider field than sculpture; it may concern itself with anything in space. Whatever can be seen can be painted: lakes, trees, clouds, houses, mountains, fields, anything that has form to the eye either in reality or in the artist's mind.

Traditional painting and sculpture are both limited in time. Each can represent its object only at a single moment of time. In life the running horse or the smiling girl does not stay the same for ten consecutive seconds; the sculptor or the painter chooses, and preserves the object at, one instant. A feeling or an illusion of movement may be created, so that we are conscious of the action that is taking place or is about to take place. In El Greco's *Resurrection* (Color Plate 6), Christ seems to be really rising out of a mass of bodies. In Botticelli's *Birth of Venus* (Color Plate 12), the goddess is being blown to the shore. Even in Ghirlandajo's *Old Man and Boy* (Color Plate 11), we feel that it is just for a moment that the figures will be in these positions, that one or both will move very soon. In each case the artist is showing the characteristic motion or gesture of the person about to move; we feel that the next second there will be movement; but the scene as presented is still—the action does not change.

Early in this century there was a great deal of talk about a painting by Duchamp called *Nude Descending a Staircase* (Figure 5-7). The artist was trying to picture just what the title indicates, the appearance of a form in motion. He did this by presenting a succession of pictures of the same thing from slightly different points of view. Some modern artists, notably Picasso, have given a sense of movement to a painting by presenting at one time different aspects of a head or figure. Here, as in everything connected with art, we must admit that all standards are empirical—that is, derived from experience. Artists may do anything they can do. In other words, if Duchamp and Picasso can persuade us that we can see action in a painting and that we like to see action portrayed in that way, then painting becomes a medium for the portrayal of action.

[2] Quoted in Alfred H. Barr, Jr. (ed.), *Master of Modern Art*, 3d ed., rev. (New York: Museum of Modern Art, 1958), p. 148.

Figure 5-7. Marcel Duchamp (1887–1968), French painter. *Nude Descending a Staircase, No. 2* (1912). (Oil on canvas. Size: 58⅜ by 35⅜ inches. Philadelphia Museum of Art; collection of Louise and Walter Arensberg.)

Nude Descending a Staircase

Toe upon toe, a snowing flesh
A gold of lemon, root and rind,
She shifts in sunlight down the stairs
With nothing on. Nor on her mind.

We spy beneath the banister
A constant thresh of thigh on thigh—
Her lips imprint the swinging air
That parts to let her parts go by.

One-woman waterfall, she wears
Her slow descent like a long cape
And pausing, on the final stair
Collects her motions into shape.

—X. J. Kennedy[3]

[3] "Nude Descending a Staircase," copyright © 1960 by X. J. Kennedy from the book *Nude Descending a Staircase* by X. J. Kennedy. Reprinted by permission of Doubleday & Company, In

Literature

Painting allows a wider range of subjects than sculpture, but literature allows a wider range than painting; while painting can present anything that might be seen, literature can present anything that can be put into words. Moreover, it is not limited to a second of time, as are the visual arts. Literature can describe a situation at any given moment and can tell what happened before and after that time. Literature differs from the other arts in another respect. Since the language of literature is the same as the language of abstract thought, it can express abstract thought as the other arts cannot. Shakespeare can have Hamlet say, "There's a divinity that shapes our ends, rough-hew them how we will" (*Hamlet*, V, ii, 10–11). It is hard to image representing this idea pictorially. The sculptor or the painter may portray a thoughtful face; the musician may make one think; but none of the three can express a thought as clearly as the writer.

On the other hand, imitation through literature is less exact than imitation through either painting or sculpture. A statue of a dog may conceivably be mistaken for the living dog, but a poem about a dog will never be. And yet the poem may call to mind the characteristics of a dog better than the statue.

Music

As we have seen, music can never portray any subject clearly. And, since music can only suggest the subject, it can suggest any subject. Subjects that cannot even be put into words can be expressed in music. Vague ideas, half-formed opinions and emotions, feelings that can never be given tangible form—all these are found in music. To the extent that music permits the imagination its greatest scope, to the extent that it calls on the individual to make a totally personal, almost limitless, interpretation of and contribution to the meaning of the music—to that extent music becomes the most subjective and personal of the arts. Almost everyone has experienced the variety and richness of the response to music; and each time we listen to a composition, we may find something new, something we had not heard before.

LIMITATIONS AND POSSIBILITIES OF MEDIUM

Although artists are free to use any medium that seems right to them, they must work within the limitations of the medium. Each medium has its own possibilities and limitations. What Blake says in words in "The Sick Rose" he cannot say in engraving, and what the Greek sculptor of the statue of Zeus says in bronze cannot be said in words or in engraving.

Figure 5-8. *Orpheus and Eurydice* (ca. 430 B.C.). (Roman copy in Pentelic marble of marble original. Height: 3 feet, 10½ inches. Naples, National Museum. Photograph by Alinari/Scala.)

The limitations and possibilities of medium can be illustrate clearly if we compare the use of a single subject in several medium Take, for instance, the myth of Orpheus, the great musician wh went to the world of the dead to demand back his wife Eurydice. H request was granted on condition that he should not look at her un he had reached the upper world. But just before he arrived he look back, and his wife was lost.

This legend was the subject of a Greek relief of about the fif century before Christ (shown in Figure 5-8), though the work known only in a Roman copy. The sculptor had to choose one secon and only one from the entire story. He chose the moment just aft Orpheus had looked around, when both Orpheus and Eurydice rea ized that she must return to Hades. In that one instant he has had show all the love and longing of the lovers. The legend says th when Orpheus turned, Eurydice disappeared. Sculpture cann show a person in the act of disappearing, and therefore Hermes, t messenger of the gods, is shown waiting to take Eurydice back to t realm of Pluto.

This change in the story, however, shows how a seeming limit tion of the medium becomes an opportunity, for the sculptor show the contrast between the mortals and the gods, not in physique b in attitude. The mortals, Orpheus and Eurydice, are pathetic in the fruitless yearning and powerlessness; the god is patient, conscious the inevitability of the gods' decree, but quite detached from t sufferings of human creatures.

The story is told again by Ovid, a Latin poet who lived about t time of Christ, in his *Metamorphoses*. Since he was using word Ovid could give minute details of all kinds. He told, for instanc how the wild beasts and even the trees and rocks responded to t playing of Orpheus. He described the bad omen at the weddir when Hymen's torch smoked, and how Eurydice, while runnir away from the unwelcome advances of a shepherd, was bitten by snake and died. Orpheus, inconsolable, at last made the despera resolve to seek her in Hades. Playing on his lyre, he passed all t people being tortured there. Finally, he reached the throne of Plu and Proserpine, where he declared boldy that if they would not gi him back his wife, they would have a new inhabitant of Hades, f he would not leave without Eurydice. They agreed that she might on condition that he should not look behind to see if she were follo ing. When he had almost reached the entrance, he looked back; ar she disappeared. Later, some Thracian maidens tried to captiva him, but when he refused to have anything to do with them, the tore him to bits and threw the pieces into the river.

Gluck, an eighteenth-century German composer, used the sto in his opera *Orpheus and Eurydice*. The change in medium again ne essarily involved changes in presentation. In the first place, an ope is limited in time, and singing is much slower than speaking. Therefore, the story had to be shortened; the opera begins after the death of Eurydice and ends with the departure from Hades. Moreover, it would be impossible on the stage to show the various punishments of Hades: Ixion is on a fiery wheel, the daughters of Danaüs are carrying water in a sieve, Tantalus is immersed in water up to his lips. Instead Gluck introduced bands of Furies who assail Orpheus and challenge his approach. The most interesting change comes in the return of Orpheus and Eurydice. Ovid says simply that Eurydice followed Orpheus until they were almost out in the world. Orpheus was, of course, playing on his lyre, but there is no other indication as to what was happening on the journey. Such a scene would be difficult if enacted on the stage—a man singing and a woman following in silence. Hence, Eurydice is made to talk. She asks where they are going. Why does Orpheus not look at her? Has he ceased to love her? At last she says in desperation that she would rather be back in Hades if her husband does not love her anymore. At this Orpheus can stand it no longer: he turns, and she disappears. (It is not important for our study to notice that in this version the god Amor—love—brings her to life again, saying that the lovers have suffered enough, and Orpheus and Eurydice leave Hades happily.)

PRESERVATION OF ART

Since art can be known only as it is expressed in some medium, it is lost if the medium is lost. We cannot study the architecture of Mesopotamia as we can that of Greece, for the houses were made of sun-dried brick and almost all of them have been washed away. The Angles and Saxons, when they settled in England, must have known many stories about the heroes of their native land; but only one of these stories, *Beowulf*, was written down; the others have been forgotten.

About some of the lost works of art a great deal is known. The great statue of Athena called the *Athena Parthenos*, for which the Parthenon was a shrine, was described by the historians. It was about 40 feet in height, and it was made of gold and ivory. Standing as it did in the Parthenon, lighted by the beams of the early morning sun, it must have been an object of rare beauty. But the statue itself has not been preserved; there are two known copies that are inadequate, and while we may learn various facts about the statue, we cannot experience its beauty. Other examples might be cited almost indefinitely, but the point is clear. If the medium of a work of art is gone, the art is gone. It is therefore extremely important that the medium be preserved.

In this matter of preservation we find a sharp difference between the visual and the auditory arts. The visual arts are material realitie and as such can be preserved. A painting, a statue, a building, even bit of embroidery or lace may be kept; and when we want to study we can see the original work. It may not be in as good condition a when it was made, but we can see the thing itself. In a painting b Rembrandt we see the actual paint which was put on by the artis the colors may be darkened by time, but the picture we see is th work of the artist himself. The statues of Michelangelo are the figure made by Michelangelo. In the visual arts, therefore, the problems c preservation are all problems of keeping the medium safe and i good condition: of finding paints that will not fade or darken, of see ing that houses and statues are made of materials that will endur and that they are not destroyed.

In the time arts and the combined arts (all of which include time art), the situation is entirely different. Music, literature, and dance exist in time, and time once past is gone forever. The only wa we can keep the time arts is to reproduce them. We cannot hear th song as it was sung a half-hour ago; we must sing it over again. W cannot listen today to the poem as we heard it yesterday, but we ca repeat the poem. We cannot feel the dance we did last night, but w can dance it again. The problem of preserving the time arts, there fore, is the problem of finding some means of keeping them so tha they can be reproduced.

Originally, music, literature, and dance were preserved b memory and by oral transmission. One generation taught another the grandfather told tales to his grandsons; the mother sang songs t her children and danced with them. In most countries, songs, stories and dances were handed down in this way for a long time, often fo centuries, before they were put into permanent form. Even today some of our literature, music, and dance comes to us by word o mouth. The stories we tell of Santa Claus, the verses and songs we sing in games, and the simple steps which we dance to them are learned from others, not from books. From Maine to California children sing of London Bridge and the farmer in the dell, not be cause the words have any significance for them, but because they have learned the songs from their parents and friends.

The difficulties with this kind of transmission, however, are very great. The song, story, or dance may be forgotten. Even when remembered, it does not remain the same. Someone who tells a story or sings a melody often changes it, sometimes unconsciously. The poet who does not understand one word will substitute another, familiar word. In the Kentucky mountains, songs have been pre served since the time of Shakespeare, but they are not exactly the same: words and music have changed.

Although we have many descriptions of dances in Elizabethan times, and even have books on dance, we have no certainty that the attempts we make to recreate them are accurate. Even in ballet, where the various dances were carefully choreographed with steps and movements to be very precisely performed, the dances as we now see them have been passed down to us from one dancer to another. One ballet teacher teaches them to a student who in turn becomes a teacher and teaches them to other students. Inevitably, change occurs in this process, but we have no way of knowing how little or how much.

A better way to preserve a time art is to convert it into symbols that can be kept. Hence, from the very earliest times, there have been attempts to find such symbols. The symbols for words came first; they are old. In fact, we can almost say that they are as old as history, for we know comparatively little history earlier than the symbols of written language. Moreover, these symbols are accurate and can be accurately interpreted. We know the writings of the Egyptians, the Greeks, and the Hebrews, and we know that, in the main, we are reading those writings correctly.

The symbols of music were invented much later, and hence we do not know music of as early a date as we do literature. We know that the early peoples had music and musical instruments; the Hebrews mentioned cymbals and the psaltery, and the Egyptians and the Greeks drew pictures of people with musical instruments. We knew also that the Greeks had a very elaborate musical system; they have written its laws and principles; much of our present theory derives directly from the Greeks. But none of these people had a precise way of writing the music itself, and very little has been preserved. The earliest music that can be read with any degree of accuracy is that of the Middle Ages. Before that time there were various attempts at musical notation, but either these early examples were not exact or we have not learned how to interpret them accurately. Hence, for us, the history of music is vague until about the year 1000.

More recent devices for preserving the auditory arts are the sound film, the phonograph record, and the tape recorder. These can preserve the exact tone, the exact speed, the intonation, and many other characteristics that are lost in the written symbol. They have not, however, superseded writing; music and literature are still primarily written symbols.

For the combined arts there are even yet no very good methods of preservation. In the drama and the opera we have, of course, symbols for words and for music; and we can take photographs of stage sets and actors, of singers and dancers. But for the combination of various effects that make up the theater or the opera, we have now no adequate means of preservation. The film with its sound track would seem to be a perfect means for preserving the combined arts; and it is probably the best we have today. The conditions for the making of a motion picture, however, are so different from the condi-

tions of a stage performance that it is difficult, not to say impossible
to get the same effects. Furthermore, as film is evolving now,
has become a new art rather than a means for reproducing or preserving a stage performance. It is also quite doubtful how good televisio
will be for the preservation of the combined arts. It seems to hav
great possibilities, but if we can judge by present indications, it i
evolving, like film, into an independent art.

As regards dance in particular, there have in the past been man
attempts to develop an adequate system of dance notation, but it i
only recently that a system which has wide usage and general ap
proval has come into being—Labanotation (see Figure 16-2). We d
not, of course, know how adequate future generations of dancers wil
find Labanotation in recreating the dances recorded in it. But it i
now being taught to dance students in many colleges and univers
ities; and the Dance Notation Bureau, in New York, is making grant
to assist choreographers in preserving their work by this means an
to help companies in reconstructing ballets from notated scores.

For the preservation of all the arts, there will undoubtedly b
improvements in the future. Within the past fifty years we have seer
so many changes effected by the film, the phonograph, and tele
vision that we cannot say what the future will hold. Several years
from now a library may consist almost entirely of phonograph
records, tapes, and sound films, and it may be that we shall listen to
a record of a book or magazine as naturally as we now read it. We
now have notation for dance, but future generations may look on our
previous failure to preserve dance with as great wonderment and lack
of comprehension as we have in viewing the period before writing
was invented or adequate music notation devised. But whatever may
happen in the future, for the present, opera and theater performances
are almost entirely lost, and music and literature are preserved primarily through written symbols.

The symbols of music and literature have the disadvantages of al
symbols: they are arbitrary, and they must be known to be interpreted correctly. The child and the entirely unlettered person can
each recognize a picture, but they must know how to read notes or
written words before they can get the meaning of written music or
literature. Moreover, the symbols themselves are not entirely exact.
The printed page gives only the word; one cannot tell how long it is
to be held, in what tone it should be uttered, or how much stress it is
to be given, and, unless one knows the language, the symbol does
not even give the sound. Written music is in this respect much more
exact, for it can give duration and pitch and can indicate accent. Even
so, however, it is far from accurate, and it is so technical that comparatively few can read it and even fewer can write it, whereas the
simpler symbols for language can now be read and written almost
universally.

The disadvantages of the symbol have, however, a corresponding advantage. In the auditory arts, especially in music, there is often a third person coming between the artist and the audience helping to explain to the audience what the artist is trying to say. We hear the music of the composer and the drama of the author as interpreted by the performer. Under the best circumstances, the performers themselves are artists. Reading the lines or playing the music is not to them merely a mechanical performance; it is a new interpretation, a re-creation.

This element of re-creation in the auditory arts is so important that we do not even admit the artist's right to decide on a fixed interpretation. A poet may read one of his or her poems with a certain emphasis, but anyone who wants to change that emphasis has the right to do so. A pianist may have been fortunate enough to hear a certain piece played by its composer, but nevertheless, will not hesitate to change the interpretation. In both these respects the auditory arts are in marked contrast to the visual. When a painter draws a line or puts on a color, no one has the right to change it, and there is usually no artist-interpreter to make the meaning clear. Hence it may be said that the visual arts, as we know them, are relatively exact and definite; they tend to be finished, complete, and static. The auditory arts tend to be vague and indefinite; they are always subject to various interpretations, but they are dynamic and creative.

TECHNIQUE

Technique is the ability to do *what* you want to do, *when* you want to do it, *in the way* you want to do it. Technique, in short, is the artist's control of the medium. It has to do with the way the artist uses a medium in expressing an idea, not with the value of the idea itself.

A musician's technique is the ability to make the music sound as he or she wants it to sound; a sculptor's technique is a way of handling chisel and hammer to produce the desired effect. In the same way, there are techniques of blowing glass, casting bronze, making etchings, laying bricks. The technique is perfect when it enables the artist to do just what he or she wants with the medium. Browning states this ideal when he makes Andrea del Sarto say,

I can do with my pencil what I know,
What I see, what at bottom of my heart
I wish for. . . .

    —Robert Browning, British poet (1812–1889),
      "Andrea del Sarto" (1855)

Obviously, techniques differ not only in the different arts but i various mediums of a single art; a person's technique in one mediu will be quite different from that same person's technique in anothe A painter may be a good technician in oil but a poor one in wate color. A musician may have a fine technique with the bassoon but poor one with the flute.

Technique is the actual doing of something; it is the handling material; the term *technique* is not usually applied to mental labo We speak of the technique of Botticelli in painting the picture but n of his technique in planning the composition. We notice that Miche angelo has used different techniques in *David* (Figure 3-1) and in *Th Entombment* (Figure 19-7); in the one the surface is smooth, in th other rough. But the decision that the smooth surface was right in th one case and the rough in the other was not a matter of technique

On the basis of technique the distinction is made between an a and a craft. For the artist, the technique is not the end but the mean Technique is the language of which the artist is master; throug their technique, artists are able to say what they want to say. Fo artisans, technique is the end. They are concerned only with tech niques; they do not go beyond techniques. An artisan may make a excellent copy of a picture, may make an engraving or an etchin from it. But the artisan will follow the design of the artist; the arti must make the design.

At various times, however, technique has been considered great, if not primary, importance, especially in music. It is as thoug the best singer were the one who could do the most difficult cadenza and the most amazing trills, as though it were a virtue that the son is hard to sing, not that it is beautiful music. It is interesting, course, to observe a difficult feat well done, whether it be a playe hitting a tennis ball or an acrobat hanging by the teeth. So, likewise it is interesting to hear a soprano reach a high note or to see a dance poised on one toe for an inordinately long time. Nevertheless, th real point is not whether the performer is master of a difficult bit technique but whether the passage expresses the ideas of the musi or the dance. Is the dancer merely giving an exhibition of the abilit to stand on one toe, or is that position an essential part of the dance Is the high note appropriate, or is it merely difficult? Probably th best commentary on technique is this story told of a critic: After singer's performance, an admirer said, "Was that not difficult?" an the critic replied, "Would to God it had been impossible!" Techniqu should always be the means, not the end.

Technique impinges on the question of value in art in ye another way: in the problem of whether an artist's work may b hampered by poor technique. We hear much talk of this kind: "/ good artist but poor technique!" "She has good ideas for a landscape but she cannot paint them!" "He is Milton, but mute and therefor inglorious!'' To this problem, as to all other problems in art, no immediate or summary solution may be given that will fit all cases. In the recreative or performing phases of art, technique is of great importance. A man who speaks with a monotonous voice cannot be as forceful an actor as one who has learned to control his voice. A pianist must know how to play; a singer must be able to sing. A *performer*, then, is truly hampered by poor technique.

When, however, it is a question of creative work such as painting, writing, poetry, or music—as opposed to recreative or interpretive work—we tend to take technique more for granted. Obviously, trained artists think and work like artists, no matter how, in the end, they may express themselves. They work in terms of space, form, texture, color, and other artistic ingredients, but subconsciously rather than consciously, putting together a given combination of these elements spontaneously as they react to the reality which they have observed and which has stirred them to create. Their "technique" is so deeply ingrained by that point that they no longer think about anything but expressing themselves. In this sense we may say that the artist's creative ability and technique go hand in hand.

This point is of importance in the criticism of art. In judging any work of art, it is wise to take it for granted that the artist has done what he or she wanted to do—in other words, that the artist has not been hampered by lack of technique. It is easy to look at the distortions and abstractions of Rouault or Picasso and say, "If only he

Figure 5-9. Photograph of a piano which John Cage (1912–   ), American composer, prepared for producing special sounds in pieces he composed for it. Spoons, nuts and bolts, screws, and other small objects have been pressed between and under the strings. (Photograph from Performing Artservices, Inc., New York, with the permission of John Cage.)

would learn how to draw!" or to hear the dissonances of Hindemith and say, "If only he had had a few lessons in harmony!" But such criticisms are almost always false. The artist who distorts a figure, or the composer who uses dissonances, does so to produce a certain effect. See, for example, the photograph of a piano which John Cage, a contemporary American composer, deliberately modified (Figure 5-9) for special effects he wished to achieve.

6 MEDIUMS OF THE VISUAL ARTS

ARCHITECTURE

Traditionally, the material of which a building is made has been determined by the materials native to the place where the building is erected. In Greece marble was easily available, and many of the buildings were made of marble. In Rome concrete was used because there were great quantities of an earth called *pozzuolana* which, when mixed with lime, made a hard and enduring cement. Throughout Europe limestone was easily available, and the cathedrals were built of limestone. In most sections of the United States there were heavily wooded forests, and the first houses were built by chopping down trees and putting up log cabins. In some parts of the country clay was to be had for the digging; settlers dug the clay and fired the brick where the house was to be built. In the Southwest the Indians had no stone and no way of firing brick, and so they built their houses of brick dried in the sun, *adobe*. The Eskimos built with blocks of hard snow. In most circumstances buildings have been constructed of the materials at hand.

This condition has changed, however, because new building materials are being made and architects are less dependent on local materials than they used to be. The most important of the new materials are structural steel and reinforced concrete. But many other new materials have gained wide acceptance. Plate glass makes possible huge expanses of uninterrupted windows. Glass bricks have the advantage of being translucent—that is, of letting in light—while not being transparent. There are fabricated woods made of thin

133

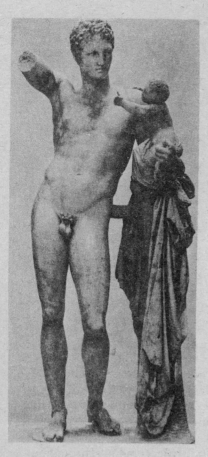

sheets of wood glued together with grain running in opposite directions to prevent warping and bending as in ordinary wood. Such fabricated woods can take their place with steel and reinforced concrete as scientific materials that lend themselves to exact calculatio. Aluminum and enameled surfaces are being tried. Linoleum, rubbe. and concrete tiles are used for floors. Plastics are being used increasingly, and we can expect other new materials in the future.

The choice of medium determines, or is determined by, the typ. of construction used in the building. For buildings in wood, th. post-and-lintel type of construction is generally used. For ston. post-and-lintel construction is used if the slabs are large; if the ston. are small, the arch is usuall employed. The arch is the typical metho. for stone construction, as post-and-lintel is for wood. Steel and rein. forced concrete, which are very strong and relatively light, can b. used in any type of construction; the type that is characteristic . them is known as "skeleton" construction. (See Chapter 14.)

SCULPTURE

Stone and Bronze

The two mediums most commonly used for sculpture are stone an. metal. Stone is durable; it resists weather, fire, and all ordinar. hazards. On the other hand, it is heavy and expensive and break. easily. Of the stones, marble is the most beautiful. It takes a hig. polish and is almost translucent. A noteworthy example of marb. sculpture is the *Hermes and Dionysus* of Praxiteles (shown in Figur. 6-1). The stone is so smooth that one wants to feel it, to run one. hand over the surface. The sculptor has followed the contours of th. body so well that one almost believes the surface would be soft an. pliable to the touch. In medieval cathedrals the figures were carve. of the material of which the church was made, usually limeston. Limestone is soft, and for that reason it does not polish well. Even i. photographs one can tell the difference between the surface of . marble statue like the *Hermes and Dionysus* and the surface of a statu. made of softer stone, such as the *King of Judah* (shown in Figure 6-. at Chartres. Granite is coarse but hard and is suitable for bold effect. In the *Adams Memorial* (Figure 4-11), Saint-Gaudens has used granit. for the background; its hard, uncompromising texture and speckle. color contrast with the soft clothing of the bronze figure.

Figure 6-1. *Above left:* Praxiteles, Greek sculptor. *Hermes and Dionysus* (ca. 350 B.C.. (Parian marble. Height: 6 feet, 11 inches. Olympia Museum, Greece. Photograph, Saul Weinberg.)

Figure 6-2. *Left: King of Judah* (twelfth century). (Stone. Above life-size. Chartre. Cathedral of Notre Dame. Photograph by Houvet.)

Figure 6-3. *The Charioteer* (ca. 475 B.C.). (Bronze with enamel and silver inlay. Height: 5 feet, 11 inches. Delphi, Museum. Photograph, Greek National Tourist Office.)

Of the metals, the one most commonly used traditionally was bronze. The processes used in making stone and bronze statues are exactly opposite. Stone statues are made by cutting away the stone until only the figures are left. For metal sculpture, the sculptor builds up the figure in clay and then has it cast in bronze.

In small statues the bronze is solid, but in large ones solid metal would be too heavy and too expensive; besides, it has a tendency to crack when it is cooled. Most bronze statues, therefore, are hollow. The process of casting bronze is a very difficult and intricate one, so difficult that it constitutes one of the disadvantages of the medium. Another drawback is that bronze is easily melted down for other uses; many a bronze statue has been poured into cannons. Its rich color, however, and the smooth texture, reflecting lights as they can be reflected only in metal, make it one of the most beautiful of all the mediums for sculpture. Moreover, it is relatively light, and the figure can support itself in many positions that would be impossible in stone. *The Charioteer* (shown in Figure 6-3) and the *Hermes and Dionysus* of Praxiteles are original Greek statues. The *Charioteer* is in bronze, the *Hermes* in marble. The charioteer stands on his own feet, and though the figure is large, it needs no other support. In the *Hermes*, however, extra support is given by a tree trunk, partially covered with a cloak, on which the god is leaning his left elbow. The marble would break if the entire weight of the statue were concentrated on the legs.

After the downfall of Greece a large number of Greek statues in bronze were destroyed, but copies in stone were made by the Romans. Since the stone would not support the figure in the position used in the bronze, stone supports, often poorly disguised, were added. This is the reason that one often sees a trunk of a tree in a copy of Greek statue where it is not expected. As an example of effective use of bronze in sculpture, consider the *Flying Horse of Kansu* (Figure 6-4). A statue such as this one of a flying horse—balanced for one timeless moment on the wing of a swallow as a hoof inadvertently touches it in flight, with head tossed to one side in alarm—is inconceivable in marble.

In modern times a variety of metals, such as forged iron, welded steel, and duraluminum, have replaced bronze, while bronze casting as an art is disappearing. For many artists, the new metals symbolize modernity. This is true of Theodore Roszak, Seymour Lipton, and the late David Smith, whose works are characterized by abstract surrealist forms. See, for example, Roszak's *Thorn Blossom* (Figure 6-8) and David Smith's *Hudson River Landscape* (Figure 6-9), discussed below.

Because of the differences in method and medium, the effects to be gained in stone and metal are very different. Stone tends to be heavy and massive but brittle, whereas metal tends to be light, tensile, and graceful.

Figure 6-4. *Flying Horse of Kansu* (excavated in Wu-Wei, Kansu, 1969). (Bronze. Height: 34½ cm.; length: 48 cm. Exhibition of Archaeological Finds of the People's Republic of China, 1975.)

Wood

Besides stone and metal, wood, terra cotta, and ivory are importa[nt] mediums for sculpture. Wood has an initial advantage in that it [is] cheap, readily available, and easy to cut. Covered with a light coat [of] gesso (plaster of Paris or gypsum mixed with glue), it can be paint[ed] or gilded. It is then described as polychromed or gilded wood. F[or] examples, see the *Kuan Yin Bodhisattva* (Figure 3-25) and *Christ a[nd] S. John* (Figure 3-10). Wood is not brittle and permits the sculptor [to] work in thin, extended forms, such as the hands of the *Kuan Yin*. It [is] capable of much fine detail and polishes well. When it is not painte[d] as in most modern sculpture, the grain of the wood can often be se[en] and, if used well, adds greatly to the effect of the whole, as in Hen[ry] Moore's *Reclining Figure* (Figure 2-5) and *Two Forms* (Figure 2-2[?]) Wood is also useful for relief sculpture.

Ivory

Ivory and terra cotta may almost be counted as lost mediums, f[or] they are used very little today, though they have been important [in] the past. As we have said, the great statue of Athena in the Pa[r]thenon was of gold and ivory. In the Boston Museum of Fine Ar[ts] is a statuette of ivory called the *Snake Goddess* (shown in Figure 6-5[?]) it dates from the little-known Aegean, or Minoan, civilization, whi[ch]

Figure 6-5. *Snake Goddess.* (Minoan, ca. 1500 B.C.). (Gold and ivory. Height: 6½ inches. Boston, Museum of Fine Arts.)

preceded the Greek. When excavations were being made in Crete, a woman interested in the Museum bought a mass of earth just as it came from the spade because it contained fragments of gold and ivory. When the pieces were put together, this little figure emerged, and it is now one of the treasures of the Museum. The snakes and the bands of her skirt are of gold. There are holes in her tiara, which would indicate that gold was wound through it also. The lady looks very modern with her small waist and full skirts. Probably she was a priestess, for she carries snakes in her hands. Certainly she was an aristocrat; her face and bearing both bear witness to a noble lineage.

From the Middle Ages on, ivory has been much used for small pieces in which very delicate carving is needed—as, for example, crosses, chess pieces, and the backs of books. Usually carvings in ivory are small, the reasons being the great expense of ivory and the difficulty of securing it in large pieces. The color of ivory is a rich, creamy yellow. Like wood, ivory cracks.

Terra Cotta

The term *terra cotta* means "baked earth." Terra cotta is made by firing clay, as in pottery. It is usually painted and covered with a heavy glaze. The great advantages of terra cotta are that it is very cheap in comparison with stone or bronze, and that brilliant colors are made possible by the glazing. Like all pottery, terra cotta is easily broken and chipped. As a medium for sculpture, terra cotta has been used at all times. Excellent examples are to be found in the work of many early peoples, notably the Greeks, the Chinese, and the Etruscans. A frequent subject in Chinese art is the lohan, a disciple of the Buddha. Uusually, as in the example shown in Figure 6-6, we find that emphasis on meditation which is characteristic of Buddhism. In the Renaissance, terra cotta was the favorite medium of successive generations of the della Robbias, a family of artists.

New Mediums

Artists at all times have experimented in new mediums, and sculptors of the present day are no exception. Henry Moore's little figure *The Bride* (not shown) is of cast lead and copper wire. Zorach's *Head of Christ* is of black porphyry (Figure 6-7). Cast stone (an artificial conglomerate of sand and silicone pressed and molded like concrete), wrought iron, aluminum, glass, and steel are other mediums used today.

This use of new and technologically derived mediums is seen in the work of such artists as Roszak, whose *Thorn Blossom* (Figure 6-8) is of steel and nickel-silver; Lipton; and, above all, David Smith. Smith, in many ways the originator of the current use of welded iron

Figure 6-6. Lohan (Chinese, Liao Dynasty, 947–1125). (Pottery, hard reddish-buff clay, green and yellow glazes. Height: 49¾ inches. Toronto, Canada, Royal Ontario Museum.)

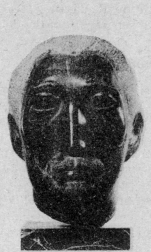

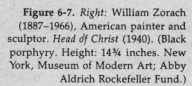

Figure 6-7. *Right:* William Zorach (1887–1966), American painter and sculptor. *Head of Christ* (1940). (Black porphyry. Height: 14¾ inches. New York, Museum of Modern Art; Abby Aldrich Rockefeller Fund.)

Figure 6-8. *Far right:* Theodore Roszak (1907–   ), American sculptor. *Thorn Blossom* (1948). (Steel and nickel-silver. Height: 33½ inches. Collection of the Whitney Museum of American Art, New York. Photograph, Geoffrey Clements.)

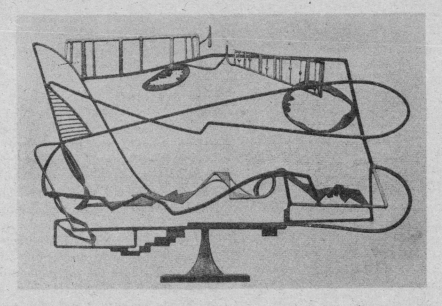

and steel for sculpture, began as a riveter in the Studebaker plant at
South Bend, Indiana. Influenced by Picasso's experiments with metal
sculpture, Smith started to do welded iron sculpture (Figure 6-9),
using a number of fanciful openwork forms whose symbols and
imagery depend on the machine itself.

PAINTING

Painting may be defined as the application of colored pigments to a
flat surface, usually canvas, paper, wood, or plaster.

Pigments

Pigments used in making colors come from different sources: clay,
coal tar, vegetable matter, etc. Some are manufactured; some are
found in nature almost as they are used. Some have been newly discovered; some have been known for a long time. Many of the pigments used today are obtained from natural sources. The reds and
browns now obtained from clay are the same reds and browns used
by the people who painted on cave walls in prehistoric times. Vege-
tables have been the source for many pigments; indigo produces blue
and madder, red. Ultramarine, which is the *blue* blue, the most expensive of all blues, was made by grinding the stone lapis lazuli.
Purple can be extracted from a shellfish, the murex.

Many pigments also have been made by the chemists. It is generally believed that the first chemical pigment was Prussian blue,

discovered in 1704. About a century later, many new pigments we
made, and in 1826 Guimet discovered a way to make ultramari
artificially. Since that time, there has been an ever increasing nu
ber of pigments made by chemical formulas.

Vehicles

The sources of many colors have been pretty much the same throug
out the generations, but the way the color is applied to the surfa
has changed. Since the colors as procured either from nature or fr
artificial sources are dry, they must be mixed with something
order to be spread on a surface. This substance, usually a fluid,
called the "vehicle." In oil painting, the colors are mixed with c
in other words, oil is the vehicle. In watercolor, water is the vehic
The vehicle determines the surface on which the paint is sprea
Canvas is not a good surface for watercolor, nor is paper a good su
face for oil. Since the pigments are essentially the same no mat
what surface or vehicle is used, a medium is commonly disti
guished by the surface and vehicle used. We do not speak of painti
in earth colors but of painting in oil or acrylic on canvas. Ea
medium determines its own brush stroke and produces its ov
effect.

Oil and acrylic   Probably the most widely used medium for painti
at the present time is oil. The vehicle is oil and the surface is usua
canvas, though various other surfaces may be used. The special a
vantage of oil is that it stays moist for a long time. The artist can wo
over what he or she has done and may change today what w
painted yesterday. The paint may be applied in any way that su
the artist: so thinly that the canvas shows through or so thick
as to produce a textured surface. The rough surface of Van Gogh
Self-Portrait in a Straw Hat may be seen even in the photograph (e
amine Figure 6-10); the paint is so thick that each stroke show
clearly. In contrast, the paint in Gauguin's *By the Sea* (Color Plate 1
has been applied smoothly, and individual brush strokes do n
show at all. In this painting, as in most of his paintings, Gaugu
added the title of the work in Tahitian directly on the canvas to e
hance the exotic subject matter, thus fusing the sounds of the Tah
tian words with the bright colors. Both pictures are on white canva
which gives them a certain brilliance.

    There are two methods of painting in oil, the direct and the i
direct. In the direct method, the paints are opaque and are appli
to the surface just as they are to look in the finished picture. In t
indirect method, the paint is put on in many thin layers of tra
parent color; the effect produced in this way is very rich a

Figure 6-10. Vincent Van Gogh (1853–
1890), Dutch painter. *Self-Portrait in a
Straw Hat* (1888–1889). (Oil on canvas,
on wood. Height: 13¾ inches. Courtesy
of the Detroit Institute of Arts. Purchase; City Appropriation.

luminous. Unfortunately, it cannot be distinguished in a photograph. The direct method is the more flexible medium of expression; the artist can use pigment very freely and express in it any fleeting thought. And, if it has not the richness of the transparent colors, it can obtain great vitality through the use of colors in high intensity. For the expressive purposes of, say, Van Gogh, the direct method was clearly more suitable. For the purposes of Rembrandt or El Greco, where the overlapping layers of paint on a dark canvas control the emergence of the light as it strikes the surface, the indirect method was more suitable.

The disadvantages of oil have to do with the preservation of the picture. Because the paint takes a long time to dry, the oil has a tendency to rise to the surface and form a film over the picture, thus dulling the colors. Moreover, it tends to become yellow, and in time the paint cracks.

Acrylic is a synthetic medium for pigments. It is clear and glasslike, but will neither yellow nor crack as oil-based pigments will. It is the most adaptable of mediums for painting; depending on the amount of water, the only thinner used, it can be used as paint or watercolor. Since it dries almost immediately, one color can be used to overpaint another to obtain an optical mixture or glaze. When it is used as an underpaint, almost any pigment-bearing vehicle can be used to overpaint it—oil, pastel, watercolor, and even wax crayon. It has greater permanence than oils on canvas since it will not crack. It can be used to paint over any surface that is not oily—cardboard, canvas, and even paper. It will not suffer change as a result of heat or humidity; thus the original colors and hues stay fast.

Watercolor   In watercolor the pigments are mixed with water and applied to a good-quality paper, pale and light in color. The paper shines through the paint and makes the color brilliant. It is difficult to produce warm, rich tones in watercolor. Changes may be made once the paint has been applied, but usually such changes tend to make the color less brilliant. In Marin's painting (Color Plate 19), the characteristic "watery" look of watercolor can be clearly seen. Watercolor is best for spontaneous, evanescent expression.

Opaque watercolor is called "gouache." It differs from the dominantly brilliant quality of translucent watercolor painting, whose major effects are caused by the light color of the paper itself. The gouache, which is made by mixing zinc white (Chinese white) with the regular watercolor paints to tone them down, is more sober in quality and therefore suitable to more dramatic purposes. These qualities may be illustrated by Picasso's *Blue Boy* (Figure 2-7), although the picture retains a certain lightness of expression and a pastel-like surface texture.

Figure 6-11. *Left:* Michelangelo (1475–1565), Italian painter, sculptor, architect, and poet. *Decorative Nude.* Detail of Sistine Chapel ceiling. (Fresco. Photograph by Alinari/Scala.)

Figure 6-12. *Right:* José Clemente Orozco (1883–1949), Mexican painter. *Modern Migration of the Spirit* (1932–1934). (Fresco, 126 inches wide, 120 inches high. Baker Library, Dartmouth College, Hanover, New Hampshire. Courtesy of the Trustees of Dartmouth College.)

Figure 6-13. Simone Martini (ca. 1284–1344), Italian painter. *Annunciation* (1333). (Tempera on wood. Height: 5 feet, 11½ inches. Florence, Uffizi Gallery. Photograph by Alinari/Scala.)

Fresco   In fresco painting a wall is prepared with successive coats of plaster. Designs are prepared in advance on large sheets of paper (cartoons), each sheet accounting for a section of the wall. The artist marks off on the wall the approximate amount that can be covered in a day's work and gives it the final coat of fresh (Italian *fresco*) plaster, to which that section of the drawing is transferred. The artist is then ready to paint. The pigment is mixed with water and applied to the wet plaster. The color dries into the plaster, and the picture thus becomes a part of the wall. Since fresco must be done quickly, it is a very exacting medium; there is no rubbing out and no changing once the design is begun. It is accordingly a medium of broad, bold outlines, usually with great simplification of form. Because of the chemical action of the plaster on the paint, only earth pigments may be used, and these colors lack intensity; there is, however, uniformity of tone with no glaring contrasts. The disadvantages of fresco are two: first, it is almost impossible to move a fresco; second, the painting, being permanently fixed to the wall, is subject to any of the disasters that may happen to the wall. If the plaster cracks or has a hole punched in it, the picture is hurt to that extent. The Sistine Chapel ceiling is in fresco; numerous cracks are clearly seen in the decorative nude shown in Figure 6-11. For many years fresco was used very little, but in recent times there has been a return to fresco painting, notably by the Mexican artists Diego Rivera and José Clemente Orozco. One of Orozco's most important works is on the walls of the Dartmouth College library: this is *Modern Migration of the Spirit* (Figure 6-12), in which, as has already been noted, the central figure is a dynamic Christ come back to earth to destroy his cross in a world filled with military equipment, where the name and the cross of Christ have been misused.

Egg tempera   Tempera and fresco were favorite mediums throughout the Middle Ages and early Renaissance, before oil was generally adopted. Tempera painting is usually done on a wooden panel that has been made very smooth with a coating of plaster called "gesso." The colors are mixed with egg yolk (with or without the white). The paint dries almost immediately. There is little blending or fusing of colors in tempera painting; the colors are laid on side by side or are superimposed. Hence the painting is composed of a large number of successive small strokes, and the effect is largely linear. It is hard to obtain rich, deep tones or dark shadows. Because tempera paint dries quickly, the artist must be precise and exact. It is a medium well designed for careful detail. The advantage of tempera is its great luminosity of tone, the colors being clear and beautiful. On the other hand, the precision needed tends to produce a certain hardness of outline. Botticelli's *Birth of Venus* (Color Plate 12) and Simone Martini's *Annunciation* (Figure 6-13) show most of the characteristics of tempera.

Figure 6-14. *Portrait of a Boy* (second century after Christ). Fayum, Lower Egypt. (Encaustic on wood panel. Size: about 10 by 16 inches. New York, Metropolitan Museum of Art; gift of Edward S. Harkness, 1917–1918.)

Encaustic Wax was used by the Egyptians for portraits painted o mummy cases. There were several ways of preparing the wax, but i general the color was mixed with warm wax and burned in. Th method was also used by the Greeks and the Romans, and it was em ployed to some extent during the Middle Ages. Paintings with wa have a definite body and a pleasing sheen which seem to show their best in portraits. *Portrait of a Boy* (Figure 6-14), dating from th second century after Christ, is an example. In recent years, paintin in wax has been revived by some modern painters, notably Dieg Rivera.

Jasper Johns, a contemporary American painter and sculptor, i *Target with Four Faces* (Figure 13-21), mixes encaustic with othe mediums.

Pastel In pastel, pigments in the form of powders are compresse lightly into sticks. Its colors are brilliant, and it is a very flexib medium, one in which very rich and varied effects may be pro duced. As a medium, however, it has never won a high place be cause no one has yet discovered a way to preserve it in its origina freshness. Even if it is covered almost at once with a fixing mediur or with a protecting surface such as glass, the chalk rubs and the pic ture loses some of its brilliance.

One of the outstanding artists in this medium is Edgar Dega (Color Plate 20). Degas used the pastel to combine drawing and colo: drawing set the figures in motion, and color dissolved the movin forms in a mist of surface tones. The French impressionists wer interested in the ability of the eye to mix juxtaposed colors so that th viewer would experience the vibrant dancing effects of light fallin on objects. Because, in this medium, the color values of the indi vidual strokes are preserved even when directly juxtaposed and d not blend as they do in oil painting, not only Degas, but Renoi Redon, Toulouse-Lautrec, Bonnard, and Matisse worked extensivel in pastels.

Illumination In the Middle Ages, when books were lettered by hand, the pages were often decorated with gold, silver, and brigh colors. Capital letters, especially, were made large and important Decorative borders were common, and frequently the artist addec miniature paintings of people or scenes. In the page from the Tickhi Psalter shown in Figure 6-15, all the capitals are emphasized, bu special attention is given the initial letter B, with which the firs Psalm begins, *"Beatus vir qui non abiit in consilio impiorum"* ("Blessec is the man that walketh not in the counsel of the ungodly"). Each half of the letter is filled with a miniature, and there are furthe miniatures at the foot of the page. These miniatures tell the story o

the anointing of David, the supposed author of the Psalms. The miniatures were made of tempera or pen and ink.

Mosaic Mosaic, stained glass, and tapestry are usually classed with painting, though the mediums are not pigment. A picture in mosaic is made by putting together small pieces of colored glass or stone, called "tesserae." These tesserae are often square. They are set in cement to hold them in place, the underside of the tesserae being roughened to make them fast in the cement. The use of stones makes simplification of design necessary. Moreover, the stones can never be set very smoothly in the cement, and hence the surface is always rough, reflecting light in many ways and creating a lively, vibrant effect. The greatest mosaics were made in the Middle Ages before painting became usual in churches. Some of the most famous are found in the church of S. Vitale at Ravenna. *Theodora and Her Attendants* (Color Plate 22) is one of the two in the church showing the Byzantine monarchs in the Offertory procession preceding the Mass. In the first (not shown), the emperor is represented carrying the bread for consecration. In the second, Theodora, his consort, is shown carrying the golden cup and the wine. (Incidentally, the Offertory procession has recently been revived in the new Catholic liturgy.) The enlargement of a portion of the mosaic (Figure 6-16) shows the tesserae clearly.

Figure 6-15. First page of the Psalms from the *Tickhill Psalter* (ca. 1310). Illuminated manuscript. Size: 12⅞ by 8 inches. New York, Spencer Collection, the New York Public Library; Astor, Lenox, and Tilden Foundations.)

Figure 6-16. "Portrait of Theodora," detail of *Theodora and Her Attendants*. (Church of S. Vitale, Ravenna. Photograph by Alinari/Scala.)

Figure 6-17. *S. Eustace Hunting* (twelfth
century), window. (Stained glass.
Height of diamond about 3 feet.
Chartres, Cathedral of Notre Dame, bay
13. Photograph by Houvet.)

Stained glass   Like the mosaic, the stained-glass window is a ki
of patchwork. It is made by combining many small pieces of color
glass which are held together by bands of lead. In a large windo
the lead is reinforced by heavy iron bars that make very hea
black lines in the picture. In the Middle Ages, when many peop
were illiterate, the glass of the church windows served as a "pictu
book" of biblical scenes. The windows at Chartres are consider
among the greatest of a great period. Our illustration shows or
section of the window of *S. Eustace* (Figure 6-17). The saint is se
riding to the hunt, his horn at his lips. At his feet are the dogs, ar
just before him the stags; behind him is an attendant urging on th
chase.

Tapestry   Tapestries are large fabrics in which a design is woven by hand. In the Middle Ages they were hung on the walls of palaces and in the cathedrals on festive occasions, both as decoration and for warmth. Being of very firm texture, they shut out the cold and helped to preserve the heat from the fireplace. In the *Unicorn in Captivity* (Figure 6-18), we see the famous *millefleur*, or "thousand-flower," background.

Figure 6-18. *The Hunt of the Unicorn: ʔe Unicorn in Captivity* (late fifteenth or early sixteenth century). (French or emish tapestry, from Chateau of Ver-uil. Silk and wool with silver and gilt hreads. Size: about 12 by 8 feet. New ork, Metropolitan Museum of Art; gift of John D. Rockefeller, Jr., 1937.)

MEDIUMS OF THE VISUAL ARTS

147

Figure 6-19. Jean August Dominique Ingres (1780–1867), French painter and pencil portraitist. *Lady and Boy* (1808). (Pencil drawing. Size: 9¾ by 7½ inches. New York, courtesy Metropolitan Museum of Art; bequest of Mrs. H. O. Havemeyer, 1929, H. O. Havemeyer Collection.)

Figure 6-20. Michelangelo. Studies for Libyan Sibyl (Figure 3-19). (Red chalk. New York, Metropolitan Museum of Art; purchase 1924, Joseph Pulitzer Bequest.)

Drawings

Drawings and prints are of special interest to the student, both for their intrinsic value and because they are comparatively inexpensive. In them, even the person of small means can afford original works.

A drawing may be a finished work, as in Ingres's *Lady and Boy* (shown in Figure 6-19); or it may be made as a study for a painting to be completed, like Michelangelo's studies for the *Libyan Sibyl* (shown in Figure 6-20). Notice Michelangelo's sketches of the big toe, and his change from the masculine face which appears in the center to the feminine face at the left.

Drawings are known chiefly by the mediums used, as pencil

Figure 6-21. Leonardo da Vinci (attributed) (1452–1519), Italian painter. *Head of a Woman*. (Silverpoint with white on bluish paper. New York, Metropolitan Museum of Art; Hewitt Fund, 1917.)

pen, silverpoint, and charcoal. *Pencil* is one of the most common because of its general utility, especially for making rapid notes. The French artist Ingres made many delicate and crisp pencil portraits as one means of support while he was living in Rome. A typical example is the *Lady and Boy*.

Silverpoint, a drawing made with a gold or silver wire on a specially prepared paper, is often very pale in tone and has little vitality but is very delicate and warmly shadowy. The difference between the line of the pencil and that of silverpoint can be seen by comparing the Ingres portrait with the *Head of a Woman*, attributed to Leonardo (Figure 6-21).

Ink makes a clear, crisp, often sketchy and spontaneous line; ink is frequently combined with a wash, as in the Rembrandt drawing *S. Peter and S. Paul at the Beautiful Gate of the Temple* (Figure 6-22).

Figure 6-22. Rembrandt Harmensz Van Rijn (1606–1669), Dutch painter. *S. Peter and S. Paul at the Beautiful Gate of the Temple*. (Pen and bistre, washed. New York, Metropolitan Museum of Art; Rogers Fund, 1911.)

Figure 6-23. Vincent Van Gogh. *Woman Cleaning a Cauldron.* (Charcoal on paper. Size: 24 by 18¼ inches. Albright-Knox Art Gallery, Buffalo, New York, Charles Clifton and Albert H. Tracy Funds.)

Bistre is a brown pigment made by mixing the soot from burning wood with a little binder.

Charcoal is one of the oldest mediums for drawing. The charcoal is made by roasting wood in a closed vessel. This medium is capable of a great variety of tones from the darkest to the very light, as is shown in Van Gogh's *Woman Cleaning a Cauldron* (Figure 6-23).

Chalk is another medium that has been used from the earliest times. It is found in white, black, and red. The red was especially desired for figure sketches like Michelangelo's sketch for the *Libyan Sibyl* (Figure 6-20). *Conté crayon* is one of the chalks; it is less waxy than the schoolroom type of crayon and much more durable than pastel. Seurat used it to produce rich shadows, great brilliancy of light, and strength of tones (Figure 6-24).

Figure 6-24. Georges Pierre Seurat (1859–1891), French painter. *The Artist's Mother* (ca. 1883). (Conté crayon on paper. Size: 12⅞ by 9½ inches. New York, Metropolitan Museum of Art, Joseph Pulitzer Bequest, 1955.

Figure 6-25. Kyosai (1831–1889), Japanese painter. *Animals, Children, and Men.* (Brush drawing. Height 10⅞ inches. New York, Metropolitan Museum of Art; Fletcher Fund, 1937.)

Drawing with a *brush* is characteristic of the Chinese and Japanese, who, it will be remembered, write with a brush instead of a pen. The brush gives very quick results and allows great freedom of handling. Kyosai's *Animals, Children, and Men* (Figure 6-25) is an example.

Often all that remains for contemporary collectors of the masters are sketches and drawings which they made as exercises or studies in the process of painting the great masterpieces we admire. But these are of great significance to us, for they are reminders of the fierce struggle and discipline which went into the finest works of art, a fact which is easy to overlook when we see only the perfection of the finished product. Such drawings from the High Renaissance represent not just casual notations or ideas, but deliberate searches for a new artistic style. Michaelangelo's studies for the *Libyan Sibyl* (Figure 6-20) are a revealing instance of this process. For the finished product, see Figure 3-19.

Prints

A print is something printed; that is, it is the impression left on paper or some other surface from an inked plate. Ordinarily the printing is in black ink on white paper. The plate is made by the artist, who usually does the printing. For these reasons a print is considered the authentic work of an artist and is signed by the artist. The number of copies that are made from any plate depends on the design, the kind of print, and the wishes of the artist. Often an artist decides on a certain number—thirty, fifty, one hundred—and destroys the plate when that number has been reached.

Figure 6-27. Karl Schmidt-Rottluff (1884–1968), German painter and printmaker. *The Miraculous Draught of Fishes* (1918). (Woodcut, Size: 5½ by 19⅝ inches. From *Kristus*, portfolio of nine woodcuts, published by Kurt Wolff, Leipzig. 1919. Collection, Museum of Modern Art, New York. Gift of Mrs. Gertrude A. Mellon.)

Figure 6-26. Albrecht Dürer (1471–1528), German printer and engraver. *The Crucifixion*. (Woodcut, New York, Metropolitan Museum of Art; gift of Henry Walters, 1917.)

There are five major types of prints: *woodcut, engraving, etching* (and related processes), *lithograph*, and the *serigraph*, or silkscreen print. Each print can be distinguished by the way the plate is made. Therefore, it is convenient to know both the kind of line characteristic of a print and the way the plate is made.

Woodcut   The woodcut, as the name implies, is made from a plate of wood. The design stands out in relief, the remaining surface of the block being cut away. A wood block prints just as the letters of a typewriter do. Since the lines of the design are of wood, they can never be very fine, and woodcuts can be identified by their firm, clear lines, usually black, such as those we see in Dürer's *Crucifixion* (Figure 6-26) and his *Four Horsemen* (Figure 5-3). The design is left standing in relief, and any part of the plate that is not cut away will print solid black. Older makers of the woodcut, like Dürer, used solid blacks very sparingly. In modern prints, such as *The Miarculous Draught of Fishes* by Schmidt-Rottluff (Figure 6-27), large areas of black are used in the design.

Color Plate 17. Georges Rouault 1871–1958), French painter. *La Sainte* *e* (1933). (Oil on paper. Size: 36 by 26 nches. © S.P.A.D.E.M., Paris, 1977.)

Color Plate 18. Paul Gauguin (1848–1903), French painter. *Fatata Te Miti (By the Sea)* (1893). (Oil on canvas. Size: 26¾ by 36 inches. Washington D.C., National Gallery of Art #1813; Chester Dale Collection.)

Color Plate 19. John Marin (1870–1953), American painter. *From the Bridge, New York City*. (Watercolor. Hartford, Connecticut, Wadsworth Atheneum.)

Color Plate 20. Edgar Degas (1834–1917), French painter. *Ballet Scene* (1907). (Pastel. Size: 30½ by 43¾ inches. Washington, D.C., National Gallery of Art, #1680; Chester Dale Collection.)

Color Plate 21. John Singer Sargent (1856–1925), American painter. *El Jaleo* (1882). (Oil on canvas. Boston, Isabella Steward Gardner Museum.)

Color Plate 22. *Theodora and Her Attendants* (ca. A.D. 525). (Mosaic. Figures slightly above life-size. Original mosaic in church of S. Vitale, Ravenna. Photograph by Scala, New York.)

Color Plate 23. *Above:* Honoré Daumier (1808–1879), French painter, caricaturist, and lithographer. *The Uprising* (1860?). (Oil on canvas. Size: 24½ by 44½ inches. Washington, D.C.; Phillips Collection.)

Color Plate 24. *Opposite page, top:* Henri Matisse (1869–1954), French painter. *Dance* (first version; 1909). (Oil on canvas. Size: 8 feet 6½ inches by 12 feet 9½ inches Collection, Museum of Modern Art, New York. Gift of Nelson A. Rockefeller in honor of Alfred Barr, Jr.)

Color Plate 25. *Opposite page, bottom:* Henri Matisse. *Dance* (second version; 1910) (Oil on canvas. Size: 8½ by 13 feet. Leningrad, Staatliche Ermtage—Hermitage Museum. Photograph by Mondadori.)

Color Plate 26. Georges Pierre Seurat (1859–1891), French painter. *Sunday on the Island of La Grande Jatte* (ca. 1886), detail. (Oil on canvas. Size: 81 by 120⅜ inches. Art Institute of Chicago; Helen Birch Bartlett Memorial Collection.)

The woodcut is made from a plate sawed parallel to the grain of the wood. The print often shows the grain. In recent years prints have been cut from linoleum as well as from wood. Sometimes these prints are called linoleum cuts, but there is so little difference between the two that ordinarily no distinction is made, and both are called woodcuts.

Colored woodcuts are made by preparing a separate block for each color to be used; only the parts to be printed in one color appear on the block of that color. The finished print, however, will show more shades than there are blocks, because one color is printed on top of another and the colors are mixed. The Japanese, especially, have excelled in this type of woodcut, though the technique has been used widely (Figure 6-28).

Engraving   An engraving is in many ways the opposite of a woodcut. In the woodcut, the parts that are to be printed solid are left standing, and the remainder of the block is cut away. In engraving, the lines of the design are cut into a metal plate; these lines are then filled with ink and transferred from the plate to the paper. The lines of an engraving are cut by hand with an instrument called a "burin," and since the copper plate is hard to cut, they are very fine, much finer than the lines of a woodcut. For the same reason they are hard and stiff, precise and formal. Shadows are made by lines either very

Figure 6-29. Martin Schongauer (1440–1491), German painter and engraver. *The Annunciation* (undated). (Engraving. Size: 6½ by 4¾ inches. Boston, Museum of Fine Arts.)

close together or crossing at regular angles. Blake's engraving *Whe The Morning Stars Sang Together* (Figure 3-14) shows the typical qua ity of the line. Other examples of engravings are Dürer's *Knigh Death, and the Devil* (Figure 5-2) and Schongauer's *Annunciatic* (Figure 6-29).

Etching Etching differs from engraving in the way the lines a made. In engraving, as we noted, the lines are cut directly in th plate by hand. In etching, the plate is covered with a coating of thin, waxlike material called a "ground." Through it the etcher draw the design. The etcher does not attempt to cut the plate itself b merely scratches through the wax, leaving the metal uncovere The plate is then put into an acid bath, and the design is *etched*, eaten, into the plate. Ink is applied to the plate, taking care that th all the etched-out lines are filled. The plate is then wiped, leaving thin film of ink, or no ink at all, on the remainder of the plate, d pending on any effects the artist wishes to attain in the backgroun "etching tone." The lines on an etched plate are made much mo easily than the lines on an engraved plate, and we see the differen in the finished print. The etched lines have the freedom of a pencile line, go in any direction, and cross at any angle. In *Why Does He Run* (Figure 6-30), Klee uses his etching needle almost like a pencil or pen.

Figure 6-30. Paul Klee (1879–1940), Swiss painter and printmaker. *Why Does He Run?* (ca. 1932). (Etching. Size: 9⅜ by 11¹³⁄₁₆ inches. © by S.P.A.D.E.M., Paris, 1977.)

Obviously neither etching nor engraving can show solid blacks as the woodcut can, and in both prints grays must be made by putting lines close together or by crisscrossing. The etched lines are very clear in Goya's *Pobrecitas* (Figure 6-31) and in Rembrandt's *Three Trees* (Figure 6-32).

Although black ink is most commonly used in etching, any color can be used. For example, Mary Cassatt, the most famous of the American impressionists, in *The Bath* (Figure 6-33), has chosen color for this intimate scene of a mother and child. Her emphasis on formal elements of pictorial design permits her to express maternal affection without sentimentality. Like many of the other impressionists, she greatly admired Japanese prints and Persian miniatures, and this interest is well adapted to etching, in which broad areas of color, flat patterns, and careful arrangement of forms in space are especially effective.

Drypoint, Mezzotint, Aquatint *Drypoint* stands halfway between engraving and etching. It is like engraving in that the lines are cut directly in the metal. It is like etching in that the needle is held as a pencil and is used freely. It merely scratches the metal. As it

Figure 6-31. Francisco Goya (1746–1828), Spanish painter. *Pobrecitas* ("Poor Little Things") from *Los Caprichos* ("Caprices") (1793–1798). (Etching and aquatint. New York, Metropolitan Museum of Art; gift of M. Knoedler and Co., 1918.)

Figure 6-32. Rembrandt. *Three Trees* (1643). (Etching. Size: about 8⅜ by 11 inches. New York, Metropolitan Museum of Art; bequest of Mrs. H. O. Mavemeyer, 1929, H. O. Havemeyer Collection.)

Figure 6-33. Mary Cassatt (1845–1926), American painter. *The Bath*. (Color etching. Photograph, Durand-Ruel, Paris.)

Figure 6-34. Francis Haden (1818–1911), English artist. *Eglamlock*. (Mezzotint. Size: 5¹⁵⁄₁₆ by 8¹⁵⁄₁₆ inches. New York, Metropolitan Museum of Art; Harris Brisbane Dick Fund, 1917.)

Figure 6-35. Goya. *Back to His Grandfather*, from *Los Caprichos*. (Aquatint. New York, Metropolitan Museum of Art; gift of M. Knoedler and Co., 1918.)

scratches, it leaves a little ridge at one side like the ridge left by a p run across a cake of soap. This ridge, called the "burr," takes the i and makes a very rich, velvety line. A similar ridge is thrown up engraving, but it is cleared away before any prints are made. Dr point can rarely be distinguished from etching in a photograph, b in the original the rough line of the drypoint is clear. In the Ren brandt etching (Figure 6-32) the heavily shaded portions at the low right are in drypoint.

Mezzotint and aquatint are two means of giving a solid tone tc print. *Mezzotint* is made on a copper plate which is artificially roug ened by an instrument known as a "rocker" or "cradle." The e graver then scrapes away more or less of the roughness in the pa that are to be light. The parts not scraped, or only partially scrape make a rich, velvety color like the burr of the drypoint. Mezzotint frequently combined with some other type of print, such as etchi or drypoint (Figure 6-34).

In *aquatint*, powdered resin is sprinkled on the plate and heat so that it adheres to the plate. When the plate is immersed in t acid, the parts not protected by the resin are bitten, and a very fi shadowy color is produced (Figure 6-35).

Lithography The lithograph is the most recent of the four comm types of print. It was discovered just before 1800, whereas woodcu engravings, and etchings go back to the fifteenth and sixteenth ce turies. It is made possible by the fact that oil and water will not mi The artist draws with a grease crayon directly on a flat, smooth sto (or a specially prepared metal plate). The stone is then dampene and ink is applied to the surface. The greasy, oily ink clings to t grease crayon marks, but not to the dampened areas. When a sheet paper is pressed against the stone, the ink on the crayon marks transferred to the paper. The stone must be reinked for each pri made, and a separate stone is required for each color. Every line shadow made on the stone, even those due to the texture or granine of the stone, is transferred to the paper; in fact, a lithograph loo very much like a charcoal, chalk, or crayon drawing on rough-su faced paper. It is the only print that can show tones shading in one another as in a drawing or a painting.

The discovery of lithography was especially welcomed by mu cians, who had to tediously make every copy of a music manuscri individually. And it was the mainstay of illustration at the beginnir of the century before the advent of photojournalism. Daumie *Strangers in Paris* (Figure 13-8) and Bellows's *Dempsey and Fir* (Figure 6-36) both show the characteristic shading of the lithograp Signac's *Port de St. Tropez II* (Figure 6-37) is an example of color lit ography.

Figure 6-37. Paul Signac (1863–1935), French painter, *Le Port de St. Tropez II* (1897–1898). (Color lithograph. Size: 17¼ by 13⅛ inches. Boston, Museum of Fine Arts.)

Figure 6-36. George Bellows (1882–1925), American painter and printmaker. *Dempsey and Firpo* (1924). Lithograph. Size: 18½ by 22⅜ inches. New York, Museum of Modern Art; Abby Aldrich Rockefeller Purchase Fund. Photograph, Museum of Modern Art.)

Serigraph The serigraph (or silkscreen) process is a method of making prints with oil instead of ink. A piece of silk is stretched on a wooden frame, and a design is imposed on that screen by stopping out (or blocking out) those areas which the artist does not want to print. A series of such frames are prepared, each one equivalent to one of the major colors in the design (this may be compared with the color woodcut process, discussed above). The sheets of paper constituting the "run" are then subjected to each of the screens in rotation, the oil colors being squeezed through the screen—or silk mesh—where the stop-out chemical has not been applied. In some cases, colors are superimposed in part on preceding colors so that a certain amout of blending is achieved. The total effect is more like a dark-toned gouache than an oil painting, but the result is a whole run of what appear to be paintings rather than prints (Figure 6-38).

The serigraph is widely used in commercial art as well as in conventional art forms. The poster, one common example of the use of serigraph, often falls between commercial and noncommercial art. It is, of course, used to advertise products, theatrical performances, concerts, motion pictures, and—most interestingly for our purposes —art exhibitions. Posters for art exhibitions are generally designed by the exhibiting artist and commercially distributed as reproductions after the exhibition closes. It is therefore possible for the

Figure 6-38. Sister Corita. *Jesus Never Fails*. (Serigraph. Size: 30 by 36 inches. New York, Brooklyn Museum; Henry L. Bateman Fund.)

average person to have a "special" silkscreen or lithographic desig (as a reproduction rather than as a signed print) made by an artist li Picasso, Calder, Rauschenberg, Kelly, Varsarely or Chagall (Figu 6-39).

As in other art forms—sculpture and painting, for example there is a marked tendency among contemporary printmakers to m the various mediums, to break down distinctions among mediun that were generally typical of traditional practice. Although, as v have just seen, it was always possible to have etching and aquati on the same plate, as in the Goya print (Figure 6-31), or etching ar drypoint, as in Rembrandt's *Three Trees* (Figure 6-32), the fact r mains that these combinations exist within the traditional fram work of etching practice—that is, lines etched into and below th surface of the plate. Generally, the five major areas—woodcut, e graving, etching (and related practices), lithograph, and serigraph remain separate fields for the traditional artist. More recently, or finds examples of such mixtures as etching and lithography, whe the artist first prepares an outline of the figure as an etched desig

Figure 6-39. Marc Chagall (1890–   ), Russian painter. *Bible/Editions Verve 33-34* (1956). (Lithograph. Size: 25 by 16¼ inches. New York, Museum of Modern Art; gift of Mourlot Frères.)

printed, for example, as a white outline, and then works out a series of woodcut-type blocks, one for each color, and applies them much as one would apply the color blocks for a Japanese woodcut print. This procedure results in a finely drawn outline of the main subject and a flatly worked-out series of bold color areas as background, combining the advantages of two different mediums on one print.

PHOTOGRAPHY

Although the principle of photography has been known since the Renaissance, it was not until the early part of the nineteenth century that a way was found to record the photographed image on a sensitized surface. By 1837, Mandé Daguerre was able to create a reproduction which had depth and texture. As the science of photography developed, the invention was used to produce works which reflected, even imitated, the subjects and styles of other visual art of the time. Many of the portraits done in the new medium of photography were especially sensitive and revealing of the character of the subjects. By the latter part of the nineteenth century, creative photographers no longer attempted to imitate older forms of art but used the new medium for new kinds of artistic expression. Among American photographers who led the way in demonstrating the creative, aesthetic possibilities in the medium were Alfred Stieglitz, Edward Steichen, Paul Strand, Edward Weston, Ansel Adams, and Imogene Cunningham. In their work they demonstrated that photography could present highly expressive views of commonplace scenes.

The Terminal (Figure 6-40) is characteristic of the "direct photography" which Steiglitz pioneered and which was to have a continuing influence on photography as an art. He referred to his photographs—taken out-of-doors, in the streets and open fields, away from the artificial, manipulated world of the studio—as "explorations of the familiar." For *The Terminal*, he is reported to have stood for hours in a raging snowstorm waiting for his subject to compose itself as he wished it and as we see it here. The sweeping strong curve of the men, horses, and tram pulls the many separate parts and aspects of the scene into a unified composition. Seen against the pattern of vertical and horizontal lines in the background, it communicates deliberate, determined movement in the snowy atmosphere enveloping the scene.

Steiglitz and his immediate followers were pioneers in establishing photography as an art. Today there are many, many others whose names are immediately associated with significant, individual ways of creating in the photographic medium. To suggest the range of subject matter and variety of approach, we can here name only a very few: Matthew Brady, Dorothea Lange, Eudora Welty, Margaret

Burke-White, Moholy-Nagy, Man Ray, Henri Cartier-Bresson, Bere nice Abbott, Frank Duncan, Richard Avedon, and Diane Arbus.

Of the newer mediums in the visual arts, none is now mo popular than the still photograph. Anyone can take a photograpl An image is recorded instantaneously and automatically. Psych logically, we feel that *any* result is the literal truth about what photographed. Indeed, it does tell *a* truth, because it records th external appearance of objects; but the surfaces of reality are alway shifting, presenting us myriad truths, different perspectives, ne patterns. The person who pushes the button on the camera is choos ing the aspect and instant of truth he or she considers important an wishes to record. However, perceiving and recording with a camer what is significant to the photographer is only the first step. Gre photographers—that is, those who raise photography to the level art—bring to their work not only the ability to sense the potenti significance of what they see, but the ability to choose a negative, a angle, a lens, and lighting best suited to capturing it on film. In th developing and printing process, they make choices as to wh values will dominate and what texture and color of photograph paper will be most effective. Finally, through a "cropping" proces they choose proportions for the photograph and the placement of th images within the proportions chosen.

The technical aspects of photography take time to learn, but mastery of them does not alone ensure significance. The photographs which continue to interest us after our first encounter with them, and which become art on a par with other visual art, are those made by persons who have developed an individual, sensitive way of seeing the world and translating this vision into the medium of the photograph.

As in all the arts, judgment as to what is great photography, what is good, what is less good, and what is insignificant is to some extent personal. However, it should be obvious that the visual elements and ways of organizing them in photographs are the same as those in the other visual arts. In general, one can say that those photographs which seem most pleasing to us over a long period have some ordering of forms, lines, colors, values, and textures which is currently expressive and revealing in connection with the subject matter. It seems to be especially true of great photographs that whatever processes have been used between the pressing of the camera button and the final result, the finished photograph is most appealing when it appears to have caught a bit of transient truth, fleeting, unposed—so that the total composition appears to be inevitable.

7 MEDIUMS OF MUSIC

Music and literature are both arts of sound. But words are not only sounds; they have meaning. In music, however, a sound is only a sound; it may be a high sound or a low sound, a long sound or a short sound; still, it is only a sound and has no meaning. There is a story told of Beethoven, who, after having played one of his piano works for a friend, was asked, "But what does it mean?" Whereupon Beethoven, without a word, played the composition again.

Music has an advantage over literature in that its symbols are understood throughout much of the world. The same musical symbols are used, whether in France, Australia, or Russia. Music and literature also differ in the way they produce sounds. In literature all sounds are produced by the human voice, whereas in music the human voice is but one of a number of instruments. Musical instruments are the means by which the composer communicates to the listener. The composer chooses the medium for any given composition according to an artistic conception. It is helpful, then, for the listener to have some understanding of the various musical instruments most frequently used in our culture and of the kinds of sounds they make.

The musical experience encompasses a three-way relationship involving the composer, the performer, and the listener. The performer is not a passive go-between; he or she interprets the music. The same composition may sound quite different when played by two performers whose interpretations differ. This is one of the most interesting aspects of music and explains why repeated hearings of the same work need not be repetitious. Two performances, even by the same performer, will never be exactly the same.

162

HOW INSTRUMENTS MAKE SOUND

Most instruments have three things in common; a vibrator, a resonator, and a system for producing and regulating fixed pitches.

Pitch will be discussed in more detail in Chapter 10. Here it will suffice to say that pitch is a special kind of sound produced by a particular kind of vibration. All sound, of course, is caused by vibrations, but sounds of definite pitch are created by regular, or periodic, vibrations. The sound produced by speaking results from irregular vibrations and is therefore of indefinite pitch, whereas that produced by singing results from regular vibrations and is therefore of definite pitch. When an object such as wire vibrates regularly 20 times per second, it produces the pitch we call middle C. When it vibrates 3,000 times per second, it produces a very high pitch. Most musical instruments have a limited range of pitches. Thus we distinguish between low instruments (that is, instruments capable of producing pitches only within a low range) and high instruments (those capable of producing pitches only within a high range). To take the human voice as an example, the female voice normally has a higher pitch range than the male voice. The piano, on the other hand, is an instrument with an extended range, including both very low and very high pitches, as well as those in between.

The vibrator is the part of the instrument which produces the regular vibrations. The resonator is any material used to amplify the vibrations so that they can be heard at a distance. Finally, since most instruments are capable of producing more than one pitch, there is a system for choosing which pitch within the range of the instrument will sound at any given moment. To use the piano as an illustration, the vibrators are the strings, the resonator is a wooden sounding board placed beneath the strings, and the means of determining pitches is a keyboard with a separate key for each of eighty-eight possible pitches.

THE PRINCIPAL MUSICAL INSTRUMENTS

There are three main kinds of instruments: instruments which are bowed, instruments which are blown, and instruments which are struck. These in turn are divided into four traditional groupings. The instruments which are bowed are the *strings*. Those which are blown fall into two groups: the *brasses*, so named because they are usually made of brass; and the *woodwinds*, so named because they were all originally made of wood. (The modern flute and piccolo are now almost always made of metal.) The fourth group, the percussion, consists of instruments which are struck.

The most common string, woodwind, and brass instruments used in Western music are listed below in order of range, from highest to lowest. Their size corresponds to their pitch, smaller instruments producing faster vibrations and thus higher sounds, and larger instruments producing slower vibrations and thus lower sounds.

Strings	Woodwinds	Brasses
Violin	Piccolo	Trumpet
Viola	Flute	French horn
Cello	Clarinet	Trombone
Bass	Oboe	Tuba
	English horn	
	Bass clarinet	
	Bassoon	
	Contrabassoon	

There are two kinds of percussion instruments: those that produce *definite* pitch, and those that produce *indefinite* pitch, or noise. Here are some of the most commonly used:

Percussion of Definite Pitch	Percussion of Indefinite Pitch
Tympani	Snare drum
Xylophone	Bass drum
Marimba	Cymbals
Chimes	Gong
Glockenspiel	Tambourine
(Harp)	Castanets
	Triangle

Strings

In string instruments (Figure 7-1), the vibrator is the string itself, made of gut or wire. The four strings of the bowed instruments vibrate when rubbed by a bow of horsehair made sticky with resin. Because the sound of a vibrating string is too small to be heard at a distance, a resonator is needed. The vibrations of the wooden box, along with the vibrating air inside the box, act as the resonator.

Pitch is determined in string instruments by the length, thickness, and tautness of the four strings. When a string is vibrated at full length, a specific tone is produced. Other pitches are made by stopping—that is, by putting one's finger at a certain point on the string and pressing it to the fingerboard. This shortens the length of string that vibrates and so raises the pitch. A great many tones can thus be made from each of the four strings.

Figure 7-1. String instruments. (The drawings of musical instruments are by Robin Rice.)

VIOLIN VIOLA VIOLINCELLO DOUBLE-BASS

Woodwinds

In the woodwinds (Figure 7-2), vibrators are of two kinds, a column of air and a reed. In the flute and piccolo, air blown across the opening near the head of the tube is split into two columns, part of the air going over the instrument, and part being forced through the tube. Of course the air blown across the instrument is lost, but its function is to create a steady pressure on the air being forced through the instrument. The same principal is involved in making sounds by blowing across a bottle or jug. Air is both the vibrator and the resonator. The air passing through the tube and the tube itself help to resonate the sound.

A single thin reed (now sometimes of synthetic material) is the vibrator used in the clarinet, bass clarinet, and saxophone. When air is forced into the mouthpiece, the reed flutters rapidly; and as the air is forced through the tube of the instrument, the tube becomes the resonator.

Double reeds are used by the oboe, English horn, bassoon, and contrabassoon. Air forced between the two reeds causes them to vibrate, and again the tube with the column of air passing through it is the resonator.

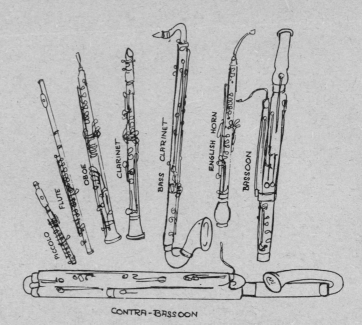

Figure 7-2. Woodwinds.

Pitch in woodwind instruments is determined by the length of the tube. The very short length of the piccolo makes it capable of playing the highest pitches in the orchestra, while the 16 feet of tubing in the contrabassoon make it the lowest pitched of all orchestral instruments.

Variety and control of pitch in woodwinds are obtained through the use of a series of holes stopped up by the performer's fingers or by the keys which shut the holes. By opening and closing these holes, the performer changes the length of tube, producing different pitches. When all the holes of the tube are closed, air passes through the entire length of the instrument and produces the lowest pitch.

In addition to the system of holes, pitch can be altered by overblowing; if the performer forces more air into the instrument than it can comfortably respond to, higher tones are produced. This technique is used in the flute, where overblowing can raise the pitch one or two octaves.

Brasses

In the brasses (Figure 7-3), the performer's lips are the vibrators. The lips are held tightly against the specially shaped mouthpiece and vibrate when air is forced through them into the instrument. The brass tube is the resonator. As in the case of the woodwinds, pitch is determined in the brass instruments by the length of tube through

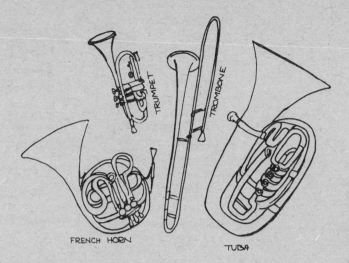

Figure 7-3. Brasses.

which the air must pass. Again, variety and control of pitch are achieved by changing the length of the tube; however, in the brass instruments, valves and sliding tubes, rather than holes, are used to do this.

Valves are used in the trumpet, horn, and tuba. When these valves are depressed, air is instantly diverted into different lengths of tube, creating different pitches. The trumpet, for example, can produce seven lengths of tube with its three valves.

The trombone has one tube fitted tightly over another: they can be telescoped in and out to lengthen the tube and change the pitch. The trombone is often popularly called the "slide trombone" because of this. Because there are no fixed valves on a trombone, the player has to rely on the ear to find the right position for the tone wanted.

Percussion Instruments

The percussion instruments are shown in Figure 7-4.

Percussion of definite pitch Tympani, or kettledrums, are large copper "kettles" with skin (or plastic) stretched over the top and tightened by "taps" around the edge. These instruments can be tuned to definite pitch by tightening or loosening the taps. Today some tympani are tuned by foot fedals, which perform the same function as taps but enable the performer to change pitch much more quickly. The vibrator is the skin of the drumhead, which the performer strikes with sticks—some soft, some hard. The resonator is the copper wall of the kettle.

Figure 7-4. Percussion instruments.

A xylophone is a series of bars of hard wood placed side by side like the keys of a piano, each bar having a different length and thus producing a different pitch. The bars are made to vibrate when struck with wooden or rubber beaters. The xylophone has no resonator.

The marimba is simply a xylophone with a resonator. Small tubes suspended under the wooden bars resonate the sound of the vibrating wood.

Chimes are tubular bells, metal tubes hung from a frame and struck with a hammer. The tube acts as a resonator.

The glockenspiel is a set of steel bars played with hammers. The sound produced by the vibrations of the bars is adequate, so that no resonator is used.

Finally, the harp is really a cross between a string instrument and a percussion instrument of definite pitch. Its strings are always plucked and they produce a silvery tone quality.

Percussion of indefinite pitch   The snare drum, or side drum, is a relatively small military instrument. Parchment is stretched over the top and bottom of a circular wooden frame, making two drumheads.

The top drumhead is beaten with two wooden sticks; the bottom drumhead has strings of gut or wire stretched across it, which give a dry, rattling sound when vibrating. Both separate strokes and long, muffled rolls are possible on the snare drum. The walls of the drum are the resonator.

The bass drum is relatively large and also has two drumheads. These are made of skin and are beaten with padded sticks. The performer can make rolls as well as single beats. The resonator, like that of the snare drum, is the wall of the drum.

Other percussion instruments of indefinite pitch have no resonator, their initial vibration being adequately loud. This is true of all the following:

The tambourine is a small wooden hoop over which skin is stretched, with metal disks on the rim. It can be shaken, hit with the hand, or banged on the knee, head, or elbow, or on some other part of the body.

Castanets are two hollowed-out pieces of hard wood which are snapped together by the hand. The two pieces may or may not be connected.

The triangle is a small steel rod bent in the shape of a triangle with one corner left open. It is suspended by a string and hit with a metal rod which is rapidly beaten against two sides.

Cymbals are two thin, slightly bowl-shaped plates of brass which can be rubbed together gently, beaten with a soft stick, or banged together violently.

The gong is a heavy metal disk hit with a padded stick.

Keyboard Instruments

The harp, as we have seen, does not fit into any one of the four instrumental groups. A similar situation exists with the keyboard instruments. Although these are normally included with the percussion group, they constitute a special set which may be considered singly. The piano, celesta, harpsichord, and organ are all keyboard instruments of definite pitch, but each has physical properties quite different from the others. The piano is basically a string instrument in which the strings are struck by hammers attached to a keyboard; the celesta, often considered a percussion instrument of definite pitch, has steel plates which are hammered; the harpsichord is a string instrument whose strings are plucked by quills or leather or brass tongues attached to the keys; and the organ is a wind instrument, its sounds being made by air forced through pipes.

RANGE

The range of an instrument is determined largely by its size. As was pointed out earlier, large objects vibrate more slowly than small ones,

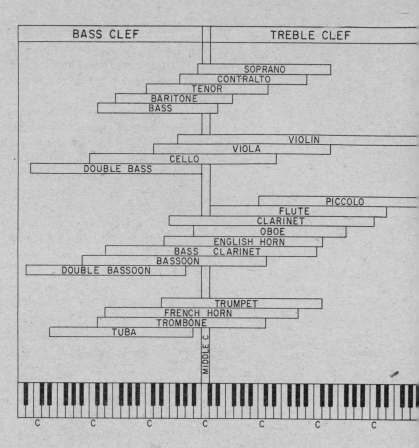

Figure 7-5. Ranges of instruments and voices.

and slower vibrations create lower tones. Small objects produce fast[er] vibrations and hence higher tones. Thus the range of a cello is low[er] than that of a violin.

The range of any voice or instrument is divided into thre[e] registers, high, middle, and low. Thus we speak of the high registe[r] of a bassoon, the middle register of a violin, the low register of [a] trumpet, etc.

To give an idea of the relative range of the instruments di[s]cussed, Figure 7-5 is a chart comparing them, along with the huma[n] voice, with the piano keyboard. The overlapping of ranges as see[n] here becomes dramatically clear. This is one of the reasons tha[t] timbre, which will be discussed next, is so important to the com[-]poser.

TIMBRE

Timbre, or tone color, is the characteristic quality of sound produce[d] by an instrument and distinguishes it from the sounds produced b[y] other kinds of instruments. Thus, although a flute and an oboe hav[e] similar ranges, they can be distinguished because they have different timbres.

When a composer thinks of a musical idea, aside from the limitations of range, he or she must think in terms of musical line, tone color, and volume—that is, the composer must imagine the instrumental sound as part of the idea. An oboe melody, for example, seems right for the oboe, though the same pitches can be played on a violin, clarinet, or trumpet. Another melody, of course, may be more suitable for the clarinet or the viola—or for that matter, any other instrument. Sometimes, however, a composer will assign the same melody first to one instrument and then to another, in order to lend it a somewhat different character in its reappearance. Great orchestrators, such as Hector Berlioz, Richard Strauss, and Igor Stravinsky, have a genius for using instruments, either singly or in combination, which can best enhance a musical idea.

There is no way to "know" the sound of any instrument other than by simply listening to it until one can say with accuracy, "That's a bassoon," or "That's a horn." Still, for those who are learning to recognize the characteristic sound of an instrument, there are a few helpful descriptive adjectives which are accepted so generally that they have become clichés. Here is a brief description of the more important instruments, with examples of music for each.

The Strings—Timbre

The strings form the backbone of the orchestra. They are largest in number and are divided into first and second violins, violas, cellos, and basses. The leading first violinist is also the concert-master; he or she is in charge of the string choir.

Some of the special effects possible on each of the string instruments, and the methods of producing them, are as follows:

Spiccato:	Making each note short and crisp by use of the bow
Saltallato:	Bouncing the bow on the string to produce light, detached tones
Martellato:	Hammering the bow on the string, making each tone separate and emphatic
Tremolo:	Making the bow quiver on the string to produce a shimmering effect
Sul ponticello:	Bowing near the bridge to produce a thin, eerie sound
Pizzicato:	Plucking the strings, making a harp-like sound

Besides these effects, double and triple stopping are possible; that is, by playing on two or three strings simultaneously, the performer can produce chords.

Violin Of all the strings, the violin is the most versatile and expressive. It has a wide range of tones which can be sustained indefinitely. It can play very quietly or loudly; it can play very slow passages or be lightning swift. Because of its expressive, voicelike quality, its range, and the special effects it can produce, the violin is a virtuoso instrument. More music has been written for it than for any other orchestral instrument. The second movement of Prokofiev's Classical Symphony has some beautiful passages for the violin choir in the upper register. The fourth movement of Brahms's Symphony No. 1 has a broad theme for violins in their lowest register. Mendelssohn's Concerto for Violin shows off the virtuosity of the solo instrument.

Viola Slightly larger than the violin, the viola has thicker strings and a heavier bow; it can be thought of as an alto violin. The viola has never been considered as much a solo instrument as the violin, being used more often for harmony than for melody. Nonetheless, it can do everything the violin can do, at a lower pitch. But the viola is best suited to passages that reveal its warm, rich tones. Walton's Concerto for Viola demonstrates this admirably.

Violoncello Commonly called the *cello*, this instrument is much larger than either the violin or viola; it has to be held between the knees of a seated performer. Its strings are thicker and heavier than those of the viola, they are tuned an octave lower, and the bow is shorter and heavier. The tone of the cello is rich and romantic, deep and full. It is a favorite instrument for solo passages. If the violin is the soprano of the string choir and the viola the alto, the cello is the tenor-baritone. A classic cello line can be found in the second movement of Beethoven's Symphony No. 5.

Double bass Known also as the *contrabass* and the *bass viol*, the *double bass* or, more simply, the *bass* is the largest member of the string family. It rests upon the floor, and the performer stands to play it. Because of its great size and the depth of its tone, it allows less agility than the other instruments in the string family and has a more limited range of expression. It is most often used as a support, supplying the bass tones for the string choir or orchestra, though occasionally it is given a solo part. In the scherzo of Beethoven's Symphony No. 5, it plays a lumbering, almost grotesque role.

In dance bands, the double bass is never bowed, but is played in a slapping fashion with the hand, not only for its tone, but to emphasize the beat.

The Woodwinds—Timbre

Unlike the string section, the woodwind section is made up of instruments which have strikingly different timbre. Whereas the cello's sound, except for its deeper range, is not radically different from that of a violin, the various woodwinds produce distinctly different tone colors. Thus this group is particularly useful for supplying timbral contrast in the orchestra.

Flute   The flute is a tube of metal approximately 27 inches long. Its sound is often called silvery, haunting, or liquid. It is very agile and can play rapid, brilliant scale passages. In its lower register the sounds are mellow and rather ethereal, but in its upper register the sound is thinner, more brilliant. One is always aware of its breathy quality. There is a beautiful flute melody in the "Dance of the Blessed Spirits" from Gluck's *Orpheus and Eurydice*.

Piccolo   This instrument is really a small flute. It is constructed like the flute and can be played by all flutists. It is approximately half the length of the flute and produces shrill and piercing tones, especially in its upper range. Because of its tiny size, it is pitched an octave above the flute and adds a sharp edge of brilliance and bite when it is heard with other instruments. Vivaldi's Concerto in C Major for Piccolo, Strings, and Cembalo is an example.

Oboe   The body of the oboe is a tube of wood which becomes larger toward the bell, or end. It is especially good in expressive solos because its sound is reedy and penetrating. The oboe's slightly nasal tone gives it a plaintive or melancholy quality, but it can also be quite lively. A good example is Vivaldi's Concerto in D Minor for Oboe, Strings, and Continuo.

English horn   Despite its name, the English horn is a large oboe. Its relationship to the oboe is roughly that of the viola to the violin. The oboe and the English horn look very much alike except that the English horn has a bulge in its bell. Its range is slightly lower, and its sound is richer and even more plaintive than the oboe's. It is usually given the slower, more expressive line to play. In Franck's Symphony in D Minor, the English horn is heard in the second movement.

Clarinet   Among woodwinds, the B-flat clarinet is perhaps the most versatile instrument. It has a very wide range, within which it produces three distinctive sounds: in its lowest register it makes rich, hollow tones sometimes called "barrel tones"; in its middle register the sound is smooth and of medium thickness; in its upper range the sound is thin and shrill.

The clarinet is capable of great expression. It can go from a barely audible sound to one quite loud, play lyrical lines with great finesse, or do rapid scale passages. For these reasons it often takes the part of the violin when orchestral music is transcribed for band. Mozart's Quintet for Clarinet and Strings is an example.

Bassoon The bassoon and contrabassoon are respectively the teno and bass of the oboe family. The bassoon has approximately 8 feet wooden tube doubled back upon itself (the contrabasson has 16), an the player supports the instrument by snapping it to a sling wor around the neck. The bassoon produces two distinct colors in i upper register: it makes a whining, nasal sound not unlike the saxo phone, whereas in its lower register the tone is gravelly, dry, an gruff. The bassoon's upper register is good for expressive solos, bu the lower register, unless for reasons of humor, is not. Rather, th register is used for bass harmony, adding a special edge to the ove all effect. In "Dragons of Alcala" from Bizet's *Carmen*, there is characteristic melody for two bassoons.

The Brasses—Timbre

Although the brasses are less agile than the strings and woodwind their assertive, penetrating sound is very useful for producin various orchestral effects, ranging in quality from great solemnity t raucous excitement. Their ability to play very loudly is also helpf in creating climaxes and for adding sudden punctuations to so passages played by the other sections.

Trumpet The trumpet has both a bright brassy sound which ca ring and pierce, and a soft, muted sound made by inserting "straight" mute (a cone-shaped piece of wood or metal) in the be of the tube. Because of its military history, it is often associated wit battle calls and is extremely effective in strident passages wher triumph or fury is intended. Purcell's Trumpet Voluntary in D is a example.

French horn Called simply the *horn*, this instrument has been de veloped from the hunting horn, and its ability to project soun across great distances is still evident. The horn normally has smooth, mellow tone, but can be made to sound very brassy. B placing a mute or a hand into the bell, the performer can get a mute sound which is both distant and haunting. By pushing the hand fa into the bell and blowing with greater force, the performer ca produce an extremely brassy, almost threatening sound.

The horn is a versatile instrument; as a solo instrument it is ver satisfactory because it can be loud or soft, lyrical or dramatic, an has a wide range. It also has the ability to blend well with every othe instrument and is often used for its full, rich tones in harmony Probably one of the best-loved horn solos is found in the secon movement of Tchaikovsky's Symphony No. 5. Mozart's Concertos fo Horn are among the most admired compositions for this instrument

Trombone   There are two kinds of trombone: tenor and bass. When we speak of the trombone, we usually mean the tenor. The two are alike in construction, but, as would be expected, the bass trombone has a lower range. The trombone's tone is rich and mellow. It can be played softly, but is more often used for dignified, grandiose melodies. When trombones play in unison, they can be overpowering, as in the overture to Wagner's *Tannhäuser*.

Tuba   This instrument is the bass of the brass choir and is therefore most often used to reinforce the harmony for the orchestra. Its sound is rather like that of the bass trombone, but fuller, richer, and more powerful. The overture to Wagner's *Die Meistersinger* has a famous tuba solo.

The Percussion Instruments—Timbre

Until the twentieth century, percussion instruments were used sparingly in the orchestra. The only ones to appear regularly in eighteenth- and nineteenth-century orchestras were the tympani, which were used primarily to supply strong accents and were normally heard in conjunction with the brasses. It is not unusual, however, for modern compositions to require very large percussion sections which are used prominently. For example, Ravel's *Rapsodie Espagnole* ("Spanish Rhapsody") requires three percussionists playing a great variety of instruments. (Percussion performers are trained to play several percussion instruments.)

COMBINATIONS OF INSTRUMENTS

Chamber Ensembles

Music written for small groups with only one player to each part is known as *chamber music*. As is true of large ensembles, there are several combinations which are frequently encountered. Most common is the string quartet, which consists of two violins, a viola, and a cello. Also popular are the piano trio (piano, violin, and cello) and the woodwind quintet (flute, oboe, clarinet, bassoon, and French horn). There is also a great deal of chamber music written for one orchestral instrument (for example, a violin) and a piano. The piano, because of its ability to sound several tones simultaneously, is particularly useful in small combinations.

The Symphony Orchestra

The most important combination of instruments is the symphony orchestra, which is composed of the four choirs discussed earlier in

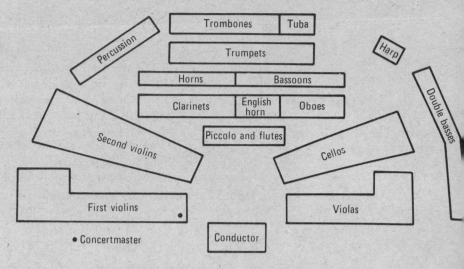

Figure 7-6. A typical seating plan of a symphony orchestra.

this chapter. Each of these choirs has an instrument or instruments which fall into the range of soprano, alto, tenor, and bass.

The number of instruments used in the orchestra varies according to the demands of the music. In the early days of its development the orchestra was much smaller than it is now. Bach's orchestra (early eighteenth century), for example, used a very small group, often consisting of no more than twenty players. Haydn's orchestra (late eighteenth century) had about forty players. By Wagner's time (the middle of the nineteenth century), it was not uncommon for or chestral pieces to require over sixty players, and by the turn of the century, in the music of Strauss and Mahler, for example, pieces were written for more than 100 players. It is apparent that an orchestra must be flexible if it is to play music from different periods. Most of the major orchestras now have approximately ninety players, but they increase the number of players in order to play compositions requiring more performers. Figure 7-6 shows a typical seating plan for an orchestra.

On the opposite page is a table which gives the typical size of the small, the medium, and the large orchestra.

Special Ensembles

It is important to keep in mind that certain mediums are particularly useful for certain kinds of music. The instruments and combinations of instruments that we have considered were developed gradually over many years to meet the requirements of particular kinds of music. There is no reason to assume, however, that they are neces-

	SIZE OF ORCHESTRA		
	SMALL	MEDIUM	LARGE
STRINGS			
First violins	8	12	16
Second violins	8	12	16
Violas	6	10	12
Cellos	4	8	10
Basses	2	4	8
WOODWINDS			
Piccolo		1	1
Flutes	2	2	2
Oboes	2	2	3
English horn		1	1
Clarinets	2	2	3
Bass clarinet		1	1
Bassoons	2	2	3
Contrabassoon		1	1
BRASSES			
Trumpets	2	3	4
French horns	2	4	6
Trombones		2	3
Tuba		1	1
PERCUSSION			
Tympani	1	1	1
Other		1	2
Harps		1	2
Total	41	71	96

sarily superior to other instruments and instrumental combinations designed for other types of music. To take a current example, the rock band is obviously better suited for the performance of rock music than the symphony orchestra. In the field of concert music too, as music evolves, composers search for new mediums more congenial to their changing musical ideas. In twentieth-century music, for example, it has become increasingly common for composers to choose "special" combinations for the unique purposes of particular compositions. Two examples are *L'Histoire du Soldat* ("The Soldier's Tale"), by Igor Stravinsky, written for clarinet, trumpet, trombone, violin, bass, percussion, and narrator; and *Le Marteau sans Maître* ("The Hammer without a Master"), by Pierre Boulez, for flute, xylophone, vibraphone, guitar, viola, various indefinite-pitch percussion instruments, and also voice.

One particularly significant trend in recent years has been the development of electronic instruments, which many contemporary composers feel are more versatile than traditional instruments and more suitable for achieving the sounds they want for their music. Karlheinz Stockhausen's *Gesang der Jünglinge* ("Song of the Youths") is an example of a composition produced electronically. In this piece the sounds are originally generated by both purely electronic means and "natural" means (a boy's voice), but all the sounds are then electronically manipulated so that the final result is a completely electronic composition.

Finally, it should be remembered that other cultures make use of instruments which are different from ours, but which, like ours, have been developed for the purposes of performing a particular kind of music. The Javanese gamelan orchestra, for example, is constituted primarily of several gonglike or chimelike instruments constructed of different kinds of materials (wood, bamboo, and metal); it has a ringing timbral quality unlike anything in Western music, and it is uniquely suited to Javanese music.

INTERPRETATION IN ENSEMBLE MUSIC

The problem of interpretation is considerably more complex in the performance of music for ensembles than in that for solo instruments, because the interpretation must be worked out in cooperation with the various performers. In chamber music the interpretation is normally arrived at through common agreement, although in some cases one player may have the main responsibility (this is frequently true of the first violinist in string quartets). In chamber music, even if one player is chiefly responsible for the interpretation, there is nevertheless no director as such during the performance. Thus the players must always listen to one another extremely carefully; precisely for this reason, many performers prefer chamber music.

In the orchestra, however, the problems of keeping all the players together and of agreeing upon an interpretation become increasingly complex. From about 1825, orchestral directors—or "conductors," as they are usually known—became regular features of all large ensembles. The conductor's importance has grown steadily until today the conductor is considered to be the most valuable and essential person in the orchestra.

The duties of today's conductor are both demanding and varied. The conductor is in charge of the personnel of the orchestra, auditions performers, and decides who will be a member of the orchestra and what part each member will play within a section.

The conductor also decides what music will be performed. The performance of obscure works, the introduction of contemporary music, or the choice of traditional works is his or her responsibility. Moreover, the conductor must decide what will make a balanced individual concert. These decisions are, of course, tempered by the proficiency of the group, the amount of rehearsal time available, the instruments and the performers the music calls for, the demands of musicians' unions, and often the taste of the public which helps to support the group.

Aside from the demands of business, the conductor must be a kind of supermusician. He or she must know thoroughly the mechanics of every instrument in the orchestra. The conductor, from the podium, reads simultaneously on the score the notes of every instrument, and should be able to detect and correct any error on the part of the performers. The conductor, therefore, must know the score perfectly and also must have knowledge of the general style of the composer whose music is being played. It is in terms of musical performance, however, that the conductor succeeds or fails, for ultimately, the kind of performance given rests upon his or her interpretation.

The following are some of the things the conductor does at a performance: sets the tempo and controls the rhythm; adjusts the volume from time to time, asking some players for softer sounds and others for more volume, so that the audience gets the correct mixture of both volume and tone color; cues the performers, making sure that each instrument enters precisely when it should; and, most important, indicates the mood of a particular motive, phrase, or section of music. It is the conductor who determines the expressive quality of the performance.

VOCAL MEDIUMS

Range

Like instruments, voices are also combined into groups, by which they fall into the four basic ranges: soprano, alto, tenor, and bass.

If each of the four parts is sung by many singers, the group is a *chorus*, or a *choir*. Choral music may be either accompanied or unaccompanied. If unaccompanied, it is known as *a cappella* music (*cappella* is the Italian word for "chapel"; thus, music "for the chapel," where in earlier times no instruments were allowed). A chorus may be accompanied by any group of instruments or by a solo keyboard instrument; it is frequently heard in combination with an orchestra. There is also music for all-male choruses and all-female choruses.

As with instrumental music, there is also music for the vocal quartet, consisting usually of one soprano, one alto, one tenor, and one bass. More prominent is the solo song with keyboard accompaniment, for which there is a large and varied literature.

In addition to the different ranges, solo voices are also cate gorized according to their timbre, or quality of sound. Thus we dis tinguish between *lyric* and *dramatic* sopranos (or altos, etc.), the lyric voice having a lighter, more flexible quality than the dramatic voice

Vocal music is a particularly attractive medium for composers for, although the human voice lacks the agility of most orchestra instruments, it more than compensates for this limitation with its expressive human quality. Moreover, the singer's performance o words as well as music, a technique obviously unavailable to instru ments, opens up an important musical dimension: the setting o texts to music.

Vocal Timbre

In group singing, voices are commonly divided into four categories, according to range. From highest to lowest they are: soprano, con tralto (or alto), tenor, and bass. Sometimes a fifth category, the baritone, is added between the tenor and bass. Soprano and con tralto are female voices; tenor, baritone, and bass are male.

In solo singing, however, and especially in art songs and opera, additional distinctions are made by names which describe timbre. This results in twelve categories of singing voice, five women's and seven men's. These voices can be identified by range, by their rela tive weight (light to heavy), and by the style of the music they sing. From highest to lowest, they are: coloratura soprano, lyric soprano, dramatic soprano, mezzo-soprano (or lyric contralto), dramatic con tralto, lyric tenor, lirico spinto tenor, dramatic tenor, lyric baritone, dramatic baritone, basso cantante (lyric bass), and basso profundo (deep bass).

A word of caution is in order here: the vocal timbre of singing voices is not so exact as that of the orchestral instruments. There are personal qualities which each singer's voice brings to bear on the music. It is sometimes difficult to decide whether the music being sung is essentially lyric or dramatic. An opera role, or even a lengthy art song, can demand both lyric and dramatic qualities. Moreover, some voices are flexible enough to sing in more than one of these categories. For example, some dramatic sopranos can also manage lyric roles, and some baritones can sing either lyric or dramatic music with equal facility. Finally, we should remember that voices change with study and maturity. Lauritz Melchior made his reputation as a dramatic tenor, although he had begun singing as a baritone.

Keeping these remarks in mind, we may look at a description of each kind of voice. The examples are from well-known operas.

Coloratura soprano This voice is the lightest in weight and is best suited to music of a florid, technical nature. There is usually an emphasis on the upper reaches of the voice, and the melodies are apt to be highly embellished. The "Indian Bell Song" from *Lakmé* is sung by a coloratura. It could easily be a flute solo.

Lyric soprano   As the name implies, this voice is one which sings lyrical music. Traditionally, the heroine of an opera is played by a lyric soprano. Her voice is of medium weight, and she is usually asked to sing a sustained melodic line, often of an emotional nature. The prayer that ends Gounod's *Faust*, "Holy Angels in Heaven Blest," is sung by a lyric soprano.

Dramatic soprano   This voice is the heaviest of soprano voices. The dramatic soprano is known for her full, clear tones, and is usually associated with roles of grand passion. The music for this voice is often heroic, with melodies of a tempestuous nature. Brünnhilde's immolation scene in Wagner's *Götterdämmerung* is an example; in it Brünnhilde greets her steed, Grane, and prepares to ride him into the fire that will end her life.

Mezzo-soprano (lyric contralto)   *Mezzo* means "middle." This voice is a lyric contralto, but the Italian name is more widely used. The mezzo-soprano has a highly colored timbre which, like the viola's, is rich and warm. She sings music of a lyric or animated character. In the opera *Mignon*, the lovely aria "Hast Thou E'er Seen the Land?" is sung by a mezzo-soprano.

Dramatic contralto   The dramatic contralto possesses the deepest and richest of women's voices. Her range is much the same as that of the mezzo-soprano, but she is known by her heavier voice and by the dramatic quality of the music she sings. In vehement passages there is normally a preoccupation with her middle and lower registers. In Wagner's *Lohengrin*, the dramatic contralto, Ortrud, is bent on ruining the hero and the heroine.

Lyric tenor   This is the lightest in weight of men's voices. The lyric tenor produces a pure, relatively thin tone best suited for music of a lyrical nature. Outside the field of opera, this voice is sometimes called an "Irish tenor" because it is so well suited to the singing of sentimental ballads and folk songs. In *The Magic Flute*, Mozart has written a cavatina requiring both expression and agility. Here the tenor, a prince, sings rapturous praises upon being shown a portrait of the beautiful Pamina.

Lirico spinto tenor   *Spinto* means "with accent." Just as the lyric tenor is often called "Irish," the lirico spinto tenor is thought of as an Italian voice because of the emphasis on *bel canto*, or beautiful singing style. His voice is richer and more powerful than that of the lyric tenor and he is most often asked to sing melodies of well-turned phrases and emotional content. The lirico spinto tenor is traditionally the hero of the opera. In most nineteenth-century operas, his role calls for an occasional high note usually sustained and adding emphasis to the passage. In Verdi's *Il Trovatore*, the hero sings of his imminent death and his love for Leonora in "Let Links Eternal Bind the Vows."

Dramatic tenor   As the name implies, music for this voice is dramatic, even heroic. The dramatic tenor therefore is often called the "heroic tenor" as well. His is the heaviest in weight of the three tenor voices. He is known for his large, opulent tones and his voice is even richer and more powerful than that of the lirico spinto. In *Lohengrin* the dramatic tenor, the hero in this opera, reveals his identity for the first time in "Lohengrin's Narrative" as the opera draws to a close.

Lyric baritone   Falling between the range of the tenor and the bass, the baritone voice is one of medium weight. The lyric baritone is most easily identified by his rich tones and by the sustained melody he most often sings. In *La Traviata*, by Verdi, the baritone, father of the unhappy hero, begs his son to forsake his love and come home to his family, in an aria called "Di Provenza."

Dramatic baritone   This voice has a wider range than that of the lyric baritone and sings music of a more emotional or dramatic intensity. In the prologue to Verdi's *Simon Boccanegra*, Simon, the hero, is trying to justify seizing power so that he will be free to marry Maria and give their daughter his name: "I Hoped to Make Myself Sublime in Your Eyes."

Basso cantante (lyric bass)   *Cantante* means "singing." This voice, then, is one which is capable of singing a broad melody. Its tones are rich and full. One of the favorite roles of lyric basses is that of Don Giovanni in Mozart's opera of the same name. "Here with Our Hands Entwining" is a charming duet in which Don Giovanni attempts to lure Zerlina away from her betrothed.

Basso profundo (deep bass)   Of all voices, this one has the heaviest weight and the deepest, richest timbre. The basso profundo sings music of an animated or dramatic character, but is also capable of sustaining a semilyrical role. Often there is an emphasis on his lowest tones. The role of Oroveso in Bellini's *Norma* was written expressly for the basso profundo. Here, Oroveso, chief of the Druids, sings that he will annihilate the enemy who has desecrated his temple in the aria "Haughty Roman."

MUSICAL EXAMPLES

There is no substitute for actually hearing the sounds produced by the various instruments and instrumental combinations. There are two recordings currently available which are designed to introduce the orchestral instruments:

The Instruments of the Orchestra (Vanguard 1017/8)
The Orchestra and Its Instruments (Folkways 3602)

In addition, a number of specific compositions illustrate clearly the timbre of the various instruments. Some of them are:

The Young Person's Guide to the Orchestra, by Benjamin Britten
Bolero, by Ravel
Nutcracker Suite, by Tchaikovsky
Peter and the Wolf, by Prokofiev
Concerto for Orchestra, by Bartók
Carnival of the Animals, by Saint-Saëns

Compositions for other mediums, such as the band and the various chamber ensembles, are also readily available on record. To list a few examples:

Serenade in C for String Orchestra, by Tchaikovsky
Symphony in B flat for Band, by Hindemith
String Quartet, Op. 18, No. 1, by Beethoven
Sonata in D Minor for Violin and Piano, Op. 103, by Brahms
Symphony of Psalms for Chorus and Orchestra, by Stravinsky
Frauenliebe und Leben, Op. 42, for Soprano and Piano, by Schumann

Other works which illustrate vocal timbre in solo are:

Coloratura Soprano
    "Sempre Libera," from Act I of *La Traviata*, by Verdi
    "Casta Diva," from Act I of *Norma*, by Bellini
Lyric Soprano
    "Voi che sapete," from Act II of *The Marriage of Figaro*, by Mozart
    "Quando m'en vo'soletta" ("Musetta's Waltz"), from Act II of *La Bohème*, by Puccini
Dramatic Soprano
    "Vissi d'arte," from Act II of *Tosca*, by Puccini
    Liebestod: "Mild und leise wie er lächelt," from Act III of *Tristan und Isolde*, by Wagner

Mezzo-soprano
  Seguidilla: "Près des ramports de Seville," from Act I of *Carmen*, by Bizet
  "Mon coeur s'ouvre à ta voix," from Act II of *Samson et Dalila*, by Saint-Saëns
Dramatic Contralto
  "Ah, mon fils," from Act II of *Le Prophete*, by Meyerbeer
  "Weiche, Wotan, Weiche" ("Erda's Warning"), from the final scene (Act I, scene 4) of *Das Rheingold*, by Wagner
Lyric Tenor
  "Il mio tesoro," from Act II (Scene 2) of *Don Giovanni*, by Mozart
  "Ecco ridente," from Act I (Scene 1) of *The Barber of Seville*, by Rossini
Lirico Spinto Tenor
  "Che gelida manina," ("Rodolfo's narrative"), from Act I of *La Bohème*, by Puccini
  "Addio alla madre," from the one-act opera *Cavellería Rusticana*, by Mascagni
Dramatic Tenor
  "Nothung! Nothung! Neidliches Schwert!" ("Forging Song"), from Act I of *Siegfried*, by Wagner
  Liebesnacht: "O sink' herneider, nacht der Liebe," a duet by Tristan and Isolde (with dramatic soprano), from Act II of *Tristan und Isolde*, by Wagner
Lyric Baritone
  "Il balen del suo sorriso," from Act II (scene 2) of *Il Trovatore*, by Verdi
  "Avant de quitter ces lieux," from Act II of *Faust*, by Gounod
Dramatic Baritone
  "Credo in un Dio crudel," from Act II of *Otello*, by Verdi
  Ode to the Evening Star: "O du mein holder abendstern," from Act III of *Tannhäuser*, by Wagner
Basso Cantante
  "Vous qui faites o'endormie," from Act IV (scene 3) of *Faust*, by Gounod
  "Some Enchanted Evening," from *South Pacific*, by Rogers
Basso Profundo
  "Hier sitz' ich zur Wacht" ("Hagen's Watch"), from Act I of *Die Götterdämmerung*, by Wagner

8 LITERATURE AND THE COMBINED ARTS

MEDIUMS IN THE TIME ARTS

Music and literature are time arts—that is, we experience them over a period of time. The medium of music is sound; the medium of literature is language. In music, the sounds are unassigned symbols; they do not refer to or signify anything outside themselves, and a sequence of sounds has only a general emotional feeling about it: the events which generated the emotions in the composer are not named. The range of events to which they may apply is not specified. One of the reasons why music is called an "international language" is that, while it often evokes similar emotional responses, it permits the individual listener to associate specific content and situations with the emotions evoked—events from personal experience or from fantasies.

In literature, on the other hand, words and their sounds have specific meanings (referents), and a sequence of them in time constitutes a grammar with a specific meaning which is logical and makes sense. Words and sequences of words, of course, have both sound and meaning. Depending upon their purposes, authors can choose words with sounds which reinforce emotionally the content they wish to convey. Thus, the poet, in carefully choosing word sounds and sequences of word sounds, approaches the conditions of music more closely than the prose writer does. For example, C. F. MacIntyre, in a note to his translation of Rilke's "Spanish Dancer" (page 201), writes, "I have got the nine *k* sounds of the original in the second stanza. These prepare the reader for the unmentioned castanets. *Kappernd* and *Schlange* really combine to *Klapperschlange*, which is *rattlesnake*."

LIMITATIONS OF THE SUBJECT IN LITERATURE

The medium of literature is language, and as we have said, language may deal with anything that can be put into words. Language has great advantage in that it is the only medium in any art which is used by everyone. Many of us do not try to draw or paint, or cannot play or sing, but we all talk. We may talk much or we may talk little, we may express our ideas easily or with difficulty, but we talk. Furthermore, we use this medium creatively. We make up new sentences to express our ideas.

The most indisputable evidence that we have of the mind's creativity is language, both spoken (or chanted) and written. In ordinary conversation one does not know what one is about to say until it is said. Every such utterance is unique and unexpected and becomes an enrichment of the whole human experience. But the greater wonder about mind and language is the remarkable ease with which an infant learns to talk. Speaking is the first certain sign of intelligence it displays in coping with its needs by manipulating the environment through the tools of vocabulary. If linguists such as Noam Chomsky are to be believed, this argues for some innate structure of mind, predisposing it toward the use of language forms that are ready to be called forth by the social environment. The ability to communicate and manipulate by tongue and hand is what is human in human beings. Art is both the creator of the social reality and a commentary on it; particularly, literature, mother of the arts, is its embodiment in a more permanent medium than the spoken word. Thus what we must say of art and creativity is that it emerges as a unique, value-laden expression, that it takes its origin from the genetic pool which fashions the brain and the dexterity or the musculature, that it finds its need gratification and approval (value) in the culture which nurtures it and of which it is the first expression, and that it characterizes the human animal. All this is true of language paramountly as a creator of social reality and per-haps—after dance—the first art.

Set against this advantage of literature as a medium is a corre-sponding disadvantage. Literature is the only art whose medium is not international. A painting in fresco loses its characteristic quality if it is copied in oil—there is an essential change—but anyone who knows it in fresco will recognize it in oil, will see that it is the same picture. In the same way, a symphony written for an orchestra loses something that is essential when it is played on the piano, and yet one recognizes it. But if a poem is translated into another language, one can have no idea what it is about without knowing the other language. To the person who knows both languages, there may be no greater difference between a poem in French and its translation into English than there is between the symphony played by the orchestra and an arrangement of that symphony for piano; but to anyone who does not know both languages one version is gibberish.

Words are symbols and therefore are incomprehensible to those who do not know them. A symbol is by nature arbitrary. It has a certain meaning because that meaning has been agreed on and for no other reason. In the story "Ali Baba and the Forty Thieves," there is no intrinsic reason why the door should open if one says, "Open sesame" rather than "Open barley" or "Open wheat"; but *sesame* was the word that had been agreed upon for that purpose, and the door would open for no other word. There is no reason why the sign "4" should stand for *four* rather than for *three* or *six*. And so it is with most words. With a small group of words, such as *bow-wow, moo-moo,* and *baa,* the sound is supposed to convey the meaning, but the number of such words is negligible, and they do not really convey any meaning. With the vast majority of words, the sound has no natural and inevitable relation to the meaning. We are accustomed to associating the sound of the word *dog* with a certain animal, but there is no essential connection between the two. The French word for dog is *chien,* the German, *Hund,* the Latin, *canis*—and there is nothing in any one of the sounds to indicate that particular animal were it not so understood by the people who speak that language.

LANGUAGE IN LITERATURE

The Languages of the World

The mediums of literature are the various languages of the world: English, French, German, Italian, Russian, Chinese, Japanese, and so on. And, as is true of all mediums of all arts, each has its own special characteristics, and what can be said in one cannot be said in another. It is said that the novelist Joseph Conrad wrote his novels in English rather than in French, a language he knew much better, because in French he could not say what he wanted to say. A modern writer on the subject of communication has said, "When I read French I need to become as a different person, with different thought; the language change bears with it a change of national character and temperament, a different history and literature."[1] In a small way all of us have experienced this change in assuming a dialect. Someone who talks as a Southerner or a New Englander assumes the character and personality of that person for that time.

A delightful account of the difficulties with a foreign language is found in Clarence Day's *Life with Father:*

I got out another Bible that Mother had lent me. This one was in French, and it sometimes shocked me deeply to read it. As my belief was that when

---

[1] Colin Cherry, *On Human Communication* (Cambridge, Mass: The M.I.T. Press, 1957), p. 70.

God had created the world he had said, "Let there be light," it seemed to
me highly irreverent to put French words in His mouth and have Him ex
claim, "Que la lumiere soit!" Imagine the Lord talking French! Aside from
few odd words in Hebrew, I took it completely for granted that God ha
never spoken anything but the most dignified English.

Instead of the children of Israel fearing lest the Lord should be wroth
the French said "les enfants d'Israel" were afraid lest "le Seigneur" shoul
be "irrité." This word "irrité" appeared everywhere in the French version
It wasn't only the Lord. Cain was "très irrité." Moïse (which seemed to me
a very jaunty way of referring to Moses) was "irrité" again and again
Everybody was "irrité." When my regular Bible, the real one, impressivel
described men as "wroth," their anger seemed to have something statel
and solemn about it. If they were full of mere irritation all the time, they wer
more like the Day family.[2]

The Question of Translations

In a very real sense no translation is ever more than an approxima
tion of the original. The sound of the original is almost always los
completely; only the sense is preserved, and the sense cannot be pu
into another language with complete accuracy. Sometimes a single
translation is made so nearly perfect that it is accepted as an adequate
rendering of the original. An example is Longfellow's translation o
Goethe's "Wanderer's Night Song":

Über allen Gipfeln
Ist Ruh
In allen Wipfein
Spürest du
Kaum einen Hauch;
Die Vögelein schweigen im Walde.
Warte nur, balde
Ruhest du auch.

    —Johann Wolfgang von Goethe
        (1749–1832, German poet, dramatist, and novelist),
        "Wanderers Nachtlied" (1780)

O'er all the hill-tops
Is quiet now,
In all the tree-tops
Hearest thou
Hardly a breath;
The birds are asleep in the trees:
Wait; soon like these
Thou too shalt rest.

    —Henry Wadsworth Longfellow (1807–1882, American poet)

[2] Clarence Day, *Life with Father.* Copyright 1935 by Clarence Day. Used by permission of Alfred
A. Knopf, Inc. (New York).

All too often, translations either fail to be good English or fail to be like the original. If it is necessary to use a translation, the best practice is to compare several versions, by different translators, for often a different translation gives a new insight into a passage. The Bible is a good book to study in this connection because there are many different translations easily available. Suppose we take the passage in Matthew when Jesus is talking about divorce; it ends with the words we all know: "What therefore God hath joined together, let no man put asunder." The disciples, however, are not satisfied and ask about the law of Moses. Moffatt's translation of their question is: "Then why did Moses lay it down that we were to divorce by giving a separation-notice?"[3] but Phillips's version is: "Then why did Moses command us to give a written divorce-notice and dismiss the woman?"[4] In the King James and Moffatt versions, the answer is that it was because of "the hardness of your hearts"; the New English Bible gives a different interpretation: "It was because you were so unteachable."[5] Phillips gives it an entirely new sense: "It was because you knew so little of the meaning of love that Moses allowed you to divorce your wives." Jesus ends this speech with the statement that adultery is the only ground for divorce, and again the disciples object and the translations differ. The King James version reads: "If the case of the man be so with his wife, it is not good to marry." Moffatt: "There is no good in marrying." The New English Bible: "If that is the position with husband and wife, it is better to refrain from marriage." Phillips: "If that is a man's position with his wife, it is not worth getting married."

Literature in English

In a text of this kind it is not safe to assume that the readers will know more than one language. Therefore, we are limiting our study of literature to one medium, English. In doing so we are obviously restricted and at a disadvantage. In the other arts we can study the work of all countries with equal ease. We can hear the music of Russia, see the sculpture of Greece, and enjoy the architecture of France and the paintings of Italy as clearly and as easily as we can those of England. In literature, on the other hand, we are confined to writings in English or to translations from other languages into English.

Fortunately, the English language is a very flexible medium, and a very wide variety of effects can be obtained in it. Fortunately, also, it is a language with a very great literature. But the fact remains that, taking up only English, we are missing other and different types of effects to be obtained in other languages.

[3] James Moffatt, *The Bible: A New Translation* (New York: Harper & Row, Publishers, 1935).
[4] *The Gospels*, translated into Modern English by J. B. Phillips (New York: Macmillan, 1952).
[5] *The New English Bible, New Testament* (Oxford and Cambridge: Delegates of the Oxford University Press and Syndics of the Cambridge University Press, 1961).

THE COMBINED ARTS

By definition, the combined arts are those which use more than one medium. The special medium of dance is the human body moving in a framed space such as a stage, a marked-out circle, or some other area; but the dancer employs music almost always, costume and lighting usually, and stage scenery sometimes. The medium of the theater is a story told in spoken dialogue and acted out on a stage; usually it also employs scenery, costumes, furniture, and lighting, and at times music. A motion picture uses not only these primary mediums as the source of images and sounds which are recorded on film and arranged in any way the director chooses; but, because of its ability to manipulate and arrange them, it goes beyond them in presenting us with such things as space larger than any stage area, the effect of simultaneous presentation of action at more than one point in time, far more complex lighting effects, and a much greater diversity of sounds, including music.

It will be noticed that all the combined arts mentioned include one time art, that is, an art in which the entire work is presented to us not all at once, but serially in a span of time, bit by bit, and which never remains completely before us for study and reflection, except in memory. From the beginning of the work to the end, it is being performed and can be experienced only as it is performed. For this reason, the combined arts are sometimes called the "performing arts."

When experiencing combined arts in performance, one cannot give equal attention to all aspects of them. When experiencing the space arts and literature, one can go back, check impressions, review a sequence in relation to another sequence. This is not so in the performed arts. The performance moves forward; one's attention is drawn with it. One reason that critics' estimates of a performance differ is that each has become accustomed to giving attention to particular aspects of it. One comes to expect that a particular critic will focus on particular aspects of, say, a film. For example, one critic may focus on the story and its human or sociological or historical significance, another on the director's style of presentation, another on the techniques used, and still another on the acting.

When studying the combined arts, it is important to see or hear the work several times to observe the way in which the sensoria components of the various arts are integrated to produce the work's distinctive qualities. When studying a film, we should attempt to attend equally to all parts of a performance. The parts to which we do not attend are influencing our responses; the parts to which we attend are influenced by our experience of the other parts. It becomes important, therefore, that we ask ourselves questions belonging uniquely to the combined arts, so as to broaden our frame for observing and responding.

Ideally, the various mediums are combined with just the right emphasis on each to make clear the idea in the mind of the artist. One of the major problems of the artist is deciding which of the mediums to stress at a particular time.

An example is found in *Hamlet*, in the scene in which Hamlet renounces Ophelia. Hamlet, a young man just returned from the university, is sorely perplexed by the condition in which he has found matters at home. His father is dead, and his mother has married again so quickly that Hamlet contemptuously says she did so to economize on the breads and meats baked for his father's funeral. Shortly afterward, he learns from a ghost that his father was murdered. Hamlet does not know whether to believe the ghost or not, and he needs help desperately. For a long time he has been in love with Ophelia, and naturally he turns to her now. But, looking into her face, he realizes that she cannot help him; so he shakes his head and leaves the room without saying a word. This might seem just the scene to be enacted on the stage. But, instead, Shakespeare uses words only. Ophelia tells her father about it:

My lord, as I was sewing in my chamber,
Lord Hamlet, with his doublet all unbrac'd,
No hat upon his head, his stockings foul'd,
Ungart'red, and down gyved to his ankle,
Pale as his shirt, his knees knocking each other,
And with a look so piteous in purport
As if he had been loosed out of hell
To speak of horrors,—he comes before me. . . .

He took me by the wrist and held me hard;
Then goes he to the length of all his arm,
And, with his other hand thus o'er his brow,
He falls to such perusal of my face
As he would draw it. Long stay'd he so.
At last, a little shaking of mine arm,
And thrice his head thus waving up and down.
He rais'd a sigh so piteous and profound
That it did seem to shatter all his bulk
And end his being. That done, he lets me go;
And, with his head over his shoulder turn'd,
He seem'd to find his way without his eyes,
For out o'doors he went without their help.
And, to the last bended their light on me.

—William Shakespeare (1564–1616, British poet and dramatist),
   Hamlet, II, i, 77–84, 87–100

The scene as described by Ophelia is so vivid that most people who read the play remember the event as one that took place on the stage. Why did Shakespeare have Ophelia merely tell about it? There probably are several reasons. One may be that in this way he could kill two birds with one stone; the father is told at the same time that we learn of the action. This would be a good but unimportant reason. A more significant consideration may be that such a scene would not be easy to enact. The most likely reason may be that Shakespeare wanted to be sure that the audience would understand the scene as he meant it to; he therefore interpreted Hamlet's visit in words.

The performing arts have much in common with other experiences—for example, a riot, a traffic accident, a drive through the country. Several senses are called upon for response—what one sees, what one hears, what one senses psychologically, what one understands of the context, etc. Each person perceives the experience from a particular point of view, abstracts from it aspects which fit into particular experience repertoire. Even reporters, who have been trained to observe details which are journalistically significant, frequently disagree on what happened in a specific dramatic incident.

One conclusion to be drawn from the above is that when planning to attend a performance of an unknown work, any knowledge and understanding of the work which can be brought to the viewing, if it will broaden one's range of attention.

To summarize, there are several important generalizations about the combined arts which have a bearing on our experiencing and enjoying them.

1. *All the combined arts involve one time art—that is, all take place within a time span.* They therefore involve a sequence of events in some type of organization. They have a beginning and they end. Between the beginning and the conclusion, the things which happen have some "organization"; experiencing them in sequence as they occur, we sense some *pattern* emerging. As further events occur, we may modify our sense of what the "pattern" is. At the conclusion, we have an overall sense of what the form of the work is. The "pattern" may appear to be one of randomness—confusion—or may be perceived as clearly carefully organized in some formal way. The organization may be narrative, like that of a novel or an opera or a drama. In other words, it may suggest or tell a story or center on some event. Or the organization may be abstract, have no specific subject matter and be organized in ways with which we have become familiar as in music which has no specified or implied subject matter. Passages of tension and relaxation, of dissonance and resolution, of nervous excitement and serenity, of intense drama and lyrical repose, of frenetic rhythm and more peaceful, unhurried rhythm are put together in sequence which, as they are heard, stimulate our feelings in one direction and then another, and then another until the piece concludes.

2. *All the combined arts are intended to be experienced in performance.* This means that the circumstances and context of the performance become a part of the experience—the competency of the performers, the adequacy of the place in which the performance is presented, the response of the audience, to name some of the more obvious ones. That this is so should be taken into account in experiencing a combined art in performance for the first time.

3. *The combined arts experienced in performance are what W. H. Auden describes as "virtuoso arts."* Apart from the virtue traditionally acclaimed for particular works and their place in the "standard *repertoire*," spectators gain pleasure from seeing them performed well, especially by "name" or established stars. While the creator's intent has validity in performance, one must also allow for imaginative recreation of a role by the artist, its integrity as a recreated "creation" and its integrity within the total performance; for example, we speak of Paul Robeson's Othello, Judith Anderson's Medea, or Marlon Brando's Stanley Kowalski.

4. *All the combined arts to a greater or lesser degree have methods of expression and principles of organization in common with music.* Thus the elements of form which characterize music may be observed in the combined arts—rhythm, tempo, intensity, dynamics, pitch, repetition, alternation, variation, etc. We sense the pattern which is emerging as we respond to them emotionally. At different points in the performance, we may feel tense, anxious, confused, released, expansive, joyful.

The mediums used in the combined arts are the mediums used in the separate arts. In this short discussion we shall attempt only to show the mediums that are used in each art and to state some of the possibilities and limitations that arise from their being combined.

Drama

Drama is usually classified as literature because the most important part of a play is the dialogue spoken by the characters. As action, however, whether presented on the stage or visualized by the mind, it involves many other mediums. There are of course the actors, for each of whom we have costume, speaking voice, and actions. For the story as a whole, we have setting and properties. The possibilities in each type of medium are almost limitless. A slight change in costume may be used to indicate that years have passed or that the person has grown richer or poorer. The accent may betray nationality or social status, and the manner of speaking may indicate character. The actor may make use of all the movements of the dancer as well as those of the ordinary person in walking, running, or standing.

We must always keep in mind that most plays were written to be performed and that, as a result, there is a world of difference between reading *Hamlet* as literature and performing it or seeing it performed. Many people find a great deal of Shakespeare relatively uninteresting if they only read it, but find that the plays come to life when they are performed well. With ancient Greek drama, the difference between reading and performing is even greater. Euripides's *Medea*, which we discussed earlier, reaches its climax as theater with the off-stage murder of the two children and an unearthly scream by the mother, whose effect no amount of reading could begin to convey and which, once heard, is never forgotten. In reading *Medea* one does not experience this emotional element; indeed, it is not present in the text but has been added by the modern actress and the director. A very instructive experience for the student would be to read this short play and then listen to the recording made by the distinguished actress Judith Anderson.

In many of the great periods of the threater, the setting has been of very little importance. In the Greek theater, for instance, the setting was the same for all plays, a street before a building. In the Elizabethan theater also, it was very simple, consisting of only a few pieces of furniture to indicate the type of room—for example, a bed for a bedroom. The Greeks and the Elizabethans, moreover, had no control over lighting; they performed their plays in the daytime with natural lighting. Now the producer has full control over the lighting of each play, and it has become common to use all sorts of settings. The producer can change both elements to suit the performance; both have become mediums for the artist just as truly as speech, action, or costume.

Since the seventeenth and eighteenth centuries, with the development of opera and theater as organized art forms with special buildings and equipment, it has been possible to do far more in the way of special effects. We can still see skillfully built equipment in the private royal theaters at, for example, Versailles in France and Drottningholm in Sweden, and in some other seventeenth- and eighteenth-century buildings. When these were built, it was already possible to achieve certain complicated effects: actors could be raised and lowered, fire could be simulated, people could be made to seem to fly, and lighting arrangements could be very sophisticated. In today's theater we can do even more with electric lighting, electronic sound, turntable stages, and other technological advances.

Dance

Before there was language to signify human needs and emotions, there was "body language" and dance. Dance as body language in which the body is the immediate signifier is the most universal and primitive form of communication. Gesture is all we know of emotion directly; emotion per se is the secret soul of art. Spontaneous movement, facial expression, and mime need only be stylized to become dance or to accompany the narrative of drama and spectacle. And when narrative is chanted, we have the beginning of opera. As we have seen, *language as spoken* is one parent of the combined arts, imposing upon them the logic of thought. Dance may be considered the other parent, nurturing them in expression of feeling and giving them grace.

Because it is the most natural form of expression in its spontaneity of gesture and mimicry, dance is the first of the arts to associate itself with religious feelings and the most likely to be ritualized and formalized as sacred. Since it is most suitably taught by marking time for its measures, such rhythmic accompaniment (witness the work song) is also a probable source of music. One of the most ancient religious texts, the Hindu Vedas, tells us of Lord Krishna (the "Supreme Personality of Godhead") instructing his followers in the arts of dance and of music. The following rendition is that of a contemporary swami; the reader should bear in mind that the dance described is spiritual, not corporeal:

As the *gopis* and Krsna danced together, a very blissful musical sound was produced from the tinkling of their bells, ornaments and bangles. It appeared that Krsna was a greenish sapphire with valuable stones. While Krsna and the *gopis* danced they displayed extraordinary features. The movements of their eybrows, their smiling, the movements of the breasts of the *gopis* and their clothes, their earrings, their cheeks, their hair with flowers—as they sang and danced these combined together to appear like clouds, thunder, snow and lightning. Krsna's bodily features appeared just like a group of clouds, their songs were like thunder, the beauty of the *gopis* appeared to be just like the lightning on the sky, and the drops of perspiration visible in their faces appeared like falling snow. In this [were] both the *gopis* and Krsna fully engaged in dancing.[7]

It will be recalled from an earlier chapter that to the Hindus, who view the world of experience not as reality but as mere appearance, it is Siva, Lord of the Dance, who presides over it (Figure 3-23). Within a ring of fire, he dances the manifest world into being; dancing still, he sustains and protects it; and in the fullness of time, he dances it to destruction and rest.

In religious rituals the dancers appropriate the costume and physical attributes of the gods, their weapons, tools, regalia, and disguises—signifying their role in myth—and reenact in mime their exploits. The Fifth Veda of the Hindus is devoted to instruction in every aspect of drama, dance, and mime—how to build theaters,

[6] Kenneth Clark, *The Nude: A Study in Ideal Form.* The A. W. Mellon Lectures in the Fine Arts, Bollingen Series XXXV: 2. Copyright © 1956 by the Trustees of the National Gallery of Art. Reprinted by permission of Princeton University Press (Princeton, N.J.), publisher of the Bollingen Series; and John Murray Publishers Ltd. (London).
[7] *Krsna, The Supreme Personality of Godhead,* A. C. Bhaktivedanta Swami Prabhupada (Los Angeles, Calif.: Bhaktivedanta Book Trust, 1970), pp. 214–215.

design costumes, act specific roles, perform traditional dances correctly, and much, much more. (The Hindus did not make the clear-cut distinctions among these arts which we have developed in Western culture.) In it there are precise instructions for the immediate personality transitions of the actor-mime in stepping from the real world of the spectator into the magic circle of art, which becomes not only a stage but the sacred dwelling place of the god and a place where the dancer becomes god. We find similar examples in Greek dances in which Dionysus communicates his divinity and the faithful partake of deity in rites and dances of enthusiasm (literally "god withinness"). Maenads were ordinary women who were worshippers of Dionysus. The little sketch from a Greek vase in Figure 16-1 shows one of them caught up in Dionysian ecstasy. And Titian, in *Bacchus and Ariadne* (Color Plate 14), depicts the god returning from India accompanied by a band of revelers who play cymbals and dance wildly behind him.

Rhythm and movement are at the very center of life. Anyone who has watched a very young baby knows the incessant random movement of the arms and legs which are its interaction with its physical and human environment. From the very moment when the human being enters the world, these are its principal means of response to both its inner and outer environments. When it is uncomfortable, the movements become agitated and stronger. When it is comfortable and contented, the movements become slower, measured, and less violent.

As the child learns to control its movements, to consciously give purposeful direction to them, the motions and rhythms become patterned to express various moods and emotional states. We have what John Martin has called "basic dance."[8] This kind of dance is universal and indeed constitutes the foundation language of dance. In this language, fast tempos and energetic, agitated, and frenetic rhythms stand at one end of a continuum expressing excitement, pleasure, anger, or sadness; and slower tempos and more deliberate, measured, graceful movements stand at the other, expressing serenity, contentment, resignation, and peacefulness.

The processes through which different cultures have shaped "basic dance" into the highly diverse characteristic dances we associate with different geographic areas and ethnic groups are very complex. An examination of them goes beyond the limitations of this book. Geography, climate, physique, religion, social environment, cultural tradition—these are but a few of the influences which affect the way people move and—more important for our purposes—the patterns and rhythms through which the movements become dance. As a result of them, we find that Oriental dancers make much use of small, slow movements, chiefly of the hands and upper body, with

[8] John Martin, *The Dance* (New York: Tudor Publishing Company, 1946), p. 6.

supple fingers bending backward, toes turned upward, and lateral movements of the head and neck. See, for example, the dancing Siva shown in Figure 3-23. African dancers tend to center their movements in the pelvic region and move to quite intricate, frequently syncopated rhythms. As Aaron Douglas reminds us (see Figure 8-2, page 199), music and dance are parts of the Negro's African heritage and have had significant influences on both music and dance in America.

Spanish dancers keep the upper part of the body rigid with arms raised, snapping fingers or playing castanets as they vigorously stamp out audible, exciting rhythms with their feet. Female Spanish dancers use long scarves and wear full, long skirts (see Sargent's *El Jaleo*, Figure 8-4 and Color Plate 21). European ballet emphasizes lightness and graceful flowing movements with toes pointed downward. The female dancer, or ballerina, at times dances on the tips of her toes (*en pointe*); and the male dancer, the *danseur noble*, prides himself on strong, vigorous leaps (elevation) and the easy grace with which he supports the ballerina in intricate steps, frequently lifting her into the air in a dramatic climax to a dance sequence. Modern dance is neither ethnic dance nor ballet (although it adapts from both at times); it emphasizes natural movements. The dancers, rather than denying or disguising the effects of gravity and the weight of the body, use them as organizing points for movements which radiate from the pelvic region.

Naturally, these are broad generalizations and may not apply to a particular dance or dancer; however, they do serve to illustrate the variety which evolves from "basic dance." The important point is that there is an elemental language of dance which is universal, a means of communication and communion. As Joost A.M. Meerloo expressed it, "The dance lives in everyone's body and mind. Somehow, by rhythmic interaction, feelings and emotions are transferred to us. These can lead us into earthbound passions or inspire the most celestial ecstasies."[9]

As a demonstration of how innate and how vital to our lives rhythm is, reflect upon what happens when you are walking along casually and are suddenly aware that your heart has skipped a beat. Immediately, you feel excitement, concern, perhaps even panic. Our empathetic responses to rhythms outside our bodies, whether they be soothing or disturbing, should therefore come as no surprise. In the introductory chapter we mentioned that there is a language of the arts which is built into us as a part of our biological and psychological nature. In none of the arts is this fact more obvious than in dance, whether it be a primitive ritual dance, a social country dance, a ballet, or the latest popular dance.

It is this spontaneous response to music and rhythm which

[9] Joost, A. M. Meerloo, *The Dance: From Ritual to Rock and Roll—Ballet to Ballroom* (New York: Chilton Company, 1960), p. 11.

George Luks captured visually in *The Spielers* (Figure 8-1). Similarly the ancient dance depicted on a Greek vase (Figure 1-6) conveys this basic response to rhythm in movements of feet and slapping of thighs which are so universal that we have no difficulty identifying with them and sensing the mood and emotions of the dancers.

Artists in all mediums have always been inspired by dance perhaps because of its primal nature, its closeness to our intuitive basic human responses and feelings. Matisse's *Dance 1* and *Dance 2* (Color Plates 24 and 25) convey the Dionysian spirit of the dance as

Figure 8-1. George Luks (1867–1933), American painter. *The Spielers* (1905). (Oil on canvas, 36 by 26 inches. Addison Gallery of American Art, Phillips Academy, Andover, Massachusetts.)

Figure 8-2. Aaron Douglas (1899–   ), American painter. First of four murals, *Aspects of Negro Life*. (Collection of the New York Public Library, Astor, Lenox and Tilden Foundations, in Countee Cullen Regional Branch.) The artist describes it: "The first of the four murals . . . indicates the African cultural background of American Negroes. Dominant in it are the strongly rhythmic arts of music, the dance and sculpture—and so the drummers, the dancers, and the carved fetish represent the exhilaration and rhythmic pulsation of life in Africa."

African Dance

The low beating of the tom-toms,
The slow beating of the tom-toms,
Low . . . slow
Slow . . . low—
Stirs your blood.

Dance!
A night-veiled girl
Whirls softly into a
Circle of light.
Whirls softly . . . slowly,
Like a wisp of smoke around the fire—
And the tom-toms beat,
And the tom-toms beat,
And the low beating of the tom-toms
Stirs your blood.

—Langston Hughes (1902–1967, American poet and novelist)[10]

an innate art form; the playfulness, the joyousness, are universal not only in the sense that they characterize all human cultures, but that they are found even in the animal kingdom. Dance is a people's native art, instructing them in their ancient culture. It has been and can be even undisciplined, spontaneous forms, primitive drama, spectacle, worship. Disciplined, it can become a solemn procession, a stately celebration, a military maneuver, a graceful ballet, a joyously shared social event, or an eloquent personal language of body movement.

Aaron Douglas recaptures the African origins of Negro culture in a scene of dance, music, and sculpture (Figure 8-2). The poet Langston Hughes evokes a similar scene in words and rhythm. George Luks shows a return to the carefree, ecstatic origins of dance in *The Spielers*. Degas found his favorite subject matter in the movements of ballet dancers (Color Plate 20 and Figure 13-7). Rodin, too, was much interested in dance. In addition to a number of pastels of Balinese dancers, which are, unfortunately, little known, he did a sculpture of Nijinsky dancing the faun to Debussy's *Afternoon of a Faun* (see page 416 and Léon Bakst's painting for the cover of a souvenir program of the ballet, Figure 16-3), and a series of sculp-

[10] Copyright 1926 by Alfred A. Knopf, Inc. (New York), and revised 1954 by Langston Hughes. Reprinted from *Selected Poems*, by Langston Hughes, by permission of Alfred A. Knopf, Inc.

In the Sistine frescoes, his most
complete work, Michelangelo shows us
Adam awakened to life at the touch of God.
He saw the climactic moment of this
episode in man's awakening. But Rodin
takes the act of creation for granted.
His Adam just rises from the dust, lifts
himself up from the soil from which he was
fashioned, his head still painfully pressed
against his left shoulder. His muscles
stretch, he begins to feel his own body, and
power of his being. But the frightful
aloneness is around him, and the inner
truth Rodin has created here is the
traumatic terror of man's awakening as
man, the prelude to his lifelong drama.

Walter Sorell[11]

Figure 8-3. August Rodin (1840–1917),
French sculptor. *The Creation of Man,*
or *Adam.* (Bronze. Metropolitan
Museum of Art, New York; gift of
Thomas F. Ryan, 1910.)

tures called simply *Dancers.* But his interest in dance and in capturing the body in movement seems apparent in other works as well, for example, in *The Creation of Man*—or *Adam,* as it is sometimes called (Figure 8-3)—where the body has, for expressive purposes, been depicted in a semirotational pull against gravity, much as is characteristic of modern dance. (Walter Sorrel, a critic and scholar of dance, comments upon this fact and contrasts the treatment of the subject in Rodin's sculpture and in Michelangelo's Sistine Chapel ceiling, Color Plate 15.) Rilke, in his "Spanish Dancer," recreates in poetry the fiery excitement of a scene the American painter Sargent caught in his most admired painting, *El Jaleo* (Figure 8-4 and Color Plate 21).

[11] The Dancer's Image: Points and Counterpoints (New York: Columbia University Press, 1971), p. 189.

;ure 8-4. John Singer Sargent (1856–
5), American painter. *El Jaleo* (1882).
(Oil on canvas. Isabella Stewart
Gardner Museum, Boston.) See also
Color Plate 22.

SPANISH TÄNZERIN

WIE in der Hand ein Schwefelzündholz, weiß,
eh es zur Flamme kommt, nach allen Seiten
zuckende Zungen streckt—: beginnt im Kreis
naher Beschauer hastig, hell und heiß
ihr runder Tanz sich zuckend auszubreiten.

Und plötzlich ist er Flamme ganz und gar.

Mit ihrem Blick entzündet sie ihr Haar
und dreht auf einmal mit gewagter Kunst
ihr ganzes Kleid in diese Feuersbrunst,
aus welcher sich, wie Schlangen, die erschrecken,
die nackten Arme wach und klappernd strecken.

Und dann: als würde ihr das Feuer knapp,
nimmt sie es ganz zusamm und wirft es ab
sehr herrisch, mit hochmütiger Gebärde
und schaut: da liegt es rasend auf der Erde
und flammt noch immer und ergibt sich nicht—.
Doch sieghaft, sicher und mit einem süßen
grüßenden Lächeln hebt sie ihr Gesicht
und stampft es aus mit kleinen festen Füßen.

—Rainer Maria Rilke (1875–1926, German poet)
(translated by C. F. MacIntyre)[12]

SPANISH DANCER

As in the hand a match glows, swiftly white
before it bursts in flame and to all sides
licks its quivering tongues: within the ring
of spectators her wheeling dance is bright,
nimble, and fervid, twitches and grows wide.

And suddenly is made of pure fire.

Now her glances kindle the dark hair;
she twirls the floating skirts with daring art
into a whirlwind of consuming flame,
from which her naked arms alertly strike,
clattering like fearful rattlesnakes.

Then, as the fire presses her too closely,
imperiously she clutches it and throws it
with haughty gestures to the floor and watches
it rage and leap with flames that will not die—
until, victorious, surely, with a sweet
greeting smile, and holding her head high,
she tramples it to death with small, firm feet.

[12] *Rainer Maria Rilke: Selected Poems with English Translations by C. F. MacIntyre* (Berkeley: University of California Press, 1966), 88f. Copyright © 1940 by C. F. MacIntyre. Reprinted by permission of the University of California Press.

Opera

Opera comprises three mediums, which in order of importance are music, drama, and spectacle. These make opera one of the most appealing of the arts, but they also make it one of the most complex and difficult. The music alone demands a full symphony orchestra, a conductor, one or more choruses, a choral conductor, and solo singers. Moreover, opera is what may well be called a "virtuoso" art. The composer writes into the opera arias and other set pieces which display the unusual talents and skills of the singer-actors who perform the leading roles.

The dramatic demands of opera begin with the libretto, or "book of words," upon which the opera is based. A good libretto gives us the essence of character and situation quickly and thoroughly. The composer who finds a librettist with whom he or she can work well is blessed. One of the happiest combinations of composer and librettist is that of Gilbert and Sullivan in the area of operetta (literally, "small opera"—and also opera light in character). In opera itself, a great combination was that of Verdi and Boito. In making Shakespeare's *Othello* into a libretto for Verdi's opera *Otello*, Boito made a number of effective changes. For example, he omitted the entire first act of the play, keeping only Othello's courtship speech, which becomes a duet between Othello and Desdemona. In the opera, Desdemona prays to the Virgin Mary before she is strangled, although that scene does not appear in the play.

In the integration of mediums as different as music and drama, compromises must be made. One is in the matter of time. For obvious reasons, singing a script takes longer than speaking it. In opera, then, quite often the dramatic action must be either slowed down or stopped altogether while a musical idea progresses. Conversely, while the dramatic action moves forward, we cannot expect to linger over a long, beautiful melody. Within this perpetual compromise there is no doubt that drama suffers more than music. Since music is the most important medium in opera, it must succeed, no matter what the fate of the dramatic action. Opera stands or falls on the quality of its music. Even an excellent libretto is inadequate if the music to which it is set is inferior. On the other hand, a trite libretto can be sustained by memorable music. Furthermore, one can forgive an opera singer whose acting ability is limited; but no matter how fine the acting, one does not forget or forgive bad singing.

Opera is the most spectacular of the theater arts. It combines a drama acted on the stage with music as the plot, which is not usually a very complicated one, unfolds. The element of spectacle in opera has always been one of its appeals. The productions are usually lavish, with elaborate sets and costumes, a large chorus, a full orchestra, and frequently a ballet. Even an opera house is much more elaborate than an ordinary theater, reflecting its heritage as an entertainment for aristocrats.

Spectacle involves anything of a visual nature which can be integrated with the opera plot. Dances which are complete works in themselves are found in many operas. Exotic sets and costumes also constitute spectacle, especially when they are changed often for the visual delight of the audience. Spectacle also occurs when there is an emphasis on the realm of nature, such as the use of fire, water, or animals in the production. Verdi's *Aïda* is an example; in the scene of the triumphal march, trumpeters on horseback, camels, chariots, and large numbers of performers can be used when the opera is staged with spectacle in mind. As Verdi matured, however, he used fewer and fewer extraneous visual effects, until in his last two operas, *Otello* and *Falstaff*, there is no spectacle: we have only the bare bones of music and drama. And although his earlier opers are still enjoyed, these two are considered his finest work. Therefore, it can be said that spectacle is not necessary to opera.

Film

We sometimes see the terms *cinema*, *moving pictures*, and *movies* used for the medium we are calling simply "film." The terms are completely interchangeable, and their use is purely a matter of personal preference.

Although film is one of the most recently developed arts, it has become one of the most familiar. Shown in local theaters, on television, and in classrooms, it is, for most of us, in one form or another a part of our daily lives. Yet, it is a medium that few of us know much about, perhaps because it is so commonplace, perhaps because it has the compelling capacity for involving us at so many levels, or perhaps because we know from our own experience that if you point a movie camera in a given direction and push a button, you make a film. We look, but we are not aware of what we are seeing and hearing. Because of this, film is one of the most rewarding mediums for study.

Film is essentially the art of the moving picture. Just as an opera stands or falls upon its music, a film stands or falls upon its visual content. Thus, motion photography is its most important medium.

In film more than in any other art, the medium and the techniques for working with it are the products of technology. It was technological development which made the contemporary film possible: the development of a sensitized negative to record an image which can be projected on a screen; the development of a camera through which the negative moves at a speed that can record a moving image which can be projected; the development of film to record color; the discovery that a sound track can be added to the margin of the negative, so that the recorded sounds will be synchronized with the projected images; the development of various kinds of lenses which enable the camera to simulate the human eye, such as the wide-angle lens and the zoom lens; the development of equipment to give the camera flexibility by raising it, lowering it, or moving it from side to side for angle shots or to physically track a moving object; the development of editing devices with which photographed material and recorded sounds can be arranged in any sequence at any speed, in order to make transitions from one shot to another in a variety of ways and to superimpose images on images or add voice or sounds. Such developments constitute the medium and tools with which the artist works.

Of course, actors, sets, special lighting, costumes, and makeup are a part of the making of most films; still, they exist only through photography. Further, they exist as the camera interprets them for us. Actually, no one of them is essential. Documentary films, such as Robert J. Flaherty's masterpiece *Nanook of the North*, are often made without them.

Because the camera is a scientific instrument capable of reproducing automatically what is presented to it, it is often unjustly dismissed as a mere recorder. But the camera can not only record precisely; it can also emphasize or minimize, distort, and create illusion. Through editing, it can present more than one time and place simultaneously, and it can show all facets of an object from changing viewpoints. It can compress both time and geography. It is difficult to remember that the camera is there at all when viewing a film, but the presence of the camera is precisely the quality that helps us gain insight into situation and character. Thus we learn not from being told, but from visual revelation.

Ideally, the director of the film is also the editor. It is the editor who selects the best shots and sequences and adds appropriate sounds and music. Putting them into an ordered relationship, the editor creates the pace and mood of the picture by giving it a feeling of continuity or discontinuity as the subject demands. The director, in a very real sense, is the composer of the film. The director who is also the editor becomes the conductor as well. Such is the case with most of the distinguished directors. The *"auteur"* theory in film criticism argues that the director stands in the same relation to a film as an author to a book. The director is responsible, or should be, for everything which appears in the completed work; thus, in all the films directed by one person, it is contended, there are similar stylistic elements whether or not they have been put there consciously and deliberately.

At every stage in the history of film as a medium, there have been artists who saw in it possibilities for a new art and who used it, formulated aesthetic principles for using it, and, indeed, produced films in it which are still considered classics. Among the early film artists are D. W. Griffith (*Birth of a Nation*, 1915), Erich Von Stroheim (*Greed*, 1929), John Ford (*Stage Coach*, 1939), and Orson Welles (*Citizen Kane*, 1941). One reads about these people and their contributions to the art, and one occasionally has an opportunity to see one of their films at an art theater or a museum, in a film history course, or in other special circumstances; but these films are not now commonly shown at regular movie theaters.

An early director and theorist one often hears mentioned is Sergei Eisenstein, whose book *The Film Scene* (1943) has an important place in the history of the art. One of his films, much admired for its effectiveness in using the new medium, is *Potemkin*. This is the story of a group of sailors on a naval ship of that name in the harbor of Odessa at the outbreak of the Russian revolution of 1905. Driven to desperation by the inhuman conditions aboard the ship and encouraged by the general political situation, the sailors mutiny against their officers. A series of quickly viewed episodes moves us from one level of action to another: a quick close-up of the face of a tyrannical officer gives us an instantaneous impression of him as a smug bourgeois; then he is seen being thrown overboard. This visual miracle— and it is such—is made possible by the technology of the film process; it is this, coupled with the artistry of the photographer, editor, and director, that allows the full emotional impact of the sailors' revolutionary act to be conveyed. In the next passage, we close in on the officer's pince-nez eyeglasses, left swinging back and forth on a projecting strut. He himself is gone, but this symbol of his bourgeois quality still trembles in the breeze. The revolution has begun. Another example from *Potemkin* is the way the implacable and apparently irresistible power of the czarist forces is projected for us in a famous scene which takes place in the city of Odessa. A squad of Russian soldiers is spread out in a line on the wide steps of the magnificent waterfront staircase; they move down in step, their rifles at the ready, sweeping everyone—rebel or not—before them. The camera gives us a momentary view of a baby's carriage rolling down the marble steps after the mother has been shot down in the indiscriminate firing.

Many of these devices, new at the time, are now quite familiar to us: the series of short episodes which become not only symbolic but cumulative in their impact; the use of close-up shots for depiction of personality; the making of symbols from ordinary objects by focusing the camera on them. But, as always in art, it is the effective, sensitive use of the medium and the techniques for working in it which gives *Potemkin* its power.

Obviously, this kind of drama and tension is not the exclusive province of the motion picture. Edgar Allan Poe's short story "The Pit and the Pendulum" is a famous example of extreme tension created in words alone. But the visual and symbolic effects created in *Potemkin* seem to call for a uniquely intense response. Perhaps this is because both sight and sound are used on the most immediate, even brutal, level. It seems to be true that what we see and hear affects us

more directly, and therefore most intensely, than what we receiv
in the form of printed words—our senses are more fully engaged.

Stanley Kubrick's *2001: A Space Odyssey* (1970), which mos
people have seen once and many people several times, illustrate
some of the possibilities inherent in the film medium. Called "
mythological documentary," it presents visually the journey c
humanity from its prehistoric anthropoid beginnings to the develop
ment of space flight and interplanetary communication, and finall
to a death and embryonic emergence in some new world somewher
in the future. The plot is so dependent on visual imagery that i
does not lend itself to detailed verbal summary. The basic organiza
tion is the cycle of birth, growth, death, and rebirth. In the firs
episode, anthropoids center their yearning and search for som
meaning in the universe on a black block which has appeare
miraculously. In the second, we find men and women in a spacecraf
developed through technological evolution, and we learn that
similar black block has been discovered on the moon. In the thir
episode, a space probe to Jupiter, king of the planets, is undertake
in search of answers to the mystery of life which will be "the mos
significant discovery in the history of science." When Jupiter ha
been reached, we see a man age, wither, and die. Following a blind
ing flash, we see an embryo staring at us through the transparen
walls of a placenta, with hints of a rebirth on Earth.

The film is best studied and experienced through analogy witl
music and the visual arts rather than with scientific exposition or th
novel. No reduction of it to rational discourse can be satisfactory
Because we are expected to "read" and respond emotionally to botl
the recognizable imagery and the abstract visual patterns, the pro
gression is slow and deliberately paced; people who are still no
visually literate sometimes find films which depend heavily on thes
forms of communication dull and confusing.

The first-person narrator is familiar to us in literature. In thi
film the camera, scanning, selecting, and focusing, is the narrator
but—and this is one of the miracles of film—identification with th
narrator, which is complex in literature, is here visually achievec
so easily and with such immediacy that we are hardly aware tha
we have yielded our eyes to the director. There is a full twenty
minutes of visual exposition before a single word is spoken. Fron
the beginning to the end, the camera scans in what seems like a con
stant swing motion—the infiniate horizon, rotating planets, the fac
of the distant earth, the graceful movements of spacecraft drifting
back and forth, the interior and exterior of the fantastic spaceship
and the satellite port. The pendulumlike motion accompanied by
music creates a sense of weightless drifting. When the motior
stops momentarily, we again become almost painfully aware o
gravity, of counterpulls and tensions.

Throughout the film Kubrick makes much use of juxtaposition and repetition of similar shapes. In the first part of the film, apelike creatures fight over a waterhole. One uses as a weapon an oblong femur bone which has been chewed clean of meat. The weapon is flung into the air; it arcs higher and higher, and turns into a spacecraft of the same shape, gliding elegantly in outer space; and through this transition, we are into the second episode of the film. There are many such shapes and motives which appear and reappear like themes in music. For example, there are four variations on the theme of food: the apes eat raw pig; the spacecraft crew drink plastic liquid and eat plastic sandwiches; the Jupiter probe crew drink plastic mush; and, in the final episode, cultivated dining takes place in an elegant eighteenth-century setting.

Music reinforces the visual narrative. The emergence of apes in the opening scene is announced by dramatic thundering music from Richard Strauss's *Thus Spake Zarathustra*. Their puzzled curiosity and awe of the black block which appears miraculously are communicated by the sound of reverberating voices reminiscent of a cathedral choir in a religious ritual. The graceful, weightless movements of spacecraft in the second episode take place to the accompaniment of the "Blue Danube Waltz." And in the final scene, as the monolith of the first scene reappears and as, in a flash of light, an infant forms and stares innocently and unseeingly at us, the dramatic declamatory music of *Thus Spake Zarathustra* is heard again as the film ends.

What little dialogue there is in the film is deliberately mechanical and emotionless—less important than the brilliance of color, advancing and receding, and the counterpoint of shapes as the imagery of the plot unfolds. Thus humanity is presented to us as insignificant in the great cosmic scheme of the universe and only Hal, the computer, may be said to have a personality.

The way in which visual imagery works in the film can be illustrated from the black rectangular slab. It appears dramatically and mysteriously in the prehistoric scene, where apes dance around it in awe. Later a replica is found on the moon, and the space probe to Jupiter is undertaken to solve the mystery of its meaning. The slab seems to represent ultimate truth, or the ultimate mystery of the universe. But why this shape? How does it communicate visually? Probably there is an association with the Mosaic tablets of the Old Testament; or with Stonehenge and other Druidical monoliths; or perhaps with "black box" exercises in which a variety of objects are sealed into the box, and students try, using all the measuring, observing, and sensing devices possible, to determine its contents, proving that even science must in some matters end in mere hypotheses and speculation. But whichever of these associations is evoked, it is probably at the unconscious, not the rational, level.

These remarks on Kubrick's film must be understood as th
merest hints of how contemporary film can be studied and enjoyed
They are in no sense a full commentary. The film experience is a
impossible to communicate in words as the hearing of music. None
theless, *2001* does illustrate some of the directions in the develop
ment of film art. In it, as in other contemporary films, time, space
movement, and sound are fused into a unified, multisensory experi
ence. In contrast with films which are little more than illustrated
acted versions of plays and novels, it exemplifies a current tren
away from traditional narrative plot and imitation of the literary arts
This film was composed rather than written. The novel version of th
scenario by Arthur C. Clarke, who worked with Kubrick on the film
appeared *after* the film—a reversal of earlier practices. Several dis
tinguished directors, such as Bergman and Fellini, make a practice o
composing directly in film with no scenario to guide them. Ther
is a story that Bob Rafelson, who directed *Five Easy Pieces* (1970), had
nc idea how to end the movie until he filmed the conclusion. Th
fact that the director, Robert Altman, edited *Nashville* from film o
improvised, acted-out situations sketched out only roughly by Joar
Tewkesbury has been much publicized. With this greater emphasi
on the visual and sound components inherent in the film medium
there is, of necessity, a greater dependence on the elements and
organizational principles of the visual arts and music for com
munication.

Critics who see a function of art as the ordering of more and
more chaos in our conscious experience find some of their best evi
dence in contemporary film art.

Over the years, the role of the director has changed from that o
administrative manager, a kind of "general" who delegated various
responsibilities to different specialists, to that of a working, creative
artist. The director today has become the filmmaker. Every image
bears the director's signature. The director composes each scene
controls the lighting, dictates the camera movements, and is deeply
involved in every aspect of the art. As a result, critics, much more
frequently than before, praise or blame the director for the quality o
a film. Audiences, too, have become conscious of the director as the
important person in filmmaking. Advertisements tout the fact that a
film was directed by one established director or another. We watch
for the release of films directed by John Schlesinger, Stanley
Kubrick, François Truffaut, Ingmar Bergman, Michelangelo An-
tonioni, Federico Fellini, Alain Resnais—to name only a few of the
current active directors—because their work has consistently shown
them to be interested in exploring and using the possibilities inherent in the medium.

Film shares with the other arts certain advantages as well as
limitations. Obviously, it can bring to life the physical appearance
and actions of any living being—human or animal—in a uniquely

factual way, anything or anyone from Picasso painting a picture to Balto the sled-dog bringing serum to an isolated northern community. It can also reproduce scenes from nature, with the camera moving about freely like our own eyes but having certain mechanical advantages that the human eye does not possess. It can take us from place to place instantaneously, create an illusion of space comparable only to the achievement of certain kinds of painting, and—most important—give impressions of different points in time through use of the flashback technique. In the 1971 version of *Death in Venice*, as has been mentioned, the director brings in a variety of early events from the life of his composer-hero to help explain his psychological problems in the fictional present. Properly handled (that is, with skillful use of close-ups, montage, flashbacks, transitional devices such as dissolves, fade-ins, fade-outs, wipes, superimpositions, jump-cuts, match-cuts, and other techniques), the camera can present the observed facts selectively to make them symbolic or to stress their importance. (The technical terms in this paragraph are explained in the Glossary.)

Several "translations" of existing literary works into filmed dramas were cited in Chapter 5 when we discussed the distinguishing characteristics of different mediums. There have been a number of very successful film adaptations of literary works. However, the great contribution of film to the world of art must be in the field of original dramas. Among the most interesting of these are the German films of the 1920s and 1930s, films of social milieu, like *The Blue Angel*, portraying pre-World War I Berlin. The protagonist in this film, an unattractive middle-aged professor, falls hopelessly in love with a cabaret singer (played by Marlene Dietrich), and his infatuation becomes a symbol of our inability to control our own destiny. The Italians, whose socially oriented realistic films are of somewhat later date (*Open City* and *The Bicycle Thief* are outstanding examples), have a long and honorable history in this area. The French also, in such films as the atmospheric *Sous les toits de Paris*, offer a characteristic combination of the romantic and the realistic. More recently they have produced a number of outstanding films of political comment. These include *La guerre est finie*, in which Yves Montand plays the role of a professional Spanish revolutionary, and—again with Montand—the more recent *Z*, a story of political repression in Greece, and *Confession*, about an anti-Soviet Czech official. Even leaving aside Montand's excellent performances, these films are important expressions of political awareness.

Film and Literature

Finally, there has appeared within the last generation or so an entirely new literary art form, the scenario. More and more, its idiom, like that of comic strips (which have similar origins in popular culture), has shaped the language and style of speech of Americans and presented their image, for better or worse, to the world. The staple of television, and the shaper of its narrative style and content is "canned film."

After World War II many eminent writers—Tennessee Williams, Truman Capote, Nathaniel West, and Aldous Huxley among others—wrote or collaborated on film scripts. Writing the scenario was often a committee affair: the author of the novel was retained as story consultant while specialists in the craft turned the novelistic idiom into a filmic visual equivalent. This method had all the merits and hazards that multiplicity of authorship suggests. But many directors—for example, Fellini and Bergman—following the tradition of D. W. Griffith, have always created their own scenarios, trusting to the inspiration of the moment and the versatility of the actors and technicians, for their realization. Other authors (such as the prolific Harold Robbins, formerly a "script doctor") write their novels essentially as paraphrased film scenarios designed to be retranslated into shooting scripts, and may even write both novel and scenario simultaneously.

Many writers who are not scenarists nevertheless use the standards of film style, with its stereotypes and conventions, to reach readers better versed in imaginative response to movies than to books. Also, both classic novels and current best-sellers, with their guaranteed box-office appeal, have long been a special genre in film fare. The appearance or the remake of a film of an established novel (*Wuthering Heights, For Whom the Bell Tolls, One Flew over the Cuckoo's Nest, Deliverance*) has frequently assured a new readership for the book.

It should be noted that the possibilities of film go far beyond this give-and-take relationship with literature; similarly the scenario as such only begins to suggest the richness that the film which is made from it can achieve. The "script" may be merely a description of shots and drawings in layout form, with notations for camera and light cues; and the accompanying dialogue that is the actual scenario may be composed almost frame by frame. Nevertheless, the scenario may be the novel of the future, as people become more and more visual and film becomes the preferred form of art.

THREE
ORGANIZATION

The great works of art are complex, but we also praise them for "having simplicity," by which we mean that they organize a wealth of meaning and form in an overall structure that clearly defines the place and function of every detail in the whole. This way of organizing a needed structure in the simplest way we call its orderliness.

—*Rudolf Arnheim**

* *Art and Visual Perception: The New Version*, Berkeley and Los Angeles: University of California Press, 1974, pp. 59–60. Copyright 1954, 1974 by The Regents of the University of California; reprinted by permission of the University of California Press.

9 ELEMENTS OF THE VISUAL ARTS

MEDIUM AND ELEMENTS

A picture, before being a war horse, a nude woman, or some anecdote, is essentially a flat surface covered by colors arranged in a certain order.
—Maurice Denis[1]

Medium and elements are together the materials the artist uses in creating a work of art. The distinction between them is easy to see but hard to define. Both answer the question: What is it made of? but from different points of view. If, for instance, we say that a building is made of brick and stone, we are talking of the medium; if we say it is made of right angles and vertical lines, we are talking of the elements. If we say that a piece of music is played on the horn, the oboe, or the piano, we are talking of the medium; if we say that it is fast or slow, or that it has a good tune or a catchy rhythm, we are talking of the elements. If we say that a picture is made of oil or watercolor, we are talking of the medium, but if we say it is made of red and green and blue, we are talking of the elements.

An element can be known only in some medium, but as an element it is independent of medium. If we see a straight line we necessarily see it as done in some medium—as a chalkline, a pencil line, or an ink line, or the line described by the corner of a house—but when we think of line we do not necessarily connect it with any medium. And so we talk of line dissociated from medium. Similarly, if we hear the song "America," we must hear it sung by some person or played on some instrument, but we think of it as a tune

---

[1] Quoted from *The Phaidon Dictionary of Twentieth Century Art* (New York: Phaidon Publishers, Inc., 1973), p. 93.

without regard to any instrument. Therefore, when we study elements, we consider them with no attention to the means by which we know them. The medium is the physical means through which we can come into contact with a work of art; the elements are its qualities or properties. Mediums are concrete; elements are abstract. The elements of the visual arts are seven:

1. Line
2. Value (light and dark)
3. Light and shadow (chiaroscuro)
4. Color
5. Texture
6. Volume
7. Space (including perspective)

The artist uses these elements in various ways and combinations to create quite different effects. Their adaptability for expressive purposes is demonstrated in two versions of Matisse's *Dance*.

In the first version (Color Plate 24), five figures are dancing in a circle on a gently undulating green hill against a blue sky. The color tones are light and cool. The bodies are depicted in slow curves and the dance takes place quite freely within the picture frame. The effect is one of relaxed, lyrical enjoyment.

The second version (Color Plate 25) was painted to be hung in the mansion of the Russian collector Sergei Vanovitch Shchukin, and was intended to reflect a more passionate, Russian temperament. Here, Matisse uses intense, dark tones of vermilion red, ultramarine blue, and emerald green instead of the more genteel colors of the "French" version. The dance takes place on a steep promontory or crest of a hill. The curves depicting the bodies are angular and contorted and the dancers writhe rhythmically and sensually within the crowded picture frame. The dance, tranquil, ordered, and dignified in the "French" version, has become impassioned, savage, and frenzied in a kind of Dionysian delirium.

As we compare the two versions, we find that the elements have been treated quite differently. We have already mentioned the contrasts of slow and sharp, angular curves, the gently rolling terrain and the steeper hilltop, the light colors and the darker ones. To these we can add the observation that in the first version (Color Plate 24) the movement is on the surface, which is left flat with no indication of perspective; in the second version (Color Plate 25) there is more anatomical detail, more overlapping of figures and some foreshortening; these and the hill which seems to jut into the sky create a sense of perspective, volume, and depth in the painting. The diagonal crossing of the stretched hands and legs creates a sense of energetic movement, excitement, ecstasy. (See Kenneth Clark's comment on the paintings on page 195.)

As we now look with greater care at the elements of the visual arts as a kind of "basic language" with which the artist works, you may find additional details which account for the differences in the emotional content of these two paintings of the same subject.

Line

Line is the simplest, most primitive, and most universal means for creating visual art. Ask a child to draw an apple, a man, or a house: the child will first draw the object in lines—that is, will try to outline it. Lines are of many different kinds. They may be broad, or so faint we can hardly see them. They may be ragged, or clear and distinct. Often lines are felt and not seen, as when an object or a person points to something we do not see. Often the felt lines are more important than the seen lines.

As a matter of fact, there is no such thing as line. What we see as lines are marks made on paper, or contours of objects. The round vase has no edge, no line, but we see one just as we see the corner of a building as a line. Or we may see shadows as lines.

Lines always have direction. They are always active. They always seem to be moving, and we follow them with our fingers, our gestures, or our eyes. Color has none of this activity. We see a wall of blue or red with no idea of motion of any kind, but whenever we see a line we begin to follow it no matter how long or winding its path.

Straight lines Lines are straight or curved; straight lines are horizontal, vertical, or diagonal. The horizontal line is primarily the line of rest and quiet, relaxation and contemplation; a long horizontal line gives a sense of infinity that is not easily obtained in any other way. Horizontal lines are found in landscapes; the quieter the landscape, the more prominent the horizontals. In Rembrandt's *Three Trees* (Figure 6-32), the sense of rest and quiet and peace derives largely from the line of the horizon.

The vertical line is the line of a tree or of a man standing, the line of chimneys and towers. The vertical line is a line of rest, but it is not the rest of relaxation we find in the horizontal. The vertical is pointed, balanced, forceful, and dynamic. The vertical is a line of potential action, though it is not acting. The early Greek bronze found at Delphi, known as *The Charioteer* (Figure 6-3), is purely vertical except for the arms, which are outstretched to hold the reins. Even a slight deviation from the vertical takes away from its force; in the caryatids of the Erechtheum (Figure 2-1), for example, each figure is perfectly straight except for one bent knee, but that break from the vertical gives a sense of relaxation. One feels that the load is not too heavy and that the maidens can easily hold up the roof for a few more centuries.

Figure 9-1. Raymond Duchamp-Villon (1876–1918), French sculptor. *The Horse* (1914). (Bronze. Size: 15¾ inches high. New York, Museum of Modern Art; Van Gogh Purchase Fund.)

The diagonal is the line of action. A man running makes a diagonal line with his body and leg; a beating rain, a tree in a hard wind, almost everything in action assumes a diagonal line. The degree of action is shown in the angle of the diagonal. The diagonal that approaches the vertical shares the force and self-sufficiency of the vertical; the diagonal that approaches the horizontal shares its abandonment. At an angle of 45 degrees the diagonal represents the maximum of action, being halfway between the independence of the vertical and the powerlessness of the horizontal. In Daumier's painting *The Uprising* (Color Plate 23), the forward movement of the mob is shown in the diagonals, especially in the upraised arm of the leader. In Duchamp-Villon's statue (Figure 9-1), the horse's head is turned to one side and its feet are drawn together for action. The energy and incipient action of the statue are derived primarily from its diagonals.

Diagonals meeting at sharp angles form jagged lines that are harsh and unpleasant; they connote confusion, disturbance, lightning, battle, war, and sudden death. In El Greco's *Purification of the Temple* (Figure 9-2), the main interest is centered on Christ and the tradespeople who are being driven away. The lines made by their arms and bodies are predominantly diagonal, meeting at acute angles. In contrast, the figures to the right of the center are quiet, being formed largely of vertical and curved lines.

Figure 9-2. El Greco (ca. 1541–1614), Spanish painter. *Purification of the Temple* (1595–1600). (Oil on canvas. Size: 41⅜ by 50 inches. Copyright Frick Collection, New York.)

216 ORGANIZATION

Color Plate 28. Jan van Eyck (1370–1440?), Flemish painter. *The Annunciation* (ca. 1425–1430). (Transferred from wood to canvas. Size: 36½ by 14⅜ inches. Washington, D.C., National Gallery of Art, #39; Mellon Collection, 1937.)

Color Plate 27. Joseph Albers (1888–1976), American painter. *Homage to the Square: Broad Call* (1967). (Oil on composition board. Size: 48 by 48 inches. The Sidney and Harriet Janis Collection, gift to the Museum of Modern Art, New York.)

Color Plate 29. Titian (1477–1576), Italian painter. *The Young Englishman* (ca. 1540–1545). (Oil on canvas. Size: 43½ by 36½ inches. Florence, Palazzo Pitti. Photograph by Alinari.)

Color Plate 30.   Edouard Manet (1832–1883), French painter. *Luncheon on the Grass.*
(Oil on canvas. Photograph by Scala, New York.)

Color Plate 31. Raphael (Raffaello Sanzio) (1483–1520), Italian painter. *School of Athens* (1509–1511): (Fresco. Figures about life-size. Vatican City, Stanza della Segnatura. Photograph by Scala, New York.)

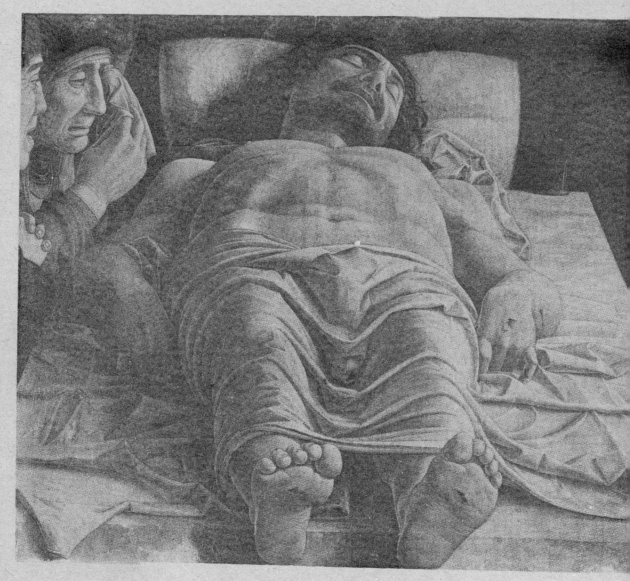

Color Plate 32. Mantegna (1431–1506), Italian painter. *Pietà* (1459). (Tempera on canvas. Size: about 32 by 26 inches. Milan, Brera Gallery. Photograph by Anderson.)

Color Plate 33. *Khusrau and His Courtiers* (Persian miniature, **sixteenth** century). King Khusrau seated **upon** his throne Herat; probably by **Mahm**ud Muzahib or one of his pupils. **From** MS of Khamsah by Mizami. (**Painted**. New York, Metropolitan Museum **of Art**, gift of Alexander Smith Cochran, 1913.)

Color Plate 34.   Paul Cézanne (1839–1906), French painter. *Still Life with Apples* (1895–1898). (Oil on canvas. Size: 27 by 36½ inches. New York, Museum of Modern Art; Lillie P. Bliss Collection.)

Figure 9-3. Vincent Van Gogh (1853–1890, Dutch painter). *La Berceuse* (*Madame Roulin Rocking the Cradle*) (1889). (Oil on canvas. Size: 36 by 38 inches. Art Institute of Chicago; Helen Birch Bartlett Memorial Collection.)

Curved lines   Curved lines show action and life and energy; they are never harsh or stern. Most of the sights to which we attach the adjective *pleasing* have curved lines: rounded hills, trees bent with fruit, curved arms and cheeks.

Curves may be single or double, slow or quick. A quick curve is an arc of a small circle, the type of curve found on a fat baby. A slow curve is an arc of a large circle, the type of a long, thin face. A single curve is but a single arc; a double curve turns back on itself in an S shape. The double slow curve is the famous "line of grace" or "line of beauty" of Hogarth. The quick curve is more exuberant than the slow curve; when used in great abundance it becomes coarse and gross.

A great deal of the elegance of Harunobu's *Lovers under Umbrella in Snow* (Figure 6-28) comes from the long single curves. In contrast, Van Gogh's *Berceuse* (Figure 9-3), with its round curves, is solid and substantial. All the curves are ample; the flowers and other ornaments in the background are circular.

Examples of the characteristics of lines are to be found everywhere. In advertisements, the shape of the letter and the quality of the line are frequently used to indicate the character of the thing advertised. For example, the lettering that advertises farm machinery may also try to suggest the product in solid, heavy, square strokes that sit flatly on the paper. Articles that are supposed to appeal to the dainty or the fastidious will be advertised in thin lines with slow curves.

Lines make shapes, and often we are conscious of line primarily as the shapes formed. In Rembrandt's *Three Trees* (Figure 6-32), we see the line of the horizon but the shape of the trees. Miró's *Painting* (Figure 9-4) is one of similar shapes. We are not sure what, if anything, they represent. We can distinguish a seated dog in the upper left, and there is a suggestion of horned cattle across the background. The whole, however, is a scene of quiet and beauty. In Albers's abstract woodcut *Aquarium* (Figure 2-4), we see large, curved black and white shapes which appear to overlap but leave us in doubt as to which is in front of the other, so that the smaller curved shapes inside the larger shapes seem to move back and forth as we change our focus on them. In *Sunday on the Island of La Grande Jatte* (Color Plate 26), Seurat has united the picture largely through the repetition of the same or similar shapes.

The curved line and the enclosed shape and surface are always suggestive of living forms (biomorphs) and processes, as the composition of Miró's *Painting* shows (Figure 9-4). The forms suggest withdrawal and return, the theme and variation of growth and de-

velopment. The presence of the curved line in the arts is universal
and is most naturally shown in dance (see Curt Sach's comment on
page 411). Matisse, in *Dance* (Color Plates 24 and 25), uses it as the
motif to epitomize the ecstatic nature of an art whose rhythms and
gestures are innate to the expression and celebration of life. For other
examples, see Henry Moore's *Two Forms* (Figure 2-2) and *Reclining
Figure* (Figure 2-5), and note especially Moore's statements concerning his sculpture (pages 33 and 40).

Value (Light and Dark)

Value has to do with the amount of light in a given painting or
graphic work of art. We may also say that *value* is the name given to
relative degrees of light, or that it indicates the degree of luminosity
—that is, the presence or absence of light. In ordinary speech the
term *light and dark* is often used instead of *value;* although this does
indicate that values go from light to dark, it is rather ambiguous in
that it does not indicate the various possible degrees of lightness or
discriminate among them. White is recognized as the highest value

and black as the lowest; a point halfway between them can be called "medium"; the point halfway between white and medium may be called "light"; and the point halfway between medium and black may be called "dark." This gives us a fairly exact scale of values:

White→light→medium→dark→black

Values that do not fit any of these points may be defined in terms of the nearer value; we may, then, speak of a value halfway between dark and medium, or of a light value very close to white.

Values in painting In architecture and sculpture, values change with the light; in painting, values are fixed. When a painter makes an area dark or light, puts in a shadow or leaves it out, it stays that way regardless of the time of year or the source of light. The painting should of course be placed where it can be seen clearly, but its essential values do not change.

In studying the values of a painting, we notice first the value tone. Is the picture predominantly light or dark? In Rembrandt's *Old Woman Cutting Her Nails* (Figure 9-5), the values are dark; in Ingres's *Lady and Boy* (Figure 6-19), they are light. And there are paintings which have an intermediate shade, an overall grayish effect, such as we see in Jan van Eyck's *Annunciation* (Color Plate 28; see the group of Color Plates following page 216), where the light is diffused.

A second question asked about contrasts in value is: Are they great or small? We have just mentioned Van Eyck's *Annunciation* as a painting with a diffused light and little contrast. Ordinarily we have greater contrasts of light and dark, as in Titian's *Young Englishman* (Color Plate 29; Color Plate 29 is in the group following page 216), where the white hands and head shine out against the dark background and the chain occupies a position halfway between them. Often an artist has a particular fondness for one set of values. Rembrandt is outstanding for his contrasts in value, as in the *Old Woman Cutting Her Nails* (Figure 9-5). In this painting, light is concentrated on head, hands, and dress, including some clothes in the background, and indeed seems to emanate from them. Any natural light source would of necessity have given greater light to the clothes and the other surfaces.

The next point to notice about values is the way they are separated one from another. Do they merge one into the other, or are they separate? Are the boundary lines blurred or distinct? In the Rembrandt we have just mentioned, boundaries are kept clear in the foreground, but in the background all sense of boundary lines is lost.

Another point to consider about values in painting is the character of the dark areas. Is there a single flat surface, or is it subtly

Figure 9-5. Rembrandt Harmensz Van Rijn (1609–1669), Dutch painter. *Old Woman Cutting Her Nails* (1658). (Oil on canvas. Size: 49⅝ by 40⅛ inches. New York, Metropolitan Museum of Art; bequest of Benjamin Altman, 1913.)

varied? This is really a matter of slight variations in value within a single tone, variations so slight as to be almost imperceptible. The shadows of Rembrandt have such variations. In the *Old Woman Cutting Her Nails* there is only a little light in the picture; the remainder of the scene is buried in darkness. But this darkness is not hard blackness against which one might strike one's head, but a soft, penetrable shadow; one feels that it is possible to see into the shadow. The effect is much the same as that produced by a small light in the large room; only a small space is clearly lighted, and the light fights against the shadows in the remainder of the space.

Light values can have important emotional connotations. If we examine various Rembrandt paintings—the reproductions in this book and other books, or (much better) some originals—we will find

Figure 9-6. Albert Pinkham Ryder (1847–1918), American painter. *The Race Track* or *Death on a Pale Horse* (ca. 1910). (Oil on canvas. Size: 28¼ by 35¼ inches. Cleveland Museum of Art; J. H. Wade Collection.)

examples of this. In both the *Man in the Gold Helmet* (Color Plate 49; this Color Plate is in the group following page 440) and the *Old Woman Cutting Her Nails* a certain mystery and grandeur have been created by the predominantly dark values. The predominantly light values of Titian's *Bacchus and Ariadne* (Color Plate 14) contribute enormously to the sense of *joie de vivre*—the joy of living—that permeates this work. Let us imagine, if we can, Ryder's *Death on a Pale Horse* (Figure 9-6) done in the light values of the Titian. If this were the case, the emotional mood would be entirely changed. It is the hazy and dark values that are largely responsible for the mood of mystery and doom; and the strong contrast between the light values of the background and the dark values of the foreground add to the mystery. (This work was inspired by a tragedy of which Ryder had personal knowledge; someone he knew had lost all his money at a racetrack and then committed suicide.)

Light and Shadow (Chiaroscuro)

Light and shadow in painting   Light and shadow or light and shade (sometimes known as *chiaroscuro*, from the Italian word for "light and dark") should be distinguished from value. Light and shadow is a means of modeling a figure in depth, a means of articulating the form. The Michelangelo painting shown in Figure 3-18 is an example. Here we see the light coming from the right side of the figure and casting a shadow on the left side, more or less in the way this actually happens in nature. Renaissance painting is rich in such examples; the painting attributed to Leonardo shown in Figure 6-21 is one.

Chiaroscuro may also be used in ways more subtle than this plastic or figure-building function. For example, let us examine Rembrandt's *Man in the Gold Helmet* (Color Plate 49) and Titian's *Young Englishman* (Color Plate 29). In the Rembrandt not only do we see the light falling on one side of a face or form; we also see the figure as a whole emerging from the darkness of the background in very gradual transitions, each one of which has its own component of light and shadow. This creates a feeling of mystery, a darkness of mood, and a sense of unexperienced depths. In the Titian painting, chiaroscuro is used to concentrate our attention on the two most expressive parts of a portrait—the face and the hands.

Light and shadow in three-dimensional art   In painting, the effects of light and shadow must be simulated; but in the three-dimensional arts (such as sculpture and many of the applied arts—pottery, armor, furniture), shadows occur naturally under almost all light conditions. The same is true of architectural design and ornament in general. A molding, whether inside or outside a building, can be seen because of the way different surfaces reflect the light. Patterns in shingles or, in the arrangement of boards or brick can hardly be seen except by means of the shadows they cast. A cornice casts a shadow on the wall below and makes a definite change in the design. An architect frequently makes a model of the building he or she is designing in order to learn the exact effects of the shadows. One of the beauties of the cathedral of Notre Dame in Paris is found in the varied carvings of the façade, and in the play of lights and shadows over them.

An artist who has not studied the effects of shadows carefully may find the finished work quite different from what was planned. French's statue of Lincoln, for example, was made in the studio with an overhead light. When it was placed in the Lincoln Memorial in Washington, all the light came from below. This lighting completely changed the expression on Lincoln's face, making it little better than a caricature, as can be seen in Figure 9-7. Fortunately the lighting could be and was easily changed, and now visitors to the Lincoln Memorial see the statue as French planned it.

In relief sculpture, light and shadow are especially important, since the design can usually be seen only in the shadows cast. In *high*

Figure 9-7. Daniel Chester French (1850–1931), American sculptor. *Abraham Lincoln* (1920), head before (right) and after (left) change of lighting. (White marble. Size: about three times life size. Washington, D.C., Lincoln Memorial. Photograph, Mrs. Margaret French Cresson.)

Figure 9-8. *Lapith and Centaur* (ca. 447–443 B.C.), metope from south-west corner of the Parthenon, Athens. (Pentelic marble. Height: 3 feet, 4 inches. Photograph, Saul Weinberg.)

Figure 9-9. *Panathenaic Procession* (fifth century, B.C.), detail of Parthenon frieze. (Pentelic marble. Height: 40 inches. London, British Museum.)

relief the figures project from the background; they are almost in the round. The shadows are deep and the lines bold and distinct, as in the metope (panel of relief sculpture) of the Parthenon (Figure 9-8). In *low relief* the figures are only slightly raised from the background. The shadows are not very deep and the lines are delicate, as in the *Panathenaic Procession* (Figure 9-9), also from the Parthenon. Therefore, a low relief should be in a dimly lighted place where the light shadows make clear the outlines of all the figures. A high relief would be in bright light, because the higher the relief, the deeper the shadows. In high relief, moreover, the design must be very simple; if there are too many figures, the shadow of one figure tends to hide its neighbor. In low relief the design may be more complicated. In the reliefs of the Parthenon, both these points were observed. The *Panathenaic Procession* is found in the frieze, which was placed on the wall of the building where it was protected from direct sunlight by a row of columns. The metopes were placed above the columns, where they received direct sunlight.

The examples given so far have had to do with rather static effects of light and shadow, dealing as they do with the placing of an object with reference to a constant light. But, as we all know, natural light changes continuously; it is alive and dynamic, and as Walter Gropius, the designer of the Bauhaus, has said, "Every object seen in the contrast of changing daylight gives a different impression each time."[2] He continues: "Imagine the surprise and animation experienced when a sunbeam, shining through a stained-glass

[2] Walter Gropius, *The Scope of Total Architecture* (New York: Harper and Row, Publishers, Inc., 1955), p. 41.

window in a cathedral, wanders slowly through the twilight of th
nave and suddenly hits the altarpiece." This constant change an
constant tension have much to do with the charm of stained-glas
windows. Not only does each window have its own color and design
but it is constantly changing.

In modern domestic architecture we have other significan
examples. Rooms may be built so that they take advantage of th
shifts in daylight through the house and in the patio and garden.

Color

All the effects obtained through line and value alone may be in
creased by the use of color. Colors may be warm or cold, advancing
or retreating, light or heavy, attractive or repulsive, in tension or in
suspension.

When we examine color we find three qualities or attributes
hue, value, and intensity. Hue is that quality by which we distinguish one color from another. The three primary hues are red, blue,
and yellow. All others can be made from them. The secondary hues
are green, violet, and orange, each being halfway between two of the
primary colors: orange is halfway between yellow and red, etc. This
relationship is easily seen on this diagram:

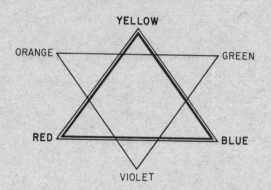

The diagram shows each hue opposite its complement. Two
hues are said to be complementary when between them they contain
the three primary colors. The complement of yellow is violet. Since
violet is made of red and blue, yellow and violet contain all the
primary colors. Complementaries intensify one another if placed
close together. Red and green, mixed, make a gray, but a red near a
green makes each color seem brighter than when alone.

Colors are either "warm" or "cool." The greens and blues on
the right of the palette, from yellow to violet, are cool; the reds and

oranges on the left of the palette, from violet to yellow, are warm. Yellow and violet are considered neither warm nor cool. The cool hues probably seem cool from their association with cool subjects in nature: green grass, green trees, blue sky, and blue or green water. The warm hues are associated with warm objects: red coals and orange fire. The cool colors are for the most part restful and quiet. The warm colors are more exciting, but we tire of them more quickly. The warm colors always seem closer than the cool colors; therefore, they are called "advancing" colors, and the cool colors are called "retreating" colors. If red, green, and blue circles are placed one beside the other, the red seems closest to the spectator, and the blue farthest away. For this reason warm colors are usually put in those parts of a picture which are nearest the spectator, and the cool colors are reserved for the distance and the shadows.

Colors can of course be known only in values. There are light blues, dark blues, medium blues. Any color may be seen at any degree of darkness, from a dark that can hardly be distinguished from black to a light that is almost white. In some colors, however, a good deal of confusion is produced by the fact that certain values have been given special names. A light red, for instance, is called "pink"; and dark yellows and oranges are called "brown."

The last attribute of color is intensity. Colors differ in intensity or vividness. Two colors may be both be blue, one just as dark as the other, but one may be more intense than the other. Powder blue is a dulled blue; old rose is a dulled red. When a hue is found in its most vivid form, it is said to be in full intensity. The same hue dulled is said to be partly neutralized. A hue completely neutralized loses its color and becomes a gray.

Though each color has certain very definite properties, it is almost never seen alone. Our perception of a color is changed by the presence of other colors. A color reflects, and changes with, all the colors around it. It looks dark beside a lighter color and light beside a darker color. A blue placed beside a violet makes the violet seem red, and a red placed beside a violet makes the violet seem blue. Delacroix was merely stating emphatically the influence of colors on one another when he said that he could paint a face of the mud from the streets if he were allowed to select the colors that were to go around it.

The impressionist painters were especially interested in the effects of natural light on color. They believed that we do not actually see forms and space; we infer them from varying intensities of light and color. Their concern was with these two factors more than with the subjects of their paintings. Seurat, for example, while a student at the Ecole des Beaux Arts, studied scientific treatises on color and optics and came to the conclusion that the retina of the eye itself will create an "optical mixture" of reflected light from adjoining colors. Experiments convinced him that these optical mixes were more lively

and produced effects closer to those of real light on objects than di
colors mixed on the palette or canvas. He proceeded, therefore,
develop a technique of painting known as "pointillism," or "div
sionism," which consisted of applying different primary colors to th
canvas in tiny brush strokes or dots so that they would in the optic
mix become the colors he wanted seen. *Sunday on the Island of L
Grande Jatte* (Color Plate 26) is one of his masterpieces. The techniqu
is very tedious and slow, and because most of his paintings are qui
large, as this one is, he completed only a few. In a small portrait c
his mother, he used this technique with conté crayons (Figur
6-24). Other impressionists interested in painting light and atmc
spheric effects on objects used the divisionist technique in modifie
forms—for example, Pissaro, Manet, and Renoir.

Painting is predominantly the art of color, but color is also im
portant in sculpture and architecture. In terra cotta, the surfaces ar
colored; and houses made of wood are usually painted. In the othe
mediums of sculpture and architecture, the color of the material i
itself a factor in the appeal of any work—the rich brown of polishe
wood or bronze, for instance, or the creamy whiteness of ivory o
marble.

Some colors have come to have specific psychological and emo
tional connotations. White is innocence and purity; blue is the colo
of heaven and truth, the color of the Virgin Mary. Red stands fo
blood and for both love and hate. Yellow represents divinity, th
sacredness of revealed truth. It also stands for degradation, treason
and deceit. Brown signifies spiritual death—the renunciation of th
world—and for this reason it is the color of the Franciscan and Capu
chin monastic orders. In modern painting, color is often used fo
itself and for its connotations without regard to the natural color o
the object painted.

Such symbolism of color we know to be largely a cultural prod
uct. But the optical and aesthetic effects of the interaction of colore
areas upon one another have been found to be empirical facts. We
have already mentioned the divisionist technique used by painters
to create optical impressions, and several painters represented in this
book have used color and spatial relationships in other ways to create
optical illusions. Such devices are used by Victor Vasarely in *Casiopé
(Color Plate 36; see the group of Color Plates following page 312),
named for the constellation Cassiopeia, and in *Vega* (Figure 10-1)
named for a brilliant star in the constellation Lyra; and by Bridge
Riley in *Shih-li* (Figure 10-2). The contemporary painter Josef Albers
experimented extensively with color, and wrote one of the authorita-
tive books on the subject, *Interaction of Color*.[4] In his paintings and

*When I paint
I think and see
first and most—color
but color as motion*

*Color not only accompanying
form of lateral extension
and after being moved
remained arrested*

*But of perpetual inner movement
as aggression—to and from the spectator
besides interaction and independence
with shape and hue and light*

*Color in a direct and frontal focus
and when closely felt
as a breathing and pulsating
—from within*

—Josef Albers[3]

[3] Eugene Gomringer (ed.), *Josef Albers: His Work as a Contribution to Visual Articulation in the
Twentieth Century* (New York: Wittenborn Art Books, Inc., 1967), frontispiece. By permission o
Wittenborn and Anni Albers.
[4] Josef Albers, *Interaction of Color* (New Haven: Yale University Press, 1963).

graphic works, Albers created spatial illusions that can be read in a number of ways. The paintings are primarily concerned with color relationships, usually within a very rigid geometric framework. *Homage to the Square: Broad Call* (Color Plate 27; Color Plates 27 to 34 follow page 216) is one of a series which uses a structure of three or four squares superimposed upon one another with the bottom, side, and top margins in a 1:2:3 ratio. Each color square reacts with the others, reciprocally affecting the apparent hues, sizes, and spatial relationships. Value contrasts are not exploited, and Albers used a large variety of commercial pigments to avoid mixing colors. The following excerpt is from Albers's "On My *Homage to the Square*":

. . . Choice of the colors used, as well as their order, is
aimed at an interaction—
influencing and changing each other forth and back.

Thus, character and feeling alter from painting to painting
without any additional "hand writing"
or, so-called, texture.

Though the underlying symmetrical and quasi-concentric
order of squares remains the same in all paintings
—in proportion and placement—
these same squares group or single themselves,
connect and separate in many different ways.

In consequence, they move forth and back, in and out,
and grow up and down and near and far, as well as enlarged and diminished.
All this, to proclaim color autonomy
as a means of a plastic organization.[5]

In *Aquarium*, a black and white woodcut (Figure 2-4), Albers also organizes shapes so that they shift to become foreground or background as we shift our focus, creating a sense of motion.

Texture

Texture has to do chiefly with the perception of touch. It is the element that appeals to our sense of the feel of things—rough or smooth, bumpy or slippery. It is the difference we feel between satin and velvet, between linen and silk, between the roughness of tweed and the smoothness of serge, between marble and bronze. Texture is first known by actually touching objects. Later it is inter-

[5] From *Josef Albers: Homage to the Square* by Kynaston L. McShine. Copyright © 1964 The International Council of The Museum of Modern Art, New York. All rights reserved. Reprinted by permission.

Figure 9-10. Aristide Maillol (1861–1944), French sculptor. *Île de France* (torso) (1910). (Bronze. Size: 42⅜ by 12¾ inches. New York, Metropolitan Museum of Art, Fletcher Fund, 1929.)

Figure 9-11. William Harnett (1848–1892), American painter. *Just Dessert* (1891). (Oil on canvas. Size: 22½ by 26¾ inches. Friends of American Art Collection, Art Institute of Chicago.)

preted by the eye without physical contact, although there is alwa a sense of contact; it is as though we had run our hands over t marble or the satin even if we have not touched it.

Texture is found in all the visual arts. In many cases, differenc in textures are due primarily to differences in medium. We know t different "feel" of brick and concrete, of shingles and smooth dressed boards, of rough and polished stone, of wood and bronz We feel the smooth bronze of Maillol's *Ile de France* (Figure 9-10) ar the rough stone of the *King of Judah* (Figure 6-2). In painting, t term *texture* is used to describe the representation of skin, clot metal, jewels, furniture, etc. In Van Eyck's *Annunciation* (Color Pla 28) we are very conscious of the heavy silk and the jewels of t angel's dress, the gold and jewels of the crown, the wood of the foc stool, the silk of the cushion on the stool, the tiles of the floor.

In the type of picture known as "still life," the representation texture may be the primary interest. As the name suggests, still li represents inanimate objects, such as flowers, fruits, and vegetable These subjects offer abundant opportunity for the display of textur and with them are combined other effects, the play of light on chin or glass, the gleam of a knife blade, the color of wine, or even the ri glow of freshly baked bread. One painter of still life is the America William Harnett. In his *Just Dessert* (Figure 9-11), he depicts the te ture of the grapes and the pewter vessels. In paintings such as th there is very little interest in subject; interest is found entirely color and texture and in their organization in the design. In Manet painting *Luncheon on the Grass* (Color Plate 30), we have the intere of still life in the basket, the rolls, and the fruits that are scattere around, while the figures remain the center of interest in the pictur

Indeed, so shocked was the public by the figures that mo people probably did not notice the effective handling of still life, the fact that Manet's chief interest as a painter seems to have been the lighting—the light as it fell against the basket, the fruit, the nud body, and the hands, and as it completely changed the color of th grass and the trees. It is difficult for us now to appreciate how scar dalous this charming scene appeared to Manet's contemporarie True, there were nude goddesses in art, for example in Giorgione *Sleeping Venus* from the Renaissance period (see Color Plate 44, in th group of Color Plates following page 440). People were even used the presentation of aristocratic nudes and goddesses engaging th spectator in eye contact; but these nudes were usually in an intimat boudoir setting, as in Goya's *Nude Maja*. Even the subject of casu female nudity in the presence of properly attired males enjoying a outdoor picnic had been treated by Giorgione in the Renaissanc The shocking thing was that Manet had seen fit to transpose th heroic and mythological subject of the naked goddess to a bohemia and, it seemed, vulgar context of artists and models on their day of

Figure 9-12. Michelangelo (1475–1564), Italian painter, sculptor, architect, and poet. *Cumaean Sibyl*, detail of Sistine Chapel ceiling (1508–1512). (Fresco. About life-size. Photograph by Alinari/Scala.)

Figure 9-13. Roman portrait (first century .c.). (Marble, about life-size. New York, Metroplitan Museum of Art; Rogers Fund, 1921.)

Figure 9-14. Profile view of Roman portrait, Figure 9-13.

Volume

Volume is often called "solidity." It is that quality of an object which enables us to know that it has thickness as well as length and breadth. As children, at first we lift and punch, pinch and squeeze objects to find if they are solid, but soon we learn to interpret solidity by sight.

If we use only our eyes, we perceive volume primarily in two ways. The first is by contour lines, that is, by outlines or shapes of objects. The second is by surface lights and shadows. When we look at Michelangelo's *Cumaean Sibyl* (Figure 9-12), we see the figure as rounded and solid. In it both ways of judging volume are found. We see the outlines of the face, the shoulder, the headdress, and we notice the subtle shadows in face and dress.

Usually the artist uses all the means available, and usually the desired effect is achieved. Not all the means are necessary, however. The Japanese give the effect of solidity through the use of line alone, as in the Harunobu print (Figure 6-28). They leave out shadows because they say that shadows are temporary and that only the permanent should be represented in painting. Their work, however, is done so skillfully that one may look at it a long time without realizing that the colors are flat and the shadows are missing. In Rembrandt's *Old Woman Cutting Her Nails* (Figure 9-5), volume is secured almost entirely through shadows.

Since painting is two-dimensional, it can only suggest volume. The shadows and contour lines are painted in and do not change. Sculpture is three-dimensional: the outlines and the shadows change with each shift in the position of the person viewing them. And we obtain not one but many different impressions from a single work, as we see in the two views of the Roman portrait shown in Figures 9-13 and 9-14. In the photographs of José de Rivera's *Construction #1* (Figure 9-15) and of Maillol's *Ile de France* (Figure 9-10), the camera shows each work from a single point of view, but we are aware that it would present a different appearance if the camera were moved. The shadows and the contour lines would both be changed. These statues by José de Rivera and Maillol also illustrate the difference in emphasis referred to earlier. *Construction #1* depends almost entirely upon linear effect, whereas in the *Ile de France*, the surface modeling in the body is all-important. These two statues illustrate another point of importance in sculpture. Maillol's not only is three-dimensional but also is solid. José de Rivera's is not solid; it seems to comprise the space within the composition as well as the material of which it is made.

Architecture, like sculpture, always exists in three dimensions. A great building, like a great statue, is seen from many points of view. As we walk around it or through it, the appearance changes with each shift in our position, and each view should be pleasing.

Space

The two arts in which space is of great importance are architectur[e] and painting. Architecture is primarily an art of space. The other ar[ts] exist in space; architecture uses space as one of its elements. We ca[n] see the exterior of a building only as it appears in space. And if w[e] are within a building, we see it as enclosing space. One of the grea[t] beauties of a building like S. Sophia (Figure 9-16) or the Church [o]

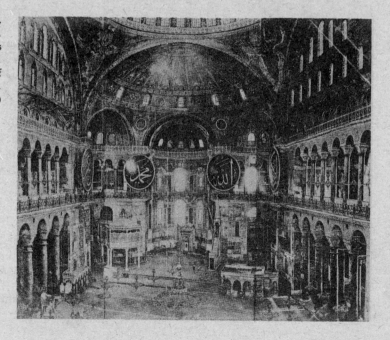

Figure 9-16. S. Sophia (Hagia Sophia), Istanbul (A.D. 532–537, restored A.D. 559, 975), interior. Anthemius of Tralles and Isidorus of Miletus, architects. (Width of nave: 108 feet, height of central dome: 180 feet. Photograph, Bettmann Archive.)

Figure 9-17. S. Apollinare in Classe, Ravenna (second quarter of sixth century). Interior looking toward apse. (Marble, mosaic, and plaster; wooden roofing. Length: 150 feet; width: 98 feet. Photograph by Alinari/Scala.)

Figure 9-18. Taj Mahal, Agra (seventeenth century). (Marble. Length: 186 feet; width: 186 feet; height: 187 feet. Temple built by Shah Jehan in memory of his wife. Photograph, Press Information Bureau, Government of India.)

S. Apollinare in Classe (Figure 9-17) comes from the sense of majesty experienced when one enters the building and feels the spaciousness of the interior. Painting does not deal with space directly as architecture does; it can only represent space on a two-dimensional surface. To the extent that it utilizes every conceivable kind of device for the simulation of space or for the creation of spatial tensions, its relation to space is perhaps far more subtle than that of any other art. The most obvious techniques for creating space in painting are the various types of perspective.

Perspective This is the technical means by which we perceive distance in painting, the means by which we are made to see the position of objects in space. There are two major types of perspective, having to do with two kinds of data on which we form opinions or make judgments about distance. These are known as "linear perspective" and "aerial perspective."

Linear perspective has to do with the direction of lines and the size of objects. Everyone has stood in the middle of a road, or on a railroad track, and noticed that the sides of the road, or the tracks, seem to rise and meet in the distance. In the same way, two parallel rows of vertical objects seem to meet in the distance, but the tops of the farther objects fall to the level of the eyes. These facts can be easily demonstrated in the photograph of the Taj Mahal (examine Figure 9-18). The lines of the pool, the paving, and the low trees rise and tend to meet, whereas the tops of the minarets fall as they recede

Figure 9-19. Colosseum, Rome (A.D. 72–82). (Travertine exterior; restorations in brick. Length: 620 feet; width: 513 feet; height: 157 feet. Photograph, Trans-World Airlines, Inc.)

and come together. If the camera is placed at one side, not between the parallel lines, the lines tend to meet just as in the example studied, but at one side. This can be clearly seen in the picture of the aqueduct at Segovia (Figure 14-10). Curved lines above the level of the eye seem to drop and those below the eye to rise, as we see in the picture of the Colosseum (Figure 9-19).

In painting, of course, lines do not vary as they do with the position of a camera; therefore, the artist must paint lines of perspective as Raphael has done in the *School of Athens* (Color Plate 31) and as Dali has done in his *Last Supper* (Figure 3-13). We notice how the lines of the pavement and the arches converge on the heads of Plato and Aristotle, the two principal figures in Raphael's scene; and how the ceiling and table lines in the Dali converge on the head of Christ.

Objects appear smaller as they recede into the distance. This is a necessary corollary of the facts we have been studying about the direction of lines, and it is illustrated in the examples already given. In the photograph of the Taj Mahal (Figure 9-18), the minarets are of equal height, but those farther away look smaller. In the *School of Athens* (Color Plate 31), the arches are painted as successively smaller. And if we study the picture, we find that Raphael has adapted the height of the men to the distance. Measured in inches, the figures of Plato and Aristotle are shorter than those of the men in front.

In Albers's *Homage to the Square: Broad Call* (Color Plate 27), the "felt" diagonal lines created by the corners of the enclosed squares and the grouping near the bottom of the picture enable us to see the painting as a tunnel or long hallway with the smallest square representing an opening or wall. Albers is here teasing our usual reading of perspective lines without confirming whether the small square is farthest from us or closest to us. Thus, he invites and evokes our participation in the work.

Foreshortening is a term of linear perspective applied mainly to the human figure. The best way to understand this device is to look at examples of it. In Mantegna's *Pietà* (Color Plate 32), the body of Christ is foreshortened.

Obviously, foreshortening is a problem only for the painter. The sculptor makes a figure of normal size. Seen from one point of view, an arm appears full-length; from another, it seems foreshortened. The arms in *The Charioteer* (Figure 6-3) are seen in full length if the statue is viewed from the side; if the statue is seen from the front, the arms are foreshortened. The painter, however, is limited to one point of view and must choose one pose for each figure. Botticelli drew the arms and legs in full length, as though he were trying to avoid the problems of foreshortening. Michelangelo, on the other hand, liked foreshortened poses for his paintings.

Aerial perspective has to do with changes in appearance due to atmosphere. Objects become lighter in color and hazier in outline as they approach the horizon. In Monet's *Waterloo Bridge* (Figure 9-20), the buildings on the horizon are so hazy that they can hardly be seen.

Accurate painting of aerial perspective is at its best in landscape painting, and among the greatest of landscape painters are the Chinese. With a few blurred outlines they give an impression of a

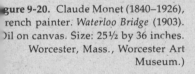

Figure 9-20. Claude Monet (1840–1926), French painter. *Waterloo Bridge* (1903). Oil on canvas. Size: 25½ by 36 inches. Worcester, Mass., Worcester Art Museum.)

foreground and a background with infinite space in between. A ver
good example is the landscape scroll of Tung Yuan shown in Fig
ure 9-21.

In Oriental pictures we find also a *diagonal perspective*; horizon
tal and vertical lines appear as diagonals, and a square appears as
diamond. There is no diminution in size as objects recede in th
picture. In the miniature *Khusrau and His Courtiers* (Color Plate 33)
we can see a good example of this kind of perspective.

Linear perspective as discussed in this chapter is primarily a
affair of the Renaissance. Artists like Raphael, Perugino, and Leon
ardo were very careful to make perspective lines clear and exact. Be
fore that time artists in general did not know realistic perspective. I
the paintings of Giotto, the buildings and landscapes that form th
background for the figures are more nearly symbols than actual pre
sentations. In his *Flight into Egypt* (Figure 9-22), the mountain an
trees are intended only to give the *idea* of mountain and trees.

Figure 9-21. Tung Yuan (Sung epoch, A.D. 960–1279), Chinese painter. Landscap
scroll (late tenth century). (Brush drawing. Size: about 1 foot, 3 inches, by 5 feet
Boston, Museum of Fine Arts.

Figure 9-22. Giotto (1266–1336), Italian painter. *Flight into Egypt* (ca. 1305). (Fresco. Height of figures: about 3½ feet. Padua, Arena Chapel. Photograph by Alinari/Scala.)

In the course of the nineteenth century, the invention and the development of photography made the skillful representation of perspective lines, or even aerial perspective, rather superfluous. The emergence of impressionist painting, with its emphasis on light and the momentary appearance of objects under that light, also diminished the importance of conventional spatial representation. With the post-impressionist movement, particularly the art of Cézanne, a new kind of space emerged, a space which was artistic rather than representational. Compare one of Cézanne's still-life pictures (Color Plate 34) with one by Harnett (Figure 9-11). In the Harnett, we are chiefly conscious of the texture of the objects; in the Cézanne, the fruit and the table are tilted toward us so that they seem to be coming out of the picture rather than going back into it like objects in conventional perspective. At the same time, the foreground objects are related very closely to the background, so that the distinction between foreground and background begins to disappear. What results

Represent nature by means of the cylinder, the sphere, the cone, all placed in perspective.

—Paul Cézanne[6]

[6] Quoted from Cézanne's letters in Theodore Rousseau, Jr., *Paul Cézanne* (New York: Harry N. Abrams, Inc. 1953).

is a new, artistic kind of space which has less to do with what we see than with the simplification of natural forms and their rearrangements into a new visual experience.

Many modern examples of tampering with perspective for an effect can be found. In the woodcut by Schmidt-Rottluff shown in Figure 6-27, the two scenes of the story are juxtaposed, and difference in size is the only indication of a difference in space. In *Melancholy and Mystery of a Street* (Color Plate 35; Color Plates 35 to 41 follow page 312), Giorgio di Chirico has changed the perspective lines to give an impression of uneasiness:

At first glance the scene looks solid enough, and yet we feel that it is about to crack along invisible seams or to drift apart in incoherent pieces. . . . The perspectives of the two colonnades negate each other. If the one to the left, which defines the horizon as lying high up, is taken as the basis of the spatial organization, the one to the right pierces the ground. Under the opposite condition the horizon lies somewhere below the center of the picture, and the rising street with the bright colonnade is only a treacherous mirage guiding the child to a plunge into nothingness.[7]

In *Vega* (Figure 10-1), Victor Vasarely uses a single motive throughout the painting—the square—but changes it in accordance with traditional devices of perspective to create the illusion of an altered picture plane.

In modern painting, a whole succession of movements has treated space as an aesthetic device which unites form, line, texture, and other elements. The earliest movements of the twentieth century—Fauvism (Matisse and others), cubism (for example, Picasso and Braque), expressionism (for example, Schmidt-Rottluff), and geometric abstraction (for example, Mondrian)—began with naturalistic space as a point of departure. Artists of these schools manipulated space in various ways: the Fauves and the expressionists, by intensifying color; the cubists, by fragmenting form and showing simultaneously facets that cannot be seen all at once in nature; the geometric painters, through tensions of form and color.

Some more recent movements, such as abstract expressionism (for example, Jackson Pollock) and color-field painting (for example, Morris Louis), are not interested in representing space. The abstract expressionists are, rather, concerned with the act of painting itself (see page 237 for a note on "action painting"); the color-field painters are interested in the impact of pure color on the observer. Other contemporary movements may maintain some illusion of space. Pop artists, such as Roy Lichtenstein, derive their subjects from such sources as contemporary advertisements (Figure 9-23) and are often

[7] Rudolf Arnheim, *Art and Visual Perception: The New Version* (Berkeley and Los Angeles: University of California Press, 1974), pp. 300–301. Copyright 1954, 1974 by The Regents of the University of California; reprinted by permission of the University of California Press.

Figure 9-23. Roy Lichtenstein 1923–   ), American painter. *Cup of Coffee* (1962). (Pencil on paper. Size: 22½ by 17½ inches. Courtesy of Mr. and Mrs. Leo Castelli; photograph by Rudolph Burckhardt.)

In "action painting," the recording on canvas of an act of creation becomes the subject and is more important to the artist than a polished, orderly work. The unretouched evidence of working the medium, of transitory, abandoned images, of dilemmas and decisions is left in the work as documentation of the artist's creative participation in it.

—James G. Rice[8]

concerned to reproduce modern objects accurately. Op artists, such as Victor Vasarely (Color Plate 36 and Figure 10-1), Bridget Riley (Figure 10-2), and Josef Albers (Color Plate 27), create illusions of spatial movement by the manipulation of geometric forms and colors, often producing images which are visually very stimulating. Op art— "optical," or "retinal" art—attempts to engage the spectator by direct appeal to a physiological response of the eye, by overloading the visual channel much as the auditory channel is overloaded by popular music of the 1960s and 1970s. Hallucinatory effects are produced by strong aesthetic stimulation in art that has no other content or meaning apart from energizing the nervous system. In contrast with the "action painting" of Pollock (Color Plate 10), where we are given the artist's creativity "in the raw," op art by the use of scientific techniques makes the spectators' eyes create new forms in geometrically programmed images. Vasarely's exercises in experimental optics are an example. Both pop art and op art, clearly, reflect the stimulation of the senses that is often characteristic of modern commerce and industry.

[8] From an unpublished work on the avant-garde in twentieth-century arts.

10 ELEMENTS OF MUSIC

Music may be said to deal with sound solely for its own sake. Yet music is not meaningless; it organizes sounds so that they assume meaning. This meaning results from the internal relationships which the sounds acquire through their use in a musical composition. One tone is made to lead to the next, with the result that the total effect seems to have meaning. This organization distinguishes music from the random sounds that we hear about us every day. Thus music can be defined as the organization of sound. The study of music is concerned with the methods composers employ to relate sounds to one another.

Before turning to these methods, it will be helpful to consider the general characteristics of sound itself. Perhaps the most important feature of musical sound is that it is experienced temporally and not spatially. When one tone moves to another, it does so only as time passes. The fact that the musical experience is essentially temporal rather than spatial is immensely important and does much to explain the unique nature of music. In other arts which deal with time, especially drama and dance, space plays an important role. But music requires the perceiver to develop the ability to listen to a sequence of events and to relate them to one another.

Musical terms used in this chapter may be found in the Glossary at the end of the book.

THE ELEMENTS OF MUSIC

The elements of music are six:

Rhythm
Melody
Harmony
Tempo
Dynamics
Timbre

Rhythm

Rhythm, the most basic of the elements, is that which gives us a sense of movement. Rhythm pervades all nature; we can sense it in the movement of the tides, in the ordered progression of the seasons, in the beating of a heart. In these rhythms there is more than repetition; we are conscious of varying degrees of emphasis or accent, which evoke both expectation and tension.

In music, rhythm is the order of movement which gives us the duration of tones and the degree of accent. By tapping out the melody of a song, we become aware of its rhythmic structure. Music concerns itself with durations which have a clearly perceptible relationship to one another. In Western music this relationship is usually based upon multiples of either two or three. In a way, musical rhythm corresponds to visual rhythm, as may be seen in Figure 10-1, where

Figure 10-1. Victor Vasarely (1908–   ), Hungarian painter. *Vega* (1957). (Size: 195 by 130 centimeters. Photograph courtesy of the artist.)

Figure 10-2. Bridget Riley (1931–   ). Cartoon for *Shih-li* (1975). (Gouache on paper, 63 by 140 inches. Courtesy of Sidney Janis Gallery, New York.)

the square is used as a basic rhythmic unit, and in Figure 10-2, wher the rhythmic upward-downward flowing of the lines creates a sens of organized movement.

Meter

Meter is a way of measuring rhythm. It is the arrangement of rhythm in a fixed, regular pattern with a uniform number of beats in uniform measures. Meter is confined to the basic underlying pulse; it i always perfectly regular like the ticking of a clock. The pulse of th meter inevitably coincides with rhythmic beats, but the number and placement of beats added to the meter by the rhythm make music so distinctive that we can often tell one piece from another merely by hearing the added beats. Example 1 shows the rhythm and meter o "Deck the Halls." When the melody is played or sung, we hear the rhythm, whereas we feel the metrical pulse.

EXAMPLE 1

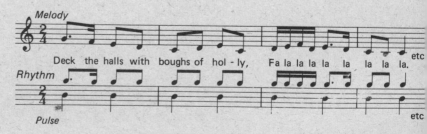

There are basically two kinds of meter: duple, as in the previous example, in which the accent falls on every other beat (ONE two, ONE two, ONE two, etc.), and triple, as in "America," in which the accent falls on every third beat (ONE two three, ONE two three: MY coun-try, 'TIS of thee, SWEET land of LIB-er-ty).

The written indication of meter is called the "time signature" and appears at the beginning of every piece of music. The numerator tells us how many basic beats there are in each measure, and the denominator tells the basic duration value of the beat. For example, in 3/4 meter (triple), which is the time signature for most waltzes, we have three quarter notes or their equivalent for each measure, and in 4/4 meter (duple), which is the time signature for marches, we have four quarter notes or their equivalent to each measure. Example 2 shows time signatures; Example 3 is a table of duration values.

EXAMPLE 2

Time Signatures

EXAMPLE 3

A dot placed after a note prolongs it by half again its length; thus ♩ . = ♩ + ♪ , or ♪ + ♪ + ♪ ; ♩ . = ♪ + ♪ , or ♪ + ♪ + ♪ . Every kind of note has a corresponding kind of rest to indicate that nothing shall be sounded.

Whole rest ▬

Half rest ▬

Quarter rest 𝄽

Eighth rest 𝄾

Sixteenth rest 𝄿

Thirty-second rest 𝅀

When using numerators not divisible by two or three, meter can be felt as a combination of duple and triple. For example, 5/4 meter can be heard as three plus two or—as the accents indicate in Example 4, a melody from Tchaikovsky's Symphony No. 6 (the *Pathétique*)—two plus three.

EXAMPLE 4

There are also multiplications of triple time that are called "compound time." The most usual are 6/8, 9/8, and 12/8, and of these three, 6/8 is the most widely used. It can be heard as duple or triple, but is considered duple because the two strong pulses in each measure dictate this feeling (ONE two three, *four* five six), the accent falling on beat 4 being weaker than that falling on beat 1. In Example 5, we have a well-known example of 6/8 meter.

EXAMPLE 5

Oh! Dear, What Can the Matter Be?

English folk song

Oh! dear! what can the mat-ter be? Dear! dear! What can the mat-ter be?
12 (3)456 1 2 3 4 5 6 12 (3)456 1 2 3 4 5 6

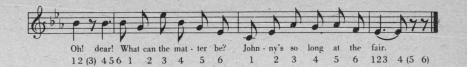

Oh! dear! What can the mat - ter be? John - ny's so long at the fair.
12 (3) 4 5 6 1 2 3 4 5 6   1 2 3 4 5 6 1 2 3 4 (5 6)

This raises the question: Why do we feel pulses when they are not explicitly stated in the music? Perhaps the answer lies in the tendency of the human mind to simplify the information it receives in order to make it more comprehensible. We seek out a common duration. The pulse represents this kind of common duration.

The beat or pulse, however, is only a part of meter. The metrical system not only groups the various durations into beats; it also groups the beats themselves into larger pulses called measures. Measures are created by accents; certain beats are stressed at regular intervals so that the other, unstressed beats seem to group themselves around the stressed ones. This can be illustrated by reciting a series of numbers: one, two, three, four, etc. In this case we have beats (if the numbers are recited regularly), but since the numbers do not group themselves into larger patterns, there are no measures. If we recite the series of numbers stressing every other number, the numbers will group themselves into larger units of two beats each: ONE two, THREE four, FIVE six, etc. In the case of the larger pattern, it seems more natural to count ONE two, ONE two, etc., thus expressing the grouping numerically. This is how measures are counted in music: the number ONE is always placed on the first, stressed, beat of each measure. However, the first note of a piece does not necessarily carry the stress; instead of beginning on the downbeat (the name given to the first beat), it may begin on an upbeat.

Free Meter

Indefinite or unmeasured meter is the chief characteristic of Gregorian chant, also called "plainsong." Irregular meter here arises naturally because the vocal melody was written to fit an existing religious text. The plainsong melody was intended to enhance the sound as well as the sense of the words sung, as in Example 6 (from the thirteenth century). Notice that the notes of longest duration fall on the word ending a natural phrase.

EXAMPLE 6

Plainsong

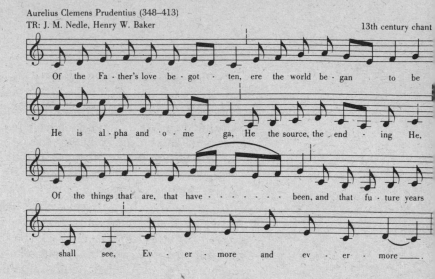

Aurelius Clemens Prudentius (348–413)
TR: J. M. Nedle, Henry W. Baker

13th century chant

Of the Fa-ther's love be-got-ten, ere the world be-gan to be

He is al-pha and o-me-ga, He the source, the end-ing He,

Of the things that are, that have . . . . . . been, and that fu-ture years

shall see, Ev-er-more and ev-er-more___

Variety in Rhythm

Variety in rhythm is one of the most compelling features of music
There are four ways in which this variety is often shown: (1) by th
addition of notes related to what has gone before, (2) by a change i
meter, which automatically makes for a change in rhythm, (3) b
evolving motives and phrases so that they seem to grow each tim
they are heard, and (4) by the manipulation of accents so that the
become syncopated.

In Haydn's second variation from the second movement of th
Surprise Symphony, a rhythmic change is made simply by doublin
the number of notes heard in the original theme, which gives
hurried, playful feeling (Example 7).

EXAMPLE 7

original theme

etc

later statement

etc

A change in meter, as in Example 8, produces a rhythmic change.

EXAMPLE 8

Andante Cantabile
from String Quartet in D, Op. 11

Peter Ilich Tchaikovsky
Russian (1840–1893)

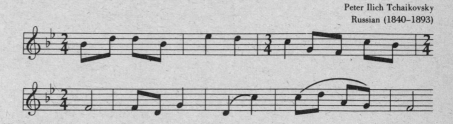

And in Example 9, from the second movement of Symphony No. 5 by Beethoven, the original melody has been altered by adding other notes and by changing their duration value.

EXAMPLE 9

Perhaps no more famous illustration of an evolving rhythmic motive can be cited than Example 10, from Beethoven's Symphony No. 5. The opening motive is the heart of the whole first movement. Notice how it has been enlarged upon.

EXAMPLE 10

The development of motives is one of the most important devices available to the composer. It provides for two qualities which are essential to musical works of extended length: unity and variety.

One of the most interesting aspects of music is its ability to combine these two contradictory qualities convincingly.

Probably the most distinctive and most used rhythmic variant is syncopation, which has to do with the irregular placement of accents. Syncopation is heard in two ways: by having an accent where it is not expected and by not having one where it is expected. If we change the accents of "Yankee Doodle," we can easily see the effect of syncopated rhythm (Example 11).

EXAMPLE 11

Example 12 shows an instance of pronounced syncopation in program music.

EXAMPLE 12

Nachtstücke (Night Visions)
(last four measures)

Robert Schumann
German (1810–1856)

Syncopation is one of the obvious features of much twentieth-century music, in which irregular rhythmic motives and phrases abound. Much of Igor Stravinsky's music makes a point of changing meter and manipulating accents so that an almost barbarous insistence is put on the shifting rhythms. This is especially true in *Le Sacre du Printemps* ("The Rite of Spring").

Nonmetric Rhythm

Much non-Western music is not metric in organization: the accents do not group themselves into a single regular pattern. The rhythmic organization of African drum music, for example, can be extremely complex and irregular. In recent Western music there has also been a tendency on the part of some composers to move toward nonmetric rhythm. Not surprisingly, the earliest efforts in this direction occurred about 1910, just at the time that the first atonal pieces appeared. Example 13, part of the "Sacrificial Dance" from Stravinsky's *Sacre du Printemps*, was composed in 1913. Although the sixteenth note functions as a pulse, the larger groupings of the pulse are quite irregular, as can be seen by the various time signatures, which frequently change from measure to measure ($3\pm2\pm3\pm3\pm2\pm2$, etc.).

EXAMPLE 13

Igor Stravinsky
Russian (1882–1971)

In recent years compositions have been written by John Cage and Karlheinz Stockhausen, among others, in which there is no longer a grouping of the durations into basic pulses. An example is Stockhausen's *Refrain*, a piece for piano, celesta, and vibraphone written in 1960. There is no sense of rhythmic pulse at all; the durations in this work seem to occur almost at random. For example, bursts of notes at very high speeds may suddenly be followed by very long, sustained tones, with no suggestion of a common denominator to help the listener group them. Clearly this music has a different rhythmic effect from that of traditional music.

Jazz Rhythm

A specific kind of rhythm is found in jazz, which is African in origin. Jazz is in duple meter and is characterized by a subtle rhythmic pulsation sometimes called "swing." Swing is what the performer does with the rhythm, which is a syncopation so flexible that it cannot be exactly notated. Jazz, then, is music which can be studied only by direct listening. It is a performer's medium. Any sound which can be made is legitimate, and use of counterpoint, variation, ornamentation, and syncopation is left to the performer. This is what gives jazz its special spontaneous quality.

MELODY

Melody is any succession of single tones which, by virtue of being placed sequentially, give a sense of continuity. Melody is heard in terms of duration and pitch. Because most melodies in Western music between 1700 and 1900 are tonal and metrical, the pitches and durations are organized so that all the pitches relate to one central tonality and all the durations relate to a basic metrical pattern. Compare this idea with its visual counterpart in Figure 10-2, where a series of like lines is produced in a measured pattern to create linear waves.

Melody may be defined as a specific ordering in time of the pitches of the scale used. Normally the notes will not appear in their scalar order, although there are exceptions to this: the hymn "Joy to the World" (Example 14) outlines a descending major scale.

EXAMPLE 14

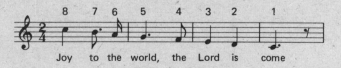

If this melody is compared with that in Example 15, we can see that the pitches occur in reverse order. Note the effect the different durations of the pitches have upon the scale. If each pitch in the melody were sung for the same length of time, it would sound like a scale, not like a melody.

In Example 15, the melody begins with an ascending major scale, then breaks off into larger intervals:

EXAMPLE 15

Mazurka, Op. 7, No. 1

Frederic Chopin
Polish (1810—1949)

Most melodies, however, do not follow the scale this closely. Thus the melody in Example 16—which, like the preceding one, is in B flat major—reorders the tones considerably. Although it begins with a scalar succession (descending from the fifth scale tone down to the second, then up to the first in the higher octave), it then uses the notes of the scale in an order which is entirely unique to this melody.

EXAMPLE 16

Tales from the Vienna Woods

Johann Strauss Jr.
Austrian (1825—1899)

When certain patterns of intervals are repeated at a differer
pitch, we have a "sequence." The sequence embodies melodic an
rhythmic repetition. There is a sequence in "America" ("Land wher
our fathers died, *land of the Pilgrims' pride"*). Example 17 shows tw
sequences following the original interval pattern without pause.

EXAMPLE 17

B Minor Mass, Agnus Dei

Johann Sebastian Bac
German (1685–1750

A · gnus   De   ·   i, qui tol · lis pec · ca · ta mun · di,

TONALITY

When all the tones of a melody have been sounded, their total rela
tionship establishes a tonality. Tonality is *key feeling;* there is one
central tone called the tonic, toward which all other tones in the
melody seem to gravitate. Tonality is expressed through the use o
scale, which is a prescribed pattern giving the number and relation
ship of tones. A scale not only chooses which tones will be used bu
also denies the use of other tones. Scales are exclusive as much as
they are inclusive. We can think of tonality as a general idea, and o
scale as specific facts to sustain the idea. A piece written in D major
for example, is based upon the major scale and its central tone is the
note D. Tonal music tends to begin and end with the central tone,
or tonic.

Scales

There are only a few scales on which most Western music is based.
They are (1) major, (2) minor, (3) pentatonic, (4) chromatic, (5) whole-
tone, and (6) twelve-tone. Each of these scales is found within the
compass of an octave, and at most only twelve different tones are
possible. The chromatic and twelve-tone scales are the only two
which make use of all twelve.

The major scale is used in a vast number of compositions and is
familiar to everyone. It is composed of eight tones (seven different
tones), the first and last of which are the tonic. The relationship of
intervals for the major scale is as shown in Example 18.

EXAMPLE 18
Major Scale

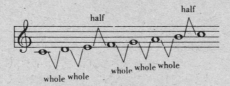

"Joy to the World" and "Deck the Halls" have been cited to show the outline of the major scale. Also in this chapter, the Strauss waltz and the second variation of Haydn's *Surprise* Symphony are major.

The minor scale also has eight tones, seven of which are different. Its interval pattern is as shown in Example 19.

EXAMPLE 19

Melodic Minor Scale

The main difference between major and minor scales is to be found in the third and sixth steps of the scale, those in the minor being lowered one-half step from their position in the major. In Example 20, by Chopin, the theme is quoted in the major and then appears immediately in the minor.

EXAMPLE 20

Valse Brillante

Frédéric Chopin
Polish (1810–1849)

The pentatonic scale (Example 21) is of Oriental origin and very ancient. As its name implies, it has five tones.

EXAMPLE 21

Pentatonic Scale

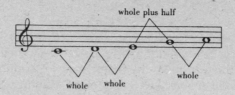

One of the many versions of the ballad "Barbara Allen" uses the pentatonic scale (Example 22). On the piano keyboard this scale can be played on the five black keys. Of course, it can also be played on all white keys, or on both black and white keys, depending on where one begins.

EXAMPLE 22

Barbara Allen

As she went on the high-way home, She heard the church-bell knell - ing, And

eve - ry stroke it struck her name, "Hard - heart - ed Bar - bara Al - len."

The chromatic scale (Example 23) uses all the twelve tones, always progressing by half steps. It is never used as the basis for an entire composition, because it seems to have no real beginning and no real end. Rather, it is used in part to add interest to music based on other scales, largely the major and the minor. Music which uses the chromatic scale is harmonically richer because of shifting tonality.

EXAMPLE 23
Chromatic Scale

all half steps

There are several famous examples of the use of this scale in vocal music: in "My Heart at Thy Sweet Voice" from the opera *Samson et Dalila,* in "To the Evening Star" from *Tannhäuser,* and in the song from *Carmen* in Example 24. The first two are in the major scale, with chromaticism in the melody; Example 24 is in the minor.

EXAMPLE 24
Love Will Like a Wild Birdling Fly
(From *Carmen*)

Georges Bizet
French (1838–1875)

Love will like a wild bird-ling fly, Ca - reer - ing whith - er⎯⎯ he may choose,
L' amour est un oi - seau re - belle Que nul ne peut⎯⎯ ap - pri - voi - ser,

The whole-tone scale (Example 25) is composed of seven tones (six different tones), each a whole tone from its nearest neighbor. It has had rather limited use, and that mostly in the late nineteenth and early twentieth centuries. This scale has an exotic, rather noncommittal sound because the feeling of tonality has been weakened, owing to the fact that each interval within the scale is alike.

EXAMPLE 25
Whole-Tone Scale

all whole steps

Debussy, who was particularly interested in experimenting with unusual scales, made fairly frequent use of the whole-tone scale, as in Example 26.

EXAMPLE 26

Préludes, Book I, No. 1
Voiles

Claude Debussy
French (1862—1918)

ATONALITY

The tendency toward increased chromaticism in the nineteenth century led some composers to abandon the idea of organizing music around one principal tone. They began to write *atonal* (nontonal) music, a term which clearly indicates how conditioned we are to tonality. The earliest atonal pieces date from about 1910. Such pieces use all twelve pitches with more or less equal emphasis.

The Twelve-Tone System

In the 1920s the composer Arnold Schöenberg devised a system of pitch organization based on the chromatic scale, but designed to give that scale a form which could relate the pitches of an atonal composition. Schöenberg arranged the twelve chromatic pitches in a series, which he called a "twelve-tone row." The series, or row, represents a specific ordering of the twelve possible pitches. The particular arrangement of pitches may vary from one composition to the next, but once a row has been devised, it becomes the standard for that piece, and the entire composition is then based upon that row.

The row may be played forward (the original form) or backward (the retrograde form); it may be inverted, by changing all ascending intervals to equivalent descending ones, and vice versa (the inversion); and the inversion may also be played backward (the retrograde inversion).

The tone row, or scale, also forms the basis for the harmony; one chord, for example, may be made from the first few tones of the row, the next from following ones, etc. Whether in melody or harmony, the use of the twelve tones is often restricted to the order in which they appear in one of the four arrangements of the established position.

In this system there is no tonic; or we might say that every note is the tonic, in which case there is no feeling of gravitation to one key, or even one central tone. For this reason the music is said to be atonal.

Examples 27 and 28 show Schöenberg's tone row and its use in one of his compositions.

EXAMPLE 27

Variations for Orchestra, Op. 31

Arnold Schöenberg
Austrian (1874—1951)

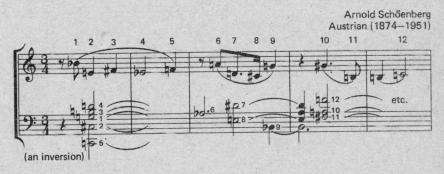

(an inversion)

EXAMPLE 28

tone row   retrograde (backward) version

1 2 3 4 5 6 7 8 9 10 11 12   12 11 10 9 8 7 6 5 4 3 2 1

inversion of tone row   retrograde inversion

1 2 3 4 5 6 7 8 9 10 11 12   12 11 10 9 8 7 6 5 4 3 2 1

(By permission of Mrs. Arnold Schöenberg)

MODES

The modes were the prevailing scales of the Middle Ages. There are seven modes, each corresponding to one of the seven tones of the major scale. The Aeolian mode has become the modern minor scale, and the Ionian mode has become the major scale. The names of the other modes are Dorian, Phrygian, Lydian, Mixolydian, and Locrian.

The use of these modes, excepting the Locrian, was very common in the religious music of the Middle Ages; therefore, they are often called the "ecclesiastic" modes. They survive largely in plainsong and in folk song, as in Example 29, in the Dorian mode. By playing this example in the key of D major (that is, by putting two sharps in the signature), we may easily hear the difference between the modal and tonal quality.

EXAMPLE 29

Henry Martin
(Dorian)

English Folk Song

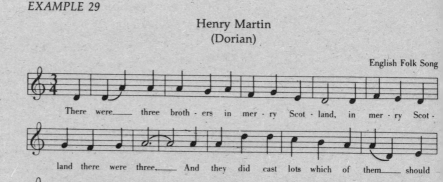

There were____ three broth-ers in mer-ry Scot-land, in mer-ry Scot-

land there were three.____ And they did cast lots which of them____ should

go____ should go____ should go, and____ turn rob-ber on the salt sea.____

COUNTERPOINT

Much folk music is monophonic, as is much medieval Western music and the music of many other cultures. Much Western concert music, however tends to have a more complex texture. If two or more melodies are played simultaneously, the texture is said to be "polyphonic." A word used interchangeably with *polyphony* is *counterpoint. Point* is an old name for *note;* hence, *counterpoint* means "note against note." Counterpoint, then, is the combination of two or more melodies (e.g., in which one is played against the other).

There are two ways to create counterpoint (or polyphony). In the first, counterpoint is created by the entrance and repetition of the same melody after it has been introduced for the first time. A piece which is constructed according to this technique is called a "round," a familiar example being "Row, Row, Row Your Boat." The melody is complete in four measures, and the entrances of the voices are one measure apart. Thus, by the fourth measure all four parts are going simultaneously, each one singing a different measure of the melody. The second way of producing counterpoint is the use of separate melodies. Let us examine these two methods in turn.

Imitation and Canon

When one voice repeats what has just been stated by another voice, this is called "imitation." And when one voice continues to imitate another exactly, it is said to be "in canon" (*canon* means "strict rule"). A good example of a canon is given in Example 30, a Franck sonata for two instruments.

EXAMPLE 30

Sonata in A Major for Violin and Piano

Cesar Franck
French (1822–1890)

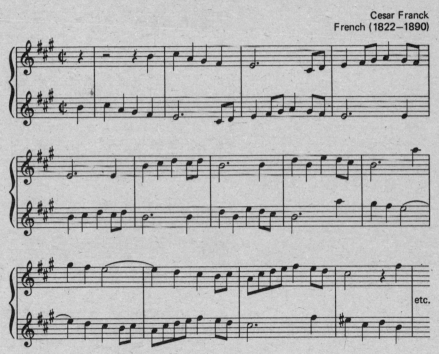

All rounds are in canon, each voice entering on the same pitch. Music in canon may be written for any number of parts, but the norm is two, three, or four.

Separate Melodies

The putting together of two separate melodies is found in both popular and classical music. Examples 31, 32, and 33, from Beethoven's Symphony No. 7, present an excellent illustration of the interweaving of two different melodies. The first time the melody is heard, it is alone (Example 31). The second time it is heard (Example 32), a new melody has been added to it, a bit lower in range; it is more melodic in character and seems almost to caress the original melody. Finally (Example 33), the two melodies are exchanged, and now the first melody appears beneath, while the second melody appears above it.

EXAMPLE 31

Symphony No. 7 in A Major
(Slow Movement)

Ludwig van Beethoven
German (1770–1827)

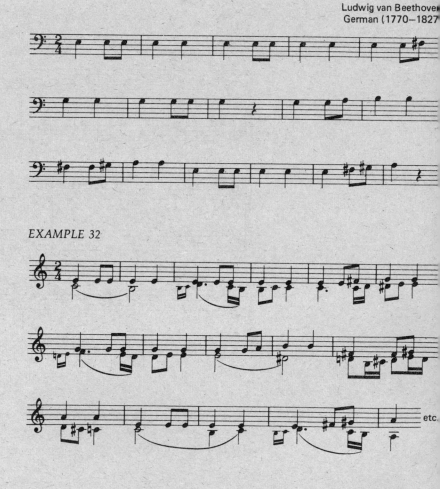

EXAMPLE 32

EXAMPLE 33

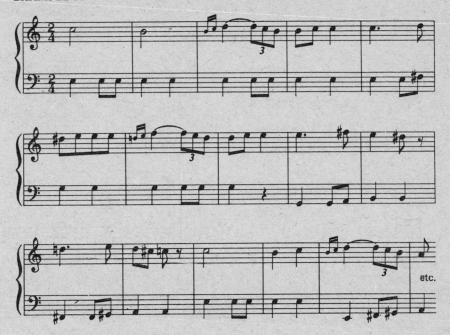

In music since the time of Bach, the tendency has been to put together two melodies that are quite different, as has been done here by Beethoven. In the great period of polyphonic music before Bach, little emphasis is found on the separate melodies as such. Instead, one is conscious only of the way the voices are woven together in a harmonic whole. This can be illustrated in almost any of the polyphonic music of Palestrina, a master of the polyphonic period. A good example is the "Christe eleison" from the *Mass: Assumpta est Maria* (Example 34, page 260).

NOTES ABOUT COUNTERPOINT

Not everyone can hear all the melodies that are woven together in polyphonic music, but we can sharpen our ears for polyphony if we listen carefully to some of the characteristics which are essential in the making of counterpoint: contrast in rhythm, contrast in direction, and contrast in pitch.

EXAMPLE 34

Mass: Assumpta est Maria

Giovanni Pierluigi da Palestrin
Italian (1514 or 1515–1594

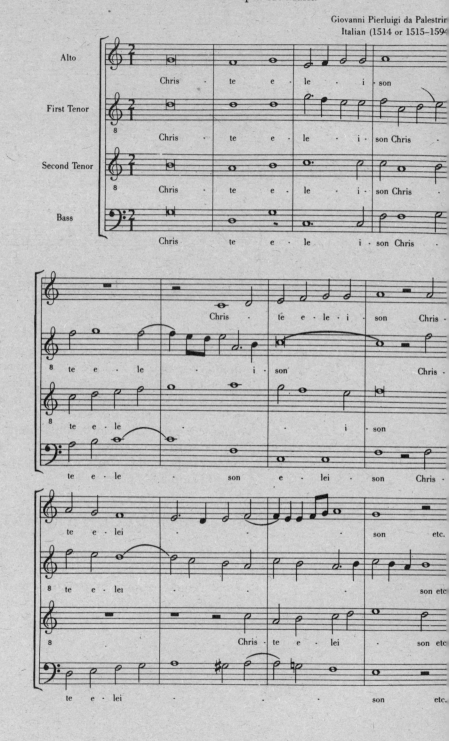

Contrast in Rhythm

Two or more voices contrast in rhythm. In Franck's Sonata for Violin and Piano, one instrument holds while the other moves. In the Two-Part Inventions by Bach, there is no waiting of one voice for the other, but when one rests the other tends to move.

Contrast in Direction

If one melody ascends while the other descends, or if one stays on one pitch while the other moves, the melodies are easily distinguished. The latter possibility is illustrated in Examples 32 and 33, where the lower notes tend to dwell on one pitch while the upper ones move.

Contrast in Pitch

One voice is usually higher than the other. In "Row, Row," the pitch goes higher in each of the first three measures. In the Bach Inventions, one voice is regularly put in the bass and the other in the treble. In Beethoven's Symphony No. 7, the secondary melody is first lower than the primary one and then above it.

HARMONY

When two or more pitches are sounded simultaneously, a chord is formed. *Harmony* refers to the relationship of the tones within the chord and the relationship of chords to one another.

The *triad* is the basic chord in the tonal system. As the name implies, there are three different pitches in a triad, and there is an interval of a third between the two lower tones and between the two upper tones. In a major triad, the bottom third is major and the upper is minor; in a minor triad, the bottom third is minor and the upper is major (Example 35).

EXAMPLE 35

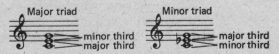

Triadic chords can be played in three positions, each position having one of the three tones of the triad as its bass, or lowest note (Example 36).

EXAMPLE 36

Triad in three positions

In tonal music, chords are derived from the major and min[e]
scales. The most important tone harmonically, as well as melodicall[y]
is the tonic, the first degree of the scale. The tonic triad (I) in a maj[e]
piece (a piece based on the major scale) is a major triad; in a min[e]
piece, it is a minor triad. Next in harmonic importance to the ton[ie]
triad is the dominant triad (V), which is built on the fifth tone of th[e]
scale. The dominant triad seems to point to the tonic, harmonicall[y]
emphasizing its role as the central pitch, much as the seventh, [or]
leading tone does melodically. Thus a V-I progression (Example 3[7])
seems to define the tonality; it produces a sense of stability an[d]
completion.

EXAMPLE 37

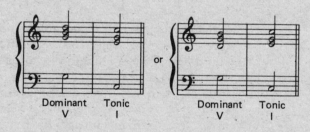

| Dominant | Tonic | | Dominant | Tonic |
| V | I | or | V | I |

If we play Example 37 backward, we hav[e] a I-V progression. In thi[s]
case we get a feeling of incompleteness, leading us to expect furthe[r]
chords until we arrive at one which will be stable and final. Suc[h]
stable progressions, which define keys, are called "cadences."

It is possible to build chords on all degrees of the scale. After th[e]
I and V chords, the most common chord is the subdominant, or I[V]
chord. There are many pieces, in fact, which are made up entirely o[f]
the chords on I, IV, and V, such as "America," "My Bonnie Lies ove[r]
the Ocean," and the traditional blues in jazz.

By using triadic chords built on the tonic, subdominant, an[d]
dominant, one can fill in the harmony for almost any simple piec[e]
of music, such as hymns or folk songs. Using Roman numerals fo[r]

the chords, here is an example of the use of tonic, subdominant, and dominant harmony:

> I   IV   I
> My Bonnie lies over the ocean,

> I   IV   V
> My Bonnie lies over the sea,

> I   IV or II   I
> My Bonnie lies over the ocean,

> IV   V   I
> Oh bring back my Bonnie to me.

In harmonically more complex music, however, it is not unusual to find chords based on all the possible degree of the scale. Diverse chords add a richness to the harmony, and can make even a very dull melody seem beautiful. This is especially true in the Chopin Prelude in E Minor (Example 41, page 267). In Example 38, which is also by Chopin, notice that the rhythmic pattern is exactly the same in each measure and that the first and last chords in each measure are mostly either tonic or dominant. Between these chords are other kinds which add richness and variety.

EXAMPLE 38

Prelude No. 20 in C minor

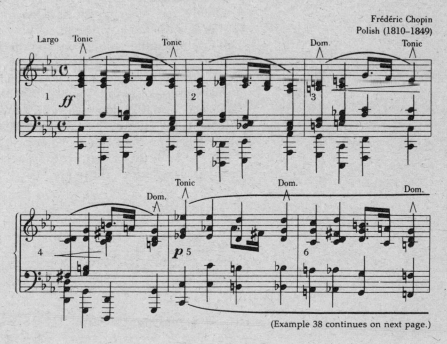

Frédéric Chopin
Polish (1810–1849)

(Example 38 continues on next page.)

EXAMPLE 38 (Continued)

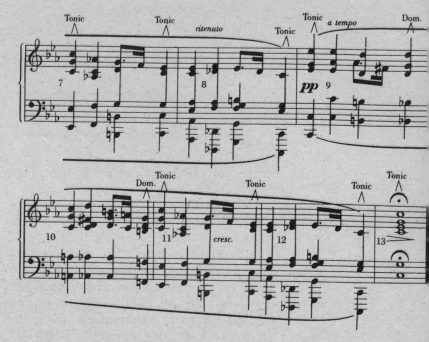

Consonance and Dissonance

Consonance in music is that which we associate with stability, rest fulness, and accord. Dissonance is that which we associate with in stability and incompleteness. Consonance and dissonance are to a large extent relative concepts, varying considerably from one musica culture to another, and even from period to period within the sam culture. In the tonal system, however, the terms are fairly clearly defined. For example, any chord which is not a triad is a dissonance and requires resolution, which is achieved when it moves to a con sonance, a triad. Likewise, any pitch in the melody which does no occur in the chord accompanying it is also dissonant. Thus, if the note B is supported by a C major chord (C-E-G), it will be dissonant and will be heard as wanting to resolve upward to C, the nearest con sonant chordal tone (Example 39).

EXAMPLE 39

It is important to realize that the terms *consonance* and *dissonance* are relative: whether a particular pitch or chord sounds consonant may well depend upon its context. Thus the note B, while dissonant when supported by a C major chord, will sound consonant if supported by a G major chord (G-B-D), which contains the pitch B as a chordal tone. Similarly, the major chord on G will sound relatively dissonant (unstable) in the key of C major (where it represents the dominant or V), but will sound consonant in the key of G major (where it represents the tonic, or I).

The importance of consonance and dissonance in the tonal system cannot be overstressed. Consonance supplies stability and is thus closely associated with the whole concept of the tonal center, which itself represents the principal stable pitch in a composition. Dissonance supplies tension. Indeed, part of the effect of arriving at the central pitch depends upon the ability of the music to move away from that pitch, thus creating instability and a need to return to the tonic later in order to reestablish stability. As a result, tonal music tends to be extremely dynamic, using changing moments of tension and relaxation in virtually limitless combinations.

There is a kind of visual equivalent of moving from consonance and clarity through dissonance and confusion to clarity again in M. C. Escher's *Sky and Water* (Figure 10-3). The images in the upper

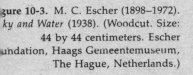

Figure 10-3. M. C. Escher (1898–1972). *Sky and Water* (1938). (Woodcut. Size: 44 by 44 centimeters. Escher Foundation, Haags Gemeentemuseum, The Hague, Netherlands.)

and lower parts of the woodcut are quite clear, but the transitional middle section is unclear and ambiguous. As our eyes move from bottom to top or from top to bottom, we begin with a comfortable feeling of knowing what we are seeing. In the middle section we are not sure what is happening, but as we proceed, the images become clear again and we experience a sense of completion. It will be noted that here, as in music, it is the ambiguous area of tension and confusion which gives the whole its significance.

Moving from a dissonance to a consonance, or moving among chords which are sometimes dissonant and sometimes consonant, produces variety, suspense, and even tension. This is the crux of harmony. Example 40 shows fairly extreme dissonance. The last chord, as we expect, is stable, sounds final, and is therefore consonant.

EXAMPLE 40

Prelude No. 15

Frédéric Chopin
(1810–1849)

Homophonic Texture

As we saw previously, polyphonic texture depends on the concept of counterpoint. Homophonic texture, on the other hand, depends on the concept of harmony, for it is a texture which consists of one melody and a chordal accompaniment. The relationship between the two, however, may vary considerably. In Example 41, the melody is above the chordal accompaniment.

EXAMPLE 41

Prelude No. 4

Frédéric Chopin
Polish (1810—1849)

The melody may also be below the accompaniment, as in Example 42.

EXAMPLE 42

Prelude No. 6

Frédéric Chopin
Polish (1810—1849)

Occasionally the melody even appears in the middle of the chordal accompaniment, as in Example 43.

EXAMPLE 43

Liebestraum

Franz Liszt
Hungarian (1811—1886)

Hearing Harmony

Hearing harmonies is primarily a matter of attentive participation. One of the best ways to begin is to listen carefully to a single voice or instrument played with an accompaniment. The solo will sing the melody while the harmonies are heard in the accompaniment. Try to hear what the accompaniment is doing. Sometimes it accompanies the melody step by step; sometimes it anticipates the melody; and sometimes it echoes it. Note what the accompaniment is doing when the solo voice is silent. Does it merely mark the time? Does it repeat the melody? Or does it go off on its own? Note also the direction of the harmony. Does it follow the line of the melody, or does the harmonic line go up when the melodic line goes down? Are the chords largely consonant, or do you hear dissonance? If there is dissonance, is it resolved? The tones of a chord may be played simultaneously as solid chords, or they may be broken or spread out in arpeggios, harplike figures. The arpeggio always gives a soft, smooth, flowing motion to the music. In the first movement of Beethoven's "Moonlight Sonata," the accompaniment is played in arpeggios. The first Prelude in Bach's *Well-tempered Clavier* is in arpeggios.

Finally, one should try to determine the place of the harmony in the total effect of the composition. A folk song, a hymn, or some other simple song, for example, needs a simple, unpretentious harmony. The beauty is in the tune, and the harmony should not distract from it. In the usual hymn or folk song, the accompaniment follows the melody exactly and inconspicuously.

On the other hand, some harmonies can give dignity and grandeur to a melody, as in Chopin's Prelude No. 20 in C minor (Example 38). The slow movement of Beethoven's *Appassionata* Sonata (Example 44) begins with a theme of the utmost loftiness and grandeur which owes its solemnity to its rich harmonies and to their being placed in the lower register of the piano.

EXAMPLE 44

Sonata Op. 57
(Slow movement)

Ludwig van Beethoven
German (1770–1827)

TEMPO

The meter in which a piece of music is written has little to do with the actual speed or tempo of the music. Notation for time and rhythm shows the duration of each note with reference to the other notes of the piece, but that is all. We can say in general that songs written with half notes as the unit of value are supposed to go more slowly than songs written in quarter notes, and songs written in eighth notes are supposed to go faster, although there is no proof that such is the case.

In general, we may say the pace is slow, quick, or moderate, but more commonly we use the traditional Italian terms:

grave	gravely, solemnly, slowly
largo	very slowly and broadly
adagio	very slowly
andante	moderately slowly
andantino	somewhat faster than andante
moderato	at a moderate tempo
allegretto	at a pace between moderato and allegro
allegro	fairly fast (lively)
presto	very fast
prestissimo	as fast as possible

These terms are made more exact by the addition of terms that indicate certain qualities of the music:

assai	very
con anima	with life
con moto	with motion
con spirito	with spirit
grazioso	gracefully
maestoso	majestically
dolce	softly or sweetly
con fuoco	with fire
con brio	with vivacity or spirit
molto	much
giusto	in exact tempo
ma non troppo	but not too much
vivace	with vivacity

Generally speaking, the slow tempos suggest concentration, reflection, and deep feeling, whereas the quick tempos suggest gaiety, joy, fun, vigor, excitement. An increasing speed (*accelerando*) means an increase in excitement and tension. A decreasing speed (*ritardando*) means loss of life or power; sometimes it shows relaxation and rest, sometimes exhaustion. Sudden changes in tempo often suggest like changes in mood or meaning.

DYNAMICS

The word *dynamics* refers to the degree and variation of volume and force, from soft to loud, with which the music is played. These gradations of intensity, like the notations describing tempo, are traditionally indicated by Italian words, for which abbreviations are generally used:

pp.	*pianissimo*	as softly as possible
p.	*piano*	softly
mp.	*mezzo piano*	somewhat softly
mf.	*mezzo forte*	somewhat loudly
f.	*forte*	loudly
ff.	*fortissimo*	as loudly as possible
cresc.	*crescendo*	getting louder
decresc.	*descrescendo*	getting softer
dim.	*diminuendo*	getting gradually softer
sf.	*sforzando*	abruptly loud

TIMBRE

We have discussed timbre in some detail in Chapter 7, and here it will suffice to add that the composer will mix the vocal and instrumental colors so as to enhance the work. One of the ways a composer can differentiate between melody and accompaniment is through the use of different timbres for the different textural components. Thus an accompaniment may be given to the strings while the melody is played on a flute; or in a two-part contrapuntal texture, one melody may be given to a clarinet while the other is played by the bassoon.

11 ELEMENTS OF LITERATURE— SENSE

The medium of literature is language, and language, as we know, is composed of words that are combined into sentences to express ideas, emotions, or desires. Words have both sound and meaning. The word *horse*, for instance, stands for the sound *horse* and the animal *horse*. These are usually associated and are separated only by an effort; yet they are distinct. To understand literature we must know both sound and sense. We begin with sense, or meaning.

MEANING

The first and last rule in knowing literature is that one should know what the words mean. It is always a temptation to guess when one is uncertain, but it is never safe. One of the authors remembers seeing the school for retarded children in Frankfort, Kentucky, when he was a child. People called it the "feeble-minded" institute. When he got home he told his mother that there was a sign in front of the building which said "Eleemosynary Institute." His mother asked, "Do you know the meaning of *eleemosynary?*" "Of course," he said; "it means feeble-minded." The word comes from the Latin *eleemosynarius*, "charitable." For the student who has studied foreign languares, meaning is often clear without a dictionary, as in the case of *eleemosynary*. This is especially true of Latin, because we have taken many of our words from the Latin. Often we have a Latin word and a Germanic (English) word for the same thing, as in the Latin *paternal* and the English *fatherly*, or the Latin *annual* and the English *yearly*. Usually there is a slight difference in connotation; the English is often simpler, more explicit, or more expressive of powerful emotions.

The ending of Enest Hemingway's novel *A Farewell to Arms* is an example of the simplicity of short, native words. In this passage, only three words are not of native origin: *statue, hospital,* and *hotel.* The hero's sweetheart has died, and he has driven everyone from the room.

> But after I had got them out and shut the door and turned off the light it wasn't any good. It was like saying good-by to a statue. After a while I went out and left the hospital and walked back to the hotel in the rain.

> —Ernest Hemingway (1899–1961, American novelist),
> *A Farewell to Arms* (1929)

Some words we do not know, because they are archaic. We do not use them now, or not in the same sense they once had. In the ballad "Sir Patrick Spence" (page 402) an "eldern knight" is an elderly knight, and a "braid letter" is a large letter, one which contains official directions.

Technical Terms

Technical terms belong to the general class of learned words but are distinguished as being the language of a particular profession, business, or trade. Often technical words get into the ordinary language; examples are *tuberculosis, statis, carburetor, ignition, wavelength.* A great part of this book is devoted to the technical language of the arts. In each art some of the terms have become general knowledge, whereas others have remained terms for the specialist. In architecture, for instance, *cornice, pediment, column,* and *frieze* are fairly well known; *architrave, entablature, basilica,* and *clerestory* are more likely to be familiar only to specialists.

Idiom

Idiom is an arbitrary form of expression peculiar to one language or dialect. For instance, we say, "It's starting to rain" but not "It's stopping to rain." Some English speakers would say, "Let's not wait *for* Harry" while others would say "Let's not wait *on* Harry." We do not notice an idiom if it is familiar to us and correctly used. Boswell uses an idiom that is now obsolete when he says, "They then repaired to one of the neighboring taverns. . . ."

Dialect, Provincialisms

A dialect is the language of a certain part of a country, as, for instance, the Scottish dialect or the Irish dialect. A provincialism is a word or phrase peculiar to a province or a small section of a country; for example, "Y'all hurry back now" for "Come and see us soon."

New Words

Some words we are conscious of as new: *burglarized, extradited, edu cationist, tycoon*. Some of these become part of the permanent lan guage.

New meanings are constantly being given to words, or th meanings of words change. Some of these changes have come abou very gradually and naturally over a long period of time. The wor *treacle*, which now means "molasses," comes originally from th Greek θηριον *(therion)*, which means "wild beast." This change i meaning, though startling at first, has come about very naturally; th word was first used for anything that had to do with a wild anima then it came to mean the medicine that was good for the bite of a wil animal; and, since that medicine was usually sweet and sticky, i came to mean any sweet and sticky substance; hence, molasses. In th same way the word *hound*, which originally meant any kind of dog as it does today in German *(Hund)*, came to mean only a certain type

Modern writers often put two or more words together, as *toy colored, fatbellied, everloving*.

Often one word has several different meanings. A class of stu dents knew only that the word *bar* in Tennyson's "Crossing th Bar" meant some kind of a barrier. One said he knew it was not saloon but that it was something like that. Hence Tennyson's line "And may there be no moaning of the bar / When I put out to sea' were meaningless to him. Another such word is *macaroni*. In th eighteenth century a "macaroni" was a dandy, a man who got him self dressed in the very latest fashion. And so it makes sense wher we sing of Yankee Doodle that he "stuck a feather in his cap/And called it macaroni."

Similarly, the same thing may be called by one name in Grea Britain and a different one in the United States. Thus an elevator ir America becomes a *lift* in England; similarly, gasoline becomes *petrol*

Allusions

For finding meanings of words like those we have been discussing the dictionary is a safe recourse. Even if a single word is used ir several different senses, each use is recorded in the dictionary There is no such speedy help in the case of allusions. An allusion is an indirect reference to some place, person, event, quotation, or the like; the writer usually supposes that the readers will be familiar enough with it to recognize the allusion. In Milton's sonnet "On His Blindness" (page 57), there is an allusion to the parable of the talents in Matthew 25. A little further on we find another allusion, wher Milton has Patience say:

"God doth not need
Either man's work or his own gifts. Who best
Bear his mild yoke, they serve him best. His state
Is kingly: thousands at his bidding speed,
And post o'er land and ocean without rest;
They also serve who only stand and wait."

—John Milton (1608–1674, English poet),
"On His Blindness" (ca. 1655)

This is a clear allusion to the saying of Jesus, "For my yoke is easy and my burden is light."

A reference is an *explicit* mention of the same sort of subjects that an allusion implicitly mentions. For example, Wordsworth refers directly to Greek mythology when he wishes to

Have sight of Proteus rising from the sea,
Or hear old Triton blow his wreathed horn.

—William Wordsworth (1770–1850, British poet),
"The World Is Too Much with Us" (1807)

If he had omitted the actual names "Proteus" and "Triton," he would then have been alluding to these gods, not referring to them.

Connotations

The connotations of a word are the allied meanings or associated ideas that are called to mind when the word is used. The word *father*, for instance, has always had the same meaning: the male parent. Its connotations are love, kindliness, protection, greater experience, guidance, wisdom. Not all male parents show these qualities. Some fathers are cruel, unkind, foolish; but if one wants to make it clear that a father is of this kind, one must state the fact definitely, for the connotes culture, leisure, aristocracy, the future ministers of the *spinster* originally meant "a person who spins"; now it means "an unmarried woman" and has much the same connotations as *old maid*. The cowboy herds cattle, but the word *cowboy* connotes youth, bravery, adventure, and romance; *cattle herder* is merely a person who herds cattle. *Oxford* is much more than a town or university; it connotes culture, leisure, aristocracy, the future ministers of the British Empire.

Chaucer, in describing the Pardoner in *The Canterbury Tales*, says he "had hair as yellow as wax, but smooth it hung as does hank of flax." The comparisons leave the impression that his hai was also dirty, full of foreign particles as wax and flax are likely to be and uncombed, matted together like strands of flax. When Chauce says that the Miller had, on the very tip end of his nose, "a wart, an thereon stood a tuft of hairs, red as the bristles of a sow's ears," w know more than the color of those hairs. Almost the only good thin Chaucer has to say of the Friar is that "his eyes twinkled in his hea aright, as do the stars in the frosty night"—a comparison which somehow restores a little confidence in the man. It gives him a plac in the great out-of-doors, and helps us to understand the confidenc people had in him in spite of his worldliness.

IMAGERY

Examine the following lines:

St. Agnes' Eve—Ah, bitter chill it was!
The owl, for all his feathers, was a-cold;
The hare limp'd trembling through the frozen grass,
And silent was the flock in woolly fold:
Numb were the Beadsman's fingers, while he told
His rosary, and while his frosted breath,
Like pious incense from a censer old,
Seem'd taking flight for heaven, without a death,
Past the sweet Virgin's picture, while his prayer he saith.

> —John Keats (1795–1821, English poet),
>   "The Eve of St. Agnes" (1820)

From this stanza we get a much clearer sense of cold than if we wer told that the thermometer registered 10 below zero. The difference i that Keats has managed to make us conscious of the ways we ar conscious of cold. To some people these are almost like physical ex perience, and for everyone they have a certain vividness, as the call to mind the sensations described. Sense impressions of this kin are called "images." *Imagery* is the general name for the functionin of the imagination in the production of images. We may say that a image is the mental duplication of a sense impression. The mos common kind of imagery is visual: we are made to see what th author is talking about.

William Butler Yeats's short poem "When You Are Old" is fille with the poet's own highly personal imagery:

When you are old and gray and full of sleep,
And nodding by the fire, take down this book,
And slowly read, and dream of the soft look
Your eyes had once, and of their shadows deep;

How many loved your moments of glad grace,
And loved your beauty with love false or true,
But one man loved the pilgrim soul in you,
And loved the sorrows of your changing face;

And bending down beside the glowing bars,
Murmur, a little sadly, how Love fled
And paced upon the mountains overhead
And hid his face amid a crowd of stars.

> —William Butler Yeats (1865–1939, Irish poet),
>   "When You Are Old" (1892)[1]

Imagery is not all visual. The other senses may also be "duplicated" by means of images. In the last stanza of Walt Whitman's poem "To a Locomotive in Winter," we have vivid auditory and motor images in addition to visual ones.

Fierce-throated beauty!
Roll through my chant with all thy lawless music, thy swinging lamps at
night,
Thy madly-whistled laughter, echoing, rumbling like an earthquake,
rousing all,
Law of thyself complete, thine own track firmly holding,
(No sweetness debonair of tearful harp or glib piano thine,)
Thy trills of shrieks by rocks and hills return'd,
Launch'd o'er the prairies wide, across the lakes,
To the free skies unpent and glad and strong.

> —Walt Whitman (1819–1892, American poet),
>   "To a Locomotive in Winter" (1876)

Shakespeare's little song from *Love's Labour's Lost* (quoted on page 52) is outstanding for its clear auditory images as well as its visual images: the shepherd *blows* his nail, the owl sings "*tu-whit; tu-who,*" Joan *keels* ("stirs") the *pot*, *coughing drowns* the parson's sermon, and the roasted crab apples *hiss* in the bowl.

Motor images are important for various reasons. In addition to conveying the sense of movement, for whatever reasons the poet

---

[1] From *The Collected Poems of W. B. Yeats* (New York: Macmillan, 1903; rev. ed. 1956).

may have in mind (as in Whitman's poem "To a Locomotive in Winter," quoted above), they may convey a general sense of the limitless power of nature. Shelley's "Ode to the West Wind" is an example:

O wild West Wind, thou breath of Autumn's being,
Thou, from whose unseen presence the leaves dead
Are driven, like ghosts from an enchanter fleeing,

Yellow and black, and pale, and hectic red,
Pestilence-stricken multitudes: O thou,
Who chariotest to their wintry bed

The winged seeds, where they lie cold and low,
Each like a corpse within its grave, until
Thine azure sister of the Spring shall blow

Her clarion o'er the dreaming earth, and fill
(Driving sweet buds like flocks to feed in air)
With living hues and odors plain and hill:

Wild Spirit, which art moving everywhere;
Destroyer and preserver; hear, oh hear!

> —Percy Bysshe Shelly (1792–1822, English poet),
>   "Ode to the West Wind"

In Shelley's "To a Skylark," the flight of the bird symbolizes our possible freedom from earthly bonds and from the material aspects of earthly existence:

Higher still and higher
   From the earth thou springest
Like a cloud of fire;
   The blue deep thou singest,
And singing still dost soar, and soaring ever singest.

Keats is a poet who is oustanding for both the wealth and the vividness of his imagery. He has images even of such sensations as touch, taste, smell, and temperature, which are not usually considered of first importance. In "The Eve of St. Agnes," the lover spreads before his sleeping lady a table on which are heaped all sorts of delicacies. The scene is made vivid by a touch of the smooth linen and the creamy cheese, the taste of the candied apple and the syrups flavored with cinnamon; all these things are made romantic by the fact that they have been brought from a distance, "from silken Samarcand to cedared Lebanon."

And still she slept an azure-lidded sleep;
In blanched linen, smooth, and lavendered,
While he from forth the closet brought a heap
Of candied apple, quince, and plum, and gourd;
With jellies smoother than the creamy curd,

And lucent syrops, tinct with cinnamon;
Manna and dates, in argosy transferr'd
From Fez; and spiced dainties, every one.
From silken Samarcand to cedared Lebanon.

    —Keats, "The Eve of St. Agnes" (1820)

In his "Ode to a Nightingale," Keats wants to get away from the world

. . . where men sit and hear each other groan
Where palsy shakes a few sad, last, grey hairs . . .

and he imagines himself in a garden at night; he cannot see the flowers, but he knows they are there by the smells, which are much stronger than in the day:

I cannot see what flowers are at my feet,
  Nor what soft incense hangs upon the boughs,
But, in embalmed darkness, guess each sweet
  Wherewith the seasonable month endows
The grass, the thicket, and the fruit-tree wild;
White hawthord, and the pastoral eglantine;
  Fast-fading violets cover'd up in leaves;
    And mid-May's eldest child,
The coming musk-rose, full of dewy wine,
  The murmurous haunt of flies on summer eves.

    —Keats, "Ode to a Nightingale" (1819)

In fact, any sensation can be brought clearly before the mind in imagery.

FIGURES OF SPEECH

Words, being symbols, have no meaning in themselves; their only meaning is what is given to them by convention. Moreover, a symbol can never be specific; it is always abstract or general. We call words "abstract" or "concrete" as they signify abstractions or concrete objects; we say *truth* and *honor* are abstract, *dog* and *lilac* are concrete. But these concrete words are themselves abstractions in that they stand for a whole class of objects. The dog may be any one of a large number of species, of any known color. And when we say *lilac*, we may mean any variety of lilac, in any color, or any one of the other sensations concerned with lilac: its fragrance, the shape of the flower or the leaf, the bush on which the flower grows.

Because of this indefiniteness of words, there have grown up certain deviations, or roundabout methods of expression, that attempt to make more clear the exact meaning. If, for instance, Coleridge had simply mentioned ice that was green, he would have left it to us to imagine the shade of green; but he gives the exact shade when he says:

And ice, mast-high, came floating by,
As green as emerald.

   —Samuel Taylor Coleridge (1772–1834, British poet),
      The Rime of the Ancient Mariner (1798)

But he can make us realize even more clearly the color of hair, the feeling of fear, and the sound of the departing souls by stating his point indirectly:

Her lips were red, her looks were free,
Her locks were yellow as gold:
Her skin was as white as leprosy,
The Nightmare Life-in-Death was she,
Who thicks man's blood with cold.
Fear at my heart, as at a cup,
My life-blood seemed to sip!

The souls did from their bodies fly,—
They fled to bliss or woe!
And every soul, it passed me by,
Like the whizz of my cross-bow!

   —*The Rime of the Ancient Mariner*

Indirect methods of expression like these are called "figures of speech."

Simile and Metaphor

The most common, and therefore the most important, of the figures of speech are the simile and the metaphor. Both depend upon the comparison of one thing to another. The simile puts in the word of comparison; the metaphor leaves it out. The simile says: *The ice was as green as emerald;* the metaphor says: *The ice was emerald.* The simile says: *Fear was like a monster which sipped my blood;* the metaphor says: *Fear sipped my blood.* The simile would say: *Thou, Peter, art like a rock;* the metaphor says: *Thou art Peter, and upon this rock I will build my church.*

The simile says:

The pale purple even
   Melts around thy flight
Like a star of Heaven
   In the broad daylight
Thou art unseen, but yet I hear thy shrill delight

Keen as are the arrows
   Of that silver sphere,
Whose intense lamp narrows
   In the white dawn clear
Until we hardly see—we feel that it is there.

   —Shelley, "To a Skylark" (1820)

Shelley here directly compares the skylark to a "star of Heaven in the broad daylight" and its shrill delight to "the arrows of that silver sphere"—the star.

The metaphor says:

The Lord is my shepherd;
I shall not want.
He maketh me to lie down in green pastures:
He leadeth me beside the still waters.
He restoreth my soul:
He leadeth me in the paths of righteousness for his name's sake.

   —Psalm 23: 1–3

Keats uses metaphor in the first eight lines of his sonnet "On First Looking into Chapman's Homer" when he identifies poetry with rich kingdoms. In the last six lines he uses two similes as he tries to tell how he felt when he read Chapman's translation of Homer: first like an astronomer who has discovered a new planet; and second like Cortez when he discovered the Pacific.[2]

Much have I travell'd in the realms of gold,
And many goodly states and kingdoms seen;
Round many western islands have I been
Which bards in fealty to Apollo hold.
Oft of one wide expanse had I been told
That deep-brow'd Homer ruled as his demesne;
Yet did I never breathe its pure serene
Till I heard Chapman speak out loud and bold:
Then felt I like some watcher of the skies
When a new planet swims into his ken;
Or like stout Cortez when with eagle eyes
He stared at the Pacific—and all his men
Look'd at each other with a wild surmise—
Silent, upon a peak in Darien.

—Keats, "On First Looking into Chapman's Homer" (1816)

Many of our most common expressions involve similes or metaphors. We say one person has a "heart of gold" and another is as "slow as molasses in January." Both simile and metaphor are used very commonly by all people at all times. It is hard to find a paragraph of prose or verse that does not contain either a simile or a metaphor.

Both simile and metaphor are based on comparison. In each a comparison is made of one thing to something essentially unlike it for the purpose of showing one point of resemblance. The power of either figure of speech rises, of course, from the implications and suggestions of the comparison. In "A Song for Simeon," T. S. Eliot has a simile about an old man's life:

My life is light, waiting for the death wind,
Like a feather on the back of my hand.[3]

By comparison, Eliot emphasizes the everyday character of the scene, the sense of the nearness of death in everyday life. In another very

[2] A well-known mistake. It was, of course, Balboa, not Cortez, who was the first European to look upon the Pacific Ocean.
[3] From *Collected Poems, 1909–1962*, by T. S. Eliot, copyright 1936, by Harcourt, Brace Jovanovich, Inc. (New York); copyright 1963, 1964, by T. S. Eliot. Reprinted by permission of the publishers.

famous example, Eliot compares an evening to a patient on an operating table:

Let us go then, you and I,
When the evening is spread out against the sky
Like a patient etherized upon a table.

—T. S. Eliot (1888–1965, American poet),
"The Love Song of J. Alfred Prufrock" (1917)[4]

Other Figures of Speech

Next to simile and metaphor, perhaps the most important figures of speech are *metonymy* and *synecdoche*. The two terms are often used interchangeably, because synecdoche is a broader application of metonymy. In metonymy, we use one word for another that it will logically suggest and be related to; for example, the word *sceptre* or *crown* may be used to refer to the person who carries the sceptre or wears the crown.

Synecdoche includes this use of one word to suggest another, related term; but it goes further. In synecdoche a part is used to represent the whole, or the whole to represent a part. When one says that something will "bring my gray hairs down to the grave," a part of the body is being used to represent the whole body. Similarly, one may say that "the United States won the Davis Cup," meaning that the United States tennis team won it. Here the term for the whole (the United States) refers to a part of it (the tennis team).

There are several other ways of writing classed among the figures of speech: personification, apostrophe (address), hyperbole (exaggeration), litotes (understatement), antithesis (statement of contrasts), and irony. Irony is found in an expression which says one thing but really means the opposite, as when a man announces that he has good news when in reality he has bad news.

Three types of irony have been distinguished: irony of statement, irony of situation, and dramatic irony. An example of irony of statement was given when we mentioned speaking of bad news as good news. A famous example is found in Job's cry to his so-called comforters: "No doubt but ye are the people, and wisdom shall die with you." Another is found in Antony's funeral oration in Shakespeare's *Julius Caesar:*

Brutus is an honorable man;
So are they all, all honorable men.

[4] Ibid.

Swift is one of the greatest writers of irony. In the essay which he called "A Modest Proposal for Preventing the Children of Poor People from Being a Burden to Their Parents," he suggests that the babies of the Irish should be fattened and sold for meat.

Irony of situation, as the name indicates, makes a contrast between a situation as it is thought to be and as it is. Edwin Arlington Robinson's "Richard Cory" makes such a contrast:

Whenever Richard Cory went down town,
We people on the pavement looked at him;
He was a gentleman from sole to crown,
Clean favored, and imperially slim.

And he was always quietly arrayed,
And he was always human when he talked;
But still he fluttered pulses when he said,
"Good morning," and he glittered when he walked.

And he was rich—yes, richer than a king—
And admirably schooled in every grace:
In fine, we thought that he was everything
To make us wish that we were in his place.

So on we worked, and waited for the light,
And went without the meat, and cursed the bread;
And Richard Cory, one calm summer night,
Went home and put a bullet through his head.

> —Edwin Arlington Robinson (1869–1935, American poet),
>   "Richard Cory"[5]

Dramatic irony is found when the members of the audience have knowledge not held by the characters on the stage. A characteristic example is found in *Romeo and Juliet*, when Romeo tells of his happy dream and gives his assurance that all will be well. Because the audience knows that tragedy will follow, all the lovers' optimism and good faith are overshadowed by doom.

GRAMMAR

Knowing a language is not just a matter of knowing words. To get the sense of a passage, we must know how the words fit together as

---

[5] From *The Children of the Night,* by Edwin Arlington Robinson (New York: Charles Scribner's Sons, 1897).

well as the meaning of each word. The rules which state how words should fit together make up grammar, which is a statement of the accepted sense relationships of words. Each language has its own method of expression, its own way of putting words together to make sense—in short, its own grammar.

Those of us who have always spoken English have no difficulty with the usual simple arrangement of words. But often an author cannot express an idea clearly by using only the usual, simple arrangements, and so deliberately distorts. The opening lines of *Paradise Lost* are not easy reading, but through them Milton has made us realize the magnitude of the task he has set himself, and the exalted mood in which he is beginning it.

Of Man's first disobedience, and the fruit
Of that forbidden tree whose mortal taste
Brought death into the World, and all our woe,
With loss of Eden, till one greater Man
Restore us, and regain the blissful Seat,
Sing, Heavenly Muse, that, on the secret top
Of Oreb, or of Sinai, didst inspire
That shepherd who first taught the chosen seed
In the beginning how the heavens and earth
Rose out of Chaos: or, if Sion hill
Delight thee more, and Siloa's brook that flowed
Fast by the oracle of God, I thence
Invoke thy aid to my adventurous song,
That, with no middle flight intends to soar
Above th' Aonian mount, while it pursues
Things unattempted yet in prose or rhyme.

—Milton, *Paradise Lost*, 1, 1–16 (1667)

In this and in most older writing, the relationships among words are always in accordance with the established rules of grammar, though it may be hard to get the sense because of the way words and phrases are piled on one another. In some more recent poetry, the authors do not write in complete sentences; they achieve emphasis by a reference here and an exclamation there, and leave us to put them together. We tend to associate this sort of writing with contemporary poets, but it did not originate with them, as the following examples will show. The first, by Emily Dickinson, was written about 1862; the second, by Gerard Manley Hopkins, in 1875. Notice, in the poem by Dickinson, how the thoughts are compressed and the grammar is fragmented in the middle stanza.

After great pain, a formal feeling comes—
The Nerves sit ceremonious, like Tombs—
The stiff Heart questions was it He, that bore,
And Yesterday, or Centuries before?

The Feet, mechanical, go round—
Of Ground, or Air, or Ought—
A Wooden way
Regardless grown,
A Quartz contentment, like a stone—

This is the Hour of Lead—
Remembered, if outlived,
As Freezing persons, recollect the Snow—
First—Chill—then Stupor—then the letting go—

    —Emily Dickinson (1830–1886, American poet)[6]

But how shall I . . . make me room there:
Reach me a . . . Fancy, come faster—
Strike you the sight of it? look at it loom there,
Thing that she . . . there then! the Master,
Ipse, the only one, Christ, King, Head:
He was to cure the extremity where he had cast her;
Do, deal, lord it with living and dead;
Let him ride, her pride, in his triumph, despatch and have
done with his doom there.

    —Gerard Manley Hopkins (1844–1899, British poet),
      stanza 28 of "The Wreck of the *Deutschland*"[7]

It is true, however, that modern poets have carried this tendency to greater extremes. In much recent poetry, radical liberties are taken with grammar and sentence structure. Sometimes the poets abandon grammar altogether, presenting only images and hints that create an atmosphere in sound and rhythm. In the little poem "Water Faucet," on the opposite page, there is simply *no* grammar; the words have been put together so as to physically represent the subject. Here—as in much nonrepresentational painting and sculpture—the title itself provides important information.

[6] Copyright 1929 by Martha Dickinson Bianchi. Copyright © 1957 by Mary L. Hampson. From Thomas H. Johnson (ed.), *The Complete Poems of Emily Dickinson* (Boston and Toronto: Little Brown and Company, 1960.) Used by permission of Little, Brown and Company.
[7] W. H. Gardiner and N. H. MacKenzie (eds.), *The Poems of Gerard Manley Hopkins*, 4th ed. (New York: Oxford University Press, 1967).

WATER FAUCET

Smooothooooze
Dribble
Dribbledribble

Drop.

—Anonymous[8]

Notice in the first line how the repeated vowels and the running to-gether of words give us simultaneously an image, a feeling (from saying them), and the sound of the thing referred to; and in the next two lines how rhythm, consonants, and repetition of words tell us what is happening. Notice also how important the spacing of words and lines is to our experiencing the event in a controlled sequence. While certainly not a great poem, "Water Faucet" does illustrate some devices which have become commonplace in contemporary poetry.

We have already noted, in the discussion of Hopkins's "Pied Beauty" (page 18), how words may pile up and tumble out in excite-ment. These lines from "The Windhover," another poem by Hop-kins, are a striking example:

Brute beauty and valor and act, or, air, pride, plume here
Buckle! AND the fire that breaks from thee then, a billion
Times told lovelier, more dangerous, O my chevalier![9]

Another device which takes liberties with established usage is the formation of new words, such as "wanwood" and "leafmeal" in Hopkins's "Spring and Fall" (page 10). The use of *sounds* to convey meaning is also important. You will recall C. F. MacIntyre's remark-ing that he was careful in his translation of Rilke's "Spanish Dancer" (page 210) to get the "nine *k* sounds of the original in the second stanza" in order to "prepare the reader for the unmentioned casta-nets." Here Rilke, and in turn MacIntyre, is depending entirely on sounds to inform us that the dancer is keeping rhythm with castanets and what that rhythm is. Langston Hughes in "African Dance" (page 199) depends almost entirely upon sounds and rhythm, created and

---

[8] From David R. Pichaske (ed.), *Beowulf to Beatles: Approaches to Poetry* (New York: The Free Press, a division of Macmillan Publishing Company, Inc., 1972), p. 194.
[9] Gardiner and MacKenzie, op. cit.

controlled by his spacing of words on the page, for the image in th
first stanza:

The low beating of the tom-toms,
   The slow beating of the tom-toms,
   Low . . . slow
   Slow . . . low—
Stirs your blood.

It is said of some piano pieces that they "feel good" to the fingers
when they are played—the fingers literally dance them. Just so,
there are sound patterns, combinations, which naturally feel good to
say; the lips, tongue, and ear enjoy them for their own sake. When
such patterns reinforce or act out a meaning, we experience a sense
of having shared in the creation of the poem.

These, then, are some of the devices we must be on the alert for
in reading poetry. We should read it aloud or at least hear it in our
imagination to savor the paralleling and interplay of sound, rhythm,
and meaning. And we must not read it as we do prose, expecting that
what it has to say will be given to us discursively, item following
item in logical order, until its meaning is clear. Poetry—and this is
one of the things which make it an art and set it apart from workaday
prose—is a presentational art. That is, like painting, which is also a
presentational art, it *presents* us images, sounds, bits of information,
rhythms which we take in, as we do aspects of a painting, reflect on,
synthesize, put together in some meaning. These departures from
ordinary, conventional usage of language are sometimes called
"poetic license," a term which conveys the idea that poets can do
what they will with language as long as it pleases and has meaning.
The enjoyment of art does not, as some people believe, arise automatically from putting oneself in its presence passively. Enjoyment
of art comes from active participation, and there is no art of which
this is more true than poetry.

From this discussion of words and grammar, several points of
importance emerge. The first is that it is essential to know the meanings of words and to understand their relationships. It is not necessary to know the grammatical name for any relationship. It is only a
matter of convenience that we say *John* is the subject and *Henry* is the
object in the sentence "John struck Henry" but it does matter that
we know how to indicate who got hit. And it does matter that when
we sing of "macaroni" in "Yankee Doodle," we do not think of a dish
of wheat paste and cheese.

The second point is that an author who departs from the simplest form of words and of sentence structure does so for a purpose.

The change from normal word order in literature is exactly the same as distortion in the visual arts. Good writers do not fail to write simply—or good artists to draw realistically—because they do not know how, but because they can express what they have to say better in another form. And our question here is just the same as it was in the case of distortions: Why is it done this way? In the opening lines of *Paradise Lost*, the effect is like that of an organ that begins quietly and gathers momentum until it finally bursts out into full diapason with the rolling "Sing, Heavenly Muse!" When Keats says "some watcher of the sky" instead of the more commonplace *astronomer*, he makes us think of the long, lonely hours the man spends gazing at the stars before his faith is rewarded and he sees a planet "swim into his ken."

12 ELEMENTS OF LITERATURE— SOUND

ELEMENTS OF SOUND

The sound of words is important in making the total sense, for no two words, no two sounds, ever have exactly the same meaning. In *The Two Gentlemen of Verona* there is a little song that begins:

Who is Silvia? What is she,
  That all our swains commend her?
Holy, fair, and wise is she;
  The heaven such grace did lend her,
That she might admired be.

—William Shakespeare (1564–1616, British poet and dramatist),
  The Two Gentlemen of Verona, IV, ii, 39–43 (ca. 1592)

Here the name *Silvia* ostensibly is only a name; but actually it has two important qualities. On the one hand, it suggests a wood nymph, and elusiveness. But more important, it is part of the poet's alliterative scheme, in which the letter s plays a major part—it occurs twice in line 1, once in line 2, twice in line 3, and once each in lines 4 and 5. The poet, like the painter, chooses each element carefully; if we were to change the name *Silvia* to almost any other woman's name—Alice, Peggy, Margaret, Louise, Phoebe, Laura, Hortense— the effect would be spoiled, the charm gone. Or take a single line from Milton:

And I shall shortly be with them that rest.

—John Milton (1608–1674, British poet and essayist),
Samson Agonistes, line 598 (1671)

Change the sound, keeping as nearly as possible the same sense. *Shortly* means *soon; them* has the same meaning as *those;* and *that* as *who;* in fact, *those who* is a more common English idiom than *them that.* Make the substitutions, and the line reads:

And I shall soon be with those who rest.

There is no appreciable difference in sense, but the line is no longer the same kind of poetry.

It is important, therefore, to know what effects are derived primarily from the sound of words. There are three categories under which we can study the uses of sound in literature:

1. The sound of letters and words: tone color
2. The sequence of sounds in a free pattern of accents: rhythm
3. The sequence of sounds in a fixed pattern of accents: meter

Tone Color—Definition

The literary term *tone color* is borrowed from music; the writer achieves effects somewhat comparable to those of different instruments by the sounds of the words or letters used. Compare the opening lines of Blake's "Introduction" to *Songs of Innocence* with the opening lines of "The Congo," by Vachel Lindsay, for contrast in tone color. The first seems to have the timbre of a high-pitched, sensitive, delicate instrument, such as the flute; this matches the spirit of the piece. The second has the sound of a deep, heavy instrument, like a drum or a tuba, which has an intense, insistent, powerful beat.

Piping down the valleys wild,
  Piping songs of pleasant glee,
On a cloud I saw a child,
  And he laughing said to me:

"Pipe a song about a Lamb!"
  So I piped with merry cheer.
"Piper, pipe that song again;"
  So I piped; he wept to hear.

—William Blake (1757–1827, British poet, painter, and engraver),
"Introduction" to *Songs of Innocence* (1787)

Fat black bucks in a wine-barrel room,
Barrel-house kings, with feet unstable,
Sagged and reeled and pounded on the table,
Pounded on the table,
Beat an empty barrel with the handle of a broom,
Hard as they were able,
Boom, boom, BOOM,
With a silk umbrella and the handle of a broom,
Boomlay, boomlay, boomlay, BOOM.

> —Vachel Lindsay (1879–1931, American poet),
> "The Congo," opening lines (1914)[1]

Three Types of Tone Color

All the effects of tone color depend on repetition. It may be repetition
(1) of words, (2) of sentences or phrases, or (3) of single sounds.

Repetition of words   The simplest and clearest example of tone color
is the repetition of words. The repetition of a word, though it may
become wearisome, is one of the most effective devices in literature.
In the "Introduction" to *Songs of Innocence*, for example, the reitera-
tion of the word *pipe* emphasizes the childlike quality of the verse.
  Mark Antony's famous funeral oration in Shakespeare's *Julius
Caesar* (Act III, Scene II) is a good example of the use of repetition to
achieve an effect. This is the speech beginning "Friends, Romans,
Countrymen, lend me your ears":

Here, under leave of Brutus and the rest,—
For Brutus is an honorable man;
So are they all, all honorable men,—
Come I to speak in Caesar's funeral.
He was my friend, faithful and just to me:
But Brutus says he was ambitious;
And Brutus is an honorable man.
He hath brought many captives home to Rome,
Whose ransoms did the general coffers fill:
Did this in Caesar seem ambitious?
When that the poor have cried, Caesar hath wept;
Ambition should be made of sterner stuff:
Yet Brutus says he was ambitious;
And Brutus is an honorable man. . . .

By the constant, ironic repetition of the phrases "honorable man"
and "ambitious," contrasted with Antony's version of Caesar's life,
a remarkable dramatic effect is created.

[1] By permission of Macmillan Publishing Company, Inc. (New York).

Repetition of sentences or phrases   In the device known as anaphora, a group of words or a sentence is repeated. In the last act of Shakespeare's *Merchant of Venice*, Lorenzo and Jessica have arrived at Belmont and are waiting for the return of Portia and the others. As they wait, they play a game in which they picture other lovers. Each speech begins with *In such a night*; the phrase serves as a musical motive and a constant reminder of the beauty of the scene.

Lorenzo	The moon shines bright. In such a night as this,
	When the sweet wind did gently kiss the trees
	And they did make no noise, in such a night
	Troilus methinks mounted the Troyan walls,
	And sigh'd his soul toward the Grecian tents,
	Where Cressid lay that night.
Jessica	In such a night
	Did Thisbe fearfully o'ertrip the dew,
	And saw the lion's shadow ere himself
	And ran dismay'd away.
Lorenzo	In such a night
	Stood Dido with a willow in her hand
	Upon the wild sea banks, and waft her love
	To come again to Carthage.
Jessica	In such a night
	Medea gathered the enchanted herbs
	That did renew old Aeson.
Lorenzo	In such a night
	Did Jessica steal from the wealthy Jew,
	And with an unthrift love did run from Venice
	As far as Belmont.
Jessica	In such a night
	Did young Lorenzo swear he lov'd her well,
	Stealing her soul with many vows of faith
	And ne'er a true one.
Lorenzo	In such a night
	Did pretty Jessica, like a little shrew
	Slander her love, and he forgave it her.
Jessica	I would out-night you, did no body come;
	But hark, I hear the footing of a man.

—Shakespeare, *The Merchant of Venice*, V, i, 1–24 (ca. 1595)

Winston Churchill's famous address to the Commons after Dunkirk, on June 4, 1940, makes constant use of the phrase *We shall fight.*

We shall go on to the end, we shall fight in France, we shall fight on the seas and oceans, we shall fight with growing confidence and growing strength in

the air, we shall defend our Island, whatever the cost may be, we shall figh
on the beaches, we shall fight on the landing grounds, we shall fight in th
fields and in the streets, we shall fight in the hills; we shall never surrende
and even if, which I do not for a moment believe, this Island or a large pa
of it were subjugated and starving, then our Empire beyond the seas, arme
and guarded by the British Fleet, would carry on the struggle, until, in God
good time, the New World, with all its power and might, steps forth to th
rescue and the liberation of the old.

> —Winston Churchill (1874–1965, British statesman),
> *Dunkirk:* Address to Commons, June 4, 1940

Ferlinghetti's poem "I Am Waiting," from the collection *A Cone*
Island of the Mind, emphasizes impatient waiting for a renaissance o
wonder by the constant repetition of the words *I am waiting*, wit
almost the effect of an orator's plea:

and I am waiting
for the American Eagle
to really spread its wings
and straighten up and fly right
and I am waiting
for the Age of Anxiety
to drop dead
and I am waiting
for the war to be fought
which will make the world safe
for anarchy
and I am waiting
for the final withering away
of all governments
and I am perpetually awaiting
a rebirth of wonder

> —Lawrence Ferlinghetti (1919–   , American poet),
> "I Am Waiting"[2]

Repetition of single sounds   Subtle examples of tone color are found
when single sounds are repeated. These sounds are usually single
letters. They are not always the same letters, however, for often two
letters have the same sound (*c*orner, *k*ick), and some single letter
have two sounds (*c*orner, *c*edar). Beside rhyme, there are three type
of tone color based on the repetition of single sounds: alliteration
assonance, and consonance.

Alliteration is the repetition of accepted sounds that begin words
*P*eter *P*iper *p*icked a *p*eck of *p*ickled *p*eppers. When used to extreme
as in the Peter Piper rhyme, alliteration, may become obnoxious; bu

---

[2] Lawrence Ferlinghetti, *A Coney Island of the Mind.* Copyright © 1958 by Lawrence Ferlinghetti
Reprinted by permission of New Directions Publishing Corporation (New York).

when well used, it is pleasing. The use of alliteration is almost universal. Here is an example:

Once upon a midnight dreary, while I pondered weak and weary,
Over many a quaint and curious volume of forgotten lore—
While I nodded, nearly napping, suddenly there there came a tapping,
As of someone gently rapping, rapping at my chamber door.
" 'Tis some visitor," I muttered, "tapping at my chamber door—
Only this and nothing more."

. . . .

Deep into that darkness peering, long I stood there wondering, fearing,
Doubting, dreaming dreams no mortal ever dared to dream before;
But the silence was unbroken, and the stillness gave no token,
And the only word there spoken was the whispered word, "Lenore!"
This I whispered, and an echo murmured back the word, "Lenore!"
    Merely this and nothing more.

. . . .

Open here I flung the shutter, when, with many a flirt and flutter
In there stepped a stately raven of the saintly days of yore.
Not the least obeisance made he; not a minute stopped or stayed he;
But, with mein of lord or lady, perched above my chamber door—
Perched upon a bust of Pallas just above my chamber door—
    Perched, and sat, and nothing more.

    —Edgar Allan Poe (1809–1848, American poet and short story writer),
      "The Raven" (1845)

In these passages from "The Raven," alliteration is liberally sprinkled throughout; *weak* and *weary; quaint* and *curious; nodded, nearly,* and *napping; doubting, dreaming,* and *dreams; dared* and *dream; silence* and *stillness,* etc. The passage from "The Congo" quoted on page 292 also has alliteration: *b*lack, *b*ucks, *b*arrel, *b*eat, *b*room, *b*oom, *b*oomlay.

    Assonance is the effect obtained from the repetition of accented vowel sounds, as in f*oo*lish, cr*oo*ning; r*a*ce, m*a*ke; fr*ee* and *ea*sy; m*a*d as a h*a*tter. The effects to be gained from assonance are delicate and varied.

Break, break, break,
    On thy cold gray stones, O Sea!
And I would that my tongue could utter
    The thoughts that arise in me.

    —Alfred, Lord Tennyson (1809–1892, British poet),
      "Break, Break, Break" (1842)

In the second line of this stanza, for example, the words do not themselves express any great grief, yet we have a sense almost of desolation. The explanation is to be found in assonance. *Oh* is universally a cry of grief and mourning; the person who cannot be consoled laments *Oh, oh, oh.* Tennyson uses the word *O* only once, but he repeats the sound two other times in the short line:

On they cold gray stones, O Sea!

In popular speech we use assonance in expressions like *time out of mind* and *slap-dash.*

Consonance is sometimes called "slant" rhyme. *Consonance* is a general term for the effects produced by the repetition of accented consonant sounds when one of them is not at the beginning of a word. Often both consonants occur at the ends of the words, as in o*dds* and en*ds* or stru*ts* and fre*ts.*

Consonance is not nearly so obvious as alliteration and is not so common, but it produces many subtle effects. In the verses from "The Raven" quoted above, we find *napping* and *tapping; dreary* and *weary; rapping* and *tapping; peering, wondering,* and *fearing; shutter* and *flutter; unbroken* and *token,* etc.

Our examples of alliteration and assonance have necessarily come from traditional poetry, particularly from the writers of the nineteenth century, who often used almost pictorial devices and exaggerated effects. Contemporary poets like Elizabeth Bishop, Delmore Schwartz, Stanley Kunitz, and Theodore Roethke create their most picturesque effects in a much less elaborate, but equally effective, manner. The passage by Elizabeth Bishop quoted on page 31, from her "Little Exercise," is as atmospheric as anything in Poe or Tennyson:

Think of the storm roaming the sky uneasily like a dog looking for a place to sleep in. Listen to it growling.

Rhyme   Two words are said to rhyme when they are identical in sound from the vowel of the accented syllable to the end, provided the sounds that precede the accented vowel are not identical. *Cry, buy; face, place; sorrow, tomorrow; running, cunning*—these words rhyme. *Wright, write, right* do not rhyme, because the letters before the accented vowel do not differ in sound. *Reason* and *pleasing* do not rhyme, because they are not identical in the syllables following the accented vowel. A rhyme is said to be "masculine" if the rhyming portion of the words is a single syllable, and "feminine" if the rhyming portion is more than one syllable. *Cry, buy* and *face, place* are masculine rhymes. *Sorrow, tomorrow,* and *cunning, running* are feminine rhymes.

Ryhme usually comes at the end of a line and follows a set pattern. Rhyme is indicated by the letters of the alphabet, *a* being used for the first rhyming word, *b* for the second, *c* for the third, etc.

My heart leaps up when I behold	*a*
A rainbow in the sky:	*b*
So was it when my life began;	*c*
So is it now I am a man,	*c*
So be it when I shall grow old	*a*
Or let me die!	*b*
The Child is father of the Man:	*c*
And I could wish my days to be	*d*
Bound each to each by natural piety.	*d*

—William Wordsworth (1770–1850, British poet), "My Heart Leaps Up" (1802)

If a poem is divided into stanzas, the same rhyme pattern will usually be used in each stanza. In the "Introduction" to *Songs of Innocence,* all the stanzas rhyme *abcb* except the first, which rhymes *abab.*

A great deal of poetry, of course, does not rhyme. There is no rhyme, for example, in the passage from Shakespeare's *Merchant of Venice* quoted on page 293.

As early as the nineteenth century, rhyme as such began to disappear from a great deal of poetry. A good example is the work of the American poet Walt Whitman, whose elegy for Abraham Lincoln, "When Lilacs Last in the Dooryard Bloomed," begins:

When lilacs last in the dooryard bloomed,
And the great star early droop'd in the western sky in the night,
I mourn'd, and yet shall mourn with ever-returning spring.

Ever-returning spring, trinity sure to me you bring,
Lilac blooming perennial and dropping star in the west,
And thought of him I love . . .

—Whitman, "When Lilacs Last in the Dooryard Bloomed" (1865, 1881)

Since the time of Whitman we have learned not to look for rhyme and to accept poetry for its other virtues and beauties, for its expression of profound and universal feelings, for its presentation of eternal truths in a new, less mannered, form. Here is an example from a contemporary poet, Stanley Kunitz, of expression of a universal emotion—the sense of loss. The lines are from Kunitz's "Father and Son":

Now in the suburbs and the falling light
I followed him, and now down sandy road
Whiter than bone-dust through the sweet
Curdle of fields, where the plums
Dropped with their load of ripeness, one by one.
Mile after mile I followed, with skimming feet,
After the secret master of my blood,
Him, steeped in the odor of ponds, whose indomitable love
Kept me in chains. Strode years; stretched into bird;
Raced through the sleeping country where I was young,
The silence unrolling before me as I came,
The night nailed like an orange to my brow.

—Stanley Kunitz (1905–   , American poet)[3]

Rhythm

Rhythm as defined in *A Prosody Handbook*, by Karl Shapiro and Robert Beum, is "the total quality of a line's motion, and is the product of several elements, not of stress and quantity alone." Shapiro and Beum say later, "Probably no two lines of poetry, and no two sentences of prose, have exactly the same rhythm."[4] Rhythm is found in all literature, as in all music; and it is the same in literature as in music.

To a certain extent all speech is rhythmic, for it is grouped in phrases; only a child just learning to read gives the same emphasis to every word. However, some speech is more rhythmic than other speech; the term *rhythmic* is usually reserved for that speech which excites the ear.

Compare the rhythms of these three examples. In the first, one has a disagreeable sense of being constantly jerked up; one cannot get into the swing of the sentence; there are no pauses. But the passages from Carlyle and Stevenson are, in contrast, very rhythmic.

Mr. Davies does not let his learning cause him to treat the paintings as material only to be studied by the Egyptologist with a critical and scientific eye.

[3] From *Selected Poems: 1928–1958* by Stanley Kunitz. Copyright © 1958 by Stanley Kunitz. By permission of Little, Brown and Company (Boston) in association with the Atlantic Monthly Press.
[4] Karl Shapiro and Robert Beum, *A Prosody Handbook* (New York: Harper and Row, 1965), p. 60.

The young spirit has awakened out of Eternity, and knows not what we mean by Time; as yet Time is no fast-hurrying stream, but a sportful sunlit ocean; years to the child are as ages. . . . Sleep on, thou fair Child, for thy long rough journey is at hand! A little while, and thou too shalt sleep no more, but thy very dreams shall be mimic battles; thou too, with old Arnauld, wilt have to say in stern patience: "Rest? Rest? Shall I not have all Eternity to rest in?"

—Thomas Carlyle (1795–1881, English philosopher and essayist),
  Sartor Resartus(1833)

And as we dwell, we living things, in our isle of terror and under the imminent hand of death, God forbid it should be man the erected, the reasoner, the wise in his own eyes—God forbid it should be man that wearies in well-doing, that despairs of unrewarded effort, or utters the language of complaint. Let it be enough for faith, that the whole creation groans in mortal frailty, strives with unconquerable constancy: Surely not all in vain.

—Robert Louis Stevenson (1850–1894, Scottish poet, novelist, and
  essayist), *Pulvis et Umbra*

These examples are prose, but rhythm is of course found in poetry as well. Often the phrase is practically identical to the line, as in the following:

Shall I, wasting in despair,
Die, because a woman's fair?
Or make pale my cheeks with care,
'Cause another's rosy are?
Be she fairer than the day.
Or the flowery meads in May!
  If she be not so to me,
  What care I how fair she be?

—George Wither (1588–1667, British poet),
  "Shall I Wasting in Despair"

More often, however, the phrase is not the same as the line. It may end in the middle of a line, or it may carry over from line to line. Note how Tennyson varies the rhythmic effects in the last lines of "Ulysses":

Come, my friends.
'Tis not too late to seek a newer world.
Push off, and sitting well in order smite
The sounding furrows; for my purpose holds

To sail beyond the sunset, and the baths
Of all the western stars, until I die.
It may be that the gulfs will wash us down;
It may be we shall touch the Happy Isles,
And see the great Achilles, whom we knew.
Tho' much is taken, much abides; and tho'
We are not now that strength which in old days
Moved earth and heaven, that which we are, we are,—
One equal temper of heroic hearts,
Made weak by time and fate, but strong in will
To strive, to seek, to find, and not to yield.

—Tennyson, "Ulysses" (1842)

Meter

English is a language of pronounced word accent. Words of more than one syllable have at least one accent. Words such as *dismay*, *avoid*, *content* have the accent on the second syllable. A few words of two syllables, such as *baseball* and *blackbird*, have accents on both syllables. *November, lemonade, vertical, butterfly* have three syllables each. In *November*, the accent is on the second syllable, in *lemonade* on the third, and in *vertical* on the first. *Butterfly* has accents on the first and third syllables. *Commemorate* has four syllables, with a primary accent on the second syllable and a secondary accent on the last syllable.

Sometimes a poet puts words together so that these accents come in a regular order. Take, for instance, the lines quoted from Tennyson's "Ulysses." The accented and unaccented syllables tend to alternate—first an unaccented, then an accented syllable. The last two lines are absolutely regular:

Made weak by time and fate, but strong in will
To strive, to seek, to find, and not to yield.

This pattern is not kept with absolute regularity throughout the poem, but it is sufficiently regular for us to recognize it.

Any such regular recurrence of accent is called "meter." The meter in which an unaccented syllable is followed by an accented syllable is known as *iambic*. It is so common as almost to be the universal meter of English poetry, but there are other meters. The accent may come on the first syllable instead of the second, as here:

Jenny kissed me when we met,
   Jumping from the chair she sat in;

Time; you thief, who love to get
  Sweets into your list, put that in:
Say I'm weary, say I'm sad,
  Say that health and wealth have missed me,
Say I'm growing old, but add,
  Jenny kissed me.

> —Leigh Hunt (1784–1859, British journalist, essayist, and poet),
> "Rondeau" (1838)

Or the accent may fall on every third instead of every second syllable. It may fall on the third, sixth, and ninth syllables, as in "Annabel Lee":

It was many and many a year ago,
  In a kingdom by the sea,
That a maiden there lived, whom you may know
  By the name of Annabel Lee;
And this maiden she lived with no other thought
  Than to love and be loved by me.

> —Poe, "Annabel Lee" (1849)

It may come on the first, fourth, and seventh syllables, as in these lines:

Just for a handful of silver he left us,
  Just for a riband to stick in his coat—
Found the one gift of which fortune bereft us,
  Lost all the others she lets us devote . . .

> —Robert Browning (1812–1889, British poet),
> "The Lost Leader" (1845)

Each of these meters is identified by the pattern of accented and unaccented syllables, and the unit is called a "foot."

Types of feet The names and symbols of the meters may be tabulated with ∪ for an unaccented syllable, and / for an accented one.

Iambic: ∪ /

∪ / ∪ / ∪ /
To strive, to seek, to find

Trochaic: / ∪

/ ∪ / ∪
Jenny kissed me

Anapestic: ∪ ∪ /

∪ ∪ / ∪ ∪ / ∪ ∪ / ∪ /
It was many and many a year ago

Dactylic: / ∪ ∪

/ ∪ ∪ / ∪ ∪ / ∪
Just for a handful of silver

A spondaic foot, called a "spondee," is composed of two accented syllables. For obvious reasons the spondee cannot be used in an entire poem or even in an entire line. It is one of the important ways of introducing variety. It emphasizes by slowing up the speed of the line. Milton, for instance, uses spondees in *Paradise Lost* to stress the enormous size of Satan:

So stretched out huge in length the Arch-*Fiend lay*.

—Milton, *Paradise Lost*, I, 209 (1667)

And in "Ulysses," Tennyson emphasizes the slow passage of time by substituting spondees for iambs:

The long *day wanes;* the slow *moon climbs;* the deep
Moans round with many voices.

The length of a line is named according to the number of feet in it.

One foot—Monometer
Two feet—Dimeter
Three feet—Trimeter
Four feet—Tetrameter
Five feet—Pentameter
Six feet—Hexameter
Seven feet—Heptameter
Eight feet—Octameter

Trimeter, tetrameter, and pentameter are the line lengths most commonly used. The lines just quoted from "Ulysses" are pentameter; "The Lost Leader" is in tetrameter; "Rondeau" is in tetrameter until the last line, which is dimeter; "Annabel Lee" alternates tetrameter and trimeter. Ordinarily a line is designated by the kind of foot and the number of feet in a line, as iambic tetrameter, spondaic pentameter, etc.

As we have already pointed out, many of the traditional devices of poetry—the assonantal and consonantal relationships, the intricate rhyming schemes—are not much used in contemporary poetry. The same can be said of the various metrical devices just examined; many modern poets do not use them. The rhythms of the contemporary poet are likely to be subtler, more personal. The metrical schemes in the tortured poetry of Delmore Schwartz are an example of modern usage; another example is this shocking short poem by Randall Jarrell:

From my mother's sleep I fell into the State,
And I hunched in its belly till my wet fur froze.
Six miles from earth, loosed from its dream of life,
I woke to black flak and the nightmare fighters.
When I died they washed me out of the turret with a hose.

—Randall Jarrell (1914–1965, American poet),
"The Death of the Ball Turret Gunner" (1945)[5]

The reader will have noticed that Jarrell's poem, although the meter is not regular, does contain a rhyme; and it should be mentioned that many traditional poetic devices are still to be found, so that an understanding of them remains useful in approaching contemporary as well as older poetry.

VERSE FORM

In traditional poetry, a poet usually decides on a kind of meter, a line length, and a rhyme scheme and sticks pretty closely to that combination throughout the poem. This is called the "verse form." Since the passage we read from "Ulysses" is in iambic pentameter without rhyme, we expect the entire poem to be in that verse form, and it is. Similarly, we expect Poe to keep to stanzas of six lines of anapestic verse alternating tetrameter and trimeter, with the even lines rhyming.

[5] Reprinted with the permission of Farrar, Straus and Giroux, Inc. (New York), from *The Complete Poems* by Randall Jarrell, copyright 1945 by Randall Jarrell, copyright renewed 1973 by Mary von Schrader Jarrell.

Traditional Forms

A traditional poet may make a new verse form but usually does not. Some forms have been used so much that they have been given names by which they may be easily identified. The number of named forms is too great for a complete list to be given here, but a few of the more common terms are these:

I. General terms
  A. *Couplet:* any stanza of two lines.
  B. *Triplet:* any stanza of three lines.
  C. *Quatrain:* any stanza of four lines.
II. Specific terms
  A. *Ballad meter:* four lines of iambic verse alternating tetrameter and trimeter. Rhyme *abab,* or *abcb.* Commonly used in ballads. Also called "common meter" from its use in hymns. Traditionally the most popular of all quatrains.

She dwelt among the untrodden ways
  Beside the springs of Dove,
A Maid whom there were none to praise
  And very few to love:

A violet by a mossy stone
  Half hidden from the eye!
—Fair as a star, when only one
  Is shining in the sky.

She lived unknown, and few could know
  When Lucy ceased to be;
But she is in her grave, and, oh,
  The difference to me!

　　　—Wordsworth, "Lucy" (1800)

  B. *Sonnet:* fourteen lines of iambic pentameter. The sonnet is one of the most elegant and subtle poetic forms. Within the short space of its fourteen lines, the poet can project an emotional universe. This form is the product of the late Middle Ages in Italy (Petrarch, in the fourteenth century) and the early seventeenth century in England (the age of Shakespeare). Ordinarily, the poet states an idea in the first eight lines (the octave) and gives an explanation or an answer in the last six (the sestet). There are two types of sonnet, distinguished by their rhymes.

    1. Italian, or Petrarchan: *abba abba* (octave); *cde cde* or *cdcdcd* (sestet).

The world is too much with us: late and soon,
Getting and spending, we lay waste our powers.
Little we see in Nature that is ours;
We have given our hearts away, a sordid boon!
This Sea that bares her bosom to the moon;
The winds that will be howling at all hours,
And are up-gathered now like sleeping flowers;
For this, for everything, we are out of tune;
It moves us not.—Great God! I'd rather be
A Pagan suckled in a creed outworn;
So might I, standing on this pleasant lea,
Have glimpses that would make me less forlorn;
Have sight of Proteus rising from the sea;
Or hear old Triton blow his wreathed horn.

—Wordsworth, "The World Is Too Much with Us" (1807)

2. English, or Shakespearean: three quatrains with alternating
rhyme and a couplet.

Let me not to the marriage of true minds
Admit impediments. Love is not love
Which alters when it alteration finds,
Or bends with the remover to remove.

Oh, no! it is an ever-fixèd mark
That looks on tempests and is never shaken;
It is the star to every wand'ring bark,
Whose worth's unknown, although his height be taken.

Love's not Time's fool, though rosy lips and cheeks
Within his bending sickle's compass come;
Love alters not with his brief hours and weeks,
But bears it out even to the edge of doom.

If this be error and upon me proved,
I never writ, nor no man ever loved.

—Shakespeare, Sonnet 116 (published 1609)

C. *Spenserian stanza:* eight lines of iambic pentameter followed by
one of iambic hexameter. Rhyme *abab bcbcc*. A graceful verse
invented by Spenser for *The Faerie Queene*.

And more to lulle him in his slumber soft,
A trickling streame from high rock tumbling downe,
And ever-drizling raine upon the loft,

Mixt with a murmuring winde, much like the sowne
Of swarming Bees, did cast him in a swowne.
No other noyse, nor peoples troublous cryes,
As still are wont t'annoy the walled towne,
Might there be heard; but carlesse Quiet lyes
Wrapt in eternall silence farre from enimyes.

> —Edmund Spenser (1552–1599, British poet),
> *The Faerie Queen*, I, i, 41 (1590)

D. *Blank verse:* unrhymed iambic pentameter.

When I see birches bend to left and right
Across the line of straighter darker trees,
I like to think some boy's been swinging them.
But swinging doesn't bend them down to stay . . .

> —Robert Frost (1875–1963, American poet),
> from "Birches" (1916)[6]

Other Types of Verse

Accentual verse   This is verse that holds to a fixed number of accents
in a line. Old English poetry was of this type; there were usually four
accents to each line. In the second section of "Ash-Wednesday,"
T. S. Eliot has used this meter successfully, two accents to a line:

Lady of silences
Calm and distressed
Torn and most whole
Rose of memory
Rose of forgetfulness.

> —T. S. Eliot (1888–1965, American poet),
> "Ash-Wednesday" (1930)[7]

Free verse   Free verse is built on the rhythm of phrase. Its unit is
the strophe, a separate section of extended movement within a poem.
Unlike the stanza, which is a group of lines repeating a given met-

[6] From *The Poetry of Robert Frost* edited by Edward Connery Lathem. Copyright 1916, 1923, 1938,
© 1967, 1969 by Holt, Rinehart and Winston. Copyright 1936, 1944, 1951 by Robert Frost. Copyright © 1964 by Lesley Frost Ballantine. Reprinted by permission of Holt, Rinehart and Winston,
Publishers. (New York).
[7] From *Collected Poems 1909–1962* by T. S. Eliot, copyright 1936 by Harcourt, Brace Jovanovich, Inc.
(New York); copyright 1963, 1964 by T. S. Eliot. Reprinted by permission of the publishers.

rical pattern, the strophe does not have to be any fixed length. It is composed of a number of phrases subtly balanced so as to constitute a complete cadence. Whitman's "When Lilacs Last in the Dooryard Bloomed," from which we have already quoted two opening verses of three lines each (page 297), continues with a five-line verse:

O powerful western fallen star!
O shades of night—O moody tearful night!
O great star disappear'd—O the black murk that hides the star!
O cruel hands that hold me powerless—O helpless soul of me!
O harsh surrounding cloud that will not free my soul.

By now we can take it for granted that great poetry need not have alliteration, assonance, rhyme, traditional regular rhythms, or even fixed stanza patterns. Here, not only does Whitman give us a five-line stanza after two three-line stanzas; he continues with units having six lines, eight, seven, thirteen, etc. Each strophe seems to have a different emotional quality and a purpose of its own, and the poet is free to use whatever form is most suitable at different stages of the poem.

Hebrew meter   Hebrew meter is often classed with free verse; it is based on parallelism of phrases, one clause or phrase being balanced against another of similar structure. It is, of course, found most conspicuously in the Bible.

Purge me with hyssop, and I shall be clean;
Wash me, and I shall be whiter than snow.
Make me to hear joy and gladness;
That the bones which thou hast broken may rejoice.
Hide thy face from my sins,
And blot out all mine iniquities.
Create in me a clean heart, O God:
And renew a right spirit within me.
Cast me not away from thy presence;
And take not thy holy spirit from me.
   —Psalm 51:7–11

The haiku and the tanka   The haiku and the tanka, two Japanese forms, are based on syllable count. The haiku contains seventeen syllables in three lines of five, seven, and five syllables. The tanka contains thirty-one syllables in five lines of five, seven, five, seven, and seven syllables. Naturally they cannot be translated into English

of the same count. The poet Issa (1763–1828) wrote this haiku afte
the death of his only child.

The world of dew
Is a world of dew and yet,
And yet.[8]

All haiku, like this poem, are concentrated on a single vivid momen
The following haiku by Onitsura (1661–1738) is more humorous, an
expresses the universal desire to write poetry on a beautiful even
ing.

Is there, I wonder,
A man without pen in hand—
The moon tonight![9]

Bashō (1644–1694), who is generally considered Japan's greatest poet
said that a haiku should have both change and permanence. It shoul
look for the virtues of the old and at the same time express the pres
ent, a modern solution. One of his best-known haiku is this one:

The ancient pond
A frog leaps in
The sound of the water.[10]

The tanka is similar, though longer. This one is by the Empero
Gotoba (1180–1239):

When I look far out
The mountain slopes are hazy
Minase River—
Why did I think that only in autumn
The evenings could be lovely?[11]

[8] Donald Keene, *Japanese Literature: An Introduction for Western Readers* (New York: Grove Press
1955), p. 21. Reprinted by permission of Grove Press, Inc.; and Georges Borchardt, Inc., 145 Eas
52 Street, New York, N.Y. Copyright © 1955 by Donald Keene.
[9] *Ibid.*, p. 26.
[10] *Ibid.*, p. 39.
[11] *Ibib.*, p. 36.

13 ORGANIZATION IN THE VISUAL ARTS

A work of art reveals its meanings only insofar as it is regarded as an autonomous creation, that is, insofar as we accept its mode of being—*that of an artistic creation*—and do not reduce it to one of its constituent elements . . . or to one of its subsequent uses.

—Mircea Eliade[1]

WHAT IS ORGANIZATION?

It has been said that human beings are most godlike in their demand for order. We are constantly trying to transform chaos into a world of order. The mind is confused, if not balked, when it cannot find some order. The "order" in a work of art is its organization. In our study thus far we have been considering the elements found in works of art, but the elements are only the materials used by the artist. Now we begin to study the ways elements are combined to make a whole.

The primary demands made of any organization are two: (1) It must make sense, and (2) it must be interesting. The first of these demands has to do with the arrangement of parts, the overall design or plan of a work. Plan might be called the "skeleton" of the work of art. Plan covers the entire work—whether it be a symphony that lasts an hour or a song that is over in a minute, whether it be a novel of a thousand pages or a poem of two lines, whether it be the ceiling of a large chapel or the picture on a postage stamp. Whatever the size or the medium, we demand an orderly arrangement of parts which reflects a plan.

[1] "History of Religions and a New Humanism," *History of Religions*, vol. 1, no. 1, Summer 1961, p. 4. By permission of Mircea Eliade and the University of Chicago Press.

The names by which we identify plans differ in the various arts. In music, we usually speak of "forms"—rondo, sonata, minuet, etc.—whereas in literature we talk of "types," such as novel, essay, and epic. In the visual arts there are no generally accepted names as such, but we may describe plans by obvious terms, such as "pyramidal" and "symmetrical."

Plan is essential because it holds the work together, but it is not interesting as such. Two works following identical plans may differ widely in interest and value. The sonnet form has been used in very great poems, but the same form is found in poems of no value. The value of a rondo does not come from the rondo form, but from the music written in that form. In any of the arts, interest comes from the way the form is used—from the elements of which the plan is made and from their interrelations. This may be called the "organic structure" of the work. If the plan is compared with a skeleton, the organic structure corresponds to the flesh and blood with which the skeleton is covered. Another analogy for organization is an orchestra. The different elements play with and against one another as do the instruments of an orchestra; and so this organic structure or organic unity of a work of art is sometimes called its "orchestration."

For organic structure there is one rule that holds, in all the arts—that of unity and variety, or repetition and contrast. The elements used must be repeated enough to become familiar but varied enough in character to provide contrast. In this way we have the satisfaction of recognizing the familiar coupled with the surprise or tension of the unfamiliar. One of the most beautiful passages in Handel's *Messiah* comes in the singing of the contralto solo "He shall feed His flock," which is followed immediately by the soprano solo "Come unto Him, all ye that labor." The tune is the same, but the soprano sings it a fourth higher. With the differences in words and in pitch, not only is the song not repetitious, but many hearers do not even know they are hearing the same tune.

BASIC PLANS IN THE VISUAL ARTS

In the traditional visual arts, plan is simply the arrangement of the parts, with one place given special attention as the center of interest. In Raphael's *Sistine Madonna* (Color Plate 37 and Figure 13-1a), the plan consists of four groups: the Madonna and the Child at the top of the canvas in the center, S. Sixtus on the left (with the papal crown at his feet to identify him), S. Barbara on the right (the building which identifies her as the patron of buildings is barely seen above her right shoulder), and, at the bottom of the picture, two cherubs. The iconography of the Lady presenting the infant Christ to the veneration of the faithful derives from the formal and regal style of imperial Byzantium. Since Giotto's time (see Color Plate 16 for an example of

Figure 13-1a. Raphael. *Sistine Madonna* (ca. 1515). (Oil on canvas. Height: 8 feet, 8½ inches. Dresden Gallery, Alinari/Scala.) See also Color Plate 37.

Figure 13-1b. Organization of lines and figures in the *Sistine Madonna*, Figure 13-1*a* and Color Plate 37. (Drawing by Gordon Gilkey.)

Giotto's work), the subject of mother and child had begun to acquire a more accessible aspect (for example, see Color Plate 38) until we have the very human, universally appealing, figures of popular piety exemplified by the *Sistine Madonna*.

To see this work freshly, we should examine it in some detail. The formal structure (the symmetrical plan is diagramed in Figure 13-1*b*) consists of implied lines and the disposition of the figures in strict symmetry, and by the "visual link" between the human and the divine personages (the eye follows the direction of S. Sixtus's gaze) and the alternation of earthly and celestial hues.

Because plan in the visual arts is obvious, there are no well
established names for types of plan, and hence we do not need any
assistance in determining types. There are, however, a few obvious
arrangements which are used repeatedly. The two most common are
the pyramidal and the symmetrical plans; the vertical plan and the
radial plan are less frequently used.

Pyramidal Plan

The pyramid is almost as common in painting as the symmetrical
plan is in architecture. The broad base gives a sense of solidity, and
the apex gives emphasis. It is the natural shape for a portrait. In the
portrait *Madame Cézanne in the Conservatory* (Figure 13-2), the
woman's skirt makes the base of the pyramid and her head the apex.
The pyramidal plan is often used in representations of the Virgin, as
in Giorgione's *Castelfranco Madonna* (Color Plate 38). The Madonna,
though dressed as a simple peasant, is seated on high at the apex of
the triangle; S. Liberale and S. Francis are at the corners. In the *Tomb
of Giuliano de' Medici* (Figure 13-3) the figures form a pyramid.

Figure 13-2. Paul Cézanne (1839–1906), French
painter. *Madame Cézanne in the Conservatory* (1891).
(Oil on canvas. Size: 36½ by 28½ inches. The
Metropolitan Museum of Art, New York; bequest
of Stephen C. Clark, 1960.)

Figure 13-3. Michelangelo (1475–1564), Italian
painter, sculptor, architect, and poet. *Tomb of
Giuliano de' Medici* (ca. 1523–1533). (Marble. Height
about 20 feet. Florence, Church of S. Lorenzo, New
Sacristy. Photograph by Alinari/Scala.)

Color Plate 35. Giorgio di Chirico (1888–), Italian painter and printmaker. *Melancholy and Mystery of a Street* (1914). (Oil on canvas. Size: 34⅜ by 28⅛ inches. Collection of Stanley R. Resor.)

Color Plate 36. Victor Vasarely (1908–), Hungarian artist. *Casiopée* (1957). © S.P.A.D.E.M., Paris, 1977.

Color Plate 37. Raphael (1483–1520), Italian painter. *Sistine Madonna* (ca. 1515). (Oil on canvas. Height: 8 feet, 8½ inches. Dresden Gallery. Photograph by Scala, New York.)

Color Plate 39. Jan van Eyck (1370–1440?), Flemish painter. *Jan Arnolfini and His Wife* (1434). (Oil on wood. Height: 2 feet, 9¼ inches. Reproduced by courtesy of the Trustees, National Gallery, London.)

Color Plate 40. Fra Angelico (1387–1455), Italian painter. *Annunciation* (ca. 1440). (Fresco. Figure three-fourths life-size. Florence, S. Marco Dormitory. Photograph by Scala, New York.)

VIRGINIS INTACTE CVM VENERIS ANTE FIGVRAM PRETEREVNDO CAVE NE SILEATVR AVE

Color Plate 41. Jacob van Ruisdael (1628–1682), Dutch painter. *The Mill.* (Size: 2 feet, 9 inches by 3 feet, 4 inches. Amsterdam, Rijksmuseum.)

Figure 13-4. Thomas Eakins (1844–1916), American painter and sculptor. *The Thinker* (1900). (Oil on canvas. Height: 6 feet, 10 inches. New York, Metropolitan Museum of Art; Purchase, Kennedy Fund, 1917.)

Symmetrical Plan

The two sides of this plan are similar and relatively equal. This is a favorite plan in architecture, where the two sides are identical, as in the Vendramin Palace (Figure 13-25). It is also a favorite in paintings and statues, as in the *Annunciation* by Simone Martini (Figure 6-13) and the *Ludovisi Throne* (Figure 5-5).

Vertical Plan

The vertical plan consists of a single vertical figure or other object. Monuments frequently follow this plan, as do some modern skyscrapers—the Seagram Building in New York (Figure 13-22), for example. The vertical plan is used a great deal in sculpture, especially in statues of a single figure, like Michelangelo's *David* (Figure 3-1). It is not so common in painting as in sculpture, but it is sometimes used for full-length single figures, as in Eakins's *Thinker* (Figure 13-4).

Radial Plan

In the radial plan the lines of the picture form radii which meet at a point in the center. In Leonadro's *Last Supper* (Figure 13-5), all the lines of the ceiling and walls, as well as the hands and faces of the twelve disciples, point to the head of Christ. Leonadro puts his point of focus directly in the center of the picture. In the *Death of S. Francis*

Figure 13-5. Leonardo da Vinci (1452–1519), Italian painter, sculptor, and architect. *The Last Supper* (1495–1498). (Tempera on plaster. Figures above life size. Milan, S. Maria delle Grazie. Photograph by Alinari/Scala.)

Figure 13-6. Giotto (1266–1336), Italian painter. *Death of S. Francis* (ca. 1325). (Fresco. Figures about life size. Florence, S. Croce, Bardi Chapel. Photograph by Alinari/Scala.)

(Figure 13-6), Giotto uses a similar organization, but with the foc point at one side. The lines of the painting—the heads and bodies the saint's followers, as well as lines of the banner—all converge o the head of S. Francis. The one exception is the soul of the sain which looks ahead as it is being carried through the air.

Plan in Abstract Art

Plan is often harder to see in abstract and nonobjective art, becaus these arts are not representational. The organization is based en tirely on the repetition and variety of the elements. One color balanced against another color, one line against another. The abstra expressionist painting by Jackson Pollock shown in Color Plate 1 is unified only in terms of its centrifugal movement. The artist is n interested in developing a "center of interest" in the tradition sense, or in creating a traditional balance, but rather wants to pr duce a record of the act of creativity. The art which results is unifie only intuitively, not planned in the traditional way. Morris Louis, contemporary color-field painter, creates a unity which consists of th total impression of one color area and the artist's preoccupation wit it: here again, the formal plan is not traditional. However, in th work of Mondrian (Color Plates 3 and 5) we can see formal plan use without subject: the various forms and colors are present for thei own sake, not as representations of anything else, and the relation ship among them is planned also for its own sake. It can be said c much abstract art that the artists are interested in formal aspects t the point where they have abandoned subject in order to concentrat exclusively on form.

BALANCE

As we look at various arrangements or plans in any art, we instinctively demand balance. No matter how the various parts are put together, we want that sense of equilibrium which we call "balance." Some people are nervous if they see a picture hanging crooked, and most of us have little satisfaction in looking at the Leaning Tower of Pisa, though we know it has stood for centuries.

There is a painting by Degas of two ballet girls, *Dancers Practicing at the Bar* (Figure 13-7). The two girls are nearly symmetrical; each is poised on one leg, and the raised legs point in opposite directions. The figures are on a diagonal line in the upper right-hand corner of the picture; all the interest points to this one spot. To balance the two dancers, Degas puts a watering can on the otherwise bare floor. This watering can is essential. If we take out the can or if we narrow the picture, the girls are no longer secure at their bar; the plan becomes unbalanced.

One of the most important ways of getting balance is by control of the direction of lines. One line points in one direction, another in the opposite direction; and from the two we get a sense of balance. In Giotto's *Flight into Egypt* (Figure 9-22), for example, the entire motion of the picture is left to right until we come to the figure of S. Joseph, which stops us and turns us back. In Daumier's *Strangers*

Figure 13-7. Edgar Degas (1834–1917), French painter. *Dancers Practicing at the Bar* (1877). (Oil on canvas. Size: about 29½ by 30½ inches. New York, Metropolitan Museum of Art; bequest of Mrs. H. O. Havemeyer, 1929; H. O. Havemeyer Collection.)

Figure 13-8. Honoré Daumier (1808–1879), French painter and etcher. *Strangers in Paris.* (Lithograph. Size: 8½ by 7 inches. New York, Metropolitan Museum of Art; Rogers Fund, 1922.)

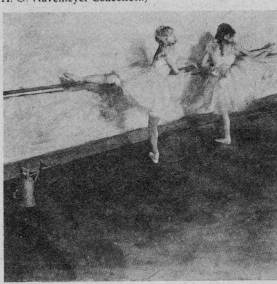

Figure 13-9. El Greco (ca. 1541–1614), Spanish painter. *S. Jerome* (ca. 1596–1600). (Oil on canvas. Size 42½ by .24¼ inches. Copyright Frick Collection, New York.)

in Paris (Figure 13-8), the couple in the distance are moving in on direction; the couple in the foreground are not moving, but the direction of their heads and umbrella is in the opposite direction. In Greco's *S. Jerome* (Figure 13-9), the eyes, head, and beard point to th right, the arms and book to the left. If the picture is cut off just belo the shoulders, the beard seems to be blown as if by a breeze. Wi the opposing motion of the hands and book, the whole is given liv ing, breathing balance.

Theoretically, every detail is necessary in a well-designed con position; if the balance is perfect, a change in a single detail w upset it. This principle may be more theory than fact, but it is inte esting to try to determine the role played by some detail of a pictur In Jan van Eyck's painting *Jan Arnolfini and His Wife* (Colo Plate 39) we have an interesting illustration. This is obviously a po trait study. The two figures are placed side by side, the man on th left, the woman on the right. Between them are the mirror on th wall and the chandelier. The light of the window, the man's fac and his hand are balanced by the white of the woman's face, he headdress, and the long cuff on her sleeve. All is regular and as should be except, apparently, for some slippers on the floor near th man. But those slippers are necessary for the balance of the pictur Their irregular line balances the irregular line of the white trim o the woman's skirt. Both lines of white are needed to bring the ey down to the lower half of the picture. The importance of the slippe can be judged in another way also: if we remove the slippers, th man seems to fall forward.

Asymmetrical balance is one of the beauties of landscape pain ing. In van Ruisdael's *Mill* (Color Plate 41), the asymmetry is dynami as it unifies light and dark masses, static and moving elements of th composition. Asymmetrical balance of light areas with dark masses precisely achieved in this interesting composition in which seascap landscape, and sky share the interest. Implied lines lead the eye pa the seawall and the windmill, out to the haven where the bo balances the uprights near the center and the bulky cylinder of th mill, which reflects a comparable amount of light. Note also that, i compensation for the curved line and short uprights of the jetty join ing the land mass to the water, there is a strong implied diagon passing over the uprights from the vanes of the mill to the sails boat and that this joins the cloudscape to the seascape. The tur bulence of the clouds and the rippling of the water appear to set th vanes of the mill and the sails of the boat in gentle motion, so tha one can almost feel an offshore breeze.

Whenever elements or images are found close to one another i rows or in paths, a direction is established; we often speak of this a an "implied line." In Brueghel's *Parable of the Blind* (Color Plate 42 Color Plates 42 to 49 follow page 440), we are impressed by such a implied line as a downward direction. In this parable in paint, as th

Figure 13-10. Sassetta (Stefano di Giovanni) (1392–1450), Italian painter. *The Journey of the Magi.* (Tempera on wood. Size: 29 by 15¼ inches. New York, Metropolitan Museum of Art; bequest of Maitland F. Griggs, 1943.)

Figure 13-11. Myron (fifth century B.C.), Greek sculptor. *Discus Thrower* (restored) (450 B.C.). (Bronze. Height to right shoulder: 5 feet. Rome, National Museum. Photograph by Alinari/Scala.)

critic Donald Weismann remarks, the implied line "analogizes the consecutive experience of walking, stumbling and falling down."[2] In one of a series of poems on Brueghel's paintings, the American poet William Carlos Williams has recorded his responses to this work eloquently (this poem is reproduced on the same page as the painting). In Sassetta's *Journey of the Magi* (Figure 13-10), we have the joyous sense of an easy journey going down from Jerusalem to Bethlehem.

In the *Discus Thrower* by Myron (Figure 13-11), the body forms a complete half circle in the long, curved line that begins in the right hand and goes through the right arm and the body to the left foot. In this statue Myron has, as Kenneth Clark puts it, "created the enduring pattern of athletic energy." He shows the athlete "balanced in equilibrium." In Toulouse-Lautrec's *In the Circus Fernando: The Ringmaster* (Figure 13-12, page 318), the woman on the horse starts a movement that is completed in the man on the left with the whip.

PROPORTION

Proportion is the aspect of plan that has to do with the comparative size of the parts of a single work. This is a matter of *relative* size, never absolute size. A picture is not too large or too small in itself but too large for this space or too small for that. One side of a rectangle is not too long or too short except in proportion to the other. An inch is

[2] Donald L. Weismann, *The Visual Arts as Human Experience* (Englewood Cliffs, N.J.: Prentice-Hall, Inc., 1974), p. 32.

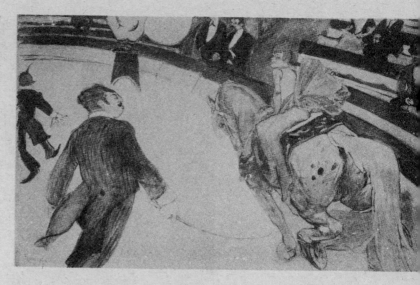

very little in computing the distance from New York City to Chicago but it is a good deal on the end of a nose.

In the visual arts, proportion at its simplest can be seen in the arrangement of objects on an indefinite surface or field, as in wall paper, carpets, and cloth. A plaid is nothing but a number of straight lines crossing at right angles; the interest of the plaid depends on the arrangement of these lines in relation to one another. In a polka dotted pattern there are two elements, the size of the dot and the space between dots. Change the size of the dots or the space between them—i.e., change the proportions—and the pattern is changed radically.

Such patterns offer simple problems of proportion, because the elements are judged only by their relation to one another. But problems in proportion are found wherever there is a question of relative size or length. In dress design, proportion determines the length of the sleeve or coat, the space between buttons. In interior decoration it governs the length of curtains, the height of the mantel, the size of the picture over it. The beauty of printed pages in books depends largely on the proportions used in filling the page: the space at the top and the bottom, the width of the margins, the size of the type, and the space between the lines. Proportion also determines our judgments of the beauty of the human body in life and in art. Is the head too large or too small? Are the legs and arms too long? Are the hips too large? In painting, proportion determines not only the shape of the frame—its height in comparison with its width—but also the placing of the subject in the frame, i.e., whether the center of interest is to be high or low, right or left.

What are good proportions and what are bad? This is like asking

Figure 13-13. Polyclitus (fifth century B.C.), Greek sculptor. *Doryphorus* ("Spear Bearer") (ca. 440 B.C.), Roman copy in marble of bronze original. (Height: 7 feet. Naples, Museum. Photograph by Alinari/Scala.)

When is a steak cooked enough? or, What is a long walk? People do not agree. The critic gives the ultimate answer: That is good which seems good; that is in good proportion which we find pleasing. But people have always wanted to know definite rules; accordingly, various people have tried to make exact formulas for pleasing proportions.

Polyclitus, a Greek sculptor of the fifth century B.C., wrote a treatise on the proportions for the ideal human figure, which he called *The Canon*, or "The Rule." Then he made a statue to illustrate his principles, also called *The Canon*. It is not certain just what this statue was, but it is believed to have been the *Doryphorus*, or "Spear Bearer" (Figure 13-13). Unfortunately, the original, probably in bronze, is lost, and the stone copy that is in the National Museum at Naples is not good; the copyist has had to make certain additions because of the weight of the stone—a tree stump to support the legs, and a bar between the hips and the right arm. Nevertheless, one can see the general proportions of the original. Polyclitus had a mathematical formula for the figure: the head is one-seventh the height of the entire body, and all details are worked out in terms of a fixed ratio. The basis of his technique was in the balance of tensed and relaxed body parts (*symmetria* of *stasis* and *dunamis*) representing the philosophy of the ideal. The art historian Helen Gardner says, "In the *Doryphorous*, movement . . . is disciplined through the use of an imposed system of proportions. The mighty body with its broad shoulders, thick torso, and muscular limbs, strikes us as an embodiment of the Spartan ideal of the warrior physique, the human equivalent of the Doric order."[3]

A century later, Lysippus introduced a new canon with a smaller head and a slimmer body, the head being one-eighth the height of the body. The statue that has been most commonly associated with these new proportions is the *Apoxyomenos*, or "Stirgil Bearer" (Figure 13-14, page 320), a figure of a young athlete holding the stirgil, a curved scraper which athletes used to remove oil and dust from the body after exercise. The canon of Polyclitus (which had decreed the proportion of head to body as 1:7) was reduced by Lysippus so that the head is proportionately smaller. The limbs extend out in space and control a greater dynamic volume in being designed to be seen from all angles. Quoting again from Gardner, ". . . The arms curve forward, the figure enclosing space in its reach and twisting in it, the small head is thrown into stronger perspective by the large hand interposed between it and the viewer. Lysippus said that he wishes to make men the way the eye sees them, allowing thus for accidents of perspective."[4]

[3] *Art Through the Ages*, 6th ed. (New York: Harcourt Brace Jovanovich, Inc., 1975), p. 164.
[4] *Ibid.*, p. 169.

Often proportions are changed to indicate position and powe
A king, for example, may be made larger than his subjects. In t
Palette of King Narmer, an Egyptian relief of the fourth millenniu
B.C. (Figure 13-15), we see the king dealing with his enemies. He
represented as much larger than any of the other figures. Wearing t
high, bowling-pin-shaped crown of Upper Egypt, he is about
slay an enemy as a sacrifice. Before him a hawk, symbol of the s
god Horus, protector of the king, takes into captivity a man-head
land form from which papyrus grows (a symbol of Lower Egyp
Below the king are two fallen enemies, and above are two heads
Nathor, a goddess favorably disposed to King Narmer. Similarly,
the *Laocoön* the two sons of the priest are represented as mu
smaller than their father (Figure 3-6).

Proportion has been differently applied in different times, b
generally there is a certain consistency at any one time in a giv
culture. We say, for example, that there is such a thing as Renai
sance proportion or Greek proportion. In the twentieth centur
serious art does not seem to be characterized by any one proportio
We see a variety, from the squat figures of a Dubuffet to the elo
gated figures of a Giacometti sculpture (for example, *City Squar*

Figure 13-14. Lysippus (fourth century, B.C.), Greek sculptor. *Apoxyomenos* ("Strigil Bearer") (second half of fourth century, B.C.), Roman marble after bronze original. (Height: 6 feet, 8½ inches. Rome, Vatican. Photograph by Alinari/Scala.)

Figure 13-15. *Palette of King Narmer.* (Egyptian, Second Dynasty, ca. 2900–2800 B.C.), Original, found at Kierakonpolis, now in Cairo Museum. (Slate. Height: 25 inches. Photograph, New York Metropolitan Museum of Art; Dodge Fund, 1931.)

Figure 13-16) in which the inordinately tall, thin figures make the surrounding barren space seem vast, isolated, and threatening. Fashion illustrations and illustrations for advertising and light fiction in magazines, however, are striking examples of consistent application of an artificial, idealized proportion, whose outstanding features are extreme slimness and very long legs.

THE FRAME

In an arrangement of parts, consideration must be given to the frame and the relation of the parts to the frame. Whether we look at the façade of a building, a statue, or a painting, we have a certain area or surface that is to be filled. Within this area the space should seem neither crowded nor empty. The camera offers interesting possibilities for experimentation, for, with the finder on the camera, the artist can try different types of content in different relationships to the frame. The stage illustrates another challenge; the proscenium arch offers a frame, and the problem of the director is to fill that frame agreeably with stage set, characters, and lighting. Since theater and dance are arts of both time and space, the director deals with a content that is constantly changing; at every moment, however, the stage is supposed to show a scene in which the frame is filled agreeably.

Since the design must fill the shape, the choice of shape partly determines the design of the picture. Moreover, the lines of the enclosing shape strengthen or oppose the lines of the design. In a picture that is rectangular or square, all the vertical or horizontal lines are strengthened by the lines of the frame. So powerful are these lines that an artist usually tries to cover them in some way, to fill in the corners by the use of trees or shrubbery, or in some other way to change the severe right angle to a more graceful curve. The square is difficult to work with because it is all center and corners; there is no neutral ground, as it were. We have good design in the square in the metopes from the Parthenon and in the panels of Ghiberti's "Gates of Paradise." But because of its difficulty, the square is relatively rare in art, and the rectangle is preferred. The rectangle has the advantage of being in straight lines, and yet it has much free space in the middle that is neither exact center nor corner, and in this central space the design is usually placed. If the rectangle is standing on its short side, it shares something of the strength of the vertical; if it is on its long side, it partakes of the peace of the horizontal. Most of the illustrations in this book are rectangular.

Complex shapes are not always easily filled. An illustration is found in the reliefs made by Brunelleschi and Ghiberti showing the *Sacrifice of Isaac* (Figures 13-17 and 13-18). Since these two reliefs were offered in a competition for the north gates of the Baptistery at Florence, they have the same shape, the same general treatment in high relief, and the same subject. The same figures are shown: Isaac

Figure 13-17. Filippo Brunelleschi (1377–1446), Italian sculptor and architect. *Sacrifice of Isaac* (1402). Competition for Gates of Baptistery, Florence. (Bronze. Size: about 1½ feet square. Bargello, Florence. Photograph by Alinari/Scala.)

Figure 13-18. Lorenzo Ghiberti (ca. 1378–1455), Florentine sculptor. *Sacrifice of Isaac* (1402). Competition for gates of Baptistery, Florence. (Bronze. Size; about 1½ feet square. Bargello, Florence. Photograph by Alinari/Scala.)

Figure 13-19. Douris (attributed) fifth century B.C.). *Two Women Putting Away Clothes* (ca. 470 B.C.). (Red-figured pottery cylix. Ripe archaic style. Size: 5 inches high, 12⅞ inches in diameter. New York, Metropolitan Museum of Art. Rogers Fund, 1923.)

kneeling on the altar; Abraham arrested by the angel just as he is about to kill his son; the servants of Abraham; and the ram which was the actual sacrifice. But the arrangement of the figures in the two compositions is entirely different. Brunelleschi has put Isaac in the center and crowded the other figures into the corners; the scene is confused. Ghiberti has divided the relief in two by a diagonal line, with Abraham and Isaac on one side and the servants on the other. His plan is clearer, simpler, and better.

The circle is a difficult shape. It is always the same; the eye tends to go around and around it without stopping, and there is a general tendency for a picture to seem to roll over if it is in a circular frame. Some of the best examples may be obtained from Greek vase painting. The cylix, or drinking cup, was ordinarily ornamented on the inside; hence the Greek artists had many opportunities to try their hand at filling a circular shape, and they often succeeded admirably. A favorite cylix painting shows two women putting away their clothes. It is attributed to Douris (Figure 13-19).

Raphael's famous *Madonna of the Chair* (Figure 13-20) is a good example of the Renaissance use of the circular composition. Where the Greek vase painter had to fill an already existing form, Raphael has chosen to integrate the figures of this scene by forcing them into the outline of the circle. The left side and head of the Madonna follow the circle, as do the back of the child and the arrangement of the youthful S. John the Baptist. The closeness and intimacy thus con-

Figure 13-20. Raphael (1483–1520), Italian painter. *Madonna of the Chair* (1514–1515). (Panel. Diameter: 28 inches. Galleria Pitti, Florence.)

Figure 13-21. Jasper Johns (1930–   ),
American painter and sculptor.
Target with Four Faces (1955).
(Encaustic on newspaper on canvas,
26 by 26 inches, surmounted by four
plaster faces in a wooden frame, 3¾
by 26 inches with hinged front.
Collection, Museum of Modern Art,
New York; gift of Mr. and Mrs.
Robert C. Scull.)

veyed by the artist are enhanced by the intertwining of the arms of
the mother and child, the feet moving left to conform to the circle

It is interesting to compare these two works with a modern pic
ture in the same shape—Jasper Johns's *Target with Four Faces* (Figure
13-21). Here the subject itself has dictated the circular outline.

The lunette, or half moon, is largely associated with architecture
and sculpture. It is found most often in the tympanum, or sculptured
space over a door. (We studied an example in the tympanum a
Chartres.) It has the rich curve of the circle but is held steady by it
horizontal base.

Architecture is conceived as a three-dimensional entity, and its
primary purpose is the defining and enclosing of space. But because
we generally encounter a building head on, it presents a two-dimen
sional, enframed surface to our eyes. Thus the façade of the Par
thenon (Figure 13-26) is a repeated vertical rhythm of columns
which make the building appear taller. The balanced horizontals and
verticals of Notre Dame de Paris (Figure 14-24) result in a controlled
calm. Modern office buildings like the Seagram Building (Figure
13-22) present a front and a side frame within which the vertical
motif dominates and gives these buildings their special character. A
variant of this type is seen in the Inland Steel Building (Figure 13-23)
which presents a much greater variety of enframements and visual
interest for the spectator. In the United Nations Secretariat building
(Figure 13-24) we have both a variety of enframements and a playing
off of mass against mass.

UNITY AND VARIETY

So far we have said little about unity and variety, but it can be seen
in any one of the examples we have used. Take the *Sistine Madonna*
(Color Plate 37). It seems simply made, as though anyone could put
the various parts together, but it is worthwhile to see what devices
Raphael has used. The lines of the painting are predominantly
curves, as we see in the small diagram. Then, the figures are also
unified by their glances. The Pope looks to the Virgin, who looks to
the saint, who looks in turn to the *putti* (cherubs) below, a seemingly
obvious and at first glance naive use of repetition.

The Vendramin Palace on the Grand Canal in Venice (Figure
13-25) is an interesting study in repetition and variety. It was built
by the Vendramin family at the end of the fifteenth century. To this

Figure 13-22. Ludwig Mies van der Rohe and Philip Johnson, American architects.
Seagram Building, New York (1957). (Bronze. 38 stories. Photograph used by
permission of Joseph E. Seagram and Sons, Inc.)

Figure 13-23. Skidmore, Owings, and Merrill, contemporary American architects. Inland Steel Building, Chicago. (1958). (Steel and glass. Main building: 19 stories; tower: 25 stories. Photograph, Bill Hedrich, Hedrich-Blessing, Chicago.)

Figure 13-24. United Nations buildings (1948–1950). General view of permanent headquarters, New York, from the north. (Glass panels, marble piers, and aluminum. General Assembly Building in foreground: Auditorium 380 feet long, 160 feet wide. Marble and glass Secretariat, 39 stories. Extreme right, part of the Library. Wallace K. Harrison, Director of Planning. Photograph, United Nations.)

Figure 13-25. Pietro Lombardo (ca. 1435–1515), Italian architect. Palazzo Vendramin-Calergi, Venice (1481–1509). (Marble. Length: about 80 feet; height: about 65 feet. Photograph by Alinari/Scala.)

palace Richard Wagner retired in 1882, and there he died a year later. One is impressed first by the repetition; the façade of the building shows a single grouping of windows repeated many times. There is, however, no lack of variety; the doorway takes the place of the central window on the first floor, and the place of the two end windows is left blank except for small openings. The first and second stories are separated by a balustrade, the second and third by a cornice. Moreover, the columns separating the windows are varied; those on the first floor are pilasters, undecorated except for a molding at the side; those of the second story are round and grooved; and those of the third story are round without grooves. The most important device for securing variety, however, is in the arrangement of the windows. The three central windows are grouped together, but the end window is set off by a narrow panel with two engaged columns. This motive, repeated at the corner of the building, brings a distinct relief in the long line of windows; it is a breathing space, as it were, that makes the façade seem easy and comfortable.

In a cathedral like that of Pisa (Figure 14-16), we trace the many repetitions and variations of the round arch. In the Egyptian temple (Figure 14-4), the sequence of rooms one after the other makes a subtle progression in darkness, from the open court at the front through the shadows of the hypostyle hall with its columns to the dark, mysterious chamber of the priest.

These ways of producing variety are fairly obvious. More subtle is the means used in the Parthenon (Figures 13-26 and 13-27). At first

Figure 13-26. Parthenon, Athens (447–432 B.C.). (Embassy of Greece. Photograph by Greek National Tourist Office.)

glance the building seems to show nothing but repetition, no variety except in the alternation of triglyphs and metopes in the frieze. In the Parthenon, however, there are many subtle variations that do not strike the observer at once. The columns are smaller at the top than at the bottom; about one third of the way up the shaft of the column there is a slight swelling, or convex curve, known as the *entasis* of the column. Moreover, the columns incline at a very slight angle; it has been calculated that the corner columns are slightly larger than the others and are placed closer together. The steps and the entablature both rise in a very slight convex curve.

It has been suggested that by means of such refinements the Greeks were attempting to counteract certain optical illusions. Two long parallel lines tend to look hollow or to approach each other in a concave curve; hence the slight curve outward was introduced in the columns. A column seen against the sky looks slighter than one seen against the background of a building; hence the corner columns were larger and closer together. This, of course, cannot be proved; nor does it matter whether the architects introduced these changes to correct optical illusions or whether they used them merely as a means of giving variety to the building and so improving its appearance. It is certain, however, that these changes were intentional. Similar refinements have been introduced in many buildings—S. Mark's in Venice and Low Library of Columbia University in New York City are two examples. And it is certain that much of the beauty of the buildings is due to the lack of stiffness, the sense of a unified, almost breathing whole, resulting from these slight variations from the exact rule.

Repetition in sculpture and painting is normally not so exact as the repetition that is characteristic of the industrial arts and architecture. In architecture, one half of a building may be, and often is just like the other half; but in a picture or a statue the two sides cannot be the same. For instance, the artist who wants to repeat the line of a woman's hair may repeat it not as hair but as a cloud or tree or scarf. This kind of repetition, therefore, is not obvious. We see the cloud as cloud or the tree as tree, and we do not see that it is repeating the line of the woman's hair. In the *Annunciation* of Fra Angelico (Figure 13-28*a* and Color Plate 40), for example, the curve of the angel's body repeats the curve of the Virgin's body (see the diagram in Figure 13-28*b*). The round curve of the Virgin's halo is repeated in the neckline of her dress, the stool on which she is seated, and the arches above her head. The arches on the side of the angel are seen in perspective, and they repeat the shape of the angel's wing until the whole seems to be alive with the motion of wings. To stabilize the curves and to give variety, Fra Angelico has introduced many straight lines—in the columns, the fence, the trees, and even the doorway, beyond which there is a rectangular window.

In Vermeer's *Young Woman with a Water Jug* (Color Plate 43), the composition is worked out primarily in terms of the straight lines of the map and the slow curve which we find in the young woman's cape. In the Medici tomb (Figure 13-3), we find repetition of lines in the bodies of the three figures. In the figure of Night the arm and the head make a complete half circle, and this curve is repeated in the curves of the body.

In *The Young Englishman* (Color Plate 29), Titian has made his design primarily in the three white spots of the head and two hands. It is, however, united in repeated circles of head, beard, and chain, with circular lines in the lace at neck and hands. There is also an interesting study in values.

It is interesting to see how these principles of formal design may be applied to contemporary art. As was noted when we discussed plan, the various formal elements are used to widely different degrees in different kinds of modern art: a Mondrian, we suggested, is planned far more traditionally than a Pollock. It is perhaps helpful to think of various works of visual art as forming a sort of continuum. In all art which is at all representational, there is a certain amount of tension between form and content. That is, we look at a painting as a picture of something but also as a design, as colors placed on a flat surface. Similarly, we see a statue as a representation of something but also as a piece of material which is a shape. When the work of art is very realistic—that is, very like the object it represents or pictures—then it requires an act of will on the part of the viewer to see it purely as a formal design. This is what we have been doing in the preceding paragraphs: saying "This is not a woman's head but the apex of a pyramid," and the like. When a work of art is not particularly realistic, we can see it as a design much more easily; indeed,

Figure 13-28a. Fra Angelico (1387–1455), Italian painter. *Annunciation* (a. 1440). (Fresco, figures three-fourths life-size. Florence, S. Marco Dormitory. Scala New York/Florence.) See also Color Plate 40.

Figure 13-28b. Drawing of the *Annunciation* (Figure 13-28a and Color Plate 40). (Gordon Gilkey.)

we may have to perform an act of will to see it as a representation at all. In certain impressionist paintings, one must stand at a certain angle and concentrate in a certain way to make the "picture" emerge. In some post-impressionist and cubist paintings—like Duchamp's *Nude Descending a Staircase* (Figure 5-7)—it is not difficult to see the representation and the design simultaneously, for they are of equal interest. In Mondrian's *Broadway Boogie Woogie* (Color Plate 5), representation is of far less importance than formal design. What has happened in a painting like this—indeed, in much of abstract art—is that the artist has become interested in form almost to the exclusion of content. Without the title, there would be no content at all, simply a formal design existing entirely for its own sake, because it is interesting and aesthetically satisfying by itself.

A great deal of modern abstract art seems to have this character. When we look at it and try to analyze it, we cannot speak of "this arm" balancing "that foot" or "the apple in the bowl" placed in the central point formed by "the table and the corner of the chair." We must adjust our way of describing what we see; we must say that "the dark oblong in the upper right" is balanced against "the red splash to the left of center." But what we are doing is no different, essentially. A design, a sculptural shape, an arrangement of colors will often contain much the same formal aspects as a picture of a bowl of apples, or a statue of an athlete, or a picture of waves breaking on the shore. When we are discussing organization alone, it is not really important whether the artist has chosen to make the design stand for some object in the "real world" or whether the design has been created for its own sake. Even a Jackson Pollock painting, which at first glance may seem to be totally unorganized, must be an aesthetically satisfying arrangement if it is to deserve the name of a work of art. Analyzing such a work is difficult; it is not easy to say exactly how balance is achieved, or how repetition and variety are produced. But a good work of art, no matter how far it departs from tradition, will not look unbalanced, or dull, or confused, or out of proportion. It will satisfy the viewers, not make them uneasy or displeased. Eventually, one may see even in nonrepresentational art a certain emotional content: a design which is purely a design may yet be ominous or serene, tranquil or violent, sweet or harsh; and one can respond just as fully to such a design as to a representation of a mother and child, a battle, or a vase of roses. And if this occurs, one must learn again to filter out the "content" in order to be able to analyze the organization as such.

14 ORGANIZATION IN ARCHITECTURE

A building, whatever else it may be, is a practical thing which must be measured by the standards of its own era rather than ours.

Of all the arts, architecture is the only one used in one way or another by everyone. It is difficult not to be interested in where one may be living, working, worshiping, or even ultimately entombed. Looking about us today, we notice a wide variety of styles, a situation that often creates some confusion if we are not aware of what we are looking at. But such variety has always existed, since buildings survive the time of their construction and live into succeeding periods of design. The modern museum on upper Fifth Avenue in New York, designed by Frank Lloyd Wright for the Guggenheim family (Figure 14-1), contrasts startlingly with the surrounding apartment houses of only one generation earlier. Conversely, the mid-nineteenth-century Trinity Church in downtown New York (Figure 14-2) was engulfed first by the skyscrapers of the early twentieth century and then by commercial structures designed and built since World War II.

It is because so much of the culture and values of particular periods is embedded in the characteristic architectural styles of those periods that we now take a rather long look at various types of buildings as they have evolved through history.

EGYPTIAN ARCHITECTURE (4000–2280 B.C.)

Egyptian architecture is closely bound up with religion. The *ka*, or "vital force," was dependent upon the human body for its life; if the body was destroyed, the ka ceased to exist. Hence, pyramids were

Figure 14-1. Frank Lloyd Wright (1869–1959), American architect. Solomon R. Guggenheim Museum, New York. (Photograph, Solomon R. Guggenheim Museum.)

Figure 14-2. Trinity Church, New York. (Museum of the City of New York; The Byron Collection.)

Figure 14-3. Pyramids of Giza (ca. 2700–200 B.C.). (Photograph by Trans-World Airlines, Inc.)

Figure 14-4. Temple of Horus, Edfu, Egypt, pylon seen from first court started by Ptolemy III, third century B.C.). (Sandstone. Height: about 100 feet. Photograph by Stoedtner.)

built to preserve the body, that the ka might be safe. The most striking group of pyramids is at Giza, where there are the great pyramids of Khufu, Khafre, and Menkure (Figure 14-3).

Great as the pyramids were, however, they did not protect their dead from robbers and marauders, and later tombs were cut in rocky cliffs. A temple adjoined each tomb, and, as the tombs were made more inaccessible, these temples developed independently. The great temples are those at Karnak, Edfu, and Luxor. They followed the same basic plan. First was the *pylon*, a huge gateway covering the entire front of the building (Figure 14-4). The temple itself, as we have said when discussing the adaptation of plan to function, was composed of a series of halls. In one of these halls the roof was supported by rows of columns (*hypostyle*). In the temple at Karnak and in some of the other temples, the center columns are higher than those next to the wall, thus making a *clerestory* for the light to enter (Figure 14-5).

Figure 14-5. Temple of Amon, Karnak, Egypt (ca. 1300 B.C.). Hypostyle hall. (Red-brown sandstone. Height of columns in middle aisles: 69 feet; width of capital at top: 22 feet; height of columns in side of aisles: 42½ feet. Model in Metropolitan Museum of Art, New York. Purchase, 1890, Levi Hale Willard Bequest. Photograph, Metropolitan Museum of Art.)

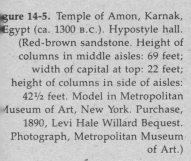

Egyptian columns are primarily of two types, the flower and the bud. In the flower columns, the flower makes a wide, bell-shaped capital. In the bud columns, the uppermost part of the capital is smaller than the lower, like the bud of a flower. The model of the hypostyle hall at Karnak shows the clerestory and the columns; the central columns have flower capitals, the aisle columns, bud.

An outstanding characteristic of Egyptian art is its size. This is probably due to the nature of the country, for in the desert everything is swallowed up, and only the very large stands out in the wide stretches of sand. But even with this environment in mind one can hardly grasp the enormous size of Egyptian buildings. The columns of the Great Hall at Karnak are large enough for a hundred people to stand on top of each capital.[1] The Great Hall itself is 338 feet wide and 170 feet deep, furnishing a floor area about equal to that of the Cathedral of Notre Dame in Paris, although this is only a single hall of the temple.[2] The pyramid of Khufu at Giza is 480 feet in length and covers about 13 acres.[3]

MESOPOTAMIAN ARCHITECTURE

Of all the great palaces and temples of the Mesopotamians, Chaldeans, Babylonians, and Assyrians, very few examples are left; the brick, either unbaked or only partially baked, has crumbled away. The distinguishing characteristic is the *ziggurat*, or tower, built at successive levels, with ramps leading from one platform to the next. In many respects the ziggurat is like the modern building with setbacks. Because of the use of brick, however, the Assyrians developed the arch and its multiple, the canopy-shaped vault—destined to be among the most important and influential devices in the history of architecture.

GREEK ARCHITECTURE (1100–100 B.C.)

Greek architecture in its most characteristic form is found in the temple, a low building of post-and-lintel construction like that of the Egyptian temple. In this type of construction, two upright pieces, *posts*, are surmounted by a horizontal piece, the *lintel*, long enough to reach from one to the other. This is the simplest and earliest type of construction, and it is more commonly used than any other. Barns are good examples, since the beams are exposed and can be seen. Post-and-lintel construction is well adapted to wood, because

[1] James Henry Breasted, *The Conquest of Civilization* (New York: Harper and Row, Publishers, Inc., 1926), plate IX, p. 98.
[2] Ibid., fig. 61, p. 96.
[3] Ibid., p. 64.

Figure 14-6. Temple of Apollo, Old Corinth (sixth century B.C.). (Porous nestone, originally covered in stucco. Height of columns: 23⅔ feet. Photograph, Office of Press and Information, Embassy of Greece.)

wooden beams are strong and are able to uphold the weight of a roof; at the same time they are long, so that a large building may be erected. However, wooden beams are not permanent; they may burn, rot, or be eaten by insects. Stone lintels, in comparison, are enduring; but they cannot be obtained in as great lengths, and they stand much less weight than wood; therefore, in stone buildings the distance between posts must be small. A typical example of post-and-lintel construction is found in the ruins of the Temple of Apollo at Old Corinth (Figure 14-6). A more familiar example is the Parthenon (Figures 13-26 and 13-27).

The typical Greek temple had columns in front and often at the

Figure 14-7. The Doric order.
(Drawing by Thad Suits.)

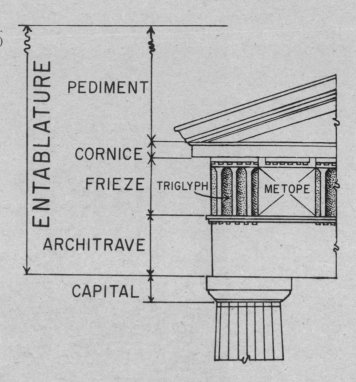

back also. Sometimes the entire building was surrounded by a row
of columns, with a double row of columns in the front and back of
the building and a single row at each side. The Parthenon belongs
to this class. In the pure Greek style, all columns are fluted.

There are three styles, or "orders," of Greek architecture: Doric,
Ionic, and Corinthian. The Doric (Figure 14-7) is seen in the Temple
of Apollo at Old Corinth and in the Parthenon, one of the greatest
temples ever built. The Doric column has no base; the bottom of the
column rests on the top step. The capital is very plain; it is a flat
block, or slab, joined to the column by a simple convex curve and
looking something like a cushion. The frieze is divided into *triglyphs*
and *metopes*; the triglyph is a square slab having two vertical grooves
(or glyphs) in the middle and a half groove at each end; the metope,
which alternates with the triglyph, is also square. Metopes are often
carved, as in the Parthenon (see Figure 9-8).

The Ionic column is taller and more slender than the Doric type.
It has a base, and the capital is ornamented with scrolls, or volutes,
on each side. In the Ionic order, the frieze is continuous instead of
being divided into triglyphs and metopes. The architrave below the
frieze is stepped; that is, it is divided horizontally into three parts,
each being set in slightly. The greatest example of the Ionic order is
the Erechtheum (Figure 2-1), which is unfinished and, unlike most
Greek temples, irregular in shape. Like all examples of the Ionic order

Figure 14-8. Temple of Athena Niké, Athens (ca. 435 B.C.). (Pentelic marble. Size: 18½ by 27 feet. Photograph, Greek National Tourist Office.)

in general, the Erectheum is characterized by great elegance and grace. The Ionic column is found also in the little Temple of Athena Niké at Athens (Figure 14-8).

The Corinthian column is distinguished from the Ionic by still greater height and by its capital, which shows two rows of acanthus leaves with volutes rising from them. The Corinthian, although an authentic Greek order, was last to be developed and was not so much used as the Doric and the Ionic. The Temple of Zeus at Athens (second century B.C.) has Corinthian capitals (Figure 14-9).

Figure 14-9. Temple of Olympian Zeus, Athens (174 B.C.–A.D. 130). (Pentelic marble. Height of column: 6½ feet. Photograph, Greek National Tourist Office.)

Figure 14-10. Segovia aqueduct (first century after Christ). (Granite. Length: 2,700 feet; height: 102 feet. Photograph, Spanish National Tourist Office.)

ROMAN ARCHITECTURE (1000 B.C.–A.D. 400)

Roman architecture follows the general lines of the Greek, with sig nificant changes. The temple is no longer the typical building equally important are civic buildings, baths, law courts, amph theaters, aqueducts, and bridges.

Structurally, the most important innovation of the Romans wa the arch, which they used widely although they had not invented i Next to the post and lintel, arch construction is historically of greates importance. An arch is made of wedge-shaped stones that are ar ranged with the small side of the wedge turned down toward th opening. When the stones have been put in place by means of scar folding or centering, their shape keeps them from falling, as we ca see in the aqueduct of Segovia (Figure 14-10). Each stone of the arch by its weight, exerts constant pressure on the stones on each side c it, and the arch is held in position only by an exact balancing of thes pressures. If that balance is upset, the arch collapses. As the ol Arabic proverb has it, "An arch never sleeps." In the thirteenth century cathedral of Beauvais, in France, the arched vaults of th nave collapsed because the building was raised too high and th upper structure therefore exercised too much downward pressure o them. The dome of S. Sophia (Hagia Sophia) in Istanbul (sixth cen tury after Christ) collapsed the first time it was erected, killing a larg

Figure 14-11. Pantheon, Rome (A.D. 120–124; portico A.D. 202). (Brick, mortar, and concrete, originally faced on the exterior with pentelic marble and stucco. Height of columns: 46½ feet. Photograph, Italian Government Travel Office.)

number of workers. It was an expensive lesson for the builders, who were successful in their next attempt.

Another characteristic of Roman architecture is the flat, round dome that covers an entire building, as in the Pantheon (Figures 14-11 and 14-12).

When the Romans used the same designs as the Greeks, they did not use them in exactly the same way. Roman columns are taller and thinner, and often, as in the Pantheon, they are not fluted. The

Figure 14-12. Pantheon, Rome (A.D. 20–124), interior. (Cement dome; wall decoration and pavement of marble and porphyry. Diameter of rotunda: 42 feet. Photograph by Alinari/Scala.)

Corinthian column was used extensively, as was the composite column, an invention of the Romans made by combining the Ionic volutes with the Corinthian acanthus-circled bell. The orders were not kept separate, but were stacked, or superimposed, as in the Colosseum (Figure 9-19), where those on the first floor are Doric, those on the second are Ionic, and those on the third are Corinthian. Moreover, the elements borrowed from the Greeks were sometimes used only as ornaments, whereas the Greeks had used them structurally. In the Colosseum, again, the columns between the arches and the entablature above them are not essential to the structure of the building; this is seen in that part of the building from which the outer layer of concrete has been torn away; the columns are missing, but the arches stand as before.

BYZANTINE ARCHITECTURE
(A.D. 200–1453; GOLDEN AGE—SIXTH CENTURY AFTER CHRIST)

During the Middle Ages, religion again took an important place; the most important buildings were the church and the cathedral. But architecture developed on different lines in the East and in the West.

Eastern, or Byzantine, architecture takes its name from Byzantium, later called Constantinople and now known as Istanbul. Byzantine architecture is characterized by a great central dome with half domes grouped around it. The dome, which is rather flat, reminds one of the Pantheon but is fitted to the building in a different way. In the Pantheon the round dome just covers the round building. In the Byzantine building the dome has to be fitted to a square area, and the space between the arches and the dome is filled by curved triangles (pendentives) on which the dome rests. This gives greater height and makes the interior more spacious and inspiring. A dome supported in this way is called a "dome on pendentives."

The greatest example of Byzantine architecture is S. Sophia (Church of the Divine Wisdom) in Istanbul (Figure 9-16). The Byzantine type has been widely used for the churches in Russia, for Mohammedan mosques, and for Jewish synagogues.

WESTERN ARCHITECTURE IN THE MIDDLE AGES
(A.D. 400–1500)

During the medieval period, Western architecture passed through three stages of development known as Early Christian, Romanesque, and Gothic. These three styles developed one out of another: the Romanesque was an outgrowth of the Early Christian, and the Gothic of the Romanesque. As in all such cases, there is never any sharp line

Figure 14-13. Basilica. Perspective cross section of an early Christian basilica. (Drawing by Thad Suits.)

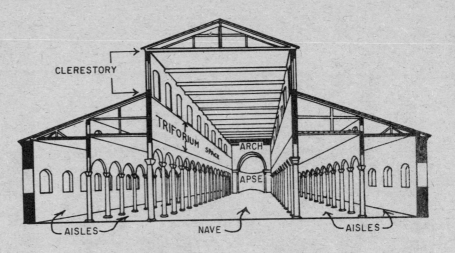

to be drawn between styles; there is never a time when one can say definitely that before that time all buildings are one style and after that time they are another. Accordingly, we shall trace the development of the styles by discussing their prominent characteristics.

In basic plan, the three Western styles follow the general type of the Roman basilica, a long rectangular building divided by pillars into a central nave and aisles (Figure 14-13). Sometimes there is one aisle on each side of the nave; sometimes there are two. Often the nave is higher than the aisles, and, therefore, there is the opportunity for clerestory lighting. Between the clerestory windows and the columns there is necessarily a space in which there can be no windows because of the roof over the aisles. This space, which was later used for the triforium, was decorated differently in different periods and is one of the significant features in determining the style of a building. At one end was a semicircular apse, which was used for the high altar. It was traditionally at the east, and that part of the church was known as the "choir."

In the early churches the building was one simple rectangle with an apse. Later, the plan was adapted to the shape of a cross by the addition of cross aisles between the nave and the choir. The arms thus made are known as "transepts." Directly opposite the high alter —i.e., at the west—was the main entrance.

Early Christian Architecture (A.D. 400–700)

The early Christian church, of which S. Apollinare in Classe at Ravenna (Figure 9-17) is an example, does not have transepts; the clerestory is heavy and the windows are small. The columns separating the nave from the aisles follow the Roman orders with flat lintels or round arches between them. The interiors of Early Christian churches were often decorated with mosaics, as in S. Apollinare.

ORGANIZATION IN ARCHITECTURE

341

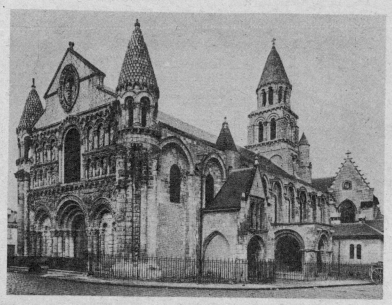

Figure 14-14. Notre Dame la Grande, Poitiers (eleventh century), side view showing facade. (Caisse Nationale des Monuments et des Sites Historiques, Archives Photographiques, Paris.)

Figure 14-15. Notre Dame la Grande, Poitiers (eleventh century), close-up of façade. (Caisse Nationale des Monuments et des Sites Historiques, Archives Photographiques, Paris.)

Romanesque Architecture (Eleventh and Twelfth Centuries)

Romanesque architecture is an extension and development of the Early Christian basilica exemplified by S. Apollinare in Classe. Examples are Notre Dame la Grande at Poitiers (exterior shown in Figures 14-14 and 14-15) and the Abbaye-aux-Dames (interior shown in Figure 14-17) at Caen, in France. Where the Early Christian style is structurally light, with a simple, lightweight, flat wooden roof, the Romanesque has very heavy walls with small window openings and a heavy stone roof arched or vaulted inside. In this respect it resembles the Roman style—hence the name *Romanesque* ("Romanish"). Although the plan is still that of the basilica, with a wide nave and narrower and lower side aisles, it does have transepts (crossings) partway down the nave. These crossings offer additional entrances on the north and south sides of the building, which, like all churches, is oriented from west to east, from the setting to the rising sun. Romanesque churches, unlike Early Christian churches, are ornamented with sculptured portals.

This heavy style appeared in France, Germany, Spain, and indeed all of Europe with the exception of Italy. In Italy a lighter style had developed, based on the basilica, and it persisted throughout the Romanesque and even the Gothic period. A typical instance of

Figure 14-16. *Above:* Busketus and Rainaldus, architects. Cathedral and Leaning Tower, Pisa (1063–1100). (White, black, and colored marbles and some stone. Length: 312 feet; width: 106 feet. Photograph, Italian Government Travel Office.)

Figure 14-17. *Right:* Abbaye-aux-Dames, or "La Trinité," Caen (ca. second half of eleventh century, remodeled twelfth century), interior, looking toward choir. Stone. Average width of middle aisle: about 26 feet; height: about 52 feet. Photograph, Stoedtner.)

Figure 14-18. Groin vault. (Drawing by Thad Suits.)

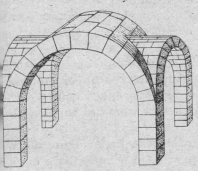

this light basilica style is the cathedral at Pisa, with the famous Leaning Tower (Figure 14-16); the delicate arcades and colorful marble stand in remarkable contrast to the powerful external and internal arches of Romanesque stone buildings. The cathedral at Pisa still has the earlier flat wooden roof rather than the heavy stone canopy or vault that is typical of Romanesque architecture.

The Romanesque style is seen in all its force in the interior of the Abbaye-aux-Dames at Caen (Figure 14-17), where magnificent stone vaulting covers the nave. Notre Dame la Grande at Poitiers has a simple continuous canopy of stone made up of a succession of individual round arches; but here the nave is divided into sections or bays, each one covered with a groin vault. A groin vault is made up of two short barrel vaults at right angles to each other, the short side facing the side aisle and raising the vault to let in light, the wider side facing the axes of the nave itself (see Figure 14-18). Later, it was discovered that diagonal arches or ribs could be built that would support the entire weight of the roof. The space between the ribs could then be filled in with lighter material. This system, known as "ribbed vaulting," is the chief characteristic of Romanesque and Gothic architecture. This construction also made a change in the columns; the ribs of the ceiling had to be supported at the base and were therefore carried down to the floor. A number of these ribs made a pier or column.

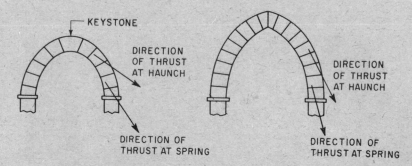

Figure 14-19. Direction of thrust in the round arch and the pointed arch. (Drawing by Thad Suits.)

Gothic Architecture (1194–1500)

As the Gothic developed from the Romanesque, the buildings became larger and taller—a change that was made possible by the use of the pointed arch. The thrust of an arch changes with its shape (Figure 14-19 illustrates thrust in the round and the pointed arch). In general, the flatter the arch, the greater the thrust; and the steeper the arch, the more nearly the thrust is absorbed in the vertical wall. With the pointed arch, therefore, buildings could be made higher than with the round arch.

With the higher buildings came a new type of buttress. The general shape of the exterior of a cathedral can be clearly seen in the basilica (Figure 14-13), with its central nave rising above the aisles on each side. In Early Christian churches, no extra support was needed for the central section, but as churches grew larger and taller during the Romanesque period, it was found necessary to reinforce this part of the building. If a solid buttress were put up, however, it would cut off the aisles below.

Accordingly, a plan was devised of making a buttress at the aisle wall from which a half arch was stretched out over the aisle to support the vault of the nave (Figure 14-20). Sometimes just one such arch was sufficient; sometimes, as at Amiens (interior, Figure 14-21), two were used, one above the other. These are called "flying buttresses." The lower buttress leans against the point where the vault springs inward and needs additional support; the upper buttress leans against the point where the vaulting curves inward and where it would tend to burst outward if its weight were not counterbalanced by the higher buttress.

The photograph of the apse of Notre Dame at Paris (Figure 14-22) shows the flying buttresses as they are actually seen. Perhaps more

Figure 14-20. Amiens Cathedral (begun 1220), perspective cross section. (Drawing by Thad Suits after Viollet-le-Duc.)

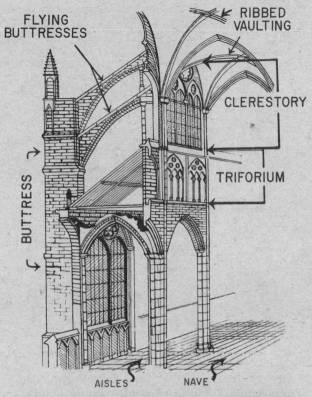

FLYING BUTTRESSES

RIBBED VAULTING

CLERESTORY

BUTTRESS

TRIFORIUM

AISLES   NAVE

Figure 14-21. Amiens Cathedral, interior. (Stone. Height: 147 feet; width of middle aisle: 43 feet. Caisse Nationale des Monuments et des Sites Historiques, Paris. Photograph, Clarence Ward.)

Figure 14-22. Cathedral of Notre Dame, Paris (twelfth and thirteenth centuries), view of apse, showing the flying buttresses. (Length: about 415 feet; height of flèche: about 310 feet. Caisse Nationale des Monuments et des Sites Historiques, Paris. Photograph, Clarence Ward.)

Figure 14-23. Chartres Cathedral (twelfth and thirteenth centuries), west, or "Royal," portal. (Stone. Height of royal ancestors: 20 feet, 6 inches; width of west portal: ca. 50 feet. Caisse Nationale des Monuments et des Sites Historiques, Paris. Photograph by Houvet.)

than any other characteristic of Gothic architecture, they seem t contribute to its mood of soaring aspiration.

In the Romanesque cathedral, several small windows were com bined in a compound arch; in the Gothic, this process was continue until the arches appeared only as stone tracery. Eventually the win dows became so large that the walls ceased to have any function a walls; the roof was supported by the huge buttresses and the enti wall space was given over to stained-glass windows. The triforiu space was regularly filled with small arches, and the rose windo became large and important. The doorways changed too. In th Romanesque church the façade sometimes had one doorway, som times three. The Gothic façade regularly had three doorways. Eac was made with multiple orders, like the Romanesque, though th arch, of course, was pointed. The decorations, also, were much mo elaborate. In the Romanesque, they were relatively simple molding with or without carvings of conventional designs, figures, animal or fruit. In the Gothic, the human figure became the characterist decoration, a recessed doorway being filled with rows of saints kings.

The west, or "Royal," portal of Chartres Cathedral (Figure 14-2 is an excellent example of early Gothic. It was finished in the middle of the twelfth century and is generally recognized as transitional work, though by common consent it is classed as Gothic. As is usual in Gothic, there are three doorways, with a lintel and a tympanum over each. Sculpture forms the only decoration. The three portals are treated as a single unit proclaiming the majesty and omnipotence of Christ.

In the tympanum above the central doorway is shown the second coming of Christ when he is to judge the quick and the dead. His right hand is raised in blessing; in his left hand he holds a book. Around him the four Evangelists are represented by their symbols. On the lintel below are the twelve Apostles.

The tympanum and the lintels over the right door celebrate the birth of Christ. In the first (lower) lintel are represented the Annunciation, the Visitation, and the birth of Jesus. Mary is lying on a couch and the child is above her in a manger. Joseph stands at Mary's head, and on beyond are angels and shepherds. The second lintel shows the presentation in the temple. In the tympanum Mary is seen in her glory, the infant in her arms. On each side is an angel swinging a censer.

In the tympanum to the doorway on the left is shown the Ascension. Christ on a cloud is being supported by two angels. On the lower lintel are the Apostles; between them and Christ are four angels who look as though they might be leaning toward the Apostles while they say:

Ye men of Galilee, why stand ye gazing up into heaven? this same Jesus, which is taken up from you into heaven, shall so come in like manner as ye have seen him go into heaven.

—Acts 1:11

On either side of the doorways are statues of kings and queens. They are commonly supposed to be the ancestors of Christ, as told in the first chapter of Matthew; hence the name "Royal" for this portal. They are richly clad in embroidered robes, and each carries some index to his or her work or character—a book, a scepter, a scroll; many wear crowns.

These kings and queens are remarkably elongaged. Each stands by a column and is stiffly posed with arms close to the body and never projecting beyond that contour. As Helen Gardner says: "They grow from the columns they rest on—this is what the artist was striving for—to use the human figure to adorn a column and yet not lose the feeling of the column."[4]

[4] Helen Gardner, *Art through the Ages*, 2d ed. (New York: Harcourt, Brace and Company, 1936), p. 314.

Figure 14-24. Cathedral of Notre Dame, Paris. (Diameter of rose windows: 42 feet; height of towers: 223 feet. Photograph, Trans-World Airlines, Inc.)

Figure 14-25. Chartres Cathedral. (Width of façade: 156 feet; height of north tower: 378 feet. Caisse Nationale des Monuments e des Sites Historiques, Paris. Photograph, Houvet.)

In general shape the façade of a Gothic cathedral is a rectangle resting on the short side, and the great height is emphasized by the two towers that usually complete the design. In Notre Dame at Paris (Figure 14-24) the towers are square and relatively short, but in many other cathedrals, such as Chartres (Figure 14-25), the towers are tall and pointed.

The Gothic cathedral often took centuries to build, with the result that the same style was not used throughout a building. Part of a building may be in Romanesque, part in early Gothic, and another part in late Gothic. As the ideas of architecture changed, the building itself changed. In the cathedral at Chartres, the towers are not the same; the older tower is shorter, more solid, and more substantial than the younger one.

The Gothic style in architecture is known, and rightly known, primarily for its cathedrals and churches. There are also, however, many beautiful palaces, especially in Venice, where the light tracery is reflected in the water of the canals. One of the favorite examples is known as the Cà d'Oro (Figure 14-26). It was built in the fifteenth century.

Figure 14-26. Cà d'Oro, Venice (1422–ca. 1440). (Photograph by Alinari/Scala.)

RENAISSANCE ARCHITECTURE
(FIFTEENTH AND SIXTEENTH CENTURIES)

In Renaissance architecture the cathedral, or temple, is no longe
the only typical building; secular architecture comes to the fore, as i
Roman times. Although Renaissance architecture is a return to th
ideals of the Greeks and Romans, it is not a slavish imitation, bu
rather a free use of the materials found in classic architecture. Th
designers got their ideas from Greece and Rome, but they used thes
ideas freely, according to their own tastes, in a way that was origina
For example, in the Medici-Riccardi Palace at Florence (Figure 4-13
designed by Michelozzo, we find the round arches of the Roman.
On the first floor a single arch occupies the space of two arches on th
second and third floors. In the upper floors, the window space
filled with the compound arch of the Romanesque. At the top of th
building there is a large cornice, heavy enough to crown the who
mass of the building. There is also a molding, or "stringcourse," tha
separates one story from the other.

In the Palace of the Senate at Rome (Figure 14-27), designed b
Michelangelo, we find the stringcourse and the cornice, this tim
surmounted by a balustrade. In addition, each large window has i
own post-and-lintel system. The windows are decorated with ped
ments; some are triangular, some are rounded. The classical ru
would have been only one pediment for one building, and th
pediment would have been in scale with the building. Between th
windows are flat columns called "pilasters."

The overhanging cornice, the stringcourse, the pilaster, and th

Figure 14-27. Michelangelo (1475–1564), Italian painter, sculptor, architect, and poet. Palace of the Senate, Rome (begun 1538). (Photograph, Anderson/Scala.)

Figure 14-28. Michelangelo. S. Peter's basilica, Vatican City (1547–1564), apse and dome. (Stone. Height of dome: 435 feet. Photograph, Italian Government Travel Office.)

ornamental pediment are characteristic features of the Renaissance style. Another feature is the dome on a drum. The Roman dome was so low that it could hardly be seen from the outside. In Renaissance architecture the dome was made small, and it was raised high on a circular drum and surmounted with a lantern. The curve of the dome was changed, too; it was made much steeper, and its sides were ribbed, as we see in the dome of S. Peter's (Figure 14-28).

In the smaller building, whether residence, church, or store, the Renaissance produced a type of symmetrical structure of great simplicity and beauty. In England it is known as the Georgian style, and in the United States as the American colonial.

BAROQUE ARCHITECTURE (1600–1750)

Baroque architecture flourished in the seventeenth century and in the opening years of the eighteenth century. It is characterized primarily as a period of elaborate sculptural ornamentation. The architectural framework remained close to that of the Renaissance, although often it was far more spacious, but it had a profusion of carved decoration. Columns and entablatures were decorated with garlands of flowers and fruit, shells and waves. Often alcoves were built into the wall to receive statues, thus making a pattern in light and dark. Surfaces were frequently curves. The churches of this period no longer use the Gothic nave and aisles; the area is filled with chapels which take the place of the aisles. They often have domes or cupolas, and they

Figure 14-30. Carlo Maderno (1556–1629), Italian architect. S. Peter's basilica, façade (1607–1615). (Stone. Photograph, Italian Government Travel Office.)

Figure 14-29. Francesco Borromini (1599–1667), Italian architect. S. Carlo alle Quattro Fontane, Rome (begun 1635, façade, 1667). (Photograph by Anderson/Scala.)

may or may not have spires. The Church of S. Carlo alle Quattr Fontane (Figure 14-29) is an excellent example of the love for orna ment and the movement, restlessness, and excitement of the style

Comparison of the apse and the façade of S. Peter's reveals inte esting differences in style. The apse, which was designed by Miche angelo, is a solid, unified whole, an appropriate symbol of the powe of the church. The façade, built by Maderno after the death of Miche angelo, is crowded. It covers the drum and is not entirely in stylist harmony with it. In the façade itself we see the spirit of the Baroqu in the massed columns which are doubled for the sake of ornamen the decorative pediments, the pilasters, and the heavy stringcours (Figure 14-30).

The Palace of the Senate (Figure 14-27), which has been mer tioned as an example of Renaissance style, shows definite leaning toward the Baroque in the stairway and the elaborate doorway wit ornamental carvings on each side.

NINETEENTH-CENTURY ARCHITECTURE

The nineteenth century in architecture is known as a period c eclecticism. *Eclecticism* means "freedom of choice"; in art, it mean the freedom to choose from the styles of the past. In former time architects had always used the style of their own periods. But in th nineteenth century, both architects and clients began deliberately t choose to make a building in the style of one era or another. Hence it happens that we have in almost any American city examples of a the historical styles, from the Greek onward. This self-consciousness about choice of style has produced some good and some bad results. Examples of borrowings from the past are the Gothic motifs in the Brooklyn Bridge and the Gothic-like "gingerbread" decorations on many houses.

The interest in various styles has resulted in the adoption of certain styles as suitable for certain types of building: Gothic for churches, Baroque for theaters, Renaissance for government buildings, and so on.

One objection to eclecticism is philosophical. In the course of historical development, each of the major styles has been evolved to meet the needs of its own age and to express its philosophy. The argument is that to go back arbitrarily to the style of a previous age is essentially false.

MODERN ARCHITECTURE

Skeleton Construction

Skeleton construction is a development of modern times, and most of our great modern structures are built in this way. But skeleton construction in its turn was made possible by the development of two new materials: structural steel and reinforced concrete.

Structural steel dates back to 1855, when Bessemer invented his process for the mass production of steel. As the advantages of steel became apparent, it gradually superseded cast iron. These advantages are, primarily, its resilience, strength, and reliability.

Concrete is composed of sand, crushed stone or gravel, water, and cement. When mixed, it is a semifluid which, owing to the cement, dries into a hard, stonelike substance. Forms are made in exactly the size and shape desired. The fluid concrete is poured into them; when dry, it is a solid substance of just those forms and shapes. Concrete is very strong and will stand great weight, but it will not stand strain or tension. At the end of the last century, some French engineers discovered that by adding steel rods to concrete they could give it the tensile strength it lacked; in other words, it would then withstand strain. "Reinforced concrete," as this new material is called, is thus the combination of concrete and steel. It has the strength of concrete, and like concrete it can readily be made into any shape. At the same time, it will withstand strain as steel does. It also has the advantage of being much cheaper than steel and lighter in weight.

In skeleton construction, strong but slender beams of steel or reinforced concrete form the framework of a building, and on it all the other parts are placed or hung. This type of construction has opened many new possibilities in building. First, it has made possible tall buildings, because the skeletons are strong but light. The walls

which are hung from the skeleton are merely curtains to keep ou cold and air. They may be made entirely of glass. They have n weight to speak of, and they are not essential to the strength of th building. A modern skyscraper, if built of masonry in the old fash ion, would need to have the first floors of solid stone to support th weight of the upper stories. In the building of the Inland Steel Com pany in Chicago (Figure 13-23), the columns which carry the weigh of the building are on the outside. As a result, the entire space on any floor is free of posts or pillars and, if necessary, can be used as single room.

Moreover, with skeleton construction the building may be lifte off the ground on posts so that the ground floor may be used for out door living or for a garage or driveway. Another important result of this type of construction is the fact that an opening of any size ma be spanned. Lintels of stone are necessarily short, since stone can not be cut in great lengths and will not bear strain. Lintels of woo are longer, but they are obviously limited. Since steel may be mad of any length and strength, a door or a window may be of an desired size.

Skeleton construction also allows freedom in the shape of th house. Concrete is a fluid material and can take any shape. Building of wood, brick, or stone tend to be rectangular, partly because of th difficulty of putting a roof on any but a rectangular building. Now buildings may be made of any shape: circular, round, or square. I the Guggenheim Museum in New York City (Figure 14-1), the gal leries mount in a continuous spiral. In the State Fair Arena at Ra leigh, North Carolina (Figure 14-31), the walls are two opposin parabolas of glass and concrete, with their open ends joined on th ground and their arches rising outward from each other. The aren measures 300 feet across in all directions, and there is not a singl column to obstruct the view. The arena seats about 9,000 people.

An innovative variation of skeleton construction for office high-rise buildings, usually cocooned in an envelope of facing material of glass or masonry, is represented in the John Hancock Building (Figure 4-17). This aggressive, powerfully designed structure wears its frame of giant cross-girders exposed as an exoskeleton (reminiscent of some forms of marine life or living fossils like the armadillo). Its truncated pyramid rises to a lofty 100 stories. In contrast, Lever House (Figure 4-15) is of gentle, classic design clothed in a sheath of glass and stainless steel; its envelope or skin is fabricated of qualitatively different material from the structure it wraps.

Cantilever Construction

Cantilever is a special form of steel and reinforced concrete construction. The term *cantilever* refers to any member or unit of an architectural design which projects beyond its support. The cantilever principle is often seen in bridges, where each half of the bridge is supported on one side only. The two halves meet in the center to form the bridge, but each half is entirely independent of the other. In most airplanes the wings are attached to the body in a cantilever construction. We see the principle in buildings when the upper story juts out beyond the lower. The two essentials of cantilever construction are, first, that the material used be able to stand the strain (i.e., have the necessary tensile strength), and second, that it be fastened securely at the side where it is supported. This principle, which is very old, has been much used in recent years, because the piece that projects can be larger in steel and reinforced concrete than in older materials.

The cantilever was used rather widely by the American architect Frank Lloyd Wright. In a number of houses he used the cantilever in a veranda, so that the roof projects over the porch with no columns or pillars to hold it up. In one case he designed a house projecting over a waterfall by means of cantilevered balconies. For the research building of the Johnson Wax Company (Figure 14-32),

Figure 14-32. Frank Lloyd Wright, Research and Development Tower of S. C. Johnson and Son, Inc., Racine, Wis. (1947–1950). (Brick and concrete with walls of glass tubing. Height of tower: 156 feet [50 feet underground]; each floor 40 feet square; each alternate floor 38 feet in diameter. Courtesy of Johnson Wax.)

Wright erected a tall building in which all the floors are cantilevered from one central column. The floors are alternately square and round. The whole is enclosed in glass. The central column contains elevators and tubes for air conditioning, besides all the passages for the machinery of the building, electric controls, etc.

The Everson Museum of Art (Figure 1-1), designed by I. M. Pei, is an example of the dramatic designs made possible by cantilever construction.

GEODESIC DOMES

Principles of geodesic frame construction developed by Buckminster Fuller have made possible the spanning of large areas which cannot be spanned by such traditional means as post-and-lintel construction or cantilevering. Inspired by the geometry of cojoined hexagons (six-sided figures) found in nature (e.g., protozoa and diatoms), these domed structures are built of modules ("facets" recalling the growth of crystals) whose units are triangles of tubular struts in frames. The struts are remarkably light (8½ pounds per square yard) and capable of bearing their own weight for large enclosures such as hangars, theaters, showrooms, gymnasiums, markets, factories, and offices. The module units that are repeated with their fixed arrangement are made up of six triangles whose apexes meet to form a central angle of circular arc and are joined at a variable angle, so that theoretically any curvature of sphere or hemisphere can be approximated. The whole tubular structure is then enclosed in a skin of light material, usually transparent.

The two examples of geodesic domes included in this book are the United States Pavilion at Expo 67, Montreal (Figure 1-2); and the Climatron, St. Louis, Missouri (Figure 4-16).

The United States Pavilion was constructed of steel tubes clothed in transparent acrylic; it encloses an area 250 feet in diameter. To achieve a greater height with a given area of floor space, it was necessary to construct its shell as an extended hemisphere; therefore, its floor area does not equal its greatest diameter. This shows the versatility of the geometric principle employed.

In the Climatron—a vast greenhouse in which any climatic condition can be simulated under the control of a computer system—an artificial atmosphere is created which can be either stabilized or varied for any given area inside the dome, with choice of humidity, temperature, and air flow. The operative principle here is the convection of a heated air mass of the solar bubble and the ecological systems of an air mass, such as the earth's own atmosphere, from which moisture precipitates when a critical temperature is reached.

Twentieth-Century Styles

International Style The buildings of the twentieth century fall in general into two different categories, known as the "international" style and the "organic" style. Both use the new materials, but their aims and techniques differ. The international style is recognized as a modern style by its severe horizontal and vertical lines, its reinforced concrete, its white walls and flat roofs. There are directness and simplicity in its use of materials and avoidance of ornament. The design is planned very carefully, usually with a *module*, or measure, to determine the exact proportions. The Seagram Building in New York City "is a bronze and glass shaft with every dimension, from total height to smallest bevel, determined by an arbitrary modular system."[5]

Adjectives often applied to buildings in this style are "spare," "aristocratic", and "chilly"—and indeed, many people find the style cold and forbidding. It is a design that can be imitated easily. Anyone can understand and use the structural elements. There are in this book three examples of this style: the Seagram Building, the Inland Steel Building and the United Nations Secretariat building (Figures 13-22, 13-23, and 13-24). Of these, the Seagram Building has generally been considered superior to the other two.

Organic style The organic architecture of the twentieth century is identified primarily with the work of Frank Lloyd Wright. For Wright, architecture is organic when there is organic unity in planning, structure, materials, and site. As Wright said, "I build a home for myself in southern Wisconsin: a stone, wood, and plaster building, make it as much a part of my grandfather's ground as the rocks and trees and hills there are."[6] And again: "Modern architecture, let us now say organic architecture, is a natural architecture: the architecture of nature, for nature."[7]

It is generally recognized now that, after his residences, Wright's ability showed itself best in the various buildings he designed for the Johnson Wax Company of Racine, Wisconsin. The tower of that group of buildings (Figure 14-32) has been discussed. The Administration Building (Figure 14-33) should be studied for the skill and beauty with which the various elements are harmonized. In the interior of the Administration Building, the columns are made to flare at the top, and some do not reach to the ceiling. They have a decora-

[5] John Canaday in John Ives Sewall, *A History of Western Art*, rev. ed. (New York: Holt, Rinehart and Winston, 1962).
[6] Frederick Gutheim (ed.), *Frank Lloyd Wright on Architecture: Selected Writings (1894–1940)* (New York: Grosset and Dunlap, 1941).
[7] Ibid., p. 248.

tive effect and give a sense of gaiety and freshness, like sunlight falling through the leaves of trees.

The boast of much modern architecture is that it is organic. Eclectic architecture, as we saw, was primarily decorative. The architect and the client chose a certain façade or a certain treatment of the material because they liked the looks of it, and often it had little, if any, relationship to the actual structure of the building. House plans were frequently presented as floor plans with the exterior to be finished in Gothic, classical, American colonial, or what have you. But when we say of modern architecture that it is "organic," we mean that there is organic unity in planning, structure, materials, and site; all are designed to meet exact needs. The needs of the age are many and various: factories, office buildings, laboratories, railroad stations, schools, hospitals, mass housing, airports, broadcasting stations, theaters, churches, homes, dormitories. The demands of each must be studied and met if the building is to be good.

In Chapter 4 we quoted Eero Saarinen's statement of his philosophy of architecture as an example of architectural thinking in the mid-twentieth century. Now, let us study in detail one example of a building designed for a special need, Saarinen's Stephens College Chapel (Figures 14-34 and 14-35). The chapel was intended primarily as a place for private worship. It was assumed that small functions might be held there, such as weddings, baptisms, or occasional concerts, but such occasions were not to be frequent enough to interfere with private devotions. The chapel was nondenominational; no one was to feel a stranger or unwelcome. Therefore, there were no sym-

Figure 14-34. Eero Saarinen (1910–1961), American architect. Stephens College Chapel, Columbia, Mo. finished 1956). (Brick. Size: 70 feet by 70 feet. Photograph, Marvin Kreisman.)

Figure 14-35. Eero Saarinen. Stephens College Chapel, interior. (Photograph, Marvin Kreisman.)

bols of any one faith, such as the cross or the Star of David; all the symbols were to be general.

An ambulatory around the entire auditorium is separated from the main chapel by a screen of interlaced brick, which makes a division but at the same time gives a view of the interior and the stained-glass doors beyond. The organ and choir are set behind a screen of wooden pieces, light brown and black. The ceiling is of wood in a square design.

The general effect is of simplicity and greatness. The place is small, but one has vistas of vast spaces; the room is intimate, but its many vistas are conducive to thoughts of the distant and the far away. It is the kind of place where one can get away from the perplexities of the everyday in the contemplation of the infinite.

The building as designed by Saarinen is square, foursquare, close to the earth; walls and roof make one unit, clinging to the ground and at the same time pointing up and ending in the central steeple. The walls are not interrupted by any windows, but at the entrance in the center of each side is a portico of stained glass, serving, Saarinen said, as a small lantern leading to the chapel.

The interior is simple and direct. If one were to draw diagonals from the four corners of the building, four equal triangles would be formed. One of these is designed for the organ and choir, the other three for the audience. In the exact center of the room is the altar, a plain square block. The light comes mainly from the base of the spire and falls directly on the altar.

Two other structures designed by Saarinen illustrate the great variety that appears in modern architecture as new principles of construction are adapted to provide for very different functions. The Stephens College Chapel may be considered as an architectural "frame" for a variety of religious expressions which it does not specify. In contrast, in the TWA Terminal Building (Figure 14-36), the architectural elements are organized to provide for the quite specific functions of a contemporary air terminal. Appropriately, the four large, flowing concrete shells which rest on abstract supports to enclose the functional interior are an eloquent celebration of the achievement of flight by human beings.

In the Gateway Arch for the Jefferson Westward Expansion Memorial at St. Louis, completed in 1967 (Figure 4-7), a mood of celebration and civic spirit predominates. The very size and simple elegance of this monument commemorating the role played by St. Louis in the great westward expansion have made it an immediately recognizable symbol throughout the world. The gleaming stainless steel arch, 630 feet tall, is in the form of a catenary curve, the shape formed by a chain suspended in space with the ends as far apart as the arc is high. The legs of the arch are 630 feet apart; each contains a 40-foot train which carries visitors to the top, where sixteen windows on each side provide extensive views to the east and west. The unmistakable impression is that of a gateway dramatically stated in massive simplicity. Such structures as the Gateway Arch are made possible by the imaginative, creative use of modern principles of construction and new mediums. In the Arch, the stressed-skin principle used in airplane construction is combined with elements of light, high-strength structural steel to produce a design and a magnitude that would have been impossible in other periods of our architectural history.

SUMMARY OUTLINE OF MAJOR HISTORICAL ARCHITECTURAL STYLES[8]

Egyptian (3000–1000 B.C.)

1. Mammoth rectangular plan of limestone
2. Sloping pylons with gorge molding
3. Bud and flower capitals for post-and-lintel construction
4. Clerestory in hypostyle hall
5. Monumental obelisks and sphinxes fronting pylons
6. Relief sculpture on walls and columns

Greek (600–100 B.C.)

1. Relatively small rectangular plan of marble
2. Entablature of pediment, cornice, frieze, and architrave
3. Doric, Ionic, or Corinthian capitals on fluted columns for post and lintel
4. Color and gilding on statuary and architectural details
5. Mathematical approach to symmetry
6. Refinements of proportion to create optical illusions—e.g., entasis

Roman (100 B.C.–A.D. 500)

1. Rectangular and circular plans of pozzuolana and stucco
2. Engineering principle of arch in dome on drum, barrel vaulting, and groin vaulting
3. Fluted freestanding and engaged columns and pilasters with Greek orders
4. Coffered ceilings over large spaces
5. Triangular, circular, and broken pedimentation
6. Decorative medallions and keystones

Early Christian (A.D. 300–700)

1. Roman basilica plan of center aisle, one or two side aisles, and apse
2. Plain buttressed façade, sometimes with small round window and compound arches
3. Campanile disengaged from façade
4. Square coffered ceiling
5. Interior marble and mosaics
6. Variations of Roman orders, such as basket capitals

[8] The drawings accompanying this summary are by Robin Rice.

Byzantine (A.D. 300–1000)

1. Greek cross plan, walls surfaced in patterned brick in meander, fret, or chevron
2. Great dome on pendentives buttressed by half domes
3. Plain exterior
4. Clustered colonnettes
5. Carved basket capitals
6. Interiors of colored, richly grained marble and mosaics in upper vaults

Romanesque (1000–1200)

1. Latin cross plan of local stone
2. Use of round arch and buttressed barrel vaulting and groin vaulting
3. Towers engaged to façade and large transept tower
4. Dome often over apse
5. Recessed doorways ornamented with sculpture, and large rose windows on upper levels
6. Grouped piers (clustered), thick columns, or both

Gothic (1200–1400)

1. Latin-cross plan, usually of native stone
2. Use of soaring pointed arch and ribbed vaulting with flying buttresses
3. High façade towers with gargoyles
4. Stained-glass rose and lancet windows
5. Pinnacles with crockets and finials
6. Tall, recessed doorways decorated with elongated sculptured figures

Renaissance (1400–1600)

1. Rectangular plan with combined post-and-lintel form and arch form
2. Balanced fenestration of three stories
3. Ribbed dome on drum with lantern
4. Entablature with two-story columns
5. Triangular and circular pedimentation
6. Decorative balustrades, pilasters, keystones, and quoins
7. Greek and Roman ornamentation

Baroque (1600–1700)

1. Circular plans and ornamentation; but Baroque façades frequently added to existing buildings
2. Playful in-and-out movement of curved steps and balustrading
3. Accent on sculpture above eye level
4. Overly dramatic and exuberant light-and-dark patterns
5. Broken pediments over doors and windows
6. Elaborate console brackets, crests, cartouches, clocks, and fountains

International Style (1920s–   )

1. Noneclectic with minimum ornamentation
2. New engineering principles, such as cantilevering from hillside
3. Multilevel construction
4. Greater use of glass, steel, and cement
5. New materials, such as permapane and stained aluminum
6. Emphasis, conceptually at least, on "honest" functionalism

15 FORM IN MUSIC

There are two distinct, though related, meanings of the word *form* as it is applied to music. In the first, *form* refers to the internal structure of a work, the relationship of the various musical elements (discussed in Chapter 10) in a particular piece. In this sense, because every composition is different, it has its own unique form which distinguishes it from all others.

A second meaning of *form* refers to certain formal patterns which, over the centuries, have become the basis of much Western music. These forms are based on *treatment*; repetition of musical material, repetition with contrast, repetition with variation, and repetition with development. Some of the more common of these traditional forms are song form, theme and variation, fugue, rondo, and sonata form. In this second sense, form represents not a strict and rigid mold into which the music may be poured, but a general pattern of repetition, contrast, and variation which is handled differently by different composers, or differently by the same composer in various works. It is in this second sense that musical form will be discussed here.

SONG FORM

Vocal music was the first music to develop standard forms. But although musical forms were often dependent upon the form of the text being sung, some of them, like song form, have been carried over into instrumental music as well.

There are two types of song form which are widely used: binary and ternary. Binary song form (AB), as its name implies, consists of two parts. The second part is both a contrast and a complement to the first. In binary form, some balance of design, with some related musical idea, is usually present in the two parts. It is somewhat like a question and its answer; that is, part A presents a musical idea which is resolved in part B. The two parts are usually divided by a significant pause and a dominant or tonic cadence. Brahms's famous "Lullaby" (Example 1) is binary, and part B is exactly as long as part A, each being eight measures.

EXAMPLE 1

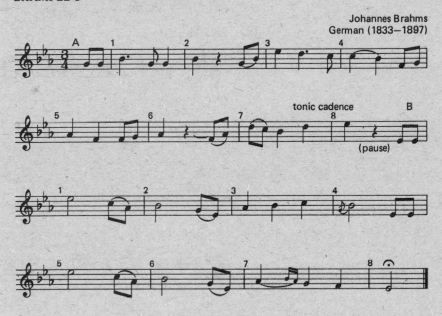

Johannes Brahms
German (1833—1897)

In this example, part A could stand alone because it ends on a tonic cadence, but part B sounds like a natural extension of it.

Not all binary forms are exactly balanced in length. In Handel's "Harmonious Blacksmith" (Example 2), part B is twice the length of part A. Here part A cannot stand alone, because it ends on a dominant cadence, which gives a feeling of incompleteness. Part B begins with the tonic and, after going through the dominant, ends on the tonic, which makes it sound finished or complete.

Sometimes part B quotes, either at the beginning or the end, a section of part A. In Example 3 we have an exact quotation of the second four measures of part A at the end of part B (the first four measures are also repeated, but in a somewhat altered form), which gives a rounded or ABa binary. The small "a," in this case, means that only a portion, half or less, of the original A part is repeated.

EXAMPLE 2

Georg Friedrich Hände
German (1685–1759
dominant
cadence

EXAMPLE 3

Minuet

J. S. Bac
German (1685–1750

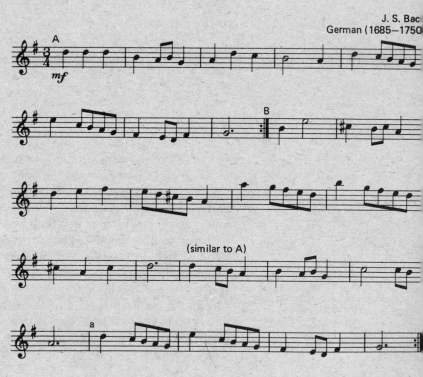

(similar to A)

Ternary song form (ABA), or three-part form, like the binary, depends on two distinct thematic sections, but in ternary form there is a full restatement of part A after part B, creating a pleasing symmetrical balance. In some music in this form, the composer, at the end of section B, will write *"da capo,"* or merely "D.C.," which means "from the head," or from the beginning—that is, "repeat part A." This saves repeating the A section in the score; obviously this is possible only if the second A section is exactly the same as the first. Example 4 is in ternary form.

EXAMPLE 4

Plaisir d'Amour (The Joy of Love)

Jean Paul Martini
French (1706—1784)

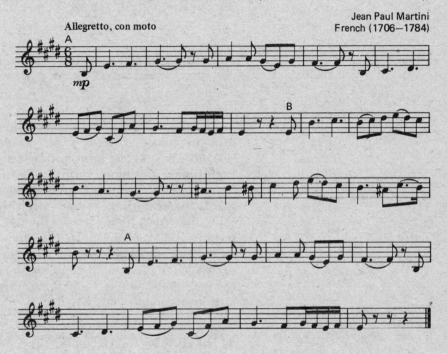

Perhaps the most widely used song form is an extended kind of ternary which is sometimes called "quatrain" form (AABA). The extension, the second A, is either an exact repetition of the first A or of such obvious similarity that we call it a second A. Ordinarily the repetition of a section of music is not of any structural significance, since it does not alter the form, which is true in this case (AABA is still basically ABA). Example 5 is an extended ternary song.

EXAMPLE 5

Drink to Me Only with Thine Eyes
(Ben Jonson, "To Celia")

Music traditional

In some pieces in song form, it may be difficult to say whether they are binary or ternary. For example, Beethoven's "Bagatelle" (Example 6) is a song form, but it seems to contain characteristics of both binary and ternary form. The first section is repeated exactly (measures 13–20) after a contrasting middle section (measures 9–12); this is characteristic of ternary form. However, the middle section is quite short (only half as long as the A section) and incapable of standing by itself; and the B section and the final A section, taken together, are repeated as a unit (as is the first A section), which tends to divide the piece into two rather than three parts. When listening, the important thing is not to force a piece into a given pattern but to attempt to understand its sense.

THEME AND VARIATIONS

One of the most popular and enduring forms in music is the theme and variation form (A, A1, A2, A3, etc.). In this form there is a constant interplay between repetition and variation, and it is the delight of both composer and listener to see how many ways there are of saying essentially the same thing.

Variations tend to progress by contrast or by increasing elaboration. In either case the variations show more use of ornamentation than the original theme. For the most part, therefore, this form is confined to a light, even witty manner of presenting a theme in sev-

Bagatelle

Ludwig van Beethoven
German (1770–1827)

eral guises. As a result, there are only a few sets of variations that could be called monumental. Two of the most famous are the Goldberg Variations by Bach and the Diabelli Variations by Beethoven.

Because the theme in the theme and variation form is usually concise and relatively simple (thus allowing for the elaboration to come), it is often itself in a binary or ternary song form. Handel's "Harmonious Blacksmith" (Example 2), mentioned earlier as an example of binary song form, is a theme for a set of five variations, which progress by increasing elaboration.

In Examples 7 through 10 we have a theme and variation form by Mozart in which the variations progress by contrast. The theme (Example 7) is binary, but only the first half of it is quoted here:

EXAMPLE 7

Theme and Variations from Sonata K331
(First Movement)

Wolfgang Amadeus Mozart
Austrian (1756–1791)

THEME (andante grazioso)

In variation I (Example 8) the melody is greatly changed by the use of syncopation and chromatic intervals. Notice that, whereas in the theme the durations of the notes are predominantly eighth and quarter notes, this variation consists largely of sixteenth notes.

EXAMPLE 8

VARIATION I

In variation IV (Example 9) the greatest change is in the texture, which is thicker, and in the range, which is higher. Here the melody flows serenely because of the stepwise rise and fall of the melodic line and the eighth notes in the melody (although the accompaniment is in sixteenths).

EXAMPLE 9

VARIATION IV

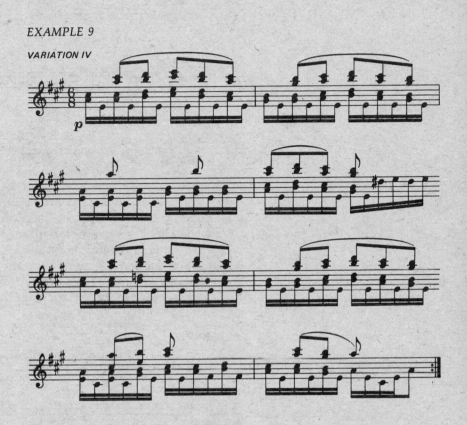

In variation VI (Example 10) changes occur in the meter, which becomes 4/4, and in the tempo, which is speeded up to *allegro*. The last half of the melody is treated quite differently from the first and acts as a finale, or grand flourish, to end the variations and bring the total form to a close.

In some variations, particularly those of the nineteenth century, greater freedom is taken. In Schumann's Symphonic Studies for piano, for example, there are only incomplete and irregular references to the theme throughout a set of short pieces (the "variations") that follow the theme.

EXAMPLE 10

VARIATION VI (allegro)

A particular kind of variation treatment is the *passacaglia*. This is a short, simple bass theme which is repeated again and again with little or no change, while in the upper voices a different variation is presented for each repetition of the bass theme. The passacaglia is in a minor key, has a triple meter, and the theme is usually eight measures long. In Example 11, for organ, the passacaglia theme is stated. It is followed by twenty variations and a fugue.

EXAMPLE 11

Passacaglia and Fugue in C minor

J. S. Bach
German (1685–1750)

FUGUE

The fugue is a kind of imitiative contrapuntal treatment of a relatively short theme. This theme is called the "subject" because it is the melodic idea on which the whole fugue is based. Although no two fugues have specifically the same design, they all have two parts in common: an exposition and a development section

In the exposition, the fugue subject is presented in the tonic by one "voice" and then imitated exactly or very closely at the interval of a fourth or fifth by one or more voices which follow one at a time. If the imitation is exact, we say that it is "real"; if only very close, it is called "tonal." When each of the voices has stated the subject, the exposition is complete. A fugue requires at least two voices, but most fugues are written for three, four, or five; rarely is one composed for six or two. However many voices appear in the exposition, that number then remains constant for the duration of the fugue.

Sometimes a countersubject is used in addition to the subject. This is the continuation of the melodic line following the subject, and is considered a countersubject only if each of the voices states it. Otherwise, whatever follows the subject is incidental counterpoint.

In the development section of the fugue, the subject is quoted in its entirety or in abbreviated form at various intervals until the end. It may also go faster (diminution), slower (augmentation), or be inverted (inversion).

Many fugues make use of the episode, which is any musical interlude not based primarily on the subject, or at least not referring to the entire subject. The purpose of the episode is to provide contrast to the theme and often to lighten the texture. Episodes are commonly used at the end of the exposition as a transition to the development section, and within the development section between entrances of the complete subject.

Stretto is another commonly used device. In stretto, the subject is announced in one voice, and before it has been completed, other voices enter, one at a time in quick succession, to imitate it. This creates an effect of overlapping. Stretto may occur at several places in the fugue, but is most commonly used at points of climax, especially near the end, where it is effective in creating tension.

Pedal point is also commonly used in fugal writing. It gets its name from music literature for the organ in which a pedal is held down while melodic and harmonic changes take place in the voices above. By common usage, however, any tone which is held for a significant length of time is called "pedal point." Like the stretto, pedal point is effective for creating tension at points of climax, especially at the end of the composition. In the fugue, pedal point tones are usually dominant or tonic.

Bach's "Little" Fugue in G minor for organ (Example 12) has four voices. These occur in a progressive downward pattern, each voice entering at a lower pitch until the fourth voice—the entrance of the subject—is stated. In outline, the "Little" Fugue looks like this:

EXPOSITION
Voice 1 (tonic): subject, countersubject, incidental counterpoint
Voice 2 (dominant): subject, countersubject, incidental counterpoint
Voice 3 (tonic): subject, countersubject, incidental counterpoint
Voice 4 (dominant): subject, countersubject, incidental counterpoint

EPISODE

DEVELOPMENT

    Return and development of subject (five times) and counter-
    subject (two times in full, two times in part)

Close with full subject

You will notice that in Example 12 there are three staves for the
organ; the organist plays the notes in the two upper staves with two
hands and plays the pedals for the notes in the bottom staff with the
feet. This piece is still performed on the organ; but it has also been
transcribed for orchestra by Leopold Stokowski. Comparing the
original version with the orchestral transcription gives a clearer idea
of the fugue form, the texture of the counterpoint, and the variety of
timbres.

EXAMPLE 12

Little Fugue in G Minor

J. S. Bach
(1685–1750)

Continuing Counterpoint

Entrance Four

etc.

MINUET AND TRIO

The minuet-trio form makes an easy introduction to the group of larger forms that use the ternary, or ABA, pattern. The first section, which is a minuet, is followed by a second, the trio, and then the minuet is heard again. Both the minuet and the trio are in 3/4 meter and are binary. The trio is used as a bridge between the two minuets; because its function is to give a sense of contrast, it is frequently in a key different from that of the minuet and contains melodies of contrasting character. Traditionally, the two parts of the first minuet are repeated, as are those of the trio; but there are no repetitions in the restatement of the minuet. This is shown in Example 13, from Mozart's *Eine Kleine Nachtmusik* ("A Little Night Music"). In outline the form looks like this:

A: Minuet—AABaBa (binary, repeated)
B: Trio—CCDCDC (binary, repeated)
A: Minuet—ABa (binary, once only)

EXAMPLE 13

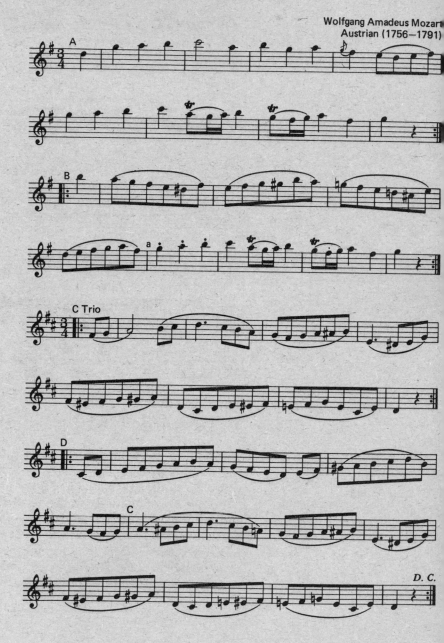

Wolfgang Amadeus Mozart
Austrian (1756–1791)

RONDO

The *rondo* is also an outgrowth of ABA form, but it is more extended. The main theme, or *refrain*, which is usually a full binary form, alternates with the other themes, called "episodes." The episodes provide contrast to the refrain and also give variety in range, texture, and character between restatements of the refrain; they are most often in different keys. The rondo always begins and ends with the main theme.

The shortest possible rondo would be ABABA, or more commonly, ABACA. There are numerous rondo designs, the one most often used being ABACA or ABACABA, which is as exactly balanced as an arch. Within these designs, the treatment may vary. In some rondos, the episodes are developments of musical ideas found in the refrain. In others, the reappearance of the refrain is varied, much as it would be in variation form. In still others, when the refrain occurs in restatement, it may be in abbreviated form.

For some obscure reason, many rondos which are the second movements of sonatas or symphonies are not labeled as rondos by the composers but merely given mood and tempo markings. Example 14 is the rondo of the second movement of Mozart's *Eine Kleine Nachtmusik*. The main theme (A1 and A2) is binary.

EXAMPLE 14

(Example 14 continues on page 378.)

EXAMPLE 14 (Continued)

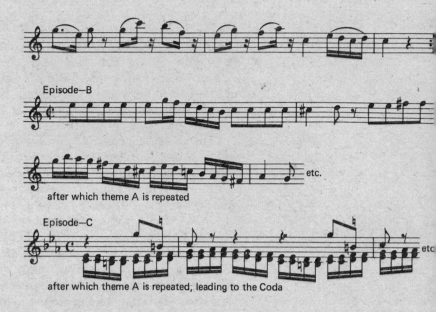

Episode—B

etc.

after which theme A is repeated

Episode—C

etc.

after which theme A is repeated, leading to the Coda

SONATA FORM

Sonata form (also known as *sonata allegro* or first-movement form) is used in the first movement of extended compositions having several movements. The form is based on two principal themes which appear in three large sections called the "exposition," "development," and "recapitulation." First-movement form is ternary in the broadest sense because the recapitulation is a restatement of the themes heard in the exposition.

The *exposition* contains two principal themes and usually several subordinate themes. The main themes, A and B, are always in different keys and are connected by extrathematic music called a "transition." The *transition*, when it links two themes in different keys, is a modulating passage—that is, a passage designed to carry the music from one tonality to another tonality.

In the *development* section, the two themes are developed in any way the composer chooses. They may appear in new keys, be quoted only in part, be extended, be compressed, or be varied in any way. Often theme A is given preferential treatment, since it is the theme that introduces the form.

The *recapitulation* is a restatement of the exposition with one important change: theme B is now heard in the same key as theme A. This allows the piece to end on the tonic, as it began.

There may or may not be a *coda* (literally, "tail") after the recapitulation. The coda is used as a flourish to put a conclusive feeling to the end and often explores some phrase or thematic idea from one of the two themes (to this extent it is reminiscent of the development section). The coda always is in the tonic key or at least ends in the tonic key. The sonata allegro form may be mapped as follows:

EXPOSITION
   Theme A, in tonic
      Transition to theme B (with modulation to key of theme B)
      Theme B, in key of dominant or other related key
      Transition
DEVELOPMENT
   Varied use of themes A and B in new keys, none of which is
   allowed to assert priority for an extended period
RECAPITULATION
   Theme A in original key (tonic)
      Transition to theme B (no modulation)
   Theme B, also in tonic

In Example 15, the first movement of Mozart's *Eine Kleine Nacht-musik*, themes A and B are binary; the parts are marked 1 and 2. The development section here is quite short.

EXAMPLE 15

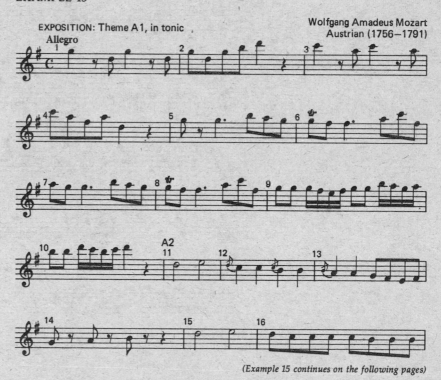

(*Example 15 continues on the following pages*)

EXAMPLE 15 (Continued)

EXAMPLE 15 (Continued)

DEVELOPMENT: Theme A in D major, modulating to

C major for second half of Theme B

modulating variously and

leading to a

transitional passage

cadence on the dominant

EXAMPLE 15 (Continued)

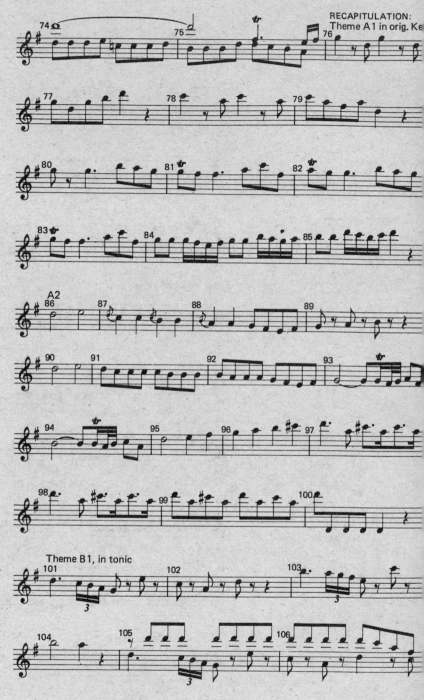

EXAMPLE 15 (Continued)

THE SUITE

One of the earliest efforts in the attempt to create instrumental music
of extended length was the suite, a collection of dances. In the seven
teenth and eighteenth centuries, there were usually five dances
known collectively as the "classical suite": (1) the *allemande*, a rather
slow dance in duple meter; (2) the *courante*, a dance of simple rhythm
and running passages in triple meter; (3) the *saraband*, a slow, stately
ceremonial dance in triple meter; (4) an optional dance, chosen by
the composer (such as gavotte, bourée, or minuet); and (5) the *gigue*,
a fast, lively dance, like the English jig, in duple meter. These dances
were held together as a unit in two ways: they were all binary and
were all in the same key.

Not all suites follow the organization of the classical suite. For
instance, in Bach's Suite No. 2 in B minor for Flute and Strings, the
dances include a rondo, a saraband, a bourée (a French dance), a
polonaise (a Polish dance), a minuet. Furthermore, this suite opens
with an overture and ends with a badinerie, a piece of playful music.

The modern suite has no necessary connection with dance forms.
It is a collection of separate pieces which have been put together because of some unifying idea, not necessarily musical. Bizet, for instance, linked excerpts from his opera in his *Carmen Suite*. Ravel's
suite *Le Tombeau de Couperin* ("In Memory of Couperin") tries to
evoke the spirit of former times. Rimsky-Korsakov based his symphonic suite *Scheherazade* on *The Arabian Nights' Entertainment*.
Prokofiev wrote a suite on the adventures of an imaginary figure,
Lieutenant Kije.

THE SONATA

Sonata is the name given to a lengthy and intricate composition made
up of a series of movements which are connected by tonality and
thematic content, and which are characterized by the use of specific
forms. In the sonata, which was developed after the suite, there may
be three or four movements for which there is a definite, though
flexible, tradition about the form each of them takes.

The first movement of the sonata is usually in sonata allegro
form, which is the most complex of the movements; and as its tempo
marking indicates, it is fairly fast. The name *sonata* is used because
the sonata allegro form is its most characteristic movement.

The second and fourth movements often use either a rondo form
or a theme and variation treatment of a song form. The second movement is generally in a slow tempo; the fourth movement is usually
fast but may be slow.

The third movement is traditionally a dance movement in either minuet-trio or scherzo-trio form. It is usually the shortest. When a sonata has only three movements, the dance movement is omitted.

Sonata, Concerto, String Quartet, Symphony

Sonata, concerto, string quartet, and *symphony* are terms which distinguish the instrumentation of the sonata for various groups.

When only one or two instruments are involved, the series of movements is known as a sonata, as in "sonata for piano," or "sonata for piano and clarinet."

The concerto is a sonata for a solo instrument and symphony orchestra. The name of the instrument featured is included in the title of the composition, as in "concerto for oboe," and "concerto for French horn." The concerto grosso is a sonata for several solo instruments and orchestra.

The string quartet is a sonata for four string instruments—two violins, one viola, and one cello.

The symphony is a sonata for the entire symphony orchestra. Traditionally, the first movement of a symphony is labeled "sonata allegro," but the second and fourth movements are labeled only by tempo. When present, the dance movement is labeled "minuet," "scherzo," "waltz," etc.

FREE FORMS

There are also musical composition which do not conform to one of the standard patterns. This is not to say, however, that they are devoid of form. On the contrary, they are as carefully structured as the standard forms; it is just that they tend to develop shapes unique to themselves. Some of the names of such compositions are noted in the following paragraphs.

Prelude   The term *prelude* originally referred to a piece meant to be played before something else, such as the preludes of Bach (which precede more complex, contrapuntal pieces, called "fugues") and the "Prelude to Lohengrin" by Wagner (which precedes his opera *Lohengrin*). But the word has now become less definite. The Preludes of Chopin, for instance, are not preludes to anything, but independent pieces. The word now enjoys both meanings: a piece to be played before something else, and a separate piece.

Impromptu   This name is really a contradiction in terms, for an impromptu purports to be extemporaneous, which it obviously cannot be, since it is written down and published. However, it has connotations of spontaneity and of rather slight organization.

Nocturne   The nocturne is a piece which is supposed to suggest the atmosphere of night. The best-known examples are those for the piano by Chopin.

Etude   The étude is a technical study, usually of great difficulty. I became important at the time of Chopin and Liszt (nineteenth century), who were virtuoso pianists as well as composers.

PROGRAM MUSIC

In Chapter 2, program music was defined as music with subject matter, and little needs to be added to that discussion. However, we may note that program music generally falls into three classes: the imitative, the descriptive, and the narrative.

Imitative music imitates the actual sound of the subject, as in Rimsky-Korsakov's "Flight of the Bumblebee."

Descriptive music is typified by Beethoven's Symphony No. 6 called the *Pastoral* Symphony. The work describes a day in the country, with a festive gathering of country people. Their pleasure is interrupted by a storm which soon subsides, and the festivities are resumed. Beethoven's own program, usually printed with the symphony, is as follows:

> *Pastoral Symphony*, or a recollection of country life (more an expression of feeling than a portrayal):
>
> 1. *Allegro ma non troppo*—The cheerful feelings aroused by arrival in the country
> 2. *Andante molto mosso*—Scene by the brook
> 3. *Allegro*—Peasants' merrymaking
> 4. *Allegro*—Storm
> 5. *Allegretto*—Shepherd's song: glad and thankful feelings after the storm

This type of program music also includes compositions which try to distill the feeling or atmosphere of a scene, for example, Debussy's "Claire de Lune," which suggests moonlight, and his "Afternoon of a Faun," which evokes forest scenes.

Narrative music attempts to tell a story, or at least give a musical impression of the story. One example is "The Sorcerer's Apprentice," by Dukas, which tells the old story of the person who activates a magic charm and then cannot stop its influence. A common type of narrative music is the *symphonic poem* or *tone poem*, an orchestral work based upon a story taken from literature. It is of the length and complexity of a symphony but has no prescribed form. The tone poems of Richard Strauss, such as *Don Juan* and *Till Eulenspiegel's Merry Pranks*, are well-known examples of this type.

GENRE

The word *genre* refers not to the particular form of a piece, but rather to the general type of music to which the piece belongs. Thus we distinguish between such different genres as folk music and art music, popular and classical music, and vocal and instrumental music. Let us now consider some of the more common vocal genres.

FOLK MUSIC AND ART SONG

A song in the broadest sense is anything sung. *Folk songs* are the songs of the folk, or people. They are communal in that they are the property of the entire community and express the life of the community. Everybody knows them and everybody sings them. They show little trace of individual authorship, or if they ever did, these traces have been lost through the oral tradition.

An *art song*, on the other hand, is the work of a single composer and as such shows his or her individuality. The German word for song is *Lied* (plural, *Lieder*), and since many of the greatest writers of art songs were German or Austrian (for example, Schubert, Schumann, Wolff, and Brahms), we refer to their songs as *Lieder*. Each composer tries to make the music of the song fit the words chosen (which are usually from a poem written by someone else), but the song is nevertheless characteristic of the composer. A song by Schumann is not like one by Schubert. Nevertheless, certain songs by certain composers have so much of the simplicity and spontaneity of folk songs that they are accepted and sung by the people as "their" songs. They are classed as folk songs and are usually found in volumes of folk songs. Examples are the American "Swanee River" and the Bohemian "Songs My Mother Taught Me."

Folk songs are often classified according to subject as hunting songs ("John Peel"), cowboy songs ("Home on the Range"), spirituals ("Nobody Knows de Trouble I See"), etc. They are also grouped according to the country from which they come: the "Volga Boatman" is Russian, "Auld Lang Syne" is Scottish, and so on.

STROPHIC AND CONTINUOUS COMPOSITION

Folk songs and art songs follow one of two kinds of treatment. In strophic composition the same music is repeated exactly for each stanza. In "Barbara Allen," for example, the same music is used no matter whether one is singing of the "merry month of May," Barbara's scorn of her lover, or her death. The only differences that can be introduced lie in tempo, dynamics, and general expressiveness.

In continuous composition (sometimes referred to as "through-composed"), new music is adapted to each stanza of words. How ever, repetition of musical phrases or motives may be, and often is used in continuous form. Schubert's "Erlkönig" is a classic example

Wer reitet so spät durch Nacht und Wind?
Es ist der Vater mit seinem Kind.
Er hat den Knaben wohl in dem Arm,
Er fasst ihn sicher, er hält ihn warm.

Who gallops so late through wind and night?
A father bearing his son in flight;
He holds him tightly, breasting the storm,
To bear him safely and keep him warm.

Mein Sohn, was birgst du so bang dein Gesicht?
Siehst, Vater, du den Erlkönig nicht?
Den Erlenkönig mit Kron' und Schweif?
Mein Sohn, es ist ein Nebelstreif.

"My son, why bury your face thus in fear?"
"Don't you see, father, the Erl-King draw near,
The king of spirits, with crown and with shroud?"
"My son, it is a wisp of cloud."

"Du liebes Kind, komm, geh mit mir!
Gar schöne Spiele spiel' ich mit dir.
Manch' bunte Blumen sind an dem Strand,
Meine Mutter hat manch gülden Gewand."

"My darling child, come, go with me!
I'll play the finest games with thee.
The brightest flowers grow on the shore;
My mother has clothes of gold in store."

Mein Vater, mein Vater, und hörest du nicht.
Was Erlenkönig mir leise verspricht?—
Sei ruhig, bleibe ruhig, mein Kind:
In dürren Blättern säuselt der Wind.—

"My father, my father, but surely you heard
The Erl-King's whisp'ring, promising word?"
"Be quiet; there is nothing to fear:
The wind is rustling through thickets sere."

"Willst, feiner Knabe, du mit mir gehn?
Meine Töchter sollen dich warten schön;
Meine Töchter führen den nächtlichen Reihn
Und wiegen und tanzen und singen dich ein."

"Wilt thou come with me, my boy, away
Where my daughters play with thee night and day?
For my daughters shall come in the night if thou wee
And rock thee and dance thee and sing thee to sleep."

Mein Vater, mein Vater, und siehst du nicht dort
Erlkönigs Töchter am düstern Ort?—
Mein Sohn, mein Sohn, ich seh' es genau:
Es scheinen die alten Weiden so grau.—

"My father, my father, but do you not see
His daughters lurking by yon dark tree?"
"My son, my son, it is only the light
Of old willows gleaming gray through the night."

"Ich liebe dich, mich reizt deine schöne Gestalt;
Und bist du nicht willig, so brauch' ich Gewalt."
Mein Vater, mein Vater, jetzt fasst er mich an!
Erlkönig hat mir ein Leids getan!—

"I love thee so, thy beauty leaves no other course,
And if thou'rt not willing, I'll take thee by force."
"My father, my father, he drags me from you;
Erl-King has seized me, and hurts me too."

Dem Vater grauset's, er reitet geschwind,
Er hält in den Armen das ächzende Kind,
Erreicht den Hof mit Mühe und Not—
In seinen Armen das Kind war tot.

The father shudders; he spurs through the wild.
His arms strain closer the weak, moaning child.
He gains his home with toil and dread—
Clasped in his arms there, the child was dead.

   —Johann Wolfgang von Goethe (1749–1832, German poet, dramatist, and novelist),
     "Der Erlkönig" (translated by Calvin Brown)[1]

[1] Calvin Brown, *Music and Literature* (Athens, Georgia: University of Georgia Press), pp. 71–72
Courtesy of Mr. Brown and the University of Georgia Press.

In Schubert's music we hear the galloping of the horse and the thunder of the storm. The voices of the three characters are carefully differentiated: the father's voice is low, calm, assured; the child's voice is high-pitched, afraid, curious, wondering; the Erl-King's voice is pleading and ingratiating until he announces that he will take the child by force, when it becomes brusque and harsh. At the end of the song, the galloping and thunder, which have continued throughout, suddenly cease as the father arrives home and finds that the boy is dead.

Almost all folk songs are strophic. Art songs are both strophic and continuous. "Der Erlkönig" has been cited as an example of continuous composition; Schubert's "Ständchen" ("Serenade") and "Haiden-Röslein" ("Hedge-Roses") are strophic.

A special type of art song is the aria (or air), which is a set piece for solo voice taken from an opera, an oratorio, or a cantata. It may be either strophic or continuous and is frequently, although not always, of considerable technical difficulty—a sort of showpiece for the singer.

OPERA

Although opera is a combined art—combining a story (the *libretto*, or "little book"), theater, sometimes dance, and music—and is discussed with the other combined arts, the perennial appeal of an opera is its music. Opera was originally conceived (ca. 1600) as an attempt to reproduce the effect of the Greek drama in a kind of musical speech, called "recitative." The voices followed the accents and natural inflections of speech, but in musical tones. This early operative recitative is more like chant than any other form of music we hear today. The first operas were composed largely of recitatives (chanted speech) and were thus of limited musical interest. Accordingly, songs, or arias, were introduced to break the monotony: solos, duets, trios, quartets, choruses, etc. For a time drama lost its importance, and the music was everything. Then Gluck (1714–1787), whose *Orpheus and Eurydice* we discussed in Chapter 5 and who is known as the first reformer of opera, brought drama back into prominence and insisted that the singers be subordinate to the plot. At the same time, he continued to stress recitative in his operas and to include many set and separable songs and choruses. This concept of opera is also to be seen in the great operas of Verdi and Mozart. Drama is emphasized, and the music still contains some recitative; but there are also arias, duets, and choruses—that is, set pieces which can be detached from the drama and sung in concert. As examples we can cite the arias "Caro Nome" from *Rigoletto* and "Celeste Aïda" from *Aïda*, as well as the "Soldiers' Chorus" from *Faust* and the sextet from *Lucia di Lammermoor*.

A new and different kind of opera was inaugurated by Wagner (1813–1883). He attempted to make a more unified work, with music and drama of equal importance, and therefore preferred to call some of his works "music dramas" rather than operas. The voices and the orchestra combine to tell the story. In this way the orchestra, which supplies a kind of musical comment on the action of the story, becomes particularly important. The music is continuous; it is not interrupted for set arias and ensembles by the singers. The vocal line, in fact, is treated almost like an orchestral line, and often the voices are subordinate to the orchestra. The action, too, is continuous; there is no pause from the beginning of an act to the fall of the curtain.

In addition, Wagner devised a new type of musical development. The characters and many of the important objects, places, and ideas in the drama are each associated with a musical motive called a "leitmotiv." These leitmotivs represent, for example, "the sword," "the rainbow," "the ring," "the Rhine," and even such abstractions as "fate." The entrance of a character is announted by his or her theme in the orchestra, and often the music tells us what the characters themselves do not know. In *Die Walkürie*, for example, when Siegmund is lying in Hunding's house, desolate because he has no sword, the music fairly shouts the sword theme, calling our attention to the sword in the tree beside him.

There are a number of distinct types of opera, three of which are basic: *grand opera* always has a serious subject, is usually tragic, and has no spoken dialogue (an example is Verdi's *Aïda*). *Comic opera* is any opera having spoken dialogue, whether it is comic or not (Bizet's *Carmen* is an example). The term derives from that for French comic opera having spoken dialogue (*opéra comique*). The third type is *operetta*, which is synonymous with musical comedy ("musicals") or light opera. The subject may be tragic or comic, and there is spoken dialogue. Generally speaking, the music is not as ambitious as in opera, and the demands made on the musicians are much lighter (Lehar's *Merry Widow* and Rodgers and Hammerstein's *South Pacific* are examples).

THE ORATORIO

Oratorio, like grand opera, is an extended piece of music employing the resources of the orchestra, chorus, and solo singers. It differs from opera in many ways, however. The subject is usually biblical, and in many of the great oratorios, the words are taken directly from the Bible. Handel's *Messiah* and Mendelssohn's *Elijah* are outstanding examples.

Whereas operas are enacted on the stage, the oratorio is sung in concert without costume, stage sets, or lighting. The chorus and soloists for the oratorio are on the stage, and each soloist stands when performing, but the text is not acted out as it is sung. The recitative is usually of greater importance in an oratorio than in modern opera; each aria is preceded by its recitative. The choruses tend to be polyphonic in structure and, as befits the subject, are serious and powerful, like the "Hallelujah Chorus" from the *Messiah* or "The Heavens Are Telling" from Haydn's *Creation*. The choruses from an opera are likely to sound less sublime than the choruses of an oratorio. We can see this in the "Soldiers' Chorus" from *Faust*, the "Anvil Chorus" from *Il Trovatore*, and even the "Triumphal March" from *Aïda*.

The *cantata* and the *passion* are special forms of the oratorio. A cantata is a small oratorio which may be secular in subject. The subject of a passion, as the name suggests, is the agony and death of Christ. The words follow the text of one of the Gospels. Passions are not numerous. Two of the greatest are Bach's *Passion According to S. John* and *Passion According to S. Matthew*. A recent example is Penderecki's *Passion According to S. Luke*.

THE MASS

The Mass is a performance of the sacrament of the Holy Eucharist (Holy Communion), based on the words of Christ at the Last Supper when he told his disciples, regarding the bread, "Take and eat, this is my body," and, regarding the wine, "Drink, for this is my blood." With these words, the celebration of the Mass began.

The prayers of the Mass are divided into the Ordinary and the Proper. The Ordinary consists of those prayers that are constant; the Proper consists of those which change according to the feast day or the season. Here are the opening words of each of the five prayers of the Ordinary:

> Kyrie Eleison: "Lord have mercy upon us."
> Gloria in Excelsis Deo: "Glory be to God on high."
> Credo: "I believe in one God."
> Sanctus: "Holy, holy, holy."
> Agnus Dei: "O Lamb of God, that takest away the sins of the world."

From very early times the Mass has been set to music, and some of the greatest music in the world has been composed for the Mass. In this music we find illustrations of the three great periods in the history of Western music. From the earliest period (before A.D. 1000) we have Masses written in Gregorian chant, which is simple, unaccompanied melody. Disembodied, aspiring, and unworldly, these

Masses are cut off from any secular consideration. In the polyphonic period (ca. 1000–1600) we have the great Masses of Josquin and Palestrina. In the later periods (from about 1600) we have Masses by Beethoven and Mozart, and in our own day, by Stravinsky and Bernstein.

The Requiem Mass is celebrated for the repose of the dead. It gets its name from the first words of the text: "*Requiem aeternam dona eis Domine*" ("Give to them, O Lord, eternal rest"). Among requiems are those of Verdi and Mozart, and Benjamin Britten's *War Requiem*.

SUMMARY

To summarize our discussion of form, it may be said that form is the element that gives music a sense of unity, order, and coherence; it is the characteristic of music which distinguishes it from all other sound. Indeed, because musical sound lends itself to formal organization, we can account for its presence in some of the most significant artistic expression of our civilization.

16 ORGANIZATION IN LITERATURE AND THE COMBINED ARTS

THE BASIS OF PLAN IN THE TIME ARTS

Music and literature are time arts, and all the combined arts involve at least one time art. The time which elapses during our experiencing these arts from a beginning to an end is a kind of frame, and the pattern of auditory and visual materials within the frame is the organization.

Sensing the plan of organization in music (see Chapter 15) is largely a matter of memory and anticipation. We remember what we have heard, and, on the basis of that, we anticipate what is to come. In music, we know when we hear a theme that we have or have not heard it before, but we can rarely be very definite. Because our response to music is at first likely to be more emotional than rational, we do not recall the themes and arrangements easily. Hence, our memories and anticipations are not very clearly formulated.

In literature, our first responses are likely to be to the story being told or to the ideas presented. We remember events and content clearly and exactly, and we retain the entire organization in mind with very little difficulty. Therefore, we recognize and demand organization in literature. Take, for instance, this sonnet by Shakespeare:

When, in disgrace with Fortune and men's eyes,
I all alone beweep my outcast state,
And trouble deaf heaven with my bootless cries,
And look upon myself and curse my fate,
Wishing me like to one more rich in hope,

Featur'd like him, like him with friends possess'd,
Desiring this man's art, and that man's scope,
With what I most enjoy contented least;

Yet in these thoughts myself almost despising,
Haply I think on thee; and then my state,
Like to the lark at break of day arising
From sullen earth, sings hymns at heaven's gate;
For thy sweet love rememb'red such wealth brings
That then I scorn to change my state with kings.

> —William Shakespeare (1564–1616, British poet and dramatist),
>   Sonnet 29 (published 1609)

There is a decided break between the octave and the sestet. In the octave—the first eight lines—the speaker is sad and discouraged. The sestet—the last six lines—says that the speaker's heart soars when he thinks of his love. Moreover, the two quatrains of the octave are clearly differentiated. The first quatrain states the trouble generally; the second gives details. In the sestet, the quatrain relates the change of spirit, and the couplet at the end sums up the whole.

There are as many logical ways of ordering the content of a work of literature as there are of thinking. Sometimes writers begin with the least important content and go on to the most important. Sometimes they begin with the simple and go on to the difficult or complicated. Cause usually precedes effect. In Milton's sonnet "On His Blindness," the octave asks a question and the sestet gives the answer. In the Shakespearean sonnet just quoted, there is the statement of a difficulty and its solution. Ideas are arranged in the manner that will make them say what the author wants them to say. It is not necessary that the author follow any one particular plan; it is only necessary that there be a logical plan and that it be reasonably clear.

Exposition expounds, or explains. Thus it is the fundamental form for all scientific writing. In pure literature it is found chiefly in the treatise and the essay. The treatise is a longer, more thorough, and more finished study than the essay.

The word *essay* was first used by Montaigne who, writing in the sixteenth century, called his writings "*essais*," or "trials." An essay is an incomplete or partial treatment of a subject. Essays are classified according to subject, as familiar, historical, literary, philosophical.

The *familiar* essay was made popular by Charles Lamb (1775–1834) and has kept to this day many of the characteristics he gave it. It is always short and always personal. It is frequently humorous, but sometimes sad or pathetic. The subjects chosen are often trivial or fantastic; the interest lies in the presentation of a point of view that is not the usual commonsense, commonplace one. William Cowper, for instance, tells of the characteristics of a card table that had grown old in the service of his house; Lamb writes of the children he never had; Robert Louis Stevenson makes a defense of idlers. Always the writer takes a philosophic point of view; he or she is calm and enjoys the pleasures of the moment; or, if there are difficulties, the attitude taken toward them is one of acceptance and calm, not of protest.

Many books which are expository in nature do not fit into the category of either essay or treatise. Among these are books of political ideas, such as Plato's *Republic* or Machiavelli's *Prince;* statements of philosophy, such as the *Noble Truths* of Buddha or the dialogues of Plato; and statements of practical wisdom, such as the *Meditations* of Marcus Aurelius and the sayings of Epictetus. To this class also belong books of devotion, such as the *Confessions* of S. Augustine and *The Imitation of Christ* by Thomas à Kempis.

THE LYRIC

The lyric is a poem which expresses a single emotion. It is frequently short, like Landor's four-line poem "On Death":

Death stands above me, whispering low
  I know not what into my ear:
Of his strange language all I know
  Is, there is not a word of fear.

    —Walter Savage Landor (1775–1864, British poet,
      literary critic, and prose writer)

However, it may be a poem of several pages, like Wordsworth's "Ode on Intimations of Immortality." Sometimes the emotional quality is preserved in what is only a fragment, not a complete poem at all, as in these lines from Sappho:

Before the lovely queen each night
The stars in shyness hide their face
As all the earth swims soft and bright
And the full moon rides in her place.

  —Sappho (about 600 B.C., Greek lyric poet)[1]

Love and death are the two favorite subjects of lyrics, though

[1] Translated by Marjorie Carpenter.

any subject may be used. In "In My Craft or Sullen Art" (1945)
Dylan Thomas tells of his reasons for writing poetry:

In my craft or sullen art
Exercised in the still night
When only the moon rages
And the lovers lie abed
With all their griefs in their arms,
I labour by singing light
Not for ambition or bread
Or the strut and trade of charms
On the ivory stages
But for the common wages
Of their most secret heart.
Not for the proud man apart
From the raging moon I write
On these spindrift pages
Nor for the towering dead
With their nightingales and psalms
But for the lovers, their arms
Round the griefs of the ages,
Who pay no praise or wages
Nor heed my craft or art.

—Dylan Thomas (1914–1953, British poet)[2]

And Hopkins writes of God and nature in "God's Grandeur":

The world is charged with the grandeur of God.
  It will flame out, like shining from shook foil;
  It gathers to a greatness, like the ooze of oil
Crushed. Why do men then now not reck his rod?
Generations have trod, have trod;
  And all is seared with trade; bleared, smeared with toil;
  And wears man's smudge and shares man's smell: the soil
Is bare now, nor can foot feel, being shod.

And for all this, nature is never spent;
  There lives.the dearest freshness deep down things;
And though the last lights off the black West went
  Oh, morning, at the brown brink eastward, springs—
Because the Holy Ghost over the bent
  World broods with warm breast and with ah! bright wings.

—Gerard Manley Hopkins (1844–1889, British poet)[3]

[2] Reprinted from *The Poems of Dylan Thomas*, copyright 1946 by New Directions Publishing
Corporation, by permission of New Directions Publishing Corporation (New York); and from
Collected Poems of Dylan Thomas by permission of J. M. Dent and Sons, Ltd. (London), and the
Trustees for the copyrights of the late Dylan Thomas.
[3] From W. H. Gardiner and N. H. MacKenzie (eds.), *The Poems of Gerard Manley Hopkins*, 4th ed
(New York: Oxford University Press, 1967).

In the lyric we have the most pronounced use of the various devices of literature, such as assonance, alliteration, meter, rhythm, rhyme, simile, imagery, metaphor, and all the figures of speech. According to Suzanne Langer, the reason why lyric poetry draws so heavily on these devices is that it has so little content in itself. It is, she says, "usually nothing more than a thought, a vision, a word, or some other poignant emotion."[4] But because of all these devices, it becomes the form in which exact wording is most important. We want to repeat and sing to ourselves separate lines of lyric poetry such as these:

It is the blight man was born for,
It is Margaret you mourn for.

Of his strange language all I know
Is, there is not a word of fear.

Fair as a star, when only one
Is shining in the sky.

In drama and the novel one may forget *how* an event was told in the interest of the event itself, but not in the lyric.

A lyric is usually written in the first person: "Death stands above *me*," "Oh the difference to *me*," "In *my* craft or sullen art." And yet it is not in itself personal. We do not feel that we are intruding on the writer. Once the song is written, it is a song for everyone. It acquires a certain timelessness; it lives in a "sort of eternal present."[5]

I'm going out to clean the pasture spring;
I'll only stop to rake the leaves away
(And wait to watch the water clear, I may):
I sha'n't be gone long.—You come too.

I'm going out to fetch the little calf
That's standing by the mother. It's so young,
It totters when she licks it with her tongue.
I sha'n't be gone long.—You come too.

—Robert Frost (1875–1963, American poet), "The Pasture"[6]

[4] Suzanne Langer, *Feeling and Form* (New York: Charles Scribner's Sons, 1965), p. 259.
[5] Ibid., p. 268.
[6] From *The Poetry of Robert Frost* edited by Edward Connery Lathem. Copyright 1916, 1923, 1939, © 1967, 1969 by Holt, Rinehart and Winston, Copyright 1936, 1944, 1959 by Robert Frost. Copyright © 1964 by Lesley Frost Ballantine. Reprinted by permission of Holt, Rinehart and Winston, Publishers (New York).

Even when Marianne Moore writes about her father, as in "Silence," the result is not, strictly speaking, personal, but universal.

My father used to say,
"Superior people never make long visits,"
have to be shown Longfellow's grave
or the glass flowers at Harvard.
Self-reliant like the cat—
that takes its prey to privacy,
the mouse's limp tail hanging like a shoelace from its mouth—
they sometimes enjoy solitude,
and can be robbed of speech
by speech which has delighted them.
The deepest feeling always shows itself in silence;
not in silence, but restraint.
Nor was he insincere in saying, "Make my house your inn."
Inns are not residences.

—Marianne Moore (1887–1972, American poet), "Silence"[7]

NARRATIVE

The narrative probably comprises more examples of pure literature than all the other types put together, and with good reason. All the world loves a lover, and it is equally true that all the world loves a story. The formula "once upon a time" still has magic to lure us all, young and old.

Plot

The essentials of a narrative are the essentials of every story. First is action, or conflict. The narrative begins with the emergence of a situation that demands solution. Something has happened to disrupt the established order. There will be anxiety, tension, and frustration until the problem is solved. The problem itself may be of any kind—finding a dead body, as in a detective story; falling in love; spending the night in an open boat. The occasion is not limited. It may be serious or frivolous. Chaucer tells a story of three rioters who went out to hunt death and found it. Cervantes tells of the adventures of an old knight who fought windmills.

Whatever the story, it is related in a series of incidents each of which has some relation to the solution of the main problem, and each of which must be credible in terms of that problem. Each of

[7] From *Collected Poems by Marianne Moore* (New York: Macmillan, 1953). Reprinted with permission of The Macmillan Company. Copyright 1953, Marianne Moore. Copyright renewed 1963 by Marianne Moore and T. S. Eliot.

these incidents will bring new knowledge and help reach the solution. This is the *plot*.

Sometimes there are two plots that run side by side; we find this often in Shakespeare's plays. *King Lear* is a good example. In this play the two plots are bound together so that each helps the other; but in addition, one is definitely more important than the other. In Tolstoi's *Anna Karenina* the main plot is concerned with the unhappy love of Anna and Vronsky, but counter to them runs the contented life of Levin and Kitty.

A narrative is sometimes simply the "story" as it happened; it begins at the beginning and recounts the incidents in *the order in which they occurred*. In drama, however, and in the combined arts of opera, ballet, and film (which follow organizational patterns similar to drama), the plot consists of the events in the story *as the author has arranged them*. This arrangement is the organization and structure of the work.

There are certain specific materials that every plot must contain. They are generally called the "exposition," the "inciting incident," the "rising action" and "turning point," the "climax," the "falling action," and the "conclusion" or "denouement." In drama and the related combined arts, the exposition usually comes at the beginning. This is where we learn who the characters are and what the situation is, including what has happened before the work begins—in short, we are told everything we need to know about the "world" in which the action is to occur. Something happens to disturb that world, the *inciting incident*, which brings about the problem or conflict which is to become the content of the piece in the rising action which follows.

In the *rising action*, there is struggle between the forces which contend for one outcome or another; this is the conflict which the inciting event has brought about. As one force gains advantage and seems to be triumphing, we have a *turning point;* as events strengthen this advantage, we have a *climax*, which is the outcome of the conflict and the culmination of the story. This climax is the resolution of the problem or conflict posed by the inciting incident, and since it is the culmination of the excitement and anxiety generated throughout the struggle, it becomes the high point in the work. What follows as the *conclusion* or *denouement* returns us once again to a situation of stability. The order of the "world" of the narrative has been restored. It is in the denouement of dramatic works that we sometimes have the pointing up of a moral or the underlining of a message which the whole narrative has demonstrated. With the conclusion or denouement, we leave the work with a feeling that it has been brought to a satisfactory and satisfying end.

These are the elements of plot. The amount of time given to each and the order in which they are included varies greatly. Contemporary plays, for example—especially those dealing with contemporary life—are likely to reduce expository material to a minimum (particularly if the intended audience is sophisticated enough to grasp situations and character relationships quickly). Since contemporary audiences have little taste for having morals or messages pointed out to them, there may well be a very short denouement or none at all. Plays such as Samuel Beckett's *Waiting for Godot* may have no exposition and no end; they are all middle. Such a play consists of the exploration of a static pattern. It proceeds by revealing various aspects of the pattern and in the end leaves the situation just as it was at the opening of the play, but now revealed in depth.

Characters

There can be no plot without actors, and so the second requirement of a narrative is *characters*. There must be people who are concerned in the main plot; they are the characters of the story. They answer the question: Why do people do what they do? And every incident should throw light on the characters. Why did Chaucer's three rioters set out to find death, and how did the old man know where they would find it? Why did Don Quixote charge the windmill? The characters of a narrative usually are human beings. When the characters are animals, the animal names are fundamentally disguises for human beings, as the hen and the rooster in Chaucer's *Tale of the Nun's Priest*. The hen and the rooster, although essentially true to what we know of fowls, nevertheless talk and act as men and women do. Chanticleer shows all the characteristics in which a man is most like a cock, and Pertelote is the eternal feminine. George Orwell's *Animal Farm* (1946) is another example of the use of animal characters; here again these characters are human beings in animal form.

Setting

The setting gives the time and place of the action. The time is always past, always "once upon a time." Even in science fiction and other narratives set in the future, the events narrated take place at some time before the narration: that is, the *tense* is always past. The place may be any place at any time. Jules Verne writes of what happens 20,000 leagues under the sea; Butler in *Erewhon* tells of people who live in a land that is as logical as ours is illogical. Writers of all ages have told of the land of the dead.

The setting comprises not only the physical character of the place —country, city, lake, etc.—but also all the beliefs, customs, and moral and social values that make up what we usually call the "environment." No matter where it is placed, the setting should fit the action; it should be a place in which those events might take place. Ivanhoe does not belong in the world of *Tom Jones*, and Elizabeth

Bennet of *Pride and Prejudice* would not fit into the environment of *Main Street*.

Theme

Plot, characters, and setting are found in every narrative, but they are not of equal importance. Any one of the three may in some narrative be of greatest importance. In *An American Tragedy* (1926), by Theodore Dreiser, the boy is the victim of his environment. Eldridge Cleaver's *Soul on Ice* (1968) is another narrative in which environment—the penitentiary and the ghetto life which brought the narrator to it—is of utmost importance. In Stevenson's *Treasure Island* (1883), the action is most important. In Thackeray's *Vanity Fair* (1848), the characterization is most important.

All depends on the author's *theme.* This is his or her point of view or idea about the tale—what the author is trying to say in the story. It reflects the author's understanding of life. This of course is the basis by which action, characters, and setting have been determined. The author decides what kind of a character belongs in *Main Street* and draws the picture that way.

Narrator

The question "Who is telling the story?" has to do with the *narrator*. There are two favorite devices. One is the omniscient narrator, who knows everything about each character—everything the characters say, do, and think. There is never any indication as to who this narrator is or how the narrator gets this information. The other favorite device is to have the story told in the first person by some character who is actually taking part in it.

In the early days of prose fiction, the letter or journal was much liked as a way of telling the story. Richardson's *Pamela* (1740) is narrated by the heroine in the form of a series of letters to her friend. James Baldwin's nonfictional *Notes of a Native Son* (1955) is in a form very like that of a diary.

Many good techniques for writing a story have to do with the narrator or narrators. A writer need not keep the same narrator throughout the story. In Faulkner's novel *The Sound and the Fury* (1929) the first chapter is told by a half-wit. Later material is narrated by a Negro cook. At the end, Faulkner uses the omniscient narrator.

Ways of Telling a Story

Within the general framework of the narrative, there are many ways of telling a story and hence of changing the plan. Ordinarily a narrative starts at the beginning and goes through to the end. *Pride and Prejudice* begins when strangers move into the community and Elizabeth and Darcy have a chance to meet each other, and it continues through many different events until they are safely married at the end. *Vanity Fair* begins when Becky Sharp leaves boarding school as a young girl, and it carries her through all her adventures until she is an old woman.

This is the method followed in the ballad "Sir Patrick Spence." The story is presented in three scenes: the first is at the court where the king and the old knight are discussing plans for the trip; the second is on the seashore when Sir Patrick hears the message and suspects foul play; the third jumps to the ending after the lords and their ship have gone down. Except for the third stanza, however, there are no connecting links between one part and the other; the reader must guess from the context what has happened.

The king sits in Dumferling toune,
  Drinking the blude-reid wine:
"O whar will I get guid sailor,
  To sail this schip of mine?"

Up and spake an eldern knicht,
  Sat at the kings richt kne:
"Sir Patrick Spence is the best sailor,
  That sails upon the se."

The king has written a braid letter,
  And signd it wi his hand,
And sent it to Sir Patrick Spence,
  Was walking on the sand.

The first line that Sir Patrick red,
  A loud lauch lauched he;
The next line that Sir Patrick red,
  The teir blinded his ee.

"O wha is this has don this deid,
  This ill deid don to me,
To send me out this time o' the yeir,
  To sail upon the se!

"Mak hast, mak hast, my mirry men all,
  Our guid schip sails the morne:"
"O say na sae, my master deir,
  For I feir a deadlie storme.

"Late late yestreen I saw the new moone,
  Wi the auld moone in her arme,
And I feir, my deir master,
  That we will cum to harme."

O our Scots nobles wer richt laith
  To weet their cork-heild schoone;
But lang owre a' the play wer playd,
  Their hats they swam aboone.

O lang, lang may their ladies sit,
  Wi thair fans into their hand,
Or eir they se Sir Patrick Spence
  Cum sailing to the land.

O lang, lang may the ladies stand,
  Wi thair gold kems in their hair,
Waiting for thair ain deir lords,
  For they'll se thame na mair.

Haf owre, haf owre to Aberdour,
  It's fiftie fadom deip,
And thair lies guid Sir Patrick Spence,
  Wi the Scots lords at his feit.

—Anonymous, "Sir Patrick Spence"

The time sequence may, however, also be altered. William Faulkner's story *A Rose for Emily* (1930) begins with the death of Miss Emily and then goes back to tell the story of her life, her old-South aristocratic manner, and her relations with her neighbors.

Sometimes we see one character through the eyes of another, and our understanding of that character changes as our informant learns to know that person. In Henry James's *Portrait of a Lady* (1881), we see one of the main characters, Madame Merle, through the eyes of the heroine, Isabel Archer. At first, Madame Merle is glamorous; then, as Isabel begins to see her more clearly, we learn of her faults and shortcomings.

Another device is to present the story as it was known to different people. This method is used by Browning in *The Ring and the Book*. An old count is tried for the murder of his young wife, who had fled to the home of her foster parents in company with a young priest just before the birth of her son. In the twelve books of the poem, Browning tells the story as it appears to many different people—the casual bystander, the wife, the priest who helped her escape, the husband when he appears in court for the trial, the husband just before he is executed for the murder, the Pope before whom the case is tried, and others.

Again, the story may be related a long time after the events have taken place. This is the method followed by Conrad in *Youth:* Marlowe, an old man, tells about the experiences of his youth. It is also used by T. S. Eliot in "The Journey of the Magi," in which one of the wise men remembers his journey to Bethlehem. One of the advantages of this plan is that the narrator can intersperse the events with comments and explanations, criticism and evaluations.

In recent years there has been much emphasis on a new type of narrative—the "stream of consciousness" method—in which all matters are presented in an uninterrupted flow of ideas, sensations, memories, and associations, as they would be presented to the consciousness of any one person. James Joyce and Virginia Woolf are but two of a large number of modern writers who have used this method of writing.

In another modern type of narrative, there is not one sequence of events; instead, events are presented in a kaleidoscopic series of pictures focusing on different occurrences of the story. In *John Brown's Body*, for instance, Stephen Vincent Benét paints a picture of the Civil War by giving short scenes that tell what was happening to various people at various times. There is no attempt to make connections among all these scenes, but they all work together to make a unified whole which gives a composite picture.

Types of Narrative Poetry

Epic Of all the types of narrative, the *epic* is one of the most distinct. It is also one of the rarest. An epic is a long, dignified poem in lofty style; its hero is of more than ordinary strength, and his deeds are of consequence to an entire nation. The authentic, or

natural, epic is the product of an age of heroes, of a people just
emerging from barbarism, when the individual, as an individual,
performed deeds that were, or seemed to be, superhuman. In the
Iliad, Achilles and Hector fight side by side with the gods, and are by
no means inferior to them. Beowulf, in a foreign country, hears of the
damage being done by the monster Grendel and goes across the sea
to fight him.

The authentic epic probably originated as a series of songs in
praise of the hero, which were later joined into one poem. The
author or authors are often not known; if a name, such as Homer,
is attached to an epic, it is merely a name, for the poetry does not
reflect the personality of the poet. The authentic epic is, as has been
said, extremely rare. The *Iliad,* the *Odyssey, Beowulf,* the *Song of
Roland, Le Cid,* and the *Song of the Nibelungs* almost complete the list
for Western literature.

The literary, or artificial, epic is the work of a single, conscious
literary artist. We would expect it to be more common than the authentic epic, but it is not. Vergil's *Aeneid* and Milton's *Paradise Lost*
are two works that are given the title "epic" without dispute. The
literary epic has a conscious purpose. Vergil is trying to arouse in the
people a greater reverence for the gods, the country, and the family.
Milton is trying to "justify the ways of God to man."

Romance   The medieval romance is, as the name implies, a product
of the Middle Ages, being, par excellence, the literary expression of
chivalry. It has been defined as a story of love and adventure, or of
adventure for the sake of love. Spenser chooses a typical romance
subject for *The Faerie Queene.* A lady appears at the court of Arthur
asking redress for the great wrongs done to her father and mother; a
knight springs up, volunteering for the expedition. He and the lady
have many adventures, and in the end the parents are released and
the knight and the lady are married. The medieval romance is usually
in verse, though it is sometimes in prose. The fifteenth-century collection made by Malory, *Le Morte d'Arthur,* is in prose.

In the age of romanticism the romance was revived, and many
authors—Keats, Byron, Swinburne, Tennyson, and others—began to
write romantic tales of knights and ladies or other faraway, strange,
and ancient people.

The term *romance,* as distinguished from the medieval romance
or its modern revival, is used for any work of fiction in which the
emphasis is on plot, such as Stevenson's *Treasure Island.* A romance
may be either in prose or in verse.

The ballad   The ballad is a story told in song. The folk ballad is the
story of an important event, told dramatically and intended for popular singing. The subject may be any conspicuous event: the death
of a suitor, the betrayal of a sister, the hunting of the cheviot, or the

adventure of a hero. As in all folk songs, the author is of no importance, and hence is not usually known.

LORD RANDAL

"Oh where ha'e ye been, Lord Randal, my son?
Oh where ha'e ye been, my handsome young man?"
"I ha'e been to the wildwood; mother, make my bed soon,
For I'm weary wi' hunting, and fain would lie down."

"Where gat ye your dinner, Lord Randal, my son?
Where gat ye your dinner, my handsome young man?"
"I dined wi' my true-love; mother, make my bed soon,
For I'm weary wi' hunting, and fain would lie down."

"What gat ye to your dinner, Lord Randal, my son?
What gat ye to your dinner, my handsome young man?"
"I gat eels boiled in brew; mother, make my bed soon,
For I'm weary wi' hunting, and fain would lie down."

"What became of your bloodhounds, Lord Randal, my son?
What became of your bloodhounds, my handsome young man?
"Oh they swelled and they died; mother, make my bed soon,
For I'm weary wi' hunting, and fain would lie down."

"Oh I fear ye are poisoned, Lord Randal, my son!
Oh I fear ye are poisoned, my handsome young man!"
"Oh yes, I am poisoned; mother, make my bed soon,
For I'm sick at the heart, and I fain would lie down."

  —Anonymous

In most ballads, as in "Lord Randal," there is a great deal of repetition, probably because it made the singing easier. This repetition is not exact; each recurrence of a phrase carries the story forward a little. Here, for example, each question adds to our knowledge of Lord Randal's day until we know the truth in the last stanza. The ballad seldom tells a story directly from beginning to end. In "Lord Randal" we begin at the end and learn by degrees what had happened earlier. The ballad form is also used by literary artists; with them it approximates the folk song more or less closely, as in Coleridge's "Rime of the Ancient Mariner."

Prose Fiction

Novel In contrast with the romance, which deals with the strange and unusual, the spectacular and the aristocratic, the novel has to do with the relations of people to one another. It is not so much concerned with how things are done as with why they are done. I presents a series of actions which show why a character does a cer tain thing, and accomplishes this largely through showing th choices which that character makes. We learn of his or her considera tions, assertions, arguments, demonstrations, and deliberate reflec tions—the conclusions that determine thought. A story so conceivec and made alive is often more vivid than actual experience. Often lif seems "stale, flat, and unprofitable," but the interest in a novel mus not fall. The people of the book may be dull, but not the book itself It must have what Henry James called "felt life." The excellence o the novel lies in its life, in its seeming truth, its unity. If it seems to be a true picture of life, if the characters move and work and make the decisions that are true to their natures, we say the novel is true and good.

The novel is a recent form; the earliest works that belong strictly to the type are those of Richardson and Fielding in the eighteentr century. As Langer says, "The novel is peculiarly suited to formulate our modern life by taking our most pervasive interest for its theme— the evaluation and the hazards of personality." Our interest in per sonality is what makes our world different and most of its problems relatively new.

Short story The short story belongs to the same general type as the novel, but it is not simply a short novel. It differs primarily in two respects. It is usually concerned with a single crisis, whereas the novel will present many facets of the characters and events; and it is limited in its analysis of character. Faulkner, for instance, gives a complete picture of an entire family in *The Sound and Fury*, whereas in the short story "Barn Burning," he gives only the incidents that resulted in the burning of a barn.

Anecdote and novella The anecdote and the novella are sometimes distinguished from the short story and sometimes classed together with it. The *anecdote* is a short narrative giving particulars of some interesting episode or event. Often the anecdote gives details of the life of some one person, as when we repeat an incident from the life of Abraham Lincoln or Thomas Jefferson. The anecdote differs from the short story in that it lacks both the plot and the characterization of that form. The *Lives* of Plutarch are now classed as anecdotal.

The *novella* is identified in two ways. The term is most com monly used to designate a narrative that is longer than the short story though it lacks the characteristics of the novel. Many of the stories of Katherine Anne Porter are in this category. Thomas Mann's *Death in Venice* is a novella. Historically, the term is applied to narratives such as we find in the *Decameron* of Boccaccio, short narratives in which story rather than character development is emphasized.

THE COMBINED ARTS

Drama, opera, dance, and film are combined arts. That is, they make use of more than one medium (for example, drama and music, in addition to being auditory arts, are also visual arts), and, as has already been mentioned, they all make use of one time art. The combined arts are *performing* arts; that is, they are experienced in performance. Both these facts are important in considering structure in the combined arts, for these arts make use not only of the organizational principles common to the time arts—particularly music and literature—but of those used in the visual arts as well. The presence of these two kinds of organizational principles accounts for the richness of the combined arts when they are successful, but, as was pointed out in Chapter 8 (page 191), it poses a problem for the artist in deciding which organizational principles to emphasize at any particular point in the work.

Drama

Because plays can be read as well as experienced on stage, drama is classified as literature. However, as was pointed out in Chapter 8 (page 193), it is intended to be seen and heard and thus involves other mediums. It is appropriate, therefore, to consider drama as a combined art which has much in common with dance, opera, and film. All, for example, use organizational plans based upon sequences of visual and auditory stimuli. Some writers prefer to reserve the term *drama* for the written play and the term *theater* for performed drama, much as one uses the term *score* for the written libretto and *music* for the entire opera, which can be experienced only in performance. Although this distinction is not mandatory, it does serve to remind us that in reading and responding to drama, we must always bear in mind that it was intended for stage performance.

Drama, the novel, and the short story are now the outstanding forms of narrative. They are alike in following the regular requirements of narrative; in having plot, characters, settings, and theme. But they differ in many ways, the most important being the medium. The short story and the novel use only words: we know the characters only as the narrator tells us about them. The drama also is basically a story in words (a story without words is a pantomime), but the words are in dialogue and are acted out. All information is conveyed to the audience through dialogue except for what can be told through costume, stage set, and the movements and gestures of the actors. In the novel, the narrator tells what the characters are doing, whereas in drama we see and hear them as they do it.

This difference in medium demands differences in presentation.

For one thing, a play is relatively short; if it is to be interesting to th
audience, it must not be so long as to be tiring. The reading of
novel may be spread out over a winter or be finished in a few hours
but a play must be over in a short time. Three hours is the conven
tional time, though many plays are shorter or longer. There have
been many experiments with longer plays, but they have not been
very popular. Shakespeare's plays are much longer than the standarc
three hours, but in his time a play was presented continuously with
out any breaks for change of scene or costume, or any other interrup
tion; it could, therefore, be presented in about the same time as a
modern play.

Again, the pace of a play is fast; the author, being limited in
time, must get ideas across quickly and cannot put in too many details. Only the important and the essential can be brought in. Moreover, a play must always be clear. A reader who gets mixed up in a
novel can turn back and see what happened, but in a play there is no
turning back. Also, the action on the stage is always in the present.
Unlike a novel, a play cannot take place in the past tense. Even events
which are presented as a sort of flashback must be enacted as if they
are taking place in the present.

Drama differs from the novel in yet another way. Since the story
is told by the characters, there can be no comment on what is said or
done unless it be by the characters, whereas in a novel the narrator
can comment directly on the scene or the situation. Jane Austen begins Pride and Prejudice with the statement: "It is a truth universally
acknowledged, that a single man in possession of a good fortune
must be in want of a wife." In a play that statement could not stand
alone like this; it would of necessity be spoken by one of the characters and would show that individual's personality, and point of
view. Dramatic form is limited also in that the author cannot talk
directly to the audience. Ordinarily the author cannot explain in his
or her own person what has taken place or what kind of people the
characters are. Various attempts have been made to overcome this
restriction, but with limited success.

A play is customarily divided into acts. An act is part of a larger
whole but distinct and independent insofar as it has its own beginning and end. In Shakespeare's time a drama regularly had five acts;
now it will more often have two or three. Acts may or may not be
divided into scenes, each scene having its own unity and its own
place in the act and the entire play. Often, the stage directions indicate that some period of time has elapsed between the end of one act
and the beginning of the next.

In the dialogue the author must provide suggestions which will
connect any act with what went before. In Macbeth, for instance, we
are told about the hero on three different occasions before we meet
him. In the opening scene the witches name Macbeth. In the second
scene Macbeth is named again, this time as a great hero in battle. In

the third scene Macbeth is heralded by the witches as one who shall be "King hereafter."

Dramatic organization prescribes a single structure to which all plays conform to a greater or lesser degree. First is the *exposition*, which gives the audience any information it needs to know about the past. Then comes the *complication*, or rising action, which involves the protagonist in a course of action that will materially affect future developments. Soon there follows an event which decides the result of the action, whether it be good or bad. This is the *crisis*. From that point the play moves to its inevitable conclusion, known as the *denouement* ("unraveling," "falling action") or *catastrophe*. This pattern follows the general plan of a triangle, as the action rises to a climax in the crisis and falls to the catastrophe.

It goes without saying that no author would follow such a scheme slavishly; yet it is interesting how often this rule holds true. In *Romeo and Juliet*, for example, we first see Romeo winning Juliet; then, after the death of Tybalt, we have a falling action (denouement) which brings about the death of both Romeo and Juliet. In *Julius Caesar*, Brutus gains in power till the death of Caesar; when he gives Mark Antony the right to speak at Caesar's funeral, he sets his own fall in motion.

We get to know the characters primarily through what they say and do. And as we look at the characters, what they think and say must seem inevitable. Everything about a character must count— words, actions, appearance, expressions, and gestures. One should study each character for visible elements that signify mental or spiritual features. Physical features may of course conceal mental and spiritual aspects of the character. When the apparent is the opposite of the truth, we have, of course, irony.

Normally a playwright has visible evidence of character in mind to a great extent. We often accept costume, action, movement, scenery, gesture, sound, and placement of people on the stage without realizing how they came to be. Physical appearance may be significant: Shakespeare makes Falstaff large and fat; Richard III is a hunchback. Details of dress can be expressive of character: for example, Tennessee Williams in *A Streetcar Named Desire* shows Blanche's desires in the bright colors of her clothes, her use of cosmetics, her false furs, her costume jewelry—they reveal her longing to get away from painful reality. Often, however, such visible evidence is supplied by a director working with performers. Thus different productions of a play can give different interpretations of the text.

The setting is one means of emphasizing what is said in the play. First we notice the number of sets. An indoor scene naturally and inevitably portrays the world inside, whereas an outdoor scene is not limited. A play that has all the action take place in one room necessarily has a limited scene, one of limited social context, whereas one that is enacted in many places is more vigorous and has many more

approaches to life as it is lived. In the set, we notice the kind of furniture: is it in good or bad taste, old or new, primly proper or poorl
kept, in order or disorder? And there is always evidence of the spe
cial scene. A law court may give a sense of order, of tradition. Rich
fertile fields may make one think of wealth and leisure; a crowde
tenement will conjure up all the disadvantages of poverty. Again
setting may be a contribution of the director if it has not been indi
cated in detail by the playwright.

Stage directions give the author's plan for any matter that is no
told in the dialogue, and of course they cover all types of information
Recent authors have often used them very exactly. In Sean O'Casey'
Juno and the Paycock, an entire page is given to a description of th
room in which the action takes place; it is followed, after one shor
sentence, by a description of Juno, the heroine. Such description
are very telling to those who read the play but run into the danger o
making statements that can hardly be put into action on the stage. I
Juno and the Paycock, for instance, we are told that Juno has "tha
look which ultimately settles down upon the faces of the women o
the working class."

Shakespeare and the Greeks were much more chary in their di
rections for the stage. *Macbeth* has only the direction "Scotland—A
open place" before the entrance of the three witches. The classi
Greek play was performed before the palace; for the opening o
Oedipus the King, the steps of the palace are crowded with suppliant
in various attitudes of despair. Invariably, whether it is supplied b
the playwright or by those involved in producing a play, the settin
contributes to the mood of the play.

Drama and the Other Combined Arts

Because drama is the most familiar of the combined arts, we some
times bring to other combined arts, such as ballet, opera, and film
the same expectancies that we would bring to a drama. To do so
however, is to ignore the fact that each is an art in its own right with
both limitations and advantages peculiar to it. Each has developec
its own unique conventions and traditions. The action in opera
moves forward dramatically in rapid passages of recitative dialogue
but stops completely for the lyrical, musical elaboration of a high
point in the story. In ballet, the story is simple, usually a familia
one drawn from mythology, folklore, or similar materials; it is little
more than a pretext for the dancing and the music which accompany
it. In film, much of the story can be presented in visual imagery
through flashbacks and projection of interior thoughts. In this ability
to bring into unified visual focus the thoughts of the characters anc
scenes from the past, the future, or the imagination, film is closer to
the novel than to a stage presentation. Its ability to present things

visually and quickly, rather than having to evoke them through words, is peculiar to film as an art.

DANCE

"The dance antedates all other forms of art because it employs no instrument but the body itself which everyone has always with him and which, in the final analysis, is the most eloquent and responsive of all the instruments."[8] Dance is the most spontaneous and personal of all the arts—not only in its medium but also in its basic patterns of organized movement. Curt Sachs, in his *World History of the Dance*, gives examples of animals that dance: the stilt birds and the anthropoid apes. In their dances, he finds a series of the essential dance motifs: the circle and ellipse, forward and backward steps, hopping, stamping, and whirling. We cannot go into the early history of human beings without finding dance. Ancient Greek vases show many examples of dancers. The Noh dancing of Japan is centuries old.

The movements of dance may be classified under two headings: (1) movements of the body parts, such as movement of the head, arms, or torso within a certain space; (2) movement from one space to another, such as walking, running, and jumping. A dance may be performed by one dancer or by any number of performers.

Dance exists in three dimensions: time, space, and dynamics. Space, of course, determines the position of the dancer in relation to the background: in the center, to one side, in front, to the back. It also determines the posture of the body—standing, lying, crouching, stooping, running, still, etc. The time, of course, may be fast or slow, and its dynamics determine the rhythm.

In general, we distinguish between folk dance and art dance. Folk dance is part of the ethnic traditions of a country or district—Spain or Andalusia, Germany or Bavaria—in which certain melodies, rhythms, costumes, and folk symbolism are preserved. Folk dances have cultural significance and inherent beauty. The art dance, sometimes called "spectacular" dance, may be either a solo performance or a group arrangement (for example, a ballet). An art dance may or may not be related to a folk tradition. In *Petrouchka*, Igor Stravinsky, using traditional Russian folk melodies, tales, and costumes, creates a new, highly artificial, and beautiful form. Ballets like Tchaikovsky's *Swan Lake* are less directly related to folk origins. Romantic in melody and symbolic in meaning, *Swan Lake* is performed by dancers wearing the canonical and traditional ballet costumes as they have come down through the nineteenth and twentieth centuries.

Time, strength and space: these are the elements which give the dance its life. Of this trinity of elemental powers, it is space which is the realm of the dancer's real activity, which belongs to him because he himself creates it. . . . Only in its spatial embrace can the dance achieve its final and decisive effect. Only then the fleeting signs are compressed into a legible and lasting mirror image in which the message of the dance grows into what it should and must be: language—the living, artistic language of dance.

—Mary Wigman[9]

[8] John Martin, *Introduction to the Dance* (Brooklyn, N.Y.: Dance Horizons, Inc., 1965), pp. 14–15.
[9] Copyright © 1966 by Wesleyan University. Reprinted from *The Language of Dance*, by Mary Wigman, translated by Walter Sorell, by permission of Wesleyan University Press (Middletown, Conn.); pp. 11–12.

The principles of organization in dance are similar to those in music: repetition of movement, alternation of movements and body positions, theme and variations, the counterpoint dancing of one kind of step against another kind of step for rhythmic and design effects. Since spectacular dance is performed on a stage or other defined space, the principles of design are similar to those in the visual arts. Symmetry, contrast, variety, and the same use of elements for expressive purposes discussed in relation to the visual arts are elements in the transitory designs dancers make on stage. In ballet, of course, there is usually a simple narrative with exposition, conflict, climax, and denouement, as in opera and drama. The story, sometimes called simply the "pretext," is the organizational frame, but it is less important than the dancing and the music, which follow closely the principles of organization in music.

There are three main purposes for organized dancing: (1) magic or religious ritual; (2) social; (3) entertainment of an audience. Ethnic dancing falls into the first category; spectacular dances fall into the third.[10]

Ethnic Dance

The term *ethnic* is used for religious dances, dances that are designed as hymns of praise to a god or to bring on good fortune in peace or war. Probably the dances of the American Indian, such as those for rain or for good crops, are the best-known examples. The royal ballets of Cambodia and India are also excellent examples. In the early days of the Christian church, the Christian mysteries were danced by the priests. As late as the eighteenth century, the Shakers in America engaged in dances as a form of worship. Usually such religious dances are traditional; often no one knows exactly how they came into being or where they came from. They are subtle and symbolic in meaning and cannot easily be understood by someone outside the ethnic group. "It is far easier to speak a foreign language without a trace of accent than it is to dance in a foreign idiom with complete purity of style."[11] Figure 16-1 is an example of ethnic dance.

One of the best-known and most important examples of ethnic dancing is the Noh play of Japan. Though known as a "play," it is actually a composite of dance, song, and music. The Noh play is generally considered one of the highest expressions of Japanese art. It is about 600 years old. Usually there are only five or six characters in a play: the principal character and those who play opposite him or her. This principal character is always masked; some of the others may also be masked. The performance is always dignified and reserved, and it never is realistic. Weeping, for example, is indicated only by a hand at the eye. The masks and the costumes worn by the char-

Figure 16-1. "A maenad." Drawing from a black-figure kylix in the Metropolitan Museum of Art, New York. (Bellerophon Books, San Francisco, 1974.)

[10] Arnold Haskell (ed.), *Ballet* (annual), nos. 16 and 17 (New York, 1962 and 1963).
[11] John Martin, op. cit., p. 106.

acters add greatly to the beauty of the play (making masks is considered an important art in Japan). The stage is very small, with a raised passageway leading to it from the performers' dressing room through the audience, and is decorated only with branches of pine.

Traditionally, a Noh play consists of a series of short plays arranged according to an established order. The first is about the gods, the second about warriors, the third about young and beautiful women, the fourth about the antics of the mad, and the fifth about devils or gods. To relieve the suspense, farces are introduced; often a farce imitates the serious scene performed just preceding it.

Social Dance

Social, or recreational, dancing is dancing for one's own pleasure; it is usually performed by groups of people who follow definite patterns. Recreational dancing is found primarily in two forms: folk dance and ballroom dancing. Folk dance is often derived from ethnic dance. Many folk dances are still identified with particular countries: the reel, jig, and hornpipe are Irish; the sword and morris dances are English; and the Cossack dances are Russian.

Social, or ballroom, dancing is formal. It was originally made up largely of square dances like the minuet until they gave way to such round dances as the "wicked waltz." The waltz, however, could not keep its place of preeminence; it was followed by a series of dances each of which was disapproved of when it appeared—the bunny hug, turkey trot, shimmy, Charleston, and so on. Some of these changes show the strong influence of two sources, American Negro and Latin American dances. Latin American forms that have been taken over completely include the tango, samba, and mambo. The influence of black music, rhythms, and dance forms has been most striking since World War II, with such forms as the jitterbug, the twist, and various forms of rock becoming prominent in turn. Rock dances popular within the last decade or so include the monkey, chicken, mashed potato, and frug. Many rock dances do not involve bodily contact between partners; the dancers move toward and away from one another, not necessarily performing exactly the same movements. At one point in the development of rock dances, dancers were encouraged to dance to a particular melody in any way they saw fit; this produced a situation where people could, and did, dance without partners.

Spectacular Dance

Certain dances are called "spectacular" or "art" dances because they are intended to be viewed by an audience. Acrobatic dance and tap dance technically fall into this category, but the most important spectacular dances are ballet and modern dance.

Arabesque. French, "Arabian, Moorish in style.") The body is supported on one leg with the other leg raised in back, making the longest possible line. (These drawings are by Robin Rice.)

Pirouette. (French, "whirling.") A complete turn of the body on one foot.

Attitude. (French, "posture.") A posture created by Carlo Blasis, who based it on the statute of Mercury by Giovanni da Bologna. The body is supported on one leg with the other leg raised and bent.

Classical ballet Classical ballet was for many years the supreme e pression of the art of dance. More than any other dance, it is subje to a definite and prescribed discipline of body, head, legs, hand and arms. There are set positions for each of these. There are, f example, five positions or movements of the head: (1) turn, (2) i cline, (3) erect, (4) back, and (5) lowered. The language of ballet always French. Here are some examples:

> *Pas de deux*—a dance of two
> *Pas de trois*—a dance of three
> *Pas de bourrée*—running on points

As was mentioned in Chapter 8, the female, to gain lightness, worl on her toes (*pointes*), whereas the man jumps and turns in the a (this is the *entrechat*).

The subject of a ballet is most often a story, though in rece years abstract subjects have been used, as when the ballet uses symphony for the accompanying music. The ideal of ballet is beau of line, grace, and purity of execution rather than any literary co cept.

Ballet is usually thought to have developed from dances pe formed between the scenes of operas at court during the seventeen century. Because these were frequently more entertaining than th operas, they eventually became independent performances and a art form in themselves. During the eighteenth century, the *en poin* technique was developed to achieve an airy, floating quality. Certai movements were gradually developed and taught to dancers for ba let. Eventually they came to be a virtual vocabulary of movemen which all ballet dancers learn. In choreographing a ballet, the chor ographer puts them together in various ways to create passages movement. In a way, these meticulously defined movements a analogous to the vocabulary of scales, harmonies, and rhythn which composers draw upon for expressive purposes. They are st the basis of training for ballet and the vocabulary in which classic ballets are performed. A very few of the common steps and positior of ballet are shown on these pages, along with definitions. The are, of course, many, many more.

En pointe technique and reliance on these traditional steps an positions are almost the only clear distinction one can make toda between ballet and modern dance. The latter, in its insistence upon freer, natural, more personally expressive idiom, avoids *en poin* almost entirely and is averse to prescribed artificial movement however graceful and impressive they may be. Nonetheless, th mutual antipathy and disapproval of ballet and modern dance which characterized the early history of modern dance—the days Isadora Duncan, Ted Shawn, and Ruth St. Denis—are rapidly pas

ort de bras. (French, "movement of e arms.") Any movement of the ms in ballet.

briole. (French, "leap, caper.") step of elevation. The working leg is lowed by the other leg, which ats against it, sending it higher. e landing is made on the lower .

é. (French, "thrown.") A transfer weight from one foot to the other ile jumping.

ing. Today one sees a blending of the two kinds of dance. Internationally acclaimed ballet virtuosos in the classical tradition and modern dancers often perform both kinds of dance, and young dancers are almost always given training in both ballet and modern techniques.

Among the classical ballets which are most frequently performed today, and which you are most likely to see in live performance or on television, are: *Giselle* (with music by Adolph Adam), the tragic love story of a German peasant girl and Duke Albrecht; *Les Sylphides*, choreographed to music by Chopin, with customes and moods inspired by his waltzes and mazurkas, but without a plot; *The Sleeping Beauty* (with music by Tchaikovsky), based on the familiar fairy tale of the beautiful princess who is awakened from a hundred years' sleep by a kiss from Prince Charming; *Scheherazade* (music by Rimsky-Korsakov), based on a story from *The Arabian Nights; Swan Lake* (with music by Tchaikovsky), which tells the story of Prince Siegfried, who falls in love with the Swan Queen, who can take human form only at midnight; *The Nutcracker* (with music by Tchaikovsky); *Coppelia* (with music by Délibes); *Petrouchka* (with music by Stravinsky), about a puppet with a human heart who comes to life in a tragic love story during a Russian street fair; and *The Fire Bird* (with music by Stravinsky), based on Russian fairy tales which tell of a bird that rescues a prince and a maiden from the castle of a villainous magician. Figure 16-2 shows how a few moments of *The Nutcracker* appear in "Labanotation," a system for recording dance movements.

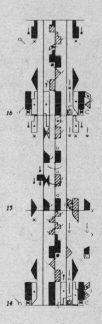

Figure 16-2. Labanotation. The symbols, read from bottom to top, represent the exact movements of the Sugar Plum Fairy during three measures (a few seconds) of the ballet *The Nutcracker.* Called "dance notation," this complex language indicates which parts of the body are moving, in what direction, and how long it takes to complete the movement. (Ford Foundation Letter, Dec. 15, 1975).

Entrechat. (French, "interweaving.") A jump in which the dancer rapidly crosses the legs before and behind one another.

Pas de chat. (French, "cat step.") A small jump resembling that of a cat, in which both knees are bent at the height of the jump.

For a closer look at ballet as a combined art, let us consider th short ballet *The Afternoon of a Faun*, which drew on the talents of famous poet, Mallarmé; a famous composer, Debussy; a famou dancer and choreographer, Nijinsky; and a well-known painter Léon Bakst. The inspiration came from Mallarmé's poem "L' Après Midi d'un Faune," which narrates the events later used in the ballet but uses them merely as an organizing principle; the poem's signifi cance lies in "the evocation of a mood and a reverie through fine spun imagery."[12] Debussy had intended to write a trilogy for orches tra based on the poem, but he completed only the *Prelude*. Nijinsky knowing the poem and Debussy's music, choreographed a balle based on them. The simple story for the ballet comes from the poem but it follows closely the organization of Debussy's tone poem.

The Faun, sated with wine, sensuously dreams as he sleeps in forest glade. He is awakened by a group of nymphs who gather abou him in curiosity. His passionate nature is aroused and he descend from his bower and advances toward them. They are startled and flee, but cautiously return. As the Faun seeks to woo them, they be come alarmed and flee again. One returns and appears almost willing to yield to his advances but then suddenly runs in panic from th stage, leaving her flimsy scarf behind her. The Faun picks it up and carries it with him to his sleeping place where, caressing and smell ing it, he falls again into voluptuous dreams.

Nijinsky adopts for his ballet the mood and events from Mal larmé's poem, but arranges them to fit the organization of Debussy' *Prelude*, which is in three-part (ABA) form. The first theme is sen suous and dreamy, with occasional hints of emotional excitemen which are interpreted in the ballet by the Faun's sensuous agitatio while dreaming. This theme gives way to a second one, with th marked rhythm of a stately dance, during the nymphs' visitation. I the closing section of the three-part composition, the first them returns and the Faun resumes his dreaming, now escalated by th scented scarf left behind by the nymph.

In developing the choreography for the ballet, Nijinsky visitec museums to study Greek bas-reliefs and black-figured vases of th sixth and fifth centuries before Christ. As a result, the ballet is chore ographed in movements which are predominantly in a two-dimen sional plane, with the hands, feet, and head in profile and with stif angular gestures simulating these archaic drawings. (See Figure 1-1 for an example, from Egypt, of the same archaic style in representing the human figure.) The costumes and stage set for the ballet wer developed by Léon Bakst, an important painter of the time, whose manner of presenting the human figure and use of colors were in fluenced by Gauguin. His design for the cover of the souvenir pro

[12] Thomas Munroe, " 'The Afternoon of a Faun' and the Interrelation of the Arts," *Journal o Aesthetics and Art Criticism*, vol. 10, no. 2, December 1951, p. 97.

Figure 16-3. Léon Bakst (1866?–1924), Russian painter. *Nijinsky in L'apres-midi d'un faune* (cover of the souvenir program, 1912). (Pencil, charcoal, watercolor, gouache, gold on cardboard. Courtesy Wadsworth Atheneum, Hartford, Conn.)

gram (1912) showed the Faun, in costume, dancing with the scarf; it is reproduced in black and white in Figure 16-3.

Nijinsky insisted that to establish the time and place as ancient Greece, the dancers should always face to the front, but with the head and feet shown in profile. His doing so was consistent with his belief that every ballet should have coherence beyond the mere formalistic pattern of taking set steps and organizing them into sequences to fit the accompanying musical forms. For each of the ballets he choreographed, he developed a basic body stance consistent with the story. For the choreography for *Le Sacre du Printemps* ("The Rite of Spring"), which has an even more primitive setting, he insisted upon a stance in which the dancers turned their toes inward (a sacrilege in the tradition of ballet), with the knees bent slightly forward, shoulders slumped, and arms dangling at the sides. The story, conceived by Igor Stravinsky, is that of a spring ritual at some prehistoric time in Russia in which primitive people worship the forces of nature. The music is dramatically evocative of a pagan religious ritual. Spring is celebrated in venerative festivities which culminate in the sacrifice of the most beautiful maiden of the tribe to ensure a favorable growing season and harvest. The ballet, in two parts, reenacts the celebration and sacrificial ritual. In an exciting climax, the chosen one separates herself from the dancing maidens and, in a wild dance which becomes more and more frenzied, dances herself to death in ecstasy. (An excerpt appears on page 247.)

It is an interesting commentary on the public's first reactions to innovations in the arts that Stravinsky's music for *Le Sacre du Printemps*, which was later to be used by Disney in his popular *Fantasia* and which has become a standard and well-liked concert piece, caused a riot among those attending the premier of the ballet in Paris in 1913; it was considered to be "a blasphemous attempt to destroy music as an art."[13]

It will be observed from the liberties which Nijinsky was taking with traditional ballet stances and movements that there was a growing discontent with these restrictive forms, a feeling that they limited expression in dance. It was not until some ten years later and in another country, however, that the complete, open revolt against them occurred.

"Modern" dance   Modern dance was in its origin primarily a revolt against the strict laws and regulations governing other dance forms, especially classical ballet. Its leader was an American, Isadora Duncan. She wanted art to be "free" and thought of her dancing as a "return to nature." As an artist she felt that she had only to "express herself." The "ideal of the dance that she saw was 'the divine expression of the human spirit through the medium of the body's movement.' "[14]

The people who followed her have been less strident in their utterances and less demanding in their claims, and thus they have produced a new purpose in dance—the expression of emotion.

Expressionist dance uses dance as a basis for direct communication between the dancer and the spectator; it is concerned less with

[13] Eric Walter White, *Stravinsky: The Composer and His Works* (Berkeley: University of California Press, 1966), p. 176.
[14] William Boletho and Isadora Duncan, quoted in Paul David Magriel (ed.), *Chronicles of the American Dance* (New York: Henry Holt and Company, 1948), p. 196.

form as such than with the meaning of life and the dancer's relation to it. "Its only aim is to impart the sensation of living, to energize the spectator into keener awareness of the vigor, of the mystery, the humor, the variety and the wonder of life."[15]

Modern dance may be said to have originated in the expressionist desire to get beneath the surface of reality. Just as Beckmann (Figure 2-13) and Kokoschka have gone beyond mere representation of a form or an emotion, modern dance, beginning with Mary Wigman in Germany after World War I, looks for essences and for meanings. In Mary Wigman's words, "Art grows out of the basic cause of existence." The idea of modern dance is not to repeat the traditional movements of the ballet, even though each interpreter might do them better than the last. It is, rather, to use the human body as an instrument. In the way the body moves, unrestrained by formalism or convention, with no emotion barred, no fact held back, the dancer can give the spectator some notion of the meaning of life.

Modern dance has existed for more than half a century, and, although it may need some word of explanation, it needs no apology at this point. In the development of the art from Mary Wigman and Isadora Duncan through Martha Graham, Hanya Holm, Anna Sokolow, and others of the middle period (1930–1945) to such contemporary artists as Merce Cunningham and Twyla Tharp, modern dance has contributed much. Classical ballet, of course, has by no means gone out of existence. There are still outstanding performances and new interpretations by such dancers as the Russian master Nureyev and the British ballerina Margot Fonteyn. Some interpreters have modernized the classical ballet for expressive or symbolic purposes: the Netherlands Dance Company and the Alvin Ailey Company are examples.

OPERA

In Chapter 15, Form in Music, we discussed the origins of opera in chanted dialogue to which were later added set musical numbers— arias, duets, trios, ensembles, choruses, and sometimes instrumental pieces to be played before the opera began or between the acts. These set vocal and instrumental numbers followed the established musical forms discussed in Chapter 15. So generalized and independent of the plot are the set numbers in some operas that they are frequently performed in concerts without the context. One thinks of such arias as the "Jewel Song" from *Faust*, "One Fine Day" from *Madame Butterfly*, and the "Habañera" from *Carmen*. However, the principal distinction between opera and other musical genres—such as the song cycle, the oratorio, the mass and the motet—is the fact that opera tells a story.

[15] John Martin, op. cit., p. 253.

The overall structure of an opera is a story which embraces th
recitative passages and the musical forms used in arias and other s
vocal pieces which make it up. As such, it requires the essentials o
all narratives: an exposition, a conflict, rising action to a turnin
point, a climax, and finally a denouement.

The stories upon which early operas were based were usuall
drawn from Greek mythology, as was the basic idea of chanting
dramatic presentation. For example, Jacopo Peri, Monteverdi, Gluck
and many others wrote operas dealing with the myth of Orpheu
and Eurydice. (See page 124 for a discussion of the story and Gluck'
handling of it.) Other myths which became popular subjects fo
operas were those of Hercules, Iphigenia, and the Trojan War.

Handling these essential elements in opera, in which the de
mands of music require that verbal content be kept to a minimum, i
the organizational problem that every composer of opera must solve
Because information is communicated much more slowly when sing
ing than when speaking, the stories of operas are usually kept fairl
simple. Moreover, the author of the libretto (the written dialogue
must allow for the musical demands. Sung dialogue—recitative—
moves the story forward much faster than the set arias and othe
pieces, which frequently use much repetition of phrases to meet th
demands of the musical form in which they are used. For this reason
the dramatic progress of an opera sometimes seems to be a series o
"starts and stops." The "stops" are the points at which set number
are used to embellish emotionally a significant point in the opera

Because the story is the organizational framework of the opera
one's enjoyment is enhanced by observing the way in which th
librettist and the composer have fulfilled the basic requirements o
plot.

FILM

Although film as an art form has much in common with some of th
other arts in its general principles of organization, the unique poten
tials of this combined art, especially its flexibility and its ability t
manipulate and combine the other arts, make it important to con
sider film as something more than a photographed record of them

The most obvious relationships of film are with narrative litera
ture, performed drama, music, and the visual arts. Because of it
ability to move back and forth through time, to change quickly from
one location to another, and to present visually materials which ar
subjective to the characters involved, film has been used for narrativ
purposes from its very beginning. Because it presents characters i
action who express themselves in dialogue, it has certain obviou

It is only through systematic and thorough exploration in the structural possibilities inherent in the cinematic parameters (rhythmic alternation, recapitulation, retrogression, gradual elimination, cyclical repetition and serial variation, thus creating structures similar to the twelve-tone scale) that film will be liberated from the old narrative forms and develop new "open" forms that will have more in common with the formal strategies of post-Debussyian music than with those of the pre-Joycean novel.

—Noel Burch[16]

[16] Noel Burch, *Theory of Film Practice* (New York: Praeger Publishers, a division of Holt, Rine
hart and Winston, 1973), p. 15.

analogies with drama; and because it uses a visual medium, it is allied to painting and the other visual arts in its modes of expression. In its complete control over the speed and rhythm in which visual and auditory material is presented to us, film has much in common with music and often draws upon it for both supportive and expressive purposes. But it is the ability to combine these, using unique principles, that constitutes the distinctiveness of film as a separate art form.

In some films, the structure and pattern seem quite simple and easily comprehended. In others, they are very complex; in experiencing them we find ourselves involved and moved deeply by individual segments, but do not sense consciously any cues or trends which alert us to the kind of structure emerging. Discounting the fact that we may be seeing an inferior production—and we should as a rule begin our consideration of works of art on the assumption that the artist had something definite in mind—there are perspectives which may be useful in helping us understand organization in film.

Film—that is, photographed moving images with or without sound—is a new medium. Because of its nature, it was at first used by artists to present traditional arts and art forms in new ways. Technically, it was a medium which could record anything seen and project it onto a large screen to be viewed in a darkened room by an audience. Since this new medium could record images of artistic creations in other mediums, it seemed natural for it to follow the patterns of expected organization structures of these. One can hardly think of a form of art or communication which early artists did not photograph "live" using the moving picture camera—operas, stage plays, lectures, circuses, sermons, paintings, buildings, comic strips, poems, etc.

Narrative continues to be the most common structure of film, but some critics feel that the constraints of the literary form hamper realization of its potential as an expressive medium. They see music, especially the "open" organic forms of contemporary music, as providing better models for creative film structure. Other critics, such as Andrew Sarris, although agreeing that the basic narratives which have become the stock in trade of entertainment films are indeed shopworn, see new areas for exploration of characterization, meaning, and the human condition in a more liberal cultural acceptance of our total, potential humanity and in our uniqueness as individuals. "The old motivational plot structure is probably dead, but that is all to the good. I think film will profit by the relaxation of taboos to the extent that new subject matter is made available to the art."[18]

Some of the taboos which have limited the subject matter of films shown to the general public at local theaters have been detailed

[17] *Four Screenplays of Ingmar Bergman* (New York: Simon and Schuster, 1960), Introduction, pp. xv–xviii.
[18] "A Symposium," *Film: 67–68* (New York: Simon and Schuster, 1968), pp. 282–289.

> *Whatever "obscenity" is, it is immeasurable as a crime and delineable only as a sin. As a sin, it is present only in the minds of some and not in the minds of others. It is entirely too subjective for legal sanction. There are as many different definitions of obscenity as there are of men; and they are as unique to the individual as are his dreams.*
>
> —Justice William O. Douglas[20]

and documented by Amos Vogel in his informed, admirably documented book *Film as a Subversive Art*.[19] Some areas of human experience which have only recently found their way into films—but not without protest—are suggested by the titles of chapters: "The Attack on Puritanism: Nudity," "The End of Sexual Taboos: Erotic and Pornographic Cinema," "Homosexuality and Other Deviations," "The First Mystery: Birth," "The Ultimate Secret: Death," "Trance and Witchcraft."

Although such taboos are frequently exploited in films of doubtful merit, more and more films are thoughtfully and effectively exploring parts of our makeup with which we are still only verbally acquainted. The potential of film for involving our emotions in ways which bypass our intellectual, verbal screening has not gone unrecognized by psychologists as a tool for bringing into consciousness things we normally hide from ourselves.

[19] *Film as a Subversive Art* (New York: Random House, 1974).
[20] Opinion rendered in *Dyson v. Stein*, 1971.

FOUR
STYLE

An art style is a particular set of selective principles. Taken as a whole, the style of a particular work of art expresses the perceptive bias of the individual artist, as conditioned by (1) his peculiar life history and (2) the context in which his life unfolds, that context being the human group to which he belongs and its culture.

—Morton H. Levine*

* "Prehistoric Art and Ideology." Reproduced by permission of the American Anthropological Association from *American Anthropologist*, vol. 59, p. 957, 1957.

17 STYLE

WHAT IS STYLE?

Style is not something which is added to a work of art. Style comes about when artists invest themselves in their works, giving their feelings and experiences forms which are satisfying to them. Style is therefore a quality which is present in every work of art, whether it be the work of a child, of an amateur who approaches art naively, or of a professional. The difference, in the end, is not between a work which has no style and a work which has style; rather, it has to do with the quality and distinctiveness, perhaps the inventiveness, of the style. Outside the arts, we are quite aware that style is deeply rooted in personality and is the sum of more or less unconscious ways of viewing the world, of articulating our ideas, and of preferences for particular kinds of experiences. For example, we speak of a person's "life-style"; not of whether a person has a life-style or not, but rather of its characteristics and qualities. Knowing this, however, we still frequently neglect to transfer this knowledge to art. We recognize immediately a friend's handwriting but somehow persist in feeling that there is something mysterious in the fact that persons familiar with art are able to recognize immediately the artist of a painting. In art as in life, style is the expression of the sum total of the personality in choosing content and giving it form which, to the artist, is pleasing and expressive and has integrity.

Rather than attempt to define style in the arts, let us try to illustrate what we mean when we speak of an artist's style. The American painter John La Farge (1855–1910) tells us in his *Considerations on Painting* how he and two other artists went out sketching in a hilly area. Although they were all painting the same hills under the same sky and atmospheric conditions, the results of their work were three distinctly different pictures. One emphasized the open sky above the hills; the others paid little attention to the sky. Each man devised his own general color scheme to achieve his own special emphasis. Although each man thought he was being true to nature, in fact each one was being true to nature in his own way.

Another story that illustrates how strikingly different results can be produced with the same subject concerns a Parisian model at the beginning of this century. For publicity purposes, she had her portrait painted by the many different artists for whom she had posed over the years. Some two dozen painters all concentrated on the same woman's features; the resulting paintings were a typical Pascin, a typical Chagall, a typical Matisse, and so on. Each man had rendered the set of features to emphasize what was typical of his own technique or manner of expression—the personality of the sitter herself was only secondary.

If painters living in the same place at the same time produce such different results, it is obvious that when the artists are of different eras, the results will be still more dissimilar. Let us compare two paintings of nudes. Giorgione's *Sleeping Venus* (Color Plate 44) is a beautiful study of a reclining figure. Two centuries later, Manet painted a similar figure in *Olympia* (Color Plate 45). Giorgione placed his figure out-of-doors and presented her sleeping. Manet opened her eyes and made her posture more erect. The effect of each painting is very different. Giorgione's is calm and idyllic, whereas Manet's is realistic, a frank picture of a courtesan, hard and cold-blooded.

We find the same sort of thing in music. Saint-Saëns and Sibelius each composed music inspired by the grace and beauty of the swan, and both used the cello as the instrument most appropriate for the swan; but again each composition reflects its composer. The work of Saint-Saëns is characteristic of Saint-Saëns, and that of Sibelius gives the mood and character of Sibelius.

The differences which we have been talking about are known as differences in *style*. Each artist works with the tools of an art—subject, medium, and organization—and the student who wants to know what style is will do well to study these tools in detail. What is the subject? How has the artist treated it? Why did the artist choose it? What are the characteristics of this use of medium? What elements does the artist prefer? Is the structure clear? Do all the parts fit together to make a whole? The student who considers such questions will soon come to feel that style is not medium, subject, and organization as such, but is rather the personality of the artist showing through them. La Farge said that he and his fellow artists were "different in the texture of their minds." The art historian Heinrich Wölfflin, talking of the paintings of two women, says of one that it is "not . . . less skilfully drawn, but . . . it is felt differently." The best definitions of style identify it with personality. This is essentially Buffon's famous definition: "The style is the man."

SOME CHARACTERISTICS OF STYLE

When we say that style is personality, we do not mean that the artist necessarily obtrudes himself or herself into the work of art. The work is personal and shows the artist's personality, but not because of intent by the artist. Each of the two paintings of nudes we mentioned above bears the imprint of the artist's personality, but this is not what the artists intended to show: they concentrated on portraying the subject, and because they expressed themselves honestly, we learn about them as well as about the subject. Paradoxically, impersonal art is personal.

Since style is a reflection of personality, it follows that when the personality changes, the style changes. An individual does not have the same personality at all times. For example, one's personality as an adolescent is different from one's personality in middle age or old age. And so it is with style. The style of Beethoven is different from the style of Mozart, and the style of Beethoven as a young man is different from his style in his middle period or his style in his last period. The style of Shakespeare is not the same as that of Marlowe or Beaumont, and Shakespeare's early style is different from his later style.

Often we hear that a young artist is working in someone else's style. For instance, the early symphonies of Beethoven are said to be in the style of Mozart; the early plays of Shakespeare are said to be in the style of Marlowe. It is true that, in these cases, Mozart and Marlowe were the models whom Beethoven and Shakespeare, respectively, followed, as a child learning to speak follows the tone and the pronunciation of the father and mother. But it is more accurate to note that even when working in the style of older men, Beethoven and Shakespeare still produced works which are recognizable as their own.

But people mature; an artist undergoes the influences of peers and social climate. Not only is there a change in the "personal signature" of the artist who is maturing from apprentice to master, but there may be a prevailing new direction in the arts themselves. When the artist is in the forefront or avant-garde of his or her culture—when values and their literary, graphic, and musical expression are in a state of flux—we have a Picasso in our time, a Mozart in the age of the Baroque, and a Shakespeare in the English Renaissance. The artist reveals and shapes what is important to his or her generation.

Picasso's *Old Guitarist* (Figure 2-6, 1903), *Blue Boy* (Figure 2-7, 1905), and *Fernande* (Figure 2-8, 1909) belong to different periods in the artist's growth and show the direction painting was taking in one decade toward increasing abstraction, which is most trenchantly epitomized in *Ma Jolie* (Figure 2-9, 1911–1912).

Shakespeare as an apprentice in his craft wrote:

Her lily hand her rosy cheek lies under,
  Cozening the pillow of a lawful kiss;
Who therefore angry, seems to part in sunder,
  Swelling on either side to want his bliss;
Between whose hills her head entombed is:
  Where like a virtuous monument, she lies
  To be admired of lewed unhallowed eyes.

—William Shakespeare (1564–1616, British poet and dramatist),
  from *The Rape of Lucrece* (1594)

This is the florid, artificial court language of the Italianate south; b
at the same time, Shakespeare was writing the more spontaneou
Romeo and Juliet for the stage, and in it we see that his art was freein
itself from aristocratic "airs" to speak the natural language of th
people. For example, when Romeo is banished from Verona—an
from Juliet—he says:

'Tis Torture, and not mercy: heaven is here
Where Juliet lives; and every cat, and dog,
And little mouse, every unworthy thing,
Live here in heaven, and may look on her;
But Romeo may not.

—Shakespeare, *Romeo and Juliet*, III, iii, 30–36 (ca. 1593)

Figure 17-1. Bernardino Luini (ca. 1465–1532), Italian painter. *Holy Family* (undated). (Oil on wood panel. Size: 27⅝ by 24¾ inches. Milan, Pinacoteca Ambrosiana. Photograph, Biblioteca Ambrosiana.)

The work of "schools" presents an interesting situation. An a
tist creates something that is good; it is recognized as good, an
it has an influence over other artists of the time. Soon there arises
"school" of artists who are carrying on the tradition of the maste
Especially is this true in the visual arts. We have a school of Bott
celli, a school of Scopas, a school of Cézanne. The work of the scho
has all the obvious characteristics of the master; at first glance it m
even be mistaken for his or her work, and it is only on careful stud
that one may be able to distinguish the work of the school from th
of the master. Because the school picks up the obvious characteristi
of the master, the work is simpler, and it is at first glance easier
grasp and more attractive than the original. Many a person immed
ately likes the winsome Madonnas of Luini (Figure 17-1) and learr
only later to like the greater Madonnas of Luini's master Leonard
(Color Plate 46).

STYLE AND STYLES

So far we have talked of style as individual, and in the last analysis it is always individual. It is the way a particular person living at a particular time does that thing by which he or she is known. Just as no person is ever an exact duplicate of any other person, the style of any person is not exactly like that of any other person. Still, people are alike in a great many respects, and we soon begin grouping them together under certain headings to show their likenesses. Similarly, we may find likenesses among the styles of various individuals. We speak of a British style or an American style, a humorous style or a poetic style, a journalistic or a scientific style, a medieval or a Renaissance style. A *style* in this sense is a recognition of certain qualities in which the works of individuals are similar.

The Historical Styles

The historical styles arise because of the similarities among people living in the same place at the same time. These people speak the same language, dress alike, have the same manners and customs, and share the same ideas; and their work reflects this community of interests. Thus we have the style of Elizabethan England, the style of the Italian Renaissance, a Chinese style, an early Greek style, a late Greek style, and so on.

Styles Based on Attitudes and Ideas

Besides the historical styles, there are also styles which arise as a result of similar attitudes and ideas. There are many examples of styles in this category: naturalism, realism, impressionism, expressionism, abstract expressionism, surrealism, cubism, the picaresque novel, the problem novel, Puritanism, imagism, and others. Many of these styles have not lasted very long, because the ideas they reflect, or the problems they deal with, have ceased to be of importance. The following passage, by John Canaday, is a vivid example of how styles come and go. It is from an article written by Canaday when he resigned as art critic for *The New York Times* (a post he had held for seventeen years) in order to devote more time to writing:

In 1959, Abstract Expressionism was at the zenith of its popularity, to such an extent that an unknown artist trying to exhibit in New York couldn't find a gallery unless he was painting in a mode derived from one or another member of the New York School. Willem de Kooning, Mark Rothko, Robert Motherwell, Barnett Newman, Clyfford Still, and their successful colleagues were already beginning to be referred to as "the new Academy" instead of the avant-garde, a term already beginning to lose viability except as an historical reference. . . . In 1959, for a critic to question the validity of Abstract

Expressionism as the ultimate art form was to inspire obscene mail, threat ening phone calls, and outraged letters to the editor signed by eminer artists, curators, collectors, and critics demanding his discharge as a Ne anderthal throwback.

As things turned out, the idea that Abstract Expressionism might b riding for a fall was more advanced than atavistic. Artists, led by a few rebel from the school (such as Frank Stella in one direction and Richard Dieben korn in another), began taking the situation into their own hands. Today th strongest contender for the title of Latest Thing in the mixed scene of 1976 i Abstract Expressionism's antithesis, Photorealism, along with several vari ants. In between we have had Pop art, which was the major revolution o the period, as well as Op art, Minimal art, Conceptual art, Earth art, Colo Field painting, Systemic Abstraction, Post-constructivism, and a lot o others, genuine and specious, rising and falling, overlapping and inter breeding, and still going on, with museums, commercial galleries, and ar publications deciding which portions of a vast overproduction the publi should be instructed to enjoy.[1]

There are, however, two categories of style which have been o importance for centuries. They are: (1) the classic and the romantic and (2) the tragic and the comic. We will consider the classic and th romantic now; the tragic and the comic will be discussed in Chap ter 18.

Classicism and Romanticism

The distinction between classicism and romanticism, though one o the clearest and most basic distinctions in art and one almost un erringly recognizable, does not lend itself easily to exact descriptior or definition. The confusion is made worse by the fact that the word themselves have shifted in meaning a great deal. *Classic* should mear nothing more than "belonging to a certain class." But by a proces analogous to that whereby we say that a man has taste when w mean he has good taste, *classic* came to mean "belonging to the firs class of excellence, the best." And the word is still used in that sens when we speak of the *classics* of English literature. Then, since fo many years Graeco-Roman culture was considered the best, the worc *classic* came to be associated only with Greek and Latin authors, sc that even today in the schools the "classics" are Greek and Latir works. When, however, we use the word *classic* or *classicism* as op posed to *romantic* or *romanticism*, we do not mean any of these defini tions but a fourth. The word *classic* came to connote the qualities tha were supposed to characterize Greek and Latin authors: clarity, sim plicity, restraint, objectivity, and balance.

The word *romantic* is also used in various ways. It should mear nothing more than "pertaining to or descended from things Romar

[1] *The New York Times*, Aug. 8, 1976, section 2, p. 1, column 7. © 1976 by The New York Time Company. Reprinted by permission.

or Latin," a usage that survives in the term *romance languages*—French, Spanish, Italian, Portuguese. The word came into use in the Middle Ages to distinguish the vernacular from the literary Latin. And, by a process of change very like what happened to the word *classic*, the words *romance* and *romantic* came to mean the literature of France, Spain, Italy, and Portugal at that time. The most outstanding type of literature was the tale of chivalry, which is still known as the "romance," and the word is kept for all narratives with emphasis on plot, as when we speak of Scott's novels as romances. *Romantic* then, came to describe the qualities found in the medieval romance: love of the remote and indefinite; escape from reality; lack of restraint in form and emotions; and a preference for picturesqueness, grandeur, or passion, rather than finish and proportion.

Classicism and romanticism are thus fundamentally in opposition; what is classic is not romantic, and what is romantic is not in that respect classic. The classic is restrained; the romantic is not restrained. The classic is more real; it is concerned with an idealization of the everyday; the romantic is unreal, concerned with the fantastic, the strange, the unusual. The classic is finished, perfect; it has great beauty of form; the romantic is unfinished, imperfect, and often careless as regards form. The classic is simple; the romantic is complex. The classic is objective; the romantic is subjective. The classic is finite, concerned only with projects that can be realized and accomplished; the romantic is infinite, concerned with plans that can never be realized, affecting "thoughts co-equal with the clouds." The classic is like an arrow shot from the bow that goes straight to the mark; the romantic is like a sailboat that tacks to one side and then to the other, reaching its destination by heading away from the mark.

The difference between the two can be seen most clearly in the great art of each type. The Greek temple, for example, is classic, and the medieval cathedral is romantic. Both are religious edifices, but they show an enormous difference in the attitudes that created them, a difference far deeper than the dissimilarities of construction and mechanics. The Greek temple is hard, bright, exact, calm, and complete; the walls and the columns are low enough to stand of their own strength; the lintels and the roof are simple, sane, and sensible. Nothing more is attempted than can be accomplished, and the result is a perfect building, finished and finite. Anyone can understand its main construction at a glance.

The Gothic cathedral, on the other hand, is not self-contained but is built on the principle of balance. The openings are not made with lintels but are arched. One stone holds in place only by its relation to the other stones. The walls will not stand alone; they must be buttressed. As the walls go higher, the arches become more pointed, the roof becomes more pointed, and the buttresses are strengthened with pinnacles and flying buttresses, the whole so carefully and cleverly balanced that a fault in one stone might cause a side or even

Figure 17-2. Chartres Cathedral, view of ambulatory from south transept. (Caisse Nationale des Monuments et des Sites Historiques, Paris. Photograph, Harry H. Hillberry.)

the entire building to collapse. And the whole cannot be grasped a a glance; one is conscious only of its great complexity, its enormou variety, its striving upward and beyond.

The Greek temple might be as solid as a statue, for all the feelin, we have of its interior; the inside does not matter; it has no mor character than the inside of a box. But with the cathedral, on th other hand, the outside sends us inevitably within. And inside w find a mystery in light and dark, a spiritual experience of unlimitec space which is the essence both of the Gothic and of romanticisn (Figure 17-2). Compare the Greek temple (Figures 13-26 and 13-27)

The difference between classicism and romanticism can also b seen clearly in music. Haydn and Mozart are typical composers of th classic school. The emotions are often subordinated to the form used. Beethoven followed Haydn and Mozart in his early works; hi early symphonies, notably the second and the fourth, are classic. Bu his more characteristic symphonies, such as the fifth and ninth, ar romantic. The music is personal and emotional; it is not containec and perfect, but exuberant, exultant, and free.

The difference, again, is clearly demonstrated if we examine two pieces of sculpture: the Greek *Hegeso Stele* (Figure 4-10) and the American *Adams Memorial* by Saint-Gaudens (Figure 4-11). Both are tombstones. The Greek stele (an upright slab) shows us Hegeso with her servant; the two are watching intently as Hegeso lifts a jewel from the box. It is a simple scene of everyday life, treated quietly and impersonally. On the other hand, the Adams monument wraps us at once in mystery and questioning. A robed and hooded figure is seated before a severe granite slab. Is it a man or a woman? What does it mean? Is it supposed to symbolize death? Or grief? Our attention is no longer centered on the object itself, as it was with the stele of Hegeso; the object now serves as a point of departure for our emotions and questionings.

Another demonstration of the difference between the classic and the romantic viewpoint may be seen in a comparison of the *Spear Bearer* of Polyclitus (Figure 13-13), from the fifth century B.C., with a later work of the Hellenistic age, the Laocoön (Figure 3-6). The *Spear Bearer* is an idealization of the male figure, and although it draws on "facts" about humankind as a whole, the result is a sort of summing up of what is most desirable in the male body. The man is serene and calm, almost godlike in his self-assurance as he proceeds into the arena with his lance. This dignified and glorified person might be considered the artist's ideal of humanity. The *Laocoön*, on the other hand, presents a highly emotional situation. A Trojan priest is punished by the gods for advising the defenders of Troy not to admit the horse of the Greek besiegers into the city. Not only is he himself to die; he must also watch as his two sons are overwhelmed by serpents. The emotions of these three figures are expressed in their anguished expressions and strained muscles; such emotional elements are not present in the *Spear Bearer*. Since the human figures of the *Laocoön* are seen at the moment of greatest possible strain, they are not idealized in the same sense that the *Spear Bearer* is. Another difference is that the *Spear Bearer* is simple whereas the *Laocoön* is complicated. It can be seen, then, that the classic and romantic approaches to art are not determined by historical period. An artist at any time may use classical or romantic qualities to achieve a desired purpose.

The difference also appears, of course, in literature. The classic drama, for example, deals with godlike emotions and carries them above the plane of humanity. Euripides's *Medea*, which we have discussed earlier, presents a woman who takes revenge on her husband by an act which has the character of fate: she murders their children. This terrifying act is, however, done off-stage; as a result of this restraint, is the *meaning* of the act, rather than the emotions causing it or produced by it, which is of utmost importance. This is characteristically classic. Let us compare this drama with Shakespeare's *Hamlet*. Here, the meaning is uncertain when Hamlet kills the king:

the *emotion* is foremost, because the characters have been presented to us in all their humanity and we have become involved with their feelings. This is characteristically romantic.

The difference is fundamentally a difference of attitude, which may be found in all types of art. We may see it illustrated also in two love poems. The first, by Landor, is classic; the second, by Shelley, is romantic.

Ah, what avails the sceptred race,
  Ah, what the form divine!
What every virtue, every grace!
  Rose Aylmer, all were thine.
Rose Aylmer, whom these wakeful eyes
  May weep, but never see,
A night of memories and of sighs
  I consecrate to thee.

    —Walter Savage Landor (1775–1864, British poet),
     "Rose Aylmer"

I arise from dreams of thee
In the first sweet sleep of night,
When the winds are breathing low,
And the stars are shining bright:
I arise from dreams of thee,
And a spirit in my feet
Hath led me—who knows how?
To thy chamber window, Sweet!

The wandering airs they faint
On the dark, the silent stream—
The Champak odours fail
Like sweet thoughts in a dream;
The nightingale's complaint,
It dies upon her heart;—
As I must on thine,
Oh! beloved as thou art!

Oh lift me from the grass!
I die! I faint! I fail!
Let thy love in kisses rain
On my lips and eyelids pale.
My cheek is cold and white, alas!
My heart beats loud and fast;—
Oh! press it to thine own again,
Where it will break at last.

    —Percy Bysshe Shelley (1792–1822, British poet),
     "The Indian Serenade"

We find the difference also in acting. May years ago Sara Bernhardt was starring in a classic drama, Racine's *Phèdre*. The story tells how Theseus, in his old age, married Phaedra. She fell in love with his son Hippolytus, who combined all the virtues of his father with youth and beauty that matched her own. Hippolytus, though he returned the love of Phaedra, would have nothing to do with his father's wife. In one scene Phaedra makes passionate love to Hippolytus. In the production by Sarah Bernhardt and her company Hippolytus stood apparently unmoved through the time that Phaedra was wooing him; at last she turned away in desperation, and as she turned, Hippolytus took one step forward, with his arms outstretched, showing in this one movement all the love which was in his own heart but which honor had kept him from making known. If this gesture of Hippolytus is compared with what we may call the usual theatrical portrayal of love, with its emphasis on the embrace and passionate words, we see again the difference between the classic and the romantic. Here it is not a difference in the amount of feeling expressed, but in the manner of expression.

Between the two extremities of pure classicism and pure romanticism there are, as always, many gradations. We can almost never say that any work of art is entirely classic or romantic; a work usually tends toward one or the other. The work of any artist is likely to be predominantly classic or romantic, although almost any artist will show both tendencies. Shakespeare is romantic in most of his plays, but quite classic in *Othello*.

Classicism and romanticism are an opposition present in all art of all ages. Although it is a mistake to say that any period is exclusively classic or romantic, we may discern times when either classicism or romanticism is distinctly ascendant. Classicism predominated in Greece of the fifth century before Christ, for example, and in eighteenth-century Europe; romanticism predominated in the Gothic period and the nineteenth century.

It may be noted also that, just as some periods lean toward classicism or toward romanticism, so, of the various arts, some are more essentially classic or romantic than others. Figure painting may be either classic or romantic, but landscape painting tends to be romantic. The distant view is naturally vague and mysterious (see Color Plate 41 for an example); and even when a composition concentrates on a nearby scene, it is not limited and self-contained—landscape, by its nature, leads one on and on; one wants to know what is over the river, beyond the tree, on the other side of the hill. Poussin is known as a classic painter, but his landscapes are classic only in the sense that they are intellectually conceived and planned; in other respects they are romantic. El Greco, in his *View of Toledo*, has heightened the romantic aspects of the scene by his use of light and cloud; the landscape is gloomy and menacing as well as mysterious and romantic (Color Plate 47).

Sculpture is by nature exact, precise, well defined, and balanced. The effects most natural to it are therefore classic, and a people of marked classic tendencies, like the Greeks, find in sculpture one of their best means of expression. It can, however, be romantic, as we have seen in the *Adams Memorial* and the *Laocoön*. Nevertheless, the classic seems the more appropriate style for sculpture, and most sculpture tends to be classic in feeling. Music, on the other hand, is by nature vague, elusive, evocative, emotional. The effects most natural for it are therefore romantic, and music can express in a few bars all the yearning and poignancy that it takes the profoundest efforts of the other arts to express. Today we often hear it said that the truest or best music is the "absolute" music of the eighteenth and twentieth centuries, which is objective and without emotion, devoted to purely formal beauty. Although it is true that a classic master such as Bach represents a pinnacle of musical achievement, it must not be forgotten that even his music often has emotional content. Contemporary music like that of Anton Webern is perhaps a more strict example of lack of emotion. But these instances are relatively rare. Most music throughout the ages, even where it is without subject and not deliberately emotional, is always evocative and mood-filled.

Finally, we should perhaps insert a word of warning that classicism and romanticism are not in themselves good or bad; they are merely different points of view and must be judged on their own merits. The good in the classic is poised, serene, and balanced; the bad in the classic is cold, overformal, and lifeless. The good in the romantic is rich and full of emotion; the bad in the romantic is gushing and undisciplined. Either can be a complete approach to art; neither without the other is a complete approach to reality.

18 THE TRAGIC AND THE COMIC

THE KINSHIP OF TRAGEDY AND COMEDY

It has been said that tragedy is life viewed close at hand, and comedy is life viewed at a distance. It has also been said that life is comedy to the person who thinks and tragedy to the one who feels. In other words, the same situation may seem tragic to one and comic to another, or tragic at one time and comic at another. Pieter Brueghel painted a picture illustrating one of the parables of Jesus: "Can the blind lead the blind? Shall they not both fall into the ditch?" (Color Plate 42). The old men in this picture might be inmates of any workhouse or poor farm. Each is trying to keep in touch with the one in front of him by holding onto his shoulder or by touching him with his stick. But the one in front has stumbled and the others are falling. To some viewers the grotesque positions they assume as they try to keep balance are comic; to others, tragic.

The close connection between the comic and the tragic is very well illustrated by the fact that certain characters formerly considered comic are now considered tragic. There is no question that Shylock, in *The Merchant of Venice*, was originally considered a comic character; now he is tragic. We feel only sympathy for the old man when we hear him say:

In the Rialto you have rated me
About my moneys and my usances.
Still have I borne it with a patient shrug,
For suff'rance is the badge of all our tribe.
You call me misbeliever, cut-throat dog,
And spit upon my Jewish gaberdine,

And all for use of that which is mine own.
Well then, it now appears you need my help.
Go to, then! You come to me, and you say,
"Shylock, we would have moneys;" you say so—
You, that did void your rheum upon my beard
And foot me as you spurn a stranger cur
Over your threshold; moneys is your suit.
What should I say to you? Should I not say,
"Hath a dog money? Is it possible
A cur can lend three thousand ducats?" Or
Shall I bend low and in a bondsman's key,
With bated breath and whisp'ring humbleness,
Say this:
"Fair sir, you spat on me on Wednesday last;
You spurn'd me such a day; another time
You call'd me dog; and for these courtesies
I'll lend you thus much moneys"?

—William Shakespeare (1564–1616, British poet and dramatist),
The Merchant of Venice, I, iii, 108–130 (ca. 1595)

THE FUNDAMENTAL TYPES OF COMEDY AND TRAGEDY

The fundamental types of comedy and tragedy may be seen in various alternative attitudes toward an old joke. If a man about to sit down has his chair pulled out from under him, there are, in general, four possibilities: (1) The man sits on the floor, and we laugh. This is comic, but a comedy of situation only; we are amused because the man on the floor is in a situation in which he did not expect to be. The man himself does not matter. (2) The man, falling to the floor, breaks his back. This is obviously tragedy, not comedy; but again it is a tragedy of situation because it does not matter in either of these cases who the man is. The situation gives the scene its character. (3) We laugh, but at the person who pulled out the chair. We are amused that anyone should think such a thing is funny. We are laughing, in this case, not at a situation but at a person; in other words, this is comedy of character rather than of situation. (4) From comedy of character to tragedy of character is only a step. Instead of laughing at the person who has such a depraved sence of humor, we feel it is tragic that anyone who is living in a civilized community should find such a trick amusing.

Comedy and tragedy of situation are also called "low comedy" and "low tragedy"; comedy and tragedy of character, "high comedy" and "high tragedy." Low comedy is the basis for slapstick comedy and farce—the comedy that results from the throwing of custard pies or from the big feet of Charlie Chaplin. Low tragedy is the essence of melodrama. One is interested in the events that occur because they are exciting—a train wreck, an explosion, a race, a hunt for a criminal. In low comedy and low tragedy the characters are not individuals but types—the hero, the heroine, the villain, etc. In high comedy and high tragedy the people are individuals.

Shakespeare's *Comedy of Errors* is comedy of situation. This play deals with twin masters who have twin servants. To make the confusion worse, both the masters are named Antipholus and both the servants are named Dromio. The masters, who have been separated since birth, find themselves in Ephesus, and naturally there are many amusing situations as masters and servants are mixed up, until at last their identity is discovered and their relationship established. There is nothing comic in the twin masters or in the twin servants as such. The comedy lies in the situations which arise because they are confused with one another.

The French comedy of Molière and the English comedy of Ben Jonson, on the other hand, present comedy of character almost without comedy of situation. For example, the miser Volpone, in Ben Jonson's play of that name, pretends to be very ill; his greedy friends bring rich gifts, each one hoping to ingratiate himself so as to be the sick man's heir. When Volpone has gotten all their gifts, he resumes his usual state of health. There is nothing comic in this situation; we are amused only by the characters.

Ordinarily a dramatist uses elements of both high and low drama; the preponderance of one or the other determines the character of the play. In *Hamlet,* for instance, many elements of the plot are frankly melodramatic. To enumerate: the guards are watching at midnight when they see a ghost; the hero kills a man through a curtain; there is a fight in an open grave; drinks are poisoned and the wrong person gets the poison; swords are exchanged and a man is killed with his own poisoned sword. All this is melodrama. The high drama is concerned with what takes place in the minds of the people, and so great is this interest that we are surprised when we realize how much melodrama the play also contains.

Shakespeare's comedies, in general, are not comedies in the strict sense of the word; the plot in a Shakespearean comedy is not itself usually a comic plot but rather a pleasant, gay story which does not take life very seriously. In *Twelfth Night,* for instance, the plot tells how Viola, learning that she is near the estate of a duke (Orsino) of whom she has heard much, decides to assume the guise of a boy and enter the duke's service in the hope that she may win him and marry him. She does both. It is a pleasant tale, not a comic one. In the development of the story, however, Shakespeare uses both comedy of character and comedy of situation.

THE BASIS OF COMEDY

The chief source of the comic is the incongruous, the unexpected. We expect one thing but find another. If one man pulls a chair out from under another, the joke lies in the fact that the second sits on the floor when he expected to sit on the chair. It is unexpectedness that makes for comedy in this speech by the nurse in *Romeo and Juliet:*

Your love says, like an honest gentleman, and a courteous, and a kind, and a handsome, and I warrant, a virtuous,—Where is your Mother?

—Shakespeare, *Romeo and Juliet*, II, v, 56–69 (ca. 1593)

Juliet has sent the nurse to find out from Romeo whether she is to be married that day. The nurse has returned with the news, and Juliet wants to know. But the nurse is hot and tired and out of humor because of the long trip she has had. At last she begins to tell the message from Romeo, but when she comes to the word *virtuous*, she is reminded of the nature of the alliance she is promoting and breaks off with the question "Where is your mother?" It is the contrast between what we expect and what we receive that is comic.

   In comedy of character, it is the difference between what persons think they are and the persons we think them to be that is funny. There is a famous passage in *Much Ado about Nothing* where Dogberry swears in the guards to check their loyalty. There is nothing funny in the situation itself: the comedy comes from Dogberry's pomposity; he thinks he is better than he is.

Dogberry	Are you good men and true?
Verges	Yea, or else it were pity but they should suffer salvation, body and soul.
Dogberry	Nay, that were a punishment too good for them, if they should have any allegiance in them, being chosen for the Prince's watch.
Verges	Well, give them their charge, neighbour Dogberry.
Dogberry	First, who think you the most desartless man to be constable?
First Watch	Hugh Oatcake, sir, or George Seacole; for they can write and read.
Dogberry	Come hither, neighbour Seacole. God hath bless'd you with a good name. To be a well-favoured man is the gift of fortune, but to write and read comes by nature.

   —Shakespeare, *Much Ado about Nothing*, III, iii, 1–22 (ca. 1599)

It is obvious that Dogberry is a pompous fool, and also that he has a very good opinion of himself: therein lies the comedy.

Color Plate 42. Pieter Brueghel the Elder (ca. 1525–1569, Flemish painter). *Parable of the Blind* (1568). (Tempera on canvas. Height: 2 feet, 10 inches. Naples, National Museum. Photograph by Alinari.)

The Parable of the Blind

This horrible but superb painting
the parable of the blind
without a red

in the composition shows a group
of beggars leading
each other diagonally downward

across the canvas
from one side
to stumble finally into a bog

where the picture
and the composition ends back
of which no seeing man

is represented the unshaven
features of the des-
titute with their few

pitiful possessions a basin
to wash in a peasant
cottage is seen and a church spire

the faces are raised
as toward the light
there is no detail extraneous

to the composition one
follows the others stick in
hand triumphant to disaster

Color Plate 43.   Jan Vermeer (1632–1675), Dutch painter. *Young Woman with a Water Jug*. (Oil on canvas. Size: 18 by 16 inches. New York, Metropolitan Museum of Art; gift of Henry G. Marquand, 1889.)

Color Plate 44.   Giorgione (ca. 1478–1510), Italian painter; landscape by Titian. *Sleeping Venus* (ca. 1505). (Oil on canvas. Height: 3 feet, 6¾ inches. Dresden, Museum. Photograph by Alinari.)

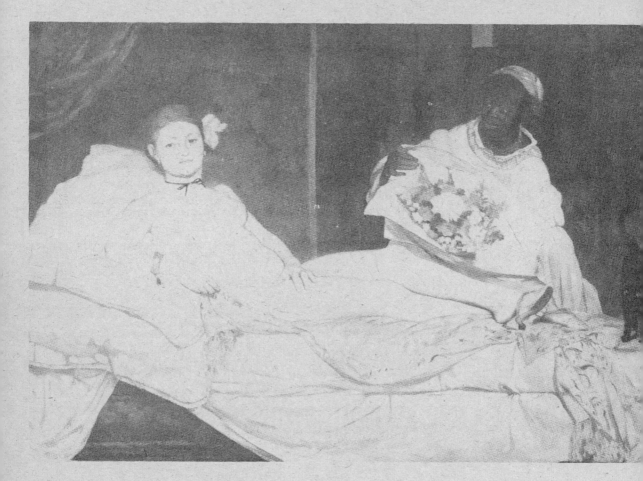

Color Plate 45. Edouard Manet (1832–1883), French painter. *Olympia* (1863). (Oil on canvas. Height: 4 feet, 2 inches. Paris, Louvre. Photograph by Scala, New York.)

Color Plate 46. Leonardo da Vinci (1452–1519), Italian painter. *Madonna and S. Anne* (1506–1510). (Oil on canvas. Size: 4 feet, 7 inches by 4 feet, 2 inches. Paris, Louvre. Photograph by Scala, New York.)

Color Plate 48. Piero della Francesca (ca. 1410–1492), Italian painter. *The Resurrection of Christ* (1460). (Fresco. Figures life-size. Borgo San Sepolcro, Palazzo del Comune. Photograph by Scala, New York.)

Color Plate 47. *Opposite page:* El Greco (1541–1614), Spanish painter. *View of Toledo* (ca. 1610). (Oil on canvas. Size: 47¾ by 32¾ inches. New York, Metropolitan Museum of Art; bequest of Mrs. H. O. Havemeyer, 1929, H. O. Havemeyer Collection.)

Color Plate 49. Rembrandt Harmensz van Rijn (1606–1669), Dutch painter. *Man in the Gold Helmet*. (Oil on canvas. Height: 2 feet, 2½ inches. Bildarchiv Preussischer Kulturbesitz, Berlin.)

Another type of comedy results from an unexpected twist in a situation: for example, someone may appear in the wrong kind of costume or in no costume, or give a stupid or incoherent account of something—in other words, there may be a departure from what is generally accepted as normal behavior. Of course the uenexpected is not, as such, comic; there is nothing comic in having an unexpected attack of ptomaine poisoning, or in getting a letter one has not expected; but if one is expecting to learn whether she is to be married, and hears the question "Where is your mother?" the difference between what one expects and what one hears *is* comic. Sometimes the standard is given; more often it is implied; but in any case we expect a standard, and we find it amusing when the actual deviates from it.

It is this measurement against a standard which has induced us to think of the abnormal as funny. Deformity, insanity, and pain have frequently been considered comic and have been regularly used for low comedy. The fool, the hunchback, and the midget were accepted as comic characters of the court; as such they are prominent in Velázquez's paintings of court scenes. In the Elizabethan drama, choruses of madmen were sometimes introduced for comic effects. Drunkenness was widely considered a cause of laughter and is still so considered in many cases. Children laugh if they see a cat having fits. In these cases the abnormal is measured against the standard of the normal and found funny.

CHARACTERISTICS OF THE COMIC

Comedy is primarily intellectual. The perception of the comic depends on the recognition of the difference between the normal and the actual. If one does not know the standard or does not perceive the deviation from the standard, one does not see the comedy in a situation. It is for this reason that jokes are tricky and that there are so many limitations on them. Comedy is highly specialized in its appeal. The people of one country do not like the jokes of another country. There is the American joke, the English joke, the French joke, the German joke. Even the sexes differ in their appreciation of comedy; women do not appreciate all the jokes of men, nor do men appreciate all the jokes appealing to women.

Comedy, moreover, is detached. We cannot laugh at anything that is very close to us. Even when we laugh at ourselves, we must, as it were, get away from ourselves in order to laugh. When a boy is suffering from puppy love, he cannot laugh at himself; but when he has recovered from the attack, he can. There is thus something impersonal about the comic. It implies a degree of insensibility on the part of the audience; we cannot sympathize too much if we are going to laugh. If we are distressed about the nurse's fatigue or her concern over Romeo's being a virtuous young man, we cannot laugh when she interrupts her tale: "Your love says, . . . Where is your mother?"

Because comedy is detached, we laugh at all sorts of things in the world of comedy that we do not find funny in everyday life: the man who does not pay his bills, the woman who deceives her husband, the young boy suffering from puppy love. In *Arsenic and Old Lace*, a delightful American comedy, two gentle old ladies are in the habit of administering arsenic in elderberry wine to the lonely old men they meet, because they feel sorry for them. The men are then buried in the basement by a brother, who believes he is Teddy Roosevelt and thinks this digging is part of the work on the Panama Canal. In real life we would demand that something be done; it would be no excuse that the old ladies are insane. Nor would it be possible to keep the whole thing quiet, as is done in the play. In short, there would be consequences. In the play there are none: the plot seems to take place in a vacuum. Evil in comedy is not evil but something to be laughed at.

Because comedy is intellectual and depends on perception, the comic always has in it a feeling of superiority. The person who sees the joke feels superior to the one who does not, and frequently patronizing. There is a bond between people who like the same joke. Sustaining comedy is like walking a tightrope. Artists usually veer to one side or the other; and they take sides with or against their characters—they are either sympathetic or critical. If the author is sympathetic, the writing becomes humorous; if critical, it becomes satirical.

HUMOR AND SATIRE

Humor is a matter of spirit rather than of words. It is kindly; it is sympathetic. Usually it has in it something of extravagance. The author, looking at the extravagant characters, smiles with tolerant indulgence. In this way we love Falstaff while we smile at the extravagance of his statements:

Bardolph, am I not fallen away vilely since this last action? do I not bate? do I not dwindle? Why, my skin hangs about me like an old lady's loose gown; I am withered like an old apple-john. Well, I'll repent, and that suddenly, while I am in some liking; I shall be out of heart shortly, and then I shall have no strength to repent. An I have not forgotten what the inside of a church is made of, I am a peppercorn, a brewer's horse. The inside of a church! Company, villainous company, hath been the spoil of me.

—Shakespeare, *Henry IV*, Part I, III, iii, 1–11 (1592)

When Orlando, in *As You Like It*, protests that he will die if he does not win Rosalind, she reminds him of famous lovers, none of whom died of love: the brains of Troilus were beaten out with a club; Leander died of a cramp while swimming the Hellespont, and so on. She ends with a summary for all time:

But these are all lies: men have died from time to time, and worms have eaten them, but not for love.

—Shakespeare, *As You Like It*, IV, i, 106–108 (1600)

Because we know Rosalind, and realize how much she is in love with Orlando and how gallantly and cleverly she is carrying on her game with him, we find the words humorous, but had they been spoken by another, we might have found them cynical.

Satire aims, or least pretends to aim, at improvement. The satirist sees the vices and faults of the human race, and exposes them in a comic manner in order to call them to attention. To this end, the satirist may use any device. Swift uses allegory in *Gulliver's Travels*, where he is satirizing the littleness of human beings. On his first voyage Gulliver goes into the land of the Lilliputians, a people who are only a few inches in height. Here he is amazed at the cunning and the foolishness of the little people. The test of the politician's ability to hold office, for example, is his skill in walking a rope. And the Lilliputians are in a great agony of disagreement and even fight a war to decide at which end an egg should be broken. Those who believe it should be broken at the big end are called the Big-endians; others, who are just as strong in their faith that it should be broken at the little end, are called the Little-endians. The point of all this becomes apparent: it is that human politics and disputes are equally ridiculous.

WIT

Wit is a general name for those forms of the comic which have to do with words. Like all other forms of the comic, wit may be based on incongruity. We may expect one word, for example, and hear another. Under the heading of wit come spoonerisms, malapropisms, puns, epigrams, and parody.

The *spoonerism*, named for one of its most distinguished exponents, the Reverend W. A. Spooner of Oxford, is the accidental transposition of the initial letters of two or more words. Spooner might have said he had just received a "blushing crow," when he meant a "crushing blow"; the English poets Keats and Shelley would have become Sheets and Kelly.

The *malapropism*, named for Mrs. Malaprop in *The Rivals*, is the ludicrous misuse of a word for one resembling it—for example, "contagious countries" for "contiguous countries."

Observe me, Sir Anthony, I would by no means wish a daughter of mine to be a progeny of learning; I don't think so much learning becomes a young woman. For instance, I would never let her meddle with Greek, or Hebrew, or Algebra, or simony, of fluxions, or paradoxes, or such inflammatory branches of learning—neither would it be necessary for her to handle any of your mathematical, astronomical, diabolical instruments.—But Sir Anthony, I would send her, at nine years old, to a boarding-school in order to learn a little ingenuity and artifice. Then, sir, she should have supercilious knowledge in accounts; and as she grew up, I would have her instructed in geometry, that she might know something of the contagious countries;—but above all, Sir Anthony, she should be mistress of orthodoxy, that she might not misspell and mispronounce words so shamefully as girls usually do; and likewise that she might reprehend the true meaning of what she is saying.—This, Sir Anthony, is what I would have a woman know; and I don't think there is a superstitious article in it.

> —Richard Sheridan (1751–1816, Irish-born British playwright),
> *The Rivals* (1775)

A *pun* is a play on words which have the same sound or similar sounds but different meanings. A serious pun is that on "grave" in Mercutio's speech in *Romeo and Juliet:*

Romeo   Courage, man; the hurt cannot be much.
Mercutio No, 'tis not so deep as a well, nor so wide as a church-door; but 'tis enough, 'twill serve. Ask for me tomorrow, and you shall find me a grave man. I am pepper'd, I warrant, for this world.

> —Shakespeare, *Romeo and Juliet*, III, i, 99–102 (ca. 1593)

James Joyce's "Lawn Tennyson" is a delightful pun (the reference is to lawn tennis).[1]

The *epigram* is a condensed, pithy statement, like that of the young man in Wilde's *Lady Windermere's Fan:* "I can resist everything except temptation." Martial is one of the most famous writers of epigrams; here is an example:

I do not love thee, Doctor Fell,
The reason why I cannot tell;
But this alone I know full well,
I do not love thee, Doctor Fell.

> —Martial (ca. A.D. 40–104, Roman poet),
> "*Non Amo Te,*" trans. Tom Brown (1663–1704)

[1] David Daiches, *A Study of Literature for Readers and Critics* (Westport, Conn.: Greenwood Press, 1972, orig. 1948; paperback ed., New York: Norton, 1964), p. 44.

John Wilmot's epigram on Charles II is famous:

Here lies our Sovereign Lord the King,
Whose word no man relies on,
Who never said a foolish thing,
Nor ever did a wise one.

> —John Wilmot, Earl of Rochester (1648–1680, British courtier and poet),
> "Epitaph on Charles II" (ca. 1675)

A *parody* is an imitation, usually of a very well-known work. The parody imitates the model very closely but turns the serious sense of the original into the ridiculous. Lewis Carroll was a great writer of parodies. He made nonsense of "How Doth the Little Busy Bee Improve Each Shining Hour," a preachy poem, in this version:

How doth the little crocodile
  Improve his shining tail,
And pour the waters of the Nile
  On every golden scale!

> —Lewis Carroll (1832–1898, British mathematician and writer),
> *Alice in Wonderland*

And "Twinkle, Twinkle, Little Star" becomes:

Twinkle, twinkle, little bat!
How I wonder what you're at!
Up above the world you fly,
Like a tea-tray in the sky.[2]

THE NATURE OF THE TRAGIC

Tragedy implies an unhappy or unfortunate ending to a series of events; usually it means death. But it is not just any kind of death; if an old man of eighty dies after an illness of months or years, his death is not called tragic. Tragedy implies a sudden reversal in prospects, a drop from a high estate to a low one. In the great traditional tragedies, the hero or heroine is usually of royal, or at least noble, blood, so as to make the change in position all the more telling. Lear is a king; Hamlet is a prince; Agamemnon is a king and leader of all the Greek armies in the Trojan War. Moreover, the tragic hero or heroine is an exceptionally fine person. Othello comes from "men of

[2] Ibid., p. 205.

royal siege," and he is cherished by all the people of Venice. Macbeth is no average general; he is unusually brave, courageous, and devoted; he is "brave Macbeth," "Valour's minion." The tragic hero or heroine is always a person of merit, usually of outstanding merit. We admire and respect such a character for virtues that are above the ordinary. When, therefore, we see his or her fall, there is something catastrophic about it. We almost cannot believe that a person so great or fine could come to such an end. Yet at the same time the fall seems inevitable. In high tragedy the ending must follow necessarily from the events and the character of the hero or heroine.

The necessity for the death of the protagonist—the hero or heroine—is clearly defined and distinguished in the two great types of tragedy, the Greek and Shakespearean. With the Greeks, the necessity was primarily religious in character. The protagonist does something that is against the law, and so must suffer. In the play called by her name, Antigone hears the decree of the ruler, Creon, that her brother should not be buried. This is a horrible sentence, since, according to the Greek religion, the funeral rites determined the position of the dead in the next world. Antigone therefore refuses to obey the decree, and buries her brother; by doing so, she violates the law and incurs death.

In Shakespearean tragedy, this necessity is found in character; because the protagonist is a certain kind of person, he or she must fall. Othello's personality, his background, his idealism, his ignorance of Venice, and even the secrecy and hurry of his wedding make the murder of Desdemona inevitable. The real cause of the tragedy is in Othello.

But even though the protagonist fails, tragedy is never fatalistic or pessimistic, nor does it leave one with a sense of frustration. We know that the protagonist has failed, and we realize that this had to happen; but there is no sense of despair or desolation. We feel even more strongly the essential values of life: love, justice, truth, goodness. In *Othello,* Iago is the only one of the important characters left alive when the play is over, but we do not admire him as a clever schemer; we hate him with all the power we have, and we love and admire even more the goodness we saw in the lives of Othello, Desdemona, and Emilia. When Antigone tells her sister she has planned to bury her brother and asks for her help, Ismene objects: it is against the law, they are but women, it is no use to attempt the impossible. But Antigone goes right on:

I'll neither urge thee, nor, if now thou'dst help
My doing, should I thank thee for thine aid.
Do thou after thy kind; thy choice is made;
I'll bury him; doing this, so let me die. . . .
But leave me, and the folly that is mine,

This worst to suffer—not the worst—since still
A worse remains, no noble death to die.

> —Sophocles (495–406 B.C., Greek dramatist),
> *Antigone*, 74–77, 102–104 (ca. 442 B.C.), trans. Robert Whitelaw

Antigone is killed, as she knew she would be, but there is no question that she has played the nobler part, and that it is better to die for what is right than to live knowing that wrong is being done.

In tragedy we know that the protagonist will not be saved and cannot be saved. There is no possibility of a happy ending. At the same time, however, we know that the values with which the protagonist is identified are not lost, and we feel triumphant in that assurance. Tragedy leaves one in a state of grief but also of positive exaltation. It is a strange combination, and if we add the fact that in tragedy these emotions are felt keenly, we have the reason why tragedy is considered the greatest of all literary forms. The pain of tragedy is great, so great it can hardly be endured. And the protagonists of tragedy suffer; indeed, Othello, Antigone, Oedipus, and Lear are great because they suffer. "It is by our power to suffer, above all," says Edith Hamilton, "that we are of more value than the sparrows."[3] Because we have the power to suffer, we can feel both the pain of the hero or heroine and our own joy and exaltation in the dramatic resolution of the story.

Tragedy is, then, almost the exact opposite of comedy. Comedy is intellectual; tragedy is emotional. Comedy depends on the unexpected, the incongruous; tragedy demands a sense of inevitability. Comedy lives in a world of trivial values where there are no consequences; tragedy, in a world where every deed brings its consequences and values are triumphant.

TRAGEDY IN THE PRESENT DAY

Tragedy as written by the Greeks and by Shakespeare is generally recognized as one of the highest phases of literary art, but it is not common today. To all intents and purposes it has not existed since the eighteenth century. Perhaps the reason for this has to do with the fact that at this time the middle class began to emerge as the dominant group in modern society. Monarchy and nobility became less important, and noble heroes and heroines must have seemed less important as well. With the nineteenth century, moreover, there came an interest in men and women as victims not of their own characters, or of fate, but of social and economic circumstances. John Galsworthy's play *Strife*, for instance, shows a man victimized by capitalism; Henrik Ibsen's *Ghosts* shows a woman victimized by

[3] Edith Hamilton, *The Greek Way* (New York: W. W. Norton and Company, Inc., 1942), p. 233.

convention. Given the circumstances of modern society—the way impersonal forces impinge on our lives—it is perhaps dramatically false to insist on one's responsibility for his or her own fate.

There is, in fact, some debate over whether there is such a thing as a genuine modern tragedy. Arthur Miller's *Death of a Salesman* (1947) gave rise to such an argument. The protagonist, a salesman named Willy Loman, is by no means royal or noble: this is one important departure from traditional tragedy. He is, however, brought down from a happier state (conveyed through a sort of flashback device), and the sense of inevitably of his downfall is strong. Moreover, it seems that a flaw in his character is responsible for this; but it can be argued that the cause is the false values of his society.

This issue of the values of society brings up another possible reason for the failure of modern drama to produce much, if any, tragedy. In modern society there is less agreement on values than ever before. No contemporary seeing *Antigone* could doubt that the heroine's action was magnificent and ennobling. A similar situation today would be likely to strike different people in different ways: "Did she do right?" "Was her action worthwhile?" "Perhaps she should have . . ." Indeed, Willy Loman's suicide prompts just such opposed reactions: was it a noble sacrifice or a cowardly retreat? Modern life is—what a tragedy must never be—full of ambiguity.

A third factor may be mentioned, though it is questionable how much emphasis it deserves—the cheap solution, the idea that all will come out right anyway. We associate this attitude with Hollywood, but film is not the only medium that reflects it. It is, perhaps, less influential today than it was three or four decades ago, when people felt disappointed not to get a "happy ending." Today, seeing a serious drama, we tend to be braced for unhappiness. Whether this ever is, or can be, tragic remains a vexed question.

COMEDY AND TRAGEDY IN THE OTHER ARTS

Literature can deal with the intellectual more completely and more exactly than the other arts because its medium is the language of the intellect, the language of philosophy; therefore, the comic finds itself at home in literature more than in any of the other arts. This does not mean, however, that there is no comedy in music and the visual arts. In the visual arts, of course, there are paintings of comic situations; but in these, the problem of interpretation is ever present. The scene or the character that is intended as comic may not seem comic once it is painted; the picture intended to be tragic may seem comic, as we saw in Brueghel's *Parable of the Blind*. With pictures or statues of happy people having a good time there is no difficulty of interpretation, but neither is there anything comic about them.

There is a great deal of comedy in program music and in vocal music, but the comedy lives primarily in the story or in the words, not in the music itself. The music of Haydn is friendly and genial, and we are tempted to call it witty because of the way one theme or one voice repeats and answers another, but it is not really comic. A superb example is the Rondo from the Sonata in E minor. We laugh aloud when listening to it, but our laugh is one of pleasure, of joy and excitement from following the repetitions. Mozart's "Musical Joke," a parody of an inept village band playing a ridiculous composition, is comic music, but such examples are extremely rare.

The tragic, like the comic, exists primarily in the realm of literature, though it, too, is found in the other arts. Music can seem to portray tragic conflict and its resolution. Most of Beethoven's sonatas and symphonies show conflict, and one feels the exaltation of the ending. But music is disembodied unless it is associated with a story (Wagner's music dramas are superb examples of the way music may interpret and resolve the conflict of a story); and then, of course, it is not the music itself which is tragic.

Painting and sculpture are limited by the fact that they can present only a single moment of time. Hence they can show either the struggle or the peace attained after the struggle is ended, but they cannot show both. The so-called *Medusa Ludovisi* (Figure 18-1) in the Terme Museum at Rome shows the struggle but not the peace that follows: even though the figure sleeps, the tension is apparent. *The Resurrection*, by Piero della Francesca (Color Plate 48), shows the solution of struggle. It is as nearly tragic as any visual art can be. Many have seen in the face of Piero's Christ the suffering and horror of his time in hell, the sympathy that he had felt for those whom he met, and his final victory over death. Painting and sculpture at their greatest show the elements of the conflict after the conflict is ended, when the warring elements are no longer in collision but at peace.

Figure 18-1. *Medusa Ludovisi*, or *Sleeping Fury*, copy of a late Hellenistic original. (Pentelic marble. Size: about 14½ inches high. Rome, Terme Museum. Photograph, Alinari/Scala.)

19 JUDGMENT

Among the most frequent and perhaps the most justifiable questions
we all have to face when learning to recognize art are these: "How do
we know that a certain poem or picture is really good? Who is the
final judge?" The American poet Marianne Moore had something to
say about this problem:

POETRY

I, too, dislike it: there are things that are important beyond all this fiddle.
   Reading it, however, with a perfect contempt for it, one discovers in
      it after all, a place for the genuine.
      Hands that can grasp, eyes
    that can dilate, hair that can rise
       if it must, these things are important not because a

high-sounding interpretation can be put upon them but because they are
   useful. When they become so derivative as to become unintelligible,
   the same thing may be said for all of us, that we
     do not admire what
     we cannot understand: the bat
       holding on upside down or in quest of something to

eat, elephants pushing, a wild horse taking a roll, a tireless wolf under
  a tree, the immovable critic twitching his skin like a horse that feels
                              a flea, the base-
  ball fan, the statistician—
    nor is it valid
      to discriminate against "business documents and

school-books"; all these phenomena are important. One must make a
distinction
    however: when dragged into prominence by half poets, the result is not
                poetry,

nor till the poets among us can be
    "literalists of
    the imagination"—above
      insolence and triviality and can present

for inspection, imaginary gardens with real toads in them, shall we have
    it. In the meantime, if you demand on the one hand,
    the raw material of poetry in
      all its rawness and
    that which is on the other hand
      genuine, then you are interested in poetry.

    —Marianne Moore (1887–1972, American poet)[1]

THE PROBLEM OF JUDGMENT

With the study of style we have completed our formal analysis of art;
we turn now to our last topic about art: judgment. We ask of any
example, How good is it? What has the artist tried to do? How far has
he or she succeeded in accomplishing this purpose?

    This does not imply that we can in a short time form opinions of
individual works which will be permanent and lasting. The great
scholars and critics have not succeeded at that game; what is liked in
one year or one decade may be considered worthless in the next. The
only real test of value in art, perhaps, is that of time. The really good,
the truly great, artists are those who survive the centuries: Shakespeare, Sophocles, Bach, Beethoven, Michelangelo, Phidias, Rembrandt.

    Still, if we pursue the analysis of art according to the plan of
this book, we consciously or unconsciously make judgments about
individual qualities in specific works of art, and to that extent address ourselves to these questions about judgment. Not that our
analysis has said, "This is good," or "That is bad," but through the
better understanding that comes from analysis, we have learned to
know details, and as a result we have instinctively judged them
interesting or dull, superficial or significant. What remains now is to
assemble such partial judgments into a comprehensive evaluation.
To the questions already mentioned, however, we must add others

[1] From *Poems*, by Marianne Moore. Copyright 1935 by Marianne Moore. Used by permission of
The Macmillan Company (New York).

which deal with judgment alone. They are assembled here unde
three headings:

1. Sincerity
2. Breadth or depth of meaning
3. Magnitude or effectiveness

Sincerity

One of the important criteria in making a judgment is the sincerity
of the artist, or, as we say more often, the honesty of the work. We
want a work of art to be a serious expression of the author's thought
and ideas. As Marianne Moore says, we want the genuine, and we
do not care for those things "so derivative as to become unintelligible," or those other phenomena "dragged into prominence by hal
poets" or other half artists. We want in a work of art an honest
genuine piece of work.

To put the matter somewhat differently, what we look for is a
genuine expression of the artist's own personality, rather than a
shallow imitation of someone else's. We may ask: To what degree is
this work original? To what degree is its type of expression borrowed from some other work or some other artist? Michelangelo's
style and achievements, for example, were so overwhelming that i
was virtually impossible for anyone working during the sixteenth
century not to have shown his influence in one way or another
Today, Picasso is an extremely dominant figure; he has influenced
art and artists since he began to work early in this century. We have,
accordingly, expressions like "Michelangelesque" and "Picassoid"
to describe the work of artists who are followers of masters such as
these.

To the extent that an artist follows someone else *imitatively*, we
may judge his or her work unoriginal and hence inferior. Artists
who are to be respected will, even if they start from a basis of someone else's work, eventually move on to create works expressing their
own individuality. Raphael, who worked in the early sixteenth century, was such an artist. He did borrow from Michelangelo at the
beginning of his career, but he became one of the most outstanding
and individual masters of the High Renaissance period. (To appreciate this, the reader may compare the left foreground figures ir
the *School of Athens,* Color Plate 31, with *Isaiah,* Figure 3-20).

It should be pointed out that originality for its own sake is not a
good criterion of quality or of sincerity. During the latter part of the
nineteenth century, from the impressionists onward, there was ar
expression among artists: *"Epatons les bourgeois!"*—"Let us astonish
the middle class"—in other words, let us baffle them as much as we
can. Matisse, who gave classes for painters in Paris during the firs
decade of the twentieth century, once asked a student why she was
attending the course. She replied that she wanted "to do something

new." This is an understandable feeling, but the urge to do something new does not of itself make for sincere artistic expression. Our reaction to the Dada art of the period around the First World War, or the "happenings" of the 1970s, may be influenced by a feeling that the artists were motivated too greatly by the desire to shock.

Another criterion that can be applied regarding sincerity is the extent to which a work of art does or does not express the character of the age in which it was produced. This criterion is particularly useful when we approach works of art, such as the great cathedrals of the Middle Ages, which were produced by anonymous artists. We cannot talk of the sincerity of any individual architect or stonemason in connection with, say, the cathedral of Milan (Figure 19-1). We can only speak of its authenticity as a work of Gothic art—that is, the degree to which it embodies the Gothic ideal as we discussed it earlier, in our examination of the history of architecture. We may find that although the size and richness of decoration in the cathedral at Milan are indeed impressive, the building as a whole does not express the Gothic style as it was developed and perfected in northern and central France in the thirteenth century. The cathedral of Milan is, actually, an Italian adaptation of a much earlier French style, a style in which stone (in the cathedral of Milan marble is used instead) was used to produce an organic structure whose dominant feature was an emphasis on functionally related parts. The later French Gothic style, with its emphasis on verticality, symbolized the

Figure 19-1. Cathedral of Milan (mostly 1386–1522; west facade seventeenth to nineteenth centuries; most of the pinnacles, nineteenth century). (White marble. Length: about 490 feet; width: about 200 feet. Photograph, Italian Government Travel Office.)

aspirations of the faith of those who created it. The cathedral at Milan, on the other hand, was produced in a country where the Gothic style had never taken root. In Italy, the style of the simple basilica always remained the norm; the cathedral at Milan represented a bow in the direction of a fashionable but foreign style, a style that the Italians had never understood. This cathedral is, then, a highly ornamented basilica: the pointed arches, tracery, pinnacles, and other Gothic elements are added as a kind of frosting, rather than being organically related to the structure. Because of such considerations, one might find such a building out of place, not genuine, inappropriate, or unmoving.

The form in which insincerity is most often found in art is sentimentality. Sentimentality may be defined as an insincere emotion; it is interest in the effect of an action rather than in the action itself. Sentimentality is not to be confused with sentiment, which is genuine feeling. We are all sentimental when we are young; we love to think how good and noble we are and how we are not appreciated, how sorry our parents will be when we die and they recognize us as the wonderful people we really were. That is essentially the point of view in this little poem by Christina Rossetti:

When I am dead, my dearest,
   Sing no sad songs for me;
Plant thou no roses at my head,
   Nor shady cypress-tree:
Be the green grass above me
   With showers and dewdrops wet;
And if thou wilt, remember,
   And if thou wilt, forget.

I shall not see the shadows,
   I shall not feel the rain;
I shall not hear the nightingale
   Sing on, as if in pain:
And dreaming through the twilight
   That doth not rise nor set,
Haply I may remember,
   And haply may forget.

   —Christina Rossetti (1830–1894, British poet of Italian parentage),
   "Song" (1862)

The speaker seems interested in the effect of her death, and she is enjoying the melancholy prospect of being in the grave. It is essentially a romantic pose.

Similarly, in the "Good Night" from the first canto of Byron's *Childe Harold's Pilgrimage*, we sense not so much loneliness and desertion as enjoyment of the thought of being lonely and deserted

And now I'm in the world alone,
  Upon the wide, wide sea;
But why should I for others groan,
  When none will sigh for me?
Perchance my dog will whine in vain,
  Till fed by stranger hands;
But long ere I come back again
  He'd tear me where he stands.

> —Lord Byron (1788–1824, British poet),
>   *Childe Harold's Pilgrimage*, Canto I (1812)

For comparison, read the lyric "She Walks in Beauty," where Byron has his mind on the woman, not on himself—where, in other words, he is not sentimental:

She walks in beauty, like the night
  Of cloudless climes and starry skies;
And all that's best of dark and bright
  Meet in her aspect and her eyes:
Thus mellow'd to that tender light
  Which heaven to gaudy day denies.

> —"She Walks in Beauty" (1814)

It is harder to be sincere about oneself than about other people, but not impossible. Byron is sincere even about himself in the following:

And I have loved thee, Ocean! and my joy
Of youthful sports was on thy breast to be
Borne, like thy bubbles, onward. From a boy
I wanton'd with thy breakers—they to me
Were a delight; and if the freshening sea
Made them a terror—'twas a pleasing fear,
For I was as it were a child of thee,
And trusted to thy billows far and near,
And laid my hand upon thy mane—as I do here.

> —*Childe Harold's Pilgrimage*, Canto IV (1818)

The examples of sentimentality given so far have been from literature, but sentimentality is found in all the arts. We are especially conscious of it in music, though we cannot explain how we recognize it. Beethoven's Sonata in C minor (or Chopin's Prelude No. 6) has in it something of self-pity, something of the spirit that finds itself an abused and sorrowful object—in short, something of sentimentality. The title by which the Beethoven piece is usually

Figure 19-2. Adolphe William Bourguereau (1825–1905), French painter. *Virgin of Consolation* (1877). (Oil on canvas. Size: about 14 feet by 11 feet, 3 inches. Strasbourg. Ville de Strasbourg, Conservation des Musées Château des Rohan. Photograph, Braun, Inc.)

Figure 19-3. Giotto (1266–1336), Italian painter. *Madonna Enthroned* (ca. 1304). (Tempera on wood. Height: 10 feet, 8½ inches. Florence, Uffizi Gallery. Photograph, Anderson/Scala. See also Color Plate 15.)

known, the *Pathétique* ("Pathetic"), is evidence of this. In compari-son, Beethoven's Symphony in C minor is entirely lacking in senti-mentality; it is open, frank, direct. It seems to show suffering, but does not enjoy the suffering.

Painting, like literature and music, is an open field for senti-mentality, and sweet, sentimental creatures are almost as common in painting as in life. In the *Virgin of Consolation* by Bouguereau (Figure 19-2), the figures are artificially posed; the Virgin, the mother at her knee, and the child lying at her feet are all designed primarily to produce a certain effect. There is no truth; it is not genuine. If this picture is compared with any of the great paintings of the Madonna the difference is clear; in Giotto's *Madonna Enthroned* (Figure 19-3), for example, the artist avoids the melodramatic, and projects calm, dignity, and nobility.

Depth of Meaning

Another criterion to apply to a work of art has to do with its depth of meaning. How much is the artist trying to do? What has been attempted?

Consider two works by Brahms. His "Lullaby," which we love to sing ("Hushabye and goodnight, with roses bedight"), is beautiful. But compare it with the magnificent final movement of his Symphony No. 1. The lullaby, although it is true and fine, lacks the breadth and depth of the symphony. Each work is supreme of its kind, but Brahms has attempted more in the symphony.

Let us examine two works of literature on the subject of war. In Hardy's short poem "The Man He Killed," an ordinary man thinks about his own experience of war:

"Had he and I but met
By some old ancient inn,
We should have sat us down to wet
Right many a nipperkin!

"But ranged as infantry,
And staring face to face,
I shot at him as he at me,
And killed him in his place.

"I shot him dead because—
Because he was my foe,
Just so: my foe of course he was;
That's clear enough; although

"He thought he'd list, perhaps,
Off-hand like—just as I—
Was out of work—had sold his traps—
No other reason why.

"Yes, quaint and curious war is!
You shoot a fellow down
You'd treat if met where any bar is,
Or help to half-a-crown!"

—Thomas Hardy (1840–1928, British novelist, short-story writer, and poet), "The Man He Killed" (1902)[2]

[2] From *Collected Poems of Thomas Hardy*. Copyright 1925 by The Macmillan Company. Used by permission of The Macmillan Company (New York).

Figure 19-4. *Niké Loosening Her Sandal* (end of fifth century B.C.) from the Temple of Athena Niké, Athens. (Pentelic marble. Height: 3 feet, 2 inches. Athens, Acropolis Museum. Photograph, Office of Press and Information, Embassy of Greece.)

Tolstoi's novel *War and Peace* comes to conclusions that are no radically different from those of Hardy's poem as far as the valu and meaning of war are concerned, but its scope is much greater Tolstoi makes us see the horrors of war year in and year out, th hopes, dreads, uncertainties, and dangers as they are stretched ou for years, until it seems that human beings can take no more.

The question of levels of meaning is another important aspect o appreciating a work of art. Some works we seem to enjoy purely o the surface level. Here are two examples: One of the reliefs from th Temple of Athena Niké in Athens is known by the title *Niké Loosen ing Her Sandal* (Figure 19-4). The goddess rests her entire weight o her left leg; the right leg is raised as she leans over to loosen the cor of her sandal. Her costume is of a soft material which falls in sof folds across her body, curve after curve all following in the sam general lines but with no two exactly alike. We have already studie a Greek vase which shows two women putting away their clothe (Figure 13-19). The figures and their clothes are balanced perfectly the space is filled but is not crowded; the bodies of the women ar graceful and each seems to complement the other, although there i little exact repetition. These are not works to make one think o ponder; one simply rejoices in the grace of the shapes in the design We do not ask why the sandal is being removed or why the clothe are being put away.

There is the same sense of untroubled enjoyment when one reads a little poem like Yeats's "Fiddler of Dooney" (1899):

When I play on my fiddle in Dooney
Folk dance like a wave of the sea;
My cousin is priest in Kilvarnet,
My brother in Mocharabuiee.

I passed my brother and cousin;
They read in their books of prayer;
I read in my book of songs
I bought at the Sligo fair.

When we come at the end of time
To Peter sitting in state,
He will smile on the three old spirits,
But call me first through the gate;

For the good are always the merry,
Save by an evil chance,
And the merry love the fiddle,
And the merry love to dance:

And when the folk there spy me,
They will all come up to me,
With "Here is the fiddler of Dooney!"
And dance like a wave of the sea.

—W. B. Yeats (1865–1939, Irish poet and playwright)[3]

This is very pleasant, and we enjoy it; we don't stop to ask if the Catholic church puts the work of the fiddler above that of the priest. The poem makes the heart dance "like a wave of the sea", it does not set the mind to puzzling. These examples are simple, clear, direct, finished, and perfect. We know them at once, and we feel we know them well. There is no hidden meaning in them.

Often, however, a work of art has more than one level of meaning. To start with an obvious instance, let us look at a poem by Robert Frost, "The Span of Life." It has only two lines:

The old dog barks backward without getting up,
I can remember when he was a pup.

—Robert Frost (1875–1963, American poet)[4]

[3] From *The Collected Poems of W. B. Yeats*. Copyright 1903 by The Macmillan Company; rev. ed., 1956. Used by permission of The Macmillan Company.
[4] From *The Poetry of Robert Frost* edited by Edward Connery Lathem. Copyright 1916, 1923, 1939, © 1967, 1969 by Holt, Rinehart and Winston. Copyright 1931, 1944, 1951 by Robert Frost. Copyright © 1964 by Lesley Frost Ballantine. Reprinted by permission of Holt, Rinehart and Winston (New York).

This is short and simple, like the examples we have just discussed, but there is a difference. Change the second line to

He was frisky and lively when he was a pup

and the poem becomes more like the three first examples—pleasant and final. In restoring the line as Frost wrote it, "I can remember when he was a pup," we find that the meaning is changed entirely. There is a sudden realization of the weakness of age, the eagerness of youth, and the shortness of life. In spite of the use of the pronoun "I," the poem seems far away and abstract. It fits the title, "The Span of Life."

From a small, simple, obvious object the poet can draw philosophical conclusions. John Ciardi in his poem "Credibility" looks at an ant and sees in it universal significance.

Who could believe an ant in theory?
a giraffe in blueprint?
Ten thousand doctors of what's possible
could reason half the jungle out of being.
I speak of love, and something more,
to say we are the thing that proves itself
not against reason, but impossibly true,
and therefore to teach reason reason.

—John Ciardi (1916–   , American poet)[5]

Muriel Rukeyser interviews a Zen Buddhist and captures the essence of an obscure philosophy in her poem "Fragile."

I think of the image brought into my room
Of the sage and the thin young man who flickers and asks.
He is asking about the moment when the Buddha
Offers the lotus, a flower held out as declaration.
"Isn't that fragile?" he asks.   The sage answers:
"I speak to you.   You speak to me.   Is that fragile?"

—Muriel Rukeyser (1913–   , American poet)[6]

We find the same sort of thing in two short poems by Robert Browning, "Meeting at Night" and "Parting at Morning." The first is a

[5] From *In Fact* (New Brunswick, N.J.: Rutgers University Press, 1962). Copyright 1962, Rutgers, the State University. Reprinted by permission of John Ciardi.
[6] From *Waterlily Fire* (New York: Macmillan, 1962). Reprinted by permission of Monica McCall, International Creative Management. Copyright © 1962 by Muriel Rukeyser.

vivid description of the meeting of two lovers, the eagerness hardly to be borne as the lover makes his way to the house where his loved one is awaiting him. The images are very clear: gray sea, long black land, yellow half-moon large and low, tap on pane, scratch of match, warm sea-scented beach.

The grey sea and the long black land;
And the yellow half-moon large and low;
And the startled little waves that leap
In fiery ringlets from their sleep,
As I gain the cove with pushing prow,
And quench its speed i' the slushy sand.

Then a mile of warm sea-scented beach;
Three fields to cross till a farm appears;
A tap at the pane, the quick sharp scratch
And blue spurt of a lighted match,
And a voice less loud, through its joys and fears,
Than the two hearts beating each to each!

> —Robert Browning (1812–1889, British poet),
> "Meeting at Night"

Here is the second poem ("him" in the third line refers to the sun):

Round the cape of a sudden came the sea,
And the sun looked over the mountain's rim:
And straight was a path of gold for him,
And the need of a world of men for me.

> —Browning, "Parting at Morning"

Each of the two poems has its own meaning, clear and exact when taken by itself. Each describes a situation. But the meaning changes when they are taken together, as Browning put them. Together, they say that the "need of a world of men" is a greater, higher appeal than that of "two hearts beating each to each." This prods us to thought: Why is this conclusion reached? We start to go below the surface of the poem to find what underlies it.

"Ozymandias" is nothing if it is only a description of a ruined monument.

I met a traveller from an antique land
Who said: Two vast and trunkless legs of stone
Stand in the desert . . . Near them, on the sand,
Half sunk, a shattered visage lies, whose frown,

And wrinkled lip, and sneer of cold command,
Tell that its sculptor well those passions read
Which yet survive, stamped on these lifeless things,
The hand that mocked them, and the heart that fed:
And on the pedestal these words appear:
"My name is Ozymandias, king of kings:
Look on my works, ye Mighty, and despair!"
Nothing beside remains. Round the decay
Of that colossal wreck, boundless and bare
The lone and level sands stretch far away.

   —Percy Bysshe Shelley (1792–1822, British poet),
     "Ozymandias" (1817)

What is important is not the surface but the point being made on the second level—that of irony. The theme is presented not explicitly, but in the unstated contrast between the king's proud words and the desolation that makes them ridiculous.

In the visual arts, the existence of levels of meaning may be illustrated by good portraiture. A good portrait shows more than what can be seen at any time and by anyone. It shows the person inside the face, as it were; looking at it, we may seem to know what the person hoped and feared. In Rembrandt's *Man in the Gold Helmet* (Color Plate 49) we see first the beauty of the helmet, its rich chasing; then we notice the rich garments. The exterior details show a man who has apparently all that money and power can bring him. The face is a great contrast to the rich garments. It is tired. stern, kind; it seems to be the face of a man who has known hard work, who has had to make hard decisions and take the consequences; a man who has had so much wealth that it means nothing to him; a man who can be trusted to see truth and deal fairly with it.

In *Early Sunday Morning* (Figure 19-5) Hopper has given us more

Figure 19-5. Edward Hopper (1882–1967, American painter). *Early Sunday Morning* (ca. 1930). (Oil on canvas. Size: 35 by 60 inches. New York, Whitney Museum of American Art.)

than a painting of a street. A sense of stillness pervades the street; we are conscious of how the delicate light of morning, the quietness of a Sunday, can touch a poor, ugly scene with beauty and dignity, and impart a sense of time suspended.

El Greco's *View of Toledo* (Color Plate 47) is a painting of a city where a storm is about to break. But beyond the natural appearance, the scene is ominous and foreboding; it is one of emotional intensity, mystery, and passion.

Magnitude or Effectiveness

Magnitude is concerned with the impact or effectiveness of a work as a whole, whether it be shallow or deep, important or unimportant, great or trivial—in short, with the quality of greatness felt in it.

For some years, one of the criteria applied was the degree to which a work met the ideal of sublimity. The source of the sublime is always a greatness of power. One feels the sublime in the ocean, in a fierce storm, in a mighty waterfall; there is no sense of greatness in a small pond or a trickling stream in a pleasant meadow. But even greater than the sublimity of physical power is the sublimity of spiritual power, the power of the Mass in B minor by Bach, or the Book of Job.

The sublime ordinarily demands a great protagonist: a person who is noble or powerful. It seems more natural to think of great emotions in great persons—kings, queens, and people in authority; hence the tradition was that heroes and heroines must be of noble birth. But greatness of rank is not essential; the highest emotions can be found even in the simplest subjects. A. C. Bradley quotes this passage from Turgenev as an example of sublimity in so little a thing as a sparrow.

I was on my way home from hunting, and was walking up the garden avenue. My dog was running in front of me.

Suddenly he slackened his pace, and began to steal forward as though he scented game ahead.

I looked along the avenue; and I saw on the ground a young sparrow, its beak edged with yellow, and its head covered with soft brown. It had fallen from the nest (a strong wind was blowing, and shaking the birches of the avenue); and there it sat and never stirred, except to stretch out its little half-grown wings in a helpless flutter.

My dog was slowly approaching it, when suddenly, darting from the tree overhead, an old black-throated sparrow dropped like a stone right before his nose and, all rumpled and flustered, with a plaintive desperate cry flung itself, once, twice, at his open jaws with their great teeth.

It would save its young one; it screened it with its own body; the tiny frame quivered with terror; the little cries grew wild and hoarse; it sank and died. It had sacrificed itself.

What a huge monster the dog must have seemed to it! And yet it could not stay up there on its safe bough. A power stronger than its own will tore it away.

My dog stood still, and then slunk back disconcerted. Plainly he too had to recognize that power. I called him to me; and a feeling of reverence came over me as I passed on.

Yes, do not laugh. It was really reverence I felt before that little heroic bird and the passionate outburst of its love.

Love, I thought, is verily stronger than death and the terror of death. By love, only by love, is life sustained and moved.[7]

Below the sublime are other degrees of magnitude, such as the grand, the beautiful, the graceful, and the pretty. By common consent, prettiness is the opposite of sublimity; it is pleasant, but it arouses no strong emotions. The grand and the sublime both have the quality of greatness; the pretty and the graceful have not. The beautiful may or may not be great.

These terms will become more meaningful if we try to apply them to definite works. Differences can be seen most easily if we contrast two subjects that are alike or two works by the same artist.

Dvořák's *Humoresque* is pretty or graceful, but his *New World Symphony* is beautiful, perhaps even great. Yeats's poem "The Second Coming" is great or beautiful; his "Fiddler of Dooney" is no more than pretty or graceful.

Turning and turning in the widening gyre
The falcon cannot hear the falconer;
Things fall apart; the center cannot hold;
Mere anarchy is loosed upon the world,
The blood-dimmed tide is loosed, and everywhere
The ceremony of innocence is drowned;
The best lack all conviction, while the worst
Are full of passionate intensity.

Surely some revelation is at hand;
Surely the Second Coming is at hand.
The Second Coming! Hardly are those words out
When a vast image out of *Spiritus Mundi*
Troubles my sight: somewhere in sands of the desert
A shape with lion body and the head of a man,
A gaze blank and pitiless as the sun,
Is moving its slow thighs, while all about it
Reel shadows of the indignant desert birds.
The darkness drops again; but now I know
That twenty centuries of stony sleep
Were vexed to nightmare by a rocking cradle,

---

[7] A. C. Bradley, "The Sublime," *Oxford Lectures on Poetry* (New York: St. Martin's Press), p. 44.

And what rough beast, its hour come round at last,
Slouches towards Bethlehem to be born?

    —Yeats, ''The Second Coming'' (1921)[8]

    Compare two great compositions by Michelangelo: the *Pietà*
(Figure 19-6) at S. Peter's in Rome, done when he was a young man,
and its counterpart *The Entombment* (Figure 19-7) in the cathedral at
Florence, done some fifty years later. Both are sincere; both are
polished. In the first, the Madonna is young, her face sweetly serious,
her head bent forward as she tries to comprehend what has happened. One hand is holding the body of Jesus, the other is left free in
a youthful gesture. In the later *Entombment*, youth and sweetness
have been left behind. The greatest change is in the face of Jesus, for

Figure 19-6. Michelangelo (1475–1564),
Italian painter, sculptor, architect,
and poet. *Pietà* (1498–1502).
Marble. Height: about 6 feet, 3 inches.
S. Peter's, Vatican City. Photograph,
Anderson/Scala.

[8] From *The Collected Poems of W. B. Yeats.* Copyright 1903 by The Macmillan Company; rev. ed.;
1956. Used by permission of The Macmillan Company (New York).

Figure 19-7. Michelangelo. *The Entombment* (ca. 1550). (Marble. Height: about 7 feet. Florence, Cathedral. Photograph, Anderson/Scala.)

he is now the Christ who has died to save the world. This agonized yet triumphant statue has elements of sublimity, whereas the lyrical and gentle *Pietà* lacks them.

The sublime arouses in one a feeling of astonishment, rapture, and awe. In comparison with its greatness, one feels one's own littleness; but, paradoxically, the attempt to share the sublime makes one greater than before. Confronted with the greatness of Socrates as we see him in Plato's account, we feel petty, and yet our attempt to understand him makes us greater than we were.

Crito, when he heard this, made a sign to the servant; and the servant went in, and remained for some time, and then returned with the jailer carrying the cup of poison. Socrates said: "You, my good friend, who are experienced in these matters, shall give me directions how I am to proceed." The man answered: "You have only to walk about until your legs are heavy, and then to lie down, and the poison will act." At the same time he handed the cup to Socrates, who in the easiest and gentlest manner, without the least fear or change of color or feature, looking at the man with all his eyes . . . as his manner was, took the cup and said: "What do you say about making a libation out of this cup to any god? May I, or not?" The man answered: "We only prepare, Socrates, just so much as we deem enough." "I understand," he said: "yet I may and must pray to the gods to prosper my journey from this to that other world—may this then, which is my prayer, be granted to me." Then holding the cup to his lips, quite readily and cheerfully he drank off the poison. And hitherto most of us had been able to control our sorrow; but now when we saw him drinking, and saw too that he had finished the draught, we could no longer forbear, and in spite of myself my own tears were flowing fast; so that I covered my face and wept over myself, for certainly I was not weeping over him, but at the thought of my own calamity in having lost such a companion. Nor was I the first, for Crito, when he found himself unable to restrain his tears, had got up and moved away, and I followed; and at that moment, Apollodorus, who had been weeping all the time, broke out into a loud cry which made cowards of us all. Socrates alone retained his calmness. "What is this strange outcry?" he said. "I sent away the women mainly in order that they might not offend in this way, for I have heard that a man should die in peace. Be quiet then, and have patience." When we heard that, we were ashamed, and refrained our tears; and he walked about until, as he said, his legs began to fail, and then he lay on his back, according to the directions, and the man who gave him the poison now and then looked at his feet and legs; and after a while he pressed his foot hard and asked him if he could feel; and he said, "No"; and then his leg, and so upwards and upwards, and showed us that he was cold and stiff. And he felt then himself, and said: "When the poison reaches the heart, that will be the end." He was beginning to grow cold about the groin, when he uncovered his face, for he had covered himself up, and said (they were his last words)—he said: "Crito, I owe a cock to Asclepius; will you remember to pay the debt?" "The debt shall be paid," said Crito; "is there anything else?" There was no answer to this question; but in a minute or two a movement was heard, and the attendants uncovered him; his eyes were set, and Crito closed his eyes and mouth.

—Plato (427?–347 B.C., Greek philosopher), *The Phaedo*,
trans. Benjamin Jowett (1817–1893, British scholar)

An excellent example of sublimity in music is the choral section of Beethoven's Ninth Symphony (1824) based on Friedrich Schiller's "Ode to Joy," a poem about the brotherhood of man. Few listeners can remain unmoved in the presence of this majestic combination of music and verse, with its full orchestra and huge chorus. Other examples are the mighty final movement of Brahms's First Symphony (1876), and the portion of Wagner's *Götterdämmerung* ("Twilight of the Gods," 1874) known as "Siegfried's Death," which begins with a spine-chilling roll of the timpani and the unearthly forest music that presages the death of the hero.

Today, sublimity is no longer the supreme criterion applied in discussing the magnitude or effectiveness of works of art. A number of factors, including the development of abstraction, have presented a challenge to traditional values and methods of judging. The term *sublime*, indeed, is not applied to modern and contemporary works although we do retain the sense that some works are characterized by "greatness," by a magnitude beyond that of other works. The murals of Orozco, the triptychs of Max Beckmann, and Picasso's *Guernica* are examples of impressive magnitude, but these works cannot properly be described as sublime. Similarly, the concept of sublime heroism no longer seems to apply, as was suggested in our discussion of the absence of traditional tragedy from modern drama.

Does this mean that the criteria we apply to modern works must be different from those applied to traditional works? We are now approaching a very complex subject, which the scope of this book will not allow us to deal with. Aestheticians—that is, scholars who devote themselves to the problem of characteristics of art and value in art—believe that there are universal criteria, that we can make exactly the same demands of all kinds of art produced at all times. Unfortunately for our purposes, the aestheticians differ on what these criteria may be. It is not even entirely clear whether there are basic irreconcilable differences among the various sets of criteria suggested, or whether the criteria might not represent different aspects of roughly similar ideas. For example, we have suggested as criteria sincerity, depth, and magnitude or effectiveness. Monroe Beardsley, a well-known American aesthetician, has suggested unity, complexity, and intensity. Are these two sets entirely incompatible? Perhaps "complexity" and "depth" are essentially the same idea; but perhaps "intensity" and "magnitude" are altogether different concepts. We have not taken up "unity"—that is, the fact that a work of art is complete in itself and totally self-contained—and Beardsley's criteria do not include "sincerity." James Joyce, speaking through the character Stephen Dedalus in *A Portrait of the Artist as a Young Man*, proposed "wholeness," "harmony," and "radiance." To what extent do these criteria agree or disagree with those we have just mentioned? Even if we decide to take it for granted that there are universal criteria, formulating them is an enormous and subtle problem. (It is also a fascinating one.) For practical purposes, it is well to know that there are, broadly speaking, two main ways of evaluating works of art. One is purely formal. Those who take this approach are interested in the physical or structural characteristics of the work: in visual art, for example, these would include form, space, color, and texture. The work of art is considered to be a combination of these formal elements. Meaning and emotion are not so important. Another approach concentrates on the way a work of art reflects the period in which it was produced, and particularly the standards which existed during that period. Following this second approach, one would try to distill from the works of an era the artistic ideal of that era, and then apply that ideal to the works of the time.

These two approaches do not necessarily produce opposed judgments about a work of art. For example, let us take each approach to Luini's *Holy Family* (Figure 17-1). First, we can see that it lacks clarity, restraint, and adequate space for the figures in it; that is, it is not pleasing as a formal design. Second, we may compare it with contemporaneous works by Leonardo, Raphael, and Michelangelo. We find in the works of these High Renaissance masters qualities which we may consider as part of the Renaissance ideal: the sculpturesque, the geometric, great control and restraint over emotional content, careful composition. These qualities do not seem to be present in the Luini. With either approach, then, we are led to the conclusion that this is not a particularly good work.

GROWTH IN JUDGMENT AND EVALUATION

The judgment each person makes of a work of art is individual and personal, just as the experience of the work of art was individual and personal. Since one person is never exactly like any other, no one's evaluation and appreciation of art will ever be exactly like that of another. Moreover, no person's judgment of any work of art will remain exactly the same. With each new experience one tends to like a work of art more or less, to find it more or less rewarding. In short, there is never one evaluation which can be embalmed and put away as final.

Not only does evaluation change with each new experience, but it changes as one comes to know the judgments of others. Both history and criticism can help us to see and hear what we have not seen and heard for ourselves, and so our experience becomes richer and deeper.

This is the greatest contribution history and criticism can make to us, but there is a secondary influence which is also of importance. History and criticism can help us in the selection of works we want to become acquainted with. No one can possibly know all the art in the world; one cannot read all the books that are printed or hear all the music that is composed and played in any one year; one can hardly know all the pictures and statues in any one of the great galleries, much less in all of them. Therefore, we use the opinions of others to help us decide what is worth looking at and listening to, to tell what has been thought good and what poor, what has been reckoned great and what mediocre.

This is especially important in the case of those artists who have become known through the ages as the very great: Dante, Homer, Rembrandt, Shakespeare, Phidias, Bach, Beethoven, Michelangelo. They cannot be known easily or at once. Therefore we do not get the immediate satisfaction we get from lesser works; we are perhaps repulsed, and we put them aside. The very great in art, as in every thing else, is difficult. Almost anything worth doing is difficult; i cannot be attained easily or without hard work. The prophecies o Isaiah and the Book of Job in the Old Testament are among the su preme examples of literature, but it is doubtful if anyone can ge very great pleasure from them without study. No one can ever appre ciate the Mass in B minor or the *Divine Comedy* on a casual hearing o a superficial reading; they need concentrated attention. When we know that they are considered among the world's great master pieces, we can prepare to give them the necessary study. The person who gives them this study will not necessarily like them; in art, as ir life, one must count on a certain number of failures. But we canno know if we will like the great works of art until we have given them the necessary attention.

Fortunately, there is little difference of opinion with regard tc the very great. About the lesser works there are many and various judgments—one person prefers this and another that—but as we ap proach those few masterpieces that can be called supremely great, the differences melt away. Hence we may approach them with greater assurance, understanding that though they demand work, they will bring their reward; the work will not be in vain. Fortu nately, also, the rewards of art, like the rewards of goodness, are open to everyone. Appreciation of art, like virtue, is not reserved for the learned but is free to the honest and sincere.

20 A FINAL WORD

The ancients, when they came to focus their analytical methods on the universe, were able to agree that it was composed of four elements—earth, air, water, and fire. Although this was a neat, logical, demonstrable conclusion, it did not satisfy their feelings, their emotional responses to it. To account for their total, holistic sense of the universe, they therefore added to these four material elements a fifth. This fifth element, the quintessence, was seen as permeating all the material universe, giving it meaning, form, being, and purpose.

And so it is with the physical and social sciences and the technologies. They can and do analyze and manipulate a kind of reality abstracted in signs and concepts, and it is for this capability that we value them. But all too often, in the end they leave us with a frustrated feeling that the very essence of being human has somehow slipped through their nets. Because the various sciences and technologies currently have ascendancy on the academic and cultural scene of the Western world, the methodologies of these disciplines—impersonal rationality, classification, objectivity, lineality—have ascendancy also, and mastery of them tends to be taken as the most important thing for human beings to attain. But it is characteristic of human nature that we have unused abilities beyond these mechanical methodologies as well as needs which cannot be met by mere facts, the purely practical, or material goods. It is to the cultivation of these abilities and to the meeting of these needs that the arts as humanities speak.

In the preceding chapters we have attempted to guide you in experiencing some of the great art of the past, our artistic heritage, and selected examples from our recent past. What of the art of the present and the future? How do the ways of looking at art, of listening to music, and of reading literature presented in these chapters apply to current art and to styles yet to be developed? What of "aleatory music," "electronic music," "musique concrête"? What about "happenings," the "theatre of the absurd," the "drama of the imagination"? What of "light sculpture," "op art," "pop art," "color-field painting," "photorealism," "found objects"?

This chapter attempts to provide a context for dealing with these and similar questions, but not by analysis of specific examples, styles, or schools. By this time, this book has provided sufficient exercise in that. It insists, rather, that now that we all, when our eyes have been opened and our senses sharpened, can with some confidence approach unfamiliar art and expand our horizons of awareness still further. This chapter suggests some broad perspectives which will be helpful.

PERSPECTIVE ONE

All art comes before the theories which explain it, the terminology which enables us to point to various aspects of it, the name which classifies it. This fact is especially important to remember as we consider the newer art forms and styles. Often we tend to approach them with the expectancies built into us from all our previous experiencing of art. When these do not correspond to what we see or hear, we tend to reject the new art completely or to judge it harshly. To give the new a chance, however, we must go beyond *sensing that it is different* to asking what the "differences" are expressing. Sometimes we may conclude that the "difference" is no more than deliberate perversity. More often we shall discover that it evokes in us new ranges of sensitivity. A good example of this is Thomas B. Hess's *Abstract Painting: Background and American Phase* (1951), which was the first attempt to explain abstract expressionism. This book made clear what the movement stood for and what it was trying to do.

PERSPECTIVE TWO

In looking at any new or unfamiliar work of art, we should interpret in their broadest sense the terms we have been using to point to various aspects of it. *Organization, order*—whatever term one uses should be thought of not as an absolute, exact description but as a continuum running from chaos at one end to geometric, mathematical forms at the other. Art always seeks some reconciliation of these opposites. The reconciliation may be toward one end of the con-

472 STYLE

tinuum or toward the other. Style is the part of art which comes into play unconsciously. In all periods there are great individuals whose personal stamp is so strong that it becomes recognizable in everything they produce. Sometimes it is so distinctive and powerful that it is copied by lesser artists and creates a "school" or "movement." At other times the style may break so completely with prevailing ones that the works of the artist, when seen in the perspective of history, do not seem to belong—that is, they do not fit into the academic generalizations about a period. Medium, too, should be broadly interpreted. In contemporary art the traditional compartmentalization of mediums has yielded to experimentation with various "intermediums"—for example, art which is between music and theater, between sculpture and painting, between sculpture and architecture. There is no right or wrong medium or any known limit to appropriate mediums. Mediums are always being found, and artists are always exploiting them to their maximum expressive potential.

PERSPECTIVE THREE

It is helpful to look at new art from the point of view of the artist as he or she slowly creates it step by step. From this point of view, from the way in which it came into being, one can consider art on a scale of homogeneity to heterogeneity. "From the moment work starts on a picture, it begins to shift slowly along a scale from extreme homogeneity (blank space) toward ever-increasing heterogeneity. Maximum heterogeneity (a mass of fuzzy detail) is not apparently visually desirable and so somewhere along this homogeneous-heterogeneous scale there is for each picture a point of optimum heterogeneity. This is the point at which the picture is considered finished."[1] Similarly, into utter silence the musician puts a sound, a succession of sounds, a harmony. The musician leaves more or less of the homogeneous silence in the composition. If greater amounts of silence are included, this can focus attention on a single sound which would otherwise be "lost" in the din of maximum heterogeneity. The music of John Cage and the sculpture of Henry Moore illustrate this phenomenon, the open spaces in the latter representing spatial silence (Figure 2-5).

You will notice that we are repeating here the poem by John Moffitt which appeared in the first chapter of this book. We have done this partly to underline the importance of the kind of "looking"

To Look at Any Thing

To look at any thing,
If you would know that thing,
You must look at it long:
To look at this green and say
"I have seen spring in these
Woods," will not do—you must
Be the thing you see:
You must be the dark snakes of
Stems and ferny plumes of leaves,
You must enter in
To the small silences between
The leaves,
You must take your time
And touch the very peace
They issue from.

—John Moffitt[2]

---

[1] Desmond Morris, *The Biology of Art*, (London: Methuen and Company, Ltd., 1962), p. 165.
[2] "To Look at Any Thing," by John Moffitt, © 1961 by John Moffitt. Reprinted from his volume *The Living Seed*, by permission of Harcourt Brace Jovanovich, Inc. (New York).

Moffitt describes as one looks at unfamiliar art. But also, as we come to the end of the book and its approach to the arts, rereading this poem will let you see how much richer the analogy between looking at things and experiencing art is at this stage in your development.

PERSPECTIVE FOUR

New art frequently seems shocking. The operas of Richard Wagner, the paintings of the impressionists during the 1870s, the public demonstrations of the Dadaists of 1916, the "happenings" mounted in the 1960s—these are only a few examples of work that was not accepted by the general public of its time. Much of what is now accepted as standard repertoire in music, and many pieces now automatically included in anthologies of literature, were at one time considered odd, distasteful, or imcomprehensible. Such rejection will continue to occur because one of the functions of art is to help us bring again into our perceptual systems things which we have been conditioned to exclude. Each of us has a personal orientation which "keeps us from seeing reality, locks us into the illusory embrace of given orientations." But "art . . . by breaking up those orientations releases us to see aspects of reality which orientations conceal from us."[3] Thus, while we may correctly think of art as an ordering and extending of relationships, we should also remember that art is a disordering of our usual ways of seeing; it omits things commonly emphasized and includes those not commonly emphasized. A function of art, therefore, is to read back into life the complexities which our orientations, our systems and abstractions, have tended to obscure and omit. The simplifications and systems necessary to functioning in our social structure tend to impoverish our full functioning as organisms. By restoring the excluded into our consciousness, art can give us back some sense of our wholeness. It is therefore, in the strict sense of the term, *consciousness-expanding* in its nature.

The one universal intention of Underground artists is to open new areas of perception by clearing away taboos, to make the secret psychic drama the collective experience. This is their revolutionary proposal, and it should be taken seriously as such; it is a utopian dream and people are jumping the wall to embrace it. Whether or not you approve depends, of course, on who you are and how well you like the life you're leading.

—Barry Farrell[4]

PERSPECTIVE FIVE

One thing the new art forms say is simple. They are revealing that the old forms are too constricting to hold our view of the world, or to hold the personal experience of the artist in our world, or to accommodate our perceptual patterns. They are saying that the same courageous freedom which produced the older art is a continuing

[3] Morse Peckham, *Beyond the Tragic Vision* (New York: George Braziller, Inc., 1962).
[4] *Life*, Feb. 17, 1967. Excerpt from "The Other Culture," by Barry Farrell for *Life*, © 1967 Time Inc. Used with permission.

Boundary lines break down. The arts move to meet each other in happenings that may presage great changes in the structure of society and in human consciousness. "Theatre takes place all the time, wherever one is."

—James B. Hall and Barry Ulanov[5]

right of the artist, that this freedom must be exercised, and that it is necessary if art is to fulfill its cultural function. The established conventions, traditions, and forms constrict. And artists who begin to feel trapped often resort to somewhat violent means of escape. Serendipity, the planned accident, chance art, and other ways of achieving random relationships have throughout history been used by artists in their search for immediacy, freshness, and individual expression. It is, however, only in our time that they have gained status as a significant phase of the creative process. The "planned-accident" type of expression is perhaps best seen in the work of Jackson Pollock (Color Plate 10).

PERSPECTIVE SIX

The arts should be viewed as continuous with other human activities contemporary with them. A new invention, medium, world view, or way of seeing things reflects the changes in science, psychology, and philosophy that have been taking place in ways frequently unnoticed by the public at large. Art is a way of making visible these changes in our thinking and feeling. It is a way of making them a part of our sensory and conscious experience. It explores their echoes and eddies in our psychic life and gives expression to them. Advances in our understanding of how we think, new insights into our ways of perceiving, have in the past influenced the arts. A question always worth asking, therefore, is: How does what is being done in the arts relate to the other human activities in which the culture is engaging? The discoveries of the past twenty years and the consequent revisions of what we know have confirmed the observation that "knowledge does not keep any better than fish." To continue as participants in our culture, therefore, it is imperative that we become competent in fishing, that is, in the attitudes of open inquiry which will continue to add to and replace our present knowledge. Already we have come to see that logic frequently leads us to go wrong with a sense of certainty, that myth is as true as history, that the world is a letter addressed "To Whom It May Concern," and that the answers it gives depend upon the questions we ask of it. If one looks for a single word to characterize the attitude toward knowing in our time, one might well choose *tentativeness*, for we have come to entertain the possibility that all knowledge is tentative, partial, and personal.

It is quite possible that these new insights have contributed to an insecurity in our time. In fact, it has been argued that one of the

---

[5] James B. Hall and Barry Ulanov, *Modern Culture and the Arts* (New York: McGraw-Hill Book Company, 1972), p. 337.

reasons we have clung with such desperateness, persistence, and inflexibility to the vision of an ordered, certain universe is that we cannot tolerate such uncertainty. To the extent that you, however, can entertain this broader view, it should be liberating, for it makes you an authority along with whatever other authorities you know. It should give you confidence and freedom in your own observing and perceiving. Whose eyes but yours can see the world you see?

While these developments may appear to set us adrift in chaos, they can and do, after the initial shock, function to expand one's sense of personal presence in a cosmos which always seems to be breaking out of our little contrived systems and orderly forms of thought.

ART IS A ROAD BACK

There is a story of the Zen master who one day when his student came to him for instruction said, "I think you are ready. Play me a song on an imaginary flute." The student sat in silent meditation before the master. "Play louder, I cannot hear it." "No, Master," replied the student, "you must listen louder." After a moment of silence, the Master said, "Go. I am no longer your teacher. You are no longer my student."

Many people are saying that we have become caught in our own thinking, that in making the machine the model of perfection and measuring our achievements in terms of it, we have become automatons dissociated from our feelings and individual responses, that we have relinquished ourselves so completely that we are willing, conspiring victims of authoritarianism. If this is true, then it is time that we ask: Is there no alternative for us? Is there no road back? Art is a road back; and, like all roads back, it is a road forward, for it leads not to a past, accomplished somewhere back there, but to the past within us. It offers a road back to experiencing, to a quickening of the senses, to a fuller realization of our humanity, and to a wholeness which is our real heritage.

GLOSSARY

Most of the terms in the following list are defined and discussed elsewhere in this book, but some are mentioned or examined only briefly. All are useful in reading about the arts and in discussing them. Cross references within the glossary are indicated by **boldface type.**

Abstract art, abstraction In a sense, any painting or sculpture can be viewed as an *abstraction*, since the artist willy-nilly *or* by design leaves out something, but we usually reserve the term *abstract art* for works in which the aesthetic value is felt to reside more in the forms and colors than in the subject matter. There are various degrees of abstraction. We may recognize the subject matter (bottles, a guitar, a cannon); but its significance seems to lie more in the colors, shapes, and organization. Some styles, such as **abstract expressionism,** hard-edge painting, and **cubism,** depend completely upon formal qualities for engaging the viewer, and have no recognizable subject matter or symbolic significance; they are sometimes called "pure" abstraction. Two other terms applied to styles in the visual arts which have no recognizable subject matter are *nonobjective* and *nonrepresentational.* Mondrian, Pollack, and Kline have quite different styles, but all are nonobjective painters— i.e., their paintings are nonrepresentational. (See also **Abstract expressionism.**)

Abstract expressionism A term first applied by his contemporaries to paintings of the Russian artist Vasily Kandinsky (Color Plates 8 and 9), who expressed emotion solely through color and nonobjective or nonrepresentational forms. Later, more generally applied to works of a group of American artists who dominated the art scene in the 1950s, among them Pollock (Color Plate 10), de Kooning (Color Plate 4), and Franz Kline (Figure 1-8). Free, spontaneous, personal expression characterized abstract expressionism as a movement. Among the many individual styles which appeared, one finds three general approaches (1) **action painting,** depending on the spontaneous interaction of artist and medium (Pollock, de Kooning, Kline); (2) the use of large, well-defined images (Gottlieb, Motherwell) or large areas of intensely interacting color, sometimes called **color-field painting** (Rothko, Frankenthaler); (3) hard-edge painting, reminiscent of the precise, geometric patterns of Mondrian (Color Plates 3 and 5) and Albers (Color Plate 27), in which hard-edged forms and carefully chosen colors were used to excite the eye in pure sensation. The color areas were evenly saturated, in contrast, for example, to the loosely brushed areas in de Kooning's paintings (Color Plate 4).

Absurd As a critical term, used to describe art in the twentieth century which expresses the disillusionment and loss of certainty characteristic of our time, through *presenting* in new art forms—not *arguing*—the senselessness of life. Its most common usage is in referring to plays written by Beckett (*Waiting for Godot, Endgame, Krapp's Last Tape*), Ionesco (*The Bald Soprano, Chairs*) Genêt (*The Balcony*), Albee (*Zoo Story*), and others. "Theater of the absurd," as such plays are called, abandons reason and discursive thought as worthless and inadequate in a world cut off from religious, metaphysical moorings. Human actions in such a world become senseless, pointless, and absurd and are presented as such.

Acrylic Plastic emulsion, soluble in water, that is both medium or vehicle and pigment. The first development in use of pigment since the Renaissance in which the vehicle or binder does not alter the character of colors and their permanence. Long-lasting, quick-drying, it can be thinned with acrylic medium or water and used as watercolor. With less thinner it can be used like oil paint, but it dries to a tougher film and adheres to any oil-free surface. Although it has been used only recently, it presumably does not fade as oils do, nor does it suffer changes as a result of climatic conditions.

Action painting A phase of **abstract expressionism.** Pollock's work (Color Plate 10) is an example. He dribbled paint on canvas to stress the physical activity over the product of art; the unconscious impulses of his hand were the only human control in the process. The spectator, surrendering attention to the flow of the lines, experiences the tension of customary perceptual habits while seeking recognizable forms and turns to meditation on the sheer expressiveness of the material itself. The artist thus induces us into the creative process instead of rewarding our passive acceptance of a finished work. De Kooning, also called an action painter, paints with no preconceived plan as to what will emerge, letting one color, one image, one line suggest the next (see Color Plate 4).

Aesthetics, aesthetic *Aesthetics* is theoretical investigation of the arts as the domain of human concerns, using philosophical, historical, educational, and psychological perspectives. More broadly conceived than in the past when canons of taste and beauty were of primary concern, aesthetics now emphasizes aspects of perception rather than the ideals or content of subject matter. In speaking of the *aesthetic* values of a work of art, one most often means stylistic effectiveness in the treatment of the subject or its moral qualities. (The term is also spelled *esthetics, esthetic.*)

Altar An elaborate table and tomblike structure that is the focus of the ritual and architectural organization of a Christian church. In **basilican** churches it is located in the **apse**; but in cruciform churches, sometimes at the crossing. See **Transepts and crossing.**

Ambulatory A covered passageway around the place of worship. In Christian churches, the side aisles which continue to the area behind the **altar** where the **liturgy** is performed in a sacred place not open to the laity. This area provided space for devotional chapels in pilgrimage churches so that the worshipers need not disturb the liturgical functions in the **sanctuary.**

Apse The vaulted semicircular recess projecting from the **nave** behind the main **altar** of basilican churches in the Romanesque and Gothic styles. In pilgrimage churches such as Canterbury Cathedral, Santiago de Compostela, and S. Peters (see Figure 14-28), the side aisles permitted direct access to the shrine without disturbing the **liturgy** in the nave. See **Basilica, Vault.**

Arabesque Ornate design deriving from Arab (Islamic) art. In Islam, representation of the human figure was forbidden lest it invite idolatry. Artists elaborated the Arabs' flowing script to incorporate the names rather than the visual forms of the holy in decorating places of worship, as can be seen in S. Sophia (Hagia Sophia, Figure 9-16). Christian Renaissance art of the fourteenth century borrowed from Spain the scroll-like decoration based on the geometrized Islamic forms of plants and animals as pure design in illuminated or decorated pages of manuscript (Figure 6-15).

Arcade A series of arches supported by columns or piers, standing free or attached to a wall as decoration. First used by the Romans but incorporated into Christian and Renaissance buildings. (See Figures 14-10, 14-13, 14-17, 14-21, and 14-26.) The term is also used for a passageway with an arched roof.

Arch A curved structure spanning an open area. Arches are constructed of wedge-shaped stones placed side by side so that they lean against one another and, because of gravity, create an unsupported curve at the top. The central stone is known as the "keystone." The Roman arch is round; the Gothic is pointed. (See Figure 14-19.)

Architectonic Possessing the qualities of structural design and the technical aspects of organization in space and time rather than subject matter, thus recalling the three-dimensional clarity of architecture. In paintings of still life or landscape, for example, the arrangement of forms and picture planes, as in Cézanne's *Still Life with Apples* (Color Plate 34), where the interest is on organization of formal elements.

Architrave The lowest section of an **entablature**; in classical architecture, it is directly above the capital of a column.

Aria A song for solo voice from an **opera, oratorio, cantata,** or anthem.

Arpeggio The sounding of the notes of a chord in succession and not simultaneously. Sometimes referred to as a "broken chord."

Art song A song of artistic origin and character whose text and accompaniment cooperate to give an expressive effect, usually that of a particular mood.

Asymmetrical plan and balance A slight imbalance suggesting the dynamism of motion, as can be seen in Botticelli's picture of Venus blown to shore by Zephyrus (Color Plate 12), despite the symmetry of the overall composition. *Balance of masses* is a compensation between unequal shapes and sizes, and between contrasts in lighting, color, and texture, as in van Ruisdael's *Mill* (Color Plate 41).

Atonality No central tonality; music written without regard to a specific key. The tones are arranged so that there is no single tonal center. Atonal music is normally dissonant. See **Tonality.**

Attribute A sign or emblem which in the tradition of an art serves to identify a subject or a type by associating the individual or type with stylized signs that indicate function. Examples are the halo and keys which are the symbols of S. Peter's spiritual power and the bump of wisdom and the eye of knowledge which identify the Buddha (Figure 3-24).

Auteur theory From the French word meaning "author." This theory, used in filmmaking and film criticism, insists that the **director** of a film has the same relationship to it as that of an author to a book. Thus, the director is (or should be) responsible for every detail which appears in the finished film, and the director's personality and personal style are (or should be) recognizable in every film he or she makes. Popularized by critics in *Cahiers du Cinema*, a French periodical, in the 1950s, the theory has influenced all film criticism and enhanced the role of director in film art.

Balustrade A decorated protective banister used at the edge of buildings and terraces. Sometimes used for purely decorative reasons at other points on an architectural structure, for example, at the edge of a roof.

Baroque Used generally as a term for the arts of the seventeenth century. The Catholic Church at the height of the Counter-Reformation laid down the specifics of an official art program intended to stimulate piety in the laity. The result was grandiose elaboration in architecture and decoration and the use of dramatic, theatrical subject matter in painting and sculpture. Thousands of artists were employed to paint altarpieces and murals on walls and ceilings. Subject matter was chosen to excite religious fervor, piety, exultation: intensely painted scenes of martyrdom, terror, damnation, and ecstasy whose message could not be missed. The style made use of large, juxtaposed areas of dark and light and of dramatic, exciting colors to fuse with the architectural decoration and to heighten the emotional appeal of the doctrinal message. (See Figure 14-29 and the text comments on it.) Rubens, in Flanders, was to evolve his own version of Baroque style for a different purpose. (See Figure 2-16.)

Bas-relief See **Relief.**

Basilica A type of Roman building used as a court of justice or place of assembly and providing the plan for Early Christian churches. (See Figure 14-13.) Rectangular in shape, it had a large central area (**nave**) and colonnaded aisles, a semicircular niche (**apse**) at one or both ends, and entrances on the sides or at one end. With the refinement of the principle of **arch** construction, the plan was abandoned for the cruciform (cross form) as more emblematic of Christian aspiration.

Binary A musical form divided into two parts, usually presenting one theme in two balanced, or complementary, parts.

Buttress, flying buttress, thrust When an arch spans a large space, the weight of the top curved portion tends to push (thrust) the supporting verticals apart. The verticals were therefore made thicker with buttresses. The pointed **arch** of **Gothic** churches provided some relief from the pressure against the side walls, since lateral thrust was lessened. But with the increasing height of the **nave,** the critical point needed reinforcement. Consequently, buttresses were constructed at some distance from the outer wall with arches extending from them to a higher point on the wall to provide the necessary counterthrust. They are called "flying buttresses." (See Figures 14-20 and 14-22.)

Cadence A point of rest or the end of a piece of music, especially a harmonic completion involving a series of chords which give a sense of tonal finality. There are several kinds of cadence, depending on the sequence of the chords used.

Camera angle The angle between the camera and the subject. A normal angle corresponds to eye level; low angle is below eye level; high angle is located above eye level.

Canon An imitative polyphonic composition in which two or more voices or parts follow one another exactly in a lapsed time sequence, most often beginning at an interval different from the first or opening part.

Cantata A choral composition having choruses, solos, and **recitatives** which may be either religious, resembling a short **oratorio,** or secular. A cantata is performed without action, scenery, or costume.

Cantilever In architecture, a lintel (see **Post-and-lintel construction**) or beam which extends beyond its support. Based on the lever principle, the beam or horizontal member can extend beyond its support on one side because it is weighted and balanced on the other. The size of the cantilevered area depends on the strength and rigidity of the horizontal member and on the weight on the other side of the support. Familiar examples are the unsupported balconies on high-rise apartments which are cantilevered slabs of reinforced concrete.

Chiaroscuro The treatment of light and shade in painting to create the illusion of volume, of solid, three-dimensional forms, as distinct from contours. Note the chiaroscuro in Titian (Color Plate 29) and in Rembrandt (Color Plate 49). **Sculpture in the round** and objects in **relief,** ceramics, and architectural structures, because of some natural unevenness of surface, lend themselves to this effect.

Choir (1) A group of orchestral instruments, usually of the same type. (2) An organized group of singers, usualy participating in church services. (3) A section of a church between the sanctuary and the nave. See **Sanctuary and choir.**

Chord A combination of three or more tones sounded simultaneously. The *common*, or basic, chord, is based on the first, third, and fifth steps of the scale.

Chromaticism Half-step interpolations of the major and minor scales. Chromatic intervals are always half-step intervals.

Classicism The opposite of **romanticism.** Used in all the arts, the term is applied to art which emphasizes or exhibits those qualities considered to be characteristic of Greek and Roman art. objectivity, restraint, reason, and clarity of form. It is disciplined and finished, and stresses universal aspects rather than personal, individual differences. For example, classical music is restrained and orderly, has well-defined forms and generally regular meters, and uses very little dissonance; the tempo and volume are fairly constant within a movement or piece. The term is also used less precisely to refer to any work of art whose excellence has been generally recognized, or to a work which has become a kind of touchstone, or measuring rod, for excellence in a particular category, as when we say, "A classic instance of . . .," or "The classic in that genre is . . .," or refer to something as "a classic."

Clerestory See **Triforium** and Figures 14-13 and 14-20.

Close-up In film, a photograph taken at close range so that details become larger than life. Sometimes used in combination with "zooming in" (see **Zoom shot**) to focus the viewer's attention on some aspect of a scene or action.

Color-field painting The use of arrangements of large areas of uniform color on a canvas of vast size so that they occupy one's entire field of vision and, in effect, become one's environment. Only the color, of course, can be reproduced in illustrations. Color-field painting, to be experienced, must be seen first hand. See **Abstract expressionism.**

Combined arts Dance, opera, drama, and film are called "combined arts" because they use the elements, conventions, and organizational patterns common to more than one medium in an art which is performed. For example, **opera** combines the talents of the music composer and performers (singers and instrumentalists), stage designers, costume designers—in short, all that can be simultaneously seen and heard under some central direction and that imparts a unity of effect of both theater and concert.

Comic opera Opera having musical numbers interspersed with spoken dialogue, whether comic or not, as opposed to grand opera, which is sung throughout—i.e., which uses sung dialogue (**recitative**). Comic opera is also known as *opera comique.* See **Opera.**

Compound time Any meter whose pattern of accents is a combination of duple and triple, as in 6/8, 5/4, 7/8, etc.

Concerto An instrumental composition, usually in sonata form with three movements, in which one or more instruments are featured against an orchestra or other accompaniment. See **Sonata.**

Consonance A stable chord or interval not demanding resolution (because the vibration rates are consonant), and giving a sense of repose. The opposite of **dissonance.**

Content See **Subject.**

Corinthian A later version of the Ionic order of Greek architecture. Its capital is more ornate, with a doubled volute arrangement of tendrils and palmettes emerging from a base of acanthus leaves, and its column is longer and more slender than the Doric or Ionian. The acanthus is a large-lobed leaf 1 to 2 feet long that lends itself to scroll decoration. See Figure 14-9, and **Ionic** and **Doric.**

Cornice In Greek architecture, the unornamented part of the entablature or the crown surmounting the **frieze,** which is the decorated portion

(See Figure 14-7.) The top horizontal element of a building, just below the roof, common in Renaissance architecture. (See Figures 14-26 and 14-27.)

Counterpoint A melody played or sung against one or more related melodies. The manipulation of note against note, producing contrapuntal style, or **polyphony.**

Crossing See **Transepts and crossing.**

Cruciform See **Transepts and crossing.**

Cubism Cézanne had admonished impressionist painters, whose work often showed a certain flatness, to analyze their subject matter into simple, geometric forms—cylinders, cones, spheres—to achieve illusions of three-dimensionality and space relationships between objects. (See Color Plate 34.) Picasso (Figure 2-8) and Braque, while abandoning the aims of the impressionists, carried this analytical method still further in what came to be known as "cubism" or "analytical cubism." Still later, they and other painters not only abstracted forms but put them together into new configurations (Figure 2-9), sometimes so that the viewer might see several views at the same time, adding a kind of temporal dimension, as though one walked around an object collecting different perspectives on it (see Figure 2-17). This fusion of abstracted forms and perspectives into new relationships is sometimes called "synthetic cubism." See also **Impressionism.**

Development The unfolding of a musical idea, theme, or subject in rhythmic, melodic, or harmonic changes. Hence, development is also the name given the part of a composition where this happens. See **Sonata-allegro form, Fugue.**

Diatonic A type of musical **scale** of eight tones with fixed intervals between them.

Director The film director is the interpreter of a shooting filmscript and is responsible to the producer for the overall quality of the film. Some theorists compare him or her to the author of a novel (the **auteur theory**) because of the opportunity to put a personal stamp on the results; but the director may have to share responsibilities with an art director, a director of photography, the scriptwriter, and the film editor unless given ultimate authority for techniques in coordinating their combined arts. See **Editing, editor.**

Dissolve In film, two successive shots which are briefly superimposed as one gradually fades in and the other fades out. See **Fade-in, fade-out; Superimposition;** and **Transitional devices.**

Dissonance An unstable **chord** or interval. Out of harmonic relation (because vibrations of the notes are dissonant), demanding resolution if completeness or consonance is desired. Sometimes called "discord." The opposite of **consonance.**

Divisionism In their concern for painting accurately the effects of light on objects and vibratory effects of atmosphere. Monet, Sisley, and Pissarro developed the technique of juxtaposing tiny strokes of primary colors so that the eye mixed them. Instead of mixing blue and yellow pigments to obtain a green, they painted small strips of blue and yellow next to each other; the result was a brighter, vibrating green. Seurat, for the same effect, applied dots or points (thus the term *pointillism*) of primary colors, in proportions to obtain the shades he wanted (Color Plate

26). Unfortunately, the effects produced by divisionism and pointillism cannot be experienced in small-scale reproductions, because the printing process disturbs the intended mix and results in a faded look, completely contrary to the artist's intenton.

Dome, dome on drum A vaulted roof in the shape of a hemisphere, like an inverted cup, supported on columns or walls. It is constructed on the **arch** principle—as if one rotated an arch (Figures 14-11 and 14-12) The cylindrical band or drum on which it is set may be pierced as a clerestory (see **Triforium**), as in S. Peter's in the Vatican (Figure 14-28) In Notre Dame in Paris, the **apse** is covered by a half dome (Figure 14-24).

Dominant The fifth step of the major and minor scales. Also, the triad based on the fifth tone.

Doric The oldest of the three Greek architectural styles or orders. It is characterized by greater simplicity than **Ionic** and **Corinthian.** (See Figures 13-26 and 13-27.) Its column is short in proportion to its diameter and has a slight convex bulge (entasis) to correct for the optical illusion of parallel columns appearing concave when seen from a distance. The **entablature** has a **frieze** decorated with bas-relief sculpture (see **Relief)** (Figure 9-9) running the length of the **cornice** or crown (Figure 14-7).

Dubbing In film, the matching of separately recorded sound to the lip movements of actors or singers on the screen. Dubbing makes possible the close-up of singers who, in projecting as they ordinarily do on stage, must show unphotogenic facial strain unnoticed in a live performance. (Also called "lip-sync.")

Duration In music, the time allotted to a given note.

Eclectic art The melding of styles, qualities, or effects in the tradition of art sometimes thought to be unoriginal in the work of an artist who affects them as mannerisms that are not his or her own. Any artist may copy an admired style more or less unconsciously; but an eclectic artist selects with no apparent principle unrelated aspects of certain predecessors' style, either in conscious or unconscious attraction to their success or esteem, and adds nothing distinctly personal. But no artist is so original that a critic cannot find some such affinities.

Editing, editor In film, *editing* is the splicing and assembling of the separate **shots** of film selected from the rushes (first shots) to match the script and to add special effects, montages, and credits. The *editor* may or may not be the **director,** depending on whether he or she (rather than some other studio official) has "final cut" rights.

Entablature The upper portion of a wall, consisting of **cornice, frieze,** and **architrave,** usually supported by columns. See Figure 14-7.

Epic A literary rendition of an oral tradition in the form of continuous narration of the exploits of the hero. The compilation of such material may be anonymous. When the epic form and style are intentionally used, as they were by Virgil, Dante, and Milton, the epic nostalgically celebrates the ethnic values of former times.

Establishing shot Any film **shot** at the beginning of a **sequence** which establishes the location, time, and situation for what is to follow. Frequently done by **panning.** Similar in function to **exposition** in drama, opera, and ballet.

Exposition In music, the first part of a form in which the composer introduces the theme or themes on which the whole composition is based, as in the exposition of a **sonata-allegro** movement or **fugue.** In drama, opera, and ballet, the early scenes which introduce the characters, time, locale, and situation on which the work focuses as it develops.

Expressionism In contrast with **impressionism,** which aimed at recording reality passively and accurately, expressionism aimed at presenting reality as passionately felt and developed ways of doing so in the various arts. In expressionist painting, for example, artists depended heavily on color, frequently in disturbing combinations, and on distortion of colors and shapes of objects to evoke feeling. The terms *expressionism* and *expressionist* are used in two ways: (1) As general terms applied to all art in which the artist gives subjective feelings and emotions precedence over representation of surface reality (expressionist painting, sculpture); imitation of life (expressionist drama, film, dance); and the traditional forms and idioms of the art (especially expressionist music, dance, painting). In this sense, one applies the terms to artists as separated in time as El Greco (Color Plate 6), Van Gogh (Color Plate 2), Rouault (Color Plate 17), and Orozco (Color Plate 13). (2) As a term referring precisely to German expressionism, a movement in the visual arts, theater, and dance which developed just before World War I, exhibiting these characteristics in rebelling against the traditional authoritarian, militaristic, patriarchal culture of that country. (See Figures 2-12, 2-13, and 6-27.) See also **Abstract expressionism.**

Façade The front exterior wall of a building, its face, and, therefore, in Gothic architecture the west side and entrance; also, other sides of a building that are decorated or emphasized architecturally.

Fade-in, fade-out In film, an image which slowly emerges from darkness or slowly disappears into it. See **Transitional devices.**

Fenestration The arrangement of windows on the **façade** of a building.

Flashback A film-editing device which interrupts the present action with one or more **shots** showing the past. The techniques of the novel, with its stream of consciousness, multiple levels, and dialogue interspersed with reminiscences, may be imitated in film by **montage** and flashback. When the time sequence of the narration is interrupted for brief allusions to previous scenes, suspense and emotional response are heightened by delaying the flow of the story.

Flying buttress. See **Buttress.**

Foot In poetry, a metrical unit, consisting of a group of syllables.

Foreshortening When a subject is seen in low perspective and nearer than normal to the picture plane, extreme distortion of the mass (foreshortening) results from displacing the vanishing point above the horizon. It is as if one were placed in the prompter's box or in the first row before a movie screen. Mantegna's body of Christ (Color Plate 32) is intended to startle with the dramatic effect of its apparent protrusion from the picture plane.

Frame (1) In theater and staged dance, the front opening of the stage; all the visual patterns created by the actors or dancers are experienced in relation to it. (2) In painting, the edges of the picture, which establish the psychological frame. Also, the wooden edging or other material used to hold the painting. (3) In film, a single shot in the filmed action—one rectangle of the film which, moving rapidly through the projector, creates the sense of movement. (4) A still print made from a film. Sometimes, in a device called a "freeze frame," the negative of a frame is reprinted and repeatedly spliced to create the effect of suspended motion or time in a film, creating a powerful emotional effect, usually reserved for the final frame.

Fresco Painting on a wet, freshly plastered wall surface with pigment ground in pure water. Used universally before the discovery of oils but now little used because of its fragility under conditions of industrially polluted air. In fresco, the pigment is bound by the lime plaster, which is alkaline; acid in polluted air interacts with it and disintegrates the medium. See *Creation of Adam* (Color Plate 15).

Frieze The central sculpture in the recessed **tympanum** in the **pediment** of a classical building, or any decorated or sculptured horizontal band. See **Cornice**.

Fugue A polyphonic composition which has three general divisions. In outline, they are: (1) an **exposition** in which a short musical subject is first stated in one voice, then repeated in other voices in turn at the interval of a fourth or fifth until all voices are heard; (2) a **development** section in which the subject reappears in various ways alternating with other musical material called "episodes"; (3) a conclusion which is a clear, full-voiced, final statement of the subject. See **Counterpoint**.

Geodesic dome A principle of **dome** construction developed by Buckminster Fuller from geodesy (an application of geometry to translate the curvature of the earth's surface to flat maps). Small, light triangles of tubing are organized around a point to form hexagons; enough hexagons joined together can approximate a hemisphere. This structure in tension is covered with a light, usually translucent, covering skin. Large areas can be covered quickly and inexpensively by geodesic domes. (See Figures 1-2 and 4-16.)

Gothic A style of religious architecture which spread throughout Europe between the twelfth and sixteenth centuries. A Gothic cathedral was structurally a monumental system of stone arches, vaults, and buttresses capable of spanning large areas and of reaching great heights (Figure 14-20). Decoration and treatment throughout emphasized vertical lines—tall, pointed arches, long, narrow windows, ribbing, finials, etc. The construction of large cathedrals was an expression of intense religious faith and a matter of community pride. The cathedrals of the Île de France (the region around Paris) are estimated to have consumed a proportion of the economy greater than the national budget consumes of ours. (See Figures 14-22 through 14-25.)

Gouache A painting medium containing a higher proportion of gum arabic than pure watercolor does. It therefore has a more opaque, less flexible base than a watercolor wash and is more likely to peel and crack when applied heavily. See **Watercolor**.

Graphic arts Originally, those arts which depend on the visual element of line, rather than color, such as drawing and engraving, and their reproduction by mechanical or photochemical means. With new technologies for reproducing color (for example, in advertising), the graphic arts now include printmaking, posters, and photography using line, tone, and color as well as typographic design.

Hard-edge painting See **Abstract expressionism.**

Harmony The sounding together of different **pitches,** especially in chord sequences. Sometimes referred to as the "vertical" aspect of musical structure. See **Melody.**

Homophony Music employing a single melody at a time. The opposite of **polyphony.** See **Counterpoint.**

Hue The name of a color, e.g., red, blue, yellow, violet.

Hypostyle From the Greek *hypostylos,* "resting on pillars." In Egyptian temples, a hall or vestibule whose roof was supported by many large columns, for example, the hypostyle hall in the Temple of Amon at Karnak (Figure 14-5). Because the columns are large and elaborately decorated, they dominate the hall and create narrow shifting perspectives of the enclosed space as one moves through them. The central pillars are taller and permit wall perforations (clerestory) to admit light. The hypostyle was later adapted for the Christian **basilica** (Figure 14-13) and the **Gothic** cathedral (Figure 14-20).

Icon The greek word for "image." Used specifically for panel paintings and mosaics made under the influence of the Greek Orthodox Church. In order to avoid the sin of idolatry in worshiping "graven images" (interpreted as lifelike representations or **sculpture in the round**), icons were purposely flat, semiabstract paintings or **mosaics** of holy personages and were considered sacred in themselves. By extension, the word is used for any image, sacred or profane, which has become specialized as a visual symbol with meanings and implications beyond itself, as in I. C. Phelps Stokes's *Iconography of Manhattan Island.*

Iconography The representation of abstract ideas and concepts through a "language" of images and pictures and their interpretation. See **Icon.**

Imagery In visual arts, the use of concrete objects and specific meanings in ways and contexts to express more than is literally presented. In literature, language devices such as metaphors, similes, metonymies, etc.

Imitation In music, repetition, either exact or only slightly modified, of a **melody,** a **phrase,** or a **motive** heard previously in another voice or part.

Impressionism The early phase of modern painting begun in the late nineteenth century in France by Monet (Figure 9-20), Sisley, and Pissarro. Characterized by a passive registration and accurate reproduction of visual impressions. The goal was to paint exactly what the eye *saw*, not what the artists *knew* about the subject. Their typical paintings were quickly recorded, transitory impressions, momentary aspects of scenes, candid views, and unpremediated gestures. They were especially interested in the vibration of light on objects, the effects of mist and fog, and other elusive atmospheric effects, and they developed a technique called **divisionism** to record them. They used unusual points of view and organizational patterns to enhance the sense of slice-of-life content. Other painters associated with the movement are Manet (Color Plates 30 and 45), Degas (Color Plate 20 and Figure 13-7), Renoir, and Cassatt (Figure 6-33). By analogy with impressionistic painting, the term is used to describe the music of Debussy and Ravel, whose compositions often have titles about clouds, moonlight, the sea, sailboats, exotic landscapes, etc., and who use hazy, shimmering, ambiguous harmo nies and unusual instrumental combinations to develop atmospheri effects that suggest the subjects rather than imitate natural sounds an movements.

Interval The **pitch** relationship of two tones. If in a **chord,** the interval i harmonic. If in successive tones, it is melodic. See **Harmony.**

Ionic A Greek classical style or order of architecture (Figure 14-8). Its col umn, more graceful if less severely geometrical than the **Doric,** has voluted capital with cushioned base or pedestal. The **volute** (a spiral scroll-like ornament) suggests a ram's horn. See **Doric** and **Corinthian**

Jazz Music with a pronounced syncopated rhythm, derived from Americar blacks who combined European melody with African dance rhythms.

Jump cut In film, an abrupt shift from one time or place of action to an other with no transitional material or devices. See **Transitional devices**

Keystone See **Arch** and Figure 14-19.

Leading tone The seventh step of the major or minor scale. Its tendency tc lead directly to the tonic explains its name.

Leitmotiv, leit motiv, or **leitmotif** Literally, German for "leading motive," a term used by Wagner for a melodic passage associated repeatedly with a person, place, thing, or idea in his operas. Used as a principle of musical construction, especially in nineteenth-century **opera.**

Libretto The text of an **opera** or other musical work. The term, literally "little book," originated in Italy when it was found that even Italians needed a printed text to follow the words sung in Italian operas.

Light and shadow See **Chiaroscuro.**

Lip-sync See **Dubbing.**

Liturgy The public rituals and services of the Christian church. The most important of them all is the **Mass** (the rite of the Eucharist), which cele brates Holy Communion.

Major Music based on the major **scale.** The term is used to describe an **interval,** a **chord,** a **melody,** or the **tonality** of a whole composition.

Major arts Sometimes called "fine arts." Those arts which have tradition ally had the most significant cultural and critical interest, such as music, literature, painting, sculpture, and architecture, and whose subjects and themes have been the aesthetic embodiment of the humanistic and religious ideals in Western culture.

Mass As a musical form, the setting of the Ordinary (or invariable) por tion of the text of the Eucharistic liturgy according to the Roman rite, consisting of the Kyrie, Gloria, Credo, Sanctus, and Agnus Dei. See **Liturgy.**

Match-cut In filmmaking, an editing technique for maintaining continuity by matching visual images in putting **shots** together. See **Editing** and **Transitional Devices.**

Measure In music, a grouping of beats made by the regular repetition of strong accents into regular units. Each measure of printed music is set off by vertical bar lines.

Media The word (the plural of **medium**) usually used to refer to electronic and print methods of mass communications, such as radio, television, newspapers, and magazines.

Medium The material basis of any art. There is no art without a medium and there is no limit to the kind of material that can be so used. In painting, *medium* refers to the various vehicles used to bind and disperse color pigment. In music, the medium is the instrument or voice used to produce the sound.

Melody A succession of single tones having some relationship within a set **scale, mode,** or rhythmic structure.

Meter The measurement of **rhythm** into patterns produced by accent (like poetic feet; see **foot**). The meter of a given musical work is written as a time signature at the beginning of the piece, as in ¾. The numerator (3) tells how many beats there are in each measure, and the denominator (4) tells the basic note value—in this instance, the quarter note.

Minimal art A term sometimes applied to painting and sculpture in the mid-twentieth century which attempted to reduce the work of art to its minimal (that is, essential) elements—flat surfaces, shapes, and colors. See **Abstract art, Abstract expressionism.**

Minor Music based on the minor **scale,** in which the third, sixth, and sometimes the seventh notes are one half tone lower than in the corresponding **major** scale. The term is used to describe an **interval,** a **chord,** a **melody,** or the **tonality** of a whole composition.

Minuet and trio A dance movement in ¾ or ⅜ meter followed by a trio which is another minuet in a related key, followed by the original minuet.

Mode Modes are **scales** first used by the Greeks and later modified and used in music of the Middle Ages, especially in the **plainsong** of the Roman Catholic Church. Our more familiar major and minor scales can begin on any tones but follow the same whole step–half step pattern; for example, all the major scales follow the pattern of the C scale (the white keys on the piano from C to C). In contrast, although modes, too, begin on any tone, the difference among the various modes is one not simply of **pitch** as in the major scales, but of the unique order in which the whole steps and half steps fall in each mode. The names of the seven modes still indicate their Greek origin: Dorian, Phrygian, Lydian, Mixolydian, Aeolean, Locrian, and Ionian. (See Chapter 10.)

Modulation A change of tonality by planned succession of chords or melodic notes.

Montage In film, separate short camera **shots,** joined together in **editing** to create a unified series. Used most frequently to quickly establish a mood or to indicate the passage of time or a change of location; also used as the film equivalent of stream-of-consciousness narration and simultaneity-of-point-of-view techniques in the novel.

Mosaic A **mural** or floor decoration made by setting small pieces of colored stone, marble, or glass (tesserae; see **tessera**) in cement. The vibrant, brilliant color effect is due to the mix of light-absorbing and light-reflecting points of the tesserae.

Motive A brief melodic or rhythmic grouping of tones, shorter than a theme. Sometimes used to represent a character, an idea, or an object in **opera** or **program music.** The motive, by virtue of its repetition and variation, is a unifying element.

Mural Any drawing, painting, or **mosaic** on a wall. Before **fresco** was introduced in the thirteenth century, mural and floor decorations consisted chiefly of mosaics. Because of its vastness and the durability of its surface, mural decoration is especially suitable for public display and is now used on exterior surfaces.

Narthex The vestibule, a smaller enclosure than the **nave** of a basilica or church, and located just in front of it. The narthex is the remnant of an outer construction called the "atrium," which was provided with a cistern for baptism.

Naturalism See **Representational art**.

Nave The main body or open space of a church, extending in the basilican plan from the porch or vestibule at one end to the **apse** at the other, or in Gothic cruciform churches, to the crossing **transepts** (Figures 14-13, 14-17).

Nonobjective art See **Abstract art, Abstract expressionism**.

Nonrepresentational See **Abstract art, Abstract expressionism**.

Octave An interval encompassing eight steps in the major and minor scales. Its vibrations double with each ascending octave tone. The first and last tones of the major and minor scales enclose an octave.

Op art A major nonobjective art style of the 1960s, depending for its interest on optical illusions and other optical phenomena. On the surface optical art seems allied with commercial advertising, display, and textile design, but it opposes the literalism of pop art's imagery. In its hard-edged aspects, it derives from Mondrian's search for pure, impersonal forms (Color Plates 3 and 5), and in its exploitation of color for visual effects, from Albers's experiments in color (Color Plate 27). There is usually an exaggerated emphasis on centrality and symmetry, as in Escher's use of images as designs (Figure 10-3) and on tricks of the eye. (See Vasarely, Color Plate 36 and Figure 10-1; and Bridget Riley, Figure 10-2). See **Abstract art, Abstract expressionism**, and **Pop art**.

Opera A dramatic work for the stage in which music (vocal and instrumental), theater (staging, costume, acting), and sometimes dance are brought together in total theater. Although the story (the libretto) and spectacle (staging, costuming) of opera contribute to our enjoyment, it is the instrumental music and the vocal **arias, recitative** passages, choruses, and ensembles which account for its continued popularity.

Operetta A light musical-dramatic work with spoken dialogue. May be farcical or serious. See **Opera**.

Oratorio A musical setting of a dramatic text, usually founded on religious scripture, with **recitatives, arias,** choruses, and orchestral accompaniment, but without action, scenery, or costume.

Organic In discussion of the arts, a term used to indicate that the interrelationships between the parts of a work of art are similar to those in life forms and processes. This specific meaning is applied metaphorically to art in which the shapes are suggestive of living forms (biomorphic) or in which the organization is suggestive of life processes (growth, evolution, following of impulse, unfolding of motive, etc.). See Figures 2-2, 2-5, 5-6, 9-4.

Organic style In architecture, a term used by Frank Lloyd Wright to describe his architectural ideal: a unity of site, structure, and the sensuous quality of materials used (ornamentation). Eero Saarinen, without using the term, articulates the aims of organic style in his statement of the principles which have guided his architectural design (see page 103, especially the next to final paragraph). In architectural criticism the term *organic* has come to stand in opposition to the rigorously functional, barren "machines for living" advocated by the Bauhaus school of architects and to the "international style," which dominated industrial and metropolitan building in the 1920s and 1930s and continues to exert a strong influence on American architects. See also page 357.

Panning In film, turning the camera on its fixed base from right or left within a single shot. Frequently used at the beginning of a film to establish the location of action to follow—e.g., the **establishing shot** may "pan" a mountain range or the San Francisco skyline to indicate the location of the story to follow.

Passion A specific kind of **oratorio** dealing with the events of the last week of Christ's life.

Pastel A medium composed of almost pure pigment with just enough binder (gum arabic) for it to be compressed into a stick and used directly on a surface as a pencil. Schoolroom chalk is a more gritty version. Because it has no liquid vehicle with distorting optical properties, the colors are well preserved; but because it leaves a dry powder on the toothed surface of the paper, it requires a fixative and some transparent cover—glass or plexiglass—to prevent smudging. The techniques of using pastels combine the virtues of quick sketching and of painting without underpainting in monochrome.

Pedal point A single tone, usually the **tonic** or **dominant**, sustained in one voice while the other voices move independently. It is usually found in the bass and acts as a drone, creating a kind of musical tension which requires resolution.

Pediment In Greek architecture, the triangle of space formed at the end of a building by the sloping roof and the **cornice** or horizontal lintel (beam).

Perspective A scheme for representing three-dimensional objects and areas on a two-dimensional plane, taking the center of the plane as a normal point of view. In linear perspective, lines beginning at each corner are converged to this central point (the vanishing point), just as the two rails on a railroad track come to a point and disappear at the horizon when we stand between them and look down the track, and as objects decrease in size when we watch them recede in space toward the horizons. In aerial perspective, distance is indicated by toning down the colors as they recede from the picture plane toward the horizon. These conventions were developed and used by Renaissance painters with great precision (see Color Plate 31). Oriental artists do not use these conventions (Color Plate 33), and many modern artists take liberties with them (Color Plate 35) or do not use them at all.

Photorealism Sometimes called "new realism." Used to characterize a tendency in painting in the 1970s to return to the **representational art** style, but to emphasize in such clinical, minute detail surfaces of the objects painted that, though they are familiar, we have a sense of never having seen them before. Commercial scenes cluttered with neon signs, the glint of glass, chrome, and other reflective surfaces such as wet streets are favored subject matter. The aggressive forcing upon us, in a hypnotic dazzle of highlights, details we do not ordinarily notice creates a sense that somehow our territorial space is violated. Richard Estes, an American painter, is a highly successful representative of this trend.

Phrase In music, a group of successive tones, which together create melodic or thematic idea. See **Tone, Melody, Theme.**

Pigment Vegetable or mineral extract which, when ground to a powder and dispersed through a vehicle, constitutes the coloring matter c paint. Pigments are not dyes which dissolve in a solvent but particles is suspension uniformly distributed and unaltered by the vehicle which adheres them to the surface. Permanence of color requires that pigmen be chemically inert and that the optical properties of the vehicle nc deteriorate.

Pilaster A flat, slender column attached to a wall as decoration. Often see on the façade of secular Renaissance buildings.

Pitch That property of a musical tone which is determined by the fre quency of vibration of the sound waves. The greater the number o vibrations, the higher the pitch. Also called "definite pitch." *Indefinit pitch* is a term for the pitch created by instruments which produce irregular vibrations, as in the snare drum or gong. Indefinite pitch is simply noise. Absolute pitch is determined by computing the numbe of vibrations per second. Reflective pitch is determined by the position of a given tone within a scale.

Plainsong Religious song in free **rhythm** (no regular meter) sung in unisor without **harmony.** Plainsong melody is modal. See **Mode.**

Plot In drama, opera, and literature, the arrangement of incidents in a story so as to maintain interest, generate tension, and progress to ar emotional climax.

Pointillism See **Divisionism.**

Polyphony Music in which two or more independent melodies sound a once. (See **Counterpoint.**) Polyphony is the opposite of **homophony.**

Pop art Art using subject matter from commercial advertisements, cartoons and mass-produced objects, and claiming to be popular art as opposec to fine art. (See Figures 3-5, 9-23, 13-21.) As a reaction to elitism in art pop art began in England in the 1950s and flourished in America in the 1960s. Despite its tongue-in-cheek attitude and ironical reinforcemen of bad taste, it was serious in its claim to be a successor to Dadaism of the 1920s. Artists associated with pop art include Andy Warhol, Claes Oldenburg, Japser Johns, Jim Dine, Robert Indiana, Robert Rauschen berg, and Roy Lichtenstein.

Post-and-lintel construction Architectural construction which uses two verticals (posts), held upright by a horizontal (lintel) which spans the space between them. The simplest and most natural architectural prin ciple, it was the basis of Egyptian and Greek architecture, as seen in Figures 14-5 and 14-6.

Postimpressionism A term applied to the styles of many artists who were influenced in one way or another by **impressionism,** but who modified it in developing personal styles. Artists most often associated with the term are Cézanne (Color Plate 34), Renoir, Van Gogh (Color Plate 2), and Gauguin (Color Plate 18). See **cubism** and **expressionism,** which developed as artists modified impressionism to meet their individual needs in redefining the role of the artist as that of making a personal "statement," rather than simply recording visual reality.

Program music Any instrumental music based on, or related to, literary or pictorial material. Program music may be narrative, descriptive, imitative, or even loosely suggestive. The programmatic content of the music may be implied by the title of the work, supplied by a poem or exposition, or sometimes explained by the composer's notes, as in Beethoven's *Pastoral* Symphony.

Pylon Architectural term from the Greek, meaning "gateway." In Egyptian temples (Figure 14-4) the entrance is flanked by high, broad trapezoids with tapered sides and capped with a cornice. The flat rectangular roof crowns the structure and incised colored hieroglyphs cover its walls. Also, any monumental structure flanking an entrance, such as an approach to a bridge. The steel latticed tower carrying electric cables is also called a pylon.

Pyramidal plan A principle of composition in the visual arts. Enforcing the perception of static lateral balance or symmetry, the pyramid gives a feeling of great weight and stability in its horizontal base, relieved by the vertical thrust of the apex. It is a monumental plan which may accommodate one or more subjects (Color Plates 37 and 38). Leonardo, in his *Madonna and S. Anne*, combines such a plan with a radiating spiral (Color Plate 46).

Radial plan A symmetrical plan of composition centering attention on the main subject while leading the eye to scan the peripheries, as in both Leonardo's and Dali's *Last Supper* (Figures 13-5 and 3-13). The main subject need not be centrally placed to focus attention where we would normally expect to find it, when sight lines or the direction of gaze of minor subjects lead the eye to it (Figure 13-8).

Realism See **Representational art.**

Recitative A kind of musical recitation in which words rather than music dictate the phrasing and overall structure. Recitative may be accompanied or unaccompanied, the latter often having occasional chords to sustain the key and to mark emphases. Recitative occurs primarily in **opera, oratorio** and **cantata.**

Relief Sculpture, carving, or molding which projects from the background plane. Relief sculpture is attached to the wall or material from which it was sculptured (Figures 5-8 and 9-9). **Sculpture in the round,** on the other hand, is free-standing and may be seen from all sides. A bas-relief, or low relief, is sculpture or ornamentation which projects very little from the background, as, for example, the designs on coins (Figure 4-12). A relief print is a print made by inking or coloring the high-standing parts of a plate or block and then transferring the ink or color to some other material by pressing. A woodcut is an example of relief print.

Representational art, realistic art, naturalistic art Total accuracy of detail or photographic likeness is of scientific rather than of aesthetic interest. Artists require an arrangement of materials in a composition, and therefore simplify them (Figures 1-9 and 1-10). They may select, simplify, or distort for strictly formal, organizational reasons or for expressive purposes; both motives are usually present. Realism and naturalism are both representational styles. Selecting subject matter in the real world of nature and experience, representational artists depict it in ways that

enable us to recognize the correspondences between the representations and their sources. *Naturalistic* is the adjective applied to visual ar
which objectively renders a transcription of nature in a medium. Har
nett (Figure 9-11), Manet (Color Plate 30), Degas (Color Plate 20), Hade
(Figure 6-34), and Bellows (Figure 6-36) are all naturalistic to some de
gree. Realism in the visual arts and literature refers to content and no
necessarily to **subject** (the things and people represented). Whateve
the subject represented, the realist tends to focus on its matter-of-fact
everyday life aspects—the unattractive, squalid, and morbid in juxta
position with the beautiful and elevating. Realism is more an attitude
than a method. It abandons both "ideal" content (**classicism**) and emo
tional, imaginative content (**romanticism**) for factual content. Realism
and naturalism are best not thought of as degrees of subject matter
but as different preferences in subjects and different attitudes expressed
in the content.

Rhythm The flow of musical movement with recurrent accents, including
placement and balance of phrases, meter, and measures. The beat of the
music.

Romanesque An architectural style derived from the Roman basilica,
adapted to the needs of a feudal society (eleventh and twelfth centuries) when every public building had to be strong enough to be easily
defended against marauders. This need accounts in part for the crude,
powerful stonework and vaulting of isolated abbey churches and for
their low profile in contrast with the more self-assertive Gothic style
which followed after the time of Charlemagne.

Romanticism The opposite of **classicism**. The adjective *romantic* is applied
to any work of art or artist whose style stresses unrestrained emotional
content over clarity of form. Romantic art concerns itself with the personal, individual, or unique over the universal. It draws its subject
matter from fantasy, the imagination, or remote, exotic places or
times. It stresses the dramatic, spectacular aspects of nature rather than
the usual or normal ones. Whereas the classicist respects traditions in
the arts and conserves them, the romanticist ignores them or rebels
against them in order to make a personal, strongly felt statement. In this
sense the word is commonly used to describe art of any period having
these characteristics. It is also used to refer specifically to art in a movement which began in Europe in the mid-eighteenth century and extended at least through the nineteenth: a period when all the arts ex-
hibited romantic tendencies. Because of the recent emphasis on the
significance of the artist's role in art—on his or her unique feelings and
vision—some critics see the many individual styles and myriad "isms"
in contemporary arts as a continuation of the romantic temperament.

Rondo An instrumental composition in which the principal theme occurs
three or more times in the same key with contrasting themes in between.

Rose window A large, round window in the west **façade** of a Gothic
church, whose design suggests the petals of a rose. At sunset, light
floods through the rose window into the **nave**. See Figure 14-24, and
Transepts.

Round An imitative, polyphonic (see **polyphony**) composition (usually
vocal) in which two or more voices follow one another exactly in a

lapsed time sequence, each voice beginning on the same tone ("at the unison"). A round is a specific kind of **canon** called "canon at the unison."

Sanctuary and choir Consecrated place of worship in a temple or church where only the celebrants are admitted to officiate in the **liturgy**. In Christian churches on the basilican plan, it is within the **apse**, and in cruciform plans under the crossing (see **Transepts**). In front of the high altar is the **choir** (def. 3). The facing stalls are reserved for lesser clergy or canons who sing the Hours of the Divine Office at regular intervals. Both areas are separated from the laity in the **nave** by a railing or, in the Greek rite, by a screen (the iconostasis) bearing venerated images.

Scale A graduated series of single **tones** arranged in order of **pitch** and according to a set scheme.

Scenario The production plan for screen narration with a plot for scenes and sequences developed from a synopsis. See **Script**.

Scene In film, a series of **shots** united by time, place, and action. In drama, a part of the play which takes place in one location. In paintings which illustrate a story, legend, or historical episode, a dramatic point of narrative or spectacle equivalent to a still print made from a frame of film. See **Frame** (defs. 3 and 4).

Script The written text of a film, play, or broadcast. In film, the master scene script develops the narration and dialogue from an outline or synopsis of the story to be produced, with new material added for special cinematic effects. The shooting script reduces all this material, together with instructions on **camera angles** and lighting details, for scene-by-scene shooting.

Sculpture in the round Free-standing sculpture (see Michelangelo's *David*, Figure 3-1) as opposed to **relief** sculpture.

Sequence A succession of repeated harmonic or melodic phrases, rising or falling within the **tonality** of the music.

Shot A film segment of many consecutive frames that appears to the viewer to represent a single uninterrupted running of the camera. An actual scene may be taken simultaneously with several cameras, filmed at different times in any sequence, or retaken. See also **Still**.

Solo One instrument or one voice, alone or featured one at a time with a musical group.

Sonata An extended composition for one or more instruments, usually in three or four movements. The first movement is almost always in **sonata-allegro form** and is moderately fast (as *allegro* indicates). The second movement is usually slower and more lyrical in nature; in music commentary, it is sometimes referred to as the "slow movement." It may be in one of several forms: sonata-allegro, **rondo**, and **theme and variations**, for example. The third movement (when there are four movements) is usually a dance form in triple meter and ternary form—almost always a **minuet-trio** in classical works, but, after Beethoven introduced it, sometimes a scherzo-trio. The fourth movement is usually a fast, triumphant finale; the form is often a rondo, sometimes a theme and variations or a sonata-allegro.

Sonata-allegro form Sometimes called "sonata form" (because of its use in the first movement of a **sonata**), or simply "first-movement form." It consists typically of three sections: a statement of two or more contrasting thematic ideas (the **exposition**), a section in which these idea are developed (the **development**), and the restatement of these idea (recapitulation). Sometimes the form uses an introduction at the begin ning and sometimes a coda at the end.

Sound track A tape, film, or part of a film on which the sound accompany ing the visuals is recorded. When the sound is marketed without the visuals on disks or tapes, it is also, by extension, called the "sound track."

Space arts Visual presentations (such as painting and sculpture) that are perceived within a framing device as a momentary experience; all the stimuli are presented at once and may be experienced and studied in any number of relationships and in any order we choose. Cf. **Time arts**.

Still In film, one **frame** from a **shot**, of the kind used for publicity pur poses.

Stretto In a **fugue**, the crowding together (e.g., the more rapid occur rence) of subject upon subject, giving the effect of overlapping.

Stringcourse A narrow masonry molding extending across the side of a building or completely around it, usually to mark the stories. Often used (as were the **balustrade** and **pilaster**) as façade decoration on secular Renaissance buildings. In addition to breaking the rush of water running down the walls, it also relieved the bare plane of the wall with shadows.

String quartet A quartet of string performers: one first violin, one second violin, one viola, and one cello. The term also implies the form of com position—the **sonata**—usually played by such a group.

Strophic In vocal music, using the same music for successive stanzas, as opposed to involving continuous (new) composition for each stanza (**through-composed**).

Subdominant The fourth step of the diatonic scale. Also, the triad based on the fourth tone.

Subject The subject of a work of art is the named or nameable objects, persons, and situations which appear in it. In nonobjective art (see **Abstract art**), there is no subject in this sense of the word. The inter action of the subject and the responses evoked by the way it is pre sented (e.g., handling of aural, visual, tactile elements) is the *content* of the work. For example, there are several paintings of the Madonna (subject) in this book. All are recognizable as such and therefore elicit in us whatever feelings we have about madonnas in general, but each is painted differently and therefore evokes particular sets of feelings. Similarly, when we are told that a film is about "a love triangle," we know the subject, but nothing of the content.

Suite Instrumental form of the seventeenth and eighteenth centuries, con sisting of a number of dance movements in the same or related keys. The dances used were primarily the *allemande, courante, saraband, bourrée, gigue, gavotte, minuet,* and *passepied*. The term *suite* is also used for a selection of music from a ballet or opera arranged for orchestra. For example, "The Nutcracker Suite" from the ballet *The Nutcracker*.

Superimposition In film, the placing of one picture **frame** over another so that the images recorded by two cameras are seen at the same time, one on top of the other. Sometimes used as a **transitional device** in going from one scene, location, or time to another.

Surrealism Literally, the "superreality," the other reality beyond that usually represented in literature and the arts. Surrealism began as a literary movement in France in the 1920s and was immediately paralleled by a movement in the visual arts. It emphasized subject matter from the unconscious (automatic writing and painting), fantasies, the irrational, and especially dreams, and sought appropriate styles and forms for communicating them. The works of de Chirico (Color Plate 35) and Dali (Figure 2-15) are examples.

Swing A steady rhythm so subtly syncopated that it cannot be exactly notated. The hallmark of certain groups called "swing bands" which, in performance, "swing" the rhythm of their music.

Symphonic poem A composition for a symphony orchestra which is less restricted in form than the traditional **symphony** and based on a poetic subject. Usually in one continuous movement with one or more principal **themes.**

Symphony A musical composition in **sonata** form for full orchestra. The term *symphony* is also used to designate the orchestra which plays these compositions.

Syncopation The displacement of accents in which weak beats are accented or strong beats are not, or both. **Jazz** is characterized by pronounced syncopation.

Technique The manner in which an artist uses the **medium** chosen for a specific work. The artist's technique expresses her or his individuality and helps to enhance the sensual qualities of the medium.

Tempera, egg A painting medium in which egg yolk (a fatty oil and an emulsion with binding and adhesive qualities) is used as a pigment binder to make paint more workable as a quick-drying and pliable film. The surface to which it is applied must be sized or made non-absorbent.

Tessera A single piece of the colored glass, stone, or glazed ceramic used in making a **mosaic.** The plural is *tesserae.*

Texture The visual cues of tactile (touch) surface qualities which may be represented in a medium by suggesting them in another medium; or those qualities of a medium presented for their own sake when they are not used representationally. Analogously, in music we speak of a blending of sounds in melody as having texture.

Theme In literature and the visual arts, a major "statement" made about the **subject,** a controlling idea. In music, a melodic phrase which is the technical subject varied in development.

Theme and variations Usually a simple, harmonized melody presented first in its original form, then repeated a number of times in a varied treatment.

Through-composed Descriptive of any vocal piece involving continuous (new) composition for each stanza. The opposite of **strophic.**

Time arts A term sometimes applied to arts which present an organized series of stimuli within a "framing" time-span and which, therefore, must be experienced in sequence as having a beginning, a middle, and an end (e.g., literature, music, all the combined arts). See **Space arts.**

Thrust See **Buttress.**

Timbre Tone color; the quality of tone which distinguishes one voice or instrument from another. The characteristic quality of sounds which enables us, for example, to know whether a melody is being played on a violin or a trumpet.

Tonality The affinity of a series of tones for one central tone called the **tonic,** or keynote. Tonality is key feeling.

Tone The audible sound of a single note (a note is a written symbol), or the quality of a musical sound.

Tone poem An orchestral composition based on, or suggesting, a poetic sentiment or image. A variety of symphonic music developed especially by Richard Strauss.

Tonic The keynote. The central or first tone of any key. The tonic is often named in the title of a composition, as in Sonata in G Major, or Symphony in D Minor. The triad based on the tonic is called the "tonic chord."

Transepts and crossing In Christian churches in the form of a cross (cruciform), the short arms of the cross are the transepts, and the area where they meet and cross the long arms is the crossing. Usually the short arms extend north and south, and are closer to the east end of the long area, the **nave.** The west end is the portal (entrance), with a decorated **façade** which contains the **rose window.** The high **altar** is at the crossing in cruciform churches. In churches on the basilican plan (see **Basilica**), it is in the recessed **sanctuary** in the **apse.**

Transitional devices Techniques and conventions for moving from one part of an artistic creation to another smoothly and unobtrusively while maintaining a sense of continuity. In film editing, such devices as **wipe, fade-in** and **fade-out, jump cut, match-cut, superimposition, dissolve.** In music, such devices as **modulation.**

Triforium, triforium gallery, clerestory In Christian architecture, the wall space above the **arcade** of the aisles and its sloping roof; sometimes decorated, sometimes pierced with windows to create a clerestory (Figure 14-13), or made into a gallery with **arches** open to the **nave** to become a triforium gallery. (See Figure 14-20.) Sometimes this space was called a "blind story" when it was not perforated in the galleried or **fenestration** plan.

Triad A chord of three tones (or notes, in written music) based on one tone called the "root," with its third and fifth ascending intervals. Triads can be arranged and played in three positions (root-third-fifth, third-fifth-root, or fifth-root-third).

Tympanum In classical architecture, the recessed face of a **pediment,** a triangular space which contained principal sculpture decoration. (See Figures 14-7 and 13-27.) In Gothic churches, the space above the lintel of a portal recessed within an **arch,** which was usually decorated with sculptured figures or designs. (See Figure 14-23.)

Value The property of colors which makes them seem light or dark, as when a painting is photographed in black and white and its colors are converted to various shades of gray. Compare the black-and-white photograph of Sargent's painting *El Jaleo* (Figure 8-4) with Color Plate 21.

Variation The modification of the elements of music, relative to what has gone before, especially in melody and rhythm. Variation is also used to mean the treatment of a whole form, as in **theme and variations.**

Vault   A roof constructed on the principle of the **arch.** A barrel vault is a series of arches covering linear or rectangular space. A groin vault is a cross of barrel vaults which permits windows to let light into the central space (Figure 14-18). See **Dome.**

Vehicle   In paint, the liquid part in which prepared pigment is mixed so that the paint can be brushed or flowed onto a surface. Its adhesive property holds the pigment and forms a film. Linseed oil is the most commonly used vehicle for painting on canvas. See **Pigment.**

Voice-over   In film, narration in words heard over the action, dialogue, music, or other sounds. Frequently used in documentary and news films where an off-camera reader makes the commentary or narration which is dubbed (see **Dubbing**) into the final **sound track.**

Volute   The scroll-shaped design characterizing the Ionic capital. See **Ionic.**

Watercolor   A painting medium composed of very finely ground pigment in a binding medium of gum arabic, with water used as a **vehicle.** The paper on which it is used must be free of acid so that it will not yellow, become brittle, or deteriorate. Also, a painting made with watercolors. See also **Gouache.**

Wipe   In editing film, a **transitional device** in which one image pushes another image off the screen, usually diagonally but sometimes vertically or horizontally.

Zoom shot   In film, a **shot** in which a zoom lens is used to bring the subject closer to, or farther from, the viewer. See **Transitional devices.**

BIBLIOGRAPHY

This bibliography is divided into five groups. The first contains the dictionaries and other volumes needed for factual reference or allusion. The second contains those volumes, such as the ones on aesthetics, which are concerned with more than one art. The third, fourth, and fifth groups are the regular classifications of the individual arts—literature, drama, and film; the visual arts; and music, opera, and dance. Biographies and collections of illustrations are kept to a minimum.

DICTIONARIES AND REFERENCES

Avery, Catherine B., ed.: *The New Century Classical Handbook*, New York, 1972.

Beaumont, Cyril: *Bibliography of Dancing*, New York, 1963.

Bibliography of Aesthetics, New York, 1963.

Chujoy, Aratde: *Dance Encyclopedia*, rev. and enlgd. ed., New York, 1967.

Cirlot, J. E.: *A Dictionary of Symbols*, trans. from the Spanish by Jack Sage, New York, 1962.

Cruden, Alexander: *Complete Concordance to the Old and New Testament . . . with . . . a Concordance to the Apocrypha*, London, 1769.

Daniel, H.: *Encyclopedia of Themes and Subjects in Painting: Mythological, Biblical, Historical and Topical*, illus., New York, 1971.

Dictionary of Art Terms and Techniques, New York, 1969.

Encyclopedia Britannica, 15th ed., Chicago, 1974.

Encyclopedia of Modern Architecture, New York, 1964.

Encyclopedia of World Art, New York, 1968.

Ferguson, George: *Signs and Symbols in Christian Art*, New York, 1959.

Frazer, James George: *The Golden Bought: A Study in Magic and Religion*, 3d ed., London, 1907–1915, 12 vols.

Gayley, Charles Mills: *Classic Myths in English Literature and in Art*, rev. ed., New York, 1939.

Gray, L. H., ed.: *Mythology of All Races*, Boston, 1916–1932, 13 vols.

Grove, George: *Grove's Dictionary of Music and Musicians*, 5th ed., New York, 1954, 10 vols.

Hackin, J.: *Asiatic Mythology: A Detailed Description and Explanation of the Mythologies of All the Great Nations of Asia*, New York, 1963.

Hamilton, Edith: *Mythology*, New York, 1971.

Harmon, N. B., ed.: *The Interpreter's Bible*, New York, 1951–1957, 12 vols.

Hastings, James, ed.: *Encyclopedia of Religion and Ethics*, Edinburgh and New York, 1908–1927, 12 vols. and index.

Interpreter's Dictionary of the Bible, New York, 1962, 4 vols.

Jacobs, Arthur: *A New Dictionary of Music*, rev. ed., Baltimore, 1960.

Larousse Encyclopedia of Modern Art, New York, 1965.

Larousse Encyclopedia of Mythology, F. Guirand, ed., London, 1959.

Lehner, Ernst: *The Picture Book of Symbols*, New York, 1956.

Maillard, Robert: *Dictionary of Modern Sculpture*, New York, 1971.

Manvell, Roger, ed.: *The International Encyclopedia of Film*, New York, 1972.

Michael, Paul, ed.: *The American Movies Reference Book: The Sound Era*, Englewood Cliffs, N.J., 1970.

Munden, Kenneth W., ed.: *The American Film Institute Catalog, Feature Films, 1921–1930*, New York, 1971, 2 vols.

Murray, Peter, and Linda Murray: *A Dictionary of Art and Artists*, rev. ed., New York, 1968.

Myers, B., and T. Copplestone, eds.: *Landmarks of the World's Art*, New York and London, 1966–1967.

Myers, B., and S. Myers: *Encyclopedia of Painting*, rev. ed., New York, 1970.

————, eds.: *Dictionary of Art*, New York, 1969, 5 vols.

New Encyclopedia of the Opera, New York, 1971.

New Film Index, New York, 1975.

Penguin Companion to American Literature, New York, 1971.

Penguin Companion to Classical, Oriental, and African Literature, New York, 1969.

Penguin Companion to English Literature, New York, 1971.

Penguin Companion to European Literature, New York, 1969.

Performing Arts Books in Print, New York, 1973.

Pickard, R. A. E.: *Dictionary of 1000 Best Films*, New York, 1971.

Pierce, James S.: *From Abacus to Zeus: A Handbook of Art History*, Englewood Cliffs, N.J., 1968.

Reader's Encyclopedia of World Drama, New York, 1969.

Standard Dictionary of Folklore, Mythology, and Legend, New York, 1949.

Whittick, Arnold: *Symbols, Signs, and Their Meaning*, Newton, Mass., 1972.

AESTHETICS AND GENERAL WORKS

Beardsley, Monroe: *Aesthetics*, New York, 1958.

Berenson, Bernard: *Aesthetics and History in the Visual Arts*, New York, 1954.

Bonnard, Andre: *Greek Civilization—From the Iliad to the Parthenon*, London 1957, 3 vols.

Bosanquet, Bernard: *Three Lectures on Aesthetics*, New York, 1963.

Burnham, Jack: *The Structure of Art*, New York, 1971.

Dewey, John: *Art as Experience*, New York, 1934.

Feldman, Edmund: *Varieties of Visual Experience: Art as Image and Idea*, New York, 1973.

Fleming, William: *Arts and Ideas: New Brief Edition*, 1974.

Goodman, Nelson: *Languages of Art*, New York, 1968.

Hamilton, Edith: *The Greek Way to Western Civilization*, New York, 1942.

Hauser, Arnold: *The Philosophy of Art History*, Cleveland and New York 1963.

Hospers, John, ed.: *Introductory Readings in Aesthetics*, New York, 1968.

Howe, Irwin: *The Idea of the Modern in Literature and the Arts*, 1967.

Knobler, Nathan: *The Visual Dialogue: An Introduction to the Appreciation of Art*, New York, 1967.

Kris, Ernest: *Psychoanalytic Explorations in Art*, New York, 1974.

Kuh, Katherine: *Break-up: The Core of Modern Art*, New York, 1965.

Langer, Susanne K.: *Feeling and Form*, New York, 1956.

————: *Philosophy in a New Key*, 3d ed., Baltimore, 1957.

————: *Problems of Art: Ten Philosophical Lectures*, New York, 1957.

Larkin, Oliver: *Art and Life in America*, New York, 1960.

Macksey, Richard, and Eugenio Donato, eds.: *The Structuralist Controversy: The Languages of Criticism and the Sciences of Man*, Baltimore, 1972.

Margolis, Joseph Z.: *The Language of Art and Art Criticism: Analytic Questions in Aesthetics*, Detroit, 1965.

Maritain, Jacques: *Creative Intuition in Art and Poetry*, New York, 1955.

Martin, David F., and Lee A. Jacobus: *The Humanities through the Arts*, New York, 1975.

Miller, William Hugh: *Introduction to Music Appreciation: An Objective Approach to Listening*, Rahway, N.J., 1961.

Murry, John M.: *The Problem of Style*, London, 1960.

Owings, Nathaniel A.: *The American Aesthetic*, New York, 1969.

Rader, Melvin: *A Modern Book of Aesthetics: An Anthology*, 4th ed., New York, 1973.

Read, Sir Herbert: *The Meaning of Art*, Baltimore, 1964.

Seldes, Gilbert: *Seven Lively Arts*, New York, 1962.

Sypher, Wylie: *Four Stages of Renaissance Style: Transformations in Art and Literature*, Garden City, N.Y., 1955.

————: *Art History: An Anthology of Modern Criticism*, New York, 1963.

World of Culture, Joseph L. Gardner, gen. ed.: Newsweek Books, New York, 1974–1978. Separate vols. on dance, music, theater, painting, architecture, the novel, opera, and poetry.

LITERATURE, DRAMA, AND FILM

Arnheim, Rudolph: *Film as Art*, 9th prtg., Berkeley, Calif., 1974.

Auerbach, Eric: *Mimesis*, Eng. trans. from the German, Princeton, N.J., 1953.

Baldry, H. C.: *Ancient Greek Literature in Its Living Context*, New York, 1968.

Barnet, Sylvan, et al.: *A Dictionary of Literary Terms*, Boston, 1962.

Bartel, Roland, with James S. Ackerman and Thayer S. Warshaw, eds.: *Biblical Images in Literature*, New York, 1975.

Baugh, Albert C., ed.: *A Literary History of England*, New York, 1958.

Beardsley, Monroe, Robert Daniel, and Glenn Leggett: *Theme and Form*, 2d ed., Englewood Cliffs, N.J., (1962), 1975.

Benét, William Rose, ed.: *The Reader's Encyclopedia*, 2d ed., New York, 1965.

Bluestone, George: *Novels into Film*, Berkeley, 1957; paperback, 1971.

Bobker, Lee R.: *Elements of Film*, 2d ed., New York, 1974.

Booth, Wayne C.: *The Rhetoric of Fiction*, Chicago, 1961.

Bradley, A. C.: *Shakespearean Tragedy*, London, 1956.

Brockett, Oscar G.: *History of the Theatre*, Boston, 1968.

————: *Perspectives on Contemporary Theatre*, Baton Rouge, La., 1971.

Bronko, Leonard Cabell: *Avant-Garde: The Experimental Theatre in France*, Berkeley, Calif., 1962.

Brooks, Cleanth: *Modern Rhetoric*, New York, 1972.

Brustein, Robert: *The Theater of Revolt*, New York, 1964.

Burch, Noel: *The Theory of Film Practice*, New York, 1973.

Chase, Richard: *The American Novel and Its Tradition*, Garden City, N.Y., 1964.

Daiches, David: *The Present Age in British Literature*, Bloomington, Ind., 1958.

————: *English Literature*, Englewood Cliffs, N.J., 1964.

————: *A Study of Literature for Readers and Critics*, New York, 1972.

Eisenstein, Sergei M.: *Film Form* and *Film Sense*, New York, 1957, 2 vols. in one.

Eliot, T. S.: *On Poetry and Poets*, New York, 1957.

Esslin, Martin: *The Theatre of the Absurd*, rev. and updated ed., New York, 1973.

Fell, John L.: *Film: An Introduction*, New York, 1975.

Film, 1967–1968, 1968–1969, etc., Annual Anthology of the National Society of Film Critics, New York.

Gassner, J., and E. Quinn: *The Reader's Encyclopedia of World Drama*, New York, 1969.

Harvey, P., ed.: *Oxford Companion to Classical Literature*, 2d ed., New York, 1937.

————: *Oxford Companion to English Literature*, 4th ed., New York, 1967.

Hatlen, Theodore W.: *Orientation to the Theater*, 2d ed., New York, 1972.

Holland, Norman: *Poems in Persons: An Introduction to the Psychoanalysis of Literature*, New York, 1973.

Huss, Roy, and Norman Silverstein: *The Film Experience: Elements of Motion Picture Art*, New York, 1972.

Jarvie, I. C.: *Movies and Society*, New York, 1970.

Jesperson, Otto: *Growth and Structure of the English Language*, 9th ed., New York, (1955), 1968.

Jinks, William: *The Celluloid Literature: Film in the Humanities*, 2d ed., Beverly Hills, Calif., 1974.

Johnson, Lincoln F.: *Film: Space, Time, Light and Sound*, New York, 1974.

Keene, Donald: *Japanese Literature: An Introduction for Western Readers*, New York, 1955.

Kernan, Alvin B.: *Character and Conflict: An Introduction to Drama*, New York, 2d ed., 1969.

Kettle, Arnold: *An Introduction to the English Novel*, New York, (1952), 1970

Kirby, E. T., ed.: *Total Theatre: A Critical Anthology*, New York, 1969.

Lattimore, Richmond: *The Poetry of Greek Tragedy*, Baltimore, 1958.

Lawson, John H.: *Film: The Creative Process: The Search for an Audio-Visual Language and Structure*, New York, 1964.

Leavis, F. R.: *The Great Tradition: A Study of the English Novel*, New York 1963.

Legouis, E., and L. Cazmian: *A History of English Literature*, 630–1914, rev ed., trans. by H. D. Irvine and W. D. MacInnes, New York, (1957) 1971, 2 vols.

Lindgren, Ernest: *The Art of the Film*, rev. ed., New York, 1963.

Literature of America, The, New York, 1971, 2 vols.

MacCann, Richard Dyer: *Film: A Montage of Theories*, New York, 1966.

Maddux, Rachel, Stirling Silliphant, and Neil D. Issacs: *Fiction into Film* Knoxville, Tenn., 1970.

Manchel, Frank: *Film Study: A Resource Guide*, Rutherford, N.J., 1973.

Mandel, Oscar: *A Definition of Tragedy*, New York, 1961.

Mast, G., and M. Cohen: *Film Theory and Criticism*, New York, 1974.

Murray, Edward: *Nine American Film Critics*, New York, 1975.

Norton Introduction to Literature, J. Paul Hunter, ed., New York 1973. 3 vols.: *Poetry, Fiction, Drama*.

Penguin Companions to Literature. (See Dictionaries and References, page 499.)

Porter, Thomas E.: *Myth and Modern American Drama*, Detroit, 1969.

Preminger, Alex: *The Princeton Encyclopedia of Poetry and Poetics*, rev. ed. Princeton, N.J., 1975.

Quiller-Couch, Arthur: *On the Art of Writing*, New York, 1961.

Reinert, Otto: *Drama: An Introductory Anthology*, Boston, (1964), 1966.

Richardson, Robert: *Literature and Film*, Bloomington, Ind., 1969.

Ross, T. J.: *Film and the Liberal Arts*, New York, 1970.

Sapir, Edward: *Language: An Introduction to the Study of Speech*, New York (1949), 1955.

Sarris, Andrew, ed.: *The Film*, New York, 1968.

Shapiro, Karl, and Robert Beum: *A Prosody Handbook*, New York, 1965.

Sontag, Susan: *Against Interpretation and Other Essays*, New York, 1966.

Stephenson, R., and J. Debrix: *The Cinema as Art*, New York, 1969.

Styan, J. L.: *The Elements of Drama*, Cambridge, England, 1967.

Thrall, William Flint, and Addison Hibbard: *A Handbook to Literature*, rev ed., New York, 1960.

Tyler, Parker: *Classics of the Foreign Film*, New York, 1962.

————: *The Three Faces of the Film*, Cranbury, N.J., 1967.

Van Ghent, Dorothy: *The English Novel: Form and Function*, New York, 1961.

Vogel, Amos: *Film as a Subversive Art*, New York, 1974.

Watt, Ian: *The Rise of the Novel*, Berkeley, Calif., 1957.

Wellek, Rene, and Austin Warren: *Theory of Literature*, 2d ed., New York, 1956.

Whitaker, Rod: *The Language of Film*, Englewood Cliffs, N.J., 1970.

Williams, Raymond: *Drama in Performance*, New York, 1968.

Wilson, Edwin: *The Theatre Experience*, New York, 1975.

Wollen, Peter: *Signs and Meaning in the Cinema*, Bloomington, Ind., 1969.

World Masterpieces (literary anthology), New York, 1966, 2 vols.

Wright, Edward A.: *A Primer for Playgoers: An Introduction to the Understanding and Appreciation of Cinema-Stage-Television*, Englewood Cliffs,
N.J., 1958.

————: *Understanding Today's Theatre*, Englewood Cliffs, N.J., 1972.

VISUAL ARTS

Arnason, H. H.: *History of Modern Art: Painting, Sculpture and Architecture*,
Englewood Cliffs, N.J., 1968.

Arnheim, Rudolf: *Visual Thinking*, Berkeley, London, 1969.

Barr, Alfred H., Jr., ed.: *Masters of Modern Art*, New York, 1954.

————: *Picasso, Fifty Years of His Art*, New York, 1946.

Battcock, Gregory, ed.: *Minimal Art: A Critical Anthology*, New York, 1968.

————: *The New Art: A Critical Anthology*, rev. ed., New York, 1973.

————: *New Ideas in Art Education: A Critical Anthology*, New York, 1973.

Batteryberry, Michael: *Twentieth Century Art*, Discovering Art Series, New
York, 1971.

————: *Chinese and Oriental Art*, Discovering Art Series, New York, 1973.

Berenson, Bernard: *The Italian Painters of the Renaissance*, New York, 1957.

Bevlin, Marjorie Elliott: *Design through Discovery*, 3d ed., New York, 1977.

Boardman, John: *Greek Art*, rev. ed., 1973.

Brion, Marcel, et al.: *Art since 1945*, abr., New York, 1962.

Burnham, Jack: *Beyond Modern Sculpture: The Effects of Science and Technology on the Sculpture of This Century*, New York, 1968.

Canaday, John: *Mainstreams of Modern Art*, New York, 1959.

————: *Keys to Art*, New York, 1963.

Christ-Janer, Albert, and Mary Mix Foley: *Modern Church Architecture*, New
York, 1962.

Clark, Kenneth: *Landscape into Art*, London, 1966.

————: *The Nude: A Study in Ideal Form*, vol. 2, Princeton, N.J., 1972.

Cleaver, Dale C.: *Art: An Introduction*, 3d ed., New York, 1977.

Constable, W. G.: *The Painter's Workshop*, New York, 1954.

Creedy, Jean, ed.: *The Social Context of Art*, New York, 1970.

David, Jacobs: *Architecture*, New York, 1974.

Doerner, Max: *The Materials of the Artist and Their Use in Painting*, rev. ed.,
trans. by Eugen Newhaus, New York, 1949.

Drexler, Arthur: *The Architecture of Japan*, New York, 1955.

Elliott, George P.: *Dorothea Lange*, Museum of Modern Art, New York, 1967.

Faulkner, Ray, and Edwin Ziegfeld: *Art Today: An Introduction to the Visual
Arts*, 5th ed., rev., New York, 1969.

Feldman, Edmund Burke: *Varieties of Visual Experience: Art as Image and
Idea*, rev. and enlgd. ed., New York, 1973.

Finch, Margaret: *Style in Art History: An Introduction to Theories of Style and
Sequence*, Metuchen, N.J., 1974.

Fletcher, Bannister: *A History of Architecture on the Comparative Method*,
rev. ed., New York, 1975.

Frankl, Paul: *Gothic Architecture*, Baltimore, 1962.

Gardner, Ernest A.: *A Handbook of Greek Sculpture*, 2d ed., New York,
(1929), 1975.

Gardner, Helen: *Art Through the Ages*, 6th ed., New York, 1975.

Geldzahler, Henry: *American Painting in the Twentieth Century*, Metropolitan Museum Publication, New York, 1965.

Gernsheim, Helmut, and Alison Gernsheim: *Concise History of Photography*, New York, 1965.

Giedion, S.: *Architecture, You and Me*, Cambridge, Mass., 1958.

————: *Space, Time, and Architecture*, 5th ed., Cambridge, Mass., 1967.

Goldwater, Robert: *Primitivism in Modern Art*, rev. ed., 1967.

————: *What Is Modern Sculpture*, New York, 1971.

Gombrich, E. H.: *The Story of Art*, 12th ed., Greenwich, Conn., 1974.

Green, Samuel M.: *American Art*, New York, 1966.

Haftmann, Werner: *Painting in the Twentieth Century*, vol. 1: *An Analysis of the Artists and Their Works*; vol. 2: *A Pictorial Survey*, New York, 1973.

Hauser, Arnold: *The Social History of Art*, New York, 1951, 2 vols.

Heller, Jules: *Printmaking Today: An Introduction to the Graphic Arts*, New York, 1958.

Herbert, Robert L.: *Modern Artists on Art*, New York, 1964.

Hitchcock, Henry Russell, and Arthur Drexler: *Built in U.S.A.: Post-War Architecture*, New York, 1953.

————: *Architecture: Nineteenth and Twentieth Centuries*, Baltimore, 1963.

————: *World Architecture*, intro. by H.R.H., New York, 1963.

————, and Philip C. Johnson: *In the Nature of Materials: The Buildings of Frank Lloyd Wright*, New York, 1942.

————: *The International Style*, 2d ed., New York, 1966.

Hunter, Sam: *American Art of the 20th Century*, New York, 1974.

Huyghe, Rene: *Ideas and Images in World Art: Dialogue with the Visible*, Abrams, New York, 1959.

————: *Art and the Spirit of Man*, New York, 1962.

Illinois University: *Contemporary American Painting and Sculpture*, Urbana, 1965.

Janson, H. W., with Dora Jane Janson: *The Picture History of Painting*, New York, 1957.

————: *A History of Art*, New York, 2d ed., 1969.

————, eds.: *Key Monuments of the History of Art (A Visual Survey)*, New York, 1962.

Jencks, Charles: *Architecture 2000: Predictions and Methods*, New York, 1971.

————, and George Baird, eds.: *Meaning in Architecture*, New York, 1970.

Kriesberg, Irving: *Art: The Visual Experience*, New York, 1964.

Le Corbusier (pseud. of Charles E. Jeanneret-Gris): *Towards A New Architecture*, trans. of 13th French ed., with intro. by Frederick Etchells, New York, 1959.

Lee, Sherman E.: *Chinese Landscape Painting*, rev. ed., New York, 1976.

————: *The Colors of Ink: Chinese Paintings and Related Ceramics from the Cleveland Museum of Art*, New York, 1974.

Lee, Sherman: *History of Far Eastern Art*, rev. ed., New York, 1974.

Loran, Erie: *Cézanne's Composition: Analysis of His Form with Diagrams and Photographs of His Motifs*, 3d ed., Berkeley, Calif., 1963.

Lyons, Nathan: *Photography in the Twentieth Century*, New York, 1967.

Male, Emile: *Religious Art from the Twelfth to the Eighteenth Century*, New York, 1963.

Malraux, André: *The Voices of Silence*, Garden City, N.Y., 1953.

Mendelowitz, Daniel M.: *A History of American Art*, New York, 1963.

Mumford, Lewis: *The Culture of Cities*, New York, 1938.

————: *Sticks and Stones*, 2d rev. ed., New York, 1955.

Myers, Bernard S.: *Fifty Great Artists*, New York, 1959.

————: *Modern Art in the Making*, 2d ed., New York, 1959.

————: *Understanding the Arts*, rev. ed., New York, 1963.

————: *The City in History*, New York, 1972.

————: *Art and Civilization*, rev. ed., New York, 1967.

————: *The German Expressionists*, New York, 1967.

Neumeyer, Alfred: *The Search for Meaning in Modern Art (Die Kunst in Unserer Zeit)*, trans. by R. Angress, Englewood Cliffs, N.J., 1965.

Newhall, Beaumont: *History of Photography from 1839 to the Present Day*, Museum of Modern Art, New York, 1964.

————, and Nancy Newhall: *Masters of Photography*, New York, 1958.

Newton, Eric: *European Painting and Sculpture*, 4th ed., Baltimore, 1960.

Paine, R. T., and Alexander Soper: *Art and Architecture of Japan*, rev. ed., Pelican History of Art Series, New York, 1975.

Panofsky, Erwin: *Meaning in the Visual Arts*, New York, (1955), 1974.

Peterdi, Gabor: *Printmaking: Methods Old and New*, New York, 1971.

Pevsner, Nikolaus: *An Outline of European Architecture*, 6th ed. rev., Baltimore, 1960.

Pierson, William H., Jr., and William H. Jordy: *American Buildings and Their Architects*, Garden City, N.Y., 1976, 4 vols.

Pope, Arthur: *The Language of Drawing and Painting*, Cambridge, Mass., (1949), 1968.

Powell, Ann: *The Origins of Western Art*, New York, 1973.

Preble, Duane: *Man Creates Art Creates Man*, Berkeley, Calif., 1973.

Read, Herbert: *A Concise History of Modern Painting*, New York, (1959), 1964.

Rewald, John: *Post-Impressionism: From Van Gogh to Gauguin*, New York, 1958.

Richards, J. M., and Elizabeth B. Mock: *An Introduction to Modern Architecture*, Baltimore, 1956.

Richter, Gisela M. A.: *The Sculpture and Sculptors of the Ancient Greeks*, 4th ed., 1970.

Robb, David M., and J. J. Garrison: *Art in the Western World*, 4th ed., New York, 1963.

Rosenberg, Harold: *The Anxious Object: Art Today and Its Audience*, New York, 1964.

————: *The Tradition of the New*, New York, 1965.

Rowland, Benjamin, Jr.: *The Art and Architecture of India*, Baltimore, 1953.

————: *Art in East and West: An Introduction Through Comparisons*, Boston, 1964.

Ruskin, Ariane, and Michael Batterberry: *Greek and Roman Art*, Discovering Art Series, New York, 1973.

Russell, John: *The Meanings of Modern Art*, New York, 1975, 12 vols.

Sandler, Irving: *The Triumph of American Painting: A History of Abstract Expressionism*, New York, 1973.

Schefold, Karl: *Myth and Legend in Early Greek Art*, New York, 1966.

Schwarz, Ira P., and Leon C. Karel: *Teaching the Related Arts: A Guide to General Education in the Arts*, Kirksville, Mo., 1973.

Scott, Geoffrey: *The Architecture of Humanism*, New York, 1974.

Seiberling, Frank: *Looking into Art*, New York, 1959.

Seitz, William C.: *The Art of Assemblage*, Museum of Modern Art Publication, New York, 1961.

Seuphor, Michel: *Dictionary of Abstract Painting*, New York, 1957.

————: *Abstract Painting: Fifty Years of Accomplishment from Kandinsky to the Present*, New York, 1962.

Sewall, John Ives: *A History of Western Art*, rev. ed., New York, 1962.

Sickman, Laurence, and A. Soper: *The Art and Architecture of China*, Baltimore, 1971.

Siren, Osvald: *The Chinese on the Art of Painting*, 3d Schocken printing, New York, (1963), 1969.

Spencer, Harold: *The Image Maker: Man and His Art*, New York, 1975.

Talbot-Rice, David: *Art of the Byzantine Era*, 1963.

Tapie, Victor-L.: *The Age of Grandeur: Baroque Art and Architecture*, trans. from the French by A. Ross Williamson, New York, 1960.

Upjohn, Everard M., Paul S. Wingert, and Jane Gaston Mahler: *History of World Art*, 2d ed., New York, 1958.

Vallier, Dora: *Abstract Art*, trans. from the French by Jonathan Griffin, New York, 1970.

Venturi, Leonello: *Painting and Painters: How to Look at a Picture from Giotto to Chagall*, New York, 1945.

Warner, Langdon: *The Enduring Art of Japan*, New York, 1958.

Watrous, James: *The Craft of Old-Master Drawings*, Madison, Wis., 1957.

Weismann, Donald L.: *The Visual Arts as Human Experience*, Englewood Cliffs, N.J., 1974.

White, Norval: *The Architecture Book*, New York, 1976.

Willetts, William: *Foundations of Chinese Art*, New York, 1965.

Wölfflin, H.: *Principles of Art History*, trans. from the 7th German ed. by M. D. Hottinger, New York, 1949.

Wright, Frank Lloyd: *The Living City*, New York, 1958.

Wu, Nelson: *Chinese and Indian Architecture*, New York, 1967.

Zigrosser, Carl: *Prints: Thirteen Illustrated Essays on the Art of the Print*, New York, 1962.

MUSIC, OPERA, AND DANCE

Apel, Willi: *Gregorian Chant*, Bloomington, Ind., 1958.

————: *Harvard Dictionary of Music*, 2d rev. ed., 1969.

Bauman, Alvin, and Charles W. Walton: *Elementary Musicianship*, 2d ed., Englewood Cliffs, N.J., 1959.

Bernstein, Martin: *An Introduction to Music*, 4th ed., Englewood Cliffs, N.J., 1972.

Chujoy, Anatole: *The New York City Ballet*, New York, 1953.

Cohen, Selma Jeanne, ed.: *The Modern Dance: Seven Statements of Belief*, Middletown, Conn., 1969.

Cooper, Grosvenor: *Learning to Listen: A Handbook for Music*, Chicago, 1957. Prepared with the humanities staff of The College at the University of Chicago.

Copland, Aaron: *Music and Imagination*, Cambridge, Mass., 1953.

Cuyler, Louise: *The Symphony: The Harbrace History of Musical Forms*, New York, 1973.

Dallin, Leon: *Listeners' Guide to Musical Understanding*, 4th ed., Dubuque, Iowa, 1977.

Daniels, Arthur, and Lavern Wagner, eds.: *Listening to Music*, New York, 1975.

DeMille, Agnes: *The Book of the Dance*, New York, 1963.

Denby, Edwin: *Dancers, Buildings, and People in the Streets*, New York, 1965.

————: *Looking at Dance*, New York, 1968.

Dixon, Madeline C.: *The Power of Dance*, New York, 1939.

Duncan, Isadora: *The Art of the Dance*, ed. Sheldon Cheney, New York, 1928.

Ewen, David: *A Complete Book of the American Musical Theater*, rev. ed., New York, 1970.

————: *Composers Since 1900, A Bibliographical and Critical Guide*, New York, 1969.

————: *Composers of Tomorrow's Music: A Non-technical Introduction to the Musical Avant-Garde Movement*, New York, 1971.

Finney, Theodore M.: *A History of Music*, rev. ed., New York, 1947.

Geiringer, Karl: *Musical Instruments*, New York, 1945.

Graham, Martha: *Martha Graham*, ed. Merle Armitage, New York, 1966.

Green, Douglass M.: *Form in Tonal Music*, New York, 1965.

Grout, Donald Jay: *Short History of Opera*, 2d ed., New York, 1965, 2 vols.

————: *A History of Western Music*, rev. ed., New York, 1973.

Grove, George: *Beethoven and His Nine Symphonies*, London, 1898.

Hadow, W. H., ed.: *The Oxford History of Music*, 2d ed., New York, 1929, 6 vols.

Halprin, Ann: "Intuition and Improvisation in Dance," *Impulse*, 1955.

Hansen, Peter S.: *An Introduction to Twentieth Century Music*, Boston, 1961.

Harman, Alec: *Man and His Music: The Story of Musical Experience in the West*, New York, 1962.

Haskell, Arnold, ed.: *Ballet* (annual), nós. 16 and 17, New York, 1962 and 1963.

Hindemith, Paul: *The Craft of Musical Composition*, part I, New York, 1942.

Hoffer, Charles R.: *The Understanding of Music*, 3d ed., Belmont, Calif., 1976.

Horst, Louis, and Carroll Russell: *Modern Dance Forms in Relation to Other Modern Arts*, San Francisco, 1961.

Howard, John Tasker, and James Lyons: *Modern Music: A Popular Guide to Greater Musical Enjoyment*, rev. ed., New York, 1957.

Humphrey, Doris: *The Art of Making Dances*, ed. Barbara Pollack, New York, 1959.

Hutchinson, Ann: *Labanotation*, New York, 1954.

Kirstein, Lincoln: *Movement and Metaphor*, New York, 1970.

Knapp, J. Merrill: *The Magic of Opera*, New York, 1972.

Lang, Paul Henry: *Music in Western Civilization*, New York, 1941.

Lawrence, Robert: *Victor Book of Ballets and Ballet Music*, New York, 1950.

Lawson, Joan: *A History of Ballet and Its Makers*, New York, 1964.

Liepmann, Klaus: *The Language of Music*, New York, 1953.

Mann, Alfred: *The Study of Fugue*, New Brunswick, N.J., 1958.

Marek, George R., ed.: *The World Treasury of Grand Opera*, New York, 1957.

Martin, John: *The Modern Dance*, New York, 1933.

————: *Introduction to the Dance*, New York, 1939.

————: *The Dance*, New York, 1946.

McDonagh, Don: *The Rise and Fall and Rise of Modern Dance*, New York, 1970.

Meyer, Leonard B.: *Emotion and Meaning in Music*, Chicago, 1956.

Mitchell, Donald: *The Language of Modern Music*, New York, 1963.

Mitchell, Ronald E.: *Opera: Dead or Alive: Production, Performance, and Enjoyment of Musical Theatre*, Madison, Wis., 1970.

Murphy, Howard A.: *Form in Music for the Listener*, Camden, N.J., 1945.

New Oxford History of Music, New York, 1963.

Newman, Ernest: *Wagner Operas*, New York, 1949.

Orrey, Leslie: *A Concise History of Opera*, New York, 1972.

Pauly, Reinhard G.: *Music and the Theater: An Introduction to Opera*, Englewood Cliffs, N.J., 1970.

Piston, Walter: *Harmony*, 3d rev. ed., New York, 1962.

Portnoy, Julius: *Music in the Life of Man*, New York, 1963.

Raffe, Walter G.: *Dictionary of the Dance*, New York, 1965.

Ratner, Leonard G.: *Music, The Listener's Art*, New York, 1957.

Reyna, Ferdinando: *A Concise History of Ballet*, New York, 1964.

Rufer, Joseph: *Composition with Twelve Notes*, trans. by Humphrey Searle, New York, 1954.

Sachs, Curt: *The History of Musical Instruments*, New York, 1940.

————: *The Wellsprings of Music*, Jaap Kunst, ed., The Hague, Netherlands, 1962.

————: *World History of the Dance*, New York, 1963.

Salazar, Adolfo: *Music in Our Time: Trends in Music since the Romantic Era*, trans. by Isabel Pope, New York, 1946.

Scholes, Percy A.: *Listener's Guide to Music*, with concertgoer's glossary and introduction by W. Henry Hadow, 10th ed., New York, 1948.

————: *Oxford Companion to Music*, 9th ed., New York, 1955.

Sessions, Roger: *The Musical Experience of Composer, Performer, Listener*, Princeton, N.J., 1950.

Sorrel, Walter: *The Dance Through the Ages*, New York, 1967.

————: *The Dancer's Image: Points and Counterpoints*, New York, 1971.

Stearns, Marshall W.: *The Story of Jazz*, New York, 1956.

Stravinsky, Igor: *The Poetics of Music*, New York, 1947.

Stringham, Edwin John: *Listening to Music Creatively*, 2d ed., New York, n.d.

Stuckenschmidt, H. H.: *Twentieth Century Music*, New York, 1973.

Tovey, Donald Francis: *Essays in Musical Analysis*, New York, 1935–1939, 6 vols.

————: *Musical Articles from the Encyclopedia Britannica*, with editorial preface by Hubert J. Foss, New York, 1944.

————: *Beethoven*, with editorial preface by Hubert J. Foss, New York, 1945.

————: *The Main Stream of Music and Other Essays*, collected, with introduction by Hubert J. Foss, New York, 1949.

Vinton, John: *Dictionary of Contemporary Music*, New York, 1974.

Wigman, Mary: *The Language of Dance*, trans. Walter Sorrel, Middletown, Conn., 1966.

Wink, Richard L., and Lois G. Williams: *Invitation to Listening: An Introduction to Music*, 2d ed.: Boston, 1976.

Wold, Milo, and Edmund Cykler: *An Introduction to Music and Art in the Western World*, 5th ed., Dubuque, Iowa, 1976.

Zuckerkandl, Victor: *The Sense of Music*, Princeton, N.J., 1959.

TEACHING
MATERIALS

ILLUSTRATIONS OF ART SUBJECTS

HARRY N. ABRAMS

(110 E. 59th St., New York 10022) Perhaps the most active art-book publisher in the United States, this company covers both traditional and modern areas in period books, monographs, original graphic art, etc.

LANDMARKS OF THE WORLD'S ART

(McGraw-Hill, Princeton Rd., Hightstown, N.J. 08520) A series of ten color-illustrated period books divided into the broadest historical segments (e.g., *The Age of Baroque, The Classical World*).

MUSEUMS OF THE WORLD

(Newsweek, Inc., 444 Madison Ave., New York 10022) A series of fifteen volumes, each devoted to an outstanding museum. All-color, plus a history of each museum and short art-historical comments on important objects in its collection.

NEW YORK GRAPHIC SOCIETY

(140 Greenwich Ave., Greenwich, Conn. 06831) The society's new illustrated catalog of color reproductions, for purchase, entitled *Fine Art Reproductions: Old and Modern Masters*, is itself a significant reference book and source of color illustrations. It includes some 2000 illustrations in full color from every period and style.

PHAIDON/DUTTON FINE ART BOOKS

(E. P. Dutton, 201 Park Ave., S., New York 10003) The Phaidon Press has for many years specialized in art books with fine reproductions. Books over the years have covered almost every aspect of art. To these have now been added the Phaidon Colour Plate Books, a series in which one large-size volume with forty-six color plates is devoted to a single artist (e.g., *Manet, El Greco, Seurat*) or to a group of painters (e.g., *Blue Rider, Flemish Painting, Abstract Painting*, etc.). The series now contains some thirty-five titles.

Phaidon volumes, in a completely new series of oversize (10½ by 15½ inches) giant art paperbacks, contain sixty-four color reproductions each. The color is of high quality and the large size makes them suitable for mounting. (A very inexpensive source of color prints for teaching purposes.) Typical titles: *The Moderns: 1945–1975* (Measham), *The Nude in Western Art* (Cormack), *Japanese Prints: From 1700–1900* (Illing).

PRAEGER PUBLISHERS

(111 Fourth Ave., New York 10003) Various series on the history of art and the history of music. Among these, such collections as *Ancient Peoples and Places* and the *Praeger World of Art* are outstanding.

SKIRA ART BOOKS

(World Publishing Co., 110 59th St., New York 10022) Publications include a number of books of art with excellent illustrations in color. Some deal with a single artist, some with a movement or a period.

TIME-LIFE LIBRARY OF ART

(Silver-Burdett Co., Morristown, N.J. 07960) Each boxed volume is devoted to one artist. Good color and black-and-white reproductions of works of artists and artists who influenced them.

UNESCO WORLD ART SERIES

(New York Graphic Society, 140 Greenwich Ave., Greenwich, Conn. 06831) A continuing series. Many volumes already published, each devoted to a specific area (e.g., Australia, the Soviet Union, Cyprus, Greece, Tunisia, Israel).

WORLD OF CULTURE

(Newsweek Books, 444 Madison Ave., New York 10022) Each volume devoted to a single art (painting, dance, architecture, opera, cinema, theater, etc.), lavishly illustrated with excellent color reproductions relating to the art from ancient times to the present.

MUSIC

SKELETON SCORES. A skeleton score shows the melodic line of a composition, with annotations which give indications of form (first theme, development, etc.), timbre, tempo, and dynamics.

The series *Symphonic Skeleton Scores* is edited and annotated by Violet Katzner (Theodore Presser Company, Bryn Mawr, Pa.). In 1977, it contained these six symphonies:
Beethoven, Symphony No. 5 in C minor
Brahms, Symphony No. 1 in C minor
Brahms, Symphony No. 3 in F major
Franck, Symphony in D minor
Mozart, Symphony in G minor
Schubert, Symphony in B minor (*Unfinished*)
Tchaikowsky, Symphony No. 4 in F minor
Tchaikowsky, Symphony No. 6 in B minor (*Pathétique*)

Scored for Listening, by Bockman and Starr (Harcourt, Brace & World, Inc., New York, 1959), contains skeleton scores for many of the compositions referred to in this volume.

CRITICAL SCORES. A critical score, through footnotes or other devices, indicates points at which there is more than one interpretation of the composer's intention. It does not show formal aspects of analysis (themes, variations, development, transitions, etc.), but it does contain the usual performance markings (e.g., tempo, dynamics).

The Norton Critical Scores (W. W. Norton & Co., Inc., New York) indicate emendations which have over the years been made in interpreting early editions. There is also a section giving what is known of the historical background of the piece, circumstances of composition, early performances, and reactions. Another section gives a detailed analysis of the music by the editor and usually by two or three other scholars. A final section consists of critical essays on the piece. A short bibliography guides the student to further material about the work and its composer. Each score in the series has been prepared by a separate editor, but the series is uniform in format and organization. The following scores are now available:

Bach, Cantata No. 4, edited by Gerhard Herz
Bach, Cantata No. 140, edited by Gerhard Herz
Beethoven, Symphony No. 5 in C minor, edited by Elliot Forbes
Berlioz, Fantastic Symphony, edited by Edward T. Cone
Chopin, Preludes, Op. 28, edited by Thomas Higgins
Debussy, Prelude to "The Afternoon of a Faun," edited by William W. Austin
Haydn, Symphony No. 103 in E-flat major, edited by Karl Geiringer
Mozart, Symphony in G minor, K. 550, edited by Nathan Broder
Mozart, Piano Concerto in C minor, K. 503, edited by Joseph Kerman
Palestrina, Pope Marcellus Mass, edited by Lewis Lockwood
Schubert, Symphony in B minor ("Unfinished"), rev., edited by Martin Chusid
Schumann, Dichterliebe, edited by Arthur Komar
Stravinsky, Petrushka, edited by Charles Hamm

MINIATURE SCORES. The miniature score gives the entire score, but in miniature; collections of miniature scores are published by E. F. Kalmus Orchestra Scores, Inc., New York, and by Penguin Books, Inc., Baltimore, Md.

LIBRETTOS. The complete words of operas, often with one or two musical excerpts, can be obtained from the Metropolitan Opera Guild (1865 Broadway, New York 10023), Fred Rullman, Inc., New York City, and Oliver Ditson Co., Boston.

OPERA SCORES. Opera score editions, containing the words and music (arranged for piano) may be ordered from the Metropolitan Opera Guild (1865 Broadway, New York 10023) or G. Schirmer, Inc. (866 Third Avenue, New York 10022). All operas in the Metropolitan's repertoire are available. For operas which are to be studied in depth, these are indispensable.

RECORDINGS FOR TEACHING. Of the various records available for teaching the elements of music and principles of analysis, perhaps none is superior to those produced by David Randolph, called *Guide to Understanding Music*, for *Stereo Review Magazine*. The sides of the four LP records are devoted to "Rhythm," "Melody," "Harmony," "The Texture of Music," "Sense and Sensation in Music," "How Music Is Unified," "Form in Music," "Words and Music," "Can Music Tell a Story or Paint a Picture?" and "Interpretation of Music." The explanations and performed examples are clear and simple. The set is candidly "designed for the person who can't read a note of music, and who has no technical training in music." For situations requiring this level of material, the set can be extremely useful.

FILMS

AN INTRODUCTION TO THE PERFORMING ARTS

This series of five films was produced specifically for educational use. Each is in color, is 27 minutes long, and is narrated by a distinguished professional who explains the art presented, with backstage scenes and examples shown in performance. The films are:

Walter Kerr on Theater. Compares film with theater and illustrates both. Includes scenes from five plays: Aeschylus's *Prometheus*, Shakespeare's *Richard III*, Oscar Wilde's *Importance of Being Earnest*, *No Place to Be Somebody*, and the Open Theatre's production of *The Serpent*.

Ballet With Edward Villella. Discusses ballet as an art. Compares nineteenth- and twentieth-century ballet and illustrates both. Features soloists Patricia McBride and Edward Villela (who narrates the film) as well as the full corps de ballet of the New York City Ballet in excerpts from George Balanchine's *Apollo* and *Jewels* and the classic *Giselle*.

Film: The Art of the Impossible. Narrated by Director Michael Ritchie who explains the filmmaker's art, showing clips from *Birth of a Nation*, *Potemkin*, *Footlight Parade*, *King Kong*, *Lawrence of Arabia*, *The African Queen*, and his own *Downhill Racer*.

The Symphony Sound. Narrated by Conductor Henry Lewis and featuring the Royal Philharmonic Orchestra. Discusses and illustrates the timbre of various instruments of the orchestra. Includes substantive excerpts from Debussy's *Afternoon of a Faun* and Beethoven's Symphony No. 5.

Opera with Henry Butler. Butler, Director of the New York Metropolitan Opera, explains the nature of opera and traces its history with performed excerpts from each period. Featured are substantive scenes from *Pagliacci* (in rehearsal and performance) and *La Traviata* (with Metropolitan Opera star Anna Moffo).

The films may be purchased from the Learning Corporation of America (711 5th Ave., New York 10022); rental inquiries should be addressed to Customer Service Department, Learning Corporation of America (1350 Ave. of the Americas, New York 10019).

There are over 100 films in this distinguished collection. All aspects and periods of painting and sculpture are covered: "Part One. From Caveman to Michelangelo," "Part Two. From Rembrandt to Art Nouveau," and "Part Three. Abstraction and After." A catalog of each part describes each film in detail with illustrations, suggests programs for putting selections from the collection together for particular purposes, and lists "complete film narrations" available. The films may be purchased or rented. The three catalogs and information are available from The Roland Collection (1925 Willow Road, Northfield, Ill. 60093).

THE HUMANITIES SERIES

Of the sixteen color films in this series, each 18 minutes long, six have been found useful in introducing the arts covered in this text. The format varies from film to film, but all six of the films listed below present the arts as fulfilling human needs and expressing human concerns, all introduce the viewer to the nature and potentials of the medium and the ways of working with it, and all portray the arts, not as static, but as evolving and changing with the culture, reflecting it and influencing it.

Architecture: Why Man Builds. Stresses the relationship of architecture to culture. Opens with a sequence in which contemporary building is intercut with quick stills of edifices from times past. In a visual array of all types of buildings from igloos to city apartments to universities, the film makes the point that the needs of the people determine what a building should be, and that architecture helps to shape the lives of people.

Literature: Legacy for the Future. Treats literature as a link with the past, as defining the present, and as leaving a legacy for the future. Stresses the different forms that literature has taken at different times in giving expression to basic human concerns.

Opera: Man, Music and Drama. Shows how opera draws together the elements of dance, costume, drama, and vocal and orchestral music to create total theater. Through a sampling of opera excerpts from all periods, the film charts the changes which opera has undergone through its history.

Painting: A Visual Record. Reveals the art of the painter from physical dealing with materials to style, historical era, and personal vision. The film shows examples from all times and cultures to demonstrate how the painter reacts to personal and social forces, and uses the elements of line, mass, color, space, shape, and movement to fashion an individual technique.

Poetry: The Essence of Being Human. Very little narration, but quite well read excerpts and entire poems accompanied by visuals. Most of the visuals are of ordinary scenes and objects which the poetry compels us to see in a different way. The selections illustrate the range of feelings—love, hate, joy, despair, hope, ecstasy—which poetry can express.

Sculpture: The Forms of Life. Stresses that sculpture, like all art, communicates a view of life. Until recently it has dealt with the outer world; now abstract thoughts, feelings, and dreamlike images are finding expression in it. Shows the materials of sculpture, a wide range of techniques, and many examples of sculpture from around the world.

The films are available for purchase or rental from McGraw-Hill Films Film Library, Dept. 410, Princeton-Hightstown Road, Hightstown, N.J 08520. A detailed descriptive brochure from which the above summaries have been condensed and adapted is available for the whole series.

POTEMKIN

A multimedia kit for an in-depth study of the famous "Odessa Steps Sequence" of Sergei Eisenstein's 1925 classic *Battleship Potemkin* is available for purchase from Learning Seed Company (145 Brentwood Drive, Palatine, Ill. 60067). The kit contains a print of the entire 10-minute "Odessa Steps Sequence," a 72-frame, sound filmstrip analyzing the techniques used in the sequence and Eisenstein's theories of expression in film, and a brief teaching guide. The kit covers such aspects of camera art as visual rhythms, composition, continuity, montage, and editing, themes, and symbols.

BASIC FILM TERMS: A VISUAL DICTIONARY

This 15-minute film defines and illustrates 46 terms necessary in analyzing and discussing film art. This feat is achieved by portraying the making of a short film from the script to the finished product. It has been very useful in humanities classes, where it can be shown once, discussed, then shown again in one class period. Available from Pyramid Films (Box 1048, Santa Monica, Calif. 90406).

YOUNG PEOPLE'S CONCERT SERIES

Films of twenty-two of the New York Philharmonic Young People's Concerts of the 1950s, with Leonard Bernstein conducting and narrating, are available from McGraw-Hill Films (1221 Ave. of the Americas, New York 10020). Of these, at least five, useful with this text, have not been superseded. The approach and information are compatible, and the narration and performed examples are clear and dependable. The films recommended are the following: *Anatomy of an Orchestra, What Does Classical Mean? What Is Impressionism? What Is Sonata Form?* and *What Is a Concerto?* (These films are each about an hour long and are in black and white. The narrated information is given in the first half of each film; the second half consists almost entirely of performed music.)

COLOR SLIDES

THE 1976 SLIDE BUYER'S GUIDE

Compiled by Nancy DeLaurier and published by The College Art Association of America (16 East 52d St., New York 10022). This is a very important, modestly priced source book for teachers of humanities. For each source listed, the Guide includes the address, the availability of a catalog, number of slides available, prices, subjects covered, and an evaluation of the quality of slides.

THE CENTER FOR HUMANITIES

(2 Holland Ave., White Plains, New York 10603) Specializes in sound-

slide sets on all aspects of visual arts, with a comprehensive teacher's guide with each set.

McGRAW-HILL, PROFESSIONAL AND REFERENCE BOOK DIVISION

(1221 Ave. of the Americas, New York 10020)

Color Slide Program of Art Enjoyment. A series of nineteen volumes, each with twenty-four slides and a historical text plus commentaries on the individual slides. Volumes cover individual periods or styles, such as *The High Renaissance, Impressionism, Between the Two Wars.*

Color Slide Program of the Great Masters. A series of fourteen volumes with twenty slides each, plus texts as above. Each volume is devoted to an individual artist; e.g., *Chagall, Picasso, Brueghel, Michelangelo.*

PROTHMANN ASSOCIATES, INC.

(650 Thomas Ave., Baldwin, New York 11510) Over 600,000 slides available, some individually, some in sets. Covers the whole range of art history. Sets coordinated with art books published by Abrams.

SANDAK, INC.

(180 Harvard Ave., Stamford, Conn. 06902) Four catalogs: architecture, sculpture, printing, and graphics. Sets available. Modern architecture well covered.

SCHOLASTIC AUDIO-VISUALS, INC.

(5 Beekman St., New York 10036) Sets on a wide range of art history. Individual slides not sold.

VISUAL RESOURCES, INC.

(One Lincoln Plaza, New York 10023) Specializes in contemporary art. Many subjects not available elsewhere.

COLOR PRINTS

For teaching the visual arts, color prints are indispensable. Advances in reproduction processes have now made them available in all sizes and prices.

One of the best guides to specific subjects and to sources are the three volumes sponsored and published by UNESCO: *Catalogue of Reproductions of Paintings Prior to 1860* (rev. and enlarged, 1968), *Catalogue of Reproductions of Paintings 1860–1969* (9th ed., rev., 1969, and *Catalogue of Reproductions of Paintings 1860–1973* (10th ed., rev., 1973). These are important reference volumes and are available in most libraries; or they may be purchased from Unipub, Inc., A Xerox Education Company (433 Murray Hill Station, New York 10016).

In addition to giving preference in its listings to "widely distributed and generally inexpensive reproductions," the international committee of experts responsible for the volumes have applied three criteria: "the fidelity of the color reproduction, the significance of the artist and the importance of the original painting." For each listing there is a small black-and-white reproduction in the catalogs, with the artist's name, places and dates of birth and death, and title and date of the painting. The process used in printing, the size, the publisher, and the price are also indicated.

At the end of the last-named book, there is an up-to-date listing of pub-

lishers of reproductions of paintings, with addresses. Some of the mor
active publishers in the field are the following:
  Graphic Arts Unlimited, Inc., 225 Fifth Ave., New York 10010.
  Harry N. Abrams, Inc., 110 East 59th St., New York 10022.
  New York Graphic Society Ltd., 140 Greenwich Ave., Greenwich
  Conn. 06831.
Quite inexpensive and useful prints may also be obtained from:
  Shorewood Reproductions, 10 E. 53d St., New York 10022.
  Poster Originals Unlimited, 16 East 78th St., New York 10021.

TAPES, CASSETTES, FILMSTRIPS

Filmstrips and tapes (reel to reel) have for several years been popular and
useful teaching aids in the humanities. Today, however, more and more
teachers are finding cassettes a flexible, inexpensive aid which may be easily
stored and made available to students in libraries. Almost all music now
recorded on disks is also available in cassette form. The Schwann catalog
now indicate which recordings are available in this format. Also, the large
and well-equipped public libraries have large lending collections which
may be useful. Some sources of all three kinds of teaching material are
listed below:

EDUCATOR'S GUIDE TO FREE TAPES, SCRIPTS, TRANSCRIPTIONS, 23d ed.
  Compiled and edited by James L. Berger. Educators Progress Service
  Inc. (Randolph, Wisconsin 53956), 1976. The Guide is issued annually
  The 1976 edition lists over 6000 audiotapes, videotapes, audiodisks
  and scripts which may be obtained free of cost (no rental service or
  sales cost) by schools, colleges, and libraries. It is available for a modest
  charge from the address given above.
    A great many of the items listed are of use in humanities classes
  There are numerous items on the visual arts (e.g., "Art of the West,"
  "Picasso," "Italian Art"), architecture (e.g., "Architecture of Louis
  Kahn," "Paolo Soleri—Arcosanti"), drama (e.g., *A Streetcar Named De
  sire, Macbeth*), dance (e.g., "Songs and Dances of the Maori," "Folk
  Dances from around the World"), music ("Puccini," "Italian Opera
  Buffa in the 18th Century"), etc.

AUDIO-TEXT CASSETTES
  Available from The Center for Cassette Studies (8110 Webb Ave., North
  Hollywood, Calif. 91605), these cassettes have been made specifically
  for instructional purposes. In the more than 6000 now available, there
  are cassettes on all aspects of the humanities. A free catalog is available
  listing each cassette with a set of questions which students should be
  able to answer after listening to it. The questions are reliable guides to
  the content. Sample titles: "The Mass," "The Symphony," "The
  Fugue," "Theatre of the Absurd," "Theatre and the Visual Arts,"
  "Survey of the American Theater," "Ted Shawn and Ruth St. Denis."
  An important fact about Audio-Text Cassettes is that "copyright
  privilege is granted schools and libraries purchasing them"; the pur
  chaser, in other words, may make as many copies of the cassettes as are
  needed for library assignments or other instructional uses.

CAEDMON RECORDS, INC.

(505 Eighth Ave., New York 10018) A good source for records and cassettes for the teaching of literature. Caedmon records and cassettes are not made exclusively for instructional purposes and do not, therefore, contain very much background or analytical or critical information. Especially noteworthy are Caedmon's LP recordings and cassettes of performed dramas, from the Greeks to the present time.

CASSETTE LECTURES AND PROGRAMS

Produced by Everett/Edwards, Inc. (Box 1060, Deland, Fla. 32720) The materials cover almost every aspect of literature and drama. They are taped lectures by authorities on the subjects covered. Lecturers include such people as Cleanth Brooks, David Daiches, Eric Heller, Laurence Perrin, and Warren French. The tapes are probably not appropriate for classroom use. Whether they are useful for library assignments will depend on the method used in teaching the humanities course.

SPOKEN ARTS

(310 North Ave., New Rochelle, New York 10801) The company produces a variety of teaching materials useful in teaching the humanities—cassettes, LP recordings, and reel-to-reel tapes. The materials are most comprehensive in the areas of literature and drama; but *The Great Composers Series: From Corelli to Stravinsky*, consisting of thirty-one cassettes, should also be noted. Cassettes may be purchased in sets or individually. Each cassette is devoted to one composer and includes brief facts about his or her life and musical development, performed examples of significant works illustrating changing musical style, and comments on the composer's place in the history of musical forms and styles. Each is narrated simply and dramatically; the musical examples are well performed; and the text is interjected quietly and informatively.

INDEX

521